Cakes

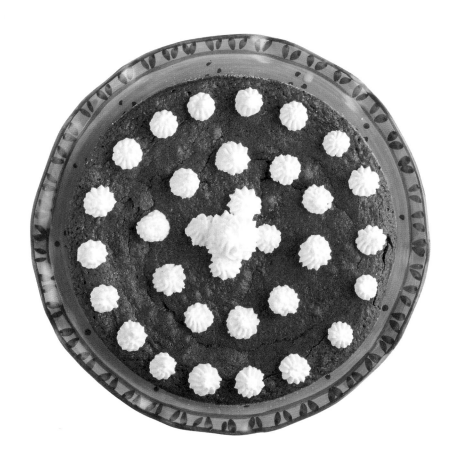

Cakes

1,001 Classic Recipes
from Around the World

Reader's Digest

THE READER'S DIGEST ASSOCIATION, INC.
PLEASANTVILLE, NEW YORK / MONTREAL

A READER'S DIGEST BOOK

This edition published by the Reader's Digest Association by arrangement with McRae Books Srl

This book was conceived, edited and designed by
McRae Books Srl
Borgo Santa Croce, 8,
50122 Florence, Italy
info@mcraebooks.com

FOR MCRAE BOOKS:
Project Director: Anne McRae
Design Director: Marco Nardi
Text: Carla Bardi, Rosalba Gioffré, Mariapaola Dettore, Sara Vignozzi
Photography: Marco Lanza, Walter Mericchi
Set Design: Rosalba Gioffrè
Test Cooks: Rachel Lee, Mollie Thomson
Layout: Laura Ottina, Paola Baldanzi
Editing: Helen Farrell

The Publishers would like to thank:

Richard Ginori (Sesto Fiorentino); Bartolini (Florence, Italy); Villeroy & Boch (Florence, Italy)
Mastrociliegia (Fiesole, Italy); Spini (Florence, Italy)

who kindly lent props for the photography.

FOR READER'S DIGEST:
U.S. Project Editors: Andrea Chesman, Miriam Rubin
Canadian Project Editor: Pamela Johnson
Australian Project Editor: Annette Carter
Project Designer: George McKeon
Executive Editor, Trade Publishing: Dolores York
Creative Director: Michele Laseau
Director, Trade Publishing: Christopher T. Reggio
Vice President & Publisher, Trade Publishing: Harold Clarke

LIBRARY OF CONGRESS CATALOGING-IN-PUBLICATION DATA
Cakes : 1,001 classic recipes from around the world/ from the editors of Reader's Digest.
    p. cm.
  ISBN: 0-7621-0403-1
  1. Cake. I. Reader's digest.

TX771.C283 2003
641.8'15--dc21   2003046869

Address any comments about *Cakes* to:
The Reader's Digest Association, Inc.
Adult Trade Publishing
Reader's Digest Road
Pleasantville, NY 10570-7000

For Reader's Digest products and information, visit our website:
www.rd.com (in the United States)
www.readersdigest.ca (in Canada)
www.readersdigest.com.au (in Australia)

Color separations: Service Lito (Persico Dosimo, Cremona)
Printed and bound in China by TIMS Printing Co. Limited

3 5 7 9 10 8 6 4 2

CONTENTS

INTRODUCTION

Adventurous cooks develop new cake recipes every day, but the art of baking cakes dates back to the time of the very earliest settled communities. Traces of small cakes, rather like modern cookies, have been found in Neolithic villages inhabited more than 10,000 years ago. The first cakes were probably baked around the time people discovered how to grind grain, thereby producing flour. It is easy to imagine a sweet-toothed ancestor experimenting with coarsely ground grain, lard, and honey, adding chopped nuts or dried fruit, flavoring the concoction with wild fennel or lemon, and delighting family and friends with her newfound confection.

Cakes gained in popularity once cooks had access to sugar. Cane sugar, which historians believe was first manufactured in India, traveled from India to Arab countries, where it was artfully combined with spices and flavorings imported from the Far East. Europe discovered sugar when the Arabs invaded Italy in the Middle Ages, and by Renaissance times, Italian pastry cooks were in great demand in aristocratic homes all over Europe. By the 17th century, many cooks were using beaten egg whites, replacing yeast to leaven cakes. The era of the light-as-air sponge cake had arrived. Europe was also the home of the café, where tea- and coffee-drinkers went to converse and dawdle over morsels of cream-filled gateaux or more substantial slices of kuchen or strudel.

These European cakes form the basis of our cake heritage. Today's cakes are refined confections, usually containing flour, sugar, and flavoring ingredients, as well as some sort of leavening, such as eggs or baking powder.

Cakes delight us not only with their taste, but also with their variety. In this book, we have gathered more than 1,001 recipes for cakes, frostings, and fillings from every corner of the globe (although the vast majority are from western Europe and the United States, where cake baking has most deliciously and variously developed). Here you will find many of your old favorites—from Devil's Food Cake and Lemon Pound Cake to New York Cheesecake and Strawberry Creamcake—alongside a host of European gateaux and tortes and a range of more exotic recipes, such as Thai Birthday Cake and New Zealand Pavlova. To provide the broadest range of delectable dessert recipes, we have been very inclusive in our definition of cakes.

Most well-stocked kitchens will already have the utensils required to bake the cakes in this book. We do suggest, though, that if you don't have one already, you invest in a good quality mixer, which will help to improve the texture of your cakes and save you some elbow grease!

In using this book, we suggest that you read the recipe you have chosen through carefully and assemble and prepare all the ingredients first. You may need to do things like browning nuts or melting butter or chocolate in advance. In many cases we have suggested that you line the baking pan with waxed paper before filling it with batter.

Baking is an exact science, and to ensure your success with these recipes, each one has been tested—some more than once. Many have been adapted to suit local tastes and modern kitchens. They are all ranked from 1 (easy) to 3 (complicated), but you will find that the majority are either easy or fairly easy (2). The recipes have been standardized to use measures, ingredients, and pans commonly found in North America. If you are baking outside of the United States, be sure to refer to the tables found at the end of the book for easy substitutions.

The recipes have been divided into 17 chapters, arranged according to their method, their ingredients, or the occasion for serving them. Never again will you lack the perfect cake recipe to serve at breakfast, with coffee or tea, as a family dessert, or as the grand finale at an elegant dinner party.

CARLA BARDI

Turn to the final chapter in this book for a dizzying array of frostings, fillings, sauces, and creams to finish your cakes. Many of the recipes have their own suggestions, while others are cross-referenced to one or more recipes in the last chapter.

BUTTER CAKES

Simple butter cakes can be frosted, filled, and layered, drizzled with sweet sugar syrups, or served with just a dusting of confectioners' sugar. Most of the recipes in this chapter are simple and quick, and the delicious cakes they make can be served at breakfast or throughout the day.

COFFEE LOAF

This simple loaf is delicious served with coffee or tea. Try it thinly sliced and buttered or, for a slightly richer offering, spread with Coffee Buttercream (see page 346) and sprinkled with some fragrant roasted coffee kernels. It is equally good made with decaffeinated coffee.

1   cup all-purpose flour
³/₄   cup granulated sugar
1   teaspoon baking powder
¹/₄   teaspoon salt
2   tablespoons freeze-dried coffee granules, dissolved in ¹/₃ cup milk
2   large eggs, lightly beaten
¹/₂   cup (1 stick) butter, melted
1   teaspoon vanilla extract

Preheat the oven to 350°F. • Butter and flour an 8¹/₂ x 4¹/₂-inch loaf pan. • Sift the flour, sugar, baking powder, and salt into a large bowl. • Beat the coffee mixture, eggs, butter, and vanilla into the dry ingredients with an electric mixer at low speed. • Spoon the batter into the prepared pan. • Bake for 35–45 minutes, or until a toothpick inserted into the center comes out clean. • Cool the loaf in the pan for 10 minutes. Turn out onto a rack to cool completely.

Makes one 8¹/₂ x 4¹/₂-inch loaf · Prep: 15 min. · Cooking: 35–45 min. · Level: 1 · Keeps: 3–4 days

◄ Tangy fresh lime cake
(see page 22)

➤ Coffee loaf

BASIC BUTTER CAKE

1½ cups all-purpose flour
1½ teaspoons baking powder
¼ teaspoon salt
1 cup (2 sticks) butter, softened
1 cup granulated sugar
2 teaspoons vanilla extract
4 large eggs, at room temperature
¾ cup milk

Preheat the oven to 350°F. • Butter and flour a 9-inch round cake pan. Line with waxed paper. Butter the paper. • Sift the flour, baking powder, and salt into a large bowl. • Beat the butter, sugar, and vanilla in a large bowl with an electric mixer at medium speed until creamy. • Add the eggs, one at a time, until just blended after each addition. • With mixer at low speed, gradually beat in the dry ingredients, alternating with the milk. • Spoon the batter into the prepared pan. • Bake for 45–55 minutes, or until a toothpick inserted into the center comes out clean. • Cool the cake in the pan for 10 minutes. Turn out onto a rack. Carefully remove the waxed paper and let cool completely.

Makes one 9-inch cake · Prep: 15 min. · Cooking: 45–55 min. · Level: 1 · Keeps: 2–3 days

CINNAMON CAKE

1½ cups all-purpose flour
2 teaspoons ground cinnamon
1½ teaspoons baking powder
¼ teaspoon salt
½ cup (1 stick) butter, softened
1 cup granulated sugar
1 teaspoon vanilla extract
2 large eggs, at room temperature
½ cup milk
¾ cup Lemon Glaze (see page 348)

Preheat the oven to 350°F. • Butter and flour a 9-inch square baking pan. • Sift the flour, cinnamon, baking powder, and salt into a large bowl. • Beat the butter, sugar, and vanilla in a large bowl with an electric mixer at medium speed until creamy. • Add the eggs, one at a time, until just blended after each addition. • With mixer at low speed, gradually beat in the dry ingredients, alternating with the milk. • Spoon the batter into the prepared pan. • Bake for 35–45 minutes, or until a toothpick inserted into the center comes out clean. • Cool the cake completely in the pan on a rack. • Drizzle with the glaze.

Makes one 9-inch cake · Prep: 20 min. · Cooking: 35–45 min. · Level: 1 · Keeps: 2–3 days

CINNAMON CRUMBLE LOAF

1½ cups all-purpose flour
½ cup granulated sugar
2 teaspoons ground cinnamon
1 teaspoon baking powder
¼ teaspoon salt
⅓ cup milk
¼ cup (½ stick) butter, melted
1 large egg, lightly beaten

CRUMBLE TOPPING

3 tablespoons cold butter, cut up
3 tablespoons granulated sugar
1 teaspoon ground cinnamon

Preheat the oven to 350°F. • Butter and flour an 8½ x 4½-inch loaf pan. • Sift the flour, sugar, cinnamon, baking powder, and salt into a large bowl. • With an electric mixer at low speed, beat in the milk, butter, and egg. • Spoon the batter into the prepared pan. • Bake for 35–45 minutes, or until a toothpick inserted into the center comes out clean. • *Crumble Topping*: Dot the butter over the cake. Sprinkle with the sugar and cinnamon. • Cool the loaf completely in the pan on a rack.

Makes one 8½ x 4½-inch loaf · Prep: 15 min. · Cooking: 35–45 min. · Level: 1 · Keeps: 3–4 days

GLAZED GOLDEN SPICE CAKE

2 cups all-purpose flour
2 teaspoons baking powder
1 teaspoon ground cinnamon
1 teaspoon ground ginger
½ teaspoon ground nutmeg
¼ teaspoon salt
1 cup (2 sticks) butter, softened
1 cup firmly packed dark brown sugar
½ cup pure maple syrup
1 teaspoon vanilla extract
4 large eggs, at room temperature
⅓ cup milk

¾ cup Lemon Glaze (see page 348)

Preheat the oven to 350°F. • Butter and flour an 11 x 7-inch baking pan. • Sift the flour,

Cinnamon crumble loaf

baking powder, cinnamon, ginger, nutmeg, and salt into a large bowl. • Beat the butter, brown sugar, maple syrup, and vanilla in a large bowl with an electric mixer at medium speed until creamy. • Add the eggs, one at a time, until just blended after each addition. • With mixer at low speed, gradually beat in the dry ingredients, alternating with the milk. • Spoon the batter into the prepared pan. • Bake for 40–50 minutes, or until the cake shrinks from the pan sides and a toothpick inserted into the center comes out clean. • Cool the cake in the pan on a rack. • Drizzle with the glaze.

Makes one 11 x 7-inch cake · Prep: 20 min. · Cooking: 40–50 min. · Level: 1 · Keeps: 3–4 days

VANILLA BUTTER CAKE

- ¹/₂ cup (1 stick) butter, cut up
- ³/₄ cup milk
- 1¹/₂ cups all-purpose flour
- 1 teaspoon baking powder
- ¹/₄ teaspoon salt
- 3 large eggs, at room temperature
- 1¹/₄ cups granulated sugar
- 1 tablespoon vanilla extract
- ³/₄ cup Lemon Glaze (see page 348)

Preheat the oven to 350°F. • Butter an 11 x 7-inch baking pan. • Place the butter and milk in a small saucepan over low heat, stirring until the butter has melted. Cool to room temperature. • Sift the flour, baking powder, and salt into a medium bowl. • Beat the eggs, sugar, and vanilla in a large bowl with an electric mixer at medium speed until pale and thick. • With mixer at low speed, gradually beat in the dry ingredients, alternating with the milk mixture. • Spoon the batter into the prepared pan. • Bake for 35–45 minutes, or until a toothpick inserted into the center comes out clean. • Cool the cake completely in the pan on a rack. • Drizzle with the glaze.

Makes one 11 x 7-inch cake · Prep: 10 min. · Cooking: 35–45 min. · Level: 1 · Keeps: 5 days

QUICK VANILLA CAKE

This cake uses oil instead of butter.

- 3 cups cake flour
- 2 teaspoons baking powder

- 1 teaspoon baking soda
- ¹/₄ teaspoon salt
- 4 large eggs, at room temperature
- ³/₄ cup granulated sugar
- 2 teaspoons vanilla extract
- ³/₄ cup vegetable oil
- 2 cups water
- 2¹/₂ cups Seven Minute Frosting (see page 348)

Preheat the oven to 350°F. • Butter and flour a 10-inch round cake pan. Line with waxed paper. Butter the paper. • Sift the flour, baking powder, baking soda, and salt into a large bowl. • Beat the eggs, sugar, and vanilla in a large bowl with an electric mixer at medium speed until pale and thick. • With mixer at low speed, gradually beat in the dry ingredients, alternating with the water and oil. • Spoon the batter into the prepared pan. Bake for 60–70 minutes, or until golden and a toothpick inserted into the center comes out clean. • Cool the cake in the pan for 10 minutes. Turn out onto a rack. Carefully remove the paper and let cool completely. • Spread the top and sides with Seven Minute Frosting.

Makes one 10-inch cake · Prep: 20 min. · Cooking: 60–70 min. · Level: 1 · Keeps: 2–3 days

BROWN SUGAR STREUSEL CAKE

BROWN SUGAR STREUSEL
- ³/₄ cup all-purpose flour
- 1 teaspoon ground cinnamon
- 1 teaspoon ground ginger
- ¹/₃ cup firmly packed brown sugar

- ¹/₃ cup butter, cut up, at room temperature

CAKE
- ¹/₂ cup (1 stick) butter, softened
- ³/₄ cup granulated sugar
- 1 teaspoon vanilla extract
- 2 large eggs, at room temperature
- 1¹/₂ cups all-purpose flour
- 1¹/₂ teaspoons baking powder
- ¹/₄ teaspoon salt
- ¹/₄ cup milk

Brown Sugar Streusel: Sift the flour, cinnamon, and ginger into a medium bowl. Stir in the brown sugar. Use a pastry blender to cut in the butter until the mixture resembles coarse crumbs. Press into a ball, wrap in plastic foil, and refrigerate for 30 minutes. • *Cake*: Preheat the oven to 350°F. • Butter and flour a 9-inch springform pan. • Beat the butter, sugar, and vanilla in a large bowl with an electric mixer at medium speed until creamy. • Add the eggs, one at a time, until just blended after each addition. • With mixer at low speed, gradually beat in the flour, baking powder, and salt, alternating with the milk. • Spoon the batter into the prepared pan. • Coarsely grate the streusel over the batter. • Bake for 35–45 minutes, or until a toothpick inserted into the center comes out clean. • Cool the cake in the pan for 10 minutes. Loosen and remove the pan sides and let cool completely.

Makes one 9-inch cake · Prep: 20 min. + 30 min. to chill · Cooking: 35–40 min. · Level: 1 · Keeps: 2 days

Brown sugar streusel cake

SANDY CAKE

- 1 cup all-purpose flour
- 1 cup cornstarch
- 1 teaspoon baking powder
- $1/4$ teaspoon salt
- $1^1/4$ cups ($2^1/2$ sticks) butter
- $1^1/2$ cups granulated sugar
- 3 large eggs, separated

Preheat the oven to 350°F. • Butter a 9-inch round cake pan. Line with waxed paper. Butter the paper. • Sift the flour, cornstarch, baking powder, and salt into a medium bowl. • Beat the butter and sugar in a large bowl with an electric mixer at medium speed until creamy. • Add the egg yolks, one at a time, until just blended after each addition. • With mixer at low speed, gradually beat in the dry ingredients. • With mixer at high speed, beat the egg whites in a medium bowl until stiff peaks form. Use a large rubber spatula to fold them into the batter. • Spoon the batter into the prepared pan. • Bake for 40–50 minutes. • Cool the cake in the pan for 20 minutes. Turn out onto a rack. Carefully remove the paper and let cool completely.

Makes one 9-inch round cake · Prep: 20 min. · Cooking: 40–50 min. · Level: 1 · Keeps: 3–4 days

BABY CAKE

- 2 cups all-purpose flour
- 2 teaspoons baking powder
- $1/4$ teaspoon salt
- $1/2$ cup (1 stick) butter, softened
- 2 cups granulated sugar
- 2 teaspoons vanilla extract
- 4 large eggs, at room temperature
- 1 cup milk

Preheat the oven to 350°F. • Butter and flour a 9-inch tube pan. • Sift the flour, baking powder, and salt into a large bowl. • Beat the butter, sugar, and vanilla in a large bowl with an electric mixer at medium speed until creamy. • Add the eggs, one at a time, until just blended after each addition. • With mixer at low speed, gradually beat in the dry ingredients, alternating with the milk. • Spoon the batter into the prepared pan. • Bake for 60–70 minutes, or until a toothpick inserted into the center comes out clean. • Cool the cake in the pan for 20 minutes. Turn out onto a rack to cool completely.

Makes one 9-inch cake · Prep: 20 min. · Cooking: 60–70 min. · Level: 1 · Keeps: 2–3 days

Sandy cake

CLOUD CAKE

Potato starch, sometimes referred to as potato flour, is found in health food stores.

- 3 large eggs
- $1/2$ cup superfine sugar
- $1/3$ cup all-purpose flour
- $1/4$ cup potato starch
- 1 tablespoon baking powder
- $1/4$ cup ($1/2$ stick) butter, melted
- 1 teaspoon vanilla extract
- confectioners' sugar, to dust
- candied cherries and lemon peel, to decorate

Preheat the oven to 350°F. • Butter and flour a deep $1^1/2$-quart ovenproof mold. • Beat the eggs and sugar in a large bowl with an electric mixer at medium speed until pale and thick. • Use a large rubber spatula to fold the flour, starch, and baking powder into the egg mixture. • Stir the butter and vanilla into the batter. • Spoon the batter into the prepared pan. • Bake for 40–45 minutes, or until a toothpick inserted into the center comes out clean. • Cool the cake completely in the pan. • Turn out onto a serving plate. • Dust with the confectioners' sugar. Arrange the cherries and lemon peel on top in a decorative manner.

Makes one $1^1/2$-quart cake · Prep: 1 hr. · Cooking: 45 min. · Level: 2 · Keeps: 2 days

APRICOT JAM CAKE

- $1^1/2$ cups all-purpose flour
- $1/2$ teaspoon baking soda
- $1/2$ teaspoon ground nutmeg
- $1/2$ teaspoon ground cinnamon
- $1/4$ teaspoon ground cloves
- $1/4$ teaspoon salt
- $1/2$ cup (1 stick) butter, softened
- 1 cup granulated sugar
- 2 large eggs, at room temperature
- $1/2$ cup buttermilk
- $1/2$ cup apricot preserves

Preheat the oven to 350°F. • Butter and flour a 9-inch square baking pan. • Sift the flour, baking soda, nutmeg, cinnamon, cloves, and salt into a medium bowl. • Beat the butter and sugar in a large bowl with an electric mixer at medium speed until creamy. • Add the eggs, one at a time, until just blended after each addition. • With mixer at low speed, gradually beat in the dry ingredients, alternating with the buttermilk and preserves. • Spoon the batter into the prepared pan. • Bake for 40–45 minutes, or until a toothpick inserted into the center comes out clean. • Cool the cake completely in the pan on a rack.

Makes one 9-inch cake · Prep: 15 min. · Cooking: 40–45 min. · Level: 1 · Keeps: 3–4 days

RASPBERRY JAM CAKE

- 2 cups all-purpose flour
- 1 teaspoon baking powder
- 1 teaspoon baking soda
- 1 teaspoon ground cinnamon
- 1 teaspoon ground nutmeg
- 1 teaspoon ground ginger
- $1/4$ teaspoon ground cloves
- $1/2$ teaspoon salt
- $1^1/2$ cups granulated sugar
- 2 cups walnuts or pecans, chopped
- 1 cup vegetable oil
- 1 cup buttermilk
- 1 cup raspberry jam
- 3 large eggs, lightly beaten
- 1 teaspoon vanilla extract
- 1 cup Mock Cream (see page 344)

Preheat the oven to 350°F. • Butter and flour two 9-inch round cake pans. • Stir together the flour, baking powder, baking soda, cinnamon, nutmeg, ginger, cloves, and salt in a large bowl. Stir in the sugar and 1 cup nuts. Add the oil, buttermilk, jam, eggs, and vanilla, and beat with an electric mixer at low speed until well mixed. • Spoon half the batter into each of the prepared pans and sprinkle with the remaining nuts. • Bake for 25–35 minutes, or until a toothpick inserted into the center comes out clean. • Cool the cakes in the pans for 10 minutes. Turn out onto racks to cool completely. • Place a cake on a serving plate and spread with the Mock Cream. Top with the remaining cake.

Makes one 9-inch cake · Prep: 20 min. · Cooking: 25–35 min. · Level: 1 · Keeps: 1–2 days

BLACK CURRANT JAM CAKE

2¼ cups all-purpose flour
 1 teaspoon baking powder
 1 teaspoon baking soda
 1 teaspoon ground cinnamon
 1 teaspoon pumpkin pie spice
 ¼ teaspoon ground cloves
 ¼ teaspoon salt
 ¾ cup (1½ sticks) butter, softened
 1 cup granulated sugar
 3 large eggs, at room temperature
 1 cup thick black currant jam
 ¼ cup milk
 ¼ cup kirsch (or other fruit liqueur)
 ¼ cup confectioners' sugar, to dust

Preheat the oven to 350°F. • Butter a 9-inch square baking pan. • Sift the flour, baking powder, baking soda, cinnamon, pumpkin pie spice, cloves, and salt into a large bowl. • Beat the butter and sugar in a large bowl with an electric mixer at medium speed until creamy. • Add the eggs, one at a time, until just blended after each addition. • With mixer at low speed, gradually beat in the jam, followed by the dry ingredients, alternating with the milk and kirsch. • Spoon the batter into the prepared pan. • Bake for 75–85 minutes, or until a toothpick inserted into the center comes out clean. • Cool the cake completely in the pan on a rack. Dust with the confectioners' sugar.

Makes one 9-inch cake · Prep: 15 min. · Cooking: 75–85 min. · Level: 1 · Keeps: 2–3 days

MACAROON RING

If it's available, use unsweetened, shredded coconut to prepare this dessert.

1½ cups all-purpose flour
 2 teaspoons baking powder
 ¼ teaspoon salt
 ½ cup (1 stick) butter
 ½ cup granulated sugar
 3 large egg yolks, at room temperature
 1 teaspoon vanilla extract
 ½ cup milk
 ½ cup raspberry jam or preserves

MACAROON TOPPING
 3 large egg whites, at room temperature
 ¼ cup granulated sugar
 ½ cup shredded coconut
 ½ teaspoon almond extract

Preheat the oven to 350°F. • Butter and flour a 9-inch tube pan. • Sift the flour, baking powder, and salt into a large bowl. • Melt the butter in a saucepan over low heat. Remove from the heat. Beat in the sugar, egg yolks, and vanilla. • Stir in the dry ingredients, alternating with the milk. • Spoon the batter into the prepared pan. • Spoon dollops of jam over the batter. • *Macaroon Topping*: Beat the egg whites in a large bowl with an electric mixer at medium speed until frothy. With mixer at high speed, gradually beat in the sugar, beating until stiff, glossy peaks form. • Use a large rubber spatula to fold in the coconut and almond extract. • Spread the topping over the batter. • Bake for 40–50 minutes, or until a toothpick inserted into the center comes out clean. • Cool the cake in the pan for 15 minutes. Turn out onto a rack. Turn top-side up and let cool completely.

Makes one 9-inch cake · Prep: 25 min. · Cooking: 40–50 min. · Level: 1 · Keeps: 4–5 days

STRAWBERRY JAM SHORTCAKE

2 cups all-purpose flour
 2 teaspoons baking powder
 ¼ teaspoon salt
 ½ cup (1 stick) cold butter, cut up
 ¾ cup granulated sugar
 1 large egg, lightly beaten
 2 tablespoons fresh lemon juice
 1 cup strawberry jam, stirred
 1 large egg white, lightly beaten
 ¼ cup slivered almonds

Preheat the oven to 350°F. • Butter and flour a 9-inch round cake pan. • Sift the flour, baking powder, and salt into a large bowl. Use a pastry blender to cut in the butter. • Stir in the sugar, then the egg. Gradually add the lemon juice, mixing until the dough is firm. Press into a ball, wrap in plastic wrap, and refrigerate for 30 minutes. • Divide the dough in two, one piece twice as big as the other (keep smaller piece chilled). Roll the larger piece of dough out on a lightly floured surface to a 12-inch round. Ease the dough into the bottom and up the sides of the prepared pan. Spread with the jam. Roll the smaller piece of dough out to a 9½-inch round. Place over the jam. Seal the edges together. • Brush the pastry with the beaten white and sprinkle with the almonds. • Bake for 40–50 minutes, or until the pastry is golden brown and flaky. • Cool the cake in the pan for 10 minutes. Turn out onto a rack and turn top-side up. Let cool completely.

Makes one 9-inch cake · Prep: 25 min. + 30 min. to chill · Cooking: 40–50 min. · Level: 1 · Keeps: 2 days

Macaroon ring

Frosted poppy seed cake

FROSTED POPPY SEED CAKE

    1   cup milk
    1/2 cup poppy seeds
    2   cups all-purpose flour
    2 1/2 teaspoons baking powder
    1/4 teaspoon salt
    3/4 cup (1 1/2 sticks) butter, softened
    1 1/2 cups granulated sugar
    2   teaspoons vanilla extract
    3   large egg whites, at room temperature

CREAM CHEESE FROSTING

    1   package (8 oz) cream cheese, softened
    4   tablespoons butter, softened
    2 1/2 cups confectioners' sugar
    2   teaspoons vanilla extract
    3   tablespoons poppy seeds, to decorate

Bring the milk to a boil in a small saucepan over medium-low heat. Remove from the heat. Stir in the poppy seeds and set aside to cool. • Preheat the oven to 350°F. • Butter and flour two 8-inch round cake pans. • Sift the flour, baking powder, and salt into a medium bowl. • Beat the butter, 1 1/4 cups of sugar, and the vanilla in a large bowl with an electric mixer at medium speed until creamy.

• With mixer at low speed, gradually beat in the dry ingredients, alternating with the milk and poppy seeds. • With mixer at medium speed, beat the egg whites in a large bowl until frothy. With mixer at high speed, gradually beat in the remaining sugar, beating until stiff, glossy peaks form. • Use a large rubber spatula to fold the beaten whites into the batter. • Spoon half the batter into each of the prepared pans. • Bake for 30–40 minutes, or until a toothpick inserted into the center comes out clean. • Cool the cakes in the pans for 10 minutes. Turn out onto racks and let cool completely. • *Cream Cheese Frosting*: With mixer at medium speed, beat the cream cheese, butter, confectioners' sugar, and vanilla until smooth. • Place one cake on a serving plate. Spread with 1/3 of the frosting. Top with the remaining cake and spread the top and sides with the remaining frosting. • To decorate: Cut 4 strips of cardboard and lay them diagonally across the cake. Sprinkle with the poppy seeds, then carefully remove the cardboard.

Makes one 8-inch cake · Prep: 35 min. · Cooking 30–40 min. · Level: 1 · Keeps: 2–3 days

ALMOND POPPY SEED LOAF

    1 1/2 cups all-purpose flour
    2   tablespoons poppy seeds
    1   teaspoon baking powder
    1/4 teaspoon salt
    1/2 cup (1 stick) butter, softened
    1   cup granulated sugar
    1/2 teaspoon almond extract
    2   large eggs, at room temperature
    1/2 cup + 1 tablespoon milk

Preheat the oven to 375°F. • Butter and flour an 8 1/2 x 4 1/2-inch loaf pan. • Sift the flour, baking powder, and salt into a medium bowl. Stir in the poppy seeds. • Beat the butter, sugar, and almond extract in a large bowl with an electric mixer at medium speed until creamy. • Add the eggs, one at a time, until just blended after each addition. • With mixer at low speed, gradually beat in the dry ingredients, alternating with the milk. • Spoon the batter into the prepared pan. • Bake for 65–75 minutes, or until golden brown and a toothpick inserted into the center comes out clean. • Cool the cake in the pan for 10 minutes. Turn out onto a rack to cool completely.

Makes one 8 1/2 x 4 1/2-inch loaf · Prep: 30 min. · Cooking: 65–75 min. · Level: 1 · Keeps: 2–3 days

PLAIN POPPY SEED CAKE

    3/4 cup milk
    1/3 cup poppy seeds
    2   cups all-purpose flour
    1   cup granulated sugar
    3/4 cup (1 1/2 sticks) butter, softened
    3   large eggs, at room temperature
    2   teaspoons almond extract
    2   teaspoons baking powder
    1/4 teaspoon salt

Place the milk and poppy seeds in a large bowl. Cover and let stand for 30 minutes. • Preheat the oven to 325°F. • Butter a 9-inch square baking pan. Line with waxed paper. Butter the paper. • Beat the flour, sugar, butter, eggs, almond extract, baking powder, and salt into the poppy seed mixture with an electric mixer at low speed until well blended. • Spoon the batter into the prepared pan. • Bake for 45–55 minutes, or until a toothpick inserted into the center comes out clean. • Cool the cake in the pan for 5 minutes. Turn out onto a rack. Carefully remove the paper and let cool completely.

Makes one 9-inch cake · Prep: 15 min. + 30 min. to stand · Cooking: 45–55 min. · Level: 1 · Keeps: 3–4 days

LEMON POPPY SEED SYRUP CAKE

- 2 cups all-purpose flour
- 2 teaspoons baking powder
- 1/4 teaspoon salt
- 1/2 cup ground almonds
- 1/3 cup poppy seeds
- 1/4 cup milk
- 3/4 cup (1 1/2 sticks) butter, softened
- 1 cup firmly packed light brown sugar
- 1 tablespoon grated lemon zest
- 3 large eggs, at room temperature
- 1/2 cup fresh lemon juice

LEMON SYRUP

- 1 cup granulated sugar
- 2/3 cup fresh lemon juice
- 1/3 cup water

Preheat the oven to 350°F. • Butter and flour a 9-inch springform pan. • Sift the flour, baking powder, and salt into a large bowl. Stir in the almonds. • Place the poppy seeds and milk in a small bowl and set aside for 15 minutes. • Beat the butter, sugar, and lemon zest in a large bowl with an electric mixer at medium speed until creamy. • Add the eggs, one at a time, until just blended after each addition. • With mixer at low speed, gradually beat in the dry ingredients, alternating with the lemon juice and poppy seed mixture. • Spoon the batter into the prepared pan. • Bake for 50–60 minutes, or until a toothpick inserted into the center comes out clean. • Cool the cake in the pan for 10 minutes. Turn out onto a rack. • *Lemon Syrup*: Heat the sugar, lemon juice, and water in a saucepan over low heat. Bring to a boil and simmer for 2 minutes. • Place the cake on the rack in a jelly-roll pan. Poke holes in the cake. Spoon the hot syrup over the warm cake. Scoop up any syrup from the pan and drizzle on the cake.

Makes one 9-inch cake · Prep: 20 min. · Cooking: 50–60 min. · Level: 1 · Keeps: 2 days

WHOLE-WHEAT LEMON CAKE

- 1 2/3 cups whole-wheat flour
- 2 teaspoons baking powder
- 1/4 teaspoon salt
- 1/3 cup almonds, finely ground
- 1/2 cup (1 stick) butter, softened
- 3/4 cup firmly packed brown sugar
- 3 tablespoons finely grated lemon zest
- 3 large eggs, at room temperature
- 3/4 cup milk
- 1/4 cup fresh lemon juice

Lemon poppy seed syrup cake

Preheat the oven to 350°F. • Butter and flour a 9-inch round cake pan. • Sift the flour, baking powder, and salt into a medium bowl. Stir in the almonds. • Beat the butter, brown sugar, and lemon zest in a large bowl with an electric mixer at medium speed until creamy. • Add the eggs, one at a time, until just blended after each addition. • With mixer at low speed, gradually beat in the dry ingredients, alternating with the milk and lemon juice. • Spoon the batter into the prepared pan. • Bake for 30–40 minutes, or until a toothpick inserted into the center comes out clean. • Cool the cake in the pan for 10 minutes. Turn out onto a rack to cool completely.

Makes one 9-inch cake · Prep: 15 min. · Cooking 30–40 min. · Level: 1 · Keeps: 2–3 days

CARAWAY SEED CAKE

- 1 1/2 cups all-purpose flour
- 1 1/2 teaspoons baking powder
- 1/4 teaspoon salt
- 2 tablespoons caraway seed
- 1/2 cup (1 stick) butter, softened
- 1 cup granulated sugar
- 1 tablespoon grated lemon zest
- 2 large eggs, at room temperature
- 1/2 cup milk
- 2 tablespoons slivered almonds (optional)

Preheat the oven to 325°F. • Butter a 9-inch square baking pan. Line with waxed paper. Butter the paper. • Sift the flour, baking powder, and salt in a medium bowl. Stir in the caraway seed. • Beat the butter, sugar, and lemon zest in a large bowl with an electric mixer at medium speed until creamy. • Add the eggs, one at a time, until just blended after each addition. • With mixer at low speed, gradually beat in the dry ingredients, alternating with the milk. • Spoon the batter into the prepared pan. Sprinkle with the slivered almonds, if desired. • Bake for 45–55 minutes, or until a toothpick inserted into the center comes out clean. • Cool the cake in the pan for 5 minutes. Turn out onto a rack. Carefully remove the paper and let cool completely.

Makes one 9-inch cake · Prep: 15 min. · Cooking: 45–55 min. · Level: 1 · Keeps: 2–3 days

French lemon crown

LEMON YOGURT CAKE

- 2 cups all-purpose flour
- 2 teaspoons baking powder
- $\frac{1}{4}$ teaspoon salt
- $\frac{1}{2}$ cup (1 stick) butter, softened
- 1 cup granulated sugar
- 1 tablespoon grated lemon zest
- 3 large eggs, separated
- 1 cup lemon-flavored yogurt

LEMON FROSTING

- 2 cups confectioners' sugar
- 3 tablespoons butter, melted
- 2–3 tablespoons fresh lemon juice
- 2 tablespoons candied lemon peel, coarsely chopped

Preheat the oven to 325°F. • Butter a 9-inch round cake pan. Line with waxed paper. Butter the paper. • Sift the flour, baking powder, and salt into a medium bowl. • Beat the butter, sugar, and lemon zest in a large bowl with an electric mixer at medium speed until creamy. • Add the egg yolks, one at a time, until just blended after each addition. • With mixer at low speed, gradually beat in the dry ingredients, alternating with the yogurt. • With mixer at high speed, beat the egg whites in a medium bowl until stiff peaks form. Use a large rubber spatula to fold them into the batter. • Spoon the batter into the prepared pan. • Bake for 35–45 minutes, or the cake shrinks from the pan sides and a toothpick inserted into the center comes out clean. • Cool the cake in the pan for 5 minutes. Turn out onto a

rack. Carefully remove the paper and let cool completely. • *Lemon Frosting*: Mix the confectioners' sugar and butter in a medium bowl. Beat in enough of the lemon juice to make a thick, spreadable frosting. Spread the top and sides of the cake with the frosting. Decorate with the lemon.

Makes one 9-inch cake · Prep: 20 min. · Cooking: 35–45 min. · Level: 1 · Keeps: 2–3 days

FRENCH LEMON CROWN

- 1$\frac{2}{3}$ cups all-purpose flour
- 2 teaspoons baking powder
- $\frac{1}{4}$ teaspoon salt
- $\frac{3}{4}$ cup (1$\frac{1}{2}$ sticks) butter, softened
- 1$\frac{1}{4}$ cups granulated sugar
- 2 tablespoons grated lemon zest
- 3 large eggs, at room temperature
- $\frac{1}{3}$ cup fresh lemon juice
- $\frac{1}{2}$ cup apricot preserves
- 1$\frac{2}{3}$ cups confectioners' sugar
  candied orange, lemon, and lime peel, cut into strips, to decorate (optional)

Preheat the oven to 400°F. • Butter and flour a 9-inch tube pan. • Sift the flour, baking powder, and salt into a medium bowl. • Beat the butter, granulated sugar, and lemon zest in a large bowl with an electric mixer at medium speed until creamy. • Add the eggs, one at a time, until just blended after each addition. • With mixer at low speed, gradually beat in the dry ingredients and 2 tablespoons lemon juice. • Spoon the batter into the prepared

pan. • Bake for 30–40 minutes, or until a toothpick inserted into the center comes out clean. • Cool the cake in the pan for 15 minutes. Turn out onto a rack to cool completely. • Warm the apricot preserves in a saucepan and spread over the cake. • Beat the confectioners' sugar and enough of the remaining lemon juice to make a thin glaze. Drizzle over the cake. • Decorate with the strips of candied peel, if desired.

Makes one 9-inch cake · Prep: 25 min. · Cooking: 30–40 min. · Level: 1 · Keeps: 4–5 days

BUTTERMILK LEMON SYRUP CAKE

Serve this wonderfully light cake with strawberries and whipped cream.

- 2 cups all-purpose flour
- 2 teaspoons baking powder
- $\frac{1}{4}$ teaspoon salt
- 1 cup (2 sticks) butter, softened
- 1$\frac{1}{4}$ cups granulated sugar
- 2 tablespoons grated lemon zest
- 3 large eggs, separated
- 1 cup buttermilk

LEMON SYRUP

- $\frac{3}{4}$ cup granulated sugar
- $\frac{1}{3}$ cup fresh lemon juice
- $\frac{1}{4}$ cup water

Preheat the oven to 350°F. • Butter and flour a 9-inch Bundt pan. • Sift the flour, baking powder, and salt into a medium bowl. • Beat the butter, sugar, and lemon zest in a large bowl with an electric mixer at medium speed until creamy. • Add the egg yolks, one at a time, until just blended after each addition. • With mixer at low speed, gradually beat in the dry ingredients, alternating with the buttermilk. • With mixer at high speed, beat the egg whites in a medium bowl until stiff peaks form. Use a large rubber spatula to fold them into the batter. • Spoon the batter into the prepared pan. • Bake for 50–60 minutes, or until a toothpick inserted into the center comes out clean. • Cool the cake in the pan for 10 minutes. Turn out onto a rack and place the rack in a jelly-roll pan. • *Lemon Syrup*: Bring the sugar, lemon juice, and water to a boil in a saucepan over low heat. Drizzle over the hot cake.

Makes one 9-inch cake · Prep: 15 min. · Cooking: 50–60 min. · Level: 1 · Keeps: 2 days

CITRUSY SOUR CREAM CAKE

- 1¼ cups all-purpose flour
- 1 teaspoon baking powder
- ½ teaspoon baking soda
- ¼ teaspoon salt
- ½ cup (1 stick) butter, softened
- 1 cup granulated sugar
- 1 tablespoon grated lemon or lime zest
- 2 large eggs, at room temperature
- ⅓ cup sour cream

CITRUS FROSTING

- ¼ cup (½ stick) butter, softened
- 1 tablespoon grated lemon or lime zest
- 1½ cups confectioners' sugar, sifted
- 3–4 tablespoons fresh lemon or lime juice

Preheat the oven to 325°F. • Butter and flour a 9-inch tube pan. • Sift the flour, baking powder, baking soda, and salt into a medium bowl. • Beat the butter, sugar, and citrus zest in a large bowl with an electric mixer at medium speed until creamy. • Add the eggs, one at a time, until just blended after each addition. • With mixer at low speed, gradually beat in the dry ingredients, alternating with the sour cream. • Spoon the batter into the prepared pan. • Bake for 35–45 minutes, or until golden and a toothpick inserted into the center comes out clean. • Cool the cake in the pan for 5 minutes. Turn out onto a rack to cool completely. • *Citrus Frosting*: With a mixer at high speed, beat the butter and citrus zest in a medium bowl until creamy. Gradually beat in the confectioners' sugar and enough citrus juice to make a spreadable frosting. • Spread the top and sides of the cake with the frosting.

Makes one 9-inch cake · Prep: 25 min. · Cooking: 35–45 min. · Level: 1 · Keeps: 2–3 days

LEMON SOUR CREAM CAKE

- 2 cups all-purpose flour
- 1½ teaspoons baking powder
- ¼ teaspoon salt
- 1 cup (2 sticks) butter, softened
- 2 cups granulated sugar
- 2 tablespoons grated lemon zest
- 6 large eggs, at room temperature
- ¾ cup sour cream
- ¼ cup confectioners' sugar, to dust

Preheat the oven to 325°F. • Butter a 13 x 9-inch baking pan. • Sift the flour, baking powder, and salt into a medium bowl. • Beat the butter, sugar, and lemon zest in a large bowl with an electric mixer at medium speed until creamy. • Add the eggs, one at a time, until just blended after each addition. • With mixer at low speed, gradually beat in the dry ingredients, alternating with the sour cream. • Spoon the batter into the prepared pan. • Bake for 40–50 minutes, or until a toothpick inserted into the center comes out clean. • Cool the cake completely in the pan on a rack. • Dust with the confectioners' sugar.

Makes one 13 x 9-inch cake · Prep: 20 min. · Cooking: 40–50 min. · Level: 1 · Keeps: 4–5 days

FROSTED LEMON BUTTER CAKE

- 2 cups all-purpose flour
- 2 teaspoons baking powder
- ¼ teaspoon salt
- ½ cup (1 stick) butter, softened
- 1 cup granulated sugar
- 1 tablespoon grated lemon zest
- 1 teaspoon lemon extract
- ½ teaspoon vanilla extract
- 3 large eggs, at room temperature
- 2 tablespoons milk

FROSTING

- 1½ cups confectioners' sugar
- 2 tablespoons butter, melted
- 1 teaspoon lemon extract
- 1–2 tablespoons fresh lemon juice

Preheat the oven to 350°F. • Butter and flour a 9-inch ring pan or savarin mold. • Sift the flour, baking powder, and salt into a medium bowl. • Beat the butter, sugar, lemon zest, lemon extract, and vanilla in a large bowl with an electric mixer at medium speed until creamy. • Add the eggs, one at a time, until just blended after each addition. • With mixer at low speed, gradually beat in the dry ingredients, alternating with the milk. • Spoon the batter into the prepared pan. • Bake for 40–50 minutes, or until a toothpick inserted into the center comes out clean. • Cool the cake in the pan for 10 minutes. Turn out onto a rack to cool completely. • *Lemon Frosting*: Mix the confectioners' sugar, butter, and lemon extract in a medium bowl. Beat in enough of the lemon juice to make a spreadable frosting. Spread the top of the cake with the frosting.

Makes one 9-inch cake · Prep: 20 min. · Cooking: 40–50 min. · Level: 1 · Keeps: 3–4 days

Frosted lemon butter cake

• Add the eggs, one at a time, until just blended after each addition. • With mixer at low speed, gradually beat in the dry ingredients, lime zest and juice, and milk. • Spoon the batter into the prepared pan. • Bake for 25–30 minutes, or until a toothpick inserted into the center comes out clean. • Cool the cake in the pan for 10 minutes. Turn out onto a rack to cool completely. • Dust with the confectioners' sugar.

Makes one 8-inch cake · Prep: 20 min. · Cooking: 25–30 min. · Level: 1 · Keeps: 3–4 days

LIME AND HONEY SYRUP CAKE

This cake should be served while still warm. It is delicious served with softly whipped cream.

- 2¹/₂ cups cake flour
- ³/₄ cup shredded coconut
- ¹/₄ cup almonds, finely ground
- 2 teaspoons baking powder
- ¹/₄ teaspoon salt
- 1 cup (2 sticks) butter, softened
- 1 cup granulated sugar
- 1 tablespoon grated lime zest
- 3 large eggs, at room temperature
- ³/₄ cup plain yogurt
- 2 tablespoons fresh lime juice

LIME AND HONEY SYRUP

- 2 limes
- ¹/₂ cup cold water
- ¹/₄ cup honey
- 4 cardamom pods, smashed with flat side of chef's knife

Preheat the oven to 350°F. • Butter and flour a 9-inch Bundt pan. • Stir together the flour, coconut, almonds, baking powder, and salt in a large bowl. • Beat the butter, sugar, and lime zest in a large bowl with an electric mixer at medium speed until creamy. • Add the eggs, one at a time, until just blended after each addition. • With mixer at low speed, gradually beat in the dry ingredients, alternating with the yogurt and lime juice. • Spoon the batter into the prepared pan. • Bake for 45–55 minutes, or until a toothpick inserted into the center comes out clean. • Cool in the pan for 10 minutes. Turn out onto a rack. Place the cake on the rack in a jelly-roll pan. • *Lime and Honey Syrup*: Peel the limes and slice the zest into thin strips. Squeeze the juice from the limes and place it in a small saucepan with the zest, water, honey, and cardamom pods. Bring to a boil over low heat and simmer for 5 minutes. Scoop out the cardamom. Poke

Lime and honey syrup cake

EASY MOIST LEMON CAKE

To make an easy variation of this cake, replace the lemon juice and zest with equal amounts of lime or orange.

- 1¹/₂ cups all-purpose flour
- ²/₃ cup granulated sugar
- 3 large eggs, at room temperature
- ¹/₂ cup (1 stick) butter, softened
- ¹/₃ cup milk
- 1 tablespoon grated lemon zest
- 1¹/₂ teaspoons baking powder
- ¹/₄ teaspoon salt

LEMON FROSTING

- 1¹/₂ cups confectioners' sugar
- 2 tablespoons butter, melted
- 2 tablespoons (approx.) fresh lemon juice
- 2 tablespoons shredded coconut (optional)

Preheat the oven to 350°F. • Butter a 9-inch square pan. • Beat the flour, sugar, eggs, butter, milk, lemon zest, baking powder, and salt in a large bowl with an electric mixer at low speed until well blended. Increase the mixer speed to medium and beat for 5 minutes more, or until pale and thick. • Spoon the batter into the prepared pan. • Bake for 40–45 minutes, or until a

toothpick inserted into the center comes out clean. • Cool the cake completely in the pan on a rack. • *Lemon Frosting*: With a wooden spoon, beat the confectioners' sugar and butter in a medium bowl. Beat in enough lemon juice to make a spreadable frosting. • Spread the cake with the frosting, and sprinkle with the coconut, if desired.

Makes one 9-inch cake · Prep: 10 min. · Cooking: 40–45 min. · Level: 1 · Keeps: 2–3 days

TANGY FRESH LIME CAKE

- 1¹/₃ cups all-purpose flour
- 1¹/₂ teaspoons baking powder
- ¹/₄ teaspoon salt
- ¹/₂ cup (1 stick) butter, softened
- ¹/₂ cup granulated sugar
- 3 large eggs, at room temperature
- 2 tablespoons grated lime zest
- 1 tablespoon fresh lime juice
- 1 tablespoon milk
- ¹/₄ cup confectioners' sugar, to dust

Preheat the oven to 350°F. • Butter and flour an 8-inch tube pan. • Sift the flour, baking powder, and salt into a medium bowl. • Beat the butter and sugar in a large bowl with an electric mixer at medium speed until creamy.

holes in the cake with a skewer. • Pour the syrup over the hot cake. Scoop up any syrup from the pan and drizzle over the cake.

Makes one 9-inch cake · Prep: 30 min. · Cooking: 45–55 min. · Level: 2 · Keeps: 1–2 days

ORANGE BUTTER CAKE WITH ALMOND-HONEY TOPPING

- 2 cups all-purpose flour
- 2 teaspoons baking powder
- $1/2$ teaspoon salt
- 1 cup (2 sticks) butter, softened
- $3/4$ cup granulated sugar
- 2 tablespoons grated orange zest
- 3 large eggs, at room temperature

ALMOND-HONEY TOPPING
- $1/4$ cup honey
- 1 cup chopped mixed candied citrus peel
- $1/2$ cup slivered almonds
- 1 teaspoon ground ginger

Preheat the oven to 375°F. • Butter a 9-inch square baking pan. • Sift the flour, baking powder, and salt into a large bowl. • Beat the butter, sugar, and orange zest in a large bowl with an electric mixer at medium speed until creamy. • Add the eggs, one at a time, until just blended after each addition. • With mixer at low speed, beat in the dry ingredients. • Spoon the batter into the prepared pan. • Bake for 30–40 minutes, or until the edges are browned and a toothpick inserted into the center comes out clean. • Cool the cake completely in the pan on a rack. • *Almond-Honey Topping*: Warm the honey in a medium saucepan over medium heat. Stir in the candied peel, almonds, and ginger. Spread the top of the cake with the topping. Cool before serving.

Makes one 9-inch cake · Prep: 20 min. · Cooking: 30–40 min. · Level: 1 · Keeps: 2–3 days

HOT MILK HONEY CAKE

- 2 cups all-purpose flour
- 2 teaspoons baking powder
- $1/4$ teaspoon salt
- 4 large eggs
- $3/4$ cup granulated sugar
- 1 cup honey, warmed
- 1 teaspoon vanilla extract
- 1 cup milk
- $1/4$ cup ($1/2$ stick) butter
- $1/4$ cup confectioners' sugar, to dust

Preheat the oven to 350°F. • Butter and flour a 9-inch springform pan. • Sift the flour, baking powder, and salt into a large bowl. • Beat the eggs, sugar, honey, and vanilla in a

Almond torte

large bowl with an electric mixer at high speed until creamy. • Bring the milk and butter to a boil in a small saucepan over medium heat. • With mixer at low speed, gradually beat in the dry ingredients, alternating with the hot milk mixture. • Spoon the batter into the prepared pan. • Bake for 30–40 minutes, or until a toothpick inserted into the center comes out clean. • Cool the cake in the pan for 10 minutes. Turn out onto a rack. Loosen and remove the pan sides. Remove the pan bottom and let cool completely. • Dust with the confectioners' sugar.

Makes one 9-inch cake · Prep: 20 min. · Cooking: 30–40 min. · Level: 1 · Keeps: 3–4 days

ALMOND TORTE

This torte is even more delicious served with a Raspberry Puree (see page 350).

- $1^1/3$ cups all-purpose flour
- $1^1/2$ teaspoons baking powder
- $1/4$ teaspoon salt
- $1/2$ cup (1 stick) butter, softened
- $3/4$ cup granulated sugar
- 1 package (7 oz) almond paste
- 4 large eggs, at room temperature
- $1/2$ teaspoon almond extract
- 1 cup heavy cream
- 2 tablespoons confectioners' sugar

Preheat the oven to 350°F. • Butter a 9-inch round cake pan. Line with waxed paper. Butter the paper. • Sift the flour, baking powder, and salt into a large bowl. • Beat the butter, sugar, and almond paste in a large bowl with an electric mixer at medium speed until creamy. • Add the eggs, one at a time, until just blended after each addition. • With mixer at low speed, gradually beat in the dry ingredients and almond extract. • Spoon the batter into the prepared pan. • Bake for 45–55 minutes, or until a toothpick inserted into the center comes out clean. • Cool the cake in the pan for 15 minutes. Turn out onto a rack. Carefully remove the paper and let cool completely. • With mixer at high speed, beat the cream and confectioners' sugar in a medium bowl until stiff. Spoon the cream over the top of the cake.

Makes one 9-inch cake · Prep: 25 min. · Cooking: 45–55 min. · Level: 1 · Keeps: 2–3 days

ALMOND BUTTER CAKE

- 3 cups all-purpose flour
- 1 tablespoon baking powder
- 1/4 teaspoon salt
- 3/4 cup (1 1/2 sticks) butter, softened
- 1 1/2 cups granulated sugar
- 1 teaspoon almond extract
- 3 large eggs, at room temperature
- 1/2 cup almonds, finely chopped
- 1/2 cup raisins
- 1 cup milk
- 1 cup Mock Cream (see page 344)
- 1/4 cup confectioners' sugar, to dust

Preheat the oven to 375°F. • Butter two 9-inch round cake pans. Line with waxed paper. Butter the paper. • Sift the flour, baking powder, and salt into a large bowl. • Beat the butter, sugar, and almond extract in a large bowl with an electric mixer at medium speed until creamy. • Add the eggs, one at a time, until just blended after each addition. • With mixer at low speed, beat in the almonds and raisins, then the dry ingredients, alternating with the milk. • Spoon half the batter into each of the prepared pans. • Bake for 25–30 minutes, or until golden and a toothpick inserted into the centers comes out clean. • Cool the cakes in the pans for 5 minutes. Turn out onto racks. Carefully remove the paper and let cool completely. • Place one cake on a serving plate and spread with Mock Cream. Place the other cake on top and dust with the confectioners' sugar.

Makes one 9-inch cake · Prep: 20 min. · Cooking: 25–30 min. · Level: 1 · Keeps: 1–2 days

HAZELNUT BUTTER CAKE

- 2 1/4 cups cake flour
- 1/2 cup hazelnuts, finely ground
- 2 1/2 teaspoons baking powder
- 1/4 teaspoon salt
- 1 1/2 cups (3 sticks) butter, softened
- 1 1/2 cups granulated sugar
- 1 teaspoon vanilla extract
- 6 large eggs, at room temperature
- 1/4 cup confectioners' sugar, to dust

Preheat the oven to 350°F. • Butter a 9 x 13-inch baking pan. • Stir together the flour, hazelnuts, baking powder, and salt in a large bowl. • Beat the butter, sugar, and vanilla in a large bowl with an electric mixer at medium speed until creamy. • Add the eggs, one at a time, until just blended after each addition. • With mixer at low speed,

gradually beat in the dry ingredients. • Spoon the batter into the prepared pan. • Bake for 60–70 minutes, or until a toothpick inserted into the center comes out clean. • Cool the cake in the pan on a rack. • Dust with the confectioners' sugar.

Makes one 9 x 13-inch cake · Prep: 15 min. · Cooking: 60–70 min. · Level: 1 · Keeps: 2–3 days

RICH BUTTER CAKE WITH HAZELNUT FROSTING

- 2 1/3 cups all-purpose flour
- 1 cup cornstarch
- 1 tablespoon baking powder
- 1/4 teaspoon salt
- 1 cup (2 sticks) unsalted butter, softened
- 1 cup granulated sugar
- 1 tablespoon grated orange zest
- 1 tablespoon grated lemon zest
- 1 teaspoon vanilla extract
- 5 large eggs, at room temperature
- 1/2 cup milk

HAZELNUT FROSTING

- 1 package (8 oz) cream cheese, softened
- 1/2 cup granulated sugar
- 2 teaspoons hazelnut oil
- 1 1/2 teaspoons rum
- 1 teaspoon vanilla extract
- 3/4 cup heavy cream
- 10 whole hazelnuts, to decorate

Preheat the oven to 350°F. • Butter and flour a 10-inch springform pan. • Stir together the flour, cornstarch, baking powder, and salt in a large bowl. • Beat the butter, sugar, orange and lemon zests and vanilla in a large bowl with an electric mixer at medium speed until

Rich butter cake with hazelnut frosting

creamy. • Add the eggs, one at a time, until just blended after each addition. • With mixer at low speed, gradually beat in the dry ingredients, alternating with the milk. • Spoon the batter into the prepared pan. • Bake for 50–60 minutes, or until a toothpick inserted into the center comes out clean. • Cool the cake in the pan on a rack for 15 minutes. Loosen and remove the pan sides. Invert the cake onto the rack. Remove the pan bottom and let cool completely. • *Hazelnut Frosting*: With mixer at medium speed, beat the cream cheese and sugar in a large bowl until smooth. • Beat in the hazelnut oil, rum, and vanilla. • With mixer at high speed, beat the cream in a medium bowl until thick. Use a large rubber spatula to fold it into the cream cheese mixture. • Split the cake horizontally. Place one layer on a serving plate and spread with 1/3 of the frosting. Top with the remaining layer. Spread the top and sides with 1/3 of the frosting. Spoon the remaining frosting into a pastry bag. Pipe a crisscross pattern over the cake. Decorate with the hazelnuts.

Makes one 10-inch cake · Prep: 40 min. · Cooking: 50–60 min. · Level: 2 · Keeps: 1–2 days

CANADIAN UPSIDE-DOWN CAKE

- 1 cup all-purpose flour
- 2 teaspoons baking powder
- 1/2 teaspoon ground cinnamon
- 1/4 teaspoon salt
- 2 tablespoons butter, softened

- ¹/₄ cup granulated sugar
- 1 large egg, at room temperature
- ¹/₂ cup milk
- 1 cup pure maple syrup
- ¹/₂ cup walnuts, finely chopped

Preheat the oven to 350°F. • Butter a 9-inch square baking pan. • Sift the flour, baking powder, cinnamon, and salt into a medium bowl. • Beat the butter, sugar, and egg in a large bowl with an electric mixer at medium speed until creamy. • With mixer at low speed, gradually beat in the dry ingredients, alternating with the milk. • Bring the maple syrup to a boil in a small saucepan over medium-low heat. Stir in the walnuts and remove from the heat. • Pour the walnut syrup into the prepared pan. Spoon large dollops of the batter over the top. Use a thin metal spatula to spread the batter; it will soften with the heat of the syrup. • Bake for 25–35 minutes, or until a toothpick inserted into the center comes out clean. • Cool the cake in the pan for 10 minutes. Turn out onto a serving plate. Serve warm.

Makes one 9-inch square cake · Prep: 30 min. · Cooking: 25–35 min. · Level: 1 · Keeps: 2–3 days

QUICK MIX BREAKFAST CAKE

- 2 cups all-purpose flour
- 2 cups granulated sugar
- 1 tablespoon baking powder
- ¹/₄ teaspoon salt
- ¹/₂ cup (1 stick) butter, melted
- 1 large ripe banana, peeled and mashed
- 1 cup plain yogurt
- 2 large eggs, separated
- 2 teaspoons vanilla extract
- ¹/₂ teaspoon almond extract

NUT FILLING

- ¹/₂ cup granulated sugar
- 1 tablespoon ground cinnamon
- 1 cup mixed nuts, chopped

Preheat the oven to 350°F. • Butter and flour a 10-inch tube pan. • Stir together the flour, 1¹/₂ cups of the sugar, baking powder, and salt in a large bowl. • With an electric mixer at medium speed, beat in the butter, banana, yogurt, egg yolks, vanilla, and almond extract. • With mixer at medium speed, beat the egg whites in a large bowl until frothy. With mixer at high speed, gradually beat in the remaining sugar, beating until stiff, glossy peaks form. Use a large rubber spatula to fold the beaten whites into the batter. • Spoon half the batter into the prepared pan. • *Nut Filling*: Mix the sugar, cinnamon, and nuts in a bowl. Sprinkle half the filling mixture over the batter in the pan. Spoon the remaining batter over the top and sprinkle with the remaining filling. • Bake for 55–65 minutes, or until a toothpick inserted into the center comes out clean. • Cool the cake in the pan for 15 minutes. Carefully turn out, turn topping-side up, and serve warm.

Makes one 10-inch tube cake · Prep: 30 min. · Cooking: 55–65 min. · Level: 1 · Keeps: 2–3 days

RISE AND SHINE BREAKFAST CAKE

- 1 cup whole-wheat flour
- 1 cup all-purpose flour
- 1 teaspoon baking powder
- ¹/₂ teaspoon baking soda
- 1 teaspoon ground cinnamon
- 1 teaspoon ground ginger
- ¹/₄ teaspoon salt
- ¹/₂ cup (1 stick) butter, softened
- ³/₄ cup firmly packed brown sugar
- 1 tablespoon grated orange zest
- 2 large eggs, at room temperature
- 1 cup plain yogurt
- 1 tablespoon fresh orange juice
- 2 cups chopped fresh peaches, nectarines, or apricots

TOPPING

- ¹/₃ cup all-purpose flour
- ¹/₄ cup firmly packed brown sugar
- 2 tablespoons butter, melted
- 1 tablespoon wheat germ
- 1 tablespoon grated orange zest
- 1 teaspoon ground cinnamon
- 1 teaspoon ground ginger

Preheat the oven to 350°F. • Butter and flour a 10-inch tube pan. • Sift both flours, baking powder, baking soda, cinnamon, ginger, and salt into a large bowl. • Beat the butter, brown sugar, and orange zest in a large bowl with an electric mixer at medium speed until creamy. • Add the eggs, one at a time, until just blended after each addition. • With mixer at low speed, gradually beat in the dry ingredients, alternating with the yogurt and orange juice. Stir in the fruit. • Spoon the batter into the prepared pan. • *Topping*: Stir all the ingredients in a medium bowl until crumbly. Sprinkle over the batter. • Bake for 55–60 minutes, or until a toothpick inserted into the center comes out clean. • Cool the cake completely in the pan on a rack. Carefully turn out of the pan and serve topping-side up.

Makes one 10-inch cake · Prep: 25 min. · Cooking: 55–60 min. · Level: 1 · Keeps: 1–2 days

BANANA CRUNCH BREAKFAST CAKE

TOPPING

- ¹/₂ cup all-purpose flour
- ¹/₂ cup firmly packed brown sugar
- 1 teaspoon ground cinnamon
- ¹/₂ teaspoon ground nutmeg
- ¹/₄ cup (¹/₂ stick) cold butter, cut up
- ¹/₂ cup almonds, coarsely chopped

CAKE

- 2 cups all-purpose flour
- 1 teaspoon baking soda
- ¹/₂ teaspoon baking powder
- ¹/₄ teaspoon salt
- ¹/₂ cup (1 stick) butter, softened
- ³/₄ cup granulated sugar
- 1 tablespoon grated orange zest
- 1 teaspoon vanilla extract
- 2 large eggs, at room temperature
- 2 large very ripe bananas, peeled and mashed
- 2 tablespoons sour cream
- ¹/₂ cup raisins

Preheat the oven to 350°F. • Butter and flour a 9-inch tube pan. • *Topping*: Stir the flour, brown sugar, cinnamon, and nutmeg in a medium bowl. Use a pastry blender to cut in the butter until the mixture resembles fine crumbs. Stir in the almonds. • *Cake*: Stir together the flour, baking soda, baking powder, and salt in a large bowl. • Beat the butter, sugar, orange zest, and vanilla in a large bowl with an electric mixer at medium speed until creamy. • Add the eggs, one at a time, until just blended after each addition. • With mixer at low speed, beat in the bananas and sour cream. Gradually beat in the dry ingredients and raisins. • Spoon the batter into the prepared pan. Sprinkle with the topping. • Bake for 25–30 minutes, or until the topping is golden brown and a toothpick inserted into the center comes out clean. • Cool the cake completely in the pan on a rack. Serve warm or at room temperature.

Makes one 9-inch cake · Prep: 25–30 min. · Cooking: 25–30 min. · Level: 1 · Keeps: 2–3 days

CINNAMON SPICE BREAKFAST CAKE

A serious breakfast cake — not too sweet, with a pleasing biscuit-like texture and spicy sugar topping.

- 2 cups all-purpose flour
- 1/3 cup firmly packed brown sugar
- 1 tablespoon baking powder
- 1/2 teaspoon salt
- 1/4 cup (1/2 stick) cold butter, cut up
- 1/2 cup milk
- 1 large egg, lightly beaten
- 1/2 cup raisins

TOPPING

- 1/4 cup granulated sugar
- 1 teaspoon ground cinnamon
- 1 teaspoon ground pumpkin pie spice
- 1 teaspoon ground ginger
- 3 tablespoons butter, melted

Preheat the oven to 375°F. • Butter and flour a 9-inch square baking pan. • Stir together the flour, brown sugar, baking powder, and salt in a large bowl. Use a pastry blender to cut in the butter until the mixture resembles fine crumbs. Stir in the milk and egg, then the raisins. The batter will be sticky and thick, like a cookie dough. • Spread the batter in the prepared pan. • *Topping*: Mix the sugar, cinnamon, pumpkin pie spice, and ginger in a small bowl. Sprinkle over the batter. Drizzle with the butter. • Bake for 30–40 minutes, or until a toothpick inserted into the center comes out clean. • Cool the cake completely in the pan on a rack.

Makes one 9-inch cake · Prep: 15 min. · Cooking: 30–40 min. · Level: 1 · Keeps: 2–3 days

CINNAMON TEA CAKE

- 1 cup all-purpose flour
- 1 teaspoon baking powder
- 1/4 teaspoon salt
- 1/4 cup (1/2 stick) butter, softened
- 1/2 cup granulated sugar
- 1 large egg, at room temperature
- 1 teaspoon vanilla extract
- 1/3 cup milk
- 2 tablespoons butter, melted
- 2 tablespoons granulated sugar
- 1 teaspoon ground cinnamon

Preheat the oven to 350°F. • Butter a 9-inch round cake pan. Line with waxed paper. Butter the paper. • Sift the flour, baking powder, and salt into a medium bowl. • Beat the butter and sugar in a large bowl with an electric mixer at medium speed until creamy. • Add the egg and vanilla, beating until just blended. • With mixer at low speed, gradually beat in the dry ingredients, alternating with the milk. • Spoon the batter into the prepared pan. • Bake for 20–30 minutes, or until pale golden brown and a toothpick inserted into the center comes out clean. • Cool in the pan for 10 minutes. Turn out onto the rack. Carefully remove the paper and turn the cake top-side up. • Brush with the butter and sprinkle with the sugar and cinnamon. Serve warm.

Makes one 9-inch cake · Prep: 15 min. · Cooking: 20–30 min. · Level: 1 · Keeps: 2–3 days

LEMON AND CINNAMON TEA CAKE

- 1 cup all-purpose flour
- 1 teaspoon baking powder
- 1/4 teaspoon salt
- 1/4 cup (1/2 stick) butter, softened
- 1 cup granulated sugar
- 2 tablespoons grated lemon zest
- 1 large egg, at room temperature
- 1/3 cup milk

SUGAR-CINNAMON TOPPING

- 4 tablespoons granulated sugar
- 2 teaspoons ground cinnamon
- 1 tablespoon butter, melted

Preheat the oven to 350°F. • Butter a 9-inch round cake pan. Line with waxed paper. Butter the paper. • Sift the flour, baking powder, and salt into a medium bowl. • Beat the butter, sugar, and lemon zest in a large bowl with an electric mixer at medium speed until creamy. Add the egg, beating until just blended. • With mixer at low speed, gradually beat in the dry ingredients, alternating with the milk. • Spoon the batter into the prepared pan. • Bake for 25–30 minutes, or until a toothpick inserted into the center comes out clean. • Turn out onto a rack. Carefully remove the paper, then turn top-side up. *Sugar-Cinnamon Topping*: Stir together the sugar and cinnamon. Brush the cake with the butter and sprinkle with the cinnamon-sugar.

Makes one 9-inch cake · Prep: 10 min. · Cooking: 25–30 min. · Level: 1 · Keeps: 2–3 days

GLAZED LEMON LOAF

Potato starch, sometimes referred to as potato flour, is found in health food stores.

- 1 cup all-purpose flour
- 1 cup potato starch
- 1/2 teaspoon baking powder
- 1/4 teaspoon salt
- 1 cup (2 sticks) butter, softened
- 2 tablespoons grated lemon zest
- 1 1/4 cups granulated sugar
- 4 large eggs, at room temperature
- 3/4 cup Lemon Glaze (see page 348)

Preheat the oven to 350°F. • Butter a 9 x 5-inch loaf pan. Line with waxed paper. Butter the paper. • Sift the flour, potato starch, baking powder, and salt into a medium bowl. • Beat the butter, sugar, and lemon zest in a large bowl with an electric mixer at medium speed until creamy. • Add the eggs, one at a time, until just blended after each addition. • With mixer at low speed, gradually beat in the dry ingredients. • Spoon the batter into the prepared pan. • Bake for 50–60 minutes, or until a toothpick inserted into the center comes out clean. • Cool the cake in the pan for 15 minutes. Turn out onto a rack. Carefully remove the paper. Drizzle the glaze over the cake while it is still warm.

Makes one 9 x 5-inch cake · Prep: 15 min. · Cooking: 50–60 min. · Level: 1 · Keeps: 2–3 days

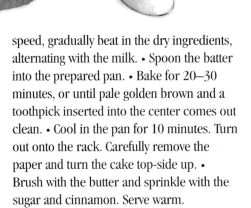

Glazed lemon loaf

HUNGARIAN TEA CAKE

2½ cups all-purpose flour
1 teaspoon ground cinnamon
1 teaspoon ground ginger
1 teaspoon ground nutmeg
¼ teaspoon salt
⅔ cup granulated sugar
⅔ cup firmly packed brown sugar
½ cup walnuts, coarsely chopped
⅔ cup cold butter, cut up
2 large eggs, at room temperature
⅔ cup milk
1 teaspoon baking powder
1 teaspoon baking soda
1 teaspoon vanilla extract

Preheat the oven to 350°F. • Butter a 13 x 9-inch baking pan. • Sift the flour, cinnamon, ginger, nutmeg, and salt into a large bowl. Stir in both sugars and the walnuts. Use a pastry blender to cut in the butter. Remove ⅔ cup of the mixture and set aside. • Beat the eggs, milk, baking powder, baking soda, and vanilla into the dry ingredients with an electric mixer at low speed. • Spoon the batter into the prepared pan. Sprinkle with the reserved topping. • Bake for 30–35 minutes, or until a toothpick inserted into the center comes out clean. • Cool the cake completely in the pan on a rack.

Makes one 13 x 9-inch cake · Prep: 15 min. · Cooking: 30–35 min. · Level: 1 · Keeps: 3 days

ITALIAN TEA CAKE

This plain, slightly dry cake is excellent served at tea with a dusting of confectioners' sugar. It is also very good for dessert with Zabaglione (see page 348).

⅔ cup all-purpose flour
⅔ cup cornstarch
1½ teaspoons baking powder
4 large eggs, at room temperature
1 cup confectioners' sugar
2 tablespoons grated lemon zest
¼ teaspoon salt
⅓ cup extra-virgin olive oil

Preheat the oven to 350°F. • Butter and flour a 9-inch springform pan. • Stir together the flour, cornstarch, and baking powder in a medium bowl. • Beat the eggs, confectioners' sugar, lemon zest, and salt in a large heatproof bowl. Fit the bowl into a saucepan of barely simmering water over low heat. (Bottom of bowl should not touch the water.) Beat constantly until the sugar has dissolved, and the mixture registers 110°–120°F on an instant-read thermometer. Remove from the heat. • Continue beating with an electric mixer at high speed until cooled, tripled in volume, and very thick. • Gradually sift in the dry ingredients, folding them in with a large rubber spatula. Fold in the olive oil until just blended. • Spoon the batter into the prepared pan. • Bake for 35–40 minutes, or until the cake is golden and a toothpick inserted into the center comes out clean. • Cool the cake in the pan for 10 minutes. Loosen and remove the pan sides. Invert the cake onto a rack. Remove the pan bottom and let cool completely.

Makes one 9-inch cake · Prep: 25 min. · Cooking: 35–40 min. · Level: 1 · Keeps: 2–3 days

CHERRY TEA CAKE

1⅓ cups all-purpose flour
1½ teaspoons baking powder
¼ teaspoon salt
½ cup (1 stick) butter, softened
¾ cup granulated sugar
¼ teaspoon almond extract
¼ teaspoon vanilla extract
4 large eggs, separated
⅓ cup milk
½ cup cherry preserves
2 cups Simple Almond Buttercream (see page 346)
16 candied cherries

Preheat the oven to 350°F. • Butter a 9-inch round cake pan. Line with waxed paper. Butter the paper. • Sift the flour, baking powder, and salt into a large bowl. • Beat the butter, sugar, almond extract, and vanilla in a large bowl with an electric mixer at medium speed until creamy. • Add the egg yolks, one at a time, until just blended after each addition. • With mixer at low speed, gradually beat in the dry ingredients, alternating with the milk. • With mixer at high speed, beat the egg whites in a large bowl until stiff peaks form. • Use a large rubber spatula to fold the beaten whites into the batter. • Spoon the batter into the prepared pan. • Bake for 30–40 minutes, or until a toothpick inserted into the center comes out clean. • Cool the cake in the pan for 10 minutes. Turn out onto a rack. Carefully remove the paper and leave to cool completely. • Split the cake horizontally. Place one cake layer on a serving plate and spread with the cherry preserves. Cover with half the buttercream. Top with the remaining layer and spread with the remaining buttercream. • Cut the cherries in half and press them into the top of the cake.

Makes one 9-inch cake · Prep: 35 min. · Cooking 30–40 min. · Level: 1 · Keeps: 2–3 days

MOIST YOGURT COFFEE CAKE

An excellent cake with a beautiful flavor and texture, and a pretty swirl of crunch throughout.

TOPPING

1 cup pecans, coarsely chopped
½ cup granulated sugar
½ cup all-purpose flour
¼ cup (½ stick) butter, melted
2 teaspoons ground cinnamon
1 teaspoon vanilla extract

CAKE

2 cups all-purpose flour
2 teaspoons baking powder
¼ teaspoon salt
½ cup (1 stick) butter, softened
1 cup granulated sugar
2 teaspoons vanilla extract
2 large eggs, at room temperature
1 cup plain yogurt

Preheat the oven to 350°F. • Butter and flour a 9-inch square baking pan. *Topping*: Stir together the pecans, sugar, flour, butter, cinnamon, and vanilla in a medium bowl. • *Cake*: Sift the flour, baking powder, and salt into a medium bowl. • Beat the butter, sugar, and vanilla in a large bowl with an electric mixer at medium speed until creamy. • Add the eggs, one at a time, until just blended after each addition. • With mixer at low speed, beat in the dry ingredients, alternating with the yogurt. • Spoon half the batter into the prepared pan. Sprinkle with half the topping. Spoon the remaining batter over and sprinkle with the remaining topping. • Bake for 55–65 minutes, or until springy to the touch and a toothpick inserted into the center comes out clean. • Cool the cake completely in the pan on a rack. Serve warm or at room temperature.

Makes one 9-inch square cake · Prep: 25 min. · Cooking: 55–65 min. · Level: 1 · Keeps: 2–3 days

ALMOND-SOUR CREAM COFFEE CAKE

If you prefer a less pronounced almond flavor, reduce the almond extract to 1 teaspoon.

- 2 cups all-purpose flour
- 2 teaspoons baking powder
- 1 teaspoon ground cinnamon
- $^1/_4$ teaspoon salt
- 2 cups granulated sugar
- 1 cup (2 sticks) butter, softened
- 2 teaspoons almond extract
- 1 teaspoon vanilla extract
- 2 large eggs, at room temperature
- 1 cup sour cream
- $^3/_4$ cup slivered almonds

Preheat the oven to 350°F. • Butter and flour a 13 x 9-inch baking pan. • Sift the flour, baking powder, cinnamon, and salt into a medium bowl. • Beat the butter, sugar, almond extract, and vanilla in a large bowl with an electric mixer at medium speed until creamy. • Add the eggs, one at a time, until just blended after each addition. • With mixer at low speed, gradually beat in the dry ingredients, alternating with the sour cream. • Spoon the batter into the prepared pan and sprinkle with the almonds. • Bake for 45–55 minutes, or until golden brown and a toothpick inserted into the center comes out clean. • Cool the cake completely in the pan on a rack.

Makes one 13 x 9-inch cake · Prep: 20 min. · Cooking: 45–55 min. · Level: 1 · Keeps: 3–4 days

OLD-FASHIONED SOUR CREAM COFFEE CAKE

TOPPING
- $^1/_3$ cup all-purpose flour
- $^1/_4$ cup firmly packed brown sugar
- 1 teaspoon ground cinnamon
- $^1/_2$ teaspoon ground nutmeg
- $^1/_4$ cup ($^1/_2$ stick) cold butter, cut up
- $^1/_2$ cup mixed nuts, chopped

CAKE
- 2 cups all-purpose flour
- 1 teaspoon baking powder
- 1 teaspoon baking soda
- 1 teaspoon ground cinnamon
- $^1/_2$ teaspoon salt
- 1 cup (2 sticks) butter, softened
- 1 cup firmly packed brown sugar
- 2 tablespoons dark molasses
- 2 teaspoons vanilla extract
- 3 large eggs, at room temperature
- 1 cup sour cream

Preheat the oven to 325°F. • Butter and flour a 13 x 9-inch baking pan. • *Topping*: Stir the flour, brown sugar, cinnamon, and

nutmeg in a medium bowl. Use a pastry blender to cut in the butter until the mixture resembles fine crumbs. Stir in the nuts. • *Cake*: Sift the flour, baking powder, baking soda, cinnamon, and salt into a large bowl. • Beat the butter, brown sugar, molasses, and vanilla in a large bowl with an electric mixer at medium speed until creamy. • Add the eggs, one at a time, until just blended after each addition. • With mixer at low speed, gradually beat in the dry ingredients, alternating with the sour cream. • Spoon the batter into the prepared pan. Sprinkle with the topping. • Bake for 50–60 minutes, or until a toothpick inserted into the center comes out clean. • Cool the cake completely in the pan on a rack.

Makes one 13 x 9-inch cake · Prep: 15 min. · Cooking: 50–60 min. · Level: 1 · Keeps: 3–4 days

CINNAMON COFFEE CAKE

The cinnamon punch is found in the topping.

- 1 cup all-purpose flour
- $^1/_2$ cup whole-wheat flour
- 1 cup firmly packed brown sugar
- 2 teaspoons baking powder
- 1 teaspoon baking soda
- $^1/_4$ teaspoon salt
- 1 cup buttermilk
- 1 large egg, at room temperature
- 2 tablespoons vegetable oil
- 2 teaspoons vanilla extract

TOPPING
- $^1/_2$ cup firmly packed brown sugar
- 1 tablespoon ground cinnamon
- 1 tablespoon butter, melted

Preheat the oven to 350°F. • Butter and flour a 9-inch square baking pan. • Stir together the flours, brown sugar, baking powder, baking soda, and salt in a large bowl, crumbling any lumps of sugar. • Beat in the buttermilk, egg, oil, and vanilla. Spoon the batter into the prepared pan. • *Topping*: Stir the brown sugar, cinnamon, and butter in a small bowl. Sprinkle over the batter. • Bake for 40–50 minutes, or until a toothpick inserted into the center comes out clean. • Cool the cake completely in the pan on a rack.

Makes one 9-inch cake · Prep: 15 min. · Cooking: 40–50 min. · Level: 1 · Keeps: 3–4 days

WALNUT CRUNCH COFFEE CAKE

CRUNCH
- $^3/_4$ cup firmly packed brown sugar
- $^1/_3$ cup all-purpose flour
- $^1/_4$ cup ($^1/_2$ stick) cold butter, cut up
- $^3/_4$ cup walnuts, coarsely chopped

CAKE
- 2 cups all-purpose flour
- 2 teaspoons baking powder
- 1 teaspoon nutmeg
- $^1/_4$ teaspoon salt
- $^1/_2$ cup (1 stick) butter, softened
- $^3/_4$ cup firmly packed brown sugar
- 1 teaspoon vanilla extract
- 4 large eggs, at room temperature
- $^3/_4$ cup buttermilk

Preheat the oven to 350°F. • Butter and flour a 9-inch Bundt pan. • *Crunch*: Stir

Walnut crunch coffee cake

the brown sugar and flour in a medium bowl. Use a pastry blender to cut in the butter until the mixture resembles fine crumbs. Stir in the walnuts. • *Cake*: Stir together the flour, baking powder, nutmeg, and salt in a medium bowl. • Beat the butter, brown sugar, and vanilla in a large bowl with an electric mixer at medium speed until creamy. • Add the eggs, one at a time, until just blended after each addition. • With mixer at low speed, gradually beat in the dry ingredients, alternating with the buttermilk. • Spoon half the batter into the prepared pan. Sprinkle with half the topping. Spoon the remaining batter over and sprinkle with the remaining topping. • Bake for 50–60 minutes, or until the topping is golden brown. • Cool the cake in the pan on a rack. Carefully turn out, turn topping-side up, and serve warm.

Makes one 9-inch cake · Prep: 20 min. · Cooking: 50–60 min. · Level: 1 · Keeps: 2–3 days

CRUNCHY CHOCOLATE CHIP COFFEE CAKE

TOPPING
- $^1/_2$ cup firmly packed brown sugar
- $^1/_2$ cup all-purpose flour
- $^1/_4$ cup ($^1/_2$ stick) cold butter, cut up
- 1 cup semisweet chocolate chips
- $^1/_2$ cup walnuts, coarsely chopped

CAKE
- $2^1/_2$ cups all-purpose flour
- 2 teaspoons baking powder
- $^1/_2$ teaspoon baking soda
- $^1/_4$ teaspoon salt
- $^3/_4$ cup ($1^1/_2$ sticks) butter, softened
- 1 package (8 oz) cream cheese, softened
- $1^1/_2$ cups granulated sugar
- 1 teaspoon vanilla extract
- 3 large eggs, at room temperature
- $^3/_4$ cup milk

Preheat the oven to 350°F. • Butter and flour a 13 x 9-inch baking pan. • *Topping*: Stir the sugar and flour in a medium bowl. Use a pastry blender to cut in the butter until the mixture resembles fine crumbs. Stir in the chocolate chips and walnuts. • *Cake*: Stir together the flour, baking powder, baking soda, and salt in a large bowl. • Beat the butter, cream cheese, sugar, and vanilla in a large bowl with an electric mixer at medium speed until creamy. • Add the eggs, one at a time, until just blended after each addition. • With mixer at low speed, gradually beat in

Crunchy chocolate chip coffee cake

the dry ingredients, alternating with the milk. • Spoon the batter into the prepared pan. Sprinkle with the topping. • Bake for 50–60 minutes, or until a toothpick inserted into the center comes out clean. • Cool the cake completely in the pan on a rack.

Makes one 13 x 9-inch cake · Prep: 20 min. · Cooking: 50–60 min. · Level: 1 · Keeps: 2–3 days

TOFFEE CRUNCH COFFEE CAKE

- 2 cups all-purpose flour
- 1 cup firmly packed brown sugar
- $^1/_2$ cup granulated sugar
- $^1/_4$ teaspoon salt
- $^1/_2$ cup (1 stick) cold butter, cut up
- 1 cup buttermilk
- 1 large egg, at room temperature
- $1^1/_2$ teaspoons vanilla extract
- 1 teaspoon baking soda
- 4 oz toffee candies (Werther's Original Toffees are a good choice), crushed in a food processor to make $^1/_2$ cup
- $^1/_2$ cup walnuts, chopped

Preheat the oven to 350°F. • Butter and flour a 9-inch square baking pan. • Stir together the flour, both sugars, and salt in a large bowl. Use a pastry blender to cut in the butter until the mixture resembles fine crumbs. • Place $^3/_4$ cup of the crumb mixture into a medium bowl and set aside. • Beat the buttermilk, egg, vanilla, and baking soda into the large bowl of crumb mixture with an electric mixer at low speed until well blended. Spoon the batter into the prepared pan. • Mix the reserved crumb mixture with the toffee and walnuts. • Sprinkle the batter

with the crumb mixture. • Bake for 60–70 minutes, or until the cake is golden brown and shrinks from the pan sides. • Cool the cake completely in the pan on a rack.

Makes one 9-inch cake · Prep: 30 min. · Cooking: 60–70 min. · Level: 1 · Keeps: 2–3 days

BUTTERSCOTCH CAKE

If you don't have butterscotch flavoring on hand, replace with the same amount of vanilla extract. The brown sugar and vanilla will create a lovely, light caramel flavor.

- $1^1/_2$ cups all-purpose flour
- 1 teaspoon baking powder
- $^1/_4$ teaspoon baking soda
- $^1/_4$ teaspoon salt
- $^1/_2$ cup (1 stick) butter, softened
- $1^1/_2$ cups firmly packed brown sugar
- 1 teaspoon butterscotch flavoring or vanilla extract
- 3 large eggs, at room temperature
- $^1/_2$ cup milk
- $^1/_4$ cup confectioners' sugar, to dust

Preheat the oven to 325°F. • Butter a 9-inch square baking pan. • Sift the flour, baking powder, baking soda, and salt into a large bowl. • Beat the butter, brown sugar, and butterscotch in a large bowl with an electric mixer at medium speed until creamy. • Add the eggs, one at a time, until just blended after each addition. • With mixer at low speed, gradually beat in the dry ingredients, alternating with the milk. • Spoon the batter into the prepared pan. • Bake for 50–60 minutes, or until a toothpick inserted into the center comes out clean. • Cool in the pan on a rack. • Dust with confectioners' sugar.

Makes one 9-inch cake · Prep: 15 min. · Cooking: 50–60 min. · Level: 1 · Keeps: 3–4 days

TOFFEE SURPRISE CAKE

- 1/3 cup firmly packed brown sugar
- 2 teaspoons ground cinnamon
- 2 cups all-purpose flour
- 2 teaspoons baking powder
- 1/4 teaspoon salt
- 1/2 cup (1 stick) butter, softened
- 1 cup granulated sugar
- 1 teaspoon vanilla extract
- 2 large eggs, at room temperature
- 1 cup sour cream
- 10 oz (1 1/4 cups) Werther's Original toffee candies, crushed
- 1/4 cup walnuts, chopped
- 1/4 cup (1/2 stick) butter, melted

Preheat the oven to 325°F. • Butter and flour a 13 x 9-inch baking pan. • Stir the brown sugar and cinnamon in a small bowl. • Sift the flour, baking powder, and salt into a medium bowl. • Beat the butter, sugar, and vanilla with an electric mixer at medium speed until creamy. • Add the eggs, one at a time, until just blended after each addition. With mixer at low speed, gradually beat in the dry ingredients, alternating with the sour cream. • Spoon half the batter into the prepared pan. Sprinkle with the cinnamon and brown sugar mixture. Spoon the remaining batter over the top. Sprinkle with the toffee and walnuts. Drizzle with the butter. • Bake for 50–60 minutes, or until golden brown and caramelized. • Cool the cake completely in the pan on a rack.

Makes one 13 x 9-inch cake · Prep: 25 min. · Cooking: 50–60 min. · Level: 1 · Keeps: 2–3 days

SWEET WINE BUTTER CAKE

- 2 cups all-purpose flour
- 2 teaspoons baking powder
- 1/4 teaspoon salt
- 3/4 cup (1 1/2 sticks) butter, softened
- 1 cup granulated sugar
- 3 large eggs
- 2 tablespoons sweet dessert wine or sherry
- 1/4 cup confectioners' sugar, to dust

Preheat the oven to 350°F. • Butter a 9-inch round cake pan. Line with waxed paper. Butter the paper. • Sift the flour, baking powder, and salt into a large bowl.

• Beat the butter and sugar in a large bowl with an electric mixer at medium speed until creamy. • Add the eggs, one at a time, until just blended after each addition. • With mixer at low speed, gradually beat in the dry ingredients, alternating with the sweet wine. • Spoon the batter into the prepared pan. • Bake for 40–50 minutes, or until golden and a toothpick inserted into the center comes out clean. • Cool the cake in the pan for 10 minutes. Turn out onto a rack. Carefully remove the paper and let cool completely. • Dust with the confectioners' sugar.

Makes one 9-inch cake · Prep: 20 min. · Cooking: 40–50 min. · Level: 1 · Keeps: 3–4 days

GINGER BUTTER CAKE

- 2 cups all-purpose flour
- 2 teaspoons baking powder
- 2 teaspoons ground ginger
- 1/4 teaspoon salt
- 3/4 cup (1 1/2 sticks) butter, softened
- 3/4 cup firmly packed brown sugar
- 1 teaspoon vanilla extract
- 3 large eggs

GINGER CREAM FILLING
- 3/4 cup heavy cream
- 2 tablespoons confectioners' sugar
- 1 teaspoon ground ginger

Preheat the oven to 350°F. • Butter and flour two 8-inch round cake pans. Line with waxed paper. Butter the paper. • Sift the flour, baking powder, ginger, and salt into a large bowl. • Beat the butter, sugar, and vanilla in a large bowl with an electric mixer at high speed until creamy. • With mixer at medium speed, add the eggs, one at a time, until just blended after each addition. • With mixer at low speed, gradually beat in the dry ingredients. • Spoon half the batter into each of the prepared pans. • Bake for 25–35 minutes, or until a toothpick inserted into the center comes out clean. • Cool the cakes in the pans for 10 minutes. Turn out onto a rack. Carefully remove the paper and let cool completely. • *Ginger Cream Filling*: With mixer at high speed, beat the cream, confectioners' sugar, and ginger in a large bowl until stiff. • Place one cake on a serving plate and spread with the cream. Top with the remaining cake.

Makes one 8-inch cake · Prep: 25 min. · Cooking: 25–35 min. · Level: 1 · Keeps: 1–2 days in the refrigerator

MARBLE CAKE

This old favorite looks lovely when baked in a tube pan.

- 2 1/4 cups all-purpose flour
- 2 1/2 teaspoons baking powder
- 1/4 teaspoon salt
- 1 cup (2 sticks) butter, softened
- 1 cup granulated sugar
- 1 teaspoon vanilla extract
- 3 large eggs, at room temperature
- 3/4 cup milk
- 1/4 cup unsweetened cocoa powder
- 1/2 teaspoon red food coloring
- 1 1/2 cups Simple Chocolate Frosting (see page 349)

Preheat the oven to 350°F. • Butter and flour a 9-inch tube pan. • Sift the flour, baking powder, and salt into a large bowl. • Beat the butter, sugar, and vanilla in a large bowl with an electric mixer at high speed until creamy. • With mixer at medium speed, add the eggs, one at a time, until just combined. • With mixer at low speed, gradually beat in the dry ingredients, alternating with the milk. • Divide the batter evenly among three small bowls. Stir the cocoa into one, and red food coloring into another. Leave one bowl plain. • Drop alternate spoonfuls of the batters into the prepared pan, swirling them together with a knife to create a marbled effect. • Bake for 40–50 minutes, or until a toothpick inserted into the center comes out clean. • Cool the cake in the pan on a rack. • Spread with the frosting.

Makes one 9-inch cake · Prep: 30 min. · Cooking: 40–50 min. · Level: 1 · Keeps: 3 days

RED AND GREEN MARBLE CAKE

- 2 cups all-purpose flour
- 2 teaspoons baking powder
- 1/4 teaspoon salt
- 3/4 cup butter, softened
- 3/4 cup granulated sugar
- 1 teaspoon vanilla extract
- 3 large eggs
- 1/2 teaspoon each almond extract, red food coloring, green food coloring

Preheat the oven to 350°F. • Butter and flour a 9-inch round cake pan. • Beat the butter, sugar, and vanilla in a large bowl with an electric mixer at high speed until creamy. • With mixer at medium speed, add the eggs, one at a time, until just blended after each addition. • With mixer at low speed, gradually beat in the dry ingredients. • Divide the batter evenly among three small bowls. Stir the almond extract into one, the red food coloring into another, and the green food coloring into the third. • Drop alternate spoonfuls of the three batters into the prepared pan, swirling them together with a knife to create a marbled effect. • Bake for 40–50 minutes, or until a toothpick inserted into the center comes out clean. • Cool the cake on a rack for 10 minutes. Turn out onto the rack to cool completely.

Makes one 9-inch cake · Prep: 30 min. · Cooking: 40–50 min. · Level: 1 · Keeps: 3 days

CINNAMON MARBLE CAKE

2⅓ cups all-purpose flour
1½ teaspoons baking powder
¼ teaspoon salt
2 cups granulated sugar
2 tablespoons unsweetened cocoa powder
2 tablespoons ground cinnamon
1 cup (2 sticks) butter, softened
1 package (8 oz) cream cheese, softened
2 teaspoons vanilla extract
4 large eggs, at room temperature
¾ cup semisweet chocolate chips

Preheat the oven to 350°F. • Butter and flour a 13 x 9-inch baking pan. • Sift the flour, baking powder, and salt into a medium bowl. • Mix ½ cup sugar, cocoa, and cinnamon in a small bowl. • Beat the butter and cream cheese in a large bowl with an electric mixer at medium speed until creamy. Gradually beat in the remaining sugar and vanilla until smooth. • Add the eggs, one at a time, until just blended after each addition. • With mixer at low speed, gradually beat in the dry ingredients. • Stir in the chocolate chips. • Spread ⅔ of the batter into the prepared pan. Sprinkle with the cocoa mixture. Spoon the remaining batter on the top and run a knife through the layers to create a marbled effect. • Bake for 40–50 minutes, or until a toothpick inserted into the center comes out clean. • Cool the cake completely in the pan on a rack.

Makes one 13 x 9-inch cake · Prep: 25 min. · Cooking: 40–50 min. · Level: 1 · Keeps: 2–3 days

Marble cake

COCOA-RASPBERRY MARBLE CAKE

1²/₃ cups all-purpose flour
1¹/₂ teaspoons baking powder
¹/₄ teaspoon salt
²/₃ cup butter, softened
³/₄ cup granulated sugar
2 large eggs, at room temperature
¹/₂ cup milk
1 teaspoon vanilla extract
¹/₄ cup unsweetened cocoa powder
¹/₂ teaspoon red food coloring

COCOA-CREAM CHEESE FROSTING

2 packages (3 oz each) cream cheese, softened
1¹/₂ cups confectioners' sugar
¹/₄ cup unsweetened cocoa powder
1 tablespoon hot milk
¹/₂ cup fresh raspberries, to decorate

Cocoa-raspberry
marble cake

Preheat the oven to 350°F. • Butter an 11 x 7-inch baking pan. Line with waxed paper. Butter the paper. • Sift the flour, baking powder, and salt into a medium bowl. • Beat the butter and sugar in a large bowl with an electric mixer at medium speed until creamy. • Add the eggs, one at a time, until just blended after each addition. • With mixer at low speed, gradually beat in the dry ingredients, alternating with the milk and vanilla. • Place half the batter in a separate bowl. Stir the cocoa into one bowl and the red food coloring into the other. • Drop alternate spoonfuls of the two batters into the prepared pan, swirling them together with a knife to create a marbled effect. • Bake for 30–40 minutes, or until a toothpick inserted into the center comes out clean. • Cool the cake in the pan for 15 minutes. Turn out onto a rack. Carefully remove the paper and let cool completely. • *Cocoa-Cream Cheese Frosting*: With mixer at medium speed, beat the cream cheese and confectioners' sugar in a large bowl until creamy. Add the cocoa and milk and beat until smooth and spreadable. Spread the top and sides of the cake with the frosting. • Decorate with the raspberries.

Makes one 11 x 7-inch cake · Prep: 30 min. · Cooking: 30–40 min. · Level: 1 · Keeps: 1–2 days

BASIC COCONUT CAKE

1²/₃ cups all-purpose flour
¹/₃ cup shredded coconut
1 cup granulated sugar
²/₃ cup almonds, finely ground
1 cup buttermilk
2 large eggs, at room temperature
1 teaspoon vanilla extract

²/₃ cup butter, melted
2 teaspoons baking powder

Preheat the oven to 350°F. • Butter an 8-inch square baking pan. Line with waxed paper. Butter the paper. • Stir together the flour, coconut, sugar, and almonds in a large bowl. Make a well in the center and stir in the buttermilk, eggs, vanilla, butter, and baking powder. • Pour the batter into the prepared pan. • Bake for 45–50 minutes, or until a toothpick inserted into the center comes out clean. • Cool the cake in the pan for 10 minutes. Turn out onto a rack to cool completely.

Makes one 8-inch cake · Prep: 25 min. · Cooking: 45–50 min. · Level: 1 · Keeps: 3–4 days

CARAMEL-FILLED COCONUT CAKE

1 cup all-purpose flour
2 teaspoons baking powder
¹/₄ teaspoon salt
¹/₂ cup shredded coconut
¹/₂ cup granulated sugar
¹/₂ cup (1 stick) butter, melted

FILLING

1 can (14 oz) sweetened condensed milk
2 tablespoons light corn syrup
¹/₄ cup firmly packed dark brown sugar
¹/₄ cup (¹/₂ stick) butter, melted

TOPPING

4 large eggs, lightly beaten
²/₃ cup superfine sugar
2³/₄ cups shredded coconut

Preheat the oven to 350°F. • Butter a 10¹/₂ x 15¹/₂-inch jelly-roll pan. • Sift the flour, baking powder, and salt into a large bowl. Stir in the coconut, granulated sugar, and butter. • Spoon the batter into the prepared pan. • Bake for 10–15 minutes, or until light golden brown. • Cool in the pan on a rack for 15 minutes. • *Filling*: Stir together

the condensed milk, corn syrup, brown sugar, and butter in a large bowl. • *Topping*: Beat the eggs and superfine sugar with an electric mixer at high speed until pale and thick. Fold in the coconut. • Use a thin metal spatula to spread the filling over the cake. Sprinkle with the topping. • Bake for 25 minutes more, or until the topping is brown. Cool completely in the pan on the rack. Cut into ¹/₂-inch thick bars to serve.

Makes 12 bars · Prep: 20 min. · Cooking: 35–40 min. · Level: 1 · Keeps: 3–4 days

COCONUT CAKE WITH BROILED COCONUT TOPPING

This recipe, minus the topping, makes a good basic cake that can be turned into a trifle or layered with a fruit or cream filling.

1¹/₂ cups all-purpose flour
1¹/₂ teaspoons baking powder
¹/₄ teaspoon salt
2 large eggs, separated
1 cup granulated sugar
1 teaspoon vanilla extract
³/₄ cup unsweetened coconut milk

COCONUT TOPPING

1 cup shredded coconut
¹/₃ cup firmly packed brown sugar
3 tablespoons butter, melted

Preheat the oven to 350°F. • Butter and flour a 9-inch springform pan. • Sift the flour, baking powder, and salt into a medium bowl. • Beat the egg yolks, sugar, and vanilla in a large bowl with an electric mixer at high speed until pale and thick. • With mixer at low speed, gradually beat in the dry ingredients, alternating with the coconut milk. • With mixer at high speed, beat the egg whites in a medium bowl until stiff peaks form. Use a rubber spatula to fold them into the batter. • Spoon the batter into prepared pan. • Bake for 45–50 minutes, or until springy to the touch and a toothpick inserted into the center comes out clean. • *Coconut Topping*: Mix the coconut, brown sugar, and butter in a small bowl. Turn on the broiler. Spread the topping over the cake as soon as it comes out of the oven. Broil the cake 6 to 8 inches from the heat source for 2–3 minutes, or until the topping is bubbly and lightly browned. Cool the cake completely in the pan on a rack. Loosen and remove the pan sides to serve.

Makes one 9-inch cake · Prep: 30 min. · Cooking: 45–50 min. · Level: 1 · Keeps: 2–3 days

LIME-GLAZED COCONUT CAKE

2	cups all-purpose flour
1	teaspoon baking powder
1/2	teaspoon baking soda
1/4	teaspoon salt
1	cup (2 sticks) butter, softened
3/4	cup granulated sugar
2	tablespoons grated lime zest
5	large eggs, separated
1/4	cup fresh lime juice
1 1/2	cups shredded coconut

LIME GLAZE

2	cups confectioners' sugar
1/4	cup (1/2 stick) butter, melted
1/2	teaspoon green food coloring (optional)
2–3	tablespoons fresh lime juice

Preheat the oven to 350°F. • Butter and flour a 13 x 9-inch baking pan. • Sift the flour, baking powder, baking soda, and salt into a medium bowl. • Beat the butter, sugar, and lime zest in a large bowl with an electric mixer at medium speed until creamy. • Add the egg yolks, one at a time, until just blended after each addition. • With mixer at low speed, gradually beat in the dry ingredients, alternating with the lime juice. • With mixer at high speed, beat the egg whites in a large bowl until stiff peaks form. • Use a large rubber spatula to fold them into the batter. Fold in the coconut. • Spoon the

batter into the prepared pan. • Bake for 20–25 minutes, or until a toothpick inserted into the center comes out clean. • Cool the cake completely in the pan on a rack. • *Lime Glaze*: Mix the confectioners' sugar, and butter in a medium bowl. Beat in the food coloring, if desired, and enough lime juice to make a fairly thin glaze. Drizzle over the cake.

Makes one 13 x 9-inch cake · Prep: 30 min. · Cooking: 20–25 min. · Level: 1 · Keeps: 1–2 days

TRICOLORED CAKE

2	cups all-purpose flour
2	teaspoons baking powder
1/4	teaspoon salt
4	large eggs, at room temperature
1	cup granulated sugar
2	tablespoons butter
1	cup + 2 tablespoons milk, warmed
1	teaspoon vanilla extract
2	teaspoons red food coloring
3	tablespoons unsweetened cocoa powder
1 1/2	cups heavy cream

VANILLA GLAZE

1 1/2	cups confectioners' sugar
1/2	teaspoon vanilla extract
2–3	tablespoons boiling water

Preheat the oven to 350°F. • Butter three 8-inch round baking pans. Line with waxed paper. Butter the waxed paper. • Sift the

flour, baking powder, and salt into a large bowl. • Beat the eggs and sugar in a large bowl with an electric mixer at medium speed until pale and thick. • Melt the butter with the milk in a medium heavy-bottomed saucepan over medium heat. Stir in the vanilla. • With mixer at low speed, gradually beat in the dry ingredients, alternating with the milk. • Divide the batter evenly among three small bowls. Stir the cocoa into one and the food coloring into another. Leave one bowl plain. • Spoon each type of batter into a separate prepared pan. • Bake for 20–25 minutes, or until a toothpick inserted into the center comes out clean. • Cool the cakes in the pans for 5 minutes. Turn out onto racks. Carefully remove the paper and let cool completely. • With mixer at medium speed, beat the cream in a large bowl until stiff. • Place the plain layer of cake on a serving plate. Spread with half the cream. Top with the pink cake and spread with the remaining cream. Top with the chocolate layer. • *Vanilla Glaze*: Beat the confectioners' sugar and vanilla with enough water to make a spreadable glaze. Drizzle over the cake.

Makes 1 cake · Prep: 40 min. · Cooking: 20–25 min. · Level: 1 · Keeps: 1–2 days

Tricolored cake

BROWN SUGAR LAYER CAKE

2²/₃ cups all-purpose flour
1 teaspoon baking soda
¹/₄ teaspoon salt
1 cup (1 stick) butter, softened
2 cups granulated sugar
1 tablespoon vanilla extract
6 large eggs, at room temperature
1 cup sour cream

BROWN SUGAR FROSTING
6 tablespoons butter
1 cup firmly packed brown sugar
³/₄ cup milk
1 tablespoon vanilla extract
2 cups confectioners' sugar

Preheat the oven to 350°F. • Butter and flour three 9-inch round cake pans. • Sift the flour, baking soda, and salt into a large bowl. • Beat the butter, sugar, and vanilla in a large bowl with an electric mixer at medium speed until creamy. • Add the eggs, one at a time, until just blended after each addition. • With mixer at low speed, gradually beat in the dry ingredients, alternating with the sour cream. • Spoon ¹/₃ of the batter into each of the prepared pans. • Bake for 25–35 minutes, until golden brown and a toothpick inserted into the center comes out clean. • Cool the cakes in the pans for 15 minutes. Turn out onto racks to cool completely. • *Brown Sugar Frosting*: Melt the butter in a large saucepan over low heat. Stir in the brown sugar and milk and simmer slowly for 5 minutes, stirring constantly. Remove from the heat and stir in the vanilla. • Beat in the confectioners' sugar until smooth. Set aside to cool. • Place one cake on a serving plate and spread with some frosting. Top with another cake and spread with frosting. Top with the remaining cake. Spread the top and sides of the cake with the remaining frosting.

Makes one 9-inch cake · Prep 30 min. · Cooking: 25–35 min. · Level: 1 · Keeps: 2–3 days

CARAMEL LAYER CAKE

You'll need a candy thermometer to prepare the caramel frosting for this cake.

3 cups all-purpose flour
2 teaspoons baking powder
1 teaspoon baking soda
¹/₄ teaspoon salt
1 cup (2 sticks) butter, softened
1¹/₂ cups firmly packed brown sugar
2 teaspoons caramel or butterscotch flavoring
5 large eggs, separated
1 cup milk

CARAMEL FROSTING
2 cups firmly packed brown sugar
1¹/₄ cups milk
5 tablespoons butter, cut up

FILLING
1 cup heavy cream
2 tablespoons granulated sugar
1 teaspoon vanilla extract

Preheat the oven to 350°F. • Butter two 9-inch round cake pans. Line with waxed paper. Butter the paper. • Sift the flour, baking powder, baking soda, and salt into a large bowl. • Beat the butter, brown sugar, and caramel flavoring in a large bowl with an electric mixer at medium speed until creamy. • Add the egg yolks, one at a time, until just blended after each addition. • With mixer at low speed, gradually beat in the dry ingredients, alternating with the milk. • With mixer at high speed, beat the egg whites in a large bowl until stiff peaks form. Use a large rubber spatula to fold them into the batter. • Spoon half the batter into each of the prepared pans. • Bake for 35–45 minutes, or until golden brown and a toothpick inserted into the center comes out clean. • Cool the cakes in the pans for 15 minutes. Turn out onto racks. Carefully remove the paper and let cool completely. • *Caramel Frosting*: Bring the brown sugar and milk to a boil in a medium saucepan over medium heat, stirring constantly until the sugar has dissolved. Continue cooking, stirring occasionally, until the mixture is thick and it registers 234°–240°F on a candy thermometer. Remove from the heat. Stir in the butter and let cool until lukewarm. (If the frosting gets cold, it won't spread). • *Filling*: With mixer at high speed, beat the cream, sugar, and vanilla in a medium bowl until stiff. • Split the cakes horizontally. Place one layer on a serving plate and spread with half the cream. Top with a second layer and spread with some frosting. Top with a third layer and spread with almost all of the remaining cream. Place the remaining layer on top. Spread the top and sides with the remaining frosting. Pipe the remaining cream in rosettes around the edges of the cake.

Makes 9-inch cake · Prep: 35 min. · Cooking: 35–45 min. · Level: 2 · Keeps: 1–2 days in the refrigerator

IRISH CREAM CAKE

2 cups all-purpose flour
1¹/₂ cups granulated sugar
2 teaspoons baking powder
¹/₄ teaspoon salt
4 oz bittersweet chocolate, coarsely chopped
¹/₂ cup vegetable oil
¹/₃ cup Irish cream liqueur
¹/₃ cup water
2 tablespoons freeze-dried coffee granules
7 large eggs, separated

COFFEE FROSTING
1 tablespoon freeze-dried coffee granules dissolved in 2 tablespoons Irish cream liqueur
3 tablespoons butter, melted
2 cups confectioners' sugar

Preheat the oven to 350°F. • Butter and flour a 10-inch tube pan. • Sift the flour, sugar, baking powder, and salt into a large bowl. • Melt the chocolate with the oil, liqueur, water, and coffee granules in a double boiler over barely simmering water. • Transfer to a large bowl and beat in the egg yolks with a wooden spoon until well blended. • Add the dry ingredients and stir until smooth. • Beat the egg whites in a large bowl with an electric mixer at high speed until stiff peaks form. Use a large rubber spatula to fold them into the batter. • Spoon the batter into the prepared pan. • Bake for 30–40 minutes, or until firm to the touch and has a slightly sugary crust. • Cool the cake in the pan for 15 minutes. Turn out onto a rack to cool completely. • *Coffee Frosting*: Beat the coffee mixture and butter into the confectioners' sugar until the frosting is thick and spreadable. Spread over the top and sides of the cake.

Makes one 10-inch cake · Prep: 20 min. · Cooking: 30–40 min. · Level: 2 · Keeps: 3 days

Irish cream cake

Coffee butter cake

mixture into the confectioners' sugar in a small bowl. • Poke holes in the cake with a skewer. Drizzle over the cake.

Makes one 9-inch cake · Prep: 30 min. · Cooking: 55–65 min. · Level: 1 · Keeps: 2–3 days

COFFEE BUTTER CAKE

    2   cups all-purpose flour
    2   teaspoons baking powder
  1/4   teaspoon salt
  2/3   cup butter, softened
    1   cup firmly packed brown sugar
    1   teaspoon vanilla extract
    2   large eggs, at room temperature
    1   tablespoon freeze-dried coffee granules dissolved in
        1/2 cup milk

COFFEE-BUTTER FROSTING

  1/2   cup (1 stick) butter, softened
 1 1/2 cups confectioners' sugar
    3   tablespoons firmly packed brown sugar
    1   tablespoon freeze-dried coffee granules dissolved
        in 1 tablespoon boiling water

Preheat the oven to 350°F. • Butter and flour an 11 x 7-inch baking pan. • Sift the flour, baking powder, and salt into a large bowl. • Beat the butter, brown sugar, and vanilla in a large bowl with an electric mixer at medium speed until creamy. • Add the eggs, one at a time, until just blended after each addition. • With mixer at low speed, gradually beat in the dry ingredients, alternating with the coffee mixture. • Spoon the batter into the prepared pan. • Bake for 30–40 minutes, or until a toothpick inserted into the center comes out clean. • Cool the cake completely in the pan on a rack. Turn out onto a serving plate. • *Coffee-Butter Frosting*: With mixer at high speed, beat the butter in a medium bowl until creamy. • With mixer at medium speed, beat in the confectioners' sugar, brown sugar, and coffee mixture until smooth. Spread the frosting over.

Makes one 11 x 7-inch cake · Prep: 30 min. · Cooking: 30–40 min. · Level: 1 · Keeps: 3–4 days

COFFEE CREAM CAKE

 1 1/3 cups all-purpose flour
    2   teaspoons baking powder
  1/4   teaspoon salt
  1/2   cup (1 stick) butter, softened
  3/4   cup granulated sugar
    3   large eggs, at room temperature
  1/2   cup cold strong coffee
 1 1/2 cups heavy cream
 1 1/2 tablespoons confectioners' sugar
    3   tablespoons Irish cream liqueur
    1   teaspoon vanilla extract

Preheat the oven to 375°F. • Butter and flour a 9-inch springform pan. • Sift the flour, baking powder, and salt into a medium bowl. • Beat the butter and granulated sugar in a large bowl with an electric mixer at medium speed until creamy. • Add the eggs, one at a time, until just blended after each addition. • With mixer at low speed, beat in the dry ingredients. • Spoon the batter into the prepared pan. • Bake for 25–30 minutes, or until golden brown and a toothpick inserted into the center comes out clean. • Cool the cake in the pan for 5 minutes. Loosen and remove the pan sides. Invert the cake onto the rack and turn the cake top-side up. Let cool until warm. Transfer to a serving plate. • Poke holes in the cake with a skewer. Drizzle with the coffee. • With mixer at high speed, beat the cream, confectioners' sugar, liqueur, and vanilla in a large bowl until stiff. Spread the top and sides of the cake with the cream.

Makes one 9-inch cake · Prep: 25 min. · Cooking: 25–30 min. · Level: 1 · Keeps: 1 day in the refrigerator

GLAZED COFFEE CAKE

    2   cups all-purpose flour
    1   teaspoon baking powder
  1/2   teaspoon baking soda
  1/4   teaspoon salt
  3/4   cup (1 1/2 sticks) butter, softened
    1   cup granulated sugar
    2   teaspoons vanilla extract
    2   large eggs, at room temperature
    1   cup sour cream
    2   tablespoons freeze-dried coffee granules dissolved
        in 1 tablespoon boiling water

GLAZE

    2   teaspoons freeze-dried coffee granules dissolved in
        1/4 cup cold strong coffee
    1   cup confectioners' sugar

Preheat the oven to 350°F. • Butter and flour a 9-inch Bundt pan. • Sift the flour, baking powder, baking soda, and salt into a large bowl. • Beat the butter, sugar, and vanilla in a large bowl with an electric mixer at medium speed until creamy. • Add the eggs, one at a time, until just blended after each addition. • With mixer at low speed, gradually beat in the dry ingredients, alternating with the sour cream. • Transfer 1/3 of the batter to a small bowl and stir in the coffee mixture. • Spoon half the plain batter into the prepared pan. Use a thin metal spatula to spread the coffee-flavored batter over. Spread the remaining batter on top. • Bake for 55–65 minutes, or until golden brown and a toothpick inserted into the center comes out clean. • Cool the cake in the pan for 15 minutes. Turn out onto a rack to cool until warm. • *Glaze*: Stir the coffee

BUTTER CAKE WITH SHERRY SAUCE

 1 1/2 cups all-purpose flour
 1 1/2 teaspoons baking powder
  1/4   teaspoon salt
  1/2   cup (1 stick) butter, softened
  3/4   cup granulated sugar
    1   teaspoon vanilla extract
    4   large eggs, at room temperature

SHERRY SAUCE
- 1 cup water
- 1 cup granulated sugar
- 1/4 cup medium dry sherry

Preheat the oven to 350°F. • Butter and flour a 9-inch round cake pan. • Sift the flour, baking powder, and salt into a medium bowl. • Beat the butter, sugar, and vanilla in a large bowl with an electric mixer at medium speed until creamy. • Add the eggs, one at a time, until just blended after each addition. • With mixer at low speed, gradually beat in the dry ingredients. • Spoon the batter into the prepared pan. • Bake for 25–30 minutes, or until golden and a toothpick inserted into the center comes out clean. • Cool the cake in the pan for 10 minutes. Turn out onto a rack and let cool completely. • *Sherry Sauce*: Bring the water and sugar to a boil in a small saucepan over medium heat, stirring constantly. Cook, without stirring, until the mixture reaches 238°F, or the soft-ball stage. Remove from the heat and let cool for 15 minutes. • Stir in the sherry. • Place the cake on the rack in a jelly-roll pan. Poke holes in the cake with a skewer. Spoon the sherry sauce over the cake. Scoop up any sauce from the pan and drizzle on the cake.

Makes one 9-inch cake · Prep: 35 min. · Cooking: 25–30 min. · Level: 1 · Keeps: 1–2 days

GINGERBREAD WITH LIME FROSTING
- 1/2 cup dark molasses
- 1/4 cup (1/2 stick) butter, cut up
- 1 cup all-purpose flour
- 3/4 cup granulated sugar
- 1 teaspoon baking powder
- 1/2 teaspoon baking soda
- 1 teaspoon ground ginger
- 1 teaspoon ground cinnamon
- 1/4 teaspoon ground cloves
- 1/4 teaspoon ground mace
- 1/4 teaspoon salt
- 1/2 cup milk
- 1 large egg, lightly beaten

LIME FROSTING
- 1/2 cup (1 stick) butter, softened
- 1 tablespoon grated lime zest
- 2 cups confectioners' sugar
- 1 tablespoon (approx) fresh lime juice

Preheat the oven to 350°F. • Butter a 9 x 5-inch loaf pan. Line with waxed paper. Butter the paper. • Stir the butter and molasses in a small saucepan over low heat until the butter has melted. Keep warm. • Stir together the flour, sugar, baking powder, baking soda, ginger, cinnamon, cloves, mace, and salt in a large bowl. With an electric mixer at low speed, gradually beat in the milk and egg. • By hand, stir the hot butter mixture into the batter. • Spoon the batter into the prepared pan. • Bake for 45–55 minutes, or until a toothpick inserted into the center comes out clean. • Cool the loaf in the pan for 15 minutes. Turn out onto a rack. Carefully remove the paper and let cool completely. • *Lime Frosting:* With mixer at medium speed, beat the butter and lime zest in a medium bowl until creamy. • With mixer at low speed, gradually beat in the confectioners' sugar and enough of the lime juice to make a thick, spreadable frosting. • Spread the frosting over the top and sides of the loaf.

Makes one 9 x 5-inch loaf · Prep: 30 min. · Cooking: 45–55 min. · Level: 1 · Keeps: 2–3 days

GINGERBREAD WITH CARAMEL FROSTING
- 2 cups all-purpose flour
- 1 tablespoon ground ginger
- 2 teaspoons baking powder
- 1/2 teaspoon baking soda
- 1/4 teaspoon salt
- 1/2 cup (1 stick) butter, softened
- 1/2 cup granulated sugar
- 2 large eggs, at room temperature
- 3/4 cup dark unsulphured molasses
- 1/2 cup milk

CARAMEL FROSTING
- 1/4 cup (1/2 stick) butter, cut up
- 1/2 cup firmly packed brown sugar
- 1/4 cup milk
- 1 1/2 cups confectioners' sugar
- 1 teaspoon vanilla extract

Preheat the oven to 350°F. • Butter and flour a 9-inch tube pan. • Sift the flour, ginger, baking powder, baking soda, and salt into a large bowl. • Beat the butter and sugar in a large bowl with an electric mixer at medium speed until creamy. • Add the eggs, one at a time, until just blended after each addition. Gradually beat in the molasses. • With mixer at low speed, gradually beat in the dry ingredients, alternating with the milk. • Spoon the batter into the prepared pan. • Bake for 50–60 minutes, or until a toothpick inserted into the center comes out clean. • Cool the cake in the pan for 15 minutes. Turn out onto a rack to cool completely. • *Caramel Frosting*: Stir the butter and brown sugar in a medium saucepan over low heat until the sugar has dissolved. Add the milk and stir for 2 minutes more. • Transfer to a medium bowl and gradually beat in the confectioners' sugar and vanilla. • Spread the top and sides of the cake with the frosting.

Makes one 9-inch cake · Prep: 20 min. · Cooking: 50–60 min. · Level: 1 · Keeps: 2–3 days

Butter cake with sherry sauce

POUND CAKES

Delicious, firm-textured, and long-lasting, the pound cake is a baker's favorite. Classic pound cakes have retained their name from the traditional content of one pound each of butter, sugar, and flour, balanced with 3 or 4 eggs. In modern kitchens, the uniformity of the pound cake has been relaxed and infused with every imaginable flavor.

POLENTA POUND CAKE

      2   cups all-purpose flour
      1   cup yellow cornmeal
    ³/₄   cup superfine sugar
      2   teaspoons baking powder
      1   teaspoon baking soda
    ¹/₄   teaspoon salt
    ¹/₄   cup solid vegetable shortening
      2   tablespoons honey
      2   teaspoons anisette
    2–3   teaspoons milk

Preheat the oven to 350°F. • Grease a 9-inch round cake pan with shortening.• Mix together the flour, cornmeal, sugar, baking powder, baking soda, and salt in a large bowl. Make a well in the center and mix in the shortening, honey, and anisette. • Gradually add enough milk to make a smooth dough. • Transfer the dough into the prepared pan and smooth the top. • Bake for 40–45 minutes, or until a toothpick inserted into the center comes out clean. • Cool the cake in the pan for 15 minutes. Turn out onto a rack to cool completely.

Makes one 9-inch cake · Prep: 30 min. · Cooking: 40–45 min. · Level: 1 · Keeps: 3–4 days

◄ Pumpkin pound cake (see page 46)

► Polenta pound cake

• Beat the butter, sugar, and vanilla in a large bowl with an electric mixer at medium speed until creamy. • Add the egg yolks, one at a time, until just blended after each addition. • With mixer at low speed, gradually beat in the dry ingredients, alternating with the milk. • With mixer at high speed, beat the egg whites in a large bowl until stiff peaks form. • Use a large rubber spatula to fold them into the batter. • Spoon the batter into the prepared pan. • Bake for 55–65 minutes, or until golden and a toothpick inserted into the center comes out clean. • Run a knife around the edges of the pan to loosen the cake. Cool the cake in the pan for 15 minutes. Turn out onto a rack to cool completely.

Makes one 9-inch cake · Prep: 15 min. · Cooking: 55–65 min. · Level: 1 · Keeps: 5–7 days

HONEY AND SPICE POUND CAKE

Fabulous at coffee or teatime.

- 2 cups all-purpose flour
- 1 teaspoon baking powder
- 1/2 teaspoon baking soda
- 1/2 teaspoon salt
- 1 cup (2 sticks) butter, softened
- 1 cup granulated sugar
- 1/3 cup honey
- 2 teaspoons vanilla extract
- 3 large eggs, at room temperature
- 3/4 cup sour cream
- 1/3 cup confectioners' sugar, to dust

FILLING

- 1 cup granulated sugar
- 2 teaspoons ground cinnamon
- 1 teaspoon ground ginger

Preheat the oven to 325°F. • Butter and flour a 10-inch Bundt pan. • Sift the flour, baking powder, baking soda, and salt into a medium bowl. • Beat the butter, sugar, honey, and vanilla in a large bowl with an electric mixer at medium speed until creamy. • Add the eggs, one at a time, until just blended after each addition. • With mixer at low speed, gradually beat in the dry ingredients, alternating with the sour cream. • Spoon half the batter into the prepared pan. • *Filling*: Mix the sugar, cinnamon, and ginger. Sprinkle over the batter in the pan. Spoon the remaining batter over. • Bake for 70–80 minutes, or until golden brown and a toothpick

Basic pound cake

BASIC POUND CAKE

Vary the flavor of this cake by changing the extracts used. Orange and coconut are a good combination, as are butterscotch and vanilla. For a different flavor, add finely grated citrus zests or a teaspoon each of ginger, nutmeg, cinnamon, and/or pumpkin pie spice. Serve with whipped cream and chopped fresh fruit.

- 3 cups all-purpose flour
- 1 teaspoon baking powder
- 1/2 teaspoon baking soda
- 1/2 teaspoon salt
- 1 cup (2 sticks) butter, softened
- 2 cups granulated sugar
- 2 teaspoons vanilla extract
- 2 teaspoons almond extract
- 5 large eggs, at room temperature
- 1 cup milk

Preheat the oven to 350°F. • Butter and flour a 10-inch tube pan. • Sift the flour, baking powder, baking soda, and salt into a large bowl. • Beat the butter, sugar, and vanilla and almond extracts in a large bowl with an electric mixer at medium speed until creamy. • Add the eggs, one at a time, until just blended after each addition. •

With mixer at low speed, gradually beat in the dry ingredients, alternating with the milk. • Spoon the batter into the prepared pan. • Bake for 50–60 minutes, or until a toothpick inserted into the center comes out clean. • Run a knife around the edges of the pan to loosen the cake. Cool the cake in the pan for 15 minutes. Turn the cake out onto a rack to cool completely.

Makes one 10-inch cake · Prep: 15 min. · Cooking: 50–60 min. · Level: 1 · Keeps: 5–6 days

YELLOW POUND CAKE

You'll love this good, simple pound cake. It's a classic.

- 2 cups all-purpose flour
- 3/4 teaspoon baking powder
- 1/4 teaspoon salt
- 1 1/2 cups (3 sticks) butter, softened
- 2 cups granulated sugar
- 1 teaspoon vanilla extract
- 5 large eggs, separated
- 1/3 cup milk

Preheat the oven to 350°F. • Butter and flour a 9-inch Bundt pan. • Sift the flour, baking powder, and salt into a large bowl.

inserted into the center comes out clean. •
Run a knife around the edges of the pan to
loosen the cake. Cool the cake in the pan
for 15 minutes. Turn out onto a rack to
cool completely. • Dust with the
confectioners' sugar.

Makes one 10-inch cake · Prep: 25 min. · Cooking:
70–80 min. · Level: 1 · Keeps: 4–5 days

MOCHA CREAM CAKE

- 2 cups all-purpose flour
- 2 tablespoons unsweetened cocoa powder
- 2 tablespoons freeze-dried coffee granules
- 2 teaspoons baking powder
- $^1/_4$ teaspoon salt
- 4 large eggs, separated
- 1 cup granulated sugar
- 1 cup (2 sticks) butter, melted
- $^1/_3$ cup milk
- 2 cups Coffee Pastry Cream (see page 346)
- 1 cup heavy cream
- 1 teaspoon freshly ground cinnamon

Preheat the oven to 350°F. • Butter and
flour a 9-inch springform pan. • Stir
together the flour, cocoa, coffee, baking
powder, and salt in a medium bowl. • Beat
the egg yolks and sugar in a large bowl
with an electric mixer at high speed until
pale and thick. • With mixer at low speed,
gradually beat in the dry ingredients,
alternating with the butter and milk. • With
mixer at high speed, beat the egg whites in
a large bowl until stiff peaks form. Use a
large rubber spatula to fold them into the
batter. • Spoon the batter into the
prepared pan. • Bake for 30–40 minutes,
or until a toothpick inserted into the
center comes out clean. • Cool the cake in
the pan for 15 minutes. Loosen and
remove the pan sides. Invert the cake onto
a rack. Loosen and remove the pan bottom
and let cool completely. • Split the cake
horizontally. Place one layer on a serving

Mocha cream cake

plate. Spread with the pastry cream. Place
the other layer on top. • With mixer at high
speed, beat the cream and cinnamon in a
medium bowl until stiff. Spread the cake
with the cream.

Makes one 9-inch round cake · Prep: 30 min. ·
Cooking: 30–40 min. · Level: 2 · Keeps: 1–2 days

MOCHA POUND CAKE

Equally good with or without the coffee glaze.

- $1^1/_3$ cups all-purpose flour
- $^2/_3$ cup unsweetened cocoa powder
- 1 teaspoon baking soda
- 2 tablespoons cold water
- $^1/_2$ cup cold strong coffee
- $^1/_2$ cup coffee-flavored liqueur
- 1 tablespoon vanilla extract
- $^3/_4$ cup (1$^1/_2$ sticks) butter, softened
- 2 cups granulated sugar
- 4 large eggs, separated

GLAZE

- $1^1/_2$ cups confectioners' sugar
- $^1/_2$ cup coffee-flavored liqueur

Preheat the oven to 325°F. • Butter and flour
a 10-inch Bundt pan. • Sift the flour and

cocoa into a medium bowl. • Dissolve the
baking soda in the water in a medium
bowl. Stir in the coffee, coffee liqueur, and
vanilla. • Beat the butter and sugar in a
large bowl with an electric mixer at
medium speed until creamy. • Add the egg
yolks, one at a time, until just blended
after each addition. • With mixer at low
speed, gradually beat in the dry
ingredients, alternating with the coffee
mixture. • With mixer at high speed, beat
the egg whites in a large bowl until stiff
peaks form. • Use a large rubber spatula
to fold them into the batter. • Spoon the
batter into the prepared pan. • Bake for
50–60 minutes, or until a toothpick
inserted into the center comes out clean. •
Run a knife around the edges of the pan to
loosen the cake. Cool the cake in the pan
for 15 minutes. Turn out onto a rack to
cool completely • *Glaze*: Beat the
confectioners' sugar and liqueur in a small
bowl until smooth. • Drizzle over the cake.

Makes one 10-inch cake · Prep: 20 min. · Cooking:
50–60 min. · Level: 1 · Keeps: 4–5 days

ALMOND POUND CAKE

    2 cups all-purpose flour
    1 teaspoon baking powder
  1/4 teaspoon salt
    1 cup almonds, finely ground
1 1/2 cups (3 sticks) butter, softened
    3 cups granulated sugar
    1 tablespoon almond extract
    1 teaspoon vanilla extract
    6 large eggs, at room temperature
    1 cup milk
  3/4 cup slivered almonds

Preheat the oven to 350°F. • Butter and flour a 10-inch Bundt pan. • Sift the flour, baking powder, and salt into a large bowl. Stir in the almonds. • Beat the butter, sugar, almond extract, and vanilla in a large bowl with an electric mixer at medium speed until creamy. • Add the eggs, one at a time, until just blended after each addition. • With mixer at low speed, gradually beat in the dry ingredients, alternating with the milk. • Spoon the batter into the prepared pan. • Sprinkle with the slivered almonds. • Bake for 75–85 minutes, or until a toothpick inserted into the center comes out clean. • Run a knife around the edges of the pan to loosen the cake. Cool the cake in the pan for 15 minutes. Turn out onto a rack to cool completely.

Makes one 10-inch cake · Prep: 20 min. · Cooking: 75–85 min. · Level: 1 · Keeps: 5–6 days

Almond pound cake

NUTTY POUND CAKE

  3/4 cup mixed nuts, coarsely chopped, such as walnuts, pecans, and hazelnuts
1 1/2 cups all-purpose flour
  1/2 teaspoon baking soda
  1/4 teaspoon salt
  3/4 cup almonds, finely ground
  3/4 cup (1 1/2 sticks) butter, softened
2 1/4 cups firmly packed brown sugar
    2 teaspoons vanilla extract
  1/2 cup sour cream
    5 large eggs, at room temperature

Preheat the oven to 350°F. • Butter and flour a 9-inch Bundt pan. Sprinkle the chopped nuts in the pan. • Sift the flour, baking soda, and salt into a large bowl. Stir in the almonds. • Beat the butter, brown sugar, and vanilla in a large bowl with an electric mixer at medium speed until creamy. Beat in the sour cream. • Add the eggs, one at a time, until just blended after each addition. • With mixer at low speed, gradually beat in the dry ingredients. • Spoon the batter into the prepared pan. • Bake for 60–65 minutes, or until a toothpick inserted into the center comes out clean. • Run a knife around the edges of the pan to loosen the cake. Cool the cake in the pan for 15 minutes. Turn out onto a rack to cool completely.

Makes one 9-inch cake · Prep: 25 min. · Cooking: 60–65 min. · Level: 1 · Keeps: 2–3 days

APPLE AND NUT POUND CAKE

    2 cups all-purpose flour
1 1/2 teaspoons ground cinnamon
1 1/2 teaspoons ground ginger
  3/4 teaspoon baking powder
  1/4 teaspoon baking soda
  1/4 teaspoon salt
    1 cup (2 sticks) butter, softened
1 1/3 cups granulated sugar
    2 large eggs, at room temperature
    2 teaspoons vanilla extract
    2 cups sweet grated peeled apple
    1 cup walnuts, coarsely chopped

Preheat the oven to 350°F. • Butter and flour a 9-inch Bundt pan. • Sift the flour, cinnamon, ginger, baking powder, baking soda, and salt into a large bowl. • Beat the butter, sugar, eggs, and vanilla in a large bowl with an electric mixer at medium speed. • With mixer at low speed, gradually beat in the dry ingredients. • By hand, stir in the apple and walnuts. • Spoon the batter into the prepared pan. • Bake for 55–65 minutes, or until a toothpick inserted into the center comes out clean. • Run a knife around the edges of the pan to loosen the cake. Cool the cake in the pan for 15 minutes. Turn out onto a rack to cool completely.

Makes one 9-inch cake · Prep: 20 min. · Cooking: 55–65 min. · Level: 1 · Keeps: 2–3 days

DATE AND NUT POUND CAKE

    3 cups all-purpose flour
    1 teaspoon baking powder
  1/2 teaspoon salt
    1 cup shredded coconut
    1 cup (2 sticks) butter, softened
    2 cups granulated sugar
    1 teaspoon vanilla extract
    1 teaspoon lemon extract
    6 large eggs, at room temperature
    1 cup milk
1 1/2 cups chopped pitted dates
    1 cup pecans, coarsely chopped

LEMON CREAM CHEESE FROSTING
    2 packages (3 oz each) cream cheese, softened
  1/4 cup (1/4 stick) butter, softened
    2 teaspoons lemon extract
    2 cups confectioners' sugar

Preheat the oven to 325°F. • Butter and flour a 10-inch tube pan. • Sift the flour, baking powder, and salt into a large bowl. Stir in the coconut. • Beat the butter, sugar, and vanilla and lemon extracts in a large bowl with an electric mixer at medium speed until creamy. • Add the eggs, one at a time, until just

blended after each addition. • With mixer at low speed, gradually beat in the dry ingredients, alternating with the milk. • By hand, stir in the dates and pecans. • Spoon the batter into the prepared pan. • Bake for 70–75 minutes, or until golden brown and a toothpick inserted into the center comes out clean. • Run a knife around the edges of the pan to loosen the cake. Cool the cake in the pan for 15 minutes. Turn out onto a rack to cool completely. • *Lemon Cream Cheese Frosting*: Beat the cream cheese, butter, and lemon extract in a medium bowl with a mixer at high speed until creamy. With mixer at low speed, gradually beat in the confectioners' sugar. • Spread with the frosting.

Makes one 10-inch cake · Prep: 30 min. · Cooking: 70–75 min. · Level: 1 · Keeps: 4–5 days

GINGER AND WALNUT POUND CAKE

Due to the high proportion of fat in pound cakes, the cakes must be completely baked. To ensure this, the toothpick must be clean, with no oily residue or sheen.

- 3/4 cup walnuts, finely chopped
- 2 1/4 cups all-purpose flour
- 2 teaspoons ground ginger
- 1 1/2 teaspoons baking powder
- 1/4 teaspoon salt
- 1 cup (2 sticks) butter, softened
- 1 1/2 cups granulated sugar
- 1 package (8 oz) cream cheese, softened
- 2 teaspoons vanilla extract
- 4 large eggs, at room temperature
- 1/2 cup coarsely chopped crystallized ginger

Preheat the oven to 325°F. • Butter and flour a 10-inch tube pan. Sprinkle the walnuts in the pan. • Sift the flour, ground ginger, baking powder, and salt into a large bowl. • Beat the butter, sugar, cream cheese, and vanilla in a large bowl with an electric mixer at medium speed until creamy. • Add the eggs, one at a time, until just blended after each addition. • With mixer at low speed, gradually beat in the dry ingredients and crystallized ginger. • Spoon the batter into the prepared pan. • Bake for 80–90 minutes, or until golden and a toothpick inserted into the center comes out clean. • Run a knife around the edges of the pan to loosen the cake. Cool the cake in the pan for 15 minutes. Turn out onto a rack to cool completely.

Makes one 10-inch cake · Prep: 20 min. · Cooking: 80–90 min. · Level: 1 · Keeps: 4–5 days

COLD-OVEN POUND CAKE

This perfectly spiced pound cake starts baking in a cold oven.

- 3 cups all-purpose flour
- 2 teaspoons pumpkin pie spice
- 3/4 teaspoon baking powder
- 1/2 teaspoon salt
- 1 cup (2 sticks) butter, softened
- 1/2 cup vegetable shortening
- 2 1/2 cups granulated sugar
- 2 teaspoons vanilla extract
- 2 teaspoons lemon extract
- 5 large eggs, at room temperature
- 1 cup milk

Butter and flour a 10-inch tube pan. • Sift the flour, pumpkin pie spice, baking powder, and salt into a large bowl. • Beat the butter, vegetable shortening, sugar, and vanilla and lemon extracts in a large bowl with an electric mixer at medium speed until creamy. • Add the eggs, one at a time, until just blended after each addition. • With mixer at low speed, gradually beat in the dry ingredients, alternating with the milk. • Spoon the batter into the prepared pan. • Set the oven temperature to 350°F and bake for 1 hour and 25–35 minutes, or until a toothpick inserted into the center comes out clean. • Run a knife around the edges of the pan to loosen the cake. Cool the cake in the pan for 15 minutes. Turn out onto a rack to cool completely.

Makes one 10-inch cake · Prep: 20 min. · Cooking: 1 hr. 25–35 min. · Level: 1 · Keeps: 4–5 days

ORANGE-FLOWER POUND CAKE

Orange-flower water is found in gourmet stores. This cake is heavenly at breakfast or teatime.

- 2 cups all-purpose flour
- 1 teaspoon baking powder
- 1/2 teaspoon salt
- 1/2 cup almonds, finely ground
- 1 cup (2 sticks) butter, softened
- 1 2/3 cups granulated sugar
- 2 teaspoons orange-flower water
- 1 teaspoon almond extract
- 5 large eggs, at room temperature
- 1/3 cup confectioners' sugar, to dust

Preheat the oven to 350°F. • Butter and flour a 9-inch tube pan. • Sift the flour, baking powder, and salt into a medium bowl. Stir in the almonds. • Beat the butter, sugar, orange-flower water, and almond extract in a large bowl with an electric

mixer at medium speed until creamy. • Add the eggs, one at a time, until just blended after each addition. • With mixer at low speed, gradually beat in the dry ingredients. • Spoon the batter into the prepared pan. • Bake for 50–60 minutes, or until golden brown and a toothpick inserted into the center comes out clean. • Run a knife around the edges of the pan to loosen the cake. Cool the cake in the pan for 15 minutes. Turn out onto a rack to cool completely. • Dust with the confectioners' sugar before serving.

Makes one 9-inch cake · Prep: 20 min. · Cooking: 50–60 min. · Level: 1 · Keeps: 4–5 days

BUTTERSCOTCH POUND CAKE

Butterscotch extract can be obtained from various sources on the Internet.

- 3 cups all-purpose flour
- 2 teaspoons baking powder
- 1/2 teaspoon baking soda
- 1/2 teaspoon salt
- 2 cups granulated sugar
- 1 cup buttermilk
- 1 cup (2 sticks) butter, melted and slightly cooled
- 4 large eggs, at room temperature
- 2 teaspoons vanilla extract
- 1 teaspoon butterscotch extract

Preheat the oven to 325°F. • Butter and flour a 10-inch Bundt pan. • Sift the flour, baking powder, baking soda, and salt into a large bowl. Stir in the sugar. • With an electric mixer at high speed, beat in the buttermilk, butter, eggs, and vanilla and butterscotch extracts. • Spoon the batter into the prepared pan. • Bake for 50–60 minutes, or until a toothpick inserted into the center comes out clean. • Cool the cake in the pan for 15 minutes. Run a knife around the edges of the pan to loosen the cake. Turn out onto a rack to cool completely.

Makes one 10-inch cake · Prep: 20 min. · Cooking: 50–60 min. · Level: 1 · Keeps: 2–3 days

CARAMEL POUND CAKE

1²/₃ cups all-purpose flour
1 teaspoon baking powder
¹/₄ teaspoon salt
1 cup (2 sticks) butter, softened
1¹/₄ cups firmly packed brown sugar
2 tablespoons corn syrup
3 large eggs
¹/₂ cup buttermilk
3 tablespoons confectioners' sugar, to dust

Preheat the oven to 350°F. • Butter and flour a 10-inch Bundt pan. • Sift the flour, baking powder, and salt into a large bowl. • Beat the butter, sugar, and corn syrup in a large bowl with an electric mixer at medium speed until creamy. • Add the eggs, one at a time, until just blended after each addition. • With mixer at low speed, gradually beat in the dry ingredients, alternating with the buttermilk. • Spoon the batter into the prepared pan. • Bake for 40–50 minutes, or until a toothpick inserted into the center comes out clean. • Run a knife around the edges of the pan to loosen the cake. Cool the cake in the pan for 10 minutes. Turn out onto a rack to cool completely. • Dust with the confectioners' sugar.

Makes one 10-inch cake · Prep: 30 min. · Cooking: 40–50 min. · Level: 1 · Keeps: 4–5 days

PEPPERMINT-FROSTED CHOCOLATE POUND CAKE

You can omit the peppermint frosting, if you prefer, but it does make this cake especially delicious.

3¹/₂ cups all-purpose flour
1 cup unsweetened cocoa powder
1 teaspoon baking powder
¹/₂ teaspoon salt
1 cup (2 sticks) butter, softened
¹/₂ cup vegetable shortening
3 cups granulated sugar
1 tablespoon vanilla extract
5 large eggs, at room temperature
1¹/₄ cups milk

PEPPERMINT FROSTING
2 cups confectioners' sugar
¹/₄ cup (¹/₂ stick) butter, softened
¹/₃ cup unsweetened cocoa powder
1 tablespoon milk
¹/₂ teaspoon peppermint extract

Preheat the oven to 350°F. • Butter and flour a 10-inch tube pan. • Sift the flour, cocoa, baking powder, and salt into a large bowl. • Beat the butter, shortening, sugar, and vanilla in a large bowl with an electric mixer at medium speed until creamy. • Add the eggs, one at a time, until just blended after each addition. • With mixer at low speed, gradually beat in the dry ingredients, alternating with the milk. • Spoon the batter into the prepared pan. • Bake for 1 hour and 35–45 minutes, or until a toothpick inserted into the center comes out clean. • Run a knife around the edges of the pan to loosen the cake. Cool the cake in the pan for 15 minutes. Turn out onto a rack to cool completely. • *Peppermint Frosting*: With mixer at medium speed, beat the confectioners' sugar and butter in a large bowl until creamy. Beat in the cocoa, milk, and peppermint extract until smooth. • Spread the top and sides of the cake with the frosting.

Makes one 10-inch cake · Prep: 25 min. · Cooking: 1 hr. 35–45 min. · Level: 1 · Keeps: 4–5 days

CHOCOLATE CHIP POUND CAKE

2¹/₂ cups all-purpose flour
1 teaspoon baking powder
¹/₂ teaspoon salt
1¹/₂ cups (3 sticks) butter, softened
2¹/₄ cups granulated sugar
2 teaspoons vanilla extract
5 large eggs, at room temperature
³/₄ cup buttermilk
1 cup semisweet chocolate chips

Preheat the oven to 350°F. • Butter and flour a 10-inch tube pan. • Sift the flour, baking powder, and salt into a large bowl. • Beat the butter, sugar, and vanilla in a large bowl with an electric mixer at medium speed until creamy. • Add the eggs, one at a time, until just blended after each addition. • With mixer at low speed, gradually beat in the dry ingredients, alternating with the buttermilk. • By hand, stir in the chocolate chips. • Spoon the batter into the prepared pan. Bake for 75–85 minutes, or until a toothpick inserted into the center comes out clean. • Run a knife around the edges of the pan to loosen the cake. Cool the cake in the pan for 15 minutes. Turn out onto a rack to cool completely.

Makes one 10-inch cake · Prep: 25 min. · Cooking: 75–85 min. · Level: 1 · Keeps: 4–5 days

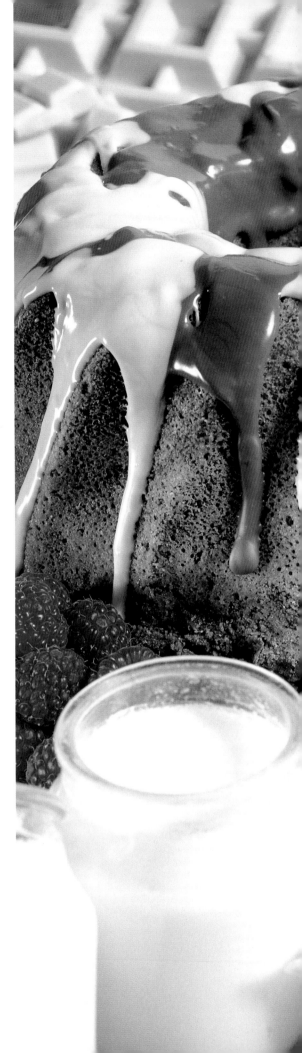

WHITE CHOCOLATE POUND CAKE

Serve with fresh raspberries to contrast with
the sweetness of the chocolate.

- 2 cups granulated sugar
- 8 oz white chocolate, coarsely chopped
- 3 cups all-purpose flour
- 1 teaspoon baking powder
- $^1/_2$ teaspoon baking soda
- $^1/_2$ teaspoon salt
- 1 cup (2 sticks) butter, at room temperature
- 2 teaspoons vanilla extract
- 1 teaspoon almond extract
- 5 large eggs, at room temperature
- 1 cup plain yogurt

GLAZE

- 4 oz white chocolate, melted
- 2 oz semisweet chocolate
  fresh raspberries, to serve (optional)

Preheat the oven to 350°F. • Butter and
flour a 10-inch Bundt pan. Sprinkle the
pan with 2 tablespoons of the sugar. •
Melt the chocolate in a double boiler
over barely simmering water. Set aside
to cool. • Sift the flour, baking powder,
baking soda, and salt into a large bowl.
• Beat the butter, remaining sugar, and
vanilla and almond extracts in a large
bowl with an electric mixer at medium
speed until creamy. • Add the eggs, one
at a time, until just blended after each
addition. • With mixer at low speed,
gradually beat in the dry ingredients,
alternating with the yogurt. • Spoon the
batter into the prepared pan. • Bake for
75–85 minutes, or until a toothpick
inserted into the center comes out
clean. • Run a knife around the edges
of the pan to loosen the cake. Cool the
cake in the pan for 15 minutes. Turn
out onto the rack to cool completely. •
Glaze: Melt each type of chocolate
separately in a double boiler over
barely simmering water. • Drizzle
alternate spoonfuls of the melted
chocolate over the cake. Serve with
raspberries, if desired.

Makes one 10-inch cake · Prep: 25 min. · Cooking:
75–85 min. · Level: 1 · Keeps: 2–3 days

White chocolate pound cake

RUM AND SPICE POUND CAKE

- 2 cups all-purpose flour
- 1 tablespoon baking powder
- 1 teaspoon ground ginger
- 1 teaspoon ground cinnamon
- 1 teaspoon ground nutmeg
- 1/4 teaspoon salt
- 1/2 cup (1 stick) butter, softened
- 1 cup granulated sugar
- 2 teaspoons rum extract
- 2 large eggs, at room temperature
- 3/4 cup milk

Preheat the oven to 350°F. • Butter and flour a 9-inch round cake pan. • Sift the flour, baking powder, cinnamon, ginger, nutmeg, and salt into a medium bowl. • Beat the butter, sugar, and rum extract in a large bowl with an electric mixer at medium speed until creamy. • Add the eggs, one at a time, until just blended after each addition. • With mixer at low speed, gradually beat in the dry ingredients, alternating with the milk. • Spoon the batter into the prepared pan. • Bake for 40–50 minutes, or until a toothpick inserted into the center comes out clean. • Run a knife around the edges of the pan to loosen the cake. Cool the cake in the pan for 15 minutes. Turn out onto a rack to cool completely.

Makes one 9-inch cake · Prep: 15 min. · Cooking: 40–50 min. · Level: 1 · Keeps: 4–5 days

APRICOT BRANDY POUND CAKE

- 3 cups all-purpose flour
- 1/2 teaspoon salt
- 1/4 teaspoon baking soda
- 1 cup (2 sticks) butter, softened
- 2 cups granulated sugar
- 1 tablespoon grated orange zest
- 6 large eggs, at room temperature
- 1 cup plain yogurt
- 1/4 cup apricot brandy

APRICOT GLAZE
- 1 cup apricot preserves
- 1/2 cup apricot brandy
- 1 teaspoon grated lemon zest

Preheat the oven to 325°F. • Butter and flour a 10-inch tube pan. • Sift the flour, salt, and baking soda into a large bowl. • Beat the butter, sugar, and orange zest in a large bowl with an electric mixer at medium speed until creamy. • Add the eggs, one at a time, until just blended after each addition. • With mixer at low speed, gradually beat in the dry ingredients, alternating with the yogurt and apricot brandy. • Spoon the

batter into the prepared pan. • Bake for 60–70 minutes, or until a toothpick inserted into the center comes out clean. • Run a knife around the edges of the pan to loosen the cake. Cool the cake in the pan for 15 minutes. Turn out onto a rack to cool completely. • *Apricot Glaze*: Mix the apricot preserves, brandy, and lemon zest in a medium saucepan and bring to a boil over medium heat. Let boil for 1 minute. Drizzle the glaze over the cake.

Makes one 10-inch cake · Prep: 25 min. · Cooking: 60–70 min. · Level: 1 · Keeps: 2–3 days

PEACH BRANDY POUND CAKE

- 2 cups all-purpose flour
- 1/2 teaspoon baking soda
- 1/2 teaspoon salt
- 2/3 cup butter, softened
- 2 cups granulated sugar
- 1 teaspoon lemon extract
- 1 teaspoon orange extract
- 1 teaspoon vanilla extract
- 4 large eggs, at room temperature
- 2/3 cup peach yogurt
- 1/3 cup peach brandy

Preheat the oven to 325°F. • Butter and flour a 9-inch Bundt pan. • Sift the flour, baking soda, and salt into a large bowl. • Beat the butter, sugar, orange, lemon, and vanilla extracts in a large bowl with an electric mixer at medium speed until creamy. • Add the eggs, one at a time, until just blended after each addition. • With mixer at low speed, gradually beat in the dry ingredients, alternating with the yogurt and brandy. • Spoon the batter into the prepared pan. • Bake for 55–65 minutes, or until golden brown and a toothpick inserted into the center comes out clean. • Run a knife around the edges of the pan to loosen the cake. Cool the cake in the pan for 15 minutes. Turn out onto a rack to cool completely.

Makes one 9-inch cake · Prep: 15 min. · Cooking: 55–65 min. · Level: 1 · Keeps: 2–3 days

PERFECT PEACH POUND CAKE

Serve this moist, yummy cake while still warm with peaches and whipped cream or vanilla (or peach) ice cream.

- 3 cups all-purpose flour
- 1 teaspoon baking soda
- 1 teaspoon ground cinnamon
- 1/2 teaspoon salt
- 1 cup (2 sticks) butter, softened
- 1 1/2 cups granulated sugar
- 2 teaspoons vanilla extract
- 3 large eggs, at room temperature
- 1 1/4 cups canned peaches, drained and coarsely chopped
- 1 cup walnuts, coarsely chopped

Preheat the oven to 325°F. • Butter and flour a 10-inch Bundt pan. • Sift the flour, baking soda, cinnamon, and salt into a large bowl • Beat the butter, sugar, and vanilla in a large bowl with an electric mixer at medium speed until creamy. • Add the eggs, one at a time, until just blended after each addition. • With mixer at low speed, gradually beat in the dry ingredients. By hand, stir in the peaches and walnuts. • Spoon the batter into the prepared pan. • Bake for 70–80 minutes, or until golden brown and a toothpick inserted into the center comes out clean. • Run a knife around the edges of the pan to loosen the cake. Cool the cake in the pan for 15 minutes. Turn out onto a rack to cool completely.

Makes one 10-inch cake · Prep: 20 min. · Cooking: 70–80 min. · Level: 1 · Keeps: 1–2 days

PUMPKIN POUND CAKE

This cake will be a lovely addition to a Thanksgiving dessert table. Serve with rum-laced heavy cream.

- 3 cups all-purpose flour
- 2 teaspoons baking powder
- 1 teaspoon baking soda
- 1 teaspoon ground cinnamon
- 1 teaspoon ground ginger
- 1 teaspoon ground nutmeg
- 1/2 teaspoon salt
- 2 1/2 cups granulated sugar
- 1 1/4 cups vegetable oil
- 4 large eggs, at room temperature
- 2 cups plain canned pumpkin
- 1/2 cup pecans, finely chopped
- 1/3 cup confectioners' sugar, to dust

Preheat the oven to 375°F. • Butter and flour a 10-inch tube pan. • Sift the flour, baking powder, baking soda, cinnamon, ginger, nutmeg, and salt into a large bowl. • Beat the sugar and oil in a large bowl with an electric mixer at medium speed until well blended. • Add the eggs, one at a time, until just blended after each addition. • With mixer at low speed, gradually beat in the pumpkin and the dry ingredients. • By hand, stir in the pecans. • Spoon the batter into the prepared pan. • Bake for 70–80 minutes, or until golden brown and a toothpick inserted into the center comes out clean. • Run a knife around the edges of the pan to loosen the cake. Cool the cake in the pan for 15 minutes. Turn out onto a rack to cool completely. • Dust with the confectioners' sugar.

Makes one 10-inch cake · Prep: 25 min. · Cooking: 70–80 min. · Level: 1 · Keeps: 2–3 days

APPLESAUCE POUND CAKE

If you plan to serve this cake for breakfast, you may prefer to omit the frosting.

3$^1/_2$ cups all-purpose flour
2 teaspoons baking soda
1 teaspoon ground cinnamon
1 teaspoon ground ginger
1 teaspoon ground nutmeg
$^1/_2$ teaspoon ground cloves
$^1/_2$ teaspoon salt
$^1/_2$ cup (1 stick) butter, softened
2 cups firmly packed brown sugar
2 large eggs, at room temperature
3 cups unsweetened applesauce
1 cup chopped, pitted dates
1 cup walnuts, chopped

FROSTING
$^1/_2$ cup (1 stick) butter, cut up
1 cup firmly packed brown sugar
$^1/_4$ cup milk
2 cups confectioners' sugar
1 teaspoon vanilla extract

Preheat the oven to 350°F. • Butter and flour a 10-inch tube pan. • Sift the flour, baking soda, cinnamon, ginger, nutmeg, cloves, and salt into a large bowl. • Beat the butter and brown sugar in a large bowl with an electric mixer at medium speed until creamy. • Add the eggs, one at a time, until just blended after each addition. • With mixer at low speed, gradually beat in the dry ingredients, alternating with the applesauce. By hand, stir in the dates and walnuts. • Spoon the batter into the prepared pan. • Bake for 80–90 minutes, or until golden brown and a toothpick inserted into the center comes out clean. • Run a knife around the edges of the pan to loosen the cake. Cool the cake in the pan for 15 minutes. Turn out onto a rack to cool completely. • *Frosting*: Place the butter and brown sugar in a small saucepan over low heat. Cook, stirring, until the butter melts and the mixture boils. Boil, stirring occasionally, for 2 minutes. • Add the milk, and stir until the mixture returns to a boil. Remove from the heat and let cool for 5 minutes. • Transfer to a large bowl and beat in the confectioners' sugar and vanilla until creamy. • Spread the top and sides of the cake with the frosting.

Makes one 10-inch cake · Prep: 20 min. · Cooking: 80–90 min. · Level: 1 · Keeps: 3–4 days

POUND CAKE WITH RASPBERRY SAUCE

A lovely, light cake—perfect for a special occasion.

3$^1/_2$ cups all-purpose flour
1 teaspoon ground nutmeg
$^1/_2$ teaspoon baking soda
$^1/_2$ teaspoon salt
2 cups (4 sticks) butter, softened
3 cups granulated sugar
2 teaspoons vanilla extract
1 teaspoon almond extract
6 large eggs, at room temperature
$^1/_2$ cup milk

RASPBERRY SAUCE
3 cups fresh raspberries, lightly mashed with a fork
$^1/_4$ cup granulated sugar
1 tablespoon crème de cassis or orange liqueur

Preheat the oven to 325°F. • Butter and flour a 10-inch tube pan. • Sift the flour, nutmeg, baking soda, and salt into a large bowl. • Beat the butter, sugar, vanilla, and almond extract in a large bowl with an electric mixer at medium speed until creamy. • Add the eggs, one at a time, until just blended after each addition. • With mixer at low speed, gradually beat in the dry ingredients, alternating with the milk. • Spoon the batter into the prepared pan. • Bake for 80–90 minutes, or until a toothpick inserted into the center comes out clean. • Run a knife around the edges of the pan to loosen the cake. Cool the cake in the pan for 15 minutes. Turn out onto a rack to cool completely. • *Raspberry Sauce*: Place the mashed raspberries, sugar, and liqueur in a medium bowl and stir until the sugar has dissolved. • Refrigerate for at least 3 hours before serving. • Drizzle the sauce over the cake, or pass the sauce on the side.

Makes one 10-inch cake · Prep: 30 min. 3 hr. to chill · Cooking: 80–90 min. · Level: 1 · Keeps: 4–5 days (before adding the sauce)

Pound cake with raspberry sauce

Yogurt cake with lemon-spice frosting

ORANGE POUND CAKE

    2   cups all-purpose flour
    2   teaspoons baking powder
  1/4   teaspoon salt
  2/3   cup butter, softened
    1   package (8 oz) cream cheese, softened
    2   tablespoons grated orange (or lime) zest
 1 3/4 cups granulated sugar
    3   large eggs, at room temperature
    2   tablespoons confectioners' sugar, to dust

Preheat the oven to 350°F. • Butter and flour a 9- or 10-inch Bundt pan. • Sift together the flour, baking powder, and salt in a large bowl. • Beat the butter, cream cheese, and zest in a large bowl with an electric mixer at medium speed until creamy. • Add the sugar and continue beating until light and fluffy. • Add the eggs, one at a time, until just blended after each addition. • With mixer at low speed, gradually beat in the dry ingredients. • Spoon the batter into the prepared pan. • Bake for 40–50 minutes, or until a toothpick inserted into the center comes out clean. • Run a knife around the edges of the pan to loosen the cake. Cool the cake in the pan for 30 minutes. Turn the cake out onto a rack to cool completely. • Dust with the confectioners' sugar.

Makes one cake · Prep: 20 min. · Cooking: 40–50 min. · Level: 1 · Keeps: 4–5 days

YOGURT CAKE WITH LEMON-SPICE FROSTING

 2 1/3 cups all-purpose flour
    1   teaspoon ground cinnamon
    1   teaspoon pumpkin pie spice
  1/2   teaspoon baking soda
  1/2   teaspoon salt
  1/2   teaspoon ground nutmeg
  1/4   teaspoon ground cloves
    1   cup (2 sticks) butter, softened
    2   cups granulated sugar
    2   teaspoons vanilla extract
    4   large eggs, at room temperature
    1   cup plain yogurt

LEMON-SPICE FROSTING
    2   cups confectioners' sugar
  1/4   cup (1/2 stick) butter, melted
    1   tablespoon fresh lemon juice
  1/2   teaspoon ground nutmeg
  1/2   teaspoon ground cinnamon

Preheat the oven to 350°F. • Butter a 13 x 9-inch baking pan. Line with waxed paper. Butter the paper. • Sift the flour, cinnamon, pumpkin pie spice, baking soda, salt, nutmeg, and cloves into a large bowl. • Beat the butter, sugar, and vanilla in a large bowl with an electric mixer at medium speed until creamy. • Add the eggs, one at a time, until just blended after each addition. • With mixer at low speed, gradually beat in the dry ingredients, alternating with the yogurt. • Spoon the batter into the prepared pan. • Bake for 55–65 minutes, or until the cake shrinks from the pan sides and a toothpick inserted into the center comes out clean. • Cool the cake in the pan for 15 minutes. Turn out onto a rack. Carefully remove the waxed paper and let cool completely. • *Lemon-Spice Frosting*: Place the confectioners' sugar, butter, 1 tablespoon of lemon juice, nutmeg, and cinnamon in a medium bowl. Beat until smooth, adding enough additional lemon juice to make a spreadable frosting. Spread the top and sides of the cake with the frosting.

Makes one 13 x 9-inch cake · Prep: 15 min. · Cooking: 55–65 min. · Level: 1 · Keeps: 4–5 days

GLAZED LEMON BUTTERMILK POUND CAKE

Excellent flavor and texture. Serve this lemony cake for your next brunch.

    3   cups all-purpose flour
  1/2   teaspoon baking powder
  1/2   teaspoon baking soda
  1/2   teaspoon salt
    1   cup (2 sticks) butter, softened
    2   cups granulated sugar
    2   tablespoons grated lemon zest
    4   large eggs, at room temperature
  3/4   cup buttermilk
    1   tablespoon fresh lemon juice

GLAZE
 1 1/2 cups confectioners' sugar
    1   tablespoon milk
    2   teaspoons fresh lemon juice

Preheat the oven to 325°F. • Butter and flour a 10-inch Bundt pan. • Sift the flour, baking powder, baking soda, and salt into a large bowl. • Beat the butter, sugar, and lemon zest in a large bowl with an electric mixer at medium speed until creamy. • Add the eggs, one at a time, until just blended after each addition. • With mixer at low speed, gradually beat in the dry ingredients, alternating with the buttermilk and lemon juice. • Spoon the batter into the prepared pan. • Bake for 75–85 minutes, or until golden brown and a toothpick inserted into the center comes out clean. • Run a knife around the edges of the pan to loosen the cake. Cool the cake in the pan for 15 minutes. Turn out onto a rack to cool completely. • *Glaze*: Beat the confectioners' sugar, milk, and lemon juice in a medium bowl until smooth. Drizzle over the cake.

Makes one 10-inch cake · Prep: 25 min. · Cooking: 75–85 min. · Level: 1 · Keeps: 4–5 days

LIME POUND CAKE

This easy-to-assemble cake has a lovely moist texture and a bright, fresh-lime flavor.

- 3 cups all-purpose flour
- 1 teaspoon baking powder
- 1/2 teaspoon salt
- 1 1/2 cups (3 sticks) butter, softened
- 3 cups granulated sugar
- 1 tablespoon grated lime zest
- 5 large eggs, at room temperature
- 1 cup evaporated milk

GLAZE

- 2 cups confectioners' sugar
- 1/4 cup (1/2 stick) butter, melted
- 1–2 tablespoons hot water
- 1 tablespoon grated lime zest

Preheat the oven to 350°F. • Butter and flour a 10-inch Bundt pan. • Sift the flour, baking powder, and salt into a large bowl. • Beat the butter, sugar, and lime zest in a large bowl with an electric mixer at medium speed until creamy. • Add the eggs, one at a time, until just blended after each addition. • With mixer at low speed, gradually beat in the dry ingredients, alternating with the evaporated milk. • Spoon the batter into the prepared pan. • Bake for 70–80 minutes, or until a toothpick inserted into the center comes out clean. • Run the knife around the edges of the pan to loosen the cake. Cool the cake in the pan for 15 minutes. Turn out onto a rack to cool completely. • *Glaze*: Beat the confectioners' sugar and butter in a medium bowl. Beat in enough of the water to make a glaze. Drizzle the cake with the glaze. Sprinkle the cake with the lime zest.

Makes one 10-inch cake · Prep: 25 min. · Cooking: 70–80 min. · Level: 1 · Keeps: 2–3 days

Lime pound cake

CITRUS AND ALMOND POUND CAKE

- 2 1/3 cups all-purpose flour
- 1/2 teaspoon baking soda
- 1/2 teaspoon salt
- 3/4 cup (1 1/2 sticks) butter, softened
- 1 package (8 oz) cream cheese, softened
- 2 1/4 cups granulated sugar
- 1 teaspoon lemon extract
- 1 teaspoon orange extract
- 1 teaspoon vanilla extract
- 5 large eggs, at room temperature

FROSTING

- 2 cups confectioners' sugar
- 1/4 cup (1/2 stick) butter, melted
- 1 tablespoon grated lemon zest
- 1 tablespoon grated orange zest
- 1–2 tablespoons fresh lemon or orange juice

Preheat the oven to 325°F. • Butter and flour a 10-inch Bundt pan. • Sift the flour, baking soda, and salt into a large bowl. • Beat the butter, cream cheese, sugar, and lemon, orange, and vanilla extracts in a large bowl with an electric mixer at medium speed until creamy. • Add the eggs, one at a time, until just blended after each addition. • With mixer at low speed, gradually beat in the dry ingredients. The batter will be quite thick. • Spoon the batter into the prepared pan. • Bake for 1 hour and 35–45 minutes, or until golden brown and a toothpick inserted into the center comes out clean. • Run a knife around the edges of the pan to loosen the cake. Cool the cake in the pan for 15 minutes. Turn out onto a rack to cool completely. • *Frosting*: Beat the confectioners' sugar, butter, and lemon and orange zests in a medium bowl. Beat in enough lemon or orange juice to make a spreadable frosting. • Spread the cake with the frosting.

Makes one 10-inch cake · Prep: 15 min. · Cooking: 1 hr. 35–45 min. · Level: 1 · Keeps: 2–3 days

LEMON-LIME POUND CAKE

3 cups all-purpose flour
1 teaspoon baking powder
1/2 teaspoon salt
1 1/2 cups (3 sticks) butter, softened
2 cups granulated sugar
1 tablespoon grated lime zest
2 teaspoons lemon extract
1 teaspoon vanilla extract
4 large eggs, at room temperature
1 cup lemon-lime-flavored soda

Preheat the oven to 325°F. • Butter and flour a 10-inch Bundt pan. • Sift the flour, baking powder, and salt into a large bowl. • Beat the butter, sugar, lime zest, lemon and vanilla extracts in a large bowl with an electric mixer at medium speed until creamy. • Add the eggs, one at a time, until just blended after each addition. • With mixer at low speed, gradually beat in the dry ingredients, alternating with the soda. • Spoon the batter into the prepared pan. • Bake for 70–80 minutes, or until the edges are golden brown, the top lightly cracked, and a toothpick inserted into the center comes out clean. • Run a knife around the edges of the pan to loosen the cake. Cool the cake in the pan for 15 minutes. Turn out onto a rack to cool completely.

Makes one 10-inch cake · Prep: 20 min. · Cooking: 70–80 min. · Level: 1 · Keeps: 5–6 days

PINEAPPLE AND GINGER POUND CAKE

This cake tastes even better the day after it has been made.

3 cups all-purpose flour
2 teaspoons ground ginger
1 teaspoon baking powder
1/2 teaspoon salt
1 cup (2 sticks) butter, softened
1 3/4 cups granulated sugar

2 teaspoons almond extract
6 large eggs, at room temperature
3/4 cup crushed pineapple, drained
1/4 cup milk
1/4 cup coarsely chopped crystallized ginger

Preheat the oven to 325°F. • Butter and flour a 10-inch tube pan. • Sift the flour, ginger, baking powder, and salt into a large bowl. • Beat the butter, sugar, and almond extract in a large bowl with an electric mixer at medium speed until creamy. • Add the eggs, one at a time, until just blended after each addition. • With mixer at low speed, gradually beat in the crushed pineapple and dry ingredients, alternating with the milk. Stir in the crystallized ginger. • Spoon the batter into the prepared pan. • Bake for 65–75 minutes, or until golden brown, the top lightly cracked, and a toothpick inserted into the center comes out clean. • Run a knife around the edges of the pan to loosen the cake. Cool the cake in the pan for 15 minutes. Turn out onto a rack to cool completely.

Makes one 10-inch cake · Prep: 15 min. · Cooking: 65–75 min. · Level: 1 · Keeps: 2–3 days

HAWAIIAN POUND CAKE

3 cups all-purpose flour
2 teaspoons baking powder
1 teaspoon ground cinnamon
1 teaspoon ground ginger
1 teaspoon ground nutmeg
1/2 teaspoon baking soda
1/2 teaspoon salt

1 cup (2 sticks) butter, softened
2 cups granulated sugar
2 teaspoons pineapple extract
2 teaspoons vanilla extract
4 large eggs, at room temperature
2 cups mashed cooked sweet potatoes, cooled to room temperature

GLAZE

2 cups confectioners' sugar
1/4 cup (1/2 stick) butter, melted
2 teaspoons pineapple extract
1–2 tablespoons hot water

Preheat the oven to 350°F. • Butter and flour a 10-inch Bundt pan. • Sift the flour, baking powder, cinnamon, ginger, nutmeg, baking soda, and salt into a large bowl. • Beat the butter, sugar, pineapple extract, and vanilla in a large bowl with an electric mixer at medium speed until creamy. • Add the eggs, one at a time, until just blended after each addition. • With mixer at low speed, gradually beat in the sweet potatoes and dry ingredients. • Spoon the batter into the prepared pan. • Bake for 70–80 minutes, or until a toothpick inserted into the center comes out clean. • Run a knife around the edges of the pan to loosen the cake. Cool the cake in the pan for 15 minutes. Turn out onto a rack to cool completely. • *Glaze*: Beat the confectioners' sugar, butter, and pineapple extract in a medium bowl until smooth. Beat in enough of the water to make a glaze. Drizzle over the cake.

Makes one 10-inch cake · Prep: 25 min. · Cooking: 70–80 min. · Level: 1 · Keeps: 2–3 days

Hawaiian pound cake

Coconut pound cake

SIX-FLAVOR POUND CAKE

- ³/₄ cup milk
- 1 teaspoon almond extract
- 1 teaspoon coconut extract
- 1 teaspoon lemon extract
- 1 teaspoon rum extract
- 1 teaspoon vanilla extract
- 2¹/₂ cups all-purpose flour
- ¹/₂ teaspoon baking powder
- ¹/₄ teaspoon salt
- ³/₄ cup (1¹/₂ sticks) butter, softened
- ¹/₃ cup vegetable oil
- 2¹/₂ cups granulated sugar
- 2 tablespoons creamy peanut butter
- 4 large eggs, at room temperature

SIX-FLAVOR GLAZE

- ¹/₂ cup granulated sugar
- ¹/₄ cup water
- 1 tablespoon peanut butter
- ¹/₂ teaspoon almond extract
- ¹/₂ teaspoon coconut extract
- ¹/₂ teaspoon lemon extract
- ¹/₂ teaspoon vanilla extract
- ¹/₂ teaspoon rum-flavored extract

Preheat the oven to 325°F. • Butter and flour a 10-inch tube pan. • Pour the milk into a small bowl with the five extracts. • Sift the flour, baking powder, and salt into a large bowl. • Beat the butter, oil, sugar, and peanut butter in a large bowl with an electric mixer at medium speed until creamy. • Add the eggs, one at a time, until just blended after each addition. • With mixer at low speed, gradually beat in the dry ingredients, alternating with the milk mixture. • Spoon the batter into the prepared pan. • Bake for 1 hour and 25–35 minutes, or until a

toothpick inserted into the center comes out clean. • Run a knife around the edges of the pan to loosen the cake. Cool the cake in the pan for 15 minutes. Turn out onto a rack to cool completely. • *Six-Flavor Glaze*: Beat the sugar, water, peanut butter, and the five extracts in a saucepan and bring to a boil over low heat. Cook, stirring constantly, until the sugar has dissolved. Set aside to cool. • Drizzle over the cake.

Makes one 10-inch cake · Prep: 25 min. · Cooking: 1 hr. 25–35 min. · Level: 1 · Keeps: 3–4 days

COCONUT POUND CAKE

- 1¹/₂ cups all-purpose flour
- 1 teaspoon baking powder
- ¹/₂ teaspoon salt
- 1¹/₄ cups shredded coconut
- ³/₄ cup (1¹/₂ sticks) butter, softened
- 1¹/₂ cups granulated sugar
- 4 large eggs, at room temperature
- ¹/₃ cup milk
- 1¹/₂ teaspoons coconut extract
- ¹/₂ cup Vanilla Frosting (see page 347)
- 18 pecans, to decorate

Preheat the oven to 350°F. • Butter and flour a 10-inch tube pan. • Sift the flour, baking powder, and salt into a large bowl. Add the coconut. • Beat the butter and sugar in a large bowl with an electric mixer at medium speed until creamy. • Add the eggs, one at a time, until just blended after each addition. • With mixer at low speed, gradually beat in the dry ingredients, alternating with the milk and coconut extract. • Spoon the batter into

the prepared pan. • Bake for 55–65 minutes, or until the cake shrinks from the pan sides and a toothpick inserted into the center comes out clean. • Run a knife around the edges of the pan to loosen the cake. Cool the cake in the pan for 15 minutes. Turn out onto a rack to cool completely. • Spread with the frosting and decorate with the pecans.

Makes one 10-inch cake · Prep: 20 min. · Cooking: 55–65 min. · Keeps: 4–5 days

BARBADOS POUND CAKE

- 2 cups all-purpose flour
- ¹/₂ teaspoon baking powder
- ¹/₂ teaspoon baking soda
- ¹/₄ teaspoon salt
- 1 cup (2 sticks) butter, softened
- 2 cups granulated sugar
- 2 teaspoons rum extract
- 1 teaspoon coconut extract
- 4 large eggs, at room temperature
- ¹/₃ cup milk
- ¹/₃ cup evaporated milk or cream

SYRUP

- ¹/₂ cup granulated sugar
- ¹/₄ cup water
- 1 teaspoon almond extract
- 1 teaspoon coconut extract
- 1 teaspoon rum extract

Preheat the oven to 325°F. • Butter and flour a 10-inch tube pan. • Sift the flour, baking powder, baking soda, and salt into a medium bowl. • Beat the butter, sugar, and rum and coconut extracts in a large bowl with an electric mixer at medium speed until creamy. • Add the eggs, one at a time, until just blended after each addition. • With mixer at low speed, gradually beat in the dry ingredients, alternating with the milk and evaporated milk. • Spoon the batter into the prepared pan. • Bake for 55–65 minutes, or until a toothpick inserted into the center comes out clean. • Run a knife around the edges of the pan to loosen the cake. Cool the cake in the pan for 15 minutes. Turn out onto a rack to cool until warm. • *Syrup*: Bring the sugar, water, and extracts to a boil in a saucepan over low heat, stirring constantly. • Place the cake on a rack in a jelly-roll pan. Poke holes all over the cake. Spoon the syrup over the cake. Scoop up any syrup from the pan and drizzle over the cake.

Makes one 10-inch cake · Prep: 15 min. · Cooking: 55–65 min. · Level: 1 · Keeps: 2–3 days

CHOCOLATE CAKES

Our word "chocolate" comes from the Mayan word xocoatl. *The ancient Mayas and Aztecs believed that cocoa seeds were brought to earth from paradise and that grinding and eating them would bring great wisdom and knowledge. Most modern chocolate fiends would agree with that!*

CHOCOLATE LAYER CAKE WITH FRESH FIGS

CHOCOLATE FILLING

- 1 cup (2 sticks) butter, softened
- 1/3 cup unsweetened cocoa powder, sifted if lumpy
- 1/3 cup confectioners' sugar
- 1 teaspoon vanilla extract
- 1 9-inch Basic Chocolate Cake (see page 56)
- 1/2 cup orange liqueur
- 1/2 cup raspberry preserves
- 12 oz bittersweet chocolate, coarsely chopped
- 8 fresh green or black figs, stemmed and halved

Chocolate Filling: Beat the butter in a large bowl with an electric mixer at medium speed until creamy. • Gradually beat in the cocoa, confectioners' sugar, and vanilla until creamy. • Split the cake in three horizontally. • Place one layer on a serving plate. Drizzle with a little liqueur and spread with the preserves. Spread with a layer of the filling. Top with another layer. Repeat until all the layers, liqueur, preserves, and filling are used, finishing with a cake layer topped with filling. • Melt the chocolate in a double boiler over barely simmering water. • Cover a work surface with waxed paper and use a pencil to mark on about twenty-five 2 x 5-inch strips. Turn the paper over. • Use a metal spatula to spread the melted chocolate to fit into the marked strips. Set aside to cool. • Trim one end of the chocolate strips so that they are the same height as the cake, and arrange them around the sides of the cake, slightly overlapping each strip. • Arrange the figs on the top of the cake.

Makes one 9-inch cake · Prep: 45 min. · Level: 2 · Keeps: 2–3 days

◄ Chocolate layer cake with truffles (see page 72)

► Chocolate layer cake with fresh figs

USING CHOCOLATE

Chocolate adds the perfect finishing touch to a cake. Whether simply melted, grated, or cut into shavings, it provides a simple sophistication to any cake.

Melting

1 Chop the chocolate coarsely on a chopping board.

2 Place the chocolate in a double boiler.

3 Melt the chocolate, stirring constantly, until smooth.

Chocolate shavings

1 Pour the chocolate onto a cold surface, preferably marble. Use a thin metal spatula to spread the chocolate thinly. Let the chocolate set and cool completely.

2 Lightly but firmly, draw a chocolate shaver, vegetable peeler, or a long sharp knife over the chocolate so it forms small shavings or curls.

3 Alternately, take a chilled block of chocolate. Use a vegetable peeler to draw firmly across the chocolate to create shavings.

Grating chocolate

Grate the chocolate, making sure that the chocolate is cold or chilled.

Types of chocolate

SEMISWEET/BITTERSWEET CHOCOLATE is made from cocoa mass, additional cocoa butter, a small amount of sugar, and vanilla. A good quality chocolate will contain 60% cocoa solids and top quality chocolate has 70% or more.

MILK CHOCOLATE is made from the same ingredients as semisweet or bittersweet chocolate but with added milk products and a much lower percentage of cocoa solids. (About 40% in good quality milk chocolate). Poorer varieties contain vegetable fat instead of cocoa butter, as well as artificial vanilla flavoring.

WHITE CHOCOLATE is made from cocoa butter and sugar, but not cocoa solids.

Chocolate leaves

1 Choose non-poisonous, blemish-free leaves, such as lemon, magnolia, or rose. Use cotton wool to lightly clean the leaves with a little water.

2 Use a brush to paint the waxy side of each leaf with melted chocolate. Let stand in a cool place to dry completely.

3 Carefully peel the leaf away from the chocolate, making sure that no green remains on the chocolate.

Piped chocolate decorations

1 Fold thick waxed paper into a triangle with a flap at the top.

2 Make the top flap into a circle and fill ¼ full with melted chocolate.

3 Cut a tiny hole at the pointed end and pipe in your desired shapes on a sheet of waxed paper.

BASIC CHOCOLATE CAKE

This recipe makes a lovely rich cake that can be served as is (or glazed or frosted), or used as a base for chocolate gâteaux and layer cakes.

- 9 oz bittersweet chocolate, coarsely chopped
- 2 cups all-purpose flour
- 1/3 cup unsweetened cocoa powder
- 2 teaspoons baking powder
- 1/2 teaspoon baking soda
- 1/4 teaspoon salt
- 1 cup (2 sticks) butter, softened
- 2 1/2 cups granulated sugar
- 4 large eggs, at room temperature
- 1/2 cup milk
- 2 tablespoons vegetable oil

Preheat the oven to 350°F. • Butter and flour a 9-inch springform pan. • Melt the chocolate in a double boiler over barely simmering water. Set aside to cool. • Sift the flour, cocoa, baking powder, baking soda, and salt into a large bowl. • Beat the butter and sugar in a large bowl with an electric mixer at medium speed until creamy. • Add the eggs, one at a time, until just blended after each addition. • With mixer at low speed, gradually beat in the dry ingredients, alternating with the chocolate, milk, and oil. • Spoon the batter into the prepared pan. • Bake for 50–60 minutes, or until a toothpick inserted into the center comes out clean. • Cool the cake in the pan on a rack for 10 minutes. Loosen and remove the pan sides and let cool completely.

Makes one 9-inch cake · Prep: 45 min. · Cooking: 50–60 min. · Level: 1 · Keeps: 3–4 days

CHOCOLATE BUTTERMILK CAKE

- 1 cup semisweet chocolate chips
- 1/3 cup water
- 1 3/4 cups cake flour
- 1 teaspoon baking soda
- 1/4 teaspoon salt
- 2/3 cup butter, softened
- 1 cup superfine sugar
- 2 teaspoons vanilla extract
- 3 large eggs
- 1 cup buttermilk

CHOCOLATE CREAM FROSTING
- 1 cup semisweet chocolate chips
- 1/3 cup honey
- 2 tablespoons water
- 1/8 teaspoon salt
- 2 cups heavy cream

Preheat the oven to 375°F. • Butter three 9-inch round cake pans. Line with parchment paper. • Melt the chocolate chips with the water in a small saucepan over low heat. Set aside to cool. • Sift the flour, baking soda, and salt into a medium bowl. • Beat the butter and sugar in a large bowl with an electric mixer at medium speed until creamy. • Add the vanilla and eggs, one at a time, until just blended after each addition. With mixer at low speed, gradually beat in the chocolate mixture, followed by the dry ingredients, alternating with the buttermilk. • Spoon the batter evenly into the prepared pans. • Bake for 20–25 minutes, or until a toothpick inserted into the center comes out clean. Cool the cakes in the pans for 15 minutes. Turn out onto racks to cool completely. • *Chocolate Cream Frosting*:

Stir the chocolate chips, honey, water, and salt in a double boiler over low heat until the chocolate has melted. Set aside to cool completely. • With mixer at medium speed, beat the cream in a medium bowl until stiff. • Use a large rubber spatula to fold the chocolate mixture into the cream mixture. Place one cake on a serving plate. Spread with the chocolate frosting. Repeat with another cake and chocolate frosting. Top with the remaining cake. Spread the top of the cake with the remaining frosting.

Makes one 9-inch cake · Prep: 20 min. · Cooking: 20–25 min. · Level: 1 · Keeps: 5 days in the refrigerator

CHOCOLATE YOGURT CAKE

- 2 1/2 cups all-purpose flour
- 2 teaspoons baking powder
- 1/4 teaspoon salt
- 6 oz semisweet chocolate, coarsely chopped
- 1/2 cup water
- 3/4 cup (1 1/2 sticks) butter, softened
- 1 3/4 cups firmly packed brown sugar
- 1 teaspoon vanilla extract
- 3 large eggs, at room temperature
- 1/2 cup plain yogurt

CHOCOLATE SOUR CREAM FROSTING
- 12 oz semisweet chocolate, coarsely chopped
- 3/4 cup sour cream
- 1 1/2 cups confectioners' sugar

FILLING
- 1 1/2 cups heavy cream
- 3 tablespoons confectioners' sugar
- 1/2 teaspoon vanilla extract
- 1 cup raspberry jelly

Preheat the oven to 350°F. • Butter two 9-inch round cake pans. Line with waxed paper. Butter the paper. • Sift the flour, baking powder, and salt into a large bowl. •

Chocolate buttermilk cake

Melt the chocolate with the water in a double boiler over barely simmering water. Set aside to cool. • Beat the butter, brown sugar, and vanilla in a large bowl with an electric mixer at medium speed until creamy. • Add the eggs, one at a time, until just blended after each addition. • With mixer at low speed, gradually beat in the chocolate mixture, followed by the yogurt and dry ingredients. • Spoon half the batter into each of the prepared pans. • Bake for 30–40 minutes, or until a toothpick inserted into the centers comes out clean. • Turn out onto racks and let cool completely. • *Filling*: With mixer at high speed, beat the cream, confectioners' sugar, and vanilla in a medium bowl until stiff. • *Chocolate Sour Cream Frosting*: Melt the chocolate in a double boiler over barely simmering water. Remove from the heat. Stir in the sour cream and confectioners' sugar. Do not let the frosting cool completely or it will be too thick to spread. • Split each cake horizontally. Place one layer on a serving plate. Spread with $1/3$ of the raspberry jam and spread with a layer of frosting. Spread with $1/3$ of the cream. Repeat with the remaining cake layers. Top with a plain cake layer. • Spread the top and sides with the remaining frosting.

Makes one 9-inch cake · Prep: 25 min. · Cooking: 30–40 min. · Level: 2 · Keeps: 1–2 days

CHOCOLATE SNACKING CAKE

$1^1/_4$ cups all-purpose flour
1 cup granulated sugar
$1/_2$ cup unsweetened cocoa powder
$1/_2$ cup (1 stick) butter, softened
$1/_2$ cup plain yogurt or sour cream
$1/_4$ cup + 2 tablespoons strong cold coffee
1 large egg, at room temperature
1 teaspoon baking powder
1 teaspoon baking soda
1 teaspoon vanilla extract
$1/_4$ teaspoon salt

Preheat the oven to 325°F. • Butter a 9-inch square baking pan. Dust the pan with cocoa. • Place all the ingredients in a food processor and process for 1–2 minutes until smooth and well blended. Or, place in a large bowl and beat with an electric mixer at low speed until just blended. • Spoon the batter into the prepared pan. • Bake for 50–60 minutes, or until a toothpick inserted

into the center comes out clean. • Cool the cake completely in the pan on a rack.

Makes one 9-inch cake · Prep: 10 min. · Cooking: 50–60 min. · Level: 1 · Keeps: 4–5 days

CHOCOLATE COFFEE CAKE

A perfect picnic or potluck cake—moist and chocolately.

2 cups all-purpose flour
1 cup unsweetened cocoa powder, sifted if lumpy
2 teaspoons baking soda
1 teaspoon baking powder
$1/_2$ teaspoon salt
$1/_2$ cup (1 stick) butter, softened
$1^1/_2$ cups granulated sugar
2 teaspoons vanilla extract
2 large eggs, at room temperature
1 cup buttermilk
$1/_2$ cup strong cold coffee
2 cups Chocolate-Walnut Frosting (see page 347)

Preheat the oven to 350°F. • Butter and flour a 13 x 9-inch baking pan. • Sift the flour, cocoa, baking soda, baking powder, and salt into a large bowl. • Beat the butter, sugar, and vanilla in a large bowl with an electric mixer at medium speed until creamy. • Add the eggs, one at a time, until just blended after each addition. • With mixer at low speed, gradually beat in the dry ingredients, alternating with the buttermilk and coffee. • Spoon the batter into the prepared pan. • Bake for 30–40 minutes, or until a toothpick inserted into the center comes out clean. • Cool the cake completely in the pan on a rack. • Spread the top with the frosting.

Makes one 13 x 9-inch cake · Prep: 30 min. · Cooking: 30–40 min. · Level: 1 · Keeps: 3–4 days

CHOCOLATE COFFEE YOGURT CAKE

$1^1/_4$ cups all-purpose flour
$1^1/_2$ teaspoons baking powder
$1/_4$ teaspoon salt
$1/_2$ cup (1 stick) butter, softened
$3/_4$ cup granulated sugar
1 teaspoon vanilla extract
2 large eggs, at room temperature
1 tablespoon freeze-dried coffee granules, dissolved in $1/_2$ cup coffee-flavored yogurt

4 oz bittersweet chocolate, grated

COFFEE FROSTING
$1/_2$ cup (1 stick) butter, softened
2 cups confectioners' sugar
2 tablespoons strong cold coffee

Preheat the oven to 350°F. • Butter a 9-inch round cake pan. Line with waxed paper. Butter the paper. • Sift the flour, baking powder, and salt into a medium bowl. • Beat the butter, sugar, and vanilla in a large bowl with an electric mixer at medium speed until creamy. • Add the eggs, one at a time, until just blended after each addition. • With mixer at low speed, gradually beat in the dry ingredients, alternating with the yogurt mixture. Stir in the chocolate. • Spoon the batter into the prepared pan. • Bake for 30–40 minutes, or until a toothpick inserted into the center comes out clean. • Cool the cake in the pan for 10 minutes. Turn out onto a rack. Carefully remove the waxed paper and let cool completely. • *Coffee Frosting*: With mixer at medium speed, beat the butter, confectioners' sugar, and coffee in a large bowl until smooth. • Spread the top and sides of the cake with the frosting.

Makes one 9-inch cake · Prep: 20 min. · Cooking: 30–40 min. · Level: 1 · Keeps: 2–3 days

CHOCOLATE CHIP OATMEAL CAKE

$1^2/_3$ cups boiling water
$1^3/_4$ cups old-fashioned rolled oats
$1/_2$ cup firmly packed dark brown sugar
1 cup granulated sugar
$1/_2$ cup (1 stick) butter, softened
2 large eggs, at room temperature
$1^1/_3$ cups all-purpose flour
1 tablespoon unsweetened cocoa powder
1 teaspoon baking soda
$1/_2$ teaspoon salt
1 cup semisweet chocolate chips
1 cup walnuts, coarsely chopped

Preheat the oven to 350°F. • Butter and flour a 10-inch round cake pan. • Stir together the water and oats in a large bowl and let rest 10 minutes. • Stir in the sugars, butter, and eggs. Mix in the flour, cocoa, baking soda, and salt. • Spoon the batter into the prepared pan. Sprinkle with the chocolate chips and walnuts. • Bake for 15–20 minutes, or until lightly browned. • Cool the cake in the pan for 15 minutes. Turn out onto a rack to cool completely.

Makes one 10-inch cake · Prep: 20 min. · Cooking: 20 min. · Level: 1 · Keeps: 3 days

CHOCOLATE CHIP CAKE

If desired, fill with Mock Cream (see page 344) and spread with Simple Chocolate Frosting (see page 349).

- 1¼ cups all-purpose flour
- ½ cup whole-wheat flour
- 2 teaspoons baking powder
- ½ teaspoon salt
- ⅔ cup butter, softened
- 1 cup firmly packed brown sugar
- ½ cup granulated sugar
- 1½ teaspoons vanilla extract
- 3 large eggs, at room temperature
- 1 cup milk
- ¾ cup semisweet chocolate chips

Preheat the oven to 350°F. • Butter two 9-inch round cake pans. Line with waxed paper. Butter the paper. • Sift the flours, baking powder, and salt into a medium bowl. • Beat the butter, the sugars, and vanilla in a large bowl with an electric mixer at medium speed until creamy. • Add the eggs, one at a time, until just blended after each addition. • With mixer at low speed, gradually beat in the dry ingredients, alternating with the milk. • By hand, stir in the chocolate chips. • Spoon half the batter into each of the prepared pans. • Bake for 25–30 minutes, or until a toothpick inserted into the center comes out clean. • Cool the cakes in pans for 10 minutes. Turn out onto racks. Carefully remove the waxed paper and let cool completely.

Makes one 9-inch cake · Prep: 20 min. · Cooking: 25–30 min. · Level: 1 · Keeps: 5 days

GRANDMA'S CHOCOLATE CAKE

- 7 oz semisweet chocolate, coarsely chopped
- ⅓ cup butter, softened
- 1 cup granulated sugar
- 2 tablespoons all-purpose flour
- 4 large egg whites, at room temperature
- ¼ teaspoon salt

Preheat the oven to 300°F. • Butter a 9 x 2-inch round cake pan. Line with waxed paper. Butter the paper and dust with cocoa. • Melt the chocolate and butter in a double boiler over barely simmering water. • Transfer to a large bowl and beat in the sugar and flour. Set aside to cool. • Beat the egg whites and salt in a large bowl with an electric mixer at high speed until stiff peaks form. Use a large rubber spatula to fold them into the cooled chocolate mixture. • Spoon the batter into the

Eggless chocolate cake

prepared pan. • Bake for 20–25 minutes. The cake should have a slight crust, but still be soft inside. • Cool the cake in the pan for 10 minutes. Turn out onto a rack to cool. Carefully remove the waxed paper and let cool completely.

Makes one 9-inch cake · Prep: 25 min. · Cooking: 20–25 min. · Level: 1 · Keeps: 1–2 days

EGGLESS CHOCOLATE CAKE

- 1½ cups all-purpose flour
- ⅓ cup unsweetened cocoa powder
- 2 teaspoons baking powder
- 1 teaspoon ground cinnamon
- ½ teaspoon ground cloves
- ¼ teaspoon salt
  pinch of ground white pepper
- 1 cup granulated sugar
- ⅔ cup butter, melted
- ½ cup milk
- ½ cup dry Marsala wine or dry sherry

FILLING
- 1¾ cups chestnut puree or fig jam
- ⅓ cup dry Marsala wine or dry sherry
- 1 cup heavy cream

Preheat the oven to 350°F. • Butter a 9-inch springform pan. • Sift the flour, sugar, cocoa, baking powder, cinnamon, cloves, salt, and white pepper into a large bowl. Stir in the sugar. • Beat in the butter, milk, and Marsala with an electric mixer at low speed. • Spoon the batter into the prepared pan. • Bake for 30–35 minutes, or until a toothpick inserted into the center comes out clean. • Cool the cake in the pan for 10 minutes. Loosen and remove the pan sides. Invert the cake onto

a rack. Loosen and remove the pan bottom and let cool completely. • Filling: Mix the jelly and Marsala in a medium bowl. • Split the cake horizontally. Place one layer on a serving plate. Spread with ⅔ of the jam. Top with the remaining layer. Spread with the remaining jelly. • With mixer at high speed, beat the cream in a medium bowl until stiff. Spread the top of the cake with the cream.

Makes one 9-inch cake · Prep: 15 min. · Cooking: 30–35 min. · Level: 1 · Keeps: 1–2 days

LOW-CAL CHOCOLATE CAKE

Fructose may be found in large supermarkets or health food stores.

- 1½ cups all-purpose flour
- 1 cup low-fat milk
- ¼ cup granulated fructose
- ⅔ cup vegetable shortening or butter
- ½ cup unsweetened cocoa powder
- 2 large eggs, at room temperature
- 1½ teaspoons baking soda
- ¼ teaspoon salt

Preheat the oven to 350°F. • Butter and flour a 9-inch square baking pan. • Beat the flour, milk, fructose, shortening, cocoa, eggs, baking soda, and salt in a large bowl with an electric mixer at low speed. • Spoon the batter into the prepared pan. • Bake for 35–45 minutes, or until a toothpick inserted into the center comes out clean. • Cool the cake completely in the pan on a rack.

Makes one 9-inch cake · Prep: 20 min. · Cooking: 35–45 min. · Level: 1 · Keeps: 3–4 days

CHOCOLATE POTATO CAKE

- 1/2 cup unsweetened cocoa powder
- 2 cups all-purpose flour
- 1 1/2 teaspoons baking powder
- 1/4 teaspoon salt
- 1/2 cup (1 stick) butter, softened
- 3/4 cup granulated sugar
- 3 large eggs, at room temperature
- 1 cup cold unseasoned mashed potato
- 1/2 cup milk
- 1 1/2 cups Simple Chocolate Frosting (see page 349)

Preheat the oven to 350°F. • Butter and flour a 10-inch tube pan. • Sift the flour, cocoa, baking powder, and salt into a medium bowl. • Beat the butter and sugar in a large bowl with an electric mixer at medium speed until creamy. • Add the eggs, one at a time, until just blended after each addition. • With mixer at low speed, gradually beat in the potato, followed by the dry ingredients, alternating with the milk.• Spoon the batter into the prepared pan. • Bake for 30–40 minutes, or until a toothpick inserted into the center comes out clean. • Cool the cake in the pan for 30 minutes. Turn out onto a rack to cool completely. • Spread the top and sides of the cake with the frosting.

Makes one 10-inch cake · Prep: 20 min. · Cooking: 30–40 min. · Level: 1 · Keeps: 2–3 days

CHOCOLATE RAISIN CAKE WITH RUM FROSTING

- 1 cup raisins
- 2 tablespoons dark rum
- 1 large egg
- 3/4 cup firmly packed dark brown sugar
- 7 oz milk chocolate, coarsely chopped
- 1/2 cup (1 stick) butter
- 1 1/4 cups all-purpose flour
- 1 teaspoon baking powder
- 1/4 teaspoon salt

RUM FUDGE FROSTING

- 4 large egg yolks
- 1/3 cup superfine sugar
- 1/4 cup light cream
- 2 teaspoons dark rum
- 2 tablespoons butter, softened
- 1 teaspoon unsweetened cocoa powder

Preheat the oven to 350°F. • Butter an 8-inch square baking pan. • Stir together the raisins and rum in a large bowl. Cover and soak for 1 hour. • Beat the egg and brown sugar in a large bowl with an electric mixer at medium speed until creamy. • Melt the chocolate and butter in a

double boiler over barely simmering water. With mixer at medium speed, beat into the egg mixture. Use a large rubber spatula to fold in the flour, baking powder, salt, and raisin mixture. • Spoon the batter into the prepared pan. • Bake for 30–35 minutes, or until firmly set. Cool completely in the pan on a rack. • *Rum Fudge Frosting*: Beat the egg yolks, superfine sugar, cream, and rum in a medium saucepan until well blended. Cook over low heat, stirring constantly with a wooden spoon, until the mixture lightly coats a metal spoon, or registers 160°F on an instant-read thermometer. Immediately plunge the pan into a bowl of ice water and stir until the egg mixture has cooled. • Beat the butter in a small bowl until creamy. Use a large rubber spatula to fold in the cocoa powder. Gradually fold the cocoa butter into the egg yolk mixture. • Cover and refrigerate for 10 minutes. • Use a thin metal spatula to spread the frosting over the cake. • Cut into squares to serve.

Makes one 8-inch cake · Prep: 15 min. + 10 min. to chill + 1 hr. to soak · Cooking: 30–35 min. · Level: 1 · Keeps: 3–4 days

PRUNE CAKE WITH HOT CHOCOLATE SAUCE

- 1 1/2 cups pitted prunes, finely chopped
- 1 cup boiling water
- 1 teaspoon baking soda
- 1 cup all-purpose flour
- 1 teaspoon baking powder
- 1/4 teaspoon salt

- 1/4 cup (1/2 stick) butter, softened
- 3/4 cup firmly packed brown sugar
- 1 teaspoon vanilla extract
- 2 large eggs, at room temperature
- 4 oz bittersweet chocolate, grated

HOT CHOCOLATE SAUCE

- 1 1/4 cups heavy cream
- 4 oz bittersweet chocolate, coarsely chopped

Preheat the oven to 350°F. • Butter and flour a 9-inch Bundt pan. • Stir the prunes, boiling water, and baking soda in a medium bowl. Soak for 10 minutes. • Sift the flour, baking powder, and salt into a medium bowl. • Beat the butter, brown sugar, and vanilla in a large bowl with an electric mixer at medium speed until creamy. • Add the eggs, one at a time, until just blended after each addition. • With mixer at low speed, gradually beat in the dry ingredients. By hand, stir in the chocolate and the prune mixture. • Spoon the batter into the prepared pan. • Bake for 50–60 minutes, or until a toothpick inserted into the center comes out clean. • Cool the cake in the pan for 10 minutes. Turn out onto a serving plate. • *Hot Chocolate Sauce*: Melt the cream and chocolate in a double boiler over barely simmering water. • Pour the sauce over the warm cake.

Makes one 9-inch cake · Prep: 25 min. · Cooking: 50–60 min. · Level: 2 · Keeps: 1–2 days

Prune cake with hot chocolate sauce

CHOCOLATE FUDGE NUT SNACKING CAKE

3 oz semisweet chocolate, coarsely chopped
3 oz milk chocolate, coarsely chopped
1/2 cup (1 stick) butter, cut up
1/2 cup firmly packed dark brown sugar
2 tablespoons honey
2 large eggs, lightly beaten
1 cup all-purpose flour
1 teaspoon baking powder
1/4 teaspoon salt
2/3 cup macadamia nuts, finely chopped

Preheat the oven to 350°F. • Butter an 8-inch square baking pan. Line with waxed paper. Butter the paper. • Melt the chocolates and butter in a double boiler over barely simmering water. Remove from the heat. • Stir in the brown sugar and honey. • Add the eggs, one at a time, until just blended after each addition. • Use a large rubber spatula to fold in the flour, baking powder, salt, and nuts. • Spoon the batter into the prepared pan. • Bake for 30–35 minutes, or until a toothpick inserted into the center comes out clean. Cool completely in the pan on a rack.

Makes one 8-inch cake · Prep: 20 min. · Cooking: 30–35 min. · Level: 1 · Keeps: 3–4 days

CHOCOLATE CREAM CHEESE AND DATE CAKE

1 1/2 cups all-purpose flour
1/2 cup unsweetened cocoa powder
2 teaspoons baking powder
1/4 teaspoon salt
1/3 cup butter, softened
5 oz cream cheese, softened
3/4 cup granulated sugar
1/2 cup firmly packed brown sugar
2 large eggs, at room temperature
3/4 cup milk
3/4 cup chopped, pitted dates

Preheat the oven to 350°F. • Butter and flour a 9-inch tube pan. • Sift the flour, cocoa, baking powder, and salt into a medium bowl. • Beat the butter, cream cheese, and sugars in a large bowl with an electric mixer at medium speed until creamy. • Add the eggs, one at a time, until

just blended after each addition. • With mixer at low speed, gradually beat in the dry ingredients, alternating with the milk. By hand, stir in the dates. • Spoon the batter into the prepared pan. • Bake for 35–40 minutes, or until a toothpick inserted into the center comes out clean. • Cool the cake in the pan for 10 minutes. Turn out onto a rack to cool completely.

Makes one 9-inch cake · Prep: 10 min. · Cooking: 35–40 min. · Level: 1 · Keeps: 3 days

CHOCOLATE PEANUT BUTTER CAKE

2 cups all-purpose flour
2 teaspoons baking powder
1/4 teaspoon salt
6 oz semisweet chocolate, coarsely chopped
1/2 cup (1 stick) butter, softened
1 3/4 cups granulated sugar
1 teaspoon vanilla extract
4 large eggs, separated
1/2 cup smooth peanut butter
1 cup milk

PEANUT BUTTER FROSTING
1 1/2 cups confectioners' sugar
1/2 cup (1 stick) butter, melted
1/2 cup smooth peanut butter

Preheat the oven to 325°F. • Butter a 9-inch square baking pan. • Sift the flour, baking powder, and salt into a large bowl. • Melt the chocolate in a double boiler over barely simmering water. Set aside to cool. • Beat the butter, sugar, and vanilla in a large bowl with an electric mixer at medium speed until creamy. • Add the egg yolks, one at a time, until just blended after each addition. • With mixer at low speed, gradually beat in the chocolate and peanut butter, followed by the dry ingredients, alternating with the milk. • With mixer at high speed, beat the egg whites in a large bowl until stiff peaks form. Use a large rubber spatula to fold them into the chocolate mixture. • Spoon the batter into the prepared pan. • Bake for 1 hour and 15–25 minutes, or until a toothpick inserted into the center comes out clean. • Cool the cake in the pan for 10 minutes. Turn out onto a rack and let cool completely. • *Peanut Butter Frosting*: With mixer at high speed, beat the confectioners' sugar, butter, and peanut butter in a large bowl until smooth. • Spread the top and sides of the cake with the frosting.

Makes one 9-inch cake · Prep: 20 min. · Cooking: 1 hr. 15–25 min. · Level: 1 · Keeps: 2–3 days

This is a very old recipe for a traditional cake made in Emilia-Romagna, in northern Italy. Ingredients for the delicious chewy cake vary from town to town and from cook to cook.

SPICED ITALIAN FRUIT CAKE WITH CHOCOLATE GLAZE

1/2 cup walnuts, coarsely chopped
1/4 cup almonds, coarsely chopped
1/4 cup hazelnuts, coarsely chopped
1/4 cup pine nuts
2/3 cup mixed candied orange and lemon peel, cut into small cubes
2 tablespoons raisins, soaked in warm water for 20 minutes
1/3 cup unsweetened cocoa powder
3 oz dark chocolate, coarsely chopped
1/2 teaspoon ground cinnamon
1/2 teaspoon ground nutmeg
1/2 teaspoon ground coriander
1/2 teaspoon ground black pepper
1/4 cup honey, warmed
2 1/3 cups all-purpose flour
1/4 teaspoon fennel seeds

GLAZE
12 oz semisweet chocolate, coarsely chopped

Preheat the oven to 325°F. • Butter and flour a 10-inch round cake pan. • Mix together the walnuts, almonds, hazelnuts, pine nuts, candied peel, raisins, cocoa, chocolate, cinnamon, nutmeg, coriander, and pepper in a large bowl. Stir in the honey, flour, and fennel seeds. • Spoon the batter into the prepared pan. • Bake for 25–30 minutes, or until light golden brown. • Cool the cake in the pan for 30 minutes. Turn out onto a rack to cool completely. • *Glaze*: Melt the chocolate in a double boiler. Set aside to cool for 10 minutes. Spread over the cake.

Makes one 10-inch cake · Prep: 1 hr. · Cooking: 25–30 min. · Level: 1 · Keeps: 5 days (and much longer without the glaze)

Spiced Italian fruit cake
with chocolate glaze

Frosted chocolate log

lightly dust a clean kitchen towel with the remaining cocoa. • Loosen the edges of the cake while still warm. Turn out onto the prepared towel. Discard the paper. Trim off the crisp edges to make even sides. From a short side, roll up the cake jelly-roll fashion. Cool the cake completely still in the towel, seam-side-down. Unroll the cake and spread with the jam, leaving a border on all sides. Reroll the cake. Stand seam-side-down. • *Frosting*: Beat the confectioners' sugar, butter, cocoa, and vanilla in a medium bowl. Add enough water to make a thick, spreadable frosting. Spread the frosting over the roll. Decorate with the whipped cream.

Makes one 10-inch roll · Prep: 20 min. · Cooking: 12–15 min. · Level: 2 · Keeps: 2 days in the refrigerator

CHOCOLATE CHIP LOAF

This cake is yummy, even without the orange frosting. Enjoyed with a cold glass of milk, it'll be a big hit with the younger members of your family.

- 1¹/₂ cups all-purpose flour
- 1 teaspoon baking powder
- ¹/₂ teaspoon baking soda
- ¹/₄ teaspoon salt
- ¹/₃ cup butter, softened
- ³/₄ cup granulated sugar
- 1 teaspoon vanilla extract
- 1 large egg, at room temperature
- 1 cup sour cream
- ³/₄ cup bittersweet or semisweet chocolate chips

ORANGE FROSTING
- 1¹/₂ cups confectioners' sugar
- 3 tablespoons butter, melted
- 1 tablespoon grated orange zest
- 2–3 tablespoons fresh orange juice

Preheat the oven to 350°F. • Butter a 9 x 5-inch loaf pan. Line with aluminum foil, letting the edges overhang. Butter the foil. • Sift the flour, baking powder, baking soda, and salt into a medium bowl. • Beat the butter, sugar, and vanilla in a large bowl with an electric mixer at medium speed until creamy. • Add the egg, beating until just blended. • With mixer at low speed, gradually beat in the dry ingredients, alternating with the sour cream. • Stir in the chocolate chips. • Spoon the batter into the prepared pan. • Bake for 45–55 minutes, or until springy to the touch and a toothpick inserted into the center comes out clean. • Cool the loaf in the pan for 5 minutes. Using the foil as a lifter, remove the loaf from the

pan. Carefully remove the foil and let cool completely on a rack. • *Orange Frosting*: Mix the confectioners' sugar, butter, and the orange zest in a medium bowl. Add enough orange juice to make a thick, spreadable frosting. • Spread the frosting over.

Makes one 9 x 5-inch loaf · Prep: 20 min. · Cooking: 45–55 min. · Level: 1 · Keeps: 2–3 days

FROSTED CHOCOLATE LOG

- 3 large eggs
- ¹/₂ cup superfine sugar
- 3 tablespoons unsweetened cocoa powder, dissolved in 2 tablespoons boiling water
- ²/₃ cup all-purpose flour
- 1 teaspoon baking powder
- 2 tablespoons butter, melted
- 6 tablespoons raspberry jam

FROSTING
- 1¹/₄ cups confectioners' sugar
- 2 tablespoons butter, softened
- 2 tablespoons unsweetened cocoa powder
- ¹/₄ teaspoon vanilla extract
- 2 tablespoons (approx.) boiling water
- ¹/₄ cup heavy cream, beaten

Preheat the oven to 375°F. • Butter and flour a 10¹/₂ x 15¹/₂-inch jelly-roll pan. Line with waxed paper. Butter the paper. • Beat the eggs and sugar with an electric mixer at high speed until pale and thick. • Beat in 1 tablespoon cocoa. • Use a large rubber spatula to fold in the flour, baking powder, and butter. • Spoon the batter into the prepared pan. • Bake for 12–15 minutes, or until a toothpick inserted into the center comes out clean. • While the cake is baking,

FROSTED CHOCOLATE LOAVES

- 2 cups all-purpose flour
- ¹/₂ cup unsweetened cocoa powder
- 2 teaspoons baking powder
- ¹/₄ teaspoon salt
- 1 cup granulated sugar
- 3 large eggs, at room temperature
- ³/₄ cup plain yogurt
- ³/₄ cup (1¹/₂ sticks) butter, melted
- 1 teaspoon vanilla extract

CHOCOLATE FROSTING
- 6 oz semisweet chocolate, coarsely chopped
- 6 tablespoons butter, cut up
- 2 cups confectioners' sugar
- 3 tablespoons plain yogurt

Preheat the oven to 350°F. • Butter two 9 x 5-inch loaf pans and dust with cocoa. • Sift the flour, cocoa, baking powder, and salt into a large bowl. Stir in the sugar. • Beat in the eggs, yogurt, butter, and vanilla with an electric mixer at low speed until just blended. • Spoon the batter into the prepared pans. • Bake for 25–35 minutes, or until a toothpick inserted into the center comes out clean. • Cool the loaves in the pans for 10 minutes. Turn out onto racks and let cool completely. • *Chocolate Frosting*: Melt the chocolate and butter in a double boiler over barely simmering water. Set aside to cool. Gradually add the confectioners' sugar and yogurt. • Spread the loaves with the frosting.

Makes two 9 x 5-inch loaves · Prep: 15 min. · Cooking: 25–35 min. · Level: 1 · Keeps: 2–3 days

RICH CHOCOLATE LOAF

    8   oz bittersweet chocolate, coarsely chopped
 1/2   cup (1 stick) unsalted butter, cut up
    4   large eggs + 1 large egg yolk
    2   large egg whites, at room temperature
    1   cup heavy cream, beaten
    1   cup fresh strawberries, hulled and sliced

Preheat the oven to 325°F. • Butter a 9 x 5-inch loaf pan. Line with waxed paper. Butter the paper. • Melt the chocolate and butter in a double boiler over barely simmering water. Set aside to cool. • Beat the eggs and egg yolk in a double boiler over barely simmering water with an electric mixer at medium speed until pale and very thick. Use a large rubber spatula to fold into the chocolate mixture. • With mixer at high speed, beat the egg whites in a medium bowl until stiff peaks form. Use a large rubber spatula to fold them into the chocolate mixture. • Spoon the batter into the prepared pan. • Place the pan in a larger pan and pour in hot water to measure 1 inch up the sides of the loaf pan. • Bake for 50–60 minutes, or until a toothpick inserted into the center comes out clean. • Cool the loaf completely in the pan on a rack. Cover and refrigerate for 12 hours. • Turn the loaf out onto a serving plate. Carefully remove the waxed paper. • Cut the loaf into thin slices with a sharp knife. Serve with the cream and strawberries.

Makes one 9 x 5-inch loaf · Prep 35 min. + 12 hr. to chill · Cooking: 50–60 min. · Level: 1 · Keeps: 2–3 days

EASY PEPPERMINT CAKE

Use any mint-fondant-filled dark chocolate thins to make this tasty cake.

    1   package (7 oz) chocolate mint candy, such as After Eight
    1   box (18 oz) yellow cake mix
    2   cups heavy cream

Freeze the chocolate candy in the freezer for 1–2 hours. • When frozen, chop the candy not too finely in a food processor. • Prepare the cake according to the instructions on the package, baking in three buttered and floured 9-inch cake pans. If package instructions do not allow for baking in three pans, reduce baking time by 5–8 minutes. • Cool the cakes in the pans for 10 minutes. Invert onto racks to cool completely. • Beat the cream in a medium bowl with an electric mixer at high speed until stiff. By hand, carefully stir in the mint candy. • Place a cake on a serving plate. Spread with 1/3 of the cream mixture. Repeat until all the cakes and cream are piled up, finishing with a layer of cream. • Refrigerate for 24 hours before serving.

Makes one 9-inch cake · Prep: 30 min. + 24 hr. to chill · Level: 1 · Keeps: 2–3 days in the refrigerator

PEPPERMINT CREAM CAKE

    4   oz dark chocolate, coarsely chopped
 1/4   cup water
1 1/4   cups all-purpose flour
    2   tablespoons unsweetened cocoa powder
    1   teaspoon baking powder
    1   teaspoon baking soda
 1/4   teaspoon salt
 1/2   cup (1 stick) butter, melted
    1   cup granulated sugar
 1/3   cup firmly packed brown sugar
    2   large eggs, at room temperature
 1/3   cup milk

PEPPERMINT FILLING

    3   cups confectioners' sugar
 1/2   cup (1 stick) butter, softened
    1   tablespoon milk
 1/2   teaspoon peppermint extract

CHOCOLATE FROSTING

    2   cups confectioners' sugar
 1/4   cup unsweetened cocoa powder
    1   tablespoon butter
 1/3   cup (approx.) hot water

Preheat the oven to 350°F. • Butter a 9-inch round cake pan. Line with waxed paper. Butter the paper. • Melt the chocolate and water in a double boiler over barely simmering water. Set aside to cool. • Sift the flour, cocoa, baking powder, baking soda, and salt into a medium bowl. • Beat the butter, and both sugars in a large bowl with an electric mixer at medium speed until creamy. • Add the eggs, one at a time, until just blended after each addition. • With mixer at low speed, gradually beat in the dry ingredients, alternating with the milk and chocolate. • Spoon the batter into the prepared pan. • Bake for 30–40 minutes, or until a toothpick inserted into the center comes out clean. • Cool the cake in the pan for 10 minutes. Turn out onto a rack. Carefully remove the waxed paper and let cool completely. • *Peppermint Filling*: With mixer at high speed, beat the confectioners' sugar and butter in a medium bowl until creamy. Stir in the milk and peppermint extract. • *Chocolate Frosting*: Stir together the confectioners' sugar and cocoa in a medium bowl. Beat in the butter and enough water to make a thick, spreadable frosting. • Split the cake horizontally. • Place one layer on a serving plate. Spread with the filling. Top with the remaining layer. Spread the top and sides with the chocolate frosting.

Makes one 9-inch cake · Prep: 40 min. · Cooking: 30–40 min. · Level: 2 · Keeps: 2–3 days

PEPPERMINT CAKE

    2   oz bittersweet chocolate, coarsely chopped
    2   cups all-purpose flour
    1   teaspoon baking soda
 1/4   teaspoon salt
 1/3   cup vegetable shortening, softened
 1/2   cup granulated sugar
    2   teaspoons vanilla extract
 1/2   teaspoon peppermint oil
    1   large egg, at room temperature
 1/2   cup milk
 1/4   cup plain yogurt
    1   cup Chocolate Peppermint Frosting (see page 350) (optional)

Preheat the oven to 350°F. • Butter and flour a 9-inch round cake pan. • Melt the chocolate in a double boiler over barely simmering water. Set aside to cool. • Sift the flour, baking soda, and salt into a medium bowl. • Beat the shortening, sugar, vanilla, and peppermint oil in a large bowl with an electric mixer at medium speed until creamy. • Add the egg, beating until just blended. • With mixer at low speed, gradually beat in the dry ingredients, alternating with the milk and yogurt. • Spoon the batter into the prepared pan. • Bake for 30–40 minutes, or until a toothpick inserted into the center comes out clean. • Cool the cake completely in the pan on a rack. • Spread with the frosting, if desired.

Makes one 9-inch cake · Prep: 20 min. · Cooking: 30–40 min. · Level: 1 · Keeps: 2–3 days

PINEAPPLE CHOCOLATE SNACKING CAKE

- 1 cup all-purpose flour
- 1/2 cup unsweetened cocoa powder
- 1 teaspoon baking powder
- 1 teaspoon ground cinnamon
- 1/4 teaspoon salt
- 3/4 cup (1 1/2 sticks) butter, softened
- 1 1/2 cups granulated sugar
- 1 teaspoon vanilla extract
- 3 large eggs, at room temperature
- 1 cup crushed drained canned pineapple
- 1/4 cup walnuts, chopped
- 2 cups Simple Chocolate Frosting (see page 349) (optional)

Preheat the oven to 350°F. • Butter and flour a 13 x 9-inch baking pan. • Sift the flour, cocoa, baking powder, cinnamon, and salt into a medium bowl. • Beat the butter, sugar, and vanilla in a large bowl with an electric mixer at medium speed until creamy. Add the eggs, one at a time, until just blended after each addition. • With mixer at low speed, gradually beat in the dry ingredients. • By hand, stir in the pineapple and walnuts. • Spoon the batter into the prepared pan. • Bake for 35–45 minutes, or until a toothpick inserted into the center comes out clean. • Cool the cake completely in the pan on a rack. • Spread with the frosting, if desired.

Makes one 13 x 9-inch cake · Prep 20 min. · Cooking: 35–45 min. · Level: 1 · Keeps: 2–3 days

CHOCOLATE CARROT CAKE

- 1 1/2 cups all-purpose flour
- 1/2 cup walnuts, chopped
- 1/2 cup raisins
- 1/3 cup shredded sweetened coconut
- 1/3 cup unsweetened cocoa powder
- 1 teaspoon ground cinnamon
- 1 teaspoon baking powder
- 1/2 teaspoon baking soda
- 1/2 teaspoon ground ginger
- 1/4 teaspoon ground nutmeg
- 1/4 teaspoon salt
- 5 oz milk chocolate, coarsely chopped
- 3 large eggs, at room temperature
- 3/4 cup firmly packed brown sugar
- 1/2 cup vegetable oil
- 3 cups finely shredded carrots

MILK CHOCOLATE FROSTING

- 6 oz milk chocolate, coarsely chopped
- 1 package (8 oz) cream cheese, softened
- 2 cups confectioners' sugar

Preheat the oven to 350°F. • Butter and flour a 13 x 9-inch baking pan. • Stir together the flour, walnuts, raisins, coconut, cocoa, baking powder, cinnamon, baking soda, ginger, nutmeg, and salt in a large bowl. • Melt the chocolate in a double boiler over barely simmering water. Set aside to cool. • Beat the eggs, sugar, and oil in a large bowl with an electric mixer at medium speed until creamy. • With mixer at low speed, gradually beat in the dry ingredients, alternating with the chocolate and carrots. • Spoon the batter into the prepared pan. • Bake for 40–50 minutes, or until a toothpick inserted into the center comes out clean. • Cool the cake completely in the pan on a rack. • *Milk Chocolate Frosting*: Melt the chocolate in a double boiler over barely simmering water. Set aside to cool. • With mixer at medium speed, beat the cream cheese and confectioners' sugar in a large bowl. Beat in the melted chocolate. Spread the top of the cake with the frosting.

Makes one 13 x 9-inch cake · Prep: 30 min. · Cooking: 40–50 min. · Level: 1 · Keeps: 2–3 days

QUICK-MIX CHOCOLATE APPLE CAKE

- 2 large tart apples (about 1 lb), coarsely grated
- 2 cups all-purpose flour
- 1 1/2 cups (3 sticks) butter, softened
- 1 1/4 cups granulated sugar
- 3 large eggs, at room temperature
- 1/3 cup unsweetened cocoa powder
- 1/3 cup water
- 2 teaspoons baking powder
- 1/2 teaspoon baking soda
- 1/4 teaspoon salt
- 2 cups Rich Chocolate Frosting (see page 349)

Preheat the oven to 350°F. • Butter a 13 x 9-inch baking pan. Line with waxed paper. Butter the paper. • Beat the apples, flour, butter, sugar, eggs, cocoa, water, baking powder, baking soda, and salt in a large bowl with an electric mixer at low speed, until just blended. • Spoon the batter into the prepared pan. • Bake for 50–60 minutes, or until a toothpick inserted into the center comes out clean. • Cool the cake in the pan for 10 minutes. Turn out onto a rack. Carefully remove the waxed paper and let cool completely. • Spread the top and sides of the cake with the frosting.

Makes one 13 x 9-inch cake · Prep: 10 min. · Cooking: 50–60 min. · Level: 1 · Keeps: 2 days

Chocolate carrot cake

Sachertorte

SACHERTORTE

 5 oz semisweet chocolate, coarsely chopped
 1/3 cup butter, softened
 1/2 cup granulated sugar
 5 large eggs, separated
 2/3 cup all-purpose flour
 1/3 cup apricot preserves

FROSTING
 1 tablespoon butter
 4 oz semisweet chocolate, coarsely chopped
 1/3 cup strong cold coffee
 2 cups confectioners' sugar
 1 tablespoon vanilla extract

Preheat the oven to 325°F. • Set out a 9-inch springform pan. • Melt the chocolate in a double boiler over barely simmering water. Set aside to cool. • Beat the butter and sugar in a large bowl with an electric mixer at medium speed until creamy. • Add the egg yolks, one at a time, until just blended after each addition. • Use a large rubber spatula to fold in the chocolate and flour. • With mixer at high speed, beat the egg whites until stiff peaks form. Fold them into the batter. • Spoon the batter into the prepared pan. • Bake for 55–60 minutes, or until a toothpick inserted into the center comes out clean. • Cool the cake in the pan for 20 minutes. Loosen and remove the pan sides and let cool completely. • Split the cake horizontally. Place one layer on a serving plate. Spread with the preserves. Top with the remaining cake. • *Frosting*: Melt the butter and chocolate in a double boiler over barely simmering water. Add the coffee, confectioners' sugar and vanilla. Beat and spread with the frosting.

Makes one 9-inch cake · Prep: 25 min. · Cooking: 60 min. · Level: 2 · Keeps: 5 days

CHOCOLATE APRICOT JAM CAKE

Serve this cake with chopped fresh fruit and whipped cream.

 1 1/4 cups all-purpose flour
 1/3 cup unsweetened cocoa powder
 1 teaspoon baking powder
 1/4 teaspoon salt
 1/2 cup (1 stick) butter, cut up
 3/4 cup granulated sugar
 1/2 cup + 2 tablespoons apricot preserves
 1/3 cup water
 2 large eggs, lightly beaten
 3–4 ripe, fresh apricots (optional)
 2 tablespoons apricot brandy

Preheat the oven to 350°F. • Butter a 9-inch springform pan. Dust with cocoa. • Sift the flour, cocoa, baking powder, and salt into a large bowl. Make a well in the center. • Place the butter, sugar, 1/2 cup preserves, and the water in a saucepan over low heat, stirring constantly, until the sugar has dissolved. • Beat the butter mixture into the dry ingredients with an electric mixer at low speed. Add the eggs, one at a time, until just blended after each addition. • Spoon the batter into the prepared pan. • Bake for 30–40 minutes, or until a toothpick inserted into the center comes out clean. • Cool the cake in the pan for 10 minutes. Loosen and remove the pan sides. Invert the cake onto a serving plate. Loosen and remove the pan bottom and let cool completely. • If using the apricots, slice them thinly and arrange on the cake. • Warm the remaining preserves and brandy in a saucepan over low heat.

Brush over the apricots or simply over the cooled cake.

Makes one 9-inch cake · Prep: 25 min. · Cooking: 30–40 min. · Level: 1 · Keeps: 2–3 days

CHOCOLATE APPLESAUCE CAKE

This very moist cake does not need to be frosted because it is sprinkled with chocolate chips and walnuts before baking.

 1 cup all-purpose flour
 2 tablespoons unsweetened cocoa powder
 3/4 teaspoon baking soda
 1/4 teaspoon salt
 1/4 cup (1/2 stick) butter, softened
 3/4 cup granulated sugar
 1 teaspoon vanilla extract
 2 large eggs, at room temperature
 1 cup unsweetened applesauce
 1/2 cup semisweet chocolate chips
 1/2 cup walnuts, chopped

Preheat the oven to 350°F. • Butter and flour an 8-inch square baking pan. • Sift the flour, cocoa, baking soda, and salt into a medium bowl. • Beat the butter, sugar, and vanilla in a large bowl with an electric mixer at medium speed until creamy. • Add the eggs, one at a time, until just blended after each addition. • With mixer at low speed, gradually beat in the dry ingredients, alternating with the applesauce. • Spoon the batter into the prepared pan. Sprinkle with the chocolate chips and walnuts. • Bake for 30–35 minutes, or until a toothpick inserted into the center comes out clean. • Cool the cake completely in the pan on a rack.

Makes one 8-inch cake · Prep: 20 min. · Cooking: 35 min. · Level: 1 · Keeps: 3–4 days

Chocolate-orange cake

EASY CHOCO-ORANGE CAKE

- 1³/₄ cups all-purpose flour
- 1¹/₂ cups granulated sugar
- ¹/₂ cup unsweetened cocoa powder
- ¹/₂ cup (1 stick) butter, softened
- 2 tablespoons grated orange zest
- ¹/₂ cup fresh orange juice
- 3 large eggs, at room temperature
- ¹/₄ cup water
- 1¹/₂ teaspoons baking powder
- ¹/₂ teaspoon baking soda
- ¹/₄ teaspoon salt

MARBLED FROSTING

- ¹/₄ cup (¹/₂ stick) butter, at room temperature
- 1 tablespoon grated orange zest
- 2 cups confectioners' sugar
- 2 tablespoons milk
- 2 tablespoons unsweetened cocoa powder, sifted if lumpy

Preheat the oven to 350°F. • Butter an 11 x 7-inch baking pan. • Beat the flour, sugar. cocoa, butter, orange zest and juice, eggs, water, baking powder, baking soda, and salt in a large bowl with an electric mixer at low speed until just blended. Increase mixer speed to medium and beat for 5 minutes, or until the batter is smooth. •

Spoon the batter into the prepared pan. • Bake for 35–45 minutes, or until a toothpick inserted into the center comes out clean. • Cool the cake completely in the pan on a rack. • *Marbled Frosting*: With mixer at high speed, beat the butter and orange zest in a large bowl until creamy. Gradually beat in the confectioners' sugar and milk. • Place half the mixture in another bowl. Stir in the cocoa. • Place spoonfuls of orange and chocolate frosting next to each other on top of the cake. Swirl them together with a knife to create a marbled effect.

Makes one 11 x 7-inch cake · Prep: 25 min. · Cooking: 35–45 min. · Level: 1 · Keeps: 2–3 days

CHOCOLATE-ORANGE CAKE

- 1²/₃ cups cake flour
- ²/₃ cup unsweetened cocoa powder
- 1¹/₂ teaspoons baking powder
- ³/₄ cup (1¹/₂ sticks) butter, softened
- ¹/₂ cup granulated sugar
- 2 large eggs
  zest of 1 orange
- ¹/₂ cup fresh orange juice
- ¹/₃ cup firmly packed dark brown sugar

FROSTING

- 1 (8 oz) package cream cheese, softened
- ¹/₂ cup confectioners' sugar
- 2 teaspoons finely grated orange zest
- ¹/₃ cup orange juice
  shredded orange zest, to decorate

Preheat the oven to 350°F. • Butter an 8-inch square baking pan. • Sift the flour, cocoa, and baking powder into a medium bowl. • Beat the butter and granulated sugar in a large bowl with an electric mixer at medium speed until creamy. Add the eggs, one at a time, until just blended after each addition. • Stir in the orange zest. • Mix the orange juice and brown sugar in a saucepan over low heat until the sugar has dissolved. Remove from the heat and set aside to cool. • With mixer at low speed, gradually beat the dry ingredients into the butter mixture, alternating with the orange mixture. • Spoon the batter into the prepared pan. • Bake for 40–45 minutes, or until a toothpick inserted into the center comes out clean. • Cool the cake in the pan for 15 minutes. Turn out onto a rack to cool completely. *Frosting*: With mixer at medium speed, beat the cream cheese, confectioners' sugar, and orange zest and juice in a large bowl until creamy. • Place the cake on a serving plate. Spread the top of the cake with the frosting. Decorate with the orange zest.

Makes one 8-inch square cake · Prep: 35 min. ·Cooking: 40–45 min. · Level: 1 · Keeps: 1–2 days

GINGER-ORANGE CHOCOLATE CAKE

- ¹/₂ cup (1 stick) butter
- 7 oz bittersweet chocolate, coarsely chopped
- 1 cup granulated sugar
- 1 tablespoon grated orange zest
- 1 tablespoon fresh orange juice
- 2 large eggs
- 1 cup all-purpose flour
- 1 teaspoon baking powder
- ¹/₄ teaspoon salt
- ¹/₃ cup candied ginger, chopped
- ¹/₃ cup mixed candied peel, chopped
  confectioners' sugar, to dust

Preheat the oven to 350°F. • Butter an 8-inch square baking pan. Line with waxed paper. Butter the paper. • Melt the chocolate and butter in a double boiler over barely simmering water. Transfer to a large bowl. Beat in the sugar and orange zest and juice with an electric mixer at medium speed until creamy. Add the eggs, one at a time, until just blended after each addition. Use a large rubber spatula to fold in the flour, baking powder, salt, ginger, and candied peel. • Spoon the batter into the prepared pan. • Bake for 45–50 minutes, or until a toothpick inserted into the center comes out clean. Cool completely in the pan on a rack. • Dust with confectioners' sugar.

Makes one 8-inch cake · Prep: 20 min. · Cooking: 45–50 min. · Level: 1 · Keeps: 3–4 days

CHOCOLATE-ORANGE MARBLE CAKE

    2   cups all-purpose flour
    2   teaspoons baking powder
  1/4   teaspoon salt
 2 1/2 oz bittersweet chocolate, coarsely chopped
  1/2   cup (1 stick) butter, softened
 1 1/2 cups granulated sugar
    2   teaspoons vanilla extract
    2   large eggs, at room temperature
  3/4   cup milk
    2   tablespoons grated orange zest

FUDGE FROSTING

    4   oz bittersweet chocolate, coarsely chopped
  1/2   cup (1 stick) butter, softened
 3 1/2 cups confectioners' sugar
  1/4   cup milk
    1   teaspoon vanilla extract
        candied orange peel, to decorate

Preheat the oven to 350°F. • Butter two 9-inch round cake pans. Line with waxed paper. Butter the paper. • Sift the flour, baking powder, and salt into a large bowl. • Melt the chocolate in a double boiler over barely simmering water. Set aside to cool. • Beat the butter, sugar, and vanilla in a large bowl with an electric mixer at medium speed until creamy. • Add the eggs, one at a time, until just blended after each addition. • With mixer at low speed, gradually beat in the dry ingredients, alternating with the milk. • Place half the batter in another bowl. Stir the chocolate into one bowl of batter and the orange zest into the other. • Drop alternating spoonfuls of the batters into the pans. Swirl the batters together with a knife to create a marbled effect. • Bake for 35–45 minutes, or until a toothpick inserted into the center comes out clean. • Cool the cakes in the pans for 10 minutes. Turn out onto racks. Carefully remove the paper and let cool completely. • *Fudge Frosting*: Melt the chocolate in a double boiler over barely simmering water. Set aside to cool. • With mixer at high

Chocolate-orange marble cake

speed, beat the butter and half the confectioners' sugar in a large bowl until creamy. Beat in the chocolate, milk, and vanilla. Beat in the remaining confectioners' sugar. • Place one cake on a serving plate. Spread with 1/3 of the frosting. Top with the remaining cake. Spread the top and sides with the remaining frosting. Decorate with the candied orange peel.

Makes one 9-inch cake · Prep: 30 min. · Cooking: 35–45 min. · Level: 1 · Keeps: 3 days

CHOCOLATE-BANANA CAKE WITH CREAM CHEESE FROSTING

    2   cups all-purpose flour
  1/2   cup unsweetened cocoa powder
 1 1/2 teaspoons baking powder
  1/2   teaspoon baking soda
  1/4   teaspoon salt
    1   cup granulated sugar
    2   large eggs, at room temperature
  3/4   cup hot water
    1   cup mashed very ripe bananas
        (about 3 large bananas)
 1 1/2 teaspoons vanilla extract

CREAM CHEESE FROSTING

    3   oz cream cheese, softened
  1/4   cup (1/2 stick) butter, softened
    1   teaspoon vanilla extract
    2   cups confectioners' sugar
  1/4   cup unsweetened cocoa powder

Preheat the oven to 350°F. • Butter a 9-inch square baking pan. Line with waxed paper. Butter the paper. • Sift the flour, cocoa, baking powder, baking soda, and salt into a large bowl. Stir in the sugar. • Beat in the eggs, water, banana and vanilla. • Spoon the batter into the prepared pan. • Bake for 35–40 minutes, or until a toothpick inserted into the center comes out clean. • Cool the cake in the pan for 10 minutes. Turn out onto a rack. Carefully remove the paper and let cool completely. • *Cream Cheese Frosting*: Beat the cream cheese, butter, and vanilla in a large bowl with an electric mixer at medium speed until creamy. With mixer at low speed, beat in the confectioners' sugar and cocoa. • Spread the cake with the frosting.

Makes one 9-inch cake · Prep: 20 min. · Cooking: 35–40 min. · Level: 1 · Keeps: 2–3 days

CHOCOLATE COFFEE LIQUEUR CAKE

This is really a warm oven-baked pudding, served with a divine sauce.

1 1/2 cups all-purpose flour
1/3 cup unsweetened cocoa powder
1 1/2 teaspoons baking powder
1/4 teaspoon salt
1/3 cup almonds, finely ground
2/3 cup butter, softened
1 cup firmly packed brown sugar
2 large eggs, at room temperature
2 tablespoons freeze-dried coffee granules, dissolved in 1/2 cup boiling water

CHOCOLATE LIQUEUR SAUCE
3/4 cup granulated sugar
3/4 cup water
1/4 cup chocolate liqueur

Preheat the oven to 350°F. • Butter and flour a 9-inch ring pan. • Sift the flour, cocoa, baking powder, and salt into a medium bowl. Stir in the almonds. • Beat the butter and brown sugar in a large bowl with an electric mixer at medium speed until creamy. • Add the eggs, one at a time, until just blended after each addition. • With mixer at low speed, gradually beat in the dry ingredients, alternating with the coffee mixture. • Spoon the batter into the prepared pan. • Bake for 30–40 minutes, or until a toothpick inserted into the center comes out clean. • Cool the cake in the pan for 15 minutes. Turn out onto a rack and cool until warm. • *Chocolate Liqueur Sauce*: Stir the sugar, water, and chocolate liqueur in a small saucepan over medium-low heat until the sugar has dissolved. Bring to a boil and simmer, stirring constantly, until reduced by half. Remove from the heat and cool for 5 minutes. • Pour the sauce over the warm cake and serve.

Makes one 9-inch cake · Prep: 25 min. · Cooking: 30–40 min. · Level: 1 · Keeps: 2–3 days

COFFEE LIQUEUR FUDGE CAKE

This cake puffs up like a big mushroom and deflates as it cools. Leave the cake on the pan bottom to serve it easily.

8 large egg whites, at room temperature
1 cup firmly packed brown sugar
1 cup (2 sticks) unsalted butter, cut up
8 oz bittersweet chocolate, coarsely chopped
3 tablespoons coffee liqueur
1 tablespoon vanilla extract
1 tablespoon strong cold coffee

Preheat the oven to 300°F. • Butter and flour a 10-inch springform pan. • Beat the egg whites with an electric mixer at medium speed until frothy. With mixer at high speed, gradually beat in the brown sugar, beating until stiff peaks form. • Melt the butter in a medium saucepan over low heat. Remove from the heat and stir in the chocolate until melted. • Use a large rubber spatula to gradually fold the liqueur, vanilla, coffee, and the chocolate mixture into the beaten whites. • Spoon the batter into the prepared pan. • Bake for 35–45 minutes, or until a toothpick inserted into the center comes out clean. • Cool the cake completely in the pan on a rack. Refrigerate for at least 3 hours, or until set before serving. Loosen and remove the pan sides to serve.

Makes one 10-inch cake · Prep 25 min. + 3 hr. to chill · Cooking: 35–45 min. · Level: 1 · Keeps: 2–3 days

CHOCOLATE RUM CAKE

A tall, attractive cake. For a fancier look, decorate with chocolate curls.

1/2 cup water
1/2 cup unsweetened cocoa powder
2 teaspoons baking soda
2 cups all-purpose flour
1/2 cup cornstarch
1/4 teaspoon salt
2/3 cup butter, softened
1 3/4 cups granulated sugar
1 1/2 teaspoons vanilla extract
2 large eggs, at room temperature
1 cup sour cream

CHOCOLATE-RUM FROSTING
2 cups confectioners' sugar
1/3 cup unsweetened cocoa powder
2/3 cup butter, melted
1 1/2 tablespoons rum
1 teaspoon vanilla extract
1–2 tablespoons milk

Preheat the oven to 350°F. • Butter and flour two 9-inch cake pans. • Stir the water, cocoa, and baking soda in a saucepan over low heat until smooth. Set aside to cool. • Sift the flour, cornstarch, and salt into a medium bowl. • Beat the butter, sugar, and vanilla in a large bowl with an electric mixer at medium speed until creamy. • Add

Chocolate coffee liqueur cake

the eggs, one at a time, until just blended after each addition. • With mixer at low speed, beat in the dry ingredients, alternating with the sour cream and cocoa mixture. • Spoon half the batter into each of the prepared pans. • Bake for 45–55 minutes, or until springy to the touch and a toothpick inserted into the center comes out clean. • Cool the cakes in the pans for 5 minutes. Turn out onto racks to cool completely. • *Chocolate-Rum Frosting*: Mix the confectioners' sugar and cocoa in a large bowl. Add the butter, rum, and vanilla. Beat in enough of the milk to make a thick, spreadable frosting. • Place a cake on a serving plate. Spread with $1/3$ of the frosting. Top with the remaining cake. Spread with the remaining frosting.

Makes one 9-inch cake · Prep: 25 min. · Cooking: 45–55 min. · Level: 1 · Keeps: 1–2 days

CHOCOLATE RUM CAKE WITH ALMOND BRITTLE

Sweet, intense, and for serious chocolate lovers, only.

ALMOND BRITTLE
$1/2$ cup granulated sugar
$1/2$ cup almonds, finely ground

CHOCOLATE RUM CAKE
8 oz bittersweet chocolate, coarsely chopped
8 oz milk chocolate, coarsely chopped
$1/4$ cup ($1/2$ stick) butter, cut up
$1/2$ cup raisins
$1/4$ cup all-purpose flour
2 tablespoons granulated sugar
2 large eggs, separated
2 tablespoons dark rum
$1/4$ teaspoon salt

Almond Brittle: Oil a cookie sheet. Place the sugar in a saucepan over medium heat, stirring constantly, until the sugar has dissolved. Bring to a boil, and cook without stirring, until a deep golden color. • Stir in the almonds and then pour onto the prepared cookie sheet. Set aside to cool. • Break into pieces or coarsely chop in a food processor. • *Chocolate Rum Cake*: Preheat the oven to 350°F. • Butter a 9-inch round cake pan. Line with waxed paper. Butter the paper. • Melt the two chocolates and butter in a double boiler over barely simmering water. Transfer to a large bowl and set aside until lukewarm. • Stir in the raisins, flour, sugar, egg yolks, and rum. • Beat the egg whites and salt in a small bowl with an

electric mixer at high speed until stiff peaks form. Use a large rubber spatula to fold them into the batter. • Spoon the batter into the prepared pan. • Bake for 10 minutes. Sprinkle with the almond brittle and bake for 10–15 minutes more. • Turn the oven off and leave the cake in the oven with the door ajar for 2 hours. • Turn out of the pan and wrap carefully in foil. • Refrigerate for at least 4 hours before serving.

Makes one 9-inch cake · Prep: 25 min. + 6 hr. to cool and chill · Cooking: 20–25 min. · Level: 1 · Keeps: 1 day

CHOCOHOLIC SUPREME

8 oz bittersweet chocolate, coarsely chopped
$2/3$ cup all-purpose flour
1 teaspoon baking powder
$1/4$ teaspoon salt
$1/3$ cup almonds, finely ground
$1/2$ cup (1 stick) butter, softened
$3/4$ cup granulated sugar
3 large eggs, separated
3 tablespoons orange liqueur

CHOCOLATE FROSTING
8 oz bittersweet chocolate, coarsely chopped
$1/2$ cup (1 stick) butter
$1/4$ cup orange marmalade
2 tablespoons orange liqueur
1 cup Chocolate Ganache (see page 350) (optional)

Preheat the oven to 350°F. • Butter and flour a 9-inch springform pan. • Melt the chocolate in a double boiler over barely simmering water. Set aside to cool. • Sift the flour, baking powder, and salt into a medium bowl. Stir in the almonds. • Beat the butter and sugar in a large bowl with an electric mixer at medium speed until creamy. • Add the egg yolks, one at a time, until just blended after each addition. • With mixer at low speed, gradually beat in the cooled chocolate, followed by the dry ingredients and the liqueur. • With mixer at high speed, beat the egg whites in a large bowl until stiff peaks form. Use a large rubber spatula to fold them into the chocolate mixture. • Spoon the batter into the prepared pan and smooth the top with a thin metal spatula. • Bake for 40–50 minutes, or until springy to the touch and a toothpick inserted into the center comes out clean. • Cool the cake in the pan for 5 minutes. Turn out onto a rack and let cool completely. • *Chocolate Frosting*: Melt the chocolate and butter in a double boiler over barely simmering water.

Set aside to cool enough to spread (make sure it doesn't set). • Warm the marmalade and liqueur in a small saucepan over low heat. • Split the cake horizontally. Place one layer on a serving plate. Spread with the marmalade and $1/3$ of the frosting. Top with the remaining layer and spread the top and sides with the remaining frosting. • Spoon the ganache into a pastry bag and decorate the top of the cake with rosettes, if desired.

Makes one 9-inch cake · Prep: 45 min. · Cooking: 40–50 min. · Level: 1 · Keeps: 2–3 days

CAROB NUT BAKE

Carob is the pod of a tree native to Syria. Although unrelated to chocolate, it has a similar flavor. It is a healthy alternative to chocolate because it does not contain caffeine. You can buy carob seeds, powder, chips, and bars in health food stores.

1 cup all-purpose flour
$1/3$ cup carob powder
1 teaspoon baking powder
$1/4$ teaspoon salt
$3/4$ cup ($1/2$ sticks) butter, softened
$1/2$ cup firmly packed brown sugar
1 teaspoon vanilla extract
4 large eggs, at room temperature
1 cup nuts, coarsely chopped
$1/4$ cup fresh orange juice

CAROB FROSTING
$1/2$ cups confectioners' sugar
$1/4$ cup carob powder
2 tablespoons butter, melted
1 tablespoon orange juice

Preheat the oven to 350°F. • Butter and flour a 9-inch square baking pan. • Sift the flour, carob, baking powder, and salt into a medium bowl • Beat the butter, brown sugar, and vanilla in a large bowl with an electric mixer at medium speed until creamy. • Add the eggs, one at a time, until just blended after each addition. • With mixer at low speed, beat in the dry ingredients and nuts, alternating with the orange juice. • Spoon the batter into the prepared pan. • Bake for 30–35 minutes, or until springy to the touch and a toothpick inserted into the center comes out clean. • Cool the cake completely in the pan on a rack. • *Carob Frosting*: Beat the confectioners' sugar, carob, butter, and orange juice in a large bowl until smooth. • Spread the cake with the frosting.

Makes one 9-inch cake · Prep: 25 min. · Cooking: 30–35 min. · Level: 1 · Keeps: 2–3 days

Repeat with the remaining cake layers. • *Frosting*: With mixer at high speed, beat the cream in a large bowl until stiff. Stir in the vanilla and remaining kirsch. Spread the top of the cake with the frosting. Decorate with cherries.

Makes one 8-inch cake · Prep: 30 min. · Cooking: 35–40 min. · Level: 2 · Keeps: 2 days in the refrigerator

CHOCOLATE SOUR CREAM CAKE WITH CHERRY LIQUEUR CREAM

1²/₃ cups all-purpose flour
1¹/₂ teaspoons baking powder
¹/₄ teaspoon salt
5 oz dark chocolate, coarsely chopped
¹/₂ cup water
¹/₂ cup (1 stick) butter, softened
1¹/₄ cups firmly packed brown sugar
2 large eggs, at room temperature
¹/₂ cup sour cream

CHERRY CREAM FILLING
1¹/₂ cups cherry jam or preserves
3 tablespoons kirsch
2 cups heavy cream

CHOCOLATE FROSTING
8 oz bittersweet chocolate, coarsely chopped
2 tablespoons butter
candied cherries, to decorate

Preheat the oven to 350°F. • Butter two 9-inch round cake pans. Line with waxed paper. Butter the paper. • Sift the flour, baking powder, and salt into a large bowl. • Melt the chocolate and water in a double boiler over barely simmering water. Set aside to cool. • Beat the butter and brown sugar in a large bowl with an electric mixer at medium speed until creamy. • Add the eggs, one at a time, until just blended after each addition. • With mixer at low speed, gradually beat in the chocolate mixture, sour cream, and dry ingredients. • Spoon half the batter into each of the prepared pans. • Bake for 45–55 minutes, or until a toothpick inserted into the centers comes out clean. • Cool the cakes in the pans for 10 minutes. Turn out onto racks. Carefully remove the waxed paper and let cool completely. • Split the cakes horizontally. • *Cherry Cream Filling*: Mix the jam and kirsch. • With mixer at high speed, beat the cream in a medium bowl until stiff. • *Chocolate Frosting*: Melt the chocolate and butter in a double boiler over barely simmering water. • Place one

Black Forest cake

BLACK FOREST CAKE

This famous cake comes from the Black Forest region in southern Germany. It is made by layering rich cherry liqueur-flavored chocolate cake with sour cherries and then topping with cherry liqueur whipped cream.

1²/₃ cups all-purpose flour
²/₃ cups unsweetened cocoa powder
1¹/₂ teaspoons baking soda
1 teaspoon salt
¹/₂ cup (1 stick) butter, softened
1¹/₂ cups superfine sugar
1 teaspoon vanilla extract
2 large eggs
1¹/₂ cups buttermilk

FILLING
¹/₂ cup kirsch
¹/₂ cup (1 stick) butter, softened
2²/₃ cups confectioners' sugar
 pinch salt
1 teaspoon strong cold coffee
2 (14 oz) cans pitted sour cherries, drained (reserve 10 cherries for decoration)

FROSTING
2 cups heavy cream
¹/₂ teaspoon vanilla extract
1 tablespoon kirsch
 chocolate shavings, to decorate (see page 54)

Preheat the oven to 350°F. • Line two 8-inch round cake pans with parchment paper. • Sift the flour, cocoa, baking soda and salt into a large bowl. • Beat the butter and sugar with an electric mixer at medium speed until creamy. Add the vanilla and eggs, one at a time, until just blended after each addition. With mixer at low speed, gradually beat in the dry ingredients, alternating with the buttermilk. • Spoon half the batter into each of the prepared pans. • Bake for 35–40 minutes, or until a toothpick inserted into the centers comes out clean. Cool the cakes in the pans for 15 minutes. Turn out onto a rack. Carefully remove the paper and let cool completely. • *Filling*: Split the cakes horizontally. Set one layer aside to use for a separate dessert. Drizzle with the kirsch. • With mixer at medium speed, beat the butter in a medium bowl until creamy. Gradually beat the confectioners' sugar, salt, and coffee until smooth. • Place one layer on a serving plate. Spread with ¹/₃ of the filling. Top with ¹/₃ of the cherries.

layer on a serving plate. Spread with ⅓ of the jam mixture and ⅓ of the whipped cream. Repeat with the remaining cake layers, finishing with a plain layer. Spread the frosting over the top and sides of the cake. Decorate with the candied cherries.

Makes one 9-inch cake · Prep: 30 min. · Cooking: 45–55 min. · Level: 2 · Keeps: 1 day in the refrigerator

OVER-THE-TOP FROZEN CHOCOLATE CAKE

A rich, fudge-like cake, equally good when made with hazelnuts instead of pecans.

- 1½ cups pecans
- ¼ cup all-purpose flour
- 1 lb semisweet chocolate, coarsely chopped
- ⅔ cup cold butter, cut up
- 1 tablespoon coffee liqueur
- 1 teaspoon vanilla extract
- 4 large eggs, at room temperature
- 2 tablespoons granulated sugar
- ¼ teaspoon salt

TOPPING
- ¾ cup heavy cream
- 3 oz bittersweet chocolate, grated

Preheat the oven to 350°F. • Butter a 9-inch springform pan. • Place the pecans and 1 tablespoon flour in a food processor and process until finely ground. • Melt the chocolate, butter, liqueur, and vanilla in a double boiler over barely simmering water. Set aside to cool. • Beat the eggs, sugar, and salt in a large bowl with an electric mixer at medium speed until pale and thick. • Stir the remaining flour, chocolate mixture, and pecans into the egg mixture. • Spoon the batter into the prepared pan. • Bake for 25–35 minutes, or until the top is set. • Cool the cake completely in the pan on a rack. • When cool, cover with foil and freeze for 12 hours. • Transfer to the refrigerator about 2 hours before serving. Loosen and remove the pan sides. *Topping*: With mixer at high speed, beat the cream in a small bowl until stiff. Spread over the cake. Sprinkle with the chocolate.

Makes one 9-inch cake · Prep: 25 min. + 12 hr. to freeze · Cooking: 25–35 min. · Level: 2 · Keeps: 2 days in the freezer

REHRUECKEN CAKE

This German cake takes its name "rack of venison" from the way in which the almonds adorn the cake, standing vertically upright.

Rehruecken cake

CAKE
- ½ cup granulated sugar
- 1 large egg + 2 large eggs, separated
- ½ teaspoon ground cinnamon
- ¼ teaspoon salt
  grated zest of ½ lemon
- ¾ cup almonds, finely ground
- 3 oz semisweet chocolate, grated
- 3 tablespoons all-purpose flour

- 3 oz semisweet chocolate, coarsely chopped
- 1 teaspoon water
- ½ cup whole almonds

Preheat the oven to 375°F. • Butter a 11 x 7-inch baking pan. Sprinkle with dried bread crumbs. • *Cake*: Beat the sugar, 1 egg and 2 egg yolks, cinnamon, salt, and grated lemon zest in a large bowl with an electric mixer at high speed until well blended. Beat in the almonds, chocolate, and flour. • Beat the egg whites in a large bowl at medium speed until stiff peaks form. • Use a large rubber spatula to fold them into the egg yolk mixture. • Spoon the batter into the prepared pan and smooth the top. • Bake for 30–35 minutes, or until a toothpick inserted into the center comes out clean. • Cool the cake in the pan for 10 minutes. Turn out onto a rack to cool completely. • Melt the chocolate and water in a double boiler over barely simmering water. • Spread the cake with the chocolate. Decorate with the almonds inserted vertically along the center of the cake. • Refrigerate until just before serving.

Makes one 11-inch cake · Prep: 70 min. · Cooking: 30–35 min. · Level: 1 · Keeps: 2–3 days

CHECKERBOARD CAKE

CAKE
- 3 oz semisweet chocolate, coarsely chopped
- 3/4 cup + 1 tablespoon butter, softened
- 1 cup granulated sugar
- 3 large eggs, separated
- 1 1/4 cups all-purpose flour
- 1 teaspoon baking powder
- 1/4 teaspoon salt
- 2/3 cup almonds, finely chopped

RUM SYRUP
- 1/4 cup granulated sugar
- 1/4 cup water
- 1/4 cup dark rum

FILLING
- 1/3 recipe Chocolate Mousse (see page 343)

- 14 oz marzipan, to decorate
- 2 tablespoons unsweetened cocoa powder
- 2 tablespoons apricot preserves
- 1 tablespoon water
- 5 oz white chocolate, coarsely chopped
- 5 oz semisweet chocolate, coarsely chopped
- 1 1/2 cups Simple Chocolate Frosting (see page 349)

Preheat the oven to 375°F. • Butter a 9-inch square baking pan. • *Cake*: Melt the chocolate in a double boiler over barely simmering water. Set aside to cool. • Beat the butter and sugar in a large bowl with an electric mixer at medium speed until creamy. • Add the egg yolks, one at a time, until just blended after each addition. • With mixer at low speed, gradually beat in the flour, baking powder, and salt. Beat in the almonds and melted chocolate. • With mixer at high speed, beat the egg whites in a large bowl until stiff, glossy peaks form. Use a large rubber spatula to fold them into the chocolate mixture. • Spoon the batter into the prepared pan. • Bake for 50–55 minutes, or until a toothpick inserted into the center comes out clean. • Cool the cake in the pan for 15 minutes. Turn out onto a rack to cool completely. • *Rum Syrup*: Bring the sugar and water to a boil in a saucepan. Continue boiling for 3 minutes, or until the sugar has dissolved. Remove from the heat and set aside to cool. • Stir in the rum. • Split the cake horizontally. • Place a layer on a chopping board. Drizzle with the rum syrup. Spread with 1/2 of the chocolate mousse. Top with the remaining layer. • Sprinkle a surface with confectioners' sugar. Knead the marzipan until malleable. Reserve 1/4 of the marzipan and set aside. • With the larger amount of marzipan, knead in the cocoa

until completely blended. Roll the marzipan out to 1/8-inch thick. • Warm the preserves and water in a saucepan over low heat until liquid. Brush the top and sides of the cake with the preserves. • Carefully cover the cake with the marzipan and press down lightly. Cut off the excess and set aside. • Transfer to a serving plate. • Melt the white chocolate in a double boiler over barely simmering water. Use a large rubber spatula to spread the chocolate on a sheet of parchment paper. Set aside to dry completely. • Dip a sharp knife in warm water and cut out thirty-two 3/4-inch white squares. • Repeat with the semisweet chocolate to make thirty-two 3/4-inch dark squares. • Refrigerate the squares until completely dry, about 1 hour. • Place the squares in an alternating pattern on the top of the cake to create a checkerboard. • Shape cocoa and plain marzipan checkers and plain decorative shapes with the remaining marzipan. • Dot the checkers with a little frosting and stick on the checkerboard top. Stick the decorative shapes to the sides of the cake with some frosting. • Spoon the remaining chocolate into a pastry bag and pipe on the cake edges in a decorative manner. • Refrigerate.

Makes one 9-inch cake · Prep: 2 hr. + 1 hr. to chill · Cooking: 50–55 min. · Level: 3 · Keeps: 1–2 days in the refrigerator

CHOCOLATE LAYER CAKE WITH TRUFFLES

TRUFFLES
- 4 oz bittersweet chocolate, coarsely chopped
- 3 tablespoons heavy cream
- 1 tablespoon unsalted butter
- 1/3 cup confectioners' sugar
- 2 tablespoons orange liqueur
- 1/3 cup unsweetened cocoa powder

CAKE
- 2 cups all-purpose flour
- 1/4 cup unsweetened cocoa powder
- 1 teaspoon baking powder
- 1/2 teaspoon baking soda
- 1/4 teaspoon salt
- 2 oz bittersweet chocolate, coarsely chopped
- 1/3 cup butter, softened
- 3/4 cup granulated sugar
- 1 package (3 oz) cream cheese, softened
- 2 large eggs, at room temperature
- 1 tablespoon orange liqueur
- 1 teaspoon vanilla extract
- 3/4 cup water

FILLING
- 8 oz bittersweet chocolate, coarsely chopped
- 1/3 cup heavy cream

FROSTING
- 5 oz bittersweet chocolate, coarsely chopped
- 10 tablespoons butter, softened

Truffles: Melt the chocolate, cream, and butter in a double boiler over barely simmering water. Stir in the confectioners' sugar and orange liqueur until smooth. • Roll spoonfuls of the mixture into marble-sized balls, dusting your hands with cocoa, if needed. Transfer to a plate and refrigerate for 30 minutes. • *Cake*: Preheat the oven to 350°F. • Butter two 9-inch springform pans. • Sift the flour, cocoa, baking powder, baking soda, and salt into a large bowl. • Melt the chocolate in a double boiler over barely simmering water. Set aside to cool. • Beat the butter, sugar, and cream cheese in a large bowl with an electric mixer at medium speed until creamy. • Add the eggs, one at a time, until just blended after each addition. • With mixer at low speed, gradually beat in the chocolate, orange liqueur, and vanilla. Beat in the dry ingredients, alternating with the water. • Spoon half the batter into each of the prepared pans. • Bake for 25–35 minutes, or until a toothpick inserted into the centers comes out clean. • Cool the cakes in the pans for 10 minutes. Loosen and remove the pan sides. Invert the cakes onto racks. Loosen and remove the pan bottoms. • *Filling*: Melt the chocolate and cream in a double boiler over barely simmering water. Set aside to cool. • *Frosting*: Melt the chocolate in a double boiler over barely simmering water. Set aside to cool. • With mixer at medium speed, beat the butter in a medium bowl until creamy. Beat the butter into the chocolate until glossy and smooth. Cover and set aside. • Split each cake horizontally. Place one layer on a serving plate. Spread with 1/3 of the filling. Repeat with 2 more layers. Top with the remaining layer. • Spread the cake with the frosting. Decorate with the truffles.

Makes one 9-inch cake · Prep: 45 min. + 30 min. to chill · Cooking: 25–35 min. · Level: 3 · Keeps: 1–2 days in the refrigerator

Checkerboard cake

RICH CHOCOLATE CAKE

This rich cake makes a great birthday cake for chocolate lovers or a special way to end a formal dinner party.

$1^2/_3$ cups self-rising flour
 $^1/_3$ cup unsweetened cocoa powder
 $^1/_2$ teaspoon baking powder
 $^3/_4$ cup ($1^1/_2$ sticks) butter, softened
 $^3/_4$ cup superfine sugar
  2 large eggs, separated
 $^1/_8$ teaspoon salt
     unsweetened cocoa powder, to dust

CHOCOLATE CREAM FROSTING
  6 oz semisweet chocolate, coarsely chopped
 $^1/_3$ cup butter
 $^1/_2$ cup sweetened condensed milk
  6 oz semisweet chocolate, coarsely grated

Preheat the oven to 350°F. • Butter and flour an 8-inch springform pan. • Sift the flour, cocoa, and baking powder into a large bowl. • Beat the butter and sugar with an electric mixer at medium speed until creamy. • Add the egg yolks, one at a time, until just blended after each addition. • With mixer at low speed, gradually beat in the dry ingredients. • With mixer at medium speed, beat the egg whites and salt until stiff peaks form. Use a large rubber spatula to fold them into the batter. • Spoon the batter into the prepared pan. • Bake for 40–45 minutes, or until a toothpick inserted into the center comes out clean. • Cool the cake in the pan for 5 minutes. Loosen and remove the pan sides. Invert onto a rack and remove the pan bottom. Let cool completely. • Dust with the cocoa powder. •

Frosting: Melt the chocolate, butter, and condensed milk in a double boiler over barely simmering water. Spoon the frosting into a pastry bag and pipe on top of the cake in a decorative manner. Decorate the sides of the cake with the grated chocolate.

Makes one 8-inch cake · Prep: 15 min. · Cooking: 40–45 min. · Level: 2 · Keeps: 2 days

RICH CHOCOLATE SNACKING CAKE

  1 cup all-purpose flour
 $^1/_2$ cup unsweetened cocoa powder, sifted if lumpy
$1^1/_2$ teaspoons baking powder
 $^1/_4$ teaspoon salt
 $^3/_4$ cup ($1^1/_2$ sticks) butter, softened
$1^1/_2$ cups granulated sugar
  2 teaspoons vanilla extract
  4 large eggs, separated
  2 oz bittersweet chocolate, grated
  1 cup plain yogurt

CHOCOLATE FROSTING
  3 oz bittersweet chocolate, coarsely chopped
  3 tablespoons butter, cut up
  1 cup confectioners' sugar
     walnut halves, to decorate

Preheat the oven to 350°F. • Butter a 9-inch square pan. Line with waxed paper. Butter the paper. • Sift the flour, cocoa, baking powder, and salt into a large bowl. • Beat the butter, sugar, and vanilla in a large bowl with an electric mixer at medium speed until creamy. • Add the egg yolks, one at a time, until just blended after each addition. • With mixer at low speed, beat in the dry ingredients and chocolate, alternating with the yogurt. • With mixer at high speed, beat

the egg whites in a large bowl until stiff peaks form. Use a large rubber spatula to fold them into the batter. • Spoon the batter into the prepared pan. • Bake for 40–50 minutes, or until a toothpick inserted into the center comes out clean. • Cool the cake completely in the pan on a rack. • *Chocolate Frosting*: Melt the chocolate and butter in a double boiler over barely simmering water. Remove from the heat and beat in the confectioners' sugar. • Spread the top of the cake with the frosting. Decorate with the walnut halves.

Makes one 9-inch cake · Prep: 35 min. · Cooking 40–50 min. · Level: 1 · Keeps: 2–3 days

GLAZED CHOCOLATE CAKE

  2 cups all-purpose flour
 $^1/_4$ cup unsweetened cocoa powder
$1^1/_2$ teaspoons baking powder
 $^1/_4$ teaspoon salt
  3 large eggs, separated
  1 cup granulated sugar
  1 cup (2 sticks) butter, melted
 $^1/_4$ teaspoon vanilla extract

CHOCOLATE GLAZE
  8 oz bittersweet chocolate, coarsely chopped
     chocolate shavings, to decorate

Preheat the oven to 350°F. • Butter a 9-inch square baking pan. Dust with cocoa. • Sift the flour, cocoa, baking powder, and salt into a medium bowl. • Beat the egg yolks and sugar in a large bowl with an electric mixer at high speed until pale and thick. • With mixer at low speed, gradually beat in

Rich chocolate cake

the butter and vanilla, followed by the dry ingredients. • With mixer at high speed, beat the egg whites in a large bowl until stiff peaks form. Use a large rubber spatula to fold them into the batter. • Spoon the batter into the prepared pan. • Bake for 35–45 minutes, or until a toothpick inserted into the center comes out clean. • Cool the cake completely in the pan on a rack. • *Chocolate Glaze*: Melt the chocolate in a double boiler over barely simmering water. Set aside to cool slightly. Pour the melted chocolate over the top of the cake, spreading with a spatula, if necessary. Decorate with chocolate shavings.

Makes one 9-inch square cake · Prep: 20 min. · Cooking: 35–45 min. · Level: 1 · Keeps: 2–3 days

Old-fashioned white chocolate cake

GLAZED CHOCOLATE CREAM CAKE

- 1 cup all-purpose flour
- $1/3$ cup unsweetened cocoa powder
- 1 teaspoon baking powder
- $1/2$ teaspoon baking soda
- $1/4$ teaspoon salt
- 1 cup granulated sugar
- 1 cup milk
- 6 tablespoons butter, softened
- 1 large egg, at room temperature
- 1 teaspoon vanilla extract

CHOCOLATE CREAM

- $1/2$ cup granulated sugar
- $1/3$ cup unsweetened cocoa powder
- 2 tablespoons cornstarch
- $1^1/2$ cups light cream
- 1 tablespoon butter
- 1 teaspoon vanilla extract

GLAZE

- 2 tablespoons water
- 1 tablespoon butter
- 1 tablespoon corn syrup
- 2 tablespoons unsweetened cocoa powder
- $2/3$ cup confectioners' sugar
- $1/2$ teaspoon vanilla extract

Preheat the oven to 350°F. • Butter a 9-inch round cake pan. Dust with cocoa. • Sift the flour, cocoa, baking powder, baking soda, and salt into a large bowl. Stir in the sugar. • Beat in the milk, butter, egg, and vanilla with an electric mixer at medium speed until well blended. • Spoon the batter into the prepared pan. • Bake for 40–50 minutes, or until a toothpick inserted into the center comes out clean. • Cool the cake in the pan for 10 minutes. Turn out onto a rack to cool

completely. • *Chocolate Cream*: Stir together the sugar, cocoa and cornstarch in a medium saucepan. Gradually stir in the cream. • Cook over medium heat, stirring constantly, until the mixture thickens and begins to boil. Boil for 1 minute, stirring constantly. Remove from the heat. • Stir in the butter and vanilla. Transfer to a bowl. Cover with plastic wrap pressed directly onto the surface. Refrigerate until cold. • *Glaze*: Bring the water, butter, and corn syrup to a boil in a medium saucepan. Remove from the heat and stir in the cocoa. Gradually beat in the confectioners' sugar and vanilla until smooth. Set aside to cool slightly. • Split the cake horizontally. • Place one layer on a serving plate. Spread with the Chocolate Cream. Top with the remaining cake. Pour the glaze over the cake, allowing some to drizzle down the sides. • Refrigerate.

Makes one 9-inch cake · Prep: 30 min. + 1 hr. to chill · Cooking: 40–50 min. · Level: 2 · Keeps: 2 days

OLD-FASHIONED WHITE CHOCOLATE CAKE

This very special cake is perfect for birthdays or other celebrations.

- 10 large eggs, separated
- $1^1/2$ cups granulated sugar
- $1^1/4$ cups ($2^1/2$ sticks) butter, melted
- 2 cups pecans, finely ground
- 2 cups almonds, finely ground
- $1/3$ cup all-purpose flour
- 1 teaspoon vanilla extract
- $1/4$ teaspoon almond extract

SYRUP

- $1^1/2$ cups water
- $3/4$ cup granulated sugar
- $1/4$ cup kirsch

- $1^1/2$ recipes White Chocolate Ganache (see page 350)
- 12 oz white chocolate, coarsely grated, to decorate

Preheat the oven to 350°F. • Butter two 9-inch round cake pans. Line with waxed paper. Butter the paper. • Beat the egg yolks and sugar in a large bowl with an electric mixer at high speed until pale and thick. • With mixer at low speed, gradually beat in the butter. • Gradually beat in the pecans, almonds, flour, vanilla, and almond extract. • With mixer at high speed, beat the egg whites in a large bowl until stiff peaks form. Use a large rubber spatula to fold them into the batter. • Spoon half the batter into each of the prepared pans. • Bake for 45–50 minutes, or until a toothpick inserted into the centers comes out clean. • Cool the cakes in the pans for 10 minutes. Turn out onto racks to cool completely. • Transfer the cakes to high-sided plates. Poke holes all over the cakes. • *Syrup*: Bring the water and sugar to a boil in a medium saucepan over medium heat. Boil for 20 minutes. Remove from the heat and stir in the kirsch. Spoon the hot syrup over the cakes. Set aside until the cakes have absorbed the syrup. • Place one layer on a serving plate. Spread with $1/3$ of the ganache. Top with the remaining layer. Spread the top and sides with the remaining ganache. • Sprinkle with the grated white chocolate.

Makes one 9-inch cake · Prep: 90 min. · Cooking: 45–50 min. · Level: 2 · Keeps: 3–4 days

HAZELNUT TORTE WITH CHOCOLATE CREAM

CHOCOLATE CREAM
- 8 oz bittersweet chocolate, coarsely chopped
- 3/4 cup heavy cream
- 1/3 cup toasted hazelnuts, finely ground

HAZELNUT TORTE
- 6 large egg whites, at room temperature
- 1/4 teaspoon salt
- 1 cup granulated sugar
- 1 1/3 cups toasted hazelnuts, finely ground
- 1/4 cup confectioners' sugar, to dust
- 1 teaspoon unsweetened cocoa powder (optional) whole hazelnuts, to decorate

Chocolate Cream: Melt the chocolate and cream in a double boiler over barely simmering water. Stir in the hazelnuts. Set aside to cool. • *Hazelnut Torte*: Preheat the oven to 400°F. • Butter and flour a baking sheet. Cut two 8-inch squares of waxed paper and place on the baking sheet. • Beat the egg whites and salt in a large bowl with an electric mixer at medium speed until frothy. With mixer at high speed, gradually beat in the sugar, beating until stiff, glossy peaks form. • Use a rubber spatula to fold the hazelnuts into the beaten whites. • Spoon the batter onto the paper, spreading them with the back of the spoon. Leave a 1/2-inch border all around the edges of the paper. • Bake for 8–10 minutes, or until a toothpick inserted into the centers comes out clean. Cool completely on a rack. • Trim the edges of the cakes so that they are straight. • Place one layer on a serving plate. Spread with the Chocolate Cream. Top with the remaining layer. • Dust with the confectioners' sugar. • If desired, place a stencil in the form of leaves on top and dust with cocoa. Decorate with the extra hazelnuts.

Makes one 13 x 8-inch cake · Prep: 40 min. · Cooking: 8–10 min. · Level: 2 · Keeps: 1–2 days

FUDGE AND NUT CRUNCH

Very rich and addictive. Serve in small pieces.

- 4 oz bittersweet chocolate, coarsely chopped
- 1/2 cup (1 stick) butter, cut up
- 1 cup water
- 1 cup old-fashioned rolled oats
- 1 cup granulated sugar
- 1 cup firmly packed brown sugar
- 3 large eggs, at room temperature
- 1/2 cup coffee liqueur
- 1/2 cup walnuts, coarsely chopped
- 1 teaspoon vanilla extract
- 2 cups all-purpose flour
- 2 teaspoons baking powder
- 1/2 teaspoon salt

TOPPING
- 1/2 cup (1 stick) cold butter, cut up
- 1 cup firmly packed brown sugar
- 1 cup walnuts, coarsely chopped
- 1/3 cup heavy cream

Preheat the oven to 350°F. • Butter and flour a 13 x 9-inch baking pan. • Melt the chocolate and butter in a double boiler over barely simmering water. • Stir in the water and bring to a boil. • Remove from the heat. Beat in the oats, both sugars, eggs, liqueur, walnuts, and vanilla. • Stir in the flour, baking powder, and salt. • Spoon the batter into the prepared pan. • Bake for 40–45 minutes, or until a toothpick inserted into the center comes out clean. Cool the cake completely in the pan on a rack. • *Topping*: Turn on the broiler. • Bring the butter, sugar, nuts, and cream to a boil in a saucepan over low heat. Cook, stirring constantly, for 2–3 minutes, or until the mixture thickens. Pour over the hot cake. Broil 4 to 6 inches from the heat source for about 5 minutes, or until the topping is lightly browned. • Cool the cake completely in the pan on a rack.

Makes one 13 x 9-inch cake · Prep: 20 min. · Cooking: 40–45 min. · Level: 1 · Keeps: 2–3 days

MARBLED CREAM CHEESE SLICE

A dense, fudgy brownie-like cake with swirls of cream cheese.

- 3 oz semisweet chocolate, coarsely chopped
- 3 tablespoons butter, cut up
- 1/3 cup butter, softened
- 1/2 cup confectioners' sugar
- 1 teaspoon vanilla extract
- 1/2 teaspoon coconut extract
- 2 large eggs, at room temperature
- 1/2 cup all-purpose flour
- 1/2 teaspoon baking powder
- 1 package (8 oz) cream cheese, softened
- 1/4 cup granulated sugar

Preheat the oven to 350°F. • Butter and flour a 9-inch square baking pan. • Melt the chocolate, and 3 tablespoons butter in a double boiler over barely simmering water. Set aside to cool. • Beat the remaining butter, confectioners' sugar, vanilla, and coconut extract in a large bowl with an electric mixer at medium speed until creamy. Add 1 egg. • With mixer at low speed, beat in the chocolate mixture, followed by the flour and baking powder. • Spoon the batter into the prepared pan. • With mixer at medium speed, beat the cream cheese and sugar in a medium bowl until smooth. • Add the remaining egg. • Spread the cream cheese mixture over the chocolate layer. Use a knife to swirl the batters together in a marble pattern. • Bake for 50–55 minutes, or until the cake shrinks from the pan sides and a toothpick inserted into the center comes out clean. • Cool the cake in the pan.

Makes one 9-inch cake · Prep: 30 min. · Cooking: 50–55 min. · Level: 1 · Keeps: 2–3 days

Hazelnut torte with chocolate cream

Viennois

followed by the dry ingredients and raisins. •
Spoon the batter into the prepared pan. •
Bake for 50–60 minutes, or until a
toothpick inserted into the center comes out
clean. • Cool the cake completely in the pan
on a rack. • *Rich Chocolate Frosting*: With
mixer at low speed, beat the confectioners'
sugar, cocoa, and butter in a large
bowl until creamy. Beat in enough of
the cream to make a thick,
spreadable frosting. Spread over
the top of the cake.

*Makes one 9-inch square cake · Prep: 35
min. · Cooking: 50–60 min. · Level: 1 ·
Keeps: 2–3 days*

CHOCOLATE PEANUT FUDGE CAKE

1½ cups all-purpose flour
⅓ cup unsweetened cocoa powder
2 teaspoons baking powder
¼ teaspoon salt
¾ cup (1½ sticks) butter, cut up
¾ cup heavy cream
¾ cup granulated sugar
4 oz bittersweet chocolate, finely chopped
⅓ cup smooth peanut butter
2 large eggs, lightly beaten

CHOCOLATE FROSTING
6 oz bittersweet chocolate, finely chopped
½ cup sweetened condensed milk
5 tablespoons butter, cut up
2 tablespoons unsweetened cocoa powder, to dust
2½ oz chocolate covered peanuts, to sprinkle

Preheat the oven to 350°F. • Butter a 9-inch
springform pan. Dust with cocoa. • Sift the
flour, cocoa, baking powder, and salt into a
large bowl. • Stir the butter, cream, sugar,
chocolate, and peanut butter in a medium
pan over low heat until the butter and
chocolate have melted and the sugar has
dissolved. • Pour the chocolate mixture into
the dry ingredients and beat with an electric
mixer at medium speed until smooth. Add
the eggs, one at a time, until just blended
after each addition. • Spoon the batter into
the prepared pan. • Bake for 40–45
minutes, or until a toothpick inserted into
the center comes out clean. • Cool the cake
in the pan for 5 minutes. Loosen and
remove the pan sides. Turn out onto a rack.
Loosen and remove the pan bottom and let
cool completely. • *Chocolate Frosting*: Stir
the chocolate, condensed milk, and butter

in a small saucepan over low heat until
melted. Set aside to cool until thick. • Split
the cake horizontally. Place one layer on a
serving plate. Spread with the frosting. Top
with the remaining layer. Spread the top
and sides with the remaining frosting. •
Dust with the cocoa and decorate with the
chocolate-covered peanuts.

*Makes one 9-inch cake · Prep: 25 min. · Cooking:
40–45 min. · Level: 1 · Keeps: 3 days*

FROSTED FUDGE CAKE

1 cup all-purpose flour
1 teaspoon baking powder
¼ teaspoon salt
5 oz bittersweet chocolate, coarsely chopped
1 cup (2 sticks) butter, softened
1 cup granulated sugar
2 teaspoons vanilla extract
4 large eggs, at room temperature
¾ cup chopped raisins

RICH CHOCOLATE FROSTING
2 cups confectioners' sugar
½ cup unsweetened cocoa powder
⅓ cup butter, softened
3–4 tablespoons heavy or light cream

Preheat the oven to 325°F. • Butter a 9-inch
square baking pan. Dust with cocoa. • Sift
the flour, baking powder, and salt into a
large bowl. Melt the chocolate in a double
boiler over barely simmering water. • Beat
the butter, sugar, and vanilla in a large bowl
with an electric mixer at medium speed
until creamy. • Add the eggs, one at a time,
until just blended after each addition. • With
mixer at low speed, beat in the chocolate,

VIENNOIS

This sinfully rich chocolate cake takes its name
from the Austrian city of Vienna, where it is served
in cafés with steaming cups of strong black coffee.

¼ cup unsweetened cocoa powder
2½ tablespoons cake flour
2½ tablespoons cornstarch
¼ teaspoon salt
1½ cups granulated sugar
8 large eggs, separated
2 cups Rich Chocolate Frosting (see page 349)
2 oz bittersweet chocolate, finely grated

Preheat the oven to 300°F. • Butter two 8-
inch round cake pans. Line with waxed
paper. Butter the paper. • Sift the cocoa,
flour, cornstarch, and salt into a medium
bowl. • Beat the sugar and egg yolks in a
large bowl with an electric mixer at high
speed until pale and thick. • With mixer at
low speed, gradually beat in the dry
ingredients • With mixer at high speed, beat
the egg whites in a large bowl until stiff peaks
form. Use a large rubber spatula to fold them
into the batter. • Spoon half the batter into
each of the prepared pans. • Bake for 20–25
minutes, or until springy to the touch and a
toothpick inserted into the center comes out
clean. • Cool the cakes in the pans for 10
minutes. Turn out onto racks. Carefully
remove the paper and let cool completely. •
Split the cakes horizontally. Place one layer
on a serving plate and spread with some
frosting. Repeat with 2 more layers. Top with
the remaining layer. Spread the top and sides
with the remaining frosting. • Sprinkle the
chocolate over the top of the cake.

*Makes one 8-inch cake · Prep: 1 hr. · Cooking 20–25
min. · Level: 2 · Keeps: 1–2 days*

Mud cake with white chocolate ganache and walnuts

FUDGE SUNDAE CAKE

Rich, chocolatey, and gooey.

1²/₃ cups all-purpose flour
1 cup unsweetened cocoa powder
1¹/₂ teaspoons baking powder
¹/₄ teaspoon salt
1¹/₄ cups granulated sugar
1 cup milk
6 tablespoons butter, melted
2 teaspoons vanilla extract
1 cup walnuts or pecans, chopped
1³/₄ cups firmly packed brown sugar
2¹/₂ cups boiling water

Preheat the oven to 350°F. • Butter a 13 x 9-inch baking pan. • Sift the flour, ¹/₂ cup cocoa, baking powder, and salt into a large bowl. Stir in the sugar. • Mix the milk, butter, and vanilla in a medium bowl. Beat the milk mixture into the dry ingredients with an electric mixer at low speed. • By hand, stir in the nuts. • Spoon the batter into the prepared pan. Place the pan on a baking sheet. Mix the brown sugar and remaining ¹/₂ cup cocoa in a medium bowl. Sprinkle over the batter and pour the water carefully over the cake. • Bake for 45–55 minutes, or until a toothpick inserted into the center comes out clean. • Serve the cake from the pan while still warm, spooning a little of the sauce that forms in the bottom of the pan over each serving.

Makes 13 x 9-inch cake · Prep: 25 min. · Cooking: 45–55 min. · Level: 1 · Keeps: 1–2 days

MUD CAKE WITH WHITE CHOCOLATE GANACHE AND WALNUTS

1 cup firmly packed brown sugar
1 cup milk
³/₄ cup (1¹/₂ sticks) butter, cut up
¹/₃ cup molasses
5 oz white chocolate, coarsely chopped
2 cups all-purpose flour
2 teaspoons baking powder
¹/₄ teaspoon salt
2 large eggs, lightly beaten
1¹/₂ cups White Chocolate Ganache (see page 350)
12 walnut halves

Preheat the oven to 325°F. • Butter a 9-inch round cake pan. Line with waxed paper. • Place the sugar, milk, butter, molasses, and chocolate in a saucepan and stir over low heat, without boiling, until smooth. • Set aside to cool. • Sift the flour, baking powder, and salt into a medium bowl. Gradually stir the dry ingredients and eggs into the sugar mixture. • Spoon the batter into the prepared pan. • Bake for 60–70 minutes, or until a toothpick inserted into the center comes out clean. • Cool the cake completely in the pan. Turn out onto a rack. Carefully remove the paper and let cool completely. • Spread with the ganache. Decorate with the walnuts.

Makes one 9-inch cake · Prep: 30 min. · Cooking: 60–70 min. · Level: 2 · Keeps: 2–3 days

GOLDEN MUD CAKE

³/₄ cup (1¹/₂ sticks) butter, cut up
5 oz white chocolate, coarsely chopped
1 cup firmly packed brown sugar
1 cup milk
¹/₃ cup corn syrup
2 cups all-purpose flour
2 teaspoons baking powder
2 large eggs, lightly beaten
1¹/₂ cups White Chocolate Ganache (see page 350)

Preheat the oven to 325°F. • Butter and flour a 9-inch springform pan. • Stir the butter, chocolate, sugar, milk, and corn syrup in a large saucepan over low heat until smooth. Do not boil. Set aside to cool. • Stir in the flour and baking powder. Beat in the eggs, one at a time, until just blended after each addition. • Spoon the batter into the prepared pan. • Bake for 70–75 minutes, or until golden brown and a toothpick inserted into the center comes out clean. • Cool the cake in the pan for 10 minutes. Loosen and remove the pan sides. Invert the cake onto a rack. Loosen and remove the pan bottom and let cool completely. • Spread the top and sides of the cake with the ganache, swirling it with a thin metal spatula to make small decorative peaks.

Makes one 9-inch cake · Prep: 25 min. · Cooking: 70–75 min. · Level: 1 · Keeps: 2–3 days

RUM MUD CAKE

Serve this very rich chocolate cake with fresh fruit, such as raspberries and strawberries or peeled and chopped fresh oranges, soaked in a mixture of sugar and orange liqueur.

14 oz bittersweet chocolate, coarsely chopped
6 large eggs, at room temperature
¹/₂ cup firmly packed brown sugar
1 cup heavy cream, beaten

¹/₃ cup dark rum
2 tablespoons unsweetened cocoa powder, to dust

Preheat the oven to 350°F. • Butter a 9-inch springform pan. Wrap the pan with heavy-duty foil. • Melt the chocolate in a double boiler over barely simmering water. Set aside to cool to warm. • Beat the eggs and brown sugar in a large bowl with an electric mixer at medium speed until creamy. • With mixer at low speed, gradually beat in the warm chocolate. Use a large rubber spatula to fold the cream and rum into the batter. • Spoon the batter into the prepared pan. • Place the springform pan in a roasting pan. Pour enough boiling water into the pan to come halfway up the side of the pan. • Bake for 25–30 minutes. Cover the springform pan with foil and bake for 30–35 minutes more, or until the cake seems set but jiggles slightly. Remove from the water bath and remove the foil cover. Cool the cake completely in the pan on a rack. • Refrigerate for at least 8 hours. Loosen and remove the pan sides. • Dust with the cocoa.

Makes one 9-inch cake · Prep: 30 min. + 8 hr. to chill · Cooking: 55–65 min. · Level: 2 · Keeps: 2–3 days

WHITE MUD CAKE

1 cup (2 sticks) butter, cut up
2 cups granulated sugar
5 oz white chocolate, coarsely chopped
1 cup milk
2 cups all-purpose flour
2 teaspoons baking powder
¹/₄ teaspoon salt
2 large eggs, lightly beaten
1 teaspoon vanilla extract
1¹/₂ cups White Chocolate Ganache (see page 350)

Preheat the oven to 325°F. • Butter a 9-inch round baking pan. Line with waxed paper. Butter the paper. • Stir the butter, sugar, chocolate, and milk in a large saucepan over low heat until smooth. Do not boil. • Set aside to cool. • Sift the flour, baking powder, and salt into a medium bowl. Gradually stir the dry ingredients, eggs, and vanilla into the saucepan. • Spoon the batter into the prepared pan. • Bake for 50–60 minutes, or until a toothpick inserted into the center comes out clean. • Cool the cake in the pan for 10 minutes. Turn out onto a rack. Carefully remove the paper and let cool completely. • Spread with the ganache.

Makes one 9-inch cake · Prep: 30 min. · Cooking: 50–60 min. · Level: 1 · Keeps: 2–3 days

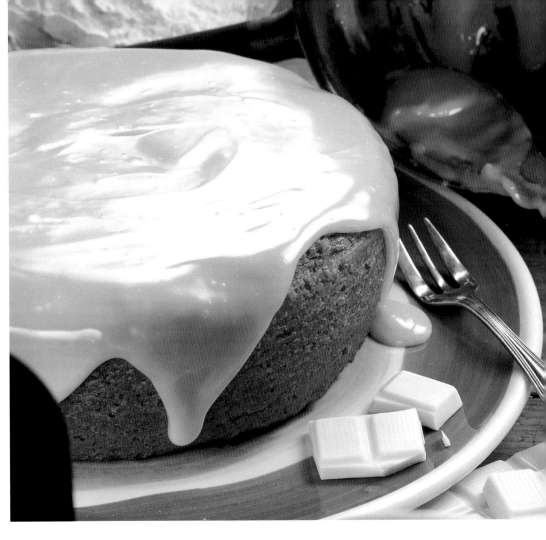

White mud cake

CHOCO-WALNUT CAKE WITH CHOCOLATE FROSTING

1¹/₄ cups granulated sugar
4 oz bittersweet chocolate, coarsely chopped
3 tablespoons water
¹/₂ cup (1 stick) butter, softened
6 large eggs, separated
¹/₄ teaspoon salt
1¹/₂ cups walnuts, finely chopped
¹/₄ cup all-purpose flour

CHOCOLATE FROSTING

4 oz bittersweet chocolate, coarsely chopped
¹/₃ cup butter, softened
2 cups confectioners' sugar
1 teaspoon vanilla extract
³/₄ cup walnuts, coarsely chopped, and walnut halves to decorate

Preheat the oven to 350°F. • Butter two 9-inch round cake pans. Line with waxed paper. Butter the paper. • Stir together the sugar, chocolate, and water in a medium saucepan over low heat until the chocolate has melted. Set aside. • Beat the butter in a large bowl with an electric mixer at medium speed until creamy. Add the egg yolks, one at a time, until just blended after each addition. • Stir in the salt, chocolate mixture, walnuts, and flour. • With mixer at high speed, beat the egg whites in a large bowl until stiff peaks form. Use a large rubber spatula to fold them into the batter. • Spoon half the batter into each of the prepared pans. • Bake for 30–40 minutes, or until a toothpick inserted into the centers comes out clean. • Cool the cakes in the pans for 10 minutes. Turn out onto racks. Carefully remove the paper and let cool completely. • Split the cakes horizontally. • *Chocolate Frosting*: Melt the chocolate in a double boiler over barely simmering water. • Beat the butter and confectioners' sugar in a small bowl. Add the chocolate and vanilla. • Place one layer on a serving plate. Spread with ¹/₃ of the frosting. Repeat with next 2 layers. Top with the remaining layer. Spread the top and sides with remaining frosting. Sprinkle the sides with the walnuts and decorate with the walnut halves.

Makes one 9-inch cake · Prep: 40 min. · Cooking: 30–40 min. · Level: 1 · Keeps: 2–3 days

Almond chocolate cake

ALMOND CHOCOLATE CAKE

- 4 large eggs, separated
- 1 cup confectioners' sugar
- 1 cup all-purpose flour
- 1/3 cup unsweetened cocoa powder
- 1/4 cup (1/2 stick) butter, melted

CHOCOLATE CREAM

- 2 large egg yolks
- 3/4 cup superfine sugar
- 1/2 cup (1 stick) butter, softened
- 1/3 cup all-purpose flour
- 3 oz dark unsweetened chocolate, grated
- 1/4 teaspoon vanilla extract
- 2 cups milk
- 1/4 cup toasted almonds

Preheat the oven to 350°F. • Butter and flour an 8-inch springform pan. • Beat the egg yolks and confectioners' sugar in a large bowl with an electric mixer at high speed until pale and thick. • Use a large rubber spatula to fold in the flour and cocoa powder. • With mixer at high speed, beat the egg whites in a large bowl until stiff peaks form. Fold them into the batter, followed by the melted butter. • Spoon the batter into the prepared pan. • Bake for 35–40 minutes, or until a toothpick inserted into the center comes out clean. • Cool the cake in the pan for 5 minutes. Loosen and remove the pan sides. Turn out onto a rack to cool completely. • *Chocolate Cream*: With mixer at medium speed, beat the egg yolks, sugar, and butter in a large saucepan until pale and thick. • Use a large rubber spatula to fold in the flour, chocolate, and vanilla. Gradually add the milk. • Place over low heat, stirring constantly with a wooden spoon until the mixture lightly coats a metal spoon or registers 160°F on an instant-read thermometer. Immediately plunge the pan into a bowl of ice water and stir until the egg

mixture has cooled. • Split the cake horizontally. Place one layer on a serving plate. Spread with half the chocolate cream. Top with the remaining layer. Spread with the remaining chocolate cream. • Sprinkle with the almonds and serve.

Makes one 8-inch cake · Prep: 30 min. · Cooking: 40–45 min. · Level: 2 · Keeps: 3 days in the refrigerator

CHOCOLATE ALMOND CAKE

- 3 cups all-purpose flour
- 1/2 cup unsweetened cocoa powder
- 2 teaspoons baking soda
- 1/2 teaspoon salt
- 2 cups granulated sugar
- 2 cups water
- 1/2 cup vegetable oil
- 1/2 teaspoon almond extract
- 2 1/2 cups Fudge Frosting (see page 347)

Preheat the oven to 350°F. • Butter and flour a 13 x 9-inch baking pan. • Sift together the flour, cocoa, baking soda, and salt in a large bowl. Stir in the sugar. • Beat in the water, oil, and almond extract with an electric mixer at low speed until blended. • Spoon the batter into the prepared pan. • Bake for 30–40 minutes, or until a toothpick inserted into the center comes out clean. • Cool the cake completely in the pan on a rack.

Makes one 13 x 9-inch cake · Prep: 15 min. · Cooking: 30–40 min. · Level: 1 · Keeps: 2–3 days

CHOCOLATE ALMOND CAKE WITH MARBLED FROSTING

- 5 oz bittersweet chocolate, coarsely chopped
- 2 cups almonds, finely ground
- 1 teaspoon baking powder
- 1 teaspoon baking soda
- 1/4 teaspoon salt
- 1/2 cup (1 stick) butter, softened
- 3/4 cup granulated sugar
- 4 large eggs, separated

MARBLED FROSTING

- 4 oz bittersweet chocolate, coarsely chopped
- 4 oz white chocolate, coarsely chopped
- 1/2 cup (1 stick) butter, cut up

Preheat the oven to 350°F. • Butter and flour a 9-inch springform pan. • Melt the chocolate in a double boiler over barely simmering water. Set aside to cool. • Stir together the almonds, baking powder, baking soda, and salt in a large bowl. • Beat the butter and sugar in a large bowl with an electric mixer at medium speed until creamy. • Add the egg yolks, one at a time, until just blended after each addition. • With mixer at low speed, beat in the chocolate and the almond mixture. • With mixer at high speed, beat the egg whites in a large bowl until stiff peaks form. Use a large rubber spatula to fold them into the batter. • Spoon the batter into the prepared pan. • Bake for 40–45 minutes, or until a toothpick inserted into the center comes out clean. • Cool the cake in the pan for 15 minutes. Loosen and remove the pan sides. Invert the cake on a rack. Loosen and remove the pan bottom and let cool completely. • *Marbled Frosting*: Melt the bittersweet chocolate and 1/4 cup butter in a double boiler over barely simmering water. Set aside to cool. Melt the white chocolate and the remaining 1/4 cup butter in the same way. • Drizzle alternate spoonfuls of the chocolates onto the cake, letting it drip down the sides. Twirl the chocolates on the top of the cake with a fork to create a marbled effect.

Makes one 9-inch cake · Prep: 25 min. · Cooking: 40–45 min. · Level: 1 · Keeps: 3–4 days

CHOCOLATE WALNUT SLICE

- 5 oz semisweet chocolate, coarsely chopped
- 1/2 cup (1 stick) butter, cut up
- 1/3 cup all-purpose flour
- 3 tablespoons unsweetened cocoa powder
- 1 teaspoon baking powder
- 1/4 teaspoon salt
- 2 large eggs, at room temperature
- 1/3 cup granulated sugar
- 1 tablespoon freeze-dried coffee granules, dissolved in 1 tablespoon hot water
- 1 tablespoon rum
- 1 tablespoon milk
- 1/2 cup walnuts, coarsely chopped
- 1/3 cup semisweet chocolate chips
- 2 tablespoons confectioners' sugar, to dust

Preheat the oven to 350°F. • Butter and flour an 8-inch square baking pan. • Melt the chocolate and butter in a double boiler over barely simmering water. Set aside to cool. • Sift the flour, cocoa, baking powder, and salt into a medium bowl. • Beat the eggs and sugar in a large bowl with an electric mixer at high speed until pale and thick. • With mixer at medium speed, beat in the chocolate mixture, then add the coffee mixture, rum, and milk. • With mixer at low speed, gradually beat in the dry ingredients. Stir in the walnuts and chocolate chips. • Spoon the batter into the prepared pan. • Bake for 25–35 minutes, or until a toothpick inserted into the center comes out clean. • Cool the cake completely in the pan on a rack. Dust with the confectioners' sugar.

Makes one 8-inch cake · Prep: 20 min. · Cooking 25–35 min. · Level: 1 · Keeps: 1–2 days

CHOCOLATE HAZELNUT CREAM CAKE

    4   oz bittersweet chocolate, coarsely chopped
 1¹/₃   cups all-purpose flour
 1¹/₂   teaspoons baking powder
   ¹/₄   teaspoon salt
    3   large eggs, separated
   ¹/₃   cup granulated sugar
   ¹/₂   teaspoon almond extract
   ¹/₂   cup heavy cream

CHOCOLATE HAZELNUT CREAM FILLING

    1   cup heavy cream
 1¹/₂   cups chocolate hazelnut cream (Nutella)
   ¹/₃   cup butter, cut up
   ¹/₄   cup unsweetened cocoa powder, to dust
        fresh raspberries, to decorate

Butter and flour two 8-inch springform pans. • Melt the chocolate in a double boiler over barely simmering water. Set aside to cool. • Sift the flour, baking powder, and salt into a medium bowl. • Beat the egg yolks, sugar, and almond extract in a medium bowl with an electric mixer at high speed until pale and thick. • With mixer at low speed, gradually beat in the dry ingredients, alternating with the chocolate and cream. • Spoon half the batter into each of the prepared pans. • Turn the oven on to 400°F and put the cakes in while the oven is still cold. Bake for 25 minutes, then turn the oven down to 300°F and bake for 15 more minutes. • Cool the cakes in the pans for 10 minutes. Loosen and remove the pan sides. Invert onto racks to cool completely. • *Chocolate Hazelnut Cream Filling*: Bring the cream to a boil in a saucepan. Remove from the heat. Stir in the chocolate hazelnut cream and butter until smooth. • Refrigerate for 30 minutes. • Split the cakes horizontally. • Place one layer on a serving plate. Spread with some of the filling. Repeat with the second layer and more filling. Top with the third layer and more filling. Finish with the remaining layer. Spread the remaining filling over the cake. • Dust with the cocoa and decorate with the raspberries.

Makes one 8-inch cake · Prep: 45 min. · Cooking: 40 min. · Level: 2 · Keeps: 2–3 days in the refrigerator

CHOCOLATE HAZELNUT CAKE

   ²/₃   cup all-purpose flour
    1   teaspoon baking powder
   ¹/₄   teaspoon salt
   ²/₃   cup butter, softened
   ³/₄   cup firmly packed brown sugar
    4   large eggs, separated
    1   cup toasted hazelnuts, finely chopped
    7   oz semisweet chocolate, coarsely chopped
   ¹/₂   cup heavy cream

FROSTING

    5   oz semisweet chocolate, coarsely chopped
    2   tablespoons light cream
   ¹/₂   teaspoon vanilla extract
    2   tablespoons hazelnuts, coarsely chopped

Preheat the oven to 350°F. • Butter and flour a 9-inch springform pan. • Sift the flour, baking powder, and salt into a medium bowl. • Beat the butter and sugar in a large bowl with an electric mixer at medium speed until creamy. Add the egg yolks, one at a time, until just blended after each addition. • With mixer at high speed, beat the egg whites in a large bowl until stiff peaks form. Use a large rubber spatula to fold them into the egg yolk mixture. Gradually fold in the dry ingredients, hazelnuts, and chocolate. • Spoon the batter into the prepared pan. • Bake for 45–50 minutes, or until a toothpick inserted into the center comes out clean. • Cool the cake in the pan for 15 minutes. Loosen and remove the pan sides. Transfer to a rack to cool completely • Split the cake horizontally. Place one layer on a serving plate. • With mixer at high speed, beat the cream in a large bowl until stiff. • Spread the cake with the cream. Top with the remaining layer. • *Frosting*: Melt the chocolate in a double boiler over barely simmering water. Add the vanilla and cream. Spread with the frosting. Decorate with the hazelnuts.

Makes one 9.inch round cake · Prep: 40 min. ·Cooking: 45–50 min. · Level: 2 · Keeps: 1–2 day

Chocolate hazelnut cream cake

and the syrup boils. Wash down the sides of the pan with a pastry brush dipped in cold water to prevent sugar crystals from forming. Cook, without stirring, until the syrup reaches 238°F, or the soft-ball stage. • Remove from the heat. Beat the syrup into the egg yolks in a slow, steady stream. Continue beating until the mixture is cool. Gradually beat in the butter. • Beat in the chocolate and vanilla until creamy. • Place one cake on a serving plate. Spread with ¹/₃ of the frosting. Top with the remaining cake. Spread with the remaining frosting.

Makes one 9-inch cake · Prep: 45 min. · Cooking 30–40 min. · Level: 1 · Keeps: 3 days in the refrigerator

OLD-FASHIONED DEVIL'S FOOD CAKE

- 5 oz semisweet chocolate
- 1 cup milk
- 1 tablespoon lemon juice
- 2 cups all-purpose flour
- 1 teaspoon baking powder
- 1 teaspoon baking soda
- ¹/₄ teaspoon salt
- ³/₄ cup granulated sugar
- ³/₄ cup firmly packed brown sugar
- ¹/₂ cup (1 stick) butter, softened
- 1 teaspoon vanilla extract
- 2 large eggs, at room temperature
- 1 teaspoon red food coloring
- ¹/₂ cup raspberry jam or preserves
- 1 cup Mock Cream (see page 344)
- 2 cups Rich Chocolate Frosting (see page 349)

Preheat the oven to 350°F. • Butter two 9-inch round cake pans. Line with waxed paper. Butter the paper. • Melt the chocolate in a double boiler over barely simmering water. Set aside to cool. • Stir together the milk and lemon juice to make sour milk. Set aside. • Sift the flour, baking powder, baking soda, and salt into a large bowl. • Beat both sugars, butter, and vanilla in a large bowl with an electric mixer at medium speed until creamy. • Add the eggs, one at a time, until just blended after each addition. • With mixer at low speed, gradually beat in the dry ingredients, food coloring, and chocolate, alternating with the sour milk. • Spoon the batter into the prepared pans. • Bake for 30–35 minutes, or until a toothpick inserted into the centers comes out clean. • Cool the cakes in the pans for 5 minutes. Turn out onto racks. Carefully remove the paper and let cool completely. • Place one cake on a serving plate. Spread with the raspberry

Devil's food cake

DEVIL'S FOOD CAKE

The frosting for this cake is time-consuming to prepare, but it's really worth the effort!

- ³/₄ cup unsweetened cocoa powder
- ¹/₂ cup boiling water
- 2 cups all-purpose flour
- 2 teaspoons baking powder
- ¹/₂ teaspoon baking soda
- ¹/₄ teaspoon salt
- ³/₄ cup (1¹/₂ sticks) butter, softened
- 2 cups granulated sugar
- 2 teaspoons vanilla extract
- 1 tablespoon chocolate or coffee liqueur
- 2 large eggs, at room temperature
- 1 cup buttermilk

FROSTING
- 8 oz bittersweet chocolate, coarsely chopped
- 6 large egg yolks
- 1 cup granulated sugar
- ¹/₂ cup water
- 1¹/₂ cups (3 sticks) butter, softened
- 2 teaspoons vanilla extract

Preheat the oven to 350°F. • Butter two 9-inch round cake pans. Line with waxed paper. Butter the paper. • Stir the cocoa and water in a small bowl until smooth. •

Sift the flour, baking powder, baking soda, and salt into a large bowl. • Beat the butter, sugar, vanilla, and liqueur in a large bowl with an electric mixer at medium speed until creamy. • Add the eggs, one at a time, until just blended after each addition. • With mixer at low speed, gradually beat in the dry ingredients, alternating with the buttermilk. Gradually beat in the cocoa mixture. • Spoon half the batter into each of the prepared pans. • Bake for 30–40 minutes, or until springy to the touch and a toothpick inserted into the centers comes out clean. • Cool the cakes in the pans for 10 minutes. Turn out onto racks. Carefully remove the paper and let cool completely. • *Frosting*: Melt the chocolate in a double boiler over barely simmering water. Set aside to cool. • With mixer at medium speed, beat the butter in a medium bowl until creamy. • Beat the egg yolks in a large bowl until pale in color. • Place the sugar and water in a medium saucepan over medium-low heat and stir until the sugar has dissolved

jam, followed by the Mock Cream. Top with the remaining cake. • Spread the top and sides with the frosting.

Makes one 9-inch cake · Prep: 45 min. · Cooking: 30–35 min. · Level: 2 · Keeps: 2–3 days in the refrigerator

CHOCOLATE SWIRL SUPREME

- 2⅓ cups all-purpose flour
- 1½ cups granulated sugar
- ⅔ cup unsweetened cocoa powder
- 2½ teaspoons baking powder
- ¼ teaspoon salt
- ¾ cup (1½ sticks) butter, softened
- 3 large eggs, at room temperature
- 1 cup milk
- ½ cup boiling water
- 1 teaspoon vanilla extract
- 1 teaspoon white vinegar

CHOCOLATE FROSTING
- ½ cup (1 stick) butter
- 4 oz bittersweet chocolate, coarsely chopped

CREAM CHEESE FROSTING
- 1 package (3 oz) cream cheese, softened
- ⅓ cup butter, softened
- 1 tablespoon honey
- 1¼ cups confectioners' sugar

Preheat the oven to 350°F. • Butter a 9-inch square baking pan. Line with waxed paper. Butter the paper. • Beat the flour, sugar, cocoa, baking powder, salt, butter, eggs, milk, water, vanilla, and vinegar in a large bowl with an electric mixer at medium speed until creamy. • Spoon the batter into the prepared pan. • Bake for 50–60 minutes, or until the cake shrinks from the pan sides and a toothpick inserted into the center comes out clean. • Cool the cake in the pan for 5 minutes. Turn out onto a rack. Carefully remove the paper and let cool completely. • *Chocolate Frosting*: Melt the chocolate and butter in a double boiler over barely simmering water. Set aside to cool enough to spread (make sure it doesn't set). • *Cream Cheese Frosting*: With mixer at medium speed, beat the cream cheese and butter in a small bowl until creamy. Add the honey and gradually beat in the confectioners' sugar. • Spoon alternate dollops of each of the frostings onto the top of the cake. Use a thin metal spatula to spread the frosting over. Use a fork to swirl the frostings together to create a marbled effect.

Makes one 9-inch cake · Prep: 45 min. · Cooking: 50–60 min. · Level: 1 · Keeps: 2–3 days

Chocolate swirl supreme

CHOCOLATE BUTTERSCOTCH CAKE

- 3 oz dark chocolate, coarsely chopped
- ⅓ cup butter, cut up
- 2 large eggs
- 1⅓ cups superfine sugar
- ½ cup butterscotch schnapps
- 1 teaspoon vanilla extract
- ½ teaspoon almond extract
- ⅔ cup all-purpose flour
- ⅓ teaspoon baking powder
- ½ teaspoon salt
- 2 oz semisweet chocolate chips
- 2 oz butterscotch chips

FROSTING
- 1 cup heavy cream
- 10 oz semisweet chocolate chips
- 2 tablespoons amaretto
- 2 tablespoons slivered almonds

Preheat the oven to 350°F. • Butter and flour two 9-inch round cake pans. • Melt the chocolate and butter in a double boiler over barely simmering water. Set aside to cool. • Beat the eggs in a large bowl with an electric mixer at high speed until pale in color. Gradually beat in the superfine sugar until pale and thick. • Use a large rubber spatula to fold in the cooled chocolate mixture. • Stir in ¼ cup schnapps, vanilla, and almond extract. • Sift the flour, baking powder, and salt into a large bowl. Gradually add the dry ingredients to the chocolate mixture. • Use a large rubber spatula to fold in the chocolate and butterscotch chips. • Spoon half the batter into each of the prepared pans. • Bake for 20–25 minutes, or until a toothpick inserted into the center comes out clean. Cool the cakes in the pans for 10 minutes. Turn out onto racks to cool completely. • *Frosting*: Bring the cream to a boil in a medium saucepan. Remove from the heat. Stir in the chocolate chips. Cover and let stand 10 minutes. • Stir in the amaretto until smooth. Place a cake on a serving plate. Drizzle with the remaining schnapps. • Spread ⅓ of the frosting over the layer. Top with the remaining cake. Spread the remaining frosting over the cake. • Decorate with the slivered almonds.

Makes one 9-inch layer cake · Prep: 20 min. Cooking: 20–25 min. · Level: 1 · Keeps: 3 days

MOIST CHOCOLATE RING WITH CREAMY CHOCOLATE SAUCE

An excellent cake with great flavor and texture. Serve as a dessert with raspberries or other fresh fruit.

1¼ cups all-purpose flour
⅓ cup unsweetened cocoa powder
1 teaspoon baking powder
1 teaspoon baking soda
¼ teaspoon salt
¾ cup granulated sugar
⅓ cup firmly packed dark brown sugar
¼ cup (½ stick) butter, melted
1 cup buttermilk
½ cup milk
2 large eggs, at room temperature
1 tablespoon freeze-dried coffee granules, dissolved in 1 tablespoon milk
1 teaspoon vanilla extract

CREAMY CHOCOLATE SAUCE
½ cup bittersweet chocolate chips
½ cup heavy cream

Preheat the oven to 350°F. • Butter a 9-inch Bundt pan. Dust with cocoa. • Sift the flour, cocoa, baking powder, baking soda, and salt into a large bowl. Stir in the sugars. • Beat the butter, buttermilk, milk, eggs, coffee mixture, and vanilla in a large bowl with an electric mixer at medium speed until well blended. With mixer at low speed, beat the butter mixture into the dry ingredients. • Spoon the batter into the prepared pan. • Bake for 40–50 minutes, or until a toothpick inserted into the center comes out clean. • Cool the cake in the pan for 15 minutes. Turn out onto a rack to cool completely. • *Creamy Chocolate Sauce*: Stir the chocolate and cream in a small saucepan over very low heat until the chocolate melts. Remove from the heat. Set aside to cool. • Spoon the sauce over the cake and serve.

Makes one 9-inch cake · Prep: 20 min. · Cooking: 40–50 min. · Level: 1 · Keeps: 2–3 days

RICH CHOCOLATE BUNDT CAKE

1 package (18 oz) dark chocolate cake mix
2 cups sour cream
3 large eggs, at room temperature
½ cup coffee-flavored liqueur
⅓ cup vegetable oil
1 package (3.9 oz) instant chocolate pudding mix
1 package (12 oz) semisweet chocolate chips

Preheat the oven to 350°F. • Butter a 10-inch Bundt pan. Dust with cocoa. • Place all the ingredients except the chocolate chips in a large bowl and beat with an electric mixer at medium speed until well blended. • Fold in the chocolate chips. The batter will be thick.• Spoon the batter into the prepared pan. • Bake for 50–60 minutes, or until a toothpick inserted into the center comes out clean. • Cool the cake in the pan for 10 minutes. Turn out onto a rack to cool completely.

Makes one 10-inch cake · Prep: 10 min. · Cooking 50–60 min. · Level: 1 · Keeps: 2–3 days

Moist chocolate ring with creamy chocolate sauce

DOUBLE CHOCOLATE BUNDT CAKE

2 cups all-purpose flour
⅓ cup unsweetened cocoa powder
1½ teaspoons baking powder
¼ teaspoon salt
⅔ cup butter, softened
¼ cup vegetable shortening
2 cups granulated sugar
3 large eggs, at room temperature
⅔ cup milk
1 teaspoon vanilla extract
¾ cup semisweet chocolate chips

Preheat the oven to 325°F. • Butter a 10-inch Bundt pan. Dust with cocoa. • Sift the flour, cocoa, baking powder, and salt into a medium bowl. • Beat the butter, shortening, and sugar in a large bowl with an electric mixer at medium speed until creamy. • Add the eggs, one at a time, until just blended after each addition. • With mixer at low speed, gradually beat in the dry ingredients, alternating with the milk and vanilla. • By hand, stir in the chocolate chips. • Spoon the batter into the prepared pan. • Bake for 55–65 minutes, or until a toothpick inserted into the center comes out clean. • Cool the cake in the pan for 10 minutes. Turn out onto a rack to cool completely.

Makes one 10-inch cake · Prep: 20 min. · Cooking: 55–65 min. · Level: 1 · Keeps: 4–5 days

GLAZED PEAR AND WHITE CHOCOLATE BUNDT CAKE

4 oz white chocolate, coarsely chopped
1½ cups all-purpose flour
1½ teaspoons baking powder
¼ teaspoon salt
½ cup (1 stick) butter, softened
½ cup granulated sugar
3 large eggs, separated
½ cup milk
1 (15¼ oz) can pear halves, drained and sliced (syrup reserved)

GLAZE
1 cup confectioners' sugar
2 tablespoons butter, melted
reserved pear syrup (see above)

Preheat the oven to 325°F. • Butter and flour a 9-inch Bundt pan. • Melt the chocolate in a double boiler over barely simmering water. Set aside to cool. • Sift the flour, baking powder, and salt into a medium bowl. • Beat the butter and sugar in a large bowl with an electric mixer at medium speed until creamy. • Add the egg yolks, one at a time, until just blended after each addition. • With mixer at low speed, gradually beat in the chocolate, followed by the dry ingredients, alternating with the milk. • With mixer at high speed, beat the egg whites in a large bowl until stiff peaks form. Use a large rubber spatula to fold them into the batter. • Spoon half the batter into the prepared pan. Top with the sliced pears. Spoon the remaining batter over the pears. • Bake for 45–55 minutes, or until a toothpick inserted into the center comes out clean. • Cool the cake in the pan for 10 minutes. Turn out onto a rack to cool completely. • *Glaze*: Mix the confectioners' sugar and butter in a medium bowl. Beat in enough of the reserved pear syrup to make a fairly thick glaze. Drizzle the glaze over the cake, letting it run down the sides.

Makes one 9-inch cake · Prep: 30 min. · Cooking: 45–55 min. · Level: 1 · Keeps: 1–2 days

CHOCOLATE ZUCCHINI BUNDT CAKE

- 2²/₃ cups all-purpose flour
- ²/₃ cup unsweetened cocoa powder
- 2¹/₂ teaspoons baking powder
- 1¹/₂ teaspoons baking soda
- 1 teaspoon ground cinnamon
- ¹/₂ teaspoon salt
- ³/₄ cup (1¹/₂ sticks) butter, softened
- 2 cups granulated sugar
- 2 teaspoons vanilla extract
- 3 large eggs, at room temperature
- 1 tablespoon grated orange zest
- 2 cups grated zucchini
- ¹/₂ cup milk
- 1 cup walnuts, chopped

Orange Vanilla Glaze (optional)

- 1 cup confectioners' sugar
- 1 tablespoon grated orange zest
- 2 teaspoons vanilla extract
- 1–2 tablespoons fresh orange juice

Preheat the oven to 350°F. • Butter and flour a 10-inch Bundt pan. • Sift the flour, cocoa, baking powder, baking soda, cinnamon, and salt into a large bowl. • Beat

the butter, sugar, and vanilla in a large bowl with an electric mixer at medium speed until creamy. • Add the eggs, one at a time, until just blended after each addition. • With mixer at low speed, gradually beat in the dry ingredients, alternating with the milk. • Spoon the batter into the prepared pan. • Bake for 55–65 minutes, or a toothpick inserted into the center comes out clean. • Cool the cake in the pan for 10 minutes. Turn out onto a rack to cool completely. • *Orange Vanilla Glaze*: Stir the confectioners' sugar, orange zest, and vanilla in a medium bowl. Stir in enough of the orange juice to make a thin glaze. Drizzle the glaze over the warm cake.

Makes one 10-inch cake · Prep: 30 min. · Cooking: 55–65 min. · Level: 1 · Keeps: 1–2 days

WHITE CHOCOLATE AND LIME BUNDT CAKE

- 5 oz white chocolate, coarsely chopped
- 2 cups all-purpose flour
- 2 teaspoons baking powder
- ¹/₄ teaspoon salt
- 1 cup (2 sticks) butter, softened
- ¹/₂ cup granulated sugar
- 1–2 tablespoons grated lime zest
- 3 large eggs, separated
- ¹/₄ cup milk

Lime Frosting

- 1 cup confectioners' sugar
- 1 tablespoon butter, melted
- 1 tablespoon grated lime zest
- 1–2 tablespoons fresh lime juice
- 4 oz white chocolate, coarsely grated

Preheat the oven to 350°F. • Butter and flour a 9-inch Bundt pan. • Melt the chocolate in a double boiler over barely simmering water. Set aside to cool. • Sift the flour, baking powder, and salt into a medium bowl. • Beat the butter, sugar, and lime zest in a large bowl with an electric mixer at medium speed until creamy. • Add the egg yolks, one at a time, until just blended after each addition. • With mixer at low speed, gradually beat in the chocolate, followed by the dry ingredients, alternating with the milk. • With mixer at high speed, beat the egg whites in a medium bowl until stiff peaks form. Use a large rubber spatula to fold them into the batter. • Spoon the batter into the prepared pan. • Bake for 40–50 minutes, or until a toothpick inserted into the center comes out clean. •

Cool the cake in the pan for 10 minutes. Turn out onto a rack to cool completely. • *Lime Frosting*: Mix the confectioners' sugar, butter, and lime zest in a large bowl. Beat in enough lime juice to make a thick, spreadable frosting. Spread the frosting over the top of the cake. Sprinkle with the grated chocolate.

Makes one 9-inch cake · Prep: 20 min. · Cooking: 40–50 min. · Level: 1 · Keeps: 2–3 days

CHOCOLATE SOUFFLÉ MOLD

- ¹/₂ cup all-purpose flour
- ¹/₄ teaspoon salt
- 1 cup milk
- ¹/₂ cup granulated sugar
- ¹/₄ cup + 2 tablespoons butter, cut up
- 4 large eggs, separated
- 4 tablespoons unsweetened cocoa powder

Preheat the oven to 375°F. • Butter a 9-inch ring mold. Dust with cocoa. • Place the flour and salt in a small bowl and stir in a little milk until smooth. • Bring the remaining milk, sugar, and butter to a boil in a medium saucepan over medium-low heat, stirring often. Beat in the flour mixture with an electric mixer at low speed until well blended. Set aside to cool. • Beat in the cocoa until smooth. • With mixer at high speed, beat the egg yolks in a large bowl until pale in color. • With mixer at high speed, beat the egg whites in a large bowl until stiff peaks form. • Stir the milk mixture into the egg yolks. Use a large rubber spatula to fold in the beaten whites. • Spoon the batter into the prepared mold. • Bake for 25–30 minutes, or until a toothpick inserted into the center comes out clean. • Cool the cake in the mold for 10 minutes. Turn out onto a rack to cool completely.

Makes one 9-inch mold · Prep: 30 min. · Cooking: 25–30 min. · Level: 1 · Keeps: 3–4 days

Place the red currants in the center of the cake in a decorative manner. • Dust with the confectioners' sugar.

Makes one 9-inch cake · Prep: 70 min. + 30. min to chill · Cooking: 35–40 min. · Level: 2 · Keeps: 1 day in the refrigerator

CHOCOLATE MOUSSE CAKE

This very rich chocolate mousse over a rich chocolate cake is topped with chocolate ganache sauce and chopped nuts. It is perfect for birthdays and other special occasions.

- $1^2/_3$ cups all-purpose flour
- $^1/_3$ cup unsweetened cocoa powder
- 2 teaspoons baking powder
- $^1/_4$ teaspoon salt
- 1 cup granulated sugar
- 1 cup lukewarm strong coffee
- $^1/_3$ cup vegetable oil
- 1 large egg, at room temperature
- 1 tablespoon vanilla extract

- 3 cups Chocolate Mousse (see page 343)

GANACHE
- 4 oz semisweet chocolate, coarsely chopped
- $^1/_4$ cup heavy cream
- 1 cup walnuts, coarsely chopped

Preheat the oven to 350°F. • Butter a 9-inch springform pan. Dust with cocoa. • Sift the flour, cocoa, baking powder, and salt into a large bowl. Stir in the sugar. • Make a well in the center and beat in the coffee, oil, egg, and vanilla with an electric mixer at medium speed. • Pour the batter into the prepared pan. • Bake for 40–45 minutes, or until a toothpick inserted into the center comes out clean. • Cool the cake completely in the pan on a rack. • Loosen and remove the pan sides. Invert the cake onto a rack. Loosen and remove the pan bottom. • Split the cake horizontally. Place one layer in a 10-inch

Mocha mousse torte

MOCHA MOUSSE TORTE

TORTE
- 6 large eggs, at room temperature
- $^3/_4$ cup granulated sugar
- $^2/_3$ cup all-purpose flour
- $^1/_3$ cup cornstarch
- $^1/_3$ cup unsweetened cocoa powder
- $^1/_3$ cup butter, melted
- $^1/_2$ teaspoon vanilla extract

RUM SYRUP
- $^1/_4$ cup granulated sugar
- 1 tablespoon water
- $^1/_4$ cup dark rum

MOUSSE FILLING
- 1 teaspoon freeze-dried coffee granules
- 2 tablespoons dark rum
- 1 cup Chocolate Mousse (see page 343)

- 1 bunch red currants, to decorate confectioners' sugar, to dust

Preheat the oven to 375°F. • Butter and flour two 9-inch round cake pans. • *Torte*: Beat the eggs and granulated sugar with an electric mixer at high speed until pale and thick. • Mix the flour, cornstarch, and cocoa in a large bowl until well blended. Use a large rubber spatula to gently fold in the egg mixture. Stir in the melted butter and vanilla. • Spoon half the batter into each of the prepared pans. • Bake for 35–40 minutes, until a toothpick inserted into the centers comes out clean. • Cool the cakes in the pans for 15 minutes. Turn out onto racks to cool completely. • *Rum Syrup*: Bring the sugar and water to a boil in a saucepan. Continue boiling for 3 minutes, or until the sugar has dissolved. Remove from the heat and set aside to cool. • Stir in the rum. • *Chocolate Mousse*: Dissolve the coffee in the rum. Fold into the mousse. Refrigerate for at least 30 minutes. • Split a cake horizontally. Place one layer on a serving plate. Sprinkle with the rum syrup. • Spread with $^1/_3$ of the chocolate mousse. Top with the remaining cake layer. Spread the top and sides of the cake with the remaining mousse. • Cut the remaining cake into small cubes. • Arrange the cake cubes over the assembled cake and press down lightly. •

springform pan. Spread with ⅓ of the chocolate mousse. Top with the remaining cake layer. Spread the remaining mousse over the top and sides of the cake. • Cover and refrigerate for 24 hours, or until completely set. • *Ganache*: Melt the chocolate and cream in a double boiler over barely simmering water. Remove from the heat. • Loosen and remove the pan sides. Gently press the chopped nuts into the side of the mousse. Drizzle with the ganache.

Makes one 10-inch cake · Prep: 1 hr. + 24 hr. to chill · Cooking: 40–45 min. · Level: 2 · Keeps: 2 days

CHOCOLATE MOUSSE SUPREME

11 oz semisweet chocolate, coarsely chopped
1 cup (2 sticks) unsalted butter, cut up
1 teaspoon freeze-dried coffee granules
10 large eggs, separated
¼ cup milk
1½ cups granulated sugar
¼ cup water
1⅛ teaspoons cream of tartar

Preheat the oven to 300°F. • Butter a 9-inch springform pan. Dust with cocoa. • Melt the chocolate, butter, and coffee granules in a double boiler over barely simmering water. Transfer to a very large bowl. Cool to lukewarm. • Whisk the egg yolks and milk in a saucepan until well blended. Cook over low heat, stirring constantly with a wooden spoon, until the mixture lightly coats a metal spoon, or registers 160°F on an instant-read thermometer. Immediately plunge the pan into a bowl of ice water and stir until the egg mixture has cooled. Transfer to a large bowl. • Use a large rubber spatula to fold the beaten yolks into the chocolate mixture. • Stir the whites, sugar, and cream of tartar in a double boiler until blended. Cook over low heat, beating constantly with a mixer at low speed until the whites register 160°F on an instant-read thermometer. Transfer to a bowl and beat at high speed until stiff peaks form. Use a large rubber spatula to fold them into the chocolate mixture • Spoon ⅔ of the mixture into the prepared pan. Cover and refrigerate the remaining mousse. • Bake for 30–40 minutes, or until just firm in the center. • Cool completely in the pan

Chocolate mousse mold

on a rack. Loosen and remove the pan sides. Place on a serving plate. Refrigerate for 1 hour. • Spread the remaining mousse over the top and sides of the cake. • Refrigerate overnight before serving.

Makes one 9-inch cake · Prep: 30 min. + 12 hr. to chill · Cooking 30–40 min. · Level: 1 · Keeps: 2 days

CHOCOLATE MOUSSE MOLD

8 oz bittersweet chocolate, coarsely chopped
¼ cup water
6 large eggs, at room temperature
¾ cup (1½ sticks) butter, softened
2 cups Chantilly Cream (see page 345)
fresh raspberries, to decorate
walnuts, to decorate

Butter an 8-inch square baking pan. • Melt the chocolate and water in a double boiler over barely simmering water. Beat in the eggs, one at a time, until just blended. Cook until the mixture lightly coats a metal spoon or it registers 160°F on an instant-read thermometer. Remove from the heat and stir in the butter. Immediately plunge

the pan into a bowl of ice water and stir until the mixture has cooled. • Use a large rubber spatula to fold 1½ cups of Chantilly Cream into the chocolate mixture. • Spoon the mixture into the prepared pan and refrigerate for 12 hours, or until set. • Cover the pan with a serving plate and carefully turn upside down. • Spoon the remaining Chantilly Cream to a pastry bag and pipe the top of the mousse. Top with the raspberries and walnuts.

Makes one 8-inch cake · Prep: 35 min. + 12 hr. to chill · Cooking:15 min. · Level: 1 · Keeps: 1–2 days in the refrigerator

Naturally sweet, fresh fruit cakes are full of fiber, providing that perfect excuse to cut just one more slice. Vegetable cakes invite the imagination and palate to merge, culminating in an array of healthy, flavorsome desserts.

FRESH FRUIT & VEGETABLE CAKES

CINNAMON BANANA LOAF

1½ cups all-purpose flour
¾ cup granulated sugar
1½ teaspoons baking powder
1 teaspoon ground cinnamon
¼ teaspoon salt
2 large very ripe bananas, peeled and sliced
2 large eggs, at room temperature
⅔ cup butter, melted
1 cup Vanilla Frosting (see page 347)

Preheat the oven to 350°F. • Butter and flour an 8½ x 4½-inch loaf pan. • Sift the flour, sugar, baking powder, cinnamon, and salt into a large bowl. • Process the bananas and eggs in a food processor until frothy. • Stir the banana mixture and butter into the flour mixture until just blended. • Spoon the batter into the prepared pan. •

Bake for 35–45 minutes, or until a toothpick inserted into the center comes out clean. • Cool the loaf in the pan for 10 minutes. Turn out onto a rack to cool completely. • Drizzle with the frosting.

Makes one 8½ x 4½-inch loaf · Prep: 15 min. · Cooking: 35–45 min. · Level: 1 · Keeps: 3–4 days

◄ Best-ever carrot and walnut cake (see page 119)

⬆ Cinnamon banana loaf

BANANA CAKE
WITH PASSION FRUIT FROSTING

- 1¾ cups all-purpose flour
- 1 teaspoon baking powder
- 1 teaspoon baking soda
- 1 teaspoon ground ginger
- ¼ teaspoon salt
- ½ cup (1 stick) butter, softened
- ¾ cup firmly packed dark brown sugar
- 3 large eggs, at room temperature
- 1¼ cups mashed very ripe bananas
- ½ cup sour cream
- ¼ cup milk

PASSION FRUIT FROSTING

- 1¾ cups (approx.) confectioners' sugar
- 3 tablespoons fresh passion fruit pulp
- 1 tablespoon butter, softened

Preheat the oven to 350°F. • Butter a 9-inch square baking pan. • Sift the flour, baking powder, baking soda, ginger, and salt into a medium bowl. • Beat the butter and brown sugar in a large bowl with an electric mixer at medium speed until creamy. • Add the eggs, one at a time, until just blended after each addition. • With mixer at low speed, gradually beat in the dry ingredients. alternating with the bananas, sour cream, and milk. • Spoon the batter into the prepared pan. • Bake for 40–50 minutes, or until a toothpick inserted into the center comes out clean. • Cool the cake completely in the pan. • *Passion Fruit Frosting*: Stir together the confectioners' sugar, passion fruit pulp, and butter in a double boiler over barely simmering water until the frosting is thick and spreadable. Add more confectioners' sugar if needed. • Spread the top of the cake with the frosting.

Makes one 9-inch cake · Prep: 30 min. · Cooking: 40–50 min. · Level: 1 · Keeps: 2–3 days

BANANA-CHOCOLATE CHIP CAKE

- 3 cups all-purpose flour
- 1 teaspoon baking powder
- 1 teaspoon baking soda
- 1 teaspoon ground cinnamon
- 1 teaspoon ground ginger
- ½ teaspoon ground allspice
- ¼ teaspoon salt
- ½ cup (1 stick) butter, softened
- 1½ cups firmly packed brown sugar
- 2 teaspoons vanilla extract
- 4 large eggs, separated
- 2½ cups mashed very ripe bananas
- 1 cup semisweet chocolate chips
- 2½ cups Fudge Frosting (see page 347) (optional)

Preheat the oven to 350°F. • Butter and flour a 9-inch tube pan. • Sift the flour, baking powder, baking soda, cinnamon, ginger, allspice, and salt into a large bowl. • Beat the butter, brown sugar, and vanilla in a large bowl with an electric mixer at medium speed until creamy. • Add the egg yolks, one at a time, until just blended after each addition. • With mixer at low speed, gradually beat in the bananas, followed by the dry ingredients and chocolate chips. • With mixer at high speed, beat the egg whites in a large bowl until stiff peaks form. Use a large rubber spatula to fold them into the batter. • Spoon the batter into the prepared pan. • Bake for 55–65 minutes, or until a toothpick inserted into the center comes out clean. • Cool the cake in the pan for 15 minutes. Turn out onto a rack to cool completely. • Spread the top and sides of the cake with Fudge Frosting, if desired.

Makes one 9-inch cake · Prep: 30 min. · Cooking: 55–65 min. · Level: 1 · Keeps: 3–4 days

WHITE CHOCOLATE AND BANANA LAYER CAKE

- 3 cups all-purpose flour
- 1½ teaspoons baking powder
- 1 teaspoon baking soda
- 1 teaspoon ground ginger
- ½ teaspoon cloves
- ½ teaspoon salt
- ⅔ cup butter, softened
- 1¼ cups firmly packed light brown sugar
- 2 teaspoons vanilla extract
- 3 large eggs, at room temperature
- 2½ cups mashed very ripe bananas
- ½ cup plain yogurt
- 1 cup white chocolate chips

FILLING

- 1 cup heavy cream
- ⅓ cup confectioners' sugar
- 1 teaspoon vanilla extract
- 1 small banana
- 1 tablespoon fresh lemon juice

Preheat the oven to 350°F. • Butter two 9-inch round cake pans. Line with waxed paper. Butter the paper. • Sift the flour, baking powder, baking soda, ginger, cloves, and salt into a large bowl. • Beat the butter, brown sugar, and vanilla in a large bowl with an electric mixer at medium speed until creamy. • Add the eggs, one at a time, until just blended after each addition. • With mixer at low speed, gradually beat in the bananas and dry ingredients, alternating with the yogurt. Stir in the chocolate chips. • Spoon half the batter into each of the prepared pans. • Bake for 25–35 minutes, or until a toothpick inserted into the center comes out clean. • Cool the cakes in the pans for 15 minutes. Turn out onto racks. Carefully remove the paper and let cool completely. • *Filling*: With mixer at high speed, beat the cream, 2 tablespoons confectioners' sugar, and vanilla in a medium bowl until stiff. • Place a cake on a serving plate. Spread with the cream. Peel, slice the banana thinly, and drizzle with the lemon juice so it doesn't discolor. Top the cream with the banana slices and cover with the remaining cake. • Dust with the remaining confectioners' sugar.

Makes one 9-inch cake · Prep: 30 min. · Cooking: 25–35 min. · Level: 1 · Keeps: 1 day in the refrigerator

FROSTED BANANA-YOGURT CAKE

- 2 cups all-purpose flour
- 1 teaspoon baking powder
- 1 teaspoon baking soda
- ¼ teaspoon salt
- ¾ cup (1½ sticks) butter, softened
- 1 cup granulated sugar
- 2 large eggs, at room temperature
- 1 cup mashed very ripe bananas
- 1 tablespoon grated lemon zest
- ¼ cup plain yogurt

YOGURT FROSTING

- 2 cups confectioners' sugar
- 2 tablespoons plain yogurt
- 1 tablespoon grated lemon zest
- 1–2 tablespoons fresh lemon juice

Preheat the oven to 350°F. • Butter a 9-inch square baking pan. Line with waxed paper. • Sift the flour, baking powder, baking soda, and salt into a large bowl. • Beat the butter and sugar in a large bowl with an electric mixer at medium speed until creamy. • Add the eggs, one at a time, until just blended after each addition. • With mixer at low speed, gradually beat in the bananas, lemon zest, and the dry ingredients, alternating with the yogurt. • Spoon the batter into the prepared pan. • Bake for 50–60 minutes, or until golden brown, springy to the touch, and a toothpick inserted into the center comes out clean. • Cool the cake in the pan for 10 minutes. Turn out onto a rack. Carefully remove the paper and let cool completely. • *Yogurt Frosting*: With mixer at low speed, beat the confectioners' sugar, yogurt, lemon zest, and 1 tablespoon lemon juice in a large bowl until smooth and spreadable. Add more lemon juice, if needed. • Spread over the top and sides of the cake.

Makes one 9-inch cake · Prep: 25 min. · Cooking: 50–60 min. · Level: 1 · Keeps: 2–3 days

CINNAMON CRUMBLE APPLE CAKE

- 3 medium tart apples (14 oz), peeled, cored, and thinly sliced
- $^1/_4$ cup fresh lemon juice
- 2 tablespoons brown sugar
- $^3/_4$ cup (1$^1/_2$ sticks) butter, softened
- $^3/_4$ cup granulated sugar
- 2 large eggs, at room temperature
- 2$^1/_4$ cups all-purpose flour
- 2 teaspoons baking powder
- $^1/_4$ teaspoon salt
- $^3/_4$ cup milk

CINNAMON CRUMBLE

- 1 cup all-purpose flour
- $^1/_2$ cup firmly packed brown sugar
- 1 tablespoon ground cinnamon
- $^1/_3$ cup cold butter, cut up
- 1 cup walnuts, coarsely chopped

Preheat the oven to 350°F. • Butter a 9-inch square baking pan. • Bring the apples, lemon juice, and brown sugar to a boil in a medium saucepan over medium heat. Cover, reduce the heat,

and simmer for about 10 minutes, or until tender. Drain well and set aside to cool • Beat the butter and granulated sugar in a large bowl with an electric mixer at medium speed until creamy. • Add the eggs, one at a time, until just blended after each addition. • With mixer at low speed, gradually beat in the flour, baking powder, and salt, alternating with the milk. • Spoon $^2/_3$ of the batter into the prepared pan. Spoon the apples over the top. Spread the remaining batter on top. • *Cinnamon Crumble*: Stir together the flour, brown sugar, and cinnamon in a large bowl. Use a pastry blender to cut in the butter until the mixture resembles coarse crumbs. Stir in the walnuts. • Sprinkle over the cake. • Bake for 40–50 minutes, or until a toothpick inserted into the center comes out clean. • Cool the cake completely in the pan on a rack.

Makes one 9-inch cake · Prep: 30 min. · Cooking: 40–50 min. · Level: 2 · Keeps: 2 days

UPSIDE-DOWN APPLE CAKE

- $^1/_3$ cup firmly packed brown sugar
- 2 large apples, peeled and cored
- 1 tablespoon fresh lemon juice
- 2 cups all-purpose flour
- 1$^1/_2$ teaspoons baking powder
- $^1/_2$ teaspoon baking soda
- 1 teaspoon ground cardamom
- 1 teaspoon ground cinnamon
- $^1/_4$ teaspoon salt
- $^3/_4$ cup (1$^1/_2$ sticks) butter, softened
- $^3/_4$ cup granulated sugar
- 1 teaspoon vanilla extract
- 2 large eggs, at room temperature
- $^1/_2$ cup milk

Preheat the oven to 350°F. • Butter a 9-inch round cake pan. • Sprinkle the pan with half the brown sugar. Slice one apple into thin rings and lay over the brown sugar. Sprinkle with the remaining brown sugar and drizzle with the lemon juice. • Sift the flour, baking powder, baking soda, cardamom, cinnamon, and salt into a medium bowl. • Beat the butter, granulated sugar, and vanilla in a large bowl with an electric mixer at medium speed until creamy. • Add the eggs, one at a time, until just blended after each addition. • With mixer at low speed, gradually beat in the dry ingredients, alternating with the milk. • Chop the remaining apple finely and stir into the batter. • Spoon the batter over the sliced apple. • Bake for 45–55 minutes, or until a toothpick inserted into the center comes out clean. • Cool the cake in the pan for 15 minutes. Turn out onto a rack. Serve the cake warm or at room temperature.

Makes one 9-inch cake · Prep: 25 min. · Cooking: 45–55 min. · Level: 1 · Keeps: 1–2 days

Upside-down apple cake

2 large eggs, at room temperature
½ cup pecans, chopped
2 large apples, peeled, cored, and thinly sliced
2–3 tablespoons apricot jam or preserves
1 tablespoon brandy

Preheat the oven to 350°F. • Butter and flour a 9-inch springform pan. • Sift the flour, custard powder, baking powder, baking soda, and salt into a medium bowl. • Beat the butter and confectioners' sugar in a large bowl with an electric mixer at medium speed until creamy. • Add the eggs, one at a time, until just blended after each addition. • With mixer at low speed, gradually beat in the pecans and dry ingredients. • Spoon the batter into the prepared pan. • Arrange the apple slices over the batter. • Bake for 40–50 minutes, or until a toothpick inserted into the center comes out clean. • Cool the cake in the pan on a rack for 10 minutes. Loosen and remove the pan sides and let cool completely. • Warm the jam and brandy in a small saucepan. Drizzle over the cake.

Makes one 9-inch cake · Prep: 20 min. · Cooking: 40–50 min. · Level: 1 · Keeps: 1–2 days

APPLE CRUMBLE CAKE WITH APRICOT GLAZE

An excellent cake that tastes every bit as good as it looks.

2 cups all-purpose flour
2 teaspoons baking powder
¼ teaspoon salt
½ cup (1 stick) butter, softened
1 cup granulated sugar
1 teaspoon vanilla extract
1 large egg, at room temperature
1 cup buttermilk
2 medium tart apples (Granny Smiths are ideal), peeled, cored, and thinly sliced

CRUMBLE
½ cup firmly packed brown sugar
3 tablespoons butter, melted
1 teaspoon ground cinnamon
½ teaspoon ground nutmeg

GLAZE
¾ cup apricot preserves
1 tablespoon fresh lemon juice

Preheat the oven to 350°F. • Butter and flour a 9-inch square baking pan. • Sift the flour, baking powder, and salt into a medium bowl. • Beat the butter, sugar, and vanilla in a large bowl with an electric mixer at medium speed until creamy. • Add the egg, beating until just blended. •

Apple pecan cake

APPLE COFFEE CAKE

2 cups all-purpose flour
1½ teaspoons baking powder
1 teaspoon ground cinnamon
½ teaspoon baking soda
¼ teaspoon salt
1 package (8 oz) cream cheese, softened
½ cup (1 stick) butter, softened
1 cup granulated sugar
1 teaspoon almond extract
3 large eggs, at room temperature
¼ cup milk

TOPPING
2 large tart apples (Granny Smiths are ideal), peeled, cored, and sliced
2 tablespoons fresh lemon juice
½ cup granulated sugar
2 tablespoons all-purpose flour
1 teaspoon ground cinnamon

Preheat the oven to 350°F. • Butter and flour a 13 x 9-inch baking pan. • Sift the flour, baking powder, cinnamon, baking soda, and salt into a large bowl. • Beat the cream cheese, butter, sugar, and the almond extract in a large bowl with an electric mixer at medium speed until

fluffy. • Add the eggs, one at a time, until just blended after each addition. • With mixer at low speed, gradually beat in the dry ingredients, alternating with the milk. • Spoon the batter into the prepared pan. • *Topping*: Place the apples in a medium bowl and toss with the lemon juice. • Mix the sugar, flour, and cinnamon in a small bowl. Add the sugar mixture to the apple slices and toss to coat well. • Arrange the apple slices over the batter. • Bake for 45–55 minutes, or until golden brown and a toothpick inserted into the center comes out clean. • Cool the cake in the pan. Serve warm.

Makes one 13 x 9-inch cake · Prep: 25 min. · Cooking: 45–55 min. · Level: 1 · Keeps: 1–2 days

APPLE PECAN CAKE

1⅓ cups all-purpose flour
⅓ cup custard powder (Bird's Imported English Dessert Mix for Custard-Style Pudding is recommended)
1 teaspoon baking powder
½ teaspoon baking soda
¼ teaspoon salt
½ cup (1 stick) butter, softened
1 cup confectioners' sugar

With mixer at low speed, gradually beat in the dry ingredients, alternating with the buttermilk. • Spoon the batter into the prepared pan. Arrange the apples on top in overlapping layers. • *Crumble*: Mix the brown sugar, butter, cinnamon, and nutmeg in a small bowl until crumbly. Sprinkle over the apples. • Bake for 55–65 minutes, or until the apples are tender, the crumble is brown, and a toothpick inserted into the center comes out clean. • Cool the cake completely in the pan on a rack. • *Glaze*: Warm the apricot preserves and lemon juice in a saucepan over low heat. Brush the cake with the glaze just before serving.

Makes one 9-inch cake · Prep: 30 min. · Cooking: 55–65 min. · Level: 1 · Keeps: 1–2 days

COUNTRY APPLE BAKE

- ½ cup (1 stick) butter, softened
- ½ cup granulated sugar
- 1½ teaspoons grated lemon zest
- 2 large eggs, at room temperature
- 1½ cups all-purpose flour
- 2 teaspoons baking powder
- ¼ teaspoon salt
- ⅓ cup milk
- 4 medium apples, peeled, cored, and halved
- 2 tablespoons fresh lemon juice
- 2 tablespoons apricot preserves

Preheat the oven to 350°F • Butter and flour a 9-inch springform pan. • Beat the butter, sugar, and lemon zest in a large bowl with an electric mixer at medium speed until creamy. • Add the eggs, one at a time, until just blended after each addition. • With mixer at low speed, gradually beat in the flour, baking powder, and salt, alternating with the milk. • Spoon the batter into the prepared pan. • Use a sharp knife to cut a grid pattern into the rounded sides of the apples. Drizzle with the lemon juice. • Arrange the apples, cut-side-up, in the batter. • Bake for 40–50 minutes, or a toothpick inserted into the batter comes out clean and the apples are tender. • Warm the apricot preserves in a small saucepan over low heat and brush over the cake. Loosen and remove the pan sides to serve. Serve warm.

Makes one 9-inch cake · Prep: 20 min. · Cooking: 40–50 min. · Level: 1 · Keeps: 1–2 days

Country apple bake

DUTCH APPLE BREAKFAST CAKE

Using homemade applesauce will give this cake a special touch.

TOPPING

- ⅔ cup all-purpose flour
- ½ cup firmly packed brown sugar
- 2 teaspoons ground cinnamon
- 1 teaspoon ground nutmeg
- ⅓ cup cold butter, cut up
- ½ cup walnuts, coarsely chopped

CAKE

- 3 cups all-purpose flour
- 2 teaspoons baking powder
- 1 teaspoon baking soda
- ½ teaspoon salt
- ½ cup (1 stick) butter, softened
- 1 cup granulated sugar
- 2 teaspoons vanilla extract
- 3 large eggs, at room temperature
- 1 cup sour cream
- ½ cup raisins
- 2½ cups applesauce

Preheat the oven to 350°F. • Butter and flour a 13 x 9-inch baking pan. • *Topping*: Stir together the flour, brown sugar, cinnamon, and nutmeg in a medium bowl. Use a pastry blender to cut in the butter until the mixture resembles fine crumbs. Stir in the walnuts. • *Cake*: Sift the flour, baking powder, baking soda, and salt into a large bowl. • Beat the butter, sugar, and vanilla in a large bowl with an electric mixer at medium speed until creamy. • Add the eggs, one at a time, until just blended after each addition. • With mixer at low speed, gradually beat in the dry ingredients, alternating with the sour cream and raisins. • Spoon the batter into the prepared pan. Top with the applesauce and sprinkle with the topping. • Bake for 50–60 minutes, or until golden brown, and a toothpick inserted into the center comes out clean. • Cool the cake completely in the pan on a rack.

Makes one 13 x 9-inch cake · Prep: 20 min. · Cooking: 50–60 min. · Level: 1 · Keeps: 1–2 days

CHOCOLATE APPLE LOAF WITH MACADAMIA NUTS

- 2 large tart apples (Granny Smiths are ideal), peeled, cored, and grated
- 1 tablespoon fresh lemon juice
- 1 cup all-purpose flour
- 1/4 cup + 1 tablespoon unsweetened cocoa powder
- 1 teaspoon baking powder
- 1/2 teaspoon baking soda
- 1/4 teaspoon salt
- 3/4 cup granulated sugar
- 1/2 cup vegetable oil
- 2 large eggs, separated
- 1/2 cup macadamia nuts, coarsely chopped
- 2 tablespoons confectioners' sugar

Preheat the oven to 350°F. • Butter a 9 x 5-inch loaf pan. Line with waxed paper. • Drizzle the apples with the lemon juice. • Sift the flour, sugar, cocoa, baking powder, baking soda, and salt into a large bowl. Stir in the sugar. • Beat in the oil and egg yolks with an electric mixer at low speed until just blended. • Stir in the apples and nuts. • With mixer at high speed, beat the egg whites in a medium bowl until stiff peaks form. Use a large rubber spatula to fold them into the batter. • Spoon the batter into the prepared pan. • Bake for 50–60 minutes, or until a toothpick inserted into the center comes out clean. • Cool the loaf in the pan for 15 minutes. Turn out onto a rack. Carefully remove the paper and let cool completely. Dust with the cocoa and remaining 1 tablespoon confectioners' sugar.

Makes one 9 x 5-inch loaf · Prep: 15 min. · Cooking: 50–60 min. · Level: 1 · Keeps: 1–2 days

APPLE AND PUMPKIN CAKE

- 2 large apples, peeled, cored, and grated
- 1 tablespoon fresh lemon juice
- 2 cups all-purpose flour
- 1 1/2 teaspoons baking powder
- 1/2 teaspoon baking soda
- 1 teaspoon ground cinnamon
- 1 teaspoon ground nutmeg
- 1/4 teaspoon salt
- 1/2 cup (1 stick) butter, softened
- 1 1/2 cups granulated sugar
- 2 large eggs, at room temperature
- 1 cup plain canned pumpkin
- 1/4 cup confectioners' sugar, to dust

Preheat the oven to 350°F. • Butter and flour a 9-inch Bundt pan. • Drizzle the apples with the lemon juice. • Sift the flour, baking powder, baking soda, cinnamon, nutmeg, and salt into a large bowl. • Beat the butter and sugar in a large bowl with an electric mixer at medium speed until creamy. • Add the eggs, one at a time, until just blended after each addition. • With mixer at low speed, gradually beat in the grated apples, pumpkin, and dry ingredients. • Spoon the batter into the prepared pan. • Bake for 50–55 minutes, or until a toothpick inserted into the center comes out clean. • Cool the cake in the pan for 10 minutes. Turn out onto a rack to cool completely. • Dust with the confectioners' sugar.

Makes one 9-inch cake · Prep: 20 min. · Cooking: 50–55 min. · Level: 1 · Keeps: 1–2 days

RHUBARB AND APPLE CAKE

Look for Bird's Custard Powder, found near the Jell-O and tapioca in the baking section of your supermarket.

CUSTARD
- 2 tablespoons custard powder
- 2 tablespoons granulated sugar
- 1 cup milk
- 1 teaspoon vanilla extract
- 1 tablespoon butter

CAKE
- 1 1/2 cups all-purpose flour
- 2 tablespoons custard powder
- 1 1/2 teaspoons baking powder
- 1/4 teaspoon salt
- 1/2 cup almonds, finely ground
- 1/2 cup (1 stick) butter, softened
- 3/4 cup granulated sugar
- 1 teaspoon vanilla extract
- 2 large eggs, at room temperature
- 1/2 cup milk

FRUIT
- 8 oz rhubarb, trimmed and sliced
- 1 large apple, peeled, cored, and thinly sliced
- 1/2 cup apricot preserves or jam, warmed

Custard: Place the custard powder and sugar in a medium saucepan. Stir in the milk and bring to a boil over medium-low heat, stirring constantly. Cook, stirring, until thickened. Remove from the heat. Transfer to a medium bowl, press a sheet of plastic wrap directly on the surface, and refrigerate until cooled. • *Cake*: Preheat the oven to 350°F. • Butter and flour a 9-inch springform pan. • Sift the flour, custard powder, baking powder, and salt into a large bowl. Stir in the almonds. • Beat the butter, sugar, and vanilla in a large bowl with an electric mixer at medium speed until creamy. • Add the eggs, one at a time, until just blended after each addition. • With mixer at low speed, gradually beat in the dry ingredients, alternating with the

Rhubarb and apple cake

milk. • Spoon half the batter into the prepared pan. Top with half the rhubarb and apple. Cover with the custard and remaining batter. Arrange the remaining rhubarb and apple on top in a decorative manner. • Bake for 50–60 minutes, or until a toothpick inserted into the center comes out clean. • Cool the cake in the pan for 10 minutes. Loosen and remove the pan sides. Brush the preserves over the warm cake. Serve warm.

Makes one 9-inch cake · Prep: 45 min. · Cooking: 50–60 min. · Level: 1 · Keeps: 2–3 days

WALNUT AND APPLE CAKE WITH MAPLE FROSTING

1¹/₂ cups all-purpose flour
2 teaspoons baking powder
1 teaspoon ground cinnamon
¹/₄ teaspoon salt
¹/₃ cup butter, softened
1 cup firmly packed brown sugar
¹/₄ cup maple-flavored syrup
3 large eggs, at room temperature
1 cup walnuts, coarsely chopped
¹/₂ cup pitted dates, finely chopped
1 cup Granny Smith apple, coarsely grated
¹/₂ cup walnut halves, toasted

MAPLE FROSTING
¹/₃ cup butter, softened
1 cup confectioners' sugar
2 tablespoons maple-flavored syrup

Preheat the oven to 350°F. • Butter a 10-inch round cake pan. Line with waxed paper. • Sift the flour, baking powder, cinnamon, and salt into a medium bowl. • Beat the butter, sugar, and syrup in a large bowl with an electric mixer at medium speed until creamy. • Add the eggs, one at a time, until just blended after each addition. • With mixer at low speed, gradually beat in the dry ingredients. • Stir in the walnuts, dates, and apple. • Spoon the batter into the prepared pan. • Bake for 45–55 minutes, or until a toothpick inserted into the center comes out clean. • Cool the cake in the pan for 10 minutes. Turn out onto a rack. Carefully remove the paper and let cool completely. • *Maple Frosting*: With mixer at high speed, beat the butter, confectioners' sugar, and syrup in a medium bowl until creamy. Spread over the top and sides of the cake and decorate with the walnuts.

Makes one 10-inch cake · Prep: 20 min. · Cooking: 45–55 min. · Level: 1 · Keeps: 2 days

APPLE, NUT, AND RAISIN CAKE

1³/₄ cups firmly packed brown sugar
1¹/₂ cups all-purpose flour
3 large eggs, at room temperature
¹/₄ cup (¹/₂ stick) butter, softened
1 teaspoon vanilla extract
1 teaspoon ground cinnamon
1 teaspoon ground nutmeg
1 teaspoon baking powder
¹/₂ teaspoon baking soda
¹/₄ teaspoon salt
2 medium tart apples, grated
1 cup walnuts, chopped
1 cup raisins

Preheat the oven to 350°F. • Butter a 9-inch square baking pan. • Beat the brown sugar, flour, eggs, butter, vanilla, cinnamon, nutmeg, baking powder, baking soda, and salt in a large bowl with an electric mixer at medium speed until well blended, about 3 minutes. • Stir in the apples, nuts, and raisins. • Spoon the batter into the prepared pan. • Bake for about 75 minutes, or until a toothpick inserted into the center comes out clean. • Cool the cake completely in the pan on a rack.

Makes one 9-inch cake · Prep: 25 min. · Cooking: 75 min. · Level: 1 · Keeps: 5 days

ORANGE AND RAISIN CAKE

1¹/₂ cups self-rising flour
¹/₂ teaspoon baking soda
¹/₄ cup (¹/₂ stick) butter, softened
¹/₂ cup superfine sugar
grated zest and juice of 1 orange
1 cup raisins
¹/₂ cup milk

Preheat the oven to 325°F. • Butter a 9 x 5-inch loaf pan. Line with waxed paper. Butter the paper. • Sift the flour and baking soda into a medium bowl. • Use your fingers to rub in the butter until the mixture resembles coarse crumbs. • Stir in the sugar, orange zest, and raisins. • Use a large rubber spatula to mix in the orange juice and milk until well blended. • Pour the batter into the prepared pan. • Bake for 65–75 minutes, or until a toothpick inserted into the center comes out clean. • Cool the cake in the pan for 15 minutes. Invert onto a rack and carefully remove the paper. Let cool completely.

Makes 9-inch cake · Prep: 20 min. · Cooking: 65–75 min. · Level: 1 · Keeps: 1 day in the freezer

LADYFINGER CREAM CAKE

about 40 ladyfingers
¹/₂ cup fruit liqueur
¹/₂ cup granulated sugar
3 tablespoons water
2 cups heavy cream
1 teaspoon vanilla extract
4 oz bittersweet chocolate, coarsely chopped
1 large peach, peeled, pitted, and cut in ¹/₄-inch cubes
fresh fruit, to decorate (optional)
¹/₂ cup confectioners' sugar

Butter a 9-inch springform pan and line the base using about half of the ladyfingers. To line the base: Trim one end of the ladyfingers so that they fit into the pan in a spokelike pattern coming from the center. Reserve the trimmings. • Sprinkle half the fruit liqueur over the ladyfinger lining. • Dissolve the sugar in the water in a small saucepan. Cook over medium-low heat until dark caramel-colored. Stir very carefully, with hand covered by a kitchen towel or oven glove, and bring to a boil. Remove from the heat and set aside to cool. • Beat the cream and vanilla with an electric mixer at high speed in a large bowl until stiff. • Melt the chocolate in a double boiler over barely simmering water until smooth. Use a large rubber spatula to fold in the cooled caramel, melted chocolate, peach, and ladyfinger trimmings. • Spoon the filling into the prepared pan and cover with the remaining ladyfingers. Trim them as you did for the base. Sprinkle the remaining liqueur over. • Refrigerate the cake overnight. • Loosen the pan sides and transfer onto a serving plate. Decorate with extra fresh fruit, if desired, and dust with the confectioners' sugar.

Makes one 9-inch cake · Prep: 30 min.+ 12 hr. to chill · Level: 1 · Keeps: 1–2 days in the refrigerator

Caramelized fresh fruit upside-down cake

CORNMEAL AND APPLE CAKE

- 1   cup (2 sticks) butter, softened
- 1   cup granulated sugar
- 1½   cups yellow cornmeal
- 1½   cups all-purpose flour
- 2   teaspoons baking powder
- ⅔   cup oil
- ½   cup white wine
- 1   apple, peeled, cored, and thinly sliced
- 2   tablespoons lemon juice
       juice of ½ lemon
- 2   tablespoons granulated sugar, to sprinkle

Preheat the oven to 350°F. • Butter a 9-inch springform pan. • Beat the butter and sugar in a large bowl with an electric mixer at medium speed until creamy. • With mixer at low speed, gradually beat in the cornmeal, flour, and baking powder, followed by the the oil and wine. • Spoon the batter into the prepared pan. • Arrange the apple over the batter. Drizzle with lemon juice and sprinkle with sugar. • Bake for 45–55 minutes, or until a toothpick inserted into the center comes out clean. • Cool the cake in the pan for 15 minutes. Loosen and remove the pan sides and let cool completely.

Makes one 9-inch cake · Prep: 20 min. · Cooking: 45–55 min. · Level: 1 · Keeps: 1–2 days

APPLE-POTATO CAKE

- 1   lb baking potatoes, such as russets or Idahos
- ¼   cup (½ stick) butter
- 1   cup all-purpose flour
- 1   teaspoon salt
- 2   large apples, peeled, cored, and chopped
- ½   cup granulated sugar
- 1   teaspoon ground cinnamon
- 1   teaspoon ground ginger
- ¼   teaspoon ground nutmeg
- ½   cup raisins
- 1   tablespoon fresh lemon juice
- ¾   cup heavy cream
- 1   tablespoon confectioners' sugar
- ½   teaspoon vanilla extract

Boil the potatoes in a large pot with enough water to cover until tender, 15–20 minutes. Drain well and leave covered in the pot for 20 minutes to sweat. Then slip off the skins. • Press the potatoes through a potato ricer into a large bowl or mash well with a potato masher, adding the butter, flour, and salt as you work. • Preheat the oven to 400°F. • Butter and flour a 10-inch springform pan. • Divide the dough in half. Roll out two rounds of equal size on a lightly floured surface to about 10 inches in diameter, ½-inch thick. • Place a potato round in the prepared pan and top with the chopped apple. • Stir together the granulated sugar, cinnamon, ginger, nutmeg, and raisins in a small bowl. Sprinkle the apple with half the sugar mixture and drizzle with the lemon juice. Top with the remaining potato round and sprinkle with the remaining sugar mixture. • Bake for 30–40 minutes, or until golden brown. • Cool the cake in the pan for 15 minutes. Loosen and remove the pan sides and let cool completely. • Beat the cream, confectioners' sugar, and vanilla in a medium bowl with an electric mixer at high speed until stiff. Decorate with the cream.

Makes one 10-inch cake · Prep: 35 min. · Cooking 30–40 min. · Level: 1 · Keeps: 2–3 days

IRISH APPLE CAKE

- 2⅓   cups all-purpose flour
- 2   teaspoons ground cinnamon
- 1½   teaspoons baking powder
- 1   teaspoon ground nutmeg
- ½   teaspoon baking soda
- ¼   teaspoon salt
- ½   cup (1 stick) butter, softened
- ¾   cup firmly packed brown sugar
- 1½   teaspoons vanilla extract
- 2   large eggs, at room temperature
- ½   cup milk
- 2   large apples, peeled, cored, and finely chopped

GLAZE

- 1   cup confectioners' sugar
- 4   teaspoons hot water
- 2   teaspoons fresh lemon juice

Preheat the oven to 350°F. • Butter and flour a 9-inch tube pan. • Stir together the flour, cinnamon, baking powder, nutmeg, baking soda, and salt in a large bowl. • Beat the butter, brown sugar, and vanilla in a large bowl with an electric mixer at medium speed until creamy. • Add the eggs, one at a time, just until blended after each addition. • With mixer at low speed, gradually beat in the dry ingredients, alternating with the milk. Stir in the apples. • Spoon the batter into the prepared pan. • Bake for 35–45 minutes, or until a toothpick inserted into the center comes out clean. • Cool the cake in the pan for 15 minutes. Turn out onto the rack to cool completely. • *Glaze*: Beat the confectioners' sugar, water, and lemon juice in a medium bowl. Drizzle over the cake.

Makes one 9-inch cake · Prep: 30 min. · Cooking: 35–45 min. · Level: 1 · Keeps: 3–4 days

CARAMELIZED FRESH FRUIT UPSIDE-DOWN CAKE

- 1⅓   cups all-purpose flour
- 1½   teaspoons baking powder
- ¼   teaspoon salt
- ¾   cup (1½ sticks) butter, softened
- 1½   cups granulated sugar
- 4   large eggs, at room temperature
- ¼   cup cold water
       apricots (10 oz), pitted and cut into quarters
- 1   large apple, peeled, cored, and cut into quarters
- 1   large pear, peeled, cored, and cut into quarters

Preheat the oven to 350°F. • Butter a 9-inch round cake pan. • Sift the flour, baking powder, and salt into a medium bowl. • Beat ½ cup butter and ¾ cup sugar in a large bowl with an electric mixer at medium speed until creamy. • Add the eggs, one at a time, until just blended after each addition. • With mixer at low speed, gradually beat in the dry ingredients. • Place the remaining sugar and water in a skillet over medium-low heat. Cook until the sugar and water are golden brown and pour into the prepared pan, tilting it to coat the bottom. • Melt the remaining butter and pour it into the pan with the caramel. Arrange the fruit over the caramel mixture. • Spoon the batter into the pan over the fruit. • Bake for 35–45 minutes, or until a toothpick inserted into the center comes out clean. • Cool the cake in the pan for 15 minutes. Invert the cake onto a serving plate. Serve warm or cool.

Makes one 9-inch cake · Prep: 30 min. · Cooking: 35–45 min. · Level: 1 · Keeps: 2–3 days

BUTTERSCOTCH APPLESAUCE CAKE

Butterscotch extract can be obtained from various sources on the Internet.

2   cups all-purpose flour
1   teaspoon baking powder
1   teaspoon baking soda
1   teaspoon ground cinnamon
$1/2$ teaspoon ground nutmeg
$1/2$ teaspoon salt
$1/2$ cup (1 stick) butter, softened
1   cup firmly packed brown sugar
1   teaspoon vanilla extract
1   teaspoon butterscotch extract
2   large eggs, at room temperature
$1^1/2$ cups unsweetened applesauce
$1/2$ cup raisins
$1/2$ cup walnuts or pecans, chopped
3   tablespoons confectioners' sugar, to dust

Preheat the oven to 350°F. • Butter a 9-inch springform pan. • Sift the flour, baking powder, baking soda, cinnamon, nutmeg, and salt into a large bowl. • Beat the butter, brown sugar, vanilla, and butterscotch extract in a large bowl with an electric mixer at medium speed until creamy. • Add the eggs, one at a time, until just blended after each addition. • With mixer at low speed, gradually beat in the dry ingredients, alternating with the applesauce. Stir in the raisins and nuts. • Spoon the batter into the prepared pan. • Bake for 50–60 minutes, or until the cake shrinks from the pan sides and a toothpick inserted into the center comes out clean. • Cool the cake in the pan on a rack for 10 minutes. Loosen and remove the pan sides and let cool completely. • Dust with the confectioners' sugar.

Makes one 9-inch cake · Prep: 25 min. · Cooking: 50–60 min. · Level: 1 · Keeps: 1–2 days

PEAR CAKE

2   lb small, ripe pears, peeled, cored, and sliced $1/4$-inch thick
3   tablespoons fresh lemon juice
$1^1/3$ cups all-purpose flour
1   tablespoon ground cinnamon
$1^1/2$ teaspoons baking powder
$1/4$ teaspoon salt
3   large eggs, at room temperature
$1^3/4$ cups granulated sugar
$1/2$ cup (1 stick) butter, melted + 3 tablespoons cold butter, cut up
$1/3$ cup dry Marsala wine

Place the pears in a bowl and drizzle with the lemon juice. • Preheat the oven to 350°F. • Butter a 9-inch springform pan. • Sift the flour, 2 teaspoons cinnamon, baking powder, and salt into a large bowl. • Beat the eggs and $3/4$ cup sugar in a large bowl with an electric mixer at high speed until pale and thick. • With mixer at low speed, gradually beat in the dry ingredients, alternating with the melted butter and wine. • Spoon half the batter into the prepared pan. Top with the pears. • Dot the pears with the cold butter and sprinkle with 3 tablespoons sugar and the remaining cinnamon. • Spoon the remaining batter over the top. Don't worry if the pears are not completely covered. Sprinkle with the remaining sugar. • Bake for 30–40 minutes, or until a toothpick inserted into

Pear cake

the center comes out clean. • Cool the cake completely in the pan on a rack. Loosen and remove the pan sides to serve.

Makes one 9-inch cake · Prep: 25 min. · Cooking: 30–40 min. · Level: 1 · Keeps: 1–2 days

LOW-FAT APPLESAUCE CAKE

2   cups all-purpose flour
$2/3$ cup granulated sugar
$1/2$ cup toasted wheat germ
2   teaspoons baking powder
$1/2$ teaspoon baking soda
1   teaspoon ground cinnamon
$1/2$ teaspoon ground cloves
$1/2$ teaspoon ground nutmeg
$1/2$ teaspoon salt
1   cup unsweetened applesauce
$1/2$ cup raisins
2   tablespoons grated orange zest
1   large egg
1   tablespoon extra-virgin olive oil
$1/2$ cup fresh orange juice

Preheat the oven to 350°F. • Butter and flour a 9-inch square cake pan. • Stir together the flour, sugar, wheat germ, baking powder, baking soda, cinnamon, cloves, nutmeg, and salt in a large bowl. • Beat in the applesauce, raisins, and orange zest with an electric mixer at low speed until well blended. • With a fork, beat the egg and oil into the orange juice. Beat the orange juice mixture into the batter. • Spoon the batter into the prepared pan. • Bake for 35–45 minutes, or until a toothpick inserted into the center comes out clean. • Cool the cake completely in the pan on a rack.

Makes one 9-inch cake · Prep: 25 min. · Cooking: 35–45 min. · Level: 1 · Keeps: 3–4 days

UPSIDE-DOWN PEAR CAKE

This cake is best served warm. It is very good with a mound of softly whipped cream or vanilla ice cream.

PEAR TOPPING

- 8 small or 6 medium firm-ripe pears, peeled, halved, and cored
- 1$\frac{1}{2}$ cups water
- $\frac{1}{4}$ cup fresh lemon juice
- 2 tablespoons butter
- $\frac{1}{2}$ cup granulated sugar

BATTER

- 1$\frac{1}{2}$ cups all-purpose flour
- 1 teaspoon baking powder
- $\frac{1}{2}$ teaspoon baking soda
- 1 teaspoon ground ginger
- 1 teaspoon pumpkin pie spice
- $\frac{1}{4}$ teaspoon salt
- $\frac{1}{2}$ cup (1 stick) butter, softened
- $\frac{3}{4}$ cup granulated sugar
- 2 tablespoons grated lemon zest
- 2 large eggs, at room temperature
- $\frac{1}{2}$ cup plain yogurt

Pear Topping: Place the pears in a bowl with the water and lemon juice. Soak for 5 minutes. Drain well and pat dry with paper towels. • Melt the butter and sugar in a large nonstick skillet over medium heat and sauté the pears. Stir gently to coat and cook for 15–20 minutes, stirring often, until tender and caramelized. Remove from the heat and let cool slightly. • *Batter*: Preheat the oven to 375°F. • Butter a 9-inch round cake pan. • Sift the flour, baking powder, baking soda, ginger, pumpkin pie spice, and salt into a large bowl. • Beat the butter, sugar, and lemon zest in a large bowl with an electric mixer at medium speed until creamy. • Add the eggs, one at a time, until just blended after each addition. • With mixer at low speed, beat in the dry ingredients, alternating with the yogurt. • Arrange the caramelized pears cut-side-up in the pan. Spoon any cooking juices over the top. • Use a thin metal spatula to spread the batter over the fruit. • Bake for 45–55 minutes, or until golden brown, springy to the touch, and a toothpick inserted into the center comes out clean. • Cool the cake in the pan for 5 minutes. Invert a serving plate over the pan and unmold the cake onto the plate. If any fruit sticks to the pan, spoon it out and replace on the cake. Serve warm.

Makes one 9-inch cake · Prep: 35 min. · Cooking: 45–55 min. · Level: 1 · Keeps: 1 day

PEAR AND HAZELNUT GÂTEAU

CAKE

- 6 large eggs, separated
- 3 tablespoons lukewarm water (105°–115°F)
- $\frac{1}{2}$ cup granulated sugar
- 1$\frac{1}{2}$ cups hazelnuts, finely ground
- 1$\frac{1}{2}$ cups almonds, finely ground
- 3 dry Italian biscotti, coarsely crumbled
- 1 teaspoon ground allspice

PEAR SYRUP

- $\frac{1}{2}$ cup water
- 2 tablespoons confectioners' sugar
- $\frac{1}{4}$ cups pear liqueur or Poire William

FILLING

- 1 lb pears, peeled, cored, and cut into quarters
- 1 tablespoon unflavored gelatin
- $\frac{3}{4}$ cups milk
- 2 tablespoons granulated sugar
- 1 teaspoon vanilla extract
- 1 large egg yolk
- 1$\frac{1}{4}$ cups heavy cream
  grated zest of 1 orange
- 1 cup mixed nuts, coarsely chopped, to decorate

Preheat the oven to 400°F. • Butter and flour a 9-inch springform pan. • Beat the egg yolks, water, and $\frac{1}{4}$ cup sugar in a large bowl with an electric mixer at high speed until pale and thick. • Beat the egg whites in a large bowl at medium speed until frothy. With mixer at high speed, gradually beat in the remaining sugar, beating until stiff, glossy peaks form. Use a large rubber spatula to fold them into the egg yolk mixture. • Stir the hazelnuts, almonds, crumbled biscotti, and allspice into the batter. • Spoon the batter into the prepared pan. • Bake for 30–35 minutes, or until a toothpick inserted into the center comes out clean. • Cool the cake in the pan for 15 minutes. Loosen and remove the pan sides. Invert the cake onto a rack. Loosen and remove the pan bottom and let cool completely. • Split the cake horizontally. • *Pear Syrup*: Mix the water, confectioners' sugar, and liqueur in a small bowl. Drizzle the syrup over the layers. Place one layer on a serving plate. • *Filling*: Arrange the pears on the cake. • Sprinkle the gelatin over the milk in a saucepan. Let stand 1 minute. • Stir over low heat until the gelatin has completely dissolved. Let cool and add the sugar, vanilla, and egg yolk until well blended. Bring to a boil over medium-high heat, stirring constantly. Set aside to cool. • With mixer at high speed, beat the cream in a large bowl until stiff. • Use a large rubber spatula to fold the cooled gelatin mixture into the cream. Spread half the filling over the pears. Top with the remaining cake layer. Spread the the top and sides of the cake with the remaining filling. • Refrigerate for 3 hours, or until set. • Sprinkle with the orange zest. Press the nuts into the sides of the cake.

Makes one 9-inch cake · Prep: 1 hr. + 3 hr. to chill · Cooking: 30–35 min. · Level: 2 · Keeps: 1 day

PEAR AND HAZELNUT CAKE

Bosc pears are a good choice for this cake. Select pears that are firm-ripe, not mushy.

TOPPING

- $\frac{1}{2}$ cup firmly packed brown sugar
- $\frac{1}{3}$ cup all-purpose flour
- 1 teaspoon ground cinnamon
- $\frac{1}{4}$ cup ($\frac{1}{2}$ stick) cold butter, cut up
- $\frac{3}{4}$ cup hazelnuts, coarsely chopped

- 1$\frac{1}{2}$ cups all-purpose flour
- 1 teaspoon baking powder
- 1 teaspoon ground cinnamon
- $\frac{1}{2}$ teaspoon baking soda
- $\frac{1}{4}$ teaspoon salt
- $\frac{1}{2}$ cup (1 stick) butter, softened
- 1 cup granulated sugar
- $\frac{1}{2}$ teaspoon lemon extract
- 2 large eggs, at room temperature
- $\frac{3}{4}$ cup sour cream
- 1$\frac{1}{2}$ cups firm-ripe pears, peeled, cored, and diced

Preheat the oven to 350°F. • Butter and flour a 13 x 9-inch baking pan. • *Topping*: Stir the brown sugar, flour, and cinnamon in a medium bowl. Use a pastry blender to cut in the butter until the mixture resembles fine crumbs. Stir in the hazelnuts. • Sift the flour, baking powder, baking soda, cinnamon, and salt into a medium bowl. • Beat the butter, sugar, and lemon extract in a large bowl with an electric mixer at medium speed until creamy. • Add the eggs, one at a time, until just blended after each addition. • With mixer at low speed, gradually beat in the dry ingredients, alternating with the sour cream. • Stir in the pears. • Spoon the batter into the prepared pan. • Sprinkle with the topping. • Bake for 55–65 minutes, or until golden brown, the cake shrinks from the pan sides, and a toothpick inserted into the center comes out clean. • Cool the cake completely in the pan on a rack.

Makes one 13 x 9-inch cake · Prep: 25 min. · Cooking: 55–65 min. · Level: 1 · Keeps: 2–3 days

Pear and hazelnut gâteau

Upside-down lemon polenta cake

FRESH FRUIT CAKE

2   large eggs, at room temperature
¹/₄ cup granulated sugar
¹/₂ cup (1 stick) butter, melted
¹/₄ cup all-purpose flour
2   tablespoons water
1   teaspoon baking powder
¹/₄ teaspoon salt
1   pear, peeled, cored, and finely chopped
1   apple, peeled, cored, and finely chopped
1   peach, peeled, cored, and finely chopped

Preheat the oven to 350°F. • Butter an 8-inch round cake pan. • Beat the eggs and sugar in a medium bowl with an electric mixer at high speed until pale and thick. • With mixer at medium speed, beat in the butter, flour, water, baking powder, and salt until smooth. • Stir in the fruit. • Spoon the batter into the prepared pan. • Bake for 25–35 minutes, or until a toothpick inserted into the center comes out clean. • Cool the cake in the pan for 15 minutes. Turn out onto a rack to cool completely.

Makes one 8-inch cake · Prep: 20 min. · Cooking: 25–35 min. · Level: 1 · Keeps: 1–2 days

UPSIDE-DOWN LEMON POLENTA CAKE

1¹/₂ cups water
1³/₄ cups granulated sugar
3   large lemons, thinly sliced
1   cup all-purpose flour
³/₄ cup polenta or yellow cornmeal
¹/₂ cup almonds, finely ground
1   teaspoon baking powder
¹/₄ teaspoon salt
¹/₂ cup (1 stick) butter, softened
1   tablespoon grated lemon zest
1   teaspoon lemon extract
3   large eggs, at room temperature
¹/₃ cup sour cream
¹/₄ cup fresh lemon juice

Preheat the oven to 350°F. • Butter and flour a 9-inch springform pan. • Heat 1¹/₄ cups water and ³/₄ cup sugar in a large skillet over medium heat until the sugar has dissolved. Bring to a boil and cook and stir for 5 minutes, or until the syrup begins to thicken. • Add the lemons and simmer for about 8 minutes, turning once, until the lemon peel is tender. • Using tongs, remove the lemon slices from the syrup and press them, overlapping, onto the bottom and sides of the prepared pan. • Return the syrup to medium heat and stir in the remaining ¹/₄ cup water. Simmer until the syrup is light gold. Carefully spoon the syrup over the lemon slices in the pan. • Stir together the flour, polenta, ground almonds, baking powder, and salt in a medium bowl. • Beat the butter, remaining sugar, lemon zest, and lemon extract in a large bowl with an electric mixer at medium speed until creamy. • Add the eggs, one at a time, until just blended after each addition. • With mixer at low speed, gradually beat in the dry ingredients, alternating with the sour cream and lemon juice. • Spoon the batter into the prepared pan. • Bake for 50–60 minutes, or until a toothpick inserted into the center comes out clean. • Cool the cake in the pan for 15 minutes. Loosen and remove the pan sides. Invert onto a serving dish. Serve warm.

Makes one 9-inch cake · Prep: 30 min. · Cooking: 50–60 min. · Level: 1 · Keeps: 1–2 days

LEMON CAKE WITH APPLE AND ALMOND TOPPING

¹/₂ cup (1 stick) butter, softened
²/₃ cup + 2 tablespoons granulated sugar
2   tablespoons grated lemon zest
2   large eggs, at room temperature
1¹/₂ cups all-purpose flour
2   teaspoons baking powder
¹/₄ teaspoon salt
¹/₃ cup milk
1   large apple, peeled, cored, and grated
¹/₂ cup slivered almonds
3   tablespoons fresh lemon juice

Preheat the oven to 350°F. • Butter and flour a 9-inch springform pan. • Beat the butter, ²/₃ cup sugar, and the lemon zest in a large bowl with an electric mixer at medium speed until creamy. • Add the eggs, one at a time, until just blended after each addition. • With mixer at low speed, gradually beat in the flour, baking powder, and salt, alternating with the milk. • Spoon the batter into the prepared pan. Sprinkle with the apple, almonds, and remaining sugar. Drizzle with the lemon juice. • Bake for 45–50 minutes, or until a toothpick inserted into the center comes out clean. • Cool the cake in the pan for 10 minutes. Loosen and remove the pan sides. Cool completely on a rack.

Makes one 9-inch cake · Prep: 15 min. · Cooking: 45–50 min. · Level: 1 · Keeps: 1 day

LEMON SHORTCAKE

LEMON FILLING

- 2 cups milk
  zest of 1 large lemon, cut in one spiral piece
- 4 large egg yolks
- 1/3 cup granulated sugar
- 3 tablespoons cornstarch
- 1 teaspoon vanilla extract

LEMON CAKE

- 2 cups all-purpose flour
- 3/4 cup granulated sugar
- 1/4 cup finely grated lemon zest
- 1 teaspoon baking powder
- 1/4 teaspoon salt
- 2/3 cup cold butter, cut up
- 1 large egg 2 large egg yolks

Lemon Filling: Heat the milk with the lemon zest until just boiling. • Beat the egg yolks, sugar, cornstarch, and vanilla in a large bowl with an electric mixer at medium speed until pale in color. • Add the milk, discarding the lemon zest, stirring constantly. • Return the mixture to the pan and cook over low heat, stirring constantly, until thick. • *Lemon Cake*: Preheat the oven to 400°F. • Butter and flour a 9-inch springform pan. • Mix the flour, sugar, 2 tablespoons lemon zest, baking powder, and salt in a large bowl. • Use a pastry blender to cut in the butter until the mixture resembles crumbs. • Stir in the egg and egg yolks until a smooth • Divide the dough into 2 pieces, one slightly larger than the other. Form into rounds. Roll out the larger piece on a lightly floured work surface until large enough to line the prepared pan. Prick all over with a fork. Sprinkle with the remaining grated lemon zest. • Spoon the Lemon Filling into the pastry shell. • Roll the remaining dough out into a 9-inch round and place it over the filling. Press down at the edges to seal. • Bake for 30–40 minutes, or until the top is golden brown. • Cool the cake in the pan on a rack. • Loosen and remove the sides of the pan and serve warm.

Makes one 9-inch cake · Prep: 30 min. · Cooking: 30–40 min. · Level: 1 · Keeps: 1–2 days

BROILED CITRUS CAKE

- 2 1/2 cups all-purpose flour
- 2 teaspoons baking powder
- 1/2 teaspoon baking soda
- 1/4 teaspoon salt
- 1/2 cup (1 stick) butter, softened

Lemon shortcake

- 1 cup firmly packed brown sugar
- 2 tablespoons grated orange zest
- 1 tablespoon grated lemon or lime zest
- 2 large eggs, at room temperature
- 1 cup buttermilk
- 1 cup raisins
- 3/4 cup pecans, chopped

CITRUS TOPPING

- 1 cup granulated sugar
- 1/4 cup + 2 tablespoons fresh orange juice
- 1/4 cup fresh lemon juice
- 1 tablespoon butter, melted
- 1 cup heavy cream, beaten

Preheat the oven to 325°F. • Butter and flour a 13 x 9-inch baking pan. • Sift the flour, baking powder, baking soda, and salt into a large bowl. • Beat the butter, brown sugar, and citrus zests in a large bowl with an electric mixer at medium speed until creamy. • Add the eggs, one at a time, until just blended after each addition. • With mixer at low speed, gradually beat in the dry ingredients, alternating with the buttermilk. Stir in the raisins and pecans. • Spoon the batter into the prepared pan. • Bake for 40–45 minutes, or until the cake shrinks from the pan sides and a toothpick inserted into the center comes out clean. • *Citrus Topping*: Stir the sugar and orange and lemon juice, and butter in a medium bowl until well blended. Spoon the topping over the cake when it comes out of the oven. Turn on the broiler. Broil 5–6 inches from the heat source for 3–5 minutes, or until golden brown and bubbly. Cool the cake completely in the pan on a rack. • Serve the cake with the cream.

Makes one 13 x 9-inch cake · Prep: 40 min. · Cooking: 45–55 min. · Level: 1 · Keeps: 1–2 days

Spicy lemon pumpkin cake

SPICY LEMON PUMPKIN CAKE

1²/₃	cups all-purpose flour
1	teaspoon baking powder
1	teaspoon ground ginger
1	teaspoon ground cinnamon
¹/₂	teaspoon baking soda
¹/₂	teaspoon ground nutmeg
¹/₄	teaspoon salt
1	cup old-fashioned rolled oats
¹/₂	cup (1 stick) butter, softened
²/₃	cup honey
1	tablespoon grated lemon zest
1	large egg, at room temperature
1	cup plain canned pumpkin
¹/₄	cup milk

CREAM CHEESE FROSTING

2	packages (3 oz each) cream cheese, softened
1	cup confectioners' sugar
1	tablespoon grated lemon zest
2–3	tablespoons fresh lemon juice

Preheat the oven to 350°F. • Butter and flour a 9-inch springform pan. • Sift the flour, baking powder, cinnamon, ginger, baking soda, nutmeg, and salt in a large bowl. Stir in the oats. • Beat the butter, honey, and lemon zest in a large bowl with an electric mixer at medium speed until creamy. • Add the egg, beating until just blended. • With mixer at low speed, gradually beat in the pumpkin and dry ingredients, alternating with the milk. • Spoon the batter into the prepared pan. • Bake for 45–55 minutes, or until a toothpick inserted into the center comes out clean. • Cool the cake in the pan for 15 minutes. Loosen and remove the pan sides. Invert the cake onto a rack. Loosen and remove the pan bottom and let cool completely. • *Cream Cheese Frosting*: With mixer at medium speed, beat the cream cheese, confectioners' sugar, and lemon zest in a large bowl until fluffy. Add enough lemon juice to make a smooth, spreadable frosting. Spread over the cake.

Makes one 9-inch cake · Prep: 25 min. · Cooking: 45–55 min. · Level: 2 · Keeps: 1–2 days

WHOLE-WHEAT ORANGE SYRUP CAKE

This cake is especially striking if made with blood oranges.

1	large navel or blood orange
1¹/₂	cups whole-wheat flour
1	teaspoon baking powder
1	teaspoon baking soda
¹/₄	teaspoon salt
¹/₂	cup (1 stick) butter, softened
³/₄	cup granulated sugar
2	large eggs, at room temperature
¹/₂	cup milk

ORANGE BUTTER SYRUP

¹/₂	cup granulated sugar
¹/₂	cup fresh orange juice
¹/₄	cup (¹/₂ stick) butter

Preheat the oven to 350°F. • Butter and flour a 9-inch tube pan. • Squeeze the orange, reserving the juice for the syrup. Place the rest of the orange in a food processor and chop finely. • Sift the whole-wheat flour, baking powder, baking soda, and salt into a medium bowl. • Beat the butter and sugar in a large bowl with an electric mixer at medium speed until creamy. • Add the eggs, one at a time, until just blended after each addition. • With mixer at low speed, gradually beat in the dry ingredients, alternating with the milk. Stir in the chopped orange. • Spoon the batter into the prepared pan. • Bake for 30–40 minutes, or until a toothpick inserted into the center comes out clean. • Cool the cake in the pan for 5 minutes. Turn onto a rack to cool. • *Orange Butter Syrup*: Stir the sugar, reserved orange juice, and butter in a saucepan over low heat until the sugar is dissolved and the butter is melted. • Place the cake on the rack on a jelly-roll pan. Poke holes in it with a skewer. Pour the syrup over the cake. Scoop any syrup from the pan and drizzle on the cake.

Makes one 9-inch cake · Prep: 25 min. · Cooking: 30–40 min. · Level: 1 · Keeps: 1–2 days

ALMOND AND ORANGE BREAKFAST CAKE

TOPPING

¹/₂	cup firmly packed brown sugar
¹/₃	cup all-purpose flour
1	teaspoon orange extract
¹/₄	cup (¹/₂ stick) cold butter, cut up
¹/₂	cup whole almonds, coarsely chopped

CAKE

1¹/₂	cups all-purpose flour
1¹/₂	teaspoons baking powder
¹/₂	teaspoon baking soda
¹/₄	teaspoon salt
¹/₂	cup almonds, finely ground
¹/₂	cup (1 stick) butter, softened
¹/₂	cup granulated sugar
1	tablespoon grated orange zest
1	teaspoon almond extract
3	large eggs, at room temperature
³/₄	cup plain yogurt
¹/₄	cup fresh orange juice

Preheat the oven to 350°F. • Butter a 9 x 13-inch baking pan. • *Topping*: Stir the brown sugar, flour, and orange extract in a medium bowl. Use a pastry blender to cut in the butter until the mixture resembles fine crumbs. Stir in the almonds. • *Cake*: Sift the flour, baking powder, baking soda, and salt in a large bowl. Stir in the ground almonds. • Beat the butter, sugar, orange zest, and almond extract in a large bowl with an electric mixer at medium speed until creamy. • Add the eggs, one at a time, until just blended after each addition. • With mixer at low speed, gradually beat in the dry ingredients, alternating with the yogurt and orange juice. • Spoon the batter into the prepared pan. Sprinkle with the topping. • Bake for 35–45 minutes, or until golden brown and a toothpick inserted into the center comes out clean. • Cool the cake completely in the pan on a rack.

Makes one 13 x 9-inch cake · Prep: 25 min. · Cooking: 35–45 min. · Level: 1 · Keeps: 1–2 days

ORANGE AND NUT LOAF

- ³/₄ cup raisins
- 1 cup warm water
- 1¹/₂ cups all-purpose flour
- 1¹/₂ teaspoons baking powder
- ¹/₄ teaspoon salt
- ¹/₂ cup milk
- 1 large egg, lightly beaten
- ¹/₃ cup butter, melted
- ¹/₃ cup orange marmalade
- 2 tablespoons brandy
- 2 tablespoons grated orange zest
- ¹/₂ cup hazelnuts, coarsely chopped
- ¹/₃ cup almonds, coarsely chopped

Plump the raisins in the water in a small bowl for 20 minutes. Drain well and pat dry with paper towels. • Preheat the oven to 350°F. • Butter an 8¹/₂ x 4¹/₂-inch loaf pan. Line the pan with foil, letting the edges overhang. Butter the foil. • Sift the flour, baking powder, and salt into a large bowl. • Beat in the milk, egg, butter, marmalade, brandy, and orange zest with an electric mixer at low speed. • Stir in the hazelnuts, almonds, and raisins. • Spoon the batter into the prepared pan. • Bake for 45–55 minutes, or until a toothpick inserted into the center comes out clean. • Cool the loaf on a rack for 10 minutes. Using the foil as a lifter, remove the loaf from the pan. Carefully remove the foil. Cool the loaf completely on a rack.

Makes one 8¹/₂ x 4¹/₂-inch loaf · Prep: 20 min. + 20 min. to soak · Cooking: 45–55 min. · Level: 1 · Keeps: 3–4 days

ALMOND AND KUMQUAT CAKE

This cake is delicious served with whipped cream. You can cook the kumquats up to two days ahead of time.

- 1¹/₄ lb fresh kumquats
- 6 large eggs, at room temperature
- 1¹/₃ cups confectioners' sugar
- 1³/₄ cups finely ground almonds
- ¹/₄ cup semolina flour
- 1 teaspoon baking powder
- 1 teaspoon vanilla extract
- ¹/₄ teaspoon salt
- ¹/₄ cup confectioners' sugar, to dust

Preheat the oven to 350°F. • Butter and flour a 9-inch springform pan. • Place the kumquats in a large saucepan. Add water to cover and bring to a boil over high heat. Reduce the heat to low, cover, and simmer for about 1 hour, or until very tender. • Drain the kumquats, let cool, then cut them in half and remove the seeds. Place the kumquats in a food processor and process until finely pureed. • Beat the eggs and confectioners' sugar in a large bowl with an electric mixer at high speed until pale and very thick. • With mixer at low speed, beat in the almonds, semolina flour, baking powder, vanilla, and salt. By hand, gently stir in the kumquats. • Spoon the batter into the prepared pan. • Bake for 50–60 minutes, or until a toothpick inserted into the center comes out clean. • Cool the cake in the pan for 15 minutes. Loosen and remove the pan sides. Invert the cake onto the rack. Loosen and remove the pan bottom and let cool completely. • Dust with the confectioners' sugar.

Makes one 9-inch cake · Prep: 30 min. · Cooking: 50–60 min. + 1 hr to cook kumquats · Level: 1 · Keeps: 2–3 days

ORANGE COCONUT CAKE WITH ORANGE FROSTING

Use blood oranges in the frosting to obtain a lovely pink-toned frosting.

- 1 cup milk
- ³/₄ cup shredded coconut
- ¹/₄ cup fresh orange juice
- ¹/₂ cup (1 stick) butter, softened
- 1 cup granulated sugar
- 2 tablespoons grated orange zest
- 2 large eggs, at room temperature
- 2 cups all-purpose flour
- 2 teaspoons baking powder
- ¹/₂ teaspoon salt

ORANGE FROSTING

- 2 cups confectioners' sugar
- 2 tablespoons butter, melted
- 1–2 tablespoons orange juice (preferably blood orange juice)

Mix the milk, coconut, and orange juice in a medium bowl. Cover and let stand at room temperature for 1 hour. • Preheat the oven to 325°F. • Butter a 9-inch round cake pan. Line with waxed paper. • Beat the butter, sugar, and orange zest in a large bowl with an electric mixer at medium speed until creamy. • Add the eggs, one at a time, until just blended after each addition. • With mixer at low speed, gradually beat in the flour, baking powder, and salt, alternating with the coconut mixture. • Spoon the batter into the prepared pan. • Bake for 40–50 minutes, or until a toothpick inserted into the center comes out clean. • Cool the cake in the pan for 10 minutes. Turn out onto a rack. Carefully remove the paper and let cool completely. • *Orange Frosting*: Mix the confectioners' sugar and butter in a medium bowl. Add enough orange juice to make a thick, spreadable frosting. • Spread over the top and sides of the cake.

Makes one 9-inch cake · Prep: 20 min. + 1 hr. to stand · Cooking: 40–50 min. · Level: 1 · Keeps: 1 day

Orange and nut loaf

Candied orange wheel cake

CANDIED ORANGE WHEEL CAKE

CANDIED ORANGES
10 oranges, thinly sliced
$^1/_2$ cup granulated sugar
$1^1/_2$ quarts cold water

$^1/_3$ cup orange liqueur
2 cups Vanilla Pastry Cream (see page 342)
$^3/_4$ cup heavy cream
1 9-inch Italian Sponge Cake (see page 157)

Simmer the oranges, sugar, and water in a large saucepan over medium-low heat for 2 hours. Let cool, cover, and set aside for 24 hours. • Line a 9-inch springform pan with aluminum foil. • Drain the oranges, reserving the syrup. • With the best-shaped orange slices, line the base and sides of the prepared pan. • Chop the remaining slices. • Stir the chopped oranges and orange liqueur into the pastry cream. • Beat the cream in a medium bowl with an electric mixer at high speed until stiff. Use a large rubber spatula to fold it into the pastry cream. • Spoon half the cream into the pan. • Split the cake horizontally. Place one

layer on top of the cream, and brush with some reserved syrup. Use a thin metal spatula to spread the remaining pastry cream. Top with the remaining cake layer and brush with more syrup. Press down lightly on the cake with your fingertips. • Refrigerate for 6 hours. • Invert onto a serving plate. Loosen the sides and carefully remove the foil.

Makes one 9-inch cake · Prep: 1 hr. 24 hr. to marinate oranges + 6 hr. to chill · Level: 3 · Keeps: 1–2 days in the refrigerator

COCONUT LEMON CAKE

3 cups all-purpose flour
4 teaspoons baking powder
$^1/_2$ teaspoon salt
$^3/_4$ cup ($1^1/_2$ sticks) butter, softened
2 cups granulated sugar
2 tablespoons grated lemon zest
3 large eggs, separated
$^1/_2$ cup freshly grated coconut or shredded coconut
$^1/_2$ cup fresh lemon juice
$^1/_2$ cup water

FILLING
4 large egg yolks
1 cup granulated sugar
$^1/_4$ cup cornstarch

2 tablespoons all-purpose flour
1 tablespoon grated lemon zest
$^1/_2$ cup fresh lemon juice
$^1/_4$ cup water
2 tablespoons butter, cut into small pieces

FROSTING
3 cups confectioners' sugar
$^1/_4$ cup ($^1/_2$ stick) butter, softened
3–4 tablespoons fresh lemon juice
$^1/_2$ cup finely grated coconut or shredded coconut

Preheat the oven to 350°F. • Butter three 9-inch round cake pans. Line with waxed paper. Butter the paper. • Sift the flour, baking powder, and salt into a large bowl. • Beat the butter, sugar, and lemon zest in a large bowl with an electric mixer at medium speed until creamy. • With mixer at medium speed, add the egg yolks, one at a time, until just blended after each addition. • With mixer at low speed, gradually beat in the dry ingredients and coconut, alternating with the lemon juice and water. • With mixer at high speed, beat the egg whites in a large bowl until stiff peaks form. Use a large rubber spatula to fold them into the batter. • Spoon $^1/_3$ of the batter into each of the prepared pans. • Bake for 25–30 minutes, or until a toothpick inserted into the center comes out clean. • Cool the cakes in the pans for 10 minutes. Turn out onto racks. Carefully remove the paper and let cool completely. • *Filling*: Beat the egg yolks and sugar in a double boiler. Beat in the cornstarch, flour, and lemon zest. Gradually add the lemon juice, water, and butter. Place over barely simmering water and cook, stirring frequently, until the mixture lightly coats a metal spoon or registers 160°F on an instant-read thermometer. Transfer to a clean bowl. Place a sheet of plastic wrap directly on the surface and refrigerate until cold. • *Frosting*: Beat the confectioners' sugar and butter in a medium bowl. Add enough of the lemon juice to make a thick, spreadable frosting. • Place one cake on a serving plate and spread with half the filling. Place another cake on top and spread with the remaining filling. Top with the remaining cake and spread with the frosting. Sprinkle with coconut. • Refrigerate for 30 minutes.

Makes one 9-inch cake · Prep: 30 min. + 30 min. to chill · Cooking: 25–30 min. · Level: 2 · Keeps: 1–2 days in the refrigerator

LIME AND COCONUT LAYER CAKE

- 2 cups all-purpose flour
- 1 teaspoon baking powder
- 1/2 teaspoon baking soda
- 1/4 teaspoon salt
- 1 cup (2 sticks) butter
- 3/4 cup granulated sugar
- 2 tablespoons finely grated lime zest
- 1/4 cup fresh lime juice
- 5 large eggs, separated
- 1 1/2 cups shredded coconut

GLAZE

- 2 cups confectioners' sugar
- 1/4 cup (1/2 stick) butter, melted
- 2–3 tablespoons fresh lime juice
- 1/2 teaspoon green food coloring (optional)

Preheat the oven to 350°F. • Butter and flour a 13 x 9-inch baking pan. • Sift the flour, baking powder, baking soda, and salt into a large bowl. • Beat the butter, sugar, and lime zest and juice in a large bowl with an electric mixer at medium speed until creamy. • Add the egg yolks, one at a time, until just blended after each addition. • With mixer at low speed, gradually beat in the dry ingredients and coconut. • With mixer at high speed, beat the egg whites in a large bowl until stiff peaks form. Use a rubber spatula to fold them into the batter. • Spoon the batter into the prepared pan. • Bake for 20–25 minutes, or until a toothpick inserted into the center comes out clean. • Cool the cake in the pan for 10 minutes. Turn out onto a rack to cool completely. • *Glaze*: Beat the confectioners' sugar and butter in a medium bowl. Add enough lime juice and food coloring (if using) to make a runny glaze. • Drizzle over the cake. • Chill for at least 1 hour before serving.

Makes one 9-inch cake · Prep: 30 min. + 1 hr to chill · Cooking: 20–25 min. · Level: 1 · Keeps: 1–2 days

COCONUT-MANGO LAYER CAKE

To make this cake, make 1 1/2 times the original amount and bake the batter in three 8-inch round cake pans.

- 1 Basic Coconut Cake, 1 1/2 times original recipe (see page 32)

TOPPING

- 2 cups heavy cream
- 1/4 cup + 2 tablespoons granulated sugar
- 1 tablespoon white rum
- 1 ripe medium mango, peeled and thinly sliced
- 1 fresh coconut, grated, reserve a couple of slices for the top, or about 1 1/2 cups shredded or coarsely grated coconut

Coconut-mango layer cake

Bake the cake and let cool. • *Topping*: Beat the cream, sugar, and rum in a large bowl with an electric mixer at high speed until stiff. • Place one cake on a serving plate. Spread with the cream. Top with some mango slices and sprinkle with the coconut. Top with another cake and spread with the cream. Top with some mango slices and sprinkle with coconut. Top with the remaining cake. Spread the top and sides with the remaining cream. Sprinkle with the remaining coconut. • Decorate with the remaining mango and the coconut slices, if using.

Makes one 8-inch cake · Prep: 35 min. · Level: 1 · Keeps: 1–2 days in the refrigerator

PACIFIC ISLAND CAKE

A wonderful cake to contribute to a bake sale. Use unsweetened coconut if you can find it.

- 2 cups all-purpose flour
- 1 teaspoon baking powder
- 1 teaspoon baking soda
- 1/4 teaspoon salt
- 3/4 cup shredded coconut
- 3/4 cup (1 1/2 sticks) butter, softened
- 1 1/2 cups granulated sugar
- 1 teaspoon coconut extract
- 3 large eggs, at room temperature
- 1 can (20 oz) crushed pineapple in its own juice, drained
- 1 cup macadamia nuts, chopped

Preheat the oven to 350°F. • Butter and flour a 10-inch Bundt pan. • Sift the flour, baking powder, baking soda, and salt into a large bowl. Stir in the coconut. • Beat the butter, sugar, and coconut extract in a large bowl with an electric mixer at medium speed until creamy. • Add the eggs, one at a time, until just blended after each addition. • With mixer at low speed, gradually beat in the dry ingredients, alternating with the pineapple. Stir in the nuts. • Spoon the batter into the prepared pan. • Bake for 65–75 minutes, or until a toothpick inserted into the center comes out clean. • Cool the cake in the pan for 10 minutes. Turn out onto a rack to cool completely.

Makes one 10-inch cake · Prep: 30 min. · Cooking: 65–75 min. · Level: 1 · Keeps: 2–3 days

FRESH GINGER AND COCONUT CAKE

- 1½ cups all-purpose flour
- 1 teaspoon baking powder
- ½ teaspoon baking soda
- ¼ teaspoon salt
- ½ cup (1 stick) butter, softened
- ¾ cup firmly packed dark brown sugar
- ¼ cup dark corn syrup
- 1 large egg, at room temperature
- ¼ cup finely minced peeled fresh ginger
- ½ cup canned coconut milk (not cream of coconut)

Preheat the oven to 350°F. • Butter a 9-inch square baking pan. • Sift the flour, baking powder, baking soda, and salt into a medium bowl. • Beat the butter, brown sugar, and corn syrup in a large bowl with an electric mixer at medium speed until creamy. • Add the egg, beating until just blended. • With mixer at low speed, gradually beat in the ginger and dry ingredients, alternating with the coconut milk. • Spoon the batter into the prepared pan. • Bake for 65–75 minutes, or until a toothpick inserted into the center comes out clean. • Cool the cake completely in the pan.

Makes one 9-inch cake · Prep: 20 min. · Cooking: 65–75 min. · Level: 2 · Keeps: 2–3 days

FROSTED COCONUT PEACH CAKE

- 1 cup (2 sticks) butter, softened
- 1¾ cups granulated sugar
- 1 teaspoon coconut extract
- 4 large eggs, at room temperature
- 2 cups shredded coconut
- ⅔ cup peach nectar
- 2½ cups all-purpose flour
- 2 teaspoons baking powder
- ½ teaspoon salt
- 2 cups Italian Buttercream (see page 346)

Preheat the oven to 350°F. • Butter and flour a 9-inch springform pan. • Beat the butter, sugar, and coconut extract in a large bowl with an electric mixer at medium speed until creamy. • Add the eggs, one at a time, until just blended after each addition. • With mixer at low speed, gradually beat in the coconut, peach nectar, flour, baking powder, and salt • Spoon the batter into the prepared pan. • Bake for 60–70 minutes, or until a toothpick inserted into the center comes out clean. • Cool completely in the pan on a rack. Loosen and remove the pan sides. • When cool, spread with the Buttercream.

Makes one 9-inch cake · Prep: 15 min. · Cooking: 60–70 min. · Level: 2 · Keeps: 2 days

COCONUT LUMBERJACK CAKE

- 3 large tart apples (Granny Smiths are ideal) (about 1 lb), peeled, cored, and grated
- 1¼ cups pitted dates, finely chopped
- 1¼ teaspoons baking soda
- 1 cup boiling water
- ½ cup (1 stick) butter, softened
- 1 cup granulated sugar
- 1 teaspoon vanilla extract
- 1 large egg, at room temperature
- 1½ cups all-purpose flour
- ¼ teaspoon salt

COCONUT TOPPING

- ⅔ cup shredded coconut
- ½ cup firmly packed brown sugar
- ½ cup milk
- ¼ cup (½ stick) butter, cut up

Preheat the oven to 350°F. • Butter an 11 x 7-inch baking pan. • Place the apples, dates, and baking soda in a large bowl. Pour in the boiling water and cover with plastic wrap. Set aside for 15 minutes. • Beat the butter, sugar, and vanilla in a large bowl with an electric mixer at medium speed until creamy. • Add the egg, beating until just blended. Beat into the apple mixture. • With mixer at low speed, gradually beat in the flour and salt. • Spoon the batter into the prepared pan. • Bake for 60 minutes (do not remove from the oven). • *Coconut Topping*: Stir the coconut, brown sugar, milk, and butter in a medium saucepan over low heat until the butter has melted and the sugar has dissolved. • After the cake has baked for 60 minutes, spread with the topping. Bake for 15 more minutes. • Turn on the broiler. Broil 5–6 inches from the heat source for 5–10 minutes, or until golden and bubbly. • Cool the cake completely in the pan on a rack.

Makes one 11 x 7-inch cake · Prep: 30 min. · Cooking: 80–90 min. · Level: 1 · Keeps: 4–5 days

PINEAPPLE CAKE WITH COCONUT TOPPING

- 1 can (14 oz) crushed pineapple
- ½ cup (1 stick) butter, softened
- 1 cup granulated sugar
- 2 large eggs, at room temperature
- 1½ cups all-purpose flour
- 2 teaspoons baking powder
- ¼ teaspoon salt

COCONUT TOPPING

- ½ cup firmly packed brown sugar
- ½ cup all-purpose flour
- ½ cup shredded coconut
- ⅓ cup butter, softened

Preheat the oven to 350°F. • Butter a 9-inch springform pan. • Drain the pineapple, reserving the juice. • Beat the butter and sugar in a large bowl with an electric mixer at medium speed until creamy. • Add the eggs, one at a time, until just blended after each addition. • With mixer at low speed, gradually beat in the flour, baking powder, and salt, alternating with the pineapple juice. • Spoon half the batter into the prepared pan and spread with the pineapple. Cover with the remaining batter. • *Coconut Topping*: Stir together the brown sugar, flour, and coconut in a medium bowl. Use a pastry blender to cut in the butter until the mixture resembles coarse crumbs. Sprinkle over the batter. • Bake for 45–55 minutes, or until a toothpick inserted into the center comes out clean. • Cool the cake in the pan for 10 minutes. Loosen and remove the pan sides. Place the cake on a rack and let cool completely.

Makes one 10-inch cake · Prep: 25 min. · Cooking: 45–55 min. · Level: 1 · Keeps: 2–3 days

PINEAPPLE WALNUT LOAF

This delicious loaf contains no butter. Serve it sliced with coffee or tea, with butter on hand for those who can't resist.

- ³/₄ cup well-drained crushed canned pineapple (squeeze out excess liquid)
- 1 large egg, lightly beaten
- 1 cup toasted walnuts, finely chopped
- 1 cup all-purpose flour
- 1 cup shredded coconut
- ¹/₂ cup firmly packed brown sugar
- ¹/₂ cup milk
- 1 teaspoon baking powder
- ¹/₄ teaspoon salt

Preheat the oven to 350°F. • Butter a 9 x 5-inch loaf pan. Line with aluminum foil, letting the edges overhang. Butter the foil. • Place the pineapple in a large bowl and stir in the egg. Stir in the flour, coconut, brown sugar, milk, baking powder, and salt. • Spoon the batter into the prepared pan. • Bake for 40–50 minutes, or until a toothpick inserted into the center comes out clean. • Cool the loaf in the pan for 10 minutes. Using the foil as a lifter, remove the loaf from the pan. Carefully remove the foil and let cool completely on a rack.

Makes one 9 x 5-inch loaf · Prep: 30 min. · Cooking: 40–50 min. · Level: 1 · Keeps: 3 days

Pineapple upside-down cake

PINEAPPLE SHEET CAKE

- 2 cups all-purpose flour
- 1¹/₂ cups granulated sugar
- 1 teaspoon baking soda
- ¹/₄ teaspoon salt
- 2¹/₂ cups crushed canned pineapple, with juice
- 2 large eggs, at room temperature
- ³/₄ cup firmly packed brown sugar
- ³/₄ cup pecans, chopped

Preheat the oven to 350°F. • Butter and flour a 13 x 9-inch baking pan. • Stir together the flour, granulated sugar, baking soda, and salt in a large bowl. Beat in the crushed pineapple and juice and eggs with an electric mixer at low speed until smooth. • Spoon the batter into the prepared pan. • Mix together the brown sugar and pecans and sprinkle evenly over the top of the cake. • Bake for 35–40 minutes, or until a toothpick inserted into the center comes out clean. • Cool the cake completely in the pan on a rack.

Makes one 13 x 9-inch cake · Prep: 25 min. · Cooking: 35–40 min. · Level: 1 · Keeps: 2–3 days

PINEAPPLE UPSIDE-DOWN CAKE

- ¹/₂ cup (1 stick) butter, softened
- 12 walnut halves, broken
- 9 rings drained canned pineapple
- ²/₃ cup granulated sugar
- 2 large eggs, at room temperature
- 1¹/₂ teaspoons baking powder
- 1 teaspoon vanilla extract
- ¹/₄ teaspoon salt
- 1¹/₂ cups all-purpose flour
- ¹/₂ cup milk

Preheat the oven to 350°F. • Melt ¹/₄ cup butter and pour into a 9-inch round cake pan. Sprinkle in the walnuts. Arrange the pineapple rings in the pan, cutting to fit, if necessary. • Beat the sugar, remaining butter, and eggs in a medium bowl with an electric mixer at medium speed until just blended. • Beat in the baking powder, vanilla, and salt. With mixer at low speed, gradually beat in the flour, alternating with the milk. The batter should be smooth and quite sticky. • Spoon the batter over the pineapple. • Bake for 40–50 minutes, or until a toothpick inserted into the center comes out clean. • Cool the cake in the pan for 20 minutes. Invert onto a serving plate.

Makes one 9-inch cake · Prep: 20 min. · Cooking: 40–50 min. · Level: 1 · Keeps: 2 days

Pineapple and banana cake

PINEAPPLE AND BANANA CAKE

1²/₃ cups all-purpose flour
2 teaspoons baking powder
¹/₂ teaspoon baking soda
¹/₄ teaspoon salt
¹/₂ cup (1 stick) butter, softened
³/₄ cup firmly packed light brown sugar
1 teaspoon vanilla extract
2 large eggs, separated
2 large very ripe bananas, peeled and mashed
2 tablespoons dark rum

TOPPING

1¹/₂ cups heavy cream
1 tablespoon granulated sugar
1 medium banana, peeled and thinly sliced
2 tablespoons fresh lemon juice
6 thin slices cored fresh pineapple, cut into quarters

Preheat the oven to 350°F. • Butter two 8-inch round cake pans. Line with waxed paper. Butter the paper. • Sift the flour, baking powder, baking soda, and salt into a medium bowl. • Beat the butter, sugar, and vanilla in a large bowl with an electric mixer at medium speed until creamy. • Add the egg yolks, one at a time, just until blended after each addition. • With mixer at low speed, gradually beat in the dry ingredients, alternating with the bananas and rum. • With mixer at high speed, beat the egg whites in a medium bowl until stiff peaks form. Use a large rubber spatula to fold them into the batter. • Spoon half the batter into each of the prepared pans. • Bake for 25–35 minutes, or until springy to the touch and a toothpick inserted into the center comes out clean. • Cool the cakes in the pans for 10 minutes. Turn out onto racks. Carefully remove the paper and let cool completely. • *Topping*: With mixer at high speed, beat the cream and sugar in a large bowl until stiff. • Drizzle the banana with the lemon juice. • Place a cake on a serving plate. Spread with ¹/₄ of the cream and cover with a layer of banana. Top with the remaining cake. Spread the cake with the remaining cream. Press the pineapple into the cream around the sides and on top of the cake. Fill the gaps on the top with the remaining banana slices.

Makes one 8-inch cake · Prep: 50 min. · Cooking: 25–35 min. · Level: 1 · Keeps: 1 day

PINEAPPLE LAYER CAKE

A new twist on an old favorite. This layer cake is baked in a loaf pan.

1 cup all-purpose flour
¹/₂ cup almonds, finely ground
1¹/₂ teaspoons baking powder
¹/₄ teaspoon salt
³/₄ cup (1¹/₂ sticks) butter, cut up
1 cup granulated sugar
¹/₂ cup apricot nectar
2 large eggs, lightly beaten
8 canned pineapple rings in heavy syrup, drained and patted dry (reserve ¹/₃ cup syrup)
2 cups heavy cream
2 tablespoons confectioners' sugar
¹/₂ cup slivered almonds

Preheat the oven to 350°F. • Butter a 9 x 5-inch loaf pan. Line with aluminum foil, letting the edges overhang. Butter the foil. • Stir together the flour, almonds, baking powder, and salt in a large bowl. • Mix the butter, granulated sugar, and apricot nectar in a medium saucepan over medium heat and stir until the butter has melted and the sugar has dissolved. Remove from the heat and let cool slightly. • Beat the butter mixture into the dry ingredients with an electric mixer at low speed. • With mixer at medium speed, add the eggs, one at a time, until just blended after each addition. • Spoon the batter into the prepared pan. • Bake for 45–50 minutes, or until golden, and a toothpick inserted into the center comes out clean. • Cool the cake in the pan for 15 minutes. Using the foil as a lifter, remove the loaf from the pan. Carefully remove the foil and let cool completely on a rack. • Coarsely chop 5 pineapple rings. • With mixer at high speed, beat the cream and confectioners' sugar in a large bowl until stiff. • Split the cake into thirds horizontally. Set aside a cake layer for the top. • Place a cake layer on a serving plate. Brush with a little pineapple syrup. Spread with ¹/₄ of the cream and sprinkle with half the chopped pineapple. Repeat with another cake layer. Top with the plain layer. Brush with some pineapple syrup. Spread the top and sides with the remaining cream. Press the slivered almonds into the sides of the cake and decorate the top with the remaining 3 pineapple rings.

Makes one 9 x 5-inch cake · Prep: 20 min. · Cooking: 45–50 min. · Level: 1 · Keeps: 1 day in the refrigerator

FROSTED PINEAPPLE GINGER CAKE

- 2 cups all-purpose flour
- 3/4 cup shredded coconut
- 2 teaspoons baking powder
- 1 teaspoon ground ginger
- 1/4 teaspoon salt
- 1/2 cup (1 stick) butter, softened
- 1 cup granulated sugar
- 2 large eggs, at room temperature
- 1/2 cup canned crushed pineapple, with some of the juice (reserve remaining juice for the frosting)

PINEAPPLE FROSTING
- 2 cups confectioners' sugar
- 2 tablespoons butter, softened
- 1 teaspoon ground ginger
- 1/4 cup pineapple juice
  chopped crystallized ginger, to decorate (optional)

Preheat the oven to 325°F. • Butter and flour a 9-inch springform pan. • Sift the flour, coconut, baking powder, ginger, and salt into a large bowl. Stir in the coconut.• Beat the butter and sugar in a large bowl with an electric mixer at medium speed until creamy. • Add the eggs, one at a time, until just blended after each addition. • With mixer at low speed, gradually beat in the dry ingredients, alternating with the pineapple. • Spoon the batter into the prepared pan. • Bake for 40–45 minutes, or until a toothpick inserted into the center comes out clean. • Cool the cake in the pan for 10 minutes. Loosen and remove the pan sides. Place the cake on a rack and let cool completely. • *Pineapple Frosting*: Mix the confectioners' sugar, butter, and ginger in a medium bowl. Add enough pineapple juice until the frosting is smooth. • Spread the top and sides of the cake with the frosting and, if desired, decorate with the crystallized ginger.

Makes one 9-inch cake · Prep: 25 min. · Cooking: 40–45 min. · Level: 1 · Keeps: 2 days

FRESH MANGO GÂTEAU

CREAMY CITRUS FILLING
- 1 tablespoon unflavored gelatin
- 1/4 cup cold water
- 2 large egg yolks
  scant 1/3 cup granulated sugar
  grated zest of 1/2 lime
- 1/2 teaspoon vanilla extract
- 2/3 cup cream cheese, softened
- 3/4 cup heavy cream

FRUIT FILLING
- 1 tablespoon unflavored gelatin
- 1 cup fresh orange juice

Fresh mango gâteau

- 1 passion fruit, peeled and pureed
  juice of 1 lime
- 1/2 cup granulated sugar
- 2 mangoes (about 10 oz each), peeled and cut into 2/3-inch slices

FROSTING
- 1/2 cup heavy cream
- 1 tablespoon superfine sugar

  Langues-de-chat (cat's tongues) or amaretto cookies, to decorate

Line an 8-inch springform pan with waxed paper. • *Creamy Citrus Filling*: Sprinkle the gelatin over the water in a small saucepan. Let stand 1 minute. Stir over low heat until the gelatin has completely dissolved. • Beat the egg yolks, sugar, and lime zest in a double boiler until well blended. Cook over low heat, until the mixture lightly coats a metal spoon or registers 160°F on an instant-read thermometer. Immediately plunge the pan in a bowl of ice water and stir until the egg mixture has cooled. Stir in the vanilla. • Use a whisk to beat the cream cheese, cream, and the gelatin mixture in a large bowl until stiff. Use a large rubber spatula to fold in the egg mixture. • Pour the mixture into the prepared pan. • Refrigerate for at least 1 hour, or until set. • *Fruit Filling*: Sprinkle the gelatin over the orange juice in a medium saucepan. Let stand 1 minute. • Stir the passion fruit, lime juice, and sugar into the orange juice mixture. Warm over medium-high heat until the sugar and gelatin have dissolved. Set aside to cool until almost set. • Mix the mango slices into the orange mixture. • Spread the fruit filling over the Creamy Citrus Filling. Refrigerate for at least 1 hour, or until set. • *Frosting*: With mixer at high speed, beat the cream and superfine sugar until stiff. • Transfer the frosting to a pastry bag. Pipe five rosettes on top of the cake and one in the center. • Arrange the cookies on top in a decorative manner. Loosen and remove the pan sides to serve.

Makes one 8-inch cake · Prep: 1 hr. + 2 hr. to chill · Level: 2 · Keeps: 1 day in the refrigerator

Fresh fruit and Champagne loaf

MANGO CREAM TART

- 4 large egg yolks
- 1/3 cup superfine sugar
- 1 tablespoon cornstarch
- 1 (10 oz) mango, peeled
- 2/3 cup light cream
- 1 lb short crust pastry (see page 280)
- 3 kiwifruit, to decorate

Preheat the oven to 375°F. • Butter and flour a 10-inch round cake pan. • Beat the egg yolks and sugar in a large bowl with an electric mixer at medium speed until pale and thick. • Stir in the cornstarch. • Place the mango in a food processor and process until pureed. Transfer to a large bowl. Use a large rubber spatula to stir in the egg mixture and cream. • Roll the pastry out on a lightly floured surface to about 1/4-inch thick. • Fit the pastry into the prepared pan. Prick all over with a fork. • Spoon the mango mixture into the pastry shell. • Bake for 40–50 minutes, or until light golden brown. • Cool completely in the pan. • Turn out onto a serving plate. Arrange the kiwifruit on top. Serve immediately.

Makes one 10-inch round cake · Prep: 1 hr. · Cooking: 40–50 min. · Level: 2 · Keeps: 1 day

FRUIT SALAD CAKE

- 2 cups all-purpose flour
- 1 1/2 teaspoons baking powder
- 1/2 teaspoon baking soda
- 1/4 teaspoon salt
- 3/4 cup granulated sugar
- 1/2 cup chopped candied pineapple
- 1/4 cup (1/2 stick) butter, cut up
- 1 tablespoon grated orange zest

- 1 tablespoon grated lemon zest
- 1/4 cup fresh orange juice
- 1/4 cup fresh lemon juice
- 1 large apple, peeled, cored, and grated
- 1/3 cup mashed very ripe bananas
- 1 large egg, lightly beaten

Preheat the oven to 350°F. • Butter a 9-inch round cake pan. Line with waxed paper. Butter the paper. • Sift the flour, baking powder, baking soda, and salt into a medium bowl. • Place the sugar, candied pineapple, butter, orange and lemon zests and juices in a medium saucepan. Stir over medium-low heat until the sugar has dissolved. • Transfer to a large bowl. Stir in the apple, banana, and egg. With mixer at low speed, gradually beat in the dry ingredients. • Spoon the batter into the prepared pan. • Bake for 50–60 minutes, or until golden brown and a toothpick inserted into the center comes out clean. • Cool the cake in the pan for 10 minutes. Turn out onto a rack. Carefully remove the paper and let cool completely.

Makes one 9-inch cake · Prep: 20 min. · Cooking: 50–60 min. · Level: 1 · Keeps: 1 day

FRESH FRUIT AND CHAMPAGNE LOAF

This "loaf" can be served as is or with Chantilly Cream (see page 345) or ice cream.

- 1/3 cup granulated sugar
- 1 orange zest, cut from the fruit in a long spiral strip
- 1 1/3 cups water
- 1 1/2 tablespoons unflavored gelatin
- 2 1/2 cups Champagne or sparkling white wine
- 1 1/4 cups mixed fresh or frozen berries, such as red or black currants, blackberries, raspberries, or strawberries

Butter a 9 x 5-inch loaf pan. • Bring the sugar, orange zest, and water to a boil in a medium saucepan over medium heat. Stir until the sugar has dissolved. Remove from the heat and set aside to cool for 1 hour. • Discard the orange zest. • Sprinkle the gelatin over 1/4 cup of the orange-flavored mixture. Let stand 1 minute. Return to the saucepan and stir over low heat until the gelatin has dissolved. Stir in the Champagne. Set aside to cool. • Spoon 1/4 of the gelatin mixture into the prepared pan. Refrigerate for 15 minutes. Cover the gelatin with 3/4 cup of the berries. Spoon half the remaining gelatin mixture over the fruit and refrigerate for 15 minutes. Cover with the remaining berries and gelatin mixture and refrigerate for 6–8 hours, or until set. • Dip the pan into hot water for about 5 seconds. Carefully turn out onto a serving plate.

Makes one 9-inch loaf · Prep: 20 min. + 6–8 hr. to chill · Cooking: 5 min. · Level: 2 · Keeps: 1–2 days in the refrigerator

FRESH FRUIT AND NUT CAKE

Use whatever fruit appeals. Peeled peaches, apricots, nectarines, strawberries, or raspberries would all be delicious.

- 1 cup all-purpose flour
- 1/2 cup whole-wheat flour
- 1 cup firmly packed brown sugar
- 1 teaspoon baking powder
- 1 teaspoon baking soda
- 1 teaspoon ground cinnamon, ginger, and nutmeg
- 1 teaspoon ground ginger
- 1 teaspoon ground nutmeg
- 3/4 cup chopped nuts, such as walnuts, peanuts, or pecans
- 1 cup very ripe mashed bananas

1 cup very ripe mashed fruit
1/2 cup vegetable oil
2 large eggs, lightly beaten

Preheat the oven to 350°F. • Butter and flour a 9-inch tube pan. • Stir together the flours, sugar, baking powder, baking soda, cinnamon, ginger, and nutmeg in a large bowl. Add the nuts. • Beat in the bananas, fruit, oil, and eggs with an electric mixer at low speed. • Spoon the batter into the prepared pan. • Bake for 50–60 minutes, or until a toothpick inserted into the center comes out clean. • Cool the cake in the pan for 10 minutes. Turn out onto a rack to cool completely.

Makes one 9-inch cake · Prep: 15 min. · Cooking: 50–60 min. · Level: 1 · Keeps: 2–3 days

RASPBERRY CAKE

1 lb frozen raspberries, thawed (reserve the juice)
1 tablespoon cornstarch
1 (8 oz) and 1 (3 oz) package cream cheese, softened
3/4 cup granulated sugar
1 tablespoon cherry brandy
2 teaspoons vanilla extract
2 cups heavy cream
2 (12 oz) packages ladyfingers
1 cup fresh raspberries, to decorate

Butter a 9-inch springform pan. • Stir the raspberry juice and cornstarch in a small saucepan over medium-low heat and, stirring constantly, bring to a boil. Remove from the heat and let cool. • Beat both packages of cream cheese, the sugar, brandy, and vanilla in a large bowl with an electric mixer at medium speed until smooth. • With mixer at high speed, beat the cream in a large bowl until stiff. Use a large rubber spatula to fold the cream into the cream cheese mixture. Fold in the thawed frozen raspberries. • Line the bottom of the prepared pan with ladyfingers, pressing them in firmly. Cut some ladyfingers in half crosswise and arrange them cut side down around the pan sides. • Spoon half the cream cheese filling into the pan. Top with a layer of ladyfingers. Spoon the remaining filling over the top, swirling it in a decorative manner with the back of a spoon. • Cover and refrigerate for at least 8 hours. Loosen and carefully remove the pan sides. Decorate with the fresh raspberries.

Makes one 9-inch cake · Prep: 25 min. + 8 hr to chill · Level: 1 · Keeps: 1–2 days

RASPBERRY BREAKFAST CAKE

1 cup fresh raspberries
1/4 cup firmly packed brown sugar
1 cup all-purpose flour
1/3 cup granulated sugar
1/2 teaspoon baking powder
1/4 teaspoon baking soda
1/4 teaspoon salt
1/2 cup plain yogurt
1 large egg, at room temperature
2 tablespoons butter, melted
1 teaspoon vanilla extract
1/4 cup sliced unblanched almonds

Preheat the oven to 350°F. • Butter an 8-inch round cake pan. • Mix the raspberries and brown sugar in a small bowl. • Stir together the flour, granulated sugar, baking powder, baking soda, and salt in a large bowl. • Beat the yogurt, egg, butter, and vanilla into the dry ingredients with an electric mixer at medium speed. • Spoon the batter into the prepared pan. Spoon over the raspberry mixture, pressing it in slightly. Sprinkle with the almonds. • Bake for 25–30 minutes, or until the edges are brown and a toothpick inserted into the center comes out clean. • Cool the cake in the pan on a rack. • Serve warm or cool.

Makes one 8-inch cake · Prep: 25 min. · Cooking: 25–30 min. · Level: 1 · Keeps: 1 day

RASPBERRY COFFEE CAKE

2 cups all-purpose flour
1 cup granulated sugar
1 tablespoon baking powder
1/2 teaspoon salt
1/2 cup (1 stick) cold butter, cut up
2 large eggs, at room temperature
1 cup milk
1 teaspoon vanilla extract
1 teaspoon almond extract
2 cups fresh or 1 1/2 cups frozen raspberries
1/2 cup hazelnuts, chopped

Preheat the oven to 350°F. • Butter a 13 x 9-inch baking pan. • Sift the flour, sugar, baking powder, and salt into a large bowl. • Use a pastry blender to cut in the butter until the mixture resembles coarse crumbs. • Beat the eggs, milk, vanilla, and almond extract in a medium bowl. • Stir the egg mixture into the dry ingredients until just blended. • Spoon the batter into the prepared pan. Sprinkle with the raspberries and the hazelnuts. • Bake for 50–60 minutes, or until a toothpick inserted into the center comes out clean. Cool the cake in the pan on a rack. Serve warm.

Makes one 13 x 9-inch cake · Prep: 25 min. · Cooking: 50–60 min. · Level: 1 · Keeps: 1–2 days

RASPBERRY PUDDING CAKE

1 1/2 cups all-purpose flour
1 1/2 teaspoons baking powder
1/2 teaspoon baking soda
1 teaspoon ground cinnamon
1 teaspoon ground nutmeg
1/4 teaspoon salt
1/2 cup (1 stick) butter, softened
3/4 cup granulated sugar
1 teaspoon vanilla extract
1 large egg, at room temperature
1/2 cup milk
2 cups raspberries
2 tablespoons fresh lemon juice

TOPPING
1/2 cup granulated sugar
1 1/2 teaspoons cornstarch
1/2 cup boiling water

Preheat the oven to 350°F. • Butter an 8-inch square baking pan. • Sift the flour, baking powder, baking soda, cinnamon, nutmeg, and salt into a medium bowl. • Beat the butter, sugar, and vanilla in a large bowl with an electric mixer at medium speed until creamy. • Add the egg, until just blended. • With mixer at low speed, gradually beat in the dry ingredients, alternating with the milk. • Sprinkle the raspberries in the prepared pan and drizzle with the lemon juice. • Spoon the batter over the raspberries. • *Topping*: Mix the sugar and cornstarch in a small bowl and sprinkle over the batter. Carefully pour the water over the top. • Bake for 40–50 minutes or until puffed and golden brown. • Cool the cake in the pan on a rack. Serve warm.

Makes one 8-inch cake · Prep: 30 min. · Cooking: 40–50 min. · Level: 1 · Keeps: 2–3 days

CRANBERRY CRUMBLE COFFEE CAKE

This cake makes a hearty family dessert, especially good for chilly wintry days. Serve warm with ice cream.

- 1/2 cup almonds, chopped
- 2 cups all-purpose flour
- 1 1/2 teaspoons baking powder
- 1/2 teaspoon baking soda
- 1/4 teaspoon salt
- 1/2 cup (1 stick) butter, softened
- 1 cup granulated sugar
- 1 teaspoon vanilla extract
- 2 large eggs, at room temperature
- 1 cup plain yogurt
- 1 cup canned whole berry cranberry sauce

TOPPING
- 1/2 cup almonds, coarsely chopped
- 1/3 cup all-purpose flour
- 1/4 cup granulated sugar
- 2 tablespoons butter, melted
- 1/2 teaspoon vanilla extract

Preheat the oven to 350°F. • Butter and flour 9-inch springform pan. • Sprinkle the almonds over the bottom of the pan. • Sift the flour, baking powder, baking soda, and salt into a medium bowl. • Beat the butter, sugar, and vanilla in a large bowl with an electric mixer at medium speed until creamy. • Add the eggs, one at a time, until just blended after each addition. • With mixer at low speed, gradually beat in the dry ingredients, alternating with the yogurt. • Spoon half the batter into the prepared pan. Top with the cranberry sauce. Spoon the remaining batter over the top. • *Topping*: Mix the almonds, flour, sugar, butter, and vanilla in a small bowl until well blended. • Sprinkle the topping over the batter. Bake for 50–60 minutes, or until browned at the sides and a toothpick inserted into the center comes out clean. • Cool the cake in the pan on a rack for 15 minutes. Loosen and remove the pan sides and let cool. Serve warm.

Makes one 9-inch cake · Prep: 25 min. · Cooking: 50–60 min. · Level: 1 · Keeps: 1–2 days

STRAWBERRY LOAF WITH HEAVENLY CREAM

- 1 1/3 cups all-purpose flour
- 1/3 cup cornstarch
- 1 teaspoon baking powder
- 1/2 teaspoon baking soda
- 1/4 teaspoon salt
- 5 oz sliced strawberries
- 1/3 cup butter, softened

- 1/2 cup confectioners' sugar
- 1 teaspoon vanilla extract
- 2 large eggs, separated

- 1 1/2 cups Heavenly Cream (see page 343)

Preheat the oven to 350°F. • Butter a 9 x 5-inch loaf pan. Line with waxed paper. Butter the paper. • Sift the flour, cornstarch, baking powder, baking soda, and salt into a medium bowl. • Puree the strawberries in a food processor until smooth. • Beat the butter, confectioners' sugar, and vanilla in a medium bowl with an electric mixer at medium speed until creamy. • Add the egg yolks, one at a time, until just blended after each addition. • With mixer at low speed, gradually beat in the dry ingredients, alternating with the pureed strawberries. • With mixer at high speed, beat the egg whites in a medium bowl until stiff peaks form. Use a large rubber spatula to fold them into the mixture. • Spoon the batter into the prepared pan. • Bake for 30–40 minutes, or until a toothpick inserted into the center comes out clean. • Cool the loaf in the pan for 10 minutes. Turn out onto a rack. Carefully remove the paper and let cool completely. • Serve thick slices of the loaf with dollops of Heavenly Cream.

Makes one 9 x 5-inch loaf · Prep: 30 min. · Cooking: 30–40 min. · Level: 1 · Keeps: 2–3 days

BLACKBERRY CRUMBLE CAKE

FILLING
- 1 lb fresh or frozen unthawed blackberries or raspberries
- 1/2 cup granulated sugar
- 1 tablespoon grated lemon zest
- 2 tablespoons fresh lemon juice
- 1/4 cup cornstarch
- 3 tablespoons water

CAKE
- 1 1/2 cups all-purpose flour
- 1 teaspoon baking powder

- 1 teaspoon ground cinnamon
- 1/4 teaspoon salt
- 1/2 cup almonds, finely ground
- 1/3 cup butter, softened
- 1/2 cup granulated sugar
- 1/2 teaspoon vanilla extract
- 1/2 teaspoon almond extract
- 1 large egg, at room temperature
- 1/2 cup walnuts, coarsely chopped

Filling: Bring the blackberries, sugar, and lemon zest and juice to a boil in a large saucepan over medium heat. Reduce the heat and simmer until the fruit is just softened, about 10 minutes. • Mix the cornstarch and water. Stir the cornstarch mixture into the fruit and cook and stir until it is thickened and bubbly. Set aside to cool. • *Cake*: Preheat the oven to 350°F. • Butter and flour a 9-inch springform pan. Sift the flour, baking powder, cinnamon, and salt in a medium bowl. Stir in the almonds. • Beat the butter, sugar, vanilla, and almond extract in a large bowl with an electric mixer at medium speed until creamy. • Add the egg, beating until just blended. • With mixer at low speed, gradually beat in the dry ingredients. The dough will be quite thick and crumbly. • Knead 2/3 of the dough briefly on a lightly floured work surface until smooth. • Press the kneaded dough into the bottom and 1-inch up the sides of the prepared pan (it will be about 1/2-inch thick). Spoon the filling into the pan. • Mix the walnuts into the remaining dough and crumble over the top. • Bake for 40–50 minutes, or until the top and sides are golden brown. • Cool the cake completely in the pan on a rack. Loosen and remove the pan sides to serve.

Makes one 9-inch cake · Prep: 35 min. · Cooking: 40–50 min. · Level: 1 · Keeps: 2–3 days

BLACKBERRY BUNDT CAKE

This cake should be served while still warm. It's superb with vanilla ice cream or slightly sweetened whipped cream.

- 1 1/2 cups all-purpose flour
- 1 3/4 cups granulated sugar
- 3/4 cup vegetable oil
- 3/4 cup plain yogurt
- 3 large eggs, lightly beaten
- 1/2 cup wheat bran
- 1/4 cup instant dry nonfat milk
- 1 teaspoon baking powder
- 1 teaspoon ground nutmeg
- 1 teaspoon ground cloves
- 1/2 teaspoon baking soda

¼ teaspoon salt
1 cup fresh or frozen unthawed blackberries
½ cup walnuts, coarsely chopped
¼ cup confectioners' sugar, to dust

Preheat the oven to 350°F. • Butter and flour a 9-inch Bundt pan. • Beat the flour, sugar, oil, yogurt, eggs, bran, nonfat milk, baking powder, nutmeg, cloves, baking soda, and salt in a large bowl with an electric mixer at low speed until well blended. • By hand, stir in the blackberries and walnuts. • Spoon the batter into the prepared pan. • Bake for 50–55 minutes, or until a toothpick inserted into the center comes out clean. • Cool the cake in the pan for 10 minutes. Turn out onto a rack. • Dust with the confectioners' sugar and serve while still warm.

Makes one 9-inch cake · Prep: 20 min. · Cooking: 50–55 min. · Level: 2 · Keeps: 1 day

BLACKBERRY BREAD PUDDING

This is a delicious way to use up day-old bread.

2 cups milk
14 oz day-old soft bread, crusts removed and torn into pieces
3 large eggs, at room temperature
2 tablespoons brandy
1¼ cups granulated sugar
¼ teaspoon salt
3 cups blackberries + extra, to decorate, rinsed and well dried
2 teaspoons cold water
1 teaspoon fresh lemon juice

Preheat the oven to 350°F. • Set out a 1 quart soufflé dish. Heat the milk in a small saucepan. Place the bread in a large bowl and pour in the milk. Beat with an electric mixer at medium speed until the bread is fairly smooth. • Add the eggs, one at a time. Beat in ½ cup + 2 tablespoons sugar, the brandy, and salt. Mix well. • Stir in the blackberries. • Place the remaining sugar and water in a small saucepan and cook and stir over medium-low heat until the sugar has dissolved. Continue cooking, without stirring, until pale gold. Remove from the heat and sprinkle with the lemon juice. Pour into a soufflé dish. Turn the dish quickly to coat the sides. • Spoon the blackberry mixture into the dish and bake for 35–40 minutes, or until firm to the touch. • Turn out of the dish onto a serving plate and decorate with blackberries.

Makes 1 bread pudding · Prep: 30 min. · Cooking: 35–40 min. · Level: 2 · Keeps: 1–2 days

BLUEBERRY CRUMBLE CAKE

If you are using frozen blueberries, do not thaw. Add them to the batter while still frozen.

CRUMBLE
½ cup all-purpose flour
½ cup granulated sugar
1 teaspoon ground cinnamon
¼ cup (½ stick) cold butter, cut up

CAKE
2 cups all-purpose flour
2 teaspoons baking powder
¼ teaspoon salt
½ cup (1 stick) butter, softened
¾ cup granulated sugar
½ teaspoon vanilla extract
2 large eggs, at room temperature
⅓ cup milk
2 cups fresh or frozen blueberries

Preheat the oven to 350°F. • Butter and flour a 13 x 9-inch baking pan. • *Crumble*: Stir together the flour, sugar, and cinnamon in a medium bowl. Use a pastry blender to cut in the butter until the mixture resembles fine crumbs. • *Cake*: Sift the flour, baking powder, and salt into a medium bowl. • Beat the butter, sugar, and vanilla in a large bowl with an electric mixer at medium speed until creamy. • Add the eggs, one at a time, until just blended after each addition. • With mixer at low speed, gradually beat in the dry ingredients, alternating with the milk. • Stir in the blueberries. • Spoon the batter into the prepared pan. • Sprinkle with the crumble. Bake for 40–50 minutes, or until a toothpick inserted into the center comes out clean. • Cool the cake completely in the pan on a rack.

Makes one 13 x 9-inch cake · Prep: 20 min. · Cooking: 40–50 min. · Level: 1 · Keeps: 3–4 days

Blackberry bread pudding

Berry fruit delight

RED CURRANT UPSIDE-DOWN CAKE

Serve this delicious tangy cake straight from the oven with vanilla ice cream.

- ³/₄ cup (1¹/₂ sticks) butter, softened
- 1¹/₄ cups firmly packed light brown sugar
- 2 cups stemmed fresh red currants
- 1 cup all-purpose flour
- 1 teaspoon baking powder
- 1 teaspoon ground nutmeg
- 1 teaspoon ground ginger
- 1 teaspoon ground cinnamon
- ¹/₄ teaspoon salt
- 3 large eggs, at room temperature
- 2 tablespoons milk

Preheat the oven to 350°F. • Butter a 9-inch round cake pan. • Melt ¹/₄ cup butter in a medium saucepan over medium heat. Stir in ¹/₂ cup brown sugar. Stir in the currants. Cook for 3–4 minutes, until the fruit is coated with the butter and sugar. • Sift the flour, baking powder, nutmeg, ginger, cinnamon, and salt into a medium bowl. • Beat the remaining butter and remaining brown sugar in a large bowl with an electric mixer at high speed until creamy. • With mixer at medium speed, add the eggs, one at a time, until just blended after each addition. • With mixer at low speed, gradually beat in the dry ingredients, alternating with the milk. • Pour the red currant mixture into the prepared pan and spread it evenly across the bottom. Spoon the batter over the top. • Bake for 40–50 minutes, or until a toothpick inserted into the center comes out clean. Invert onto a deep-sided serving plate. Serve warm.

Makes one 9-inch cake · Prep: 25 min. · Cooking: 40–50 min. · Level: 1 · Keeps: 1 day

BERRY FRUIT DELIGHT

BASE
- 2 cups all-purpose flour
- ³/₄ cup (1¹/₂ sticks) butter, softened
- 1 cup confectioners' sugar
- ¹/₈ teaspoon salt
- 1 large egg yolk, at room temperature

CHEESE FILLING
- 2 tablespoons unflavored gelatin
- ¹/₄ cup cold water
- 4 large egg yolks
- ¹/₄ cup milk
- 1 cup granulated sugar
  grated zest of 1 lemon
- 2 cups fresh ricotta cheese
- 2 cups heavy cream

FRUIT FILLING
- 1 small can (4 oz) sliced peaches, drained
- 1 cup raspberries

BEET AND CURRANT CAKE

- 1 cup (2 sticks) butter, softened
- 1 cup granulated sugar
- 1 teaspoon vanilla extract
- 4 large eggs, at room temperature
- 2 teaspoons baking powder
- ¹/₄ teaspoon salt
- 1 cup cooked, peeled beets, coarsely grated
- 1 cup currants
- 2 cups cake flour
- ¹/₄ cup confectioners' sugar, to dust

Preheat the oven to 350°F. • Butter an 11 x 7-inch baking pan. • Beat the butter, sugar, and vanilla in a large bowl with an electric mixer at high speed until creamy. • With mixer at medium speed, add the eggs, one at a time, until just blended after each addition. • Beat in the baking powder and salt. With mixer at low speed, beat in the beets, currants, and flour. • Spoon the batter into the prepared pan. • Bake for 75–85 minutes, or until a toothpick inserted into the center comes out clean. • Cool the cake completely in the pan on a rack. • Dust with confectioners' sugar just before serving.

Makes one 7 x 11-inch cake · Prep: 20 min. · Cooking: 75–85 min. · Level: 1 · Keeps: 4–5 days

BLUEBERRY COFFEE CAKE

Serve this fruit-and-crumb-filled cake while it's still warm.

TOPPING
- 1 cup firmly packed brown sugar
- ²/₃ cup all-purpose flour
- 1 teaspoon ground cinnamon
- ¹/₂ teaspoon ground nutmeg
- ¹/₂ cup (1 stick) cold butter, cut up

CAKE
- 2 cups all-purpose flour
- 1¹/₂ teaspoons baking powder
- ¹/₂ teaspoon baking soda
- ¹/₂ teaspoon ground nutmeg
- ¹/₄ teaspoon salt
- ¹/₂ cup (1 stick) butter, softened
- 1 cup granulated sugar
- 1 teaspoon vanilla extract
- 2 large eggs, at room temperature
- ¹/₂ cup milk
- 1 cup fresh blueberries

Preheat the oven to 350°F. • Butter and flour a 9-inch Bundt pan. • *Topping*: Stir together the brown sugar, flour, cinnamon, and nutmeg in a medium bowl. Use a pastry blender to cut in the butter until the mixture resembles fine crumbs. • *Cake*: Sift the flour, baking powder, baking soda, nutmeg, and salt into a large bowl. • Beat the butter, sugar, and vanilla in a large bowl with an electric mixer at medium speed until creamy. • Add the eggs, one at a time, until just blended after each addition. • With mixer at low speed, gradually beat in the dry ingredients, alternating with the milk. • Stir in the blueberries. • Spoon half the batter into the prepared pan. Sprinkle with half the topping. Spoon the remaining batter over. • Sprinkle with the remaining topping. • Bake for 55–65 minutes, or until the topping is golden brown and a toothpick inserted into the center comes out clean. • Cool the cake in the pan for 30 minutes.

Makes one 9-inch cake · Prep: 25 min. · Cooking: 55–65 min. · Level: 1 · Keeps: 1–2 days

1 cup blackberries
3/4 cup huckleberries or blueberries
3/4 cup fresh red currants

Base: Stir together the flour, butter, confectioners' sugar, salt, and egg yolk in a large bowl until the mixture just holds together. Press the dough into a disk, wrap in plastic wrap, and refrigerate for 1 hour. • *Cheese Filling*: Sprinkle the gelatin over the water in a small saucepan. Let stand 1 minute. Stir over low heat until the gelatin has completely dissolved. • Beat the egg yolks, milk, sugar, and lemon zest in a medium saucepan. Bring to a boil over medium heat. Remove from the heat and add the gelatin, stirring until well blended. • Set aside to cool, stirring occasionally. Fold in the ricotta. Refrigerate. • *Fruit Filling*: Toss together the peaches, berries, and currants in a large bowl. • Preheat the oven to 400°F. • Butter and flour a baking sheet. • Roll the dough out on a lightly floured surface to a 10 x 13-inch rectangle. Place the pastry on the prepared sheet. Prick all over with a fork. Line the pastry shell with foil and fill the foil with dried beans or pie weights. Bake for 5 minutes, then remove the foil with the beans and bake until crisp and golden brown, about 10 minutes. • Cool completely in the pan on a rack. • Spread most of the fruit (reserving some to decorate) over the cooled base. • Beat the cream in a large bowl with an electric mixer at medium speed until stiff. Stir in the cooled ricotta mixture, mixing well. • Spread over the fruit. Smooth and refrigerate for at least 4 hours or until set. • Decorate with the reserved fruit.

Makes one 10 x 13-inch cake · Prep: 2 hr. + 4 hr. · Cooking: 15 min. · Level: 2 · Keeps: 1–2 days in the refrigerator

FROZEN CHERRY GÂTEAU

1 lb short-crust pastry (see page 280)
3 1/4 cups cherry vanilla ice cream, softened
1 1/2 teaspoons butter
1 cup wild black or sour cherries, pitted
2 teaspoons granulated sugar
   juice of 1 lemon
1 tablespoon kirsch
1 1/4 cups heavy cream
1 1/4 cups canned drained sour cherries or pie cherries

Preheat the oven to 400°F. • Roll the dough out on a lightly floured surface to a 12-inch round. Fit the pastry into a 9-inch

springform pan, trimming the edges if needed. Line the pastry shell with aluminum foil and fill the foil with dried beans or pie weights. • Bake for 15 minutes. Remove the foil with the beans. • Bake for 5 minutes, or until golden and crisp. Set aside to cool completely. Refrigerate the pastry in the pan for at least 1 hour until chilled. • Spread the ice cream over the pastry 1 1/2-inch thick. Freeze for about 2 hours, or until firm. • Melt the butter in a medium skillet over medium-high heat. Stir in the wild cherries, sugar, lemon juice, and kirsch and cook until the cherries have softened. Set aside to cool completely. • Remove the pastry from the freezer. Loosen and remove the pan sides and place onto a serving plate. Spoon the cooked cherry mixture on top. • With mixer at high speed, beat the cream in a medium bowl until stiff. • Spoon the cream into a pastry bag and decorate the top. Decorate with the canned cherries and serve immediately.

Makes one 9-inch cake · Prep: 50 min. + 1 hr. to chill 2 hr. to freeze · Cooking: 20 min. · Level: 1 · Keeps: 2–3 days in the freezer

SOUR CREAM CHERRY CAKE

2 1/3 cups all-purpose flour
1 teaspoon baking powder
1 teaspoon baking soda
1/2 teaspoon ground nutmeg
1/4 teaspoon salt
1/2 cup (1 stick) butter, softened
1 cup granulated sugar
1 teaspoon vanilla extract
1 teaspoon almond extract
2 large eggs, at room temperature
1 cup sour cream
1 cup pitted and chopped dark sweet cherries
3/4 cup cherry preserves
1/4 cup confectioners' sugar, to dust

Preheat the oven to 350°F. • Butter a 13 x 9-inch baking pan. • Sift the flour, baking powder, baking soda, nutmeg, and salt into a large bowl. • Beat the butter, sugar, vanilla, and almond extract in a large bowl with an electric mixer at high speed until creamy. • With mixer at medium speed, add the eggs, one at a time, until just blended after each addition. • With mixer at low speed, gradually beat in the dry ingredients, alternating with the sour cream. Stir in the cherries and cherry preserves. • Spoon the batter into the prepared pan. • Bake for 35–45 minutes, or until golden, the cake shrinks from the pan sides, and a toothpick inserted into the center comes out clean. Cool the cake in the pan on a rack. • Serve warm. Dust with the confectioners' sugar just before serving.

Makes one 13 x 9-inch cake · Prep: 20 min. · Cooking: 35–45 min. · Level: 1 · Keeps: 1–2 days

RHUBARB COFFEE CAKE

2 cups all-purpose flour
1 teaspoon baking powder
1 teaspoon baking soda
1 teaspoon ground cinnamon (optional)
1/4 teaspoon salt
1/2 cup (1 stick) butter, softened
1 cup firmly packed brown sugar
1 teaspoon vanilla extract
2 large eggs, at room temperature
1 cup plain yogurt
1/2 cup applesauce
3 cups fresh rhubarb, coarsely chopped
3 tablespoons granulated sugar

Preheat the oven to 350°F. • Butter a 13 x 9-inch baking pan. • Sift the flour, baking powder, baking soda, cinnamon (if desired), and salt into a medium bowl. • Beat the butter, brown sugar, and vanilla in a large bowl with an electric mixer at high speed until creamy. • With mixer at medium speed, add the eggs, one at a time, until just blended after each addition. • With mixer at low speed, gradually beat in the dry ingredients, alternating with the yogurt and applesauce. Stir in the rhubarb. • Spoon the batter into the prepared pan. • Sprinkle the top with the granulated sugar. • Bake for 50–60 minutes, or until a toothpick inserted into the center comes out clean. • Cool the cake completely in the pan on a rack.

Makes one 13 x 9-inch cake · Prep: 20 min. · Cooking: 50–60 min. · Level: 1 · Keeps: 1–2 days

Upside-down plum cake

PLUM COFFEE CAKE

Make sure your springform pan is 3 inches deep, or this cake could overflow.

1 1/2 cups purple plums, peeled and chopped
1 cup granulated sugar
1 tablespoon cornstarch
2 cups all-purpose flour
2 teaspoons baking powder
1 teaspoon ground cinnamon
1 teaspoon ground ginger
1/4 teaspoon salt
1/2 cup (1 stick) butter, softened
1/2 teaspoon vanilla extract
2 large eggs, at room temperature
1/3 cup milk

TOPPING

1/4 cup granulated sugar
1 teaspoon ground cinnamon
1 teaspoon ground ginger

Preheat the oven to 350°F. • Butter and flour a 9-inch springform pan. • Mix the plums, 1/4 cup sugar, and the cornstarch in a medium bowl. • Sift the flour, baking powder, cinnamon, ginger, and salt into a medium bowl. • Beat the butter, remaining 3/4 cup sugar, and vanilla in a

large bowl with an electric mixer at high speed until creamy. • With mixer at medium speed, add the eggs, one at a time, until just blended after each addition. • With mixer at low speed, gradually beat in the dry ingredients, alternating with the milk. • Spoon half the batter into the prepared pan. Top with the plum mixture. Spoon the remaining batter over. • Topping: Mix the sugar, cinnamon, and ginger in a small bowl. Sprinkle over the batter. • Bake for 50–60 minutes, or until a toothpick inserted into the center comes out clean. • Cool the cake in the pan for 15 minutes. Loosen and remove the pan sides and let cool. Serve warm or at room temperature.

Makes one 9-inch cake · Prep: 25 min. · Cooking: 50–60 min. · Level: 1 · Keeps: 1–2 days

UPSIDE-DOWN PLUM CAKE

TOPPING

2 tablespoons butter, melted
2 tablespoons firmly packed dark brown sugar
1 teaspoon fresh lime juice
4 plums, washed and cut into 6 slices

BATTER

1 2/3 cups all-purpose flour
3/4 teaspoon baking soda
1/2 teaspoon baking powder
1/2 teaspoon ground cinnamon
1/4 teaspoon salt
1/4 teaspoon ground nutmeg
1/2 cup (1 stick) butter
1 cup granulated sugar
2 large eggs
3/4 cup milk

Preheat the oven to 350°F. • Topping: Pour the melted butter into a 10-inch round cake pan. Sprinkle with the brown sugar and arrange the plum slices on the bottom of the pan. • Batter: Sift the flour, baking soda, baking powder, cinnamon, salt, and nutmeg into a medium bowl. • Beat the butter and sugar in a large bowl with an electric mixer at medium speed until creamy. Add the eggs, one at a time, until just blended after each addition. With mixer at low speed, gradually beat the dry ingredients into the batter, alternating with the milk. • Pour the batter over the plums in the pan. • Bake for 55–65 minutes, or until a toothpick inserted into the center comes out clean. • Cool the cake in the pan for 30 minutes. Turn out onto a rack to cool completely.

Makes one 10-inch cake · Prep: 20 min. · Cooking: 55–65 min. · Level: 1 · Keeps: 3 days

POTATO GINGER CAKE

1 1/2 cups all-purpose flour
2 teaspoons ground ginger
1 teaspoon baking powder
1/2 teaspoon baking soda
1/4 teaspoon salt
3/4 cup (1 1/2 sticks) butter, softened
3/4 cup firmly packed brown sugar
1/3 cup dark corn syrup
2 large eggs, at room temperature
1 cup grated peeled raw potato
1/4 cup milk

LEMON AND GINGER FROSTING

2 teaspoons ground ginger
2 cups confectioners' sugar
2 tablespoons butter, melted
1–2 tablespoons fresh lemon juice
2 tablespoons coarsely chopped crystallized ginger (optional)

Preheat the oven to 325°F. • Butter a 13 x 9-inch baking pan. Line with waxed paper. Butter the paper. • Sift the flour, ginger, baking powder, baking soda, and salt into a medium bowl. • Beat the butter, brown sugar, and corn syrup in a large bowl with an electric mixer at medium speed until creamy. • Add the eggs, one at a time, until just blended after each addition. • With mixer at low speed, gradually beat in the potato and dry ingredients, alternating with the milk. • Spoon the batter into the prepared pan. • Bake for 50–60 minutes, or until a toothpick inserted into the center comes out clean. • Cool the cake in the pan for 10 minutes. Turn out onto a rack. Carefully remove the paper and let cool completely. • *Lemon and Ginger Frosting*: Beat the confectioners' sugar, ginger, and butter in a medium bowl. Add enough lemon juice to make a spreadable frosting. • Spread the cake with the frosting and, if desired, sprinkle with crystallized ginger.

Makes one 13 x 9-inch cake · Prep: 20 min. · Cooking: 50–60 min. · Level: 1 · Keeps: 3 days

POTATO CAKE

This cake has a mild flavor and is popular with children.

- 4   large baking potatoes, scrubbed
- 2   cups all-purpose flour
- 1   tablespoon grated lemon zest
- 2   teaspoons baking powder
- 1/4   teaspoon salt
- 1²/₃   cups ricotta cheese
- 1¹/₂   cups granulated sugar
- 4   large eggs, at room temperature
- 1/4   cup (¹/₂ stick) butter, melted
- 1/4   cup confectioners' sugar, to dust

Boil the potatoes in their skins until tender, about 30 minutes. Slip off the skins and mash while still warm. Set aside to cool. • Preheat the oven to 350°F. • Butter a 9-inch round cake pan. Line with waxed paper. • Stir together the flour, lemon zest, baking powder, and salt in a large bowl. • Beat in the mashed potatoes, ricotta, sugar, eggs, and butter with an electric mixer at low speed. • Spoon the batter into the prepared pan. • Bake for 35–45 minutes, or until a toothpick inserted into the center comes out clean. • Cool the cake in the pan for 15 minutes. Carefully remove the paper and let cool completely. Turn out onto a rack. Dust with the confectioners' sugar.

Makes one 9-inch round cake · Prep: 15 min. · Cooking: 35–45 mins. · Level: 1 · Keeps: 2–3 days

Italian potato cake

ITALIAN POTATO CAKE

- 1   lb baking potatoes, such as russet, scrubbed
- 1/4   cup all-purpose flour
- 1/2   cup (1 stick) butter, softened
- 3/4   cup granulated sugar
- 4   large eggs, separated
- 1   tablespoon grated lemon zest
- 1   teaspoon freshly grated nutmeg
- 1   teaspoon almond extract
- 3/4   cup raisins
- 1/3   cup pine nuts
  about ¹/₄ cup confectioners' sugar, to dust

Boil the potatoes in their skins in a large covered pot of boiling, salted water until tender, when pierced with a fork. Slip off the skins. Place the hot potatoes and flour in a bowl. Mash until smooth. Set aside to cool for 15 minutes. • Preheat the oven to 350°F. • Butter a 9-inch round cake pan. Line with waxed paper. • Beat the butter and sugar in a large bowl with an electric mixer at high speed until creamy. • With mixer at medium speed, add the egg yolks, one at a time, until just blended after each addition. • With mixer at low speed, beat in the potatoes,

lemon zest, nutmeg, and almond extract. Stir in the raisins and pine nuts. • With mixer at high speed, beat the egg whites in a large bowl until stiff peaks form. Use a large rubber spatula to fold the beaten whites into the batter. • Spoon the batter into the prepared pan. • Bake for 35–45 minutes, or until golden brown, and a toothpick inserted into the center comes out clean. • Cool the cake in the pan for 15 minutes. Turn out onto a rack. Carefully remove the paper and let cool completely. • Dust with the confectioners' sugar before serving.

Makes one 9-inch cake · Prep: 45 min. · Cooking: 35–45 min. · Level: 1 · Keeps: 2–3 days

PUMPKIN AND PRUNE LOAF CAKES

- 1 cup (2 sticks) butter, softened
- 1¼ cups granulated sugar
- 2 tablespoons grated orange zest
- 2 large eggs, at room temperature
- 1 cup plain canned pumpkin
- 1 cup pitted prunes, chopped
- 2 cups all-purpose flour
- 2 teaspoons baking powder
- ¼ teaspoon salt
- ½ cup milk
  confectioners' sugar, to dust

Preheat the oven to 325°F. • Butter two 8 x 4-inch loaf pans. Line with aluminum foil, letting the edges overhang. Butter the foil. • Beat the butter, sugar, and orange zest in a large bowl with an electric mixer at medium speed until creamy. • Add the eggs, one at a time, until just blended after each addition. • With mixer at low speed, gradually beat in the pumpkin, prunes, flour, baking powder, and salt, alternating with the milk. • Spoon the batter into the prepared pans. • Bake for 50–60 minutes, or until a toothpick inserted into the centers comes out clean. • Cool the loaves in the pans for 15 minutes. Using the foil as a lifter, remove the loaves from the pans. Carefully remove the foil. Cool the loaves completely on racks. Dust with the confectioners' sugar.

Makes two 8 x 4-inch loaves · Prep: 15 min. · Cooking: 50–60 min. · Level: 1 · Keeps: 2–3 days

ITALIAN PUMPKIN CAKE

- 1¼ lb peeled seeded pumpkin or butternut squash
- 2 cups all-purpose flour
- 2 teaspoons baking powder
- 1 tablespoon ground cinnamon
- ½ teaspoon ground cardamom
- ½ teaspoon ground cloves
- ½ teaspoon salt
- 1¼ cups granulated sugar
- 3 large eggs, at room temperature
- ¼ cup extra-virgin olive oil
- 1 cup raisins
- ¼ cup confectioners' sugar, to dust

Preheat the oven to 350°F. • Slice the pumpkin or squash and place in an oiled baking pan. Bake for 15–20 minutes, or until tender. Puree in a food processor. Set aside to cool. • Butter and flour a 9 x 5-inch loaf pan. • Sift the flour, baking powder, cinnamon, cardamom, cloves, and salt into a large bowl. • Beat the sugar and eggs in a large bowl with an electric mixer at high speed until pale and thick. • With mixer at low speed, gradually beat in the dry ingredients, alternating with the oil. • Stir in the pumpkin and raisins. • Spoon the batter into the prepared pan. • Bake for 50–60 minutes, or until a toothpick inserted into the center comes out clean. • Cool the cake in the pan for 10 minutes. Turn out onto a rack to cool completely. • Dust with the confectioners' sugar.

Makes one 9-inch loaf · Prep: 45–50 min. · Cooking 50–60 min. · Level: 1 · Keeps: 2–3 days

PUMPKIN BUNDT CAKE

- 3 cups all-purpose flour
- 2 teaspoons baking powder
- 2 teaspoons ground cinnamon
- 1 teaspoon baking soda
- 1 teaspoon ground allspice
- ½ teaspoon cloves
- ½ teaspoon salt
- 2 large eggs, at room temperature
- 1 cup firmly packed brown sugar
- ½ cup pure maple syrup
- ¼ cup vegetable oil
- 1 can (15 oz) plain pumpkin

Preheat the oven to 350°F . • Butter and flour a 9- or 10-inch Bundt pan. • Sift the flour, baking powder, cinnamon, baking soda, allspice, cloves, and salt into a large bowl. • Beat the eggs, brown sugar, maple syrup, and oil in a medium bowl with an electric mixer at medium speed until well blended. With mixer at low speed, beat in the pumpkin. • Stir the pumpkin mixture into the dry ingredients. • Spoon the batter into the prepared pan. • Bake for 70–80 minutes, or until a toothpick inserted into the center comes out clean. • Cool the cake in the pan for 15 minutes. Turn out onto a rack to cool completely.

Makes one 9- or 10-inch cake · Prep: 20 min. · Cooking: 70–80 min. · Level: 1 · Keeps: 2–3 days

PUMPKIN CAKE WITH ZESTY WINE SYRUP

If you prefer to use fresh pumpkin, steam or bake it until tender when pierced with a knife. Mash the pulp with a potato ricer.

- 1 cup (2 sticks) butter, softened
- 1 cup granulated sugar
- 2 tablespoons grated lemon zest
- 2 tablespoons grated lime zest
- 3 large eggs, separated
- 2 cups all-purpose flour
- 1 teaspoon baking powder
- ¼ teaspoon salt
- 1 cup plain canned pumpkin

WINE SYRUP
- ¾ cup granulated sugar
- ½ cup dry white wine
- 2 tablespoons fresh lemon zest
- 2 tablespoons fresh lime zest

Preheat the oven to 350°F. • Butter a 9-inch square baking pan. • Beat the butter, sugar, and lemon and lime zests in a large bowl with an electric mixer at medium speed until creamy. • Add the egg yolks, one at a time, until just blended after each

Italian pumpkin cake

addition. • With mixer at low speed, gradually beat in the flour, baking powder, and salt, and pumpkin. • With mixer at high speed, beat the egg whites in a medium bowl until stiff peaks form. Use a large rubber spatula to fold them into the batter. • Spoon the batter into the prepared pan. • Bake for 50–60 minutes, or until a toothpick inserted into the center comes out clean. • Cool the cake in the pan on a rack. • *Wine Syrup*: Stir together the sugar, wine, and citrus zests in a small saucepan over low heat until the sugar has dissolved. Bring to a boil and simmer for 2 minutes. • Poke holes in the cake with a skewer. Drizzle with the syrup.

Makes one 9-inch cake · Prep: 25 min. · Cooking: 50–60 min. · Level: 1 · Keeps: 2–3 days

FRENCH ALMOND AND PUMPKIN CAKE

  8 oz pumpkin, peeled and sliced

CAKE
  6 large eggs, separated
  1 cup granulated sugar
  1 teaspoon ground cinnamon
  1/4 teaspoon salt
  2 tablespoons finely grated orange zest
  2 tablespoons finely grated lemon zest
  1²/₃ cups almonds, finely ground
  1/3 cup all-purpose flour
    scant 1 cup candied orange peel, finely chopped

ORANGE TOPPING
  1/4 cup orange marmalade
  1/4 cup fresh orange juice
  2 tablespoons fresh lemon juice
  1/4 cup granulated sugar
  3/4 cup orange liqueur
  1/2 cup slivered almonds
  2 tablespoons confectioners' sugar, to dust

Boil the pumpkin until tender when pierced with a fork, about 15 minutes. Drain well. • Preheat the oven to 400°F. • *Cake*: Butter and flour a 10-inch springform pan. • Dice the cooked pumpkin into small cubes. • Beat the egg yolks, 1/4 cup sugar, cinnamon, and salt with an electric mixer at high speed until frothy. Beat in the orange and lemon zest. • With mixer at low speed, gradually beat in the almonds, flour, orange peel, and pumpkin. • With mixer at high speed, beat the egg whites until frothy. Gradually beat in the remaining sugar until stiff peaks form. •

French almond and pumpkin cake

Use a large rubber spatula to fold the beaten whites into the pumpkin mixture. • Spoon the batter into the prepared pan. • Bake for 25–30 minutes, or until a toothpick inserted into the center comes out clean. • Cool the cake in the pan for 10 minutes. Loosen and remove the pan sides. Invert the cake onto a rack to cool completely. • Split the cake horizontally, making one layer 3/4 thicker than the other. Place the thin layer on a serving plate. Spread with the marmalade. Top with the thicker layer. • Bring the citrus juices and sugar to a boil. Remove from the heat. Stir in the orange liqueur. • Prick the cake with a fork and drizzle with the syrup. Sprinkle with the slivered almonds. Dust with the confectioners' sugar.

Makes one 10-inch cake · Prep: 1 hr. + 1 hr. to rest · Cooking: 25–30 min. · Level: 2 · Keeps: 1–2 days

BEST-EVER CARROT AND WALNUT CAKE

  2¹/₃ cups all-purpose flour
  2 teaspoons ground cinnamon
  1 teaspoon baking powder
  1 teaspoon baking soda
  1 teaspoon ground ginger
  1/2 teaspoon ground nutmeg
  1/4 teaspoon ground cloves
  1/4 teaspoon salt
  1¹/₂ cups (3 sticks) butter, softened
  2 cups granulated sugar
  2 teaspoons vanilla extract
  4 large eggs, at room temperature
  3 cups grated carrots

  1¹/₂ cups chopped walnuts
  1/3 cup raisins

CREAM CHEESE FROSTING
  1 package (8 oz) cream cheese, softened
  1/3 cup butter, softened
  2¹/₂ cups confectioners' sugar
  1 tablespoon finely grated lemon zest
  2 teaspoons fresh lemon juice
    walnut halves, to decorate

Preheat the oven to 350°F. • Butter and flour a 9-inch springform pan. • Stir together the flour, cinnamon, baking powder, baking soda, ginger, nutmeg, cloves, and salt in a large bowl. • Beat the butter, sugar, and vanilla in a large bowl with an electric mixer at medium speed until creamy. • Add the eggs, one at a time, just until blended after each addition. • With mixer at low speed, gradually beat in the dry ingredients. • Stir in the carrots, walnuts, and raisins. • Spoon the batter into the prepared pan. • Bake for 45–55 minutes, or until a toothpick inserted into the center comes out clean. • Cool the cake in the pan for 10 minutes. Loosen and remove the pan sides. Invert the cake onto a rack. Loosen and remove the pan bottom and let cool completely. • *Cream Cheese Frosting*: With mixer at medium speed, beat the cream cheese, butter, confectioners' sugar, and lemon zest and juice in a large bowl until creamy. • Spread the cake with the frosting. Decorate with walnut halves.

Makes one 9-inch cake Prep: 40 min. · Cooking 45–55 min. · Level: 1 · Keeps: 2–3 days

YOGURT CARROT CAKE WITH LEMON CREAM CHEESE FROSTING

1¼ cups all-purpose flour
1 teaspoon baking powder
1 teaspoon ground cinnamon
1 teaspoon ground nutmeg
½ teaspoon baking soda
¼ teaspoon salt
1 cup firmly packed brown sugar
2 cups firmly packed grated carrots
½ cup vegetable oil
2 eggs, lightly beaten
½ cup plain yogurt
¾ cup walnuts, coarsely chopped

LEMON CREAM CHEESE FROSTING

1 package (3 oz) cream cheese, softened
2 tablespoons butter, softened
2 teaspoons grated lemon zest
1½ cups confectioners' sugar

Preheat the oven to 325°F. • Butter and flour a 10-inch tube pan. • Sift the flour, baking powder, cinnamon, nutmeg, baking soda, and salt into a large bowl. • Beat in the brown sugar and carrots with an electric mixer at medium speed. • Beat in the oil, eggs, and yogurt. Stir in the walnuts. • Spoon the batter into the prepared pan. • Bake for 45–55 minutes, or until a toothpick inserted into the center comes out clean. • Cool the cake in the pan for 15 minutes. Turn out onto a rack to cool completely. • *Lemon Cream Cheese Frosting*: Beat the cream cheese, butter, and lemon zest in a medium bowl until fluffy. Beat in the confectioners' sugar. • Spread the cake with the frosting.

Makes one 10-inch cake · Prep: 15 min. · Cooking: 45–55 min. · Level: 1 · Keeps: 3 days

SUNFLOWER CARROT CAKE WITH ORANGE CREAM CHEESE FROSTING

2½ cups all-purpose flour
2½ teaspoons baking powder
1 teaspoon ground ginger
1 teaspoon ground nutmeg
½ teaspoon baking soda
½ teaspoon salt
1 cup vegetable oil
1¼ cups firmly packed brown sugar
3 large eggs, at room temperature
3 cups firmly packed coarsely grated carrots
1 cup hazelnuts, coarsely chopped
2 tablespoons sunflower seeds

ORANGE CREAM CHEESE FROSTING

1 package (3 oz) cream cheese, softened
2 tablespoons butter, softened
1 tablespoon grated orange zest
1½ cups confectioners' sugar

Preheat the oven to 350°F. • Butter and flour a 10-inch springform pan. • Sift the flour, baking powder, ginger, nutmeg, baking soda, and salt into a large bowl. • Beat the oil, brown sugar, and eggs in a large bowl with an electric mixer at high speed until creamy. • With mixer at low speed, beat in the carrots, hazelnuts, sunflower seeds, and the dry ingredients. • Spoon the batter into the prepared pan. • Bake for 70–80 minutes, or until a toothpick inserted into the center comes out clean. • Cool in the pan for 10 minutes. Loosen and remove the pan sides. Invert the cake onto a rack. Loosen and remove the pan bottom and let cool completely. • *Orange Cream Cheese Frosting*: Beat the cream cheese, butter, and orange zest in a medium bowl until fluffy. Beat in the confectioners' sugar. Spread the cake with the frosting.

Makes one 10-inch cake · Prep: 20 min. · Cooking: 70–80 min. · Level: 1 · Keeps: 2–3 days

CARROT AND WALNUT CAKE WITH ORANGE CREAM CHEESE FROSTING

1½ cups all-purpose flour
1 teaspoon baking powder
1 teaspoon ground cinnamon
1 teaspoon ground nutmeg
½ teaspoon baking soda
¼ teaspoon salt
¾ cup (1½ sticks) butter, softened
1½ cups granulated sugar
3 large eggs, at room temperature
2 cups firmly packed grated carrots
¾ cup walnuts, coarsely chopped

ORANGE CREAM CHEESE FROSTING

1 package (3 oz) cream cheese, softened
1 tablespoon grated orange zest
2 cups confectioners' sugar
1 tablespoon fresh orange juice

Preheat the oven to 350°F. • Butter a 9-inch square baking pan. Line with waxed paper. Butter the paper. • Sift the flour, baking powder, cinnamon, nutmeg, baking soda, and salt into a large bowl. • Beat the butter and sugar in a large bowl with an electric mixer at medium speed until creamy. • Add the eggs, one at a time, until just blended after each addition. • With mixer at low speed, gradually beat in the carrots, walnuts, and dry ingredients. • Spoon the batter into the prepared pan. • Bake for 40–50 minutes, or until a toothpick inserted into the center comes out clean. • Cool the cake in the pan for 10 minutes. Turn out onto a rack. Carefully remove the paper and let cool completely. • *Orange Cream Cheese Frosting*: Beat the cream cheese and orange zest in a medium bowl. Beat in the confectioners' sugar and orange juice. • Spread the top of the cake with the frosting.

Makes one 9-inch cake · Prep: 20 min. · Cooking: 40–50 min. · Level: 1 · Keeps: 3 days

CARROT, DATE, AND WALNUT CAKE

1½ cups all-purpose flour
1½ teaspoons pumpkin pie spice
1 teaspoon baking powder
½ teaspoon baking soda
¼ teaspoon salt
½ cup (1 stick) butter, softened
1 cup granulated sugar
2 tablespoons dark corn syrup
1 teaspoon vanilla extract
2 large eggs, at room temperature
2 cups firmly packed grated carrots
1 cup pitted dates, chopped
1 cup walnuts, chopped

Preheat the oven to 350°F. • Butter and flour a 10-inch tube pan. • Sift the flour, pumpkin pie spice, baking powder, baking soda, and salt into a medium bowl. • Beat the butter, sugar, corn syrup, and vanilla in a large bowl with an electric mixer at medium speed until creamy. • Add the eggs, one at a time, until just blended after each addition. • With mixer at low speed, gradually beat in the dry ingredients. Stir in the carrots, dates, and walnuts. • Spoon the batter into the prepared pan. • Bake for about 50–60 minutes, or until a toothpick inserted into the center comes out clean. • Cool the cake in the pan for 15 minutes. Turn out onto a rack to cool completely.

Makes one 10-inch cake · Prep: 20 min. · Cooking: 50–60 min. · Level: 1 · Keeps: 5 days

QUICK CARROT AND RAISIN LOAF

2 large carrots, peeled and sliced
2 large eggs, at room temperature
¾ cup firmly packed brown sugar
½ cup (1 stick) butter, melted
1¼ cups whole-wheat flour

1/4	cup milk
1	teaspoon baking powder
1/2	teaspoon baking soda
1	teaspoon pumpkin pie spice
1/8	teaspoon salt
1	cup raisins

Preheat the oven to 350°F. • Butter a 9 x 5-inch loaf pan. Line with aluminum foil, letting the edges overhang. Butter the foil. • Process the carrots and eggs in a food processor until the carrots are finely chopped. • Add the brown sugar and butter and process until well blended. • Transfer the mixture to a large bowl. Stir in the flour, milk, baking powder, baking soda, pumpkin pie spice, salt, and raisins. • Spoon the batter into the prepared pan. • Bake for 45–55 minutes, or until a toothpick inserted into the center comes out clean. • Cool the loaf in the pan for 10 minutes. Using the foil as a lifter, remove the loaf from the pan. Carefully remove the foil. Cool the loaf completely on a rack.

Makes one 9 x 5-inch loaf · Prep: 10 min. · Cooking: 45–55 min. · Level: 1 · Keeps: 3–4 days

QUICK MIX CARROT, NUT, AND RAISIN CAKE

2	cups firmly packed grated carrots
1 1/2	cups all-purpose flour
1 1/4	cups firmly packed brown sugar
1 1/4	cups sour cream
1	cup raisins, coarsely chopped
3	large eggs, lightly beaten
3/4	cup coarsely chopped pecans
4	tablespoons butter, melted
1	tablespoon pumpkin-pie spice
1	teaspoon baking powder
1	teaspoon baking soda
1/4	teaspoon salt

Preheat the oven to 325°F. • Lightly butter a 13 x 9-inch baking pan. • Place the carrots, flour, brown sugar, sour cream, raisins, eggs, pecans, butter, pumpkin pie spice, baking powder, baking soda, and salt in a large bowl. Beat with a wooden spoon until well blended and smooth. • Spoon the batter into the prepared pan. • Bake for 60–70 minutes, or until a toothpick inserted into the center comes out clean. • Cool in the pan on a rack.

Makes one 13 x 9-inch cake · Prep: 15 min. · Cooking: 60–70 min. · Level: 1 · Keeps: 5 days

Sunflower carrot cake with orange cream cheese frosting

CARROT SPICE CAKE

1½ cups firmly packed grated carrots
1 cup raisins
1 cup granulated sugar
1 cup water
3 tablespoons butter
1 teaspoon ground cinnamon
1 teaspoon ground nutmeg
2 cups all-purpose flour
1½ teaspoons baking powder
½ teaspoon baking soda
¼ teaspoon salt
½ cup walnuts, chopped

Preheat oven to 325°F. • Butter a 13 x 9-inch baking pan. • Stir the carrot, raisins, sugar, water, butter, cinnamon, and nutmeg in a large saucepan over medium-low heat until the sugar has dissolved. Bring to a boil. Reduce the heat and simmer, uncovered, for 5 minutes. Remove from the heat and let cool to room temperature. • Sift the flour, baking powder, baking soda, and salt into a medium bowl. • Stir the dry ingredients into the carrots. Stir in the walnuts. • Spoon the batter into the prepared pan. • Bake for 30–40 minutes, or until a toothpick inserted into the center comes out clean. • Cool the cake completely in the pan on a rack.

Makes one 13 x 9-inch cake · Prep: 20 min. · Cooking: 30–40 min. · Level: 1 · Keeps: 3 days

SWISS CARROT CAKE

This Swiss classic is better served the day after it is baked. The carrots keep the cake moist as it gains flavor. The Fondant is a traditional part of the cake, but you may leave it out if you prefer.

1⅔ cups almonds, finely ground
½ cup cornstarch
2 teaspoons baking powder
½ teaspoon ground cinnamon
¼ teaspoon salt
⅛ teaspoon ground cloves
5 large eggs, separated
1¼ cups granulated sugar
2 tablespoons fresh lemon juice
3 tablespoons finely grated lemon zest
1½ cups firmly packed finely grated carrots
¼ cup kirsch

APRICOT GLAZE

½ cup apricot preserves
1 cup Fondant (see pages 348–9)

Preheat the oven to 350°F. • Butter and flour a 10-inch springform pan. • Stir together the almonds, cornstarch, baking powder, cinnamon, salt, and cloves in a large bowl. • Beat the egg yolks, sugar, and lemon juice and zest in a large bowl with an electric mixer at high speed until pale and thick. • With mixer at low speed, gradually beat in the carrots and dry ingredients, alternating with the kirsch. • With mixer at high speed, beat the egg whites in a large bowl until stiff peaks form. Use a rubber spatula to fold them into the mixture. • Spoon the batter into the prepared pan • Bake for 50–60 minutes, or until a toothpick inserted into the center comes out clean. • Cool the cake in the pan for 15 minutes. Loosen the sides and let cool on a rack. • Warm the apricot preserves in a small saucepan over low heat until runny. Pour over the cake while still warm. • Prepare the Fondant to the soft-ball stage. Pour over the center of the cake and, working quickly, spread with a thin metal spatula to cover the cake.

Makes one 10-inch cake · Prep: 40 min. · Cooking: 50–60 min. · Level: 2 · Keeps: 3–4 days

CARROT CAKE WITH GINGER CREAM CHEESE FROSTING

2½ cups all-purpose flour
2 teaspoons baking powder
1 teaspoon ground cinnamon
½ teaspoon baking soda
¼ teaspoon salt
1 cup vegetable oil
1⅓ cups firmly packed brown sugar
3 large eggs, at room temperature
3 cups firmly packed coarsely grated carrots
1 cup walnuts, coarsely chopped

GINGER CREAM CHEESE FROSTING

3 tablespoons butter, softened
1 package (3 oz) cream cheese, softened
1 tablespoon ground ginger
1½ cups confectioners' sugar
2 tablespoons coarsely chopped crystalized ginger

Preheat the oven to 350°F. • Butter a 13 x 9-inch baking pan. Line with waxed paper. Butter the paper. • Sift the flour, baking powder, cinnamon, baking soda, and salt into a medium bowl. • Beat the oil, brown sugar, and eggs in a large bowl with an electric mixer at medium speed until creamy. • With mixer at low speed, beat in the carrots and walnuts. Gradually beat in the dry ingredients. • Spoon the batter into the prepared pan. • Bake for 50–60 minutes, or until a toothpick inserted into the center comes out clean. • Cool the cake in the pan for 10 minutes. Turn out onto a rack. Carefully remove the paper and let cool completely. • *Ginger Cream Cheese Frosting*: With mixer at medium speed, beat the butter, cream cheese, and ground ginger in a large bowl. • With mixer at low speed, beat in the confectioners' sugar until smooth and fluffy. • Spread the top and sides of the cake with the frosting. Sprinkle the crystalized ginger over the top.

Makes one 13 x 9-inch cake · Prep: 20 min. · Cooking: 50–60 min. · Level: 1 · Keeps: 2 days

LOW-FAT CARROT CAKE

This cake becomes more moist and full-flavored the day after it is baked.

1½ cups all purpose flour
1½ teaspoons ground cinnamon
1 teaspoon baking powder
½ teaspoon baking soda
¼ teaspoon nutmeg
¼ teaspoon salt
½ cup firmly packed brown sugar
1 large egg, at room temperature
2 tablespoons extra-virgin olive oil
2 teaspoons vanilla extract
¼ cup plain nonfat yogurt
1½ cups firmly packed grated carrots
1 can (8 oz) crushed pineapple in its own juice, drained
2 tablespoons confectioners' sugar, to dust

Preheat the oven to 350°F. • Butter and flour a 9-inch square baking pan. • Sift the flour, cinnamon, baking powder, baking soda, nutmeg, and salt into a large bowl. • Beat the brown sugar, egg, oil, and vanilla in a large bowl with an electric mixer at medium speed until well blended. • Gradually beat in the dry ingredients, alternating with the yogurt. Stir in the carrots and pineapple. • Spoon the batter into the prepared pan. • Bake for 35–45 minutes, or until the edges are brown and a toothpick inserted into the center comes out clean. • Cool the cake completely in the pan on a rack. • Dust with the confectioners' sugar.

Makes one 9-inch cake · Prep: 35 min. · Cooking: 35–45 min. · Level: 1 · Keeps: 2–3 days

FROSTED ZUCCHINI RING

1½ cups all-purpose flour
1 teaspoon baking powder
1 teaspoon ground cinnamon
1 teaspoon ground ginger
½ teaspoon baking soda
¼ teaspoon salt
½ cup (1 stick) butter, softened
¾ cup granulated sugar
2 teaspoons vanilla extract
3 large eggs, at room temperature
1¼ cups grated zucchini
½ cup raisins
1 cup Vanilla Frosting (see page 347)
⅓ cup water
¾ cup (1½ sticks) butter, softened
2 teaspoons vanilla extract

Preheat the oven to 350°F. • Butter and flour a 9-inch ring pan. • Sift the flour, baking powder, cinnamon, ginger, baking soda, and salt into a medium bowl. • Beat the butter, sugar, and vanilla in a large bowl with an electric mixer at medium speed until creamy. • Add the eggs, one at a time, until just blended after each addition. • With mixer at low speed, gradually beat in the dry ingredients. Stir in the zucchini and raisins. • Spoon the batter into the prepared pan. • Bake for 35–45 minutes, or until golden brown and a toothpick inserted into the center comes out clean. • Cool the cake in the pan for 15 minutes. Turn out onto a rack to cool completely. • Spread the cake with the frosting.

Makes one 9-inch cake · Prep: 25 min. · Cooking: 35–45 min. · Level: 1 · Keeps: 2–3 days

FRUITY FROSTED ZUCCHINI AND APRICOT CAKE

1 cup all-purpose flour
½ cup whole-wheat flour
1 teaspoon baking powder
1 teaspoon baking soda
¼ teaspoon salt
½ cup (1 stick) butter, softened
¾ cup firmly packed brown sugar
1 tablespoon grated lemon zest
1 teaspoon lemon extract
2 large eggs, at room temperature
1½ cups coarsely grated zucchini
¼ cup dried apricots, finely chopped
¼ cup milk

FRUITY FROSTING

½ cup dried apricots, finely chopped
¾ cup water
1 package (8 oz) cream cheese, softened
1 cup confectioners' sugar
2 tablespoons fresh lemon or lime juice

Frosted zucchini ring

Preheat the oven to 350°F. • Butter a 9-inch square baking pan. Line with waxed paper. Butter the paper. • Sift the flours, baking powder, baking soda, and salt into a medium bowl. • Beat the butter, brown sugar, lemon zest, and lemon extract in a large bowl with an electric mixer at medium speed until creamy. • Add the eggs, one at a time, until just blended after each addition. • With mixer at low speed, beat in the zucchini, apricots, and dry ingredients, alternating with the milk. • Spoon the batter into the prepared pan. • Bake for 40–50 minutes, or until golden brown and a toothpick inserted into the center comes out clean. • Cool the cake in the pan for 10 minutes. Turn out onto a rack. Carefully remove the paper and let cool completely. • *Fruity Frosting*: Bring the apricots and water to a boil in a small saucepan over medium heat. Reduce the heat and simmer until the apricots are soft. Set aside to cool. • Beat the cream cheese, confectioners' sugar, and lemon juice in a large bowl. Stir in the apricot mixture. • Spread the cake with the frosting.

Makes one 9-inch cake · Prep: 25 min. · Cooking: 40–50 min. · Level: 1 · Keeps: 2–3 days

CHOCO-ORANGE ZUCCHINI CAKE

1½ cups all-purpose flour
⅓ cup unsweetened cocoa powder
1 teaspoon baking powder
¼ teaspoon salt

½ cup (1 stick) butter, softened
1¼ cups granulated sugar
1 tablespoon grated orange zest
3 large eggs, at room temperature
1 cup coarsely grated zucchini
¼ cup milk

CHOCOLATE-ORANGE FROSTING

2 cups confectioners' sugar
¼ cup unsweetened cocoa powder
2 tablespoons butter, melted
1 tablespoon grated orange zest
2 tablespoons fresh orange juice

Preheat the oven to 350°F. • Butter a 9-inch square baking pan. Line with waxed paper. • Sift the flour, cocoa, baking powder, and salt into a medium bowl. • Beat the butter, sugar, and orange zest in a large bowl with an electric mixer at medium speed until creamy • Add the eggs, one at a time, until just blended after each addition. • With mixer at low speed, gradually beat in the zucchini and dry ingredients, alternating with the milk. • Spoon the batter into the prepared pan. • Bake for 35–45 minutes, or until a toothpick inserted into the center comes out clean. • Cool the cake in the pan for 10 minutes. Turn out onto a rack. Carefully remove the paper and let cool completely. • *Frosting*: Beat the confectioners' sugar, cocoa, butter, and orange zest and juice in a large bowl. • Spread the frosting over the cake.

Makes one 9-inch cake · Prep: 20 min. · Cooking: 35–45 min. · Level: 1 · Keeps: 2–3 days

Crunchy nutty toppings, liqueur-soaked fruit, and subtle spices make these cakes irresistible to the mature palate. Or, feel free to vary the nuts and fruits used to create your specialty cakes.

DRIED FRUIT & NUT CAKES

ALMOND LOAF

1	cup all-purpose flour
1½	teaspoons baking powder
¼	teaspoon salt
⅔	cup almonds, finely chopped
¼	cup (½ stick) butter, softened
1	cup granulated sugar
1	teaspoon almond extract
3	large eggs, at room temperature

Preheat the oven to 350°F. • Butter and flour an 8½ x 4½-inch loaf pan. • Sift the flour, baking powder, and salt into a medium bowl. Stir in the almonds. • Beat the butter, sugar, and almond extract in a medium bowl with an electric mixer at medium speed until creamy. • Add the eggs, one at a time, until just blended after each addition. • With mixer at low speed, gradually beat in the dry ingredients. • Spoon the batter into the prepared pan. • Bake for 40–50 minutes, or until a toothpick inserted into the center comes out clean. • Cool the loaf in the pan for 10 minutes. Turn out onto a rack to cool completely.

Makes one 8½ x 4½-inch loaf · Prep: 15 min. · Cooking: 40–50 min. · Level: 1 · Keeps: 4–5 days

◄ Dundee cake (see page 150)

➤ Almond loaf

ALMONDS, PISTACHIOS, ETC.

Preparing nuts in your own kitchen can give a cake a whole new flavor. Freshly roasted nuts will give your cake a richness and decadence that store-prepared nuts can only imitate. Grinding and blanching nuts are simple processes that can make a difference in the final result.

Blanching and Skinning

1 Bring enough water to a boil to cover the nuts. Place the nuts in a large bowl and pour the water over. Stand 5 minutes.

Grinding

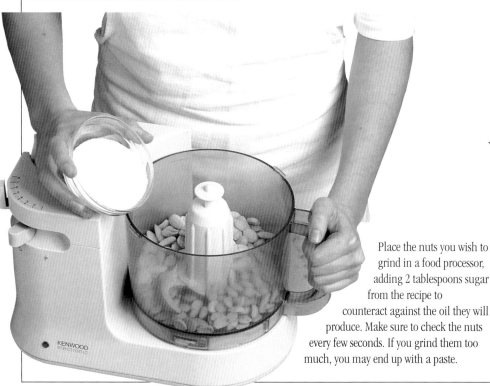

Place the nuts you wish to grind in a food processor, adding 2 tablespoons sugar from the recipe to counteract against the oil they will produce. Make sure to check the nuts every few seconds. If you grind them too much, you may end up with a paste.

2 Use a slotted spoon to scoop the nuts out of the water and place on a kitchen towel.

Toasting Almonds

Sprinkle the nuts onto a large baking sheet. Toast in a preheated 325°F oven for 7 minutes, or until lightly golden.

3 Fold the kitchen towel over and gently rub the nuts to remove the skins. Pick out the skins and use the nuts as desired.

COCONUT CAKE SUPREME

A perfect cake for St. Patrick's Day! Do not make the frosting ahead of time as it will become too hard to spread.

- 1½ cups all-purpose flour
- 1½ teaspoons baking powder
- ¼ teaspoon salt
- ¾ cup shredded coconut
- ½ cup (1 stick) butter, softened
- 1 cup granulated sugar
- 1 teaspoon coconut extract
- 2 large eggs, at room temperature
- 1 cup sour cream
- ⅓ cup milk

FROSTING

- liquid egg white equivalent to equal 2 large egg whites
- 2 cups confectioners' sugar
- 1½ cups shredded coconut
- green food coloring (optional)

Preheat the oven to 350°F. • Butter and flour a 9-inch springform pan. • Sift the flour, baking powder, and salt into a medium bowl. Stir in the coconut.• Beat the butter, sugar, and coconut extract in a large bowl with an electric mixer at medium speed until creamy.• Add the eggs, one at a time, until just blended after each addition. • With mixer at low speed, gradually beat in the dry ingredients, alternating with the sour cream and milk. • Spoon the batter into the prepared pan. • Bake for 45–55 minutes, or until a toothpick inserted into the center comes out clean. • Cool the cake in the pan for 10 minutes. Loosen and remove the pan sides and let cool completely. • *Frosting*: Beat the egg whites in a medium bowl until soft peaks form. Add in the confectioners' sugar and coconut. If desired, tint with the coloring to make a shade between pale pistachio and vivid green. • Spread the top and sides with the frosting.

Makes one 9-inch cake · Prep: 20 min. · Cooking: 45–55 min. · Level: 1 · Keeps: 5 days

COCONUT AND LIME SYRUP CAKE

- ½ cup (1 stick) butter, softened
- 1 cup granulated sugar
- 4 large eggs, at room temperature
- 1 teaspoon baking powder
- ¼ teaspoon salt
- 2 cups shredded coconut
- 1 cup all-purpose flour

LIME SYRUP

- 1 cup granulated sugar
- ⅓ cup water
- ⅓ cup fresh lime juice

Preheat the oven to 325°F. • Butter and flour a 10-inch tube pan. • Beat the butter and sugar in a large bowl with an electric mixer at medium speed until creamy.• Add the eggs, one at a time, until just blended after each addition. Beat in the baking powder and salt. • With mixer at low speed, gradually beat in the coconut and flour. • Spoon the batter into the prepared pan. • Bake for 40–50 minutes, or until a toothpick inserted into the center comes out clean. • Cool the cake in the pan for 10 minutes. Turn out onto a rack to cool. • *Lime Syrup*: Stir the sugar, water, and lime juice in a small saucepan over medium heat until the sugar has dissolved. Bring to a boil, without stirring, for 3 minutes. • Place the cake on the rack on a jelly-roll pan. Poke holes all over the cake. Pour the syrup over the top. Scoop any syrup from the pan and drizzle over the cake.

Makes one 10-inch cake · Prep: 20 min. · Cooking: 40–50 min. · Level: 1 · Keeps: 3 days

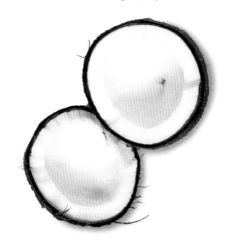

DRIED APRICOT COCONUT CAKE

- 1 cup dried apricots, chopped
- 1 cup canned apricots, chopped (reserve the juice)
- ½ cup (1 stick) butter, softened
- ¾ cup firmly packed brown sugar
- 2 large eggs, separated
- 2 teaspoons baking powder
- ¼ teaspoon salt
- 1½ cups shredded coconut
- 1½ cups all-purpose flour
- 3 tablespoons confectioners' sugar, to dust

Preheat the oven to 350°F. • Butter a 13 x 9-inch baking pan. • Mix all the apricots and juice in a small bowl. Set aside for 1 hour. • Beat the butter and brown sugar in a large bowl with an electric mixer at medium speed until creamy.• Add the egg yolks, one at a

time, until just blended after each addition. Beat in the baking powder and salt. With mixer at low speed, gradually beat in the coconut, flour, and the apricot mixture. • With mixer at high speed, beat the egg whites in a medium bowl until stiff peaks form. Use a large rubber spatula to fold the beaten whites into the batter. • Spoon the batter into the prepared pan. • Bake for 45–55 minutes, or until a toothpick inserted into the center comes out clean. • Cool the cake completely in the pan on a rack. • Dust with the confectioners' sugar.

Makes one 13 x 9-inch cake · Prep: 15 min. + 1 hr. to soak · Cooking: 45–55 min. · Level: 1 · Keeps: 5 days

COCONUT CREAM CAKE

- 1 cup (2 sticks) butter, softened
- 1½ cups granulated sugar
- 2 teaspoons vanilla extract
- 5 large eggs, separated
- 2 teaspoons baking powder
- ¼ teaspoon salt
- 2 cups all-purpose flour
- 1 cup buttermilk
- 1½ cups shredded coconut
- 1 cup macadamia nuts, coarsely chopped

FROSTING

- 1½ cups confectioners' sugar
- 1½ cups shredded coconut
- ¼ cup (½ stick) butter, melted

Preheat the oven to 350°F. • Butter a 10-inch springform pan. • Beat the butter, sugar and vanilla in a large bowl with an electric mixer at medium speed until creamy.• Add the egg yolks, one at a time, until just blended after each addition. Beat in the baking powder and salt. • With mixer at low speed, gradually beat in the flour, alternating with the buttermilk. Stir in the coconut and nuts. • With mixer at high speed, beat the egg whites in a large bowl until stiff peaks form. Use a large rubber spatula to fold the beaten whites into the batter. • Spoon the batter into the prepared pan. • Bake for 60–70 minutes, or until golden brown and a toothpick inserted into the center comes out clean. • Cool the cake in the pan for 10 minutes. Loosen and remove the pan sides and let cool completely. • *Frosting*: Beat the confectioners' sugar, coconut, and butter in a small bowl. • Spread the top and sides of the cake with the frosting.

Makes one 10-inch cake · Prep: 30 min. · Cooking: 60–70 min. · Level: 1 · Keeps: 2 days

TOASTED COCONUT CAKE WITH CARAMEL FROSTING

- 3/4 cup shredded coconut
- 1/2 cup (1 stick) butter, softened
- 3/4 cup firmly packed brown sugar
- 2 large eggs, at room temperature
- 2 tablespoons honey
- 1 1/2 teaspoons baking powder
- 1/4 teaspoon salt
- 1 1/2 cups all-purpose flour
- 1/4 cup milk

CARAMEL FROSTING

- 1/4 cup (1/2 stick) butter
- 1/2 cup firmly packed brown sugar
- 1 1/2 cups confectioners' sugar
- 2 tablespoons milk
- 2 tablespoons shredded coconut, to sprinkle

Preheat the oven to 350°F. • Butter a 9-inch square baking pan. • Toast the coconut in a skillet over medium heat, stirring often, until light golden. Set aside to cool. • Beat the butter and brown sugar in a large bowl with an electric mixer at medium speed until creamy.• Add the eggs, one at a time, until just blended after each addition. Beat in the honey, baking powder, and salt. • With mixer at low speed, gradually beat in the toasted coconut and flour, alternating with the milk. • Spoon the batter into the prepared pan. • Bake for 35–40 minutes, or until a toothpick inserted into the center comes out clean. • Cool the cake completely in the pan on a rack. • *Caramel Frosting*: Melt the butter in a medium saucepan over low heat. Add the brown sugar and cook, stirring constantly, for 3 minutes. Remove from the heat and gradually stir in the confectioners' sugar and milk. • Spread the top of the cake with the frosting and sprinkle with the coconut.

Makes one 9-inch square cake · Prep: 20 min. · Cooking: 35–40 min. · Level: 1 · Keeps: 2 days

MIXED NUT CAKE

Don't worry if you don't have all the different types of nuts on hand. Just use a combined total of 1 cup of the nuts you have in the pantry.

- 1/2 cup (1 stick) butter, softened
- 1 1/4 cups granulated sugar
- 2 tablespoons grated lemon zest
- 3 large eggs, at room temperature
- 1 1/2 cups all-purpose flour
- 1 teaspoon baking powder
- 1/2 teaspoon baking soda
- 1/4 teaspoon salt
- 1/2 cup milk
- 1/4 cup walnuts, finely chopped
- 1/4 cup almonds, finely chopped
- 1/4 cup hazelnuts, finely chopped
- 1/4 cup pistachios, finely chopped
- 1 tablespoon fresh lemon juice

NUT TOPPING

- 2 tablespoons walnuts, coarsely chopped
- 2 tablespoons slivered almonds
- 2 tablespoons pistachios, coarsely chopped
- 2 tablespoons hazelnuts, coarsely chopped
- 2 tablespoons granulated sugar

Preheat the oven to 350°F. • Butter a 9-inch square baking pan. • Beat the butter, sugar, and lemon zest in a large bowl with an electric mixer at medium speed until creamy.• Add the eggs, one at a time, until just blended after each addition.• With mixer at low speed, gradually beat in the flour, baking powder, baking soda, and salt, alternating with the milk. Stir in the nuts and lemon juice. • Spoon the batter into the prepared pan. • *Nut Topping*: Sprinkle the coarsely chopped nuts and the sugar over the batter. • Bake for 50–60 minutes, or until a toothpick inserted into the center comes out clean. • Cool the cake completely in the pan on a rack.

Makes one 9-inch cake · Prep: 25 min. · Cooking: 50–60 min. · Level: 1 · Keeps: 5–6 days

DARK CHOCOLATE ALMOND CAKE

- 5 oz bittersweet chocolate, coarsely chopped
- 2 large eggs, separated + 2 large egg yolks
- 3/4 cup granulated sugar
- 2 teaspoons baking powder
- 1/4 teaspoon salt
- 1 cup all-purpose flour
- 1/2 cup (1 stick) butter, melted
- 1/3 cup kirsch
- 1/3 cup almonds, coarsely chopped

Preheat the oven to 350°F. • Butter a 9-inch springform pan. Sprinkle the pan with cocoa. • Melt the chocolate in a double boiler over barely simmering water. Set aside to cool. • Beat the 4 egg yolks and sugar in a medium bowl with an electric mixer at high speed until pale and thick. • Beat in the baking powder and salt. • With mixer at low speed, beat in the chocolate. Gradually beat in the flour, alternating with the butter and kirsch. Stir in the almonds. • With mixer at high speed, beat the egg whites in a medium bowl until stiff peaks form. Use a large rubber spatula to fold them into the batter. • Spoon the batter into the prepared pan. • Bake for 40–45 minutes, or until a toothpick inserted into the center comes out clean. • Cool the cake in the pan for 10 minutes. Loosen and remove the pan sides and let cool completely on a rack.

Makes one 9-inch cake · Prep: 20 min. · Cooking: 40–45 min. · Level: 1 · Keeps: 2–3 days

Dark chocolate almond cake

MOCHA ALMOND CAKE

- 1/3 cup unsweetened cocoa powder
- 2 teaspoons freeze-dried coffee granules
- 1/2 cup boiling water
- 1/3 cup butter, softened
- 1 cup granulated sugar
- 1 teaspoon vanilla extract
- 2 large eggs, separated
- 1/2 cup sour cream
- 1/2 cup almonds, finely ground
- 1 cup all-purpose flour
- 1 teaspoon baking powder
- 1/4 teaspoon salt

MOCHA FROSTING

- 2 tablespoons freeze-dried coffee granules
- 2–3 tablespoons boiling water
- 2 cups confectioners' sugar
- 1/4 cup (1/2 stick) butter, softened
- 2 tablespoons unsweetened cocoa powder
- 12 walnut halves

Crumbly almond cake

Preheat the oven to 350°F. • Butter a 9-inch square baking pan. Line with waxed paper. • Dissolve the cocoa and coffee in the boiling water. • Beat the butter, sugar, and vanilla in a large bowl with an electric mixer at medium speed until creamy.• Beat in the egg yolks and sour cream. • With mixer at low speed, gradually beat in the almonds, flour, baking powder and salt, alternating with the cocoa mixture. • With mixer at high speed, beat the egg whites in a medium bowl until stiff peaks form. Use a large rubber spatula to fold them into the batter. • Spoon the batter into the prepared pan. • Bake for 40–50 minutes, or until a toothpick inserted into the center comes out clean. • Cool the cake in the pan for 5 minutes. Turn out onto a rack. Carefully remove the paper and let cool completely. • *Mocha Frosting*: Dissolve the coffee in 2 tablespoons of the boiling water in a large bowl. Beat in the confectioners' sugar, butter, and cocoa. Add enough of the remaining boiling water to make a thick, spreadable frosting. • Spread the top and sides of the cake with the frosting and decorate with the walnut halves.

Makes one 9-inch square cake · Prep: 20 min. · Cooking: 40–50 min. · Level: 1 · Keeps: 3 days

LEMON AND ALMOND TORTE

- 1/2 cup all-purpose flour
- 1 teaspoon baking powder
- 1/4 teaspoon salt
- 1 cup ground almonds
- 1/2 cup semolina flour or fine cornmeal
- 1/2 cup (1 stick) butter, softened
- 1/2 cup granulated sugar
- 2 tablespoons grated lemon zest
- 2 large eggs, at room temperature
- 1/4 cup fresh lemon juice

SYRUP

- 1/2 cup granulated sugar
- 1/2 cup fresh lemon juice
- 1/4 cup water
- 2 tablespoons brandy

Preheat the oven to 350°F. • Butter and flour a 10-inch round cake pan. • Sift the flour, baking powder, and salt into a medium bowl. Stir in the ground almonds and semolina. • Beat the butter, sugar, and lemon zest in a large bowl with an electric mixer at medium speed until creamy.• Add the eggs, one at a time, until just blended after each addition. • With mixer at low speed, gradually beat in the dry ingredients, alternating with the lemon juice. • Spoon the batter into the prepared pan. • Bake for 35–45 minutes, or until a toothpick inserted into the center comes out clean. • Cool the cake in the pan for 10 minutes. Turn out onto a rack. • *Syrup*: Stir the sugar, lemon juice, and water in a small saucepan over medium-low heat until the sugar has dissolved. Bring to a boil and reduce the heat. Simmer, without stirring, for 5 minutes. Remove from the heat and stir in the brandy. • Place the cake on the rack on a jelly-roll pan. Poke holes in the cake with a skewer. Pour the syrup over the top. Scoop any syrup from the pan and drizzle on the cake.

Makes one 10-inch round cake · Prep: 20 min. · Cooking: 35–45 min. · Level: 1 · Keeps: 3 days

CRUMBLY ALMOND CAKE

- 2 cups all-purpose flour
- 1 cup granulated sugar
- 1/4 teaspoon salt
- 2 cups almonds, finely ground
- 3/4 cup (1 1/2 sticks) cold butter, cut up
- 4 large eggs, lightly beaten

Preheat the oven to 350°F. • Butter and flour a 10-inch springform pan. • Sift the flour, sugar, and salt in a large bowl. Stir in the almonds. • Use your fingers to rub the butter and eggs into the dry ingredients, until the dough resembles large crumbs. • Transfer the dough to the prepared pan, pressing it down gently. • Bake for 35–45 minutes, or until a toothpick inserted into the center comes out clean. • Cool the cake in the pan for 10 minutes. Loosen the pan sides and let cool completely. • Serve broken into irregular diamond shapes.

Makes one 10-inch cake · Prep: 30 min. · Cooking: 35–45 min. · Level: 1 · Keeps: 3–4 days

Almond-topped cake

ALMOND-TOPPED CAKE

- 1/2 cup (1 stick) butter, softened
- 1 cup granulated sugar
- 1 teaspoon vanilla extract
- 2 large eggs, at room temperature
- 2 cups all-purpose flour
- 1 tablespoon baking powder
- 1/4 teaspoon salt
- 3/4 cup milk

ALMOND TOPPING

- 1/3 cup butter, cut up
- 1/3 cup granulated sugar
- 3/4 cup flaked almonds
- 3 tablespoons milk

Preheat the oven to 350°F. • Butter and flour a 9-inch springform pan. • Beat the butter, sugar, and vanilla in a large bowl with an electric mixer at medium speed until creamy.• Add the eggs, one at a time, until just blended after each addition.• With mixer at low speed, gradually beat in the flour, baking powder, and salt, alternating with the milk. • Spoon the batter into the prepared pan. • Bake for 40 minutes. • *Almond Topping*: Stir the butter, sugar, and almonds in a medium skillet over low heat until the butter has melted. • After the cake has baked for 40 minutes, spread with the topping. Brush with the milk• Bake for 10–15 minutes more, or until the topping is lightly browned. • Cool the cake in the pan for 10 minutes. Loosen and remove the pan sides. Place the cake on a rack to cool completely.

Makes one 9-inch cake · Prep: 30 min. · Cooking: 50–55 min. · Level: 1 · Keeps: 1–2 days

ALMOND AND GINGER TORTE

- 1 cup all-purpose flour
- 1 cup finely ground almonds
- 1 1/2 teaspoons baking powder
- 2 teaspoons ground ginger
- 1/2 teaspoon baking soda
- 1/4 teaspoon salt
- 1 cup (2 sticks) butter, softened
- 1 cup granulated sugar
- 1/2 teaspoon almond extract
- 4 large eggs, at room temperature
- 1/4 cup chopped candied ginger
- 1/3 cup milk
- 3/4 cup Lemon Glaze (see page 348) (optional)

Preheat the oven to 350°F. • Butter and flour an 11 x 7-inch baking pan. Line with waxed paper. Butter and flour the paper. • Sift the flour, almonds, baking powder, ground ginger, baking soda, and salt into a large bowl. • Beat the butter, sugar, and almond extract in a large bowl with an electric mixer at medium speed until creamy. • Add the eggs, one at a time, until just blended after each addition. • With mixer at low speed, gradually beat in the dry ingredients and chopped ginger, alternating with the milk. • Spoon the batter into the prepared pan. • Bake for 40–50 minutes, or until the cake shrinks from the pan sides and a toothpick inserted into the center comes out clean. • Cool the cake completely in the pan on a rack.

Makes one 11 x 7-inch cake · Prep: 30 min. · Cooking: 40–50 min. · Level: 1 · Keeps: 3–4 days

PRALINE BUNDT CAKE

PRALINE

- 1 1/4 cups granulated sugar
- 1 2/3 cups whole unblanched almonds, toasted

- 2 tablespoons granulated sugar
- 3 large eggs, separated
- 1/3 cup butter, melted
- 1 cup all-purpose flour
- 1/2 teaspoon baking powder
- 1/4 teaspoon salt

Praline: Line a jelly-roll pan with parchment paper. • Cook the sugar in a small saucepan over low heat until liquid and light gold. Pour into the pan and set aside to cool. • Process the cooled sugar mixture and almonds in a food processor until finely chopped. • Preheat the oven to 350°F. • Butter and flour a 9-inch Bundt pan. Sprinkle with the sugar. • Beat the egg yolks in a large bowl until pale and thick. • With mixer at low speed, beat in the butter, flour, baking powder, and salt. With mixer at medium speed, beat the egg whites in a large bowl until stiff peaks form. Use a large rubber spatula to fold them into the batter. • Stir in the chopped praline. • Spoon the batter into the prepared pan. • Bake for 30–40 minutes, or until a toothpick inserted into the center comes out clean. • Cool the cake in the pan for 15 minutes. Turn out onto a rack to cool completely.

Makes one 9-inch cake · Prep: 20 min. · Cooking: 30–40 min. · Level: 1 · Keeps: 2–3 days

BRAZIL-NUT CAKE

This cake has a delicious, crunchy exterior and a nutty texture and flavor. It will keep in an airtight cake container for up to 2 months.

- 1   lb brazil nuts, coarsely chopped
- 1   lb pitted prunes, coarsely chopped
- 1   cup halved candied cherries
- 3/4   cup all-purpose flour
- 3/4   cup granulated sugar
- 1/2   teaspoon baking powder
- 1/2   teaspoon salt
- 3   large eggs, at room temperature
- 1   tablespoon dry sherry

Preheat the oven to 350°F. • Butter a 9 x 5-inch loaf pan. Line with aluminum foil, letting the edges overhang. Butter the foil. • Place the brazil nuts, prunes, and cherries in a large bowl. • Stir in the flour, sugar, baking powder, and salt. • Beat the eggs and sherry in a medium bowl. Stir the egg mixture into the fruit mixture. • Spoon the batter into the prepared pan. • Bake for 70–80 minutes, or until dark brown and a toothpick inserted into the center comes out clean. • Cool the cake in the pan for 1 hour. Turn out onto a rack. Carefully remove the foil and let cool completely. • Store the cake well-wrapped.

Makes one 9 x 5-inch cake · Prep: 20 min. · Cooking: 70–80 min. · Level: 1 · Keeps: 1–2 months

BUCKWHEAT ALMOND CAKE

- 1   cup (2 sticks) butter, softened
- 1 1/4   cups granulated sugar
- 6   large eggs, separated
- 2   cups finely ground almonds
- 1 1/2   cups buckwheat flour
- 1/4   teaspoon salt
- 1   teaspoon vanilla extract
- 1 3/4   cups red currant jelly, warmed
- 1/4   cup confectioners' sugar, to dust

Preheat the oven to 350°F. • Butter a 9-inch round cake pan. Line with waxed paper. • Beat the butter and sugar in a large bowl with an electric mixer at medium speed until creamy.• Add the egg yolks, one at a time, until just blended after each addition. • With mixer at low speed, gradually add the almonds, buckwheat flour, salt, and vanilla. • With mixer at high speed, beat the egg whites in a large bowl until stiff. Use a large rubber spatula to fold the beaten whites into the batter. • Spoon the batter into the prepared pan. • Bake for 50–60 minutes, or until a toothpick inserted into the center

Buckwheat almond cake

comes out clean. • Cool the cake in the pan for 15 minutes. Turn out onto a rack. Carefully remove the paper and let cool completely. • Split the cake horizontally. Place a cake layer on a serving plate. Spread with the jelly. Top with the remaining cake layer. • Dust with the confectioners' sugar.

Makes one 9-inch cake · Prep: 25 min. · Cooking: 50–60 min. · Level: 1 · Keeps: 2–3 days

STREUSEL NUT CAKE

Make sure your springform pan is 3 inches deep.

STREUSEL
- 1/2   cup firmly packed brown sugar
- 2   tablespoons all-purpose flour
- 2   teaspoons ground cinnamon
- 1   cup pecans, coarsely chopped
- 1/4   cup (1/2 stick) butter, melted

- 2   cups all-purpose flour
- 1   teaspoon baking powder
- 1   teaspoon baking soda
- 1/4   teaspoon salt
- 1/2   cup (1 stick) butter, softened
- 1   cup firmly packed brown sugar
- 1   teaspoon butterscotch or rum extract

- 3   large eggs, at room temperature
- 1   cup milk

Preheat the oven to 350°F. • Butter and flour a 9-inch springform pan. • *Streusel*: Stir the brown sugar, flour, and cinnamon in a small bowl. Stir in the pecans and butter. • Sift the flour, baking powder, baking soda, and salt into a large bowl. • Beat the butter, brown sugar, and butterscotch extract in a large bowl with an electric mixer at medium speed until creamy.• Add the eggs, one at a time, until just blended after each addition. • With mixer at low speed, gradually beat in the dry ingredients, alternating with the milk. • Spoon the batter into the prepared pan. Sprinkle with the streusel. • Bake for 55–60 minutes, or until a toothpick inserted into the center comes out clean. • Cool the cake in the pan for 15 minutes. Loosen and remove the pan sides and let cool completely. Transfer the cake to the rack top-side up.

Makes one 9-inch cake · Prep: 25 min. · Cooking: 55–60 min. · Level: 1 · Keeps: 1–2 days

Hazelnut cake

HAZELNUT CAKE

Potato starch, sometimes referred to as potato flour, can be found in health food stores.

1 cup all-purpose flour
1 cup potato starch
2 teaspoons baking powder
1/4 teaspoon salt
1 1/4 cups hazelnuts, finely ground
3 large eggs, at room temperature
1 cup granulated sugar
1/2 cup (1 stick) + 2 tablespoons butter, softened
3 tablespoons rum

Preheat the oven to 350°F • Butter and flour a 9-inch springform pan. • Sift the flour, potato starch, baking powder, and salt into a medium bowl. Stir in the hazelnuts. • Beat the eggs and sugar in a large bowl with an electric mixer at high speed until pale and thick. • With mixer at medium speed, gradually beat in the butter. • With mixer at low speed, gradually add the dry ingredients and rum. • Spoon the batter into the prepared pan. • Bake for 35–40 minutes, or until a toothpick inserted into the center comes out clean. • Cool the cake in the pan for 10 minutes. Loosen and remove the pan sides and let cool completely.

Makes one 9-inch cake · Prep: 15 min. · Cooking: 35-40 min.. · Level: 1 · Keeps: 3–4 days

HAZELNUT CAKE WITH FRESH FIGS

1 cup all-purpose flour
1 teaspoon baking powder
1/2 teaspoon baking soda
1/4 teaspoon salt
scant 1 1/4 cups hazelnuts
1/2 cup (1 stick) butter, softened
3/4 cup granulated sugar
1 teaspoon vanilla extract
2 large eggs + 2 large egg yolks
8 ripe figs, green, cut in half, and stems removed

Preheat the oven to 350°F. • Butter and flour a 9-inch springform pan. • Finely chop half the hazelnuts in a food processor. Coarsely chop the remaining nuts in the food processor. • Sift the flour, baking powder, baking soda, and salt in a large bowl. Stir in the finely chopped hazelnuts. • Beat the butter, sugar, and vanilla in a large bowl with an electric mixer at medium speed until creamy. • Add the eggs and egg yolks, one at a time, until just blended after each addition. • With mixer at low speed, gradually beat in the dry ingredients. • Spoon the batter into the prepared pan. Sprinkle with the coarsely chopped nuts and arrange the figs on top, cut-side up, pressing them into the batter. • Bake for 50–60 minutes, or until a toothpick inserted into the center comes out clean. • Cool the cake in the pan for 10 minutes. Loosen and remove the pan sides. Turn out onto a rack and let cool completely.

Makes one 9-inch cake · Prep: 20 min. · Cooking 50–60 min. · Level: 1 · Keeps: 1–2 days

HAZELNUT CRUMBLE WITH RICOTTA FIG FILLING

1/2 cup (1 stick) butter, softened
1/3 cup firmly packed dark brown sugar
1 large egg
2 cups all-purpose flour
1/2 cup ground hazelnuts
1 teaspoon baking powder
1/4 teaspoon salt

RICOTTA FIG FILLING

1 2/3 cups ricotta cheese
1/2 cup superfine sugar
1/2 cup hazelnuts, finely chopped
2 tablespoons milk
1/4 cup dried figs, finely chopped

Butter a 13 x 9-inch baking pan. • Preheat the oven to 350°F. • Process the butter, brown sugar, egg, flour, hazelnuts, baking powder, and salt in a food processor until the mixture resembles fine crumbs. • Spoon half the mixture into the prepared pan, pressing it down with the back of a spoon. • *Ricotta Fig Filling*: Mix the ricotta, superfine sugar, hazelnuts, milk, and figs in a medium bowl until well blended. • Spoon the filling over. Sprinkle with the remaining crumble. • Bake for 45–50 minutes, or until light golden brown.

Makes one 12 x 8-inch cake · Prep: 15 min. · Cooking: 45–50 min. · Level: 1 · Keeps: 3–4 days

HUNGARIAN HAZELNUT TORTE

This torte has a light, nutty texture and exceptional flavor. To cut cleanly, use a sharp knife that's been dipped in hot water and wiped off.

8 oz semisweet chocolate, coarsely chopped
1 3/4 cups hazelnuts, finely ground
3/4 cup granulated sugar
3/4 cup dry white wine, such as Chablis or Chardonnay
1 tablespoon fine dry bread crumbs
6 large eggs, separated
1/4 teaspoon salt

TOPPING

1 cup heavy cream
1 tablespoon granulated sugar
1 teaspoon vanilla extract
whole hazelnuts, to decorate

Preheat the oven to 325°F. • Butter and flour a 13 x 9-inch baking pan. • Stir the chocolate, hazelnuts, sugar, wine, and bread crumbs in a large saucepan over medium-low heat until the chocolate is melted. Set aside to cool. • Beat the egg whites and salt in a large bowl with an electric mixer at high speed until stiff peaks form. • With mixer at medium speed, beat the egg yolks in a large bowl until pale. Use a large rubber spatula to fold the yolks into the chocolate mixture. • Fold in the beaten whites. • Spoon the batter into the prepared pan. • Bake for 45–55 minutes, or until a toothpick inserted into the center comes out clean. • Cool the cake completely in the pan on a rack. • *Topping*: With mixer at high speed, beat the cream, sugar, and vanilla in a medium bowl until stiff. Spread the top of the cake with the cream and decorate with the hazelnuts.

Makes one 13 x 9-inch cake · Prep: 25 min. · Cooking: 45–55 min. · Level: 1 · Keeps: 1–2 days

NUTTY CARAMEL CRUNCH

BASE

2¼ cups graham cracker crumbs
¾ cup (1½ sticks) butter, melted

CARAMEL TOPPING

⅓ cup butter, melted
1 cup sweetened condensed milk
¼ cup light corn syrup
½ cup firmly packed dark brown sugar
8 oz semisweet chocolate, coarsely chopped
¾ cup mixed nuts, finely chopped

Butter a 13 x 9-inch baking pan. • Stir together the crumbs and butter in a large bowl until well blended. Spread the mixture into the prepared pan and smooth the top. Refrigerate for at least 3 hours, or until firm. • *Caramel Topping*: Bring the butter, condensed milk, corn syrup, and brown

Hazelnut and vanilla ice cream cake

sugar to a boil in a medium saucepan over low heat. Cook, stirring constantly, until the mixture has thickened. Remove from the heat and stir in the chocolate. • Use a thin metal spatula to spread the topping over the prepared base. Sprinkle with the nuts. · Set aside to cool completely. • Refrigerate for 6 hours. • Cut into squares to serve.

Makes one 13 x 9-inch cake · Prep: 20 min. + 9 hr. to chill · Level: 1 · Keeps: 3–4 days

HAZELNUT AND VANILLA ICE CREAM CAKE

½ cup all-purpose flour
⅓ cup cornstarch
⅓ cup unsweetened cocoa powder
3 large eggs
½ cup granulated sugar
3 tablespoons butter, melted
½ teaspoon vanilla extract
chocolate leaves (or other shapes) (see page 55), to decorate

HAZELNUT ICE CREAM

4 large egg yolks
¾ cup granulated sugar
2 cups milk
1 cup toasted hazelnuts, finely ground
1 pint vanilla ice cream

Preheat the oven to 375°F. • Butter a 9-inch springform pan. • Sift the flour, cornstarch, and cocoa into a medium bowl. • Beat the eggs and sugar in a large bowl with an electric mixer at high

speed until pale and thick. • With mixer at low speed, gradually beat in the dry ingredients, alternating with the butter and vanilla. • Spoon the batter into the prepared pan. • Bake for 30–35 minutes, or until the cake is lightly browned and springy to the touch. • Cool the cake in the pan for 5 minutes. Loosen and remove the pan sides. Invert the cake onto a rack to cool completely. • *Hazelnut Ice Cream*: Beat the egg yolks, sugar, and 2 tablespoons milk in a double boiler until well blended. Stir in the remaining milk. Cook over low heat, stirring constantly, until the mixture lightly coats a metal spoon or registers 160°F on an instant-read thermometer. Immediately plunge the pan into a bowl of ice water and stir until the egg mixture has cooled. • Strain the mixture into a bowl and stir in the hazelnuts. • Pour the mixture into an ice-cream maker and follow the directions to finish the ice cream. • Trim the edges of the cake and place in an 8-inch springform pan. Cover with the hazelnut ice cream and place in the freezer until firm, about 1 hour. • Spread a layer of the vanilla ice cream and return to the freezer for at least 2 hours. • Decorate with the chocolate leaves.

Makes one 8-inch cake · Prep: 1 hr. + 3 hr. to freeze · Cooking: 30–35 min. · Level: 2 · Keeps: 1–2 days in the freezer

Pistachio cake

PISTACHIO CAKE

Slices of this unusual cake, which contains neither flour nor butter, are a beautiful green color.

1 1/2 cups pistachios
1 cup granulated sugar
3 large eggs, separated
2 tablespoons grated lemon zest
1 teaspoon baking powder
1/2 teaspoon baking soda
1/4 teaspoon salt

Preheat the oven to 350°F. • Butter a 9-inch springform pan. • Plunge the pistachios into a saucepan of boiling water for 30 seconds. Drain. Rub dry with a clean kitchen towel, then carefully peel off the inner skins. • Place the pistachios and sugar in a food processor and chop finely. • Transfer to a large bowl and stir in the egg yolks, lemon zest, baking powder, baking soda, and salt. • Beat the egg whites in a medium bowl with an electric mixer at high speed until stiff peaks form. Use a large rubber spatula to fold them into the batter. • Spoon the batter into the prepared pan. • Bake for 25–35

minutes, or until a toothpick inserted into the center comes out clean. • Cool the cake in the pan for 10 minutes. Loosen and remove the pan sides and let the cake cool completely on a rack.

Makes one 9-inch cake · Prep: 30 min. · Cooking: 25–35 min. · Level: 1 · Keeps: 3–4 days

OVERNIGHT PECAN CAKE

Prepare the batter for this delicious cake the night before. Cover the bowl with a clean kitchen towel and leave at cool room temperature overnight. Pop it into the oven the next morning while you make the coffee and breakfast is served!

2 cups all-purpose flour
2 teaspoons baking powder
1 teaspoon ground cinnamon
1/4 teaspoon salt
3/4 cup (1 1/2 sticks) butter, softened
1 cup firmly packed brown sugar
2 large eggs, at room temperature
1 cup sour cream
1/2 cup raisins

TOPPING
3/4 cup firmly packed brown sugar
3/4 cup pecans, chopped
1 teaspoon ground cinnamon
1 teaspoon ground allspice

Preheat the oven to 350°F. • Butter a 9-inch square baking pan. • Sift the flour, baking powder, cinnamon, and salt into a medium bowl. • Beat the butter and brown sugar in a large bowl with an electric mixer at medium speed until creamy.• Add the eggs, one at a time, until just blended after each addition. • With mixer at low speed, gradually beat in the dry ingredients, alternating with the sour cream. • Stir in the raisins. • Spoon the batter into the prepared pan. • *Topping*: Mix the brown sugar, pecans, cinnamon, and allspice in a small bowl. Sprinkle over the cake. • Bake for 35–45 minutes, or until a toothpick inserted into the center comes out clean. • Cool the cake in the pan on a rack. Serve warm.

Makes one 9-inch cake · Prep: 20 min. · Cooking: 35–45 min. · Level: 1 · Keeps: 2–3 days

BRANDIED PECAN CAKE WITH ORANGE SYRUP

2 cups pecans, toasted and cooled
1/2 cup (1 stick) butter, softened
1 tablespoon grated orange zest
1 cup granulated sugar
1 large egg, at room temperature
1 teaspoon baking powder
1/4 teaspoon salt
2/3 cup all-purpose flour
2 tablespoons brandy

ORANGE SYRUP
1/4 cup fresh orange juice
1/4 cup granulated sugar

Preheat the oven to 325°F. • Butter a 9-inch square baking pan. • Process the nuts in a food processor until finely ground. • Beat the butter, orange zest, sugar, and egg in a large bowl with an electric mixer at medium speed until creamy. • With mixer at low speed, beat in the flour, baking powder, salt, brandy, and ground pecans. • Spoon the batter into the prepared pan. • Bake for 50–60 minutes, or until a toothpick inserted into the center comes out clean. • *Orange Syrup*: Stir the orange juice and sugar in a small saucepan over medium heat until the sugar has dissolved. Bring to a boil and boil for 1 minute. • Pour the hot syrup over the cake in the pan. • Place the pan on a rack and let cool completely.

Makes one 9-inch cake · Prep: 20 min. · Cooking: 50–60 min. · Level: 1 · Keeps: 2 days

PECAN APPLESAUCE CAKE

- 2¹/₂ cups all-purpose flour
- 2 teaspoons baking powder
- 2 teaspoons ground cinnamon
- 1 teaspoon ground ginger
- ¹/₂ teaspoon salt
- 2 cups granulated sugar
- 1¹/₂ cups vegetable oil
- 1 cup applesauce
- 4 large eggs, separated
- 2 tablespoons hot water
- 1 cup pecans, chopped
- ¹/₃ cup confectioners' sugar, to dust

Preheat the oven to 350°F. • Butter and flour a 10-inch tube pan. • Sift the flour, baking powder, cinnamon, ginger, and salt into a large bowl. • Beat the sugar, oil, applesauce, egg yolks, and hot water in a large bowl with an electric mixer at medium speed until well blended. • With mixer at low speed, gradually beat in the dry ingredients. Stir in the pecans. • With mixer at high speed, beat the egg whites in a large bowl until stiff peaks form. Use a large rubber spatula to fold them into the batter. • Spoon the batter into the prepared pan. • Bake for 70–75 minutes, or until golden, the cake shrinks from the pan sides, and a toothpick inserted into the center comes out clean. • Cool the cake completely in the pan. Turn out onto a rack and dust with the confectioners' sugar.

Makes one 10-inch cake · Prep: 20 min. · Cooking: 70–75 min. · Level: 1 · Keeps: 2–3 days

PECAN FRUIT CAKE

- 2 cups firmly packed brown sugar
- 2 cups water
- 1¹/₂ cups dried figs, chopped
- 1¹/₂ cups raisins
- 1 cup (2 sticks) butter, cut up
- ¹/₂ cup dried apricots, chopped
- ¹/₂ cup currants
- 3 large eggs, lightly beaten
- 1 cup pecans, chopped
- 3 cups whole-wheat flour
- 1 cup toasted wheat germ
- 1 teaspoon baking powder
- 1 teaspoon baking soda
- ¹/₄ teaspoon salt

Stir the brown sugar, water, figs, raisins, butter, apricots, and currants in a saucepan over medium-low heat until the sugar has dissolved. Bring to a boil, reduce the heat to low, and simmer for 3 minutes, stirring constantly. • Set aside to cool for 1 hour. • Preheat the oven to 325°F. • Butter a 13 x 9-

Pine nut cake

inch baking pan. Line with waxed paper. • Stir the eggs, pecans, flour, wheat germ, baking powder, baking soda, and salt into the fruit mixture. • Spoon the batter into the prepared pan. • Bake for 1 hour and 40–45 minutes, or until golden brown, the cake shrinks from the pan sides, and a toothpick inserted into the center comes out clean. • Cool the cake completely in the pan. Turn out onto a rack. Carefully remove the paper.

Makes one 13 x 9-inch cake · Prep: 20 min. + 1 hr. to cool · Cooking: 1 hr. 40–45 min. · Level: 1 · Keeps: 2 weeks

PINE NUT CAKE

- 1¹/₃ cups all-purpose flour
- 1¹/₂ teaspoons baking powder
- ¹/₄ teaspoon salt
- 3 large eggs
- ³/₄ cup granulated sugar
- 1 teaspoon vanilla extract
- ²/₃ cup butter, melted
- 2 tablespoons brandy
- 1 cup pine nuts

Preheat the oven to 350°F. • Butter a 9-inch springform pan. • Sift the flour, baking powder, and salt into a medium bowl. • Beat the eggs, sugar, and vanilla in a large bowl with an electric mixer at high speed until pale and thick. • With mixer at low speed, gradually beat in the dry ingredients, alternating with the butter and brandy. Stir in the pine nuts. Spoon the batter into the prepared pan. • Bake for 35–40 minutes, or until a toothpick inserted into the center comes out clean. • Cool the cake in the pan for 10 minutes. Loosen and remove the pan sides and let cool completely.

Makes one 9-inch cake · Prep: 15 min. · Cooking: 35–40 min. · Level: 1 · Keeps: 3–4 days

bowl with an electric mixer at high speed until pale and thick. Gradually beat in the sugar. • With mixer at low speed, gradually beat in the dry ingredients, alternating with the melted butter. Stir in the walnuts. • Spoon the batter into the prepared pan. • Bake for 35–45 minutes, or until a toothpick inserted into the center comes out clean. • Cool the cake in the pan for 5 minutes. Turn out onto a rack. • *Sugar Syrup*: Stir the sugar and water in a small saucepan over low heat until the sugar has dissolved. Bring to a boil and simmer for 5 minutes. • Place the cake on the rack on a jelly-roll pan. Poke holes in the cake with a skewer. Pour the syrup over the top. Scoop any syrup from the pan and drizzle on the cake.

Makes one 10-inch cake · Prep: 20 min. · Cooking: 35–45 min. · Level: 1 · Keeps: 2–3 days

HUNGARIAN WALNUT TORTE

- 1 cup walnut halves + 8–10 halves, to decorate
- 1/2 cup granulated sugar
- 3 large eggs, separated
- 1/4 teaspoon salt

CHOCOLATE RUM FILLING
- 1/3 cup butter, softened
- 1/2 cup confectioners' sugar
- 1/3 cup unsweetened cocoa powder
- 2 tablespoons rum

MOCHA FROSTING
- 4 oz bittersweet chocolate, coarsely chopped
- 2–3 tablespoons very strong lukewarm coffee

Preheat the oven to 375°F. • Butter and flour an 8-inch springform pan. • Finely grind 1 cup walnuts in a food processor with 2 tablespoons granulated sugar. • Beat the egg yolks and remaining sugar in a medium bowl with an electric mixer at high speed until pale and thick. • With mixer at medium speed, gradually beat in the ground walnut mixture. • Beat the egg whites with the salt in a medium bowl with mixer at high speed until stiff peaks form. Use a large rubber spatula to fold them into the batter. • Spoon the batter into the prepared pan. • Bake for 25–35 minutes, or until springy to the touch and a toothpick inserted into the center comes out clean. • Cool the cake in the pan on a rack for 10 minutes, then loosen and remove the sides and invert onto the rack to cool completely. • *Chocolate Rum Filling*: Beat the butter and confectioners' sugar in

Hungarian walnut torte

CINNAMON-WALNUT BREAKFAST CAKE

TOPPING
- 1/2 cup walnuts, coarsely chopped
- 1/4 cup firmly packed brown sugar
- 1 teaspoon ground cinnamon

CAKE
- 2 cups all-purpose flour
- 1 teaspoon baking powder
- 1 teaspoon baking soda
- 1/4 teaspoon salt
- 1/2 cup (1 stick) butter, softened
- 1 cup granulated sugar
- 1 teaspoon vanilla extract
- 2 large eggs, at room temperature
- 1 cup buttermilk

Preheat the oven to 350°F. • Butter and flour a 10-inch tube pan. • *Topping*: Mix the ingredients in a small bowl and sprinkle into the prepared pan. • *Cake*: Sift the flour, baking powder, baking soda, and salt into a large bowl. • Beat the butter, sugar, and vanilla in a medium bowl with an electric mixer at medium speed until creamy. • Add the eggs, one at a time, until just blended

after each addition. • With mixer at low speed, gradually beat in the dry ingredients, alternating with the buttermilk. • Spoon the batter into the prepared pan. • Bake for 45–55 minutes, or until a toothpick inserted into the center comes out clean. • Cool the cake in the pan for 15 minutes. Turn out onto a rack and let cool completely.

Makes one 10-inch cake · Prep: 15 min. · Cooking: 45–55 min. · Level: 1 · Keeps: 3–4 days

CINNAMON-WALNUT SYRUP CAKE

- 1 cup whole-wheat flour
- 1 teaspoon baking powder
- 1 tablespoon ground cinnamon
- 1/4 teaspoon salt
- 3 large eggs, at room temperature
- 3/4 cup granulated sugar
- 2/3 cup butter, melted
- 1 cup walnuts, coarsely chopped

SUGAR SYRUP
- 1 cup granulated sugar
- 3/4 cup water

Preheat the oven to 350°F. • Butter a 10-inch round cake pan. • Sift the whole-wheat flour, baking powder, cinnamon, and salt into a medium bowl. • Beat the eggs in a large

a small bowl with mixer at medium speed until creamy. • With mixer at low speed, gradually add the cocoa and rum. • *Mocha Frosting*: Melt the chocolate with the coffee in a double boiler over barely simmering water. With a whisk, beat until smooth. Set aside to cool. • Split the cake horizontally and place one layer on a serving plate. Spread with the filling. Top with the second layer and spread with the frosting. • Decorate with the walnut halves.

Makes one 8-inch cake · Prep: 35 min. · Cooking: 25–35 min. · Level: 2 · Keeps: 1–2 days

PRUNE AND WALNUT CAKE

This cake is moist and rich the day it is baked. On days two and three, you may wish to warm it briefly in the oven and then spread the slices with a little butter before serving.

1 cup firmly packed brown sugar
1 cup pitted prunes, coarsely chopped
1 cup milk
³/₄ cup (1¹/₂ sticks) cold butter, cut up
¹/₂ cup walnuts, coarsely chopped
¹/₂ teaspoon baking soda
2 large eggs, lightly beaten
2 cups all-purpose flour
2 teaspoons baking powder
¹/₄ teaspoon salt

Preheat the oven to 350°F. • Butter a 9-inch springform pan. • Stir the brown sugar, prunes, milk, butter, and walnuts in a large saucepan over low heat. Bring to a boil and remove from the heat. • Stir in the baking soda and set aside for 10 minutes. • Beat in the eggs, flour, baking powder, and salt. • Spoon the batter into the prepared pan. • Bake for 45–55 minutes, or until a toothpick inserted into the center comes out clean. • Cool the cake in the pan for 15 minutes. Loosen and remove the pan sides and let cool completely.

Makes one 9-inch cake · Prep: 15 min. · Cooking: 45–55 min. · Level: 1 · Keeps: 2–3 days

DATE AND WALNUT LOAF

2 large eggs, separated
¹/₄ teaspoon salt
¹/₂ cup (1 stick) butter, softened
¹/₂ cup granulated sugar
2 teaspoons baking powder
1 cup all-purpose flour
¹/₄ cup + 2 tablespoons milk
2–3 tablespoons rum or brandy
1 cup pitted dates, chopped
³/₄ cup walnuts, finely chopped

Date and walnut loaf

Preheat the oven to 350°F. • Butter and flour an 8¹/₂ x 4¹/₂-inch loaf pan. • Beat the egg yolks, butter, and sugar in a large bowl with an electric mixer at high speed until pale and thick. • With mixer at low speed, gradually beat in the flour and baking powder, alternating with the milk and brandy. Stir in the dates and walnuts. With mixer at high speed, beat the egg whites and salt until stiff peaks form. • Use a large rubber spatula to fold them into the batter. • Spoon the batter into the prepared pan. • Bake for 35–45 minutes, or until a toothpick inserted into the center comes out clean. • Cool the loaf in the pan for 10 minutes. Turn out onto a rack to cool completely.

Makes one 8¹/₂ x 4¹/₂–inch loaf · Prep: 15 min. · Cooking: 35–45 min. · Level: 1 · Keeps: 3–4 days

LEMON AND WALNUT COFFEE CAKE

1¹/₂ cups all-purpose flour
¹/₃ cup firmly packed brown sugar
¹/₃ cup granulated sugar
³/₄ teaspoon baking powder
¹/₄ teaspoon baking soda
¹/₄ teaspoon salt
¹/₂ cup (1 stick) cold butter, cut up
1 cup walnuts, finely chopped
2 large eggs, at room temperature
¹/₂ cup buttermilk
1 tablespoon grated lemon zest
1 teaspoon lemon extract

Preheat the oven to 350°F. • Butter a 9-inch square baking pan. • Stir together the flour, brown sugar, granulated sugar, baking powder, baking soda, and salt in a large bowl. Use a pastry blender to cut in the butter until the mixture resembles coarse crumbs. Stir in the walnuts. • Set aside ¹/₂ cup of the mixture. • Beat the eggs, buttermilk, and lemon zest, and lemon extract in a medium bowl until well blended. • Stir the egg mixture into the dry ingredients. • Spoon the batter into the prepared pan. Sprinkle with the reserved crumb mixture. • Bake for 30–40 minutes, or until golden, and a toothpick inserted into the center comes out clean. • Cool the cake completely in the pan on a rack.

Makes one 9-inch cake · Prep: 15 min. · Cooking: 30–40 min. · Level: 1 · Keeps: 3–4 days

RAISIN CAKE
WITH WALNUT CRUNCH

WALNUT CRUNCH
- 2/3 cup all-purpose flour
- 1/3 cup firmly packed brown sugar
- 1/3 cup cold butter, cut up
- 1 cup walnuts, coarsely chopped

RAISIN CAKE
- 1 1/4 cups all-purpose flour
- 1 teaspoon baking powder
- 1/2 teaspoon baking soda
- 1/4 teaspoon salt
- 1/3 cup butter, softened
- 3/4 cup firmly packed brown sugar
- 2 tablespoons honey
- 1 teaspoon vanilla extract
- 2 large eggs, at room temperature
- 1 cup raisins
- 1/4 cup milk

Raisin-nut loaf

Walnut Crunch: Stir the flour and brown sugar in a medium bowl. Use a pastry blender to cut in the butter until the mixture resembles coarse crumbs. Stir in the walnuts. • *Raisin Cake*: Preheat the oven to 350°F. • Butter and flour a 9-inch tube pan. • Sift the flour, baking powder, baking soda, and salt into a medium bowl. • Beat the butter, brown sugar, honey, and vanilla in a large bowl with an electric mixer at medium speed until creamy.• Add the eggs, one at a time, until just blended after each addition. • With mixer at low speed, gradually beat in the raisins and dry ingredients, alternating with the milk. • Spoon the batter into the prepared pan. • Sprinkle the Walnut Crunch over the batter. • Bake for 40–50 minutes, or until a toothpick inserted into the center comes out clean. • Cool the cake in the pan for 15 minutes. Turn out onto a rack. Invert topside up and let cool completely.

Makes one 9-inch cake · Prep: 25 min. · Cooking: 40–50 min. · Level: 1 · Keeps: 2 days

RAISIN-NUT LOAF

- 3/4 cup raisins
- 1 1/2 cups warm water
- 1 1/2 cups all-purpose flour
- 1/2 cup granulated sugar
- 1 1/2 teaspoons baking powder
- 1/4 teaspoon salt
- 1/2 cup milk
- 1 large egg, lightly beaten
- 1/4 cup (1/2 stick) butter, melted
- 3/4 cup hazelnuts, finely chopped
- 1/2 cup almonds, finely chopped
- 1/4 cup mixed nuts, coarsely chopped, to decorate

Plump the raisins in the water in a small bowl for 30 minutes. Drain well and pat dry with paper towels. • Preheat the oven to 350°F. • Butter an 8 1/2 x 4 1/2-inch loaf pan. Line with aluminum foil, letting the edges overhang. Butter the foil. • Sift the flour, sugar, baking powder, and salt into a large bowl. • Beat in the milk, egg, and butter. Stir in the hazelnuts, almonds, and raisins. • Spoon the batter into the prepared pan. • Bake for 40–50 minutes, or until a toothpick inserted into the center comes out clean. • Cool the loaf in the pan on a rack for 10 minutes. Using the foil as a lifter, remove the loaf from the pan. Carefully remove the foil and let cool completely. Decorate with the chopped nuts.

Makes one 8 1/2 x 4 1/2-inch loaf · Prep: 15 min. + 30 min. to soak · Cooking: 40–50 min. · Level: 1 · Keeps: 4–5 days

RUM-RAISIN LOAF

Slice this delectable loaf thinly.

- 1 1/2 cups all-purpose flour
- 2 teaspoons baking powder
- 1/4 teaspoon salt
- 3/4 cup (1 1/2 sticks) butter, cut up
- 1/2 cup firmly packed brown sugar
- 1 cup raisins
- 2 tablespoons dark rum
- 1/2 teaspoon vanilla extract
- 3 large eggs, lightly beaten
- 2 tablespoons milk

Preheat the oven to 350°F. • Butter and flour a 9 x 5-inch loaf pan. • Sift the flour, baking powder, and salt into a large bowl. •

Melt the butter and brown sugar in a medium saucepan over low heat until the sugar has dissolved. • Remove from the heat and stir in the raisins, rum, and vanilla. • Stir the raisin mixture, eggs, and milk into the dry ingredients. • Spoon the batter into the prepared pan. • Bake for 35–40 minutes, or until a toothpick inserted into the center comes out clean. • Cool the loaf in the pan for 10 minutes. Turn out onto a rack to cool completely.

Makes one 9 x 5-inch loaf · Prep: 15 min. · Cooking: 35–40 min. · Level: 1 · Keeps: 3 days

CHERRY AND RAISIN LOAF

- 1/2 cup (1 stick) butter, softened
- 1 cup granulated sugar
- 1/2 teaspoon vanilla extract
- 3 large eggs, at room temperature
- 1/2 cup sliced candied cherries
- 1/2 cup raisins
- 2 cups all-purpose flour
- 2 teaspoons baking powder
- 1/4 teaspoon salt
- 3/4 cup milk

Preheat the oven to 350°F. • Butter two 4 1/2 x 8 1/2-inch loaf pans. Line with aluminum foil, letting the edges overhang. Butter the foil. • Beat the butter, sugar, and vanilla in a large bowl with an electric mixer at medium speed until creamy. • Add the eggs, one at a time, until just blended after each addition. • With mixer at low speed, add the cherries and raisins. Gradually beat in the flour, baking powder, and salt, alternating with the milk. • Spoon the batter into the prepared pan. • Bake for 60–70 minutes, or until a toothpick inserted into the center comes out clean. • Cool the loaves in the pans for 5 minutes. Using the foil as a lifter, remove the loaves from the pans. Carefully remove the foil. Cool the loaves completely on racks.

Makes two 4¹/₂ x 8¹/₂-inch loaves · Prep: 15 min. · Cooking: 60–70 min. · Level: 1 · Keeps: 3 days

QUICK AND EASY RAISIN LOAF

Deliciously sweet and slightly sticky, this loaf topped with whipped cream makes a luscious dessert or teatime treat. The original recipe was made with sultanas, a type of dried grape larger than a raisin. Use them if they're available.

1   lb raisins or golden raisins (sultanas)
1   cup all-purpose flour
³/₄ cup firmly packed brown sugar
¹/₂ cup (1 stick) butter, melted
2   large eggs, lightly beaten
¹/₄ cup sweet sherry
2   tablespoons orange marmalade
1   teaspoon baking powder
¹/₄ teaspoon salt

Preheat the oven to 300°F. • Butter a 9 x 5-inch loaf pan. Line with waxed paper. • Beat the raisins, flour, brown sugar, butter, eggs, sherry, marmalade, baking powder, and salt in a large bowl with an electric mixer at low speed until well blended. • Spoon the batter into the prepared pan. • Bake for 75–85 minutes, or until a toothpick inserted into the center comes out clean. • Cool the cake in the pan for 15 minutes. Turn out onto a rack to cool completely.

Makes one 9 x 5-inch loaf · Prep: 10 min. · Cooking: 75–85 min. · Level: 1 · Keeps: 5–7 days

BRANDIED RAISIN CAKE

1   lb raisins
2   cups warm water
1³/₄ cups all-purpose flour
1   teaspoon baking powder
¹/₂   teaspoon baking soda
¹/₄   teaspoon salt
²/₃   cup butter, softened
²/₃   cup firmly packed brown sugar
3   large eggs, at room temperature
3   tablespoons brandy

Plump the raisins in the water in a large bowl for 30 minutes. Drain well and pat dry with paper towels. • Preheat the oven to 325°F. • Butter a 9-inch square baking pan. Line with waxed paper. Butter the paper. • Sift the flour, baking powder, baking soda, and salt into a medium bowl. • Beat the butter and brown sugar in a large bowl with an electric mixer at medium speed until creamy.• Add the eggs, one at a time, until just blended after each addition. • With mixer at low speed, gradually beat in the dry ingredients and raisins, alternating with the brandy. • Spoon the batter into the prepared pan. • Bake for 50–60 minutes, or until a toothpick inserted into the center comes out clean. • Cool the cake completely in the pan. Turn out onto a rack. Carefully remove the paper. Store well-wrapped in foil.

Makes one 9-inch square cake · Prep: 25 min. + 30 min. to soak · Cooking: 50–60 min. · Level: 1 · Keeps: 5–6 days

ITALIAN PLUM CAKE

The original recipe for this simple loaf comes from Italy, where it is known as a "Plum Cake."

³/₄   cup raisins
3   tablespoons rum
1   cup + 2 tablespoons all-purpose flour
3   large eggs, at room temperature
¹/₂   cup granulated sugar
1   teaspoon baking powder
¹/₄   teaspoon salt
²/₃   cup mixed candied fruit, chopped
¹/₃   cup butter, melted
3   tablespoons dry Marsala wine
2   tablespoons grated lemon zest

Plump the raisins in the rum in a small bowl for at least 30 minutes. Drain well and pat dry with paper towels. Sprinkle with the 2 tablespoons flour. • Preheat the oven to 350°F. • Butter an 8¹/₂ x 4¹/₂-inch loaf pan. Line with aluminum foil, letting the edges overhang. Butter the foil. • Beat the eggs and sugar in a large bowl with an electric mixer at high speed until pale and thick. • With mixer at low speed, gradually beat in the remaining flour, baking powder, salt, candied fruit, butter, Marsala, raisins and lemon zest. • Spoon the batter into the prepared pan. • Bake for 45–55 minutes, or until a toothpick inserted into the center comes out clean. • Cool the loaf completely in the pan. Turn out onto a rack. Carefully remove the foil before serving.

Makes one 8¹/₂ x 4¹/₂-inch loaf · Prep: 20 min. + 30 min. to soak · Cooking: 45–55 min. · Level: 1 · Keeps: 4–5 days

Italian plum cake

Italian lemon-raisin cake

ITALIAN LEMON-RAISIN CAKE

- 1/2   cup raisins
- 1   cup warm water
- 1 2/3   cups all-purpose flour
- 2   teaspoons baking powder
- 1/4   teaspoon salt
- 2   large eggs, at room temperature
- 2/3   cup granulated sugar
- 1/4   cup 2 tablespoons extra-virgin olive oil
- 2   tablespoons grated lemon zest
- 1/3   cup milk

Plump the raisins in the water in a small bowl for 30 minutes. Drain well and dry with paper towels. • Preheat the oven to 350°F. • Butter a 9-inch springform pan. • Sift the flour, baking powder, and salt into a large bowl. • Beat the eggs and sugar in a large bowl with an electric mixer at high speed until pale and thick. • With mixer at medium speed, beat in the oil and lemon zest. • With mixer at low speed, gradually beat in the dry ingredients, alternating with the milk. Stir in the raisins. • Spoon the batter into the prepared pan. • Bake for 35–45 minutes, or until a toothpick inserted into the center comes out clean. • Cool the cake in the pan for 10 minutes. Loosen and remove the pan sides and cool completely on a rack.

Makes one 9-inch cake · Prep: 20 min. + 30 min. to soak · Cooking: 35–45 min. · Level: 1 · Keeps: 3–4 days

HEALTHY BRAN LOAF

- 1 1/2   cups whole-wheat flour
- 2   teaspoons baking powder
- 1/4   teaspoon salt
- 1/2   cup wheat bran
- 1/2   cup (1 stick) butter, softened
- 3/4   cup firmly packed brown sugar
- 2   large eggs, at room temperature
- 1   cup mashed very ripe bananas
- 1   cup pitted dates, chopped
- 1/2   cup walnuts, chopped
- 1/4   cup milk

Preheat the oven to 350°F. • Butter and flour two 9 x 5-inch loaf pans. • Sift the whole-wheat flour, baking powder, and salt into a medium bowl. Stir in the bran. • Beat the butter and brown sugar in a large bowl with an electric mixer at medium speed until creamy. • Add the eggs, one at a time, until just blended after each addition. • With mixer at low speed, beat in the bananas, dates, and walnuts. Gradually beat in the dry ingredients, alternating with the milk. • Spoon the batter into the prepared pans. • Bake for 45–50 minutes, or until a toothpick inserted into the centers comes out clean. • Cool the loaves in the pans for 15 minutes. Turn out onto racks to cool completely.

Makes two 9 x 5-inch loaves · Prep: 20 min. · Cooking: 45–50 min. · Level: 1 · Keeps: 3 days

BRAN APRICOT LOAVES

Prepare the cereal mixture in the evening, then bake the loaves in the morning for a healthy and delicious breakfast.

- 1 1/2   cups wheat cereal
- 1 1/2   cups milk
- 1   cup firmly packed brown sugar
- 1   cup dried apricots, coarsely chopped
- 1/4   cup honey
- 2   cups all-purpose flour
- 1 1/2   teaspoons baking powder
- 1/2   teaspoon baking soda
- 1/4   teaspoon salt

Stir the cereal, milk, brown sugar, apricots, and honey in a large bowl until well blended. Cover and refrigerate for 12 hours, or overnight. • Preheat the oven to 350°F. • Butter two 9 x 5-inch loaf pans. Line with aluminum foil, letting the edges overhang. Butter the foil. • Sift the flour, baking powder, baking soda, and salt into the cereal mixture. • Spoon the batter into the prepared pans. • Bake for 55–65 minutes, or until a toothpick inserted into the center comes out clean. • Cool the loaves in the pans for 10 minutes. Using the foil as a lifter, remove the loaves from the pans. Carefully remove the foil and let cool completely on racks.

Makes two 9 x 5-inch loaves · Prep: 15 min. + 12 hr. to stand · Cooking: 55–65 min. · Level: 1 · Keeps: 3 days

TANGY FRUIT-FILLED CAKES

- 1 1/2   cups all-purpose flour
- 1/2   cup granulated sugar
- 1/2   cup (1 stick) butter, melted

TANGY FRUIT FILLING

- 1   cup dried apricots, finely chopped
- 1/2   cup dried apples, finely chopped
- 1   cup water
- 1/4   cup granulated sugar
- 1   tablespoon freshly grated lemon zest

TOPPING

- 2   large eggs
- 1/3   cup firmly packed dark brown sugar
- 1/2   cup all-purpose flour

Preheat the oven to 350°F. • Butter a 13 x 9-inch baking pan. • Stir together the flour and sugar in a large bowl. Beat in the butter until well blended. • Spoon the batter into the prepared pan. • Bake for 20–25 minutes, or until light golden brown. Cool in the pan on a rack to room temperature. • *Fruit Filling*: Bring the apricots, apples, and water to a boil in a large saucepan over low heat. Simmer, uncovered, for 10–12 minutes, or until mixture begins to thicken. Remove from the heat and stir in the granulated sugar and lemon zest. Set aside to cool. • *Topping*: Beat the eggs and sugar in a medium bowl with an electric mixer at high speed until pale and thick. Use a large rubber spatula to fold in the flour. • Use a thin metal spatula to spread the filling over the cake. Cover with the topping. • Bake for 30 minutes more, or until well browned. Cool completely in the pan on a rack. Cut into squares to serve.

Makes one 9 x 13-inch cake · Prep: 30 min. · Cooking: 50–55 min. · Level: 1 · Keeps: 2–3 days

WHISKY LOAF

  1 cup raisins
1¹/₂ cups warm water
  6 tablespoons Scotch whisky
  2 large eggs, separated
 ¹/₄ teaspoon salt
 ³/₄ cup all-purpose flour
 ²/₃ cup granulated sugar
  1 teaspoon baking powder
  1 teaspoon ground nutmeg
 ¹/₃ cup butter, melted
  1 cup walnuts, coarsely chopped

Plump the raisins in the water in a small bowl for 30 minutes. Drain well and pat dry with paper towels. Return to the bowl and drizzle with 3 tablespoons of whisky. • Preheat the oven to 350°F. • Butter and flour an 8¹/₂ x 4¹/₂-inch loaf pan. • Beat the egg whites and salt in a medium bowl with an electric mixer at high speed until stiff peaks form. • Sift the flour, sugar, baking powder, and nutmeg into a large bowl. • With mixer at low speed, gradually beat in the egg yolks, butter, and remaining whisky. Stir in the walnuts and raisins. • Use a large rubber spatula to fold the beaten whites into the batter. • Spoon the batter into the prepared pan. • Bake for 45–55 minutes, or until a toothpick inserted into the center comes out clean. • Cool the loaf in the pan for 15 minutes. Turn out onto a rack and let cool completely.

Makes one 8¹/₂ x 4¹/₂-inch loaf · Prep: 25 min. + 20 min. to soak · Cooking: 45–55 min. · Level: 1 · Keeps: 4–5 days

DRIED FIG AND MUESLI LOAF

Muesli is a breakfast cereal made from raw or toasted nuts usually with the addition of some combination of bran, dried fruit, dried milk, and sugar. If you don't have any on hand, substitute the same quantity of granola.

1¹/₂ cups water
  1 cup dried figs, coarsely chopped
 ¹/₂ cup (1 stick) cold butter, cut up
  1 cup firmly packed brown sugar
  2 large eggs, lightly beaten
1¹/₂ cups all-purpose flour
 ³/₄ cup toasted muesli or granola
1¹/₂ teaspoons baking powder
 ¹/₄ teaspoon salt

Preheat the oven to 350°F. • Butter two 9 x 5-inch loaf pans. Line with aluminum foil, letting the edges overhang. Butter the foil. • Bring the water to a boil in a medium saucepan over high heat. Add the figs, reduce the heat to low, and simmer, uncovered, for 10 minutes. • Stir in the butter and brown sugar until the butter is melted. • Set aside to cool. • Stir in the eggs, flour, muesli, baking powder, and salt. • Spoon the batter into the prepared pans. Bake for 45–55 minutes, or until a toothpick inserted into the centers comes out clean. • Cool the loaves in the pans for 10 minutes. Using the foil as a lifter, remove the loaves from the pans. Carefully remove the foil and let cool completely on racks.

Makes two 9 x 5-inch loaves · Prep: 30 min. · Cooking: 45–55 min. · Level: 1 · Keeps: 3 days

WHOLE-WHEAT FRUIT LOAF WITH CRUNCHY PEANUT TOPPING

1¹/₂ cups whole-wheat flour
1¹/₂ teaspoons baking powder
 ¹/₂ teaspoon baking soda
 ¹/₄ teaspoon salt
  1 cup toasted wheat germ
 ³/₄ cup firmly packed dark brown sugar
  1 cup pitted dates, chopped
1¹/₄ cups milk
 ¹/₂ cup (1 stick) butter, melted
  2 large eggs, lightly beaten
  1 cup very ripe mashed bananas
 ¹/₂ cup grated carrots
 ³/₄ cup unsalted roasted peanuts, chopped

Preheat the oven to 350°F. • Butter two 8¹/₂ x 4¹/₂-inch loaf pans. Line with aluminum foil, letting the edges overhang. Butter the foil. • Sift the flour, baking powder, baking soda, and salt in a large bowl. Stir in the wheat germ, brown sugar, and dates. • Beat in the milk, butter, eggs, bananas, and carrots with an electric mixer at low speed. • Spoon half the batter into each of the prepared pans. Sprinkle with the peanuts. • Bake for 45–55 minutes, or until golden brown and a toothpick inserted into the centers comes out clean. • Cool the loaves in the pans for 10 minutes. Using the foil as a lifter, remove the loaves from the pans. Carefully remove the foil and let cool completely on racks.

Makes two 8¹/₂ x 4¹/₂-inch loaves · Prep: 20 min. · Cooking: 45–55 min. · Level: 1 · Keeps: 2–3 days

Whisky loaf

Dried fig cake

DRIED FIG CAKE

This is a traditional recipe from the Marches region in central Italy. It is very rich and nourishing.

1½ lb dried figs
½ cup extra-virgin olive oil
⅔ cup whole-wheat flour
4 oz bittersweet chocolate, coarsely chopped
½ cup honey
⅔ cup toasted walnuts, coarsely chopped
½ cup toasted almonds, coarsely chopped
⅓ cup granulated sugar
½ cup golden or dark raisins
⅓ cup candied lemon peel
3 tablespoons finely grated orange zest
½ cup sweet dessert wine or port
1 teaspoon ground nutmeg
1 teaspoon ground cinnamon

Trim the tough bits off the ends of the figs and place them in a bowl with just enough warm water to cover. Soak overnight. • Drain the figs, rinse well, and place in a saucepan with enough water to cover. Cook gently over medium heat until tender, about 30 minutes. • Preheat the oven to 350°F. • Butter a 10-inch springform pan. • Drain the figs and pat dry with paper towels. Chop coarsely and place in a large bowl. • Stir in the oil, flour, chocolate, honey, walnuts, almonds, sugar, raisins, lemon peel, orange zest, wine, nutmeg, and cinnamon until well blended. • Spoon the batter into the prepared pan. • Bake for 55–65 minutes, or until dark golden brown. • Cool the cake completely in the pan on a rack. Loosen and remove the pan sides to serve.

Makes one 10-inch cake · Prep: 2 hr. + 12 hr. to soak · Level: 1 · Keeps: 1 week

BOILED APRICOT BRANDY CAKE

A rich, moist English-Style Christmas cake with a full flavor.

1 can (15 oz) apricots in syrup
5 cups mixed dried fruit, chopped
1¼ cups firmly packed brown sugar
1 cup (2 sticks) cold butter, cut up
¼ cup apricot preserves
6 tablespoons brandy
3 large eggs, lightly beaten
2 cups all-purpose flour
1 teaspoon baking soda
¼ teaspoon salt

Drain the apricots, reserving ½ cup of the syrup. • Chop the apricots coarsely. Mix the apricots and the reserved apricot syrup in a large saucepan with the dried fruit, sugar, butter, preserves, and ¼ cup brandy. Stir over low heat until the butter has melted and the sugar dissolved. Bring to a boil and simmer, covered, for 10 minutes. Set aside to cool. • Preheat the oven to 300°F. • Butter a 9-inch square cake pan. Line with waxed paper. • Stir the eggs, flour, baking soda, and salt into the fruit mixture. • Spoon the batter into the prepared pan. • Bake for 2–2¼ hours, or until a toothpick inserted into the center comes out clean. • Brush the cake with the remaining 2 tablespoons brandy. Cool the cake completely in the pan on a rack.

Makes one 9-inch cake · Prep: 30 min. · Cooking: 2–2¼ hr. · Level: 1 · Keeps: 10 days

APRICOT LAYER CAKE

½ cup candied apricots, finely chopped
¼ cup apricot liqueur
2½ cups all-purpose flour
2 teaspoons baking powder
½ teaspoon baking soda
¼ teaspoon salt
½ cup (1 stick) butter, softened
1½ cups granulated sugar
2 teaspoons vanilla extract
3 large eggs, separated
⅔ cup sour cream

APRICOT FROSTING

½ cup candied apricots, finely chopped
¼ cup apricot liqueur
1 package (8 oz) cream cheese, softened
1 cup sour cream
1 cup confectioners' sugar
½ cup toasted slivered almonds

Preheat the oven to 350°F. • Butter a 9-inch springform pan. Line with waxed paper. Butter the paper. • Soak the apricots in a small bowl with the apricot liqueur for 15 minutes. • Sift the flour, baking powder, baking soda, and salt into a large bowl. • Beat the butter, 1 cup sugar, and vanilla in a large bowl with an electric mixer at medium speed until creamy. • Add the egg yolks, one at a time, until just blended after each addition. • With mixer at low speed, beat in the dry ingredients, alternating with the apricot mixture and sour cream. • With mixer at medium speed, beat the egg whites in a large bowl until frothy. With mixer at high speed, gradually beat in the remaining sugar, beating until stiff, glossy peaks form. Use a large rubber spatula to fold them into the batter. • Spoon the batter into the prepared pan and smooth the top. • Bake for 45–55 minutes, or until a toothpick inserted into the center comes out clean. • Cool the cake in the pan for 10 minutes. Loosen and remove the pan sides. Turn out the cake onto a rack. Carefully remove the paper and let cool completely. • *Apricot Frosting*: Soak the apricots in a small bowl with the apricot liqueur for 15 minutes. • With mixer at medium speed, beat the cream cheese and sour cream in a medium bowl until smooth. Beat in the confectioners' sugar. Stir in the apricot mixture. • Split the cake into thirds horizontally. Place one layer on a serving plate. Spread with $^1/_4$ of the frosting. Top with a second cake layer. Spread with $^1/_4$ of the frosting and top with the remaining cake layer. Spread the top and sides of the cake with the remaining frosting. • Press the slivered almonds into the sides.

Makes one 9-inch cake · Prep: 35 min. · Cooking 45–55 min. · Level: 2 · Keeps: 2–3 days

DRIED FRUIT AND BREAD PUDDING CAKE

If you like, serve the pudding with Vanilla Custard (see page 344) spooned over.

12	large slices day-old bread
1	cup pitted prunes, coarsely chopped
$^3/_4$	cup raisins
$^1/_4$	cup dried apricots, coarsely chopped
$^1/_2$	cup almonds, chopped
3	cups milk
5	large eggs
$^3/_4$	cup granulated sugar
1	teaspoon vanilla extract

Preheat the oven to 350°F. • Butter two 5 x 9-inch loaf pans. • Line the pan bottoms with the bread slices, cutting the bread so that it fits snugly into the pan. • Mix the prunes, raisins, apricots, and almonds in a large bowl. Sprinkle the bread with $^1/_3$ of the dried fruit and nuts. Repeat until all the bread and fruit are in the pans. • Warm the milk in a saucepan over medium-low heat. • Beat the eggs, sugar, and vanilla in a small bowl. Pour into the

Dried fruit and bread pudding cake

milk and mix well. • Pour the milk mixture evenly into the pans. • Wrap each pan tightly with aluminum foil. • Fill a roasting pan $^1/_3$ full with cold water. Place the pans in the water. (The water should rise to about halfway up the pan sides). • Bake for 40–50 minutes, or until the egg and milk mixture has set. • Set on serving plates and serve warm.

Makes two 5 x 9-inch loaves · Prep: 30 min. · Cooking: 40–50 min. · Level: 1 · Keeps: 1–2 days

APRICOT DATE STREUSEL CAKE

$^1/_2$	cup (1 stick) butter, softened
1	cup granulated sugar
2	teaspoons vanilla extract
3	large eggs, at room temperature
2	cups all-purpose flour
2	teaspoons baking powder
$^1/_2$	teaspoon baking soda
$^2/_3$	cup sour cream
$^1/_2$	cup dried apricots, coarsely chopped
$^1/_2$	cup pitted dates, coarsely chopped

SPICE STREUSEL

$^1/_2$	cup firmly packed brown sugar
2	tablespoons cold butter, cut up
2	tablespoons all-purpose flour
1	teaspoon ground cinnamon
1	teaspoon ground nutmeg

Preheat the oven to 350°F. • Butter and flour a 10-inch tube pan. • Beat the butter, sugar, and vanilla in a large bowl with an electric mixer at medium speed until creamy.• Add the eggs, one at a time, until just blended after each addition. • With mixer at low speed, gradually beat in the flour, baking powder, and baking soda, alternating with the sour cream. • Stir in the apricots and dates. • Spoon the batter into the prepared pan. • *Spice Streusel*: Place the brown sugar, butter, flour, cinnamon, and nutmeg in a small bowl until crumbly. Sprinkle over the batter. • Bake for 45–55 minutes, or until a toothpick inserted into the center comes out clean. • Cool the cake in the pan for 10 minutes. Turn out onto a rack crumble-side up and let cool completely.

Makes one 10-inch cake · Prep: 20 min. · Cooking: 45–55 min. · Level: 1 · Keeps: 2–3 days

FRENCH HONEY CAKE

- 7 oz bittersweet chocolate, coarsely chopped
- 2²/₃ cups all-purpose flour
- 1 tablespoon ground cinnamon
- 1 tablespoon baking powder
- ¹/₂ teaspoon salt
- 1 cup superfine sugar
- 1¹/₂ cups honey
- 1 cup cold water
- 1¹/₂ cups almonds, coarsely chopped
- 1 cup raisins
- ³/₄ cup pine nuts
- ²/₃ cup candied orange peel, chopped + candied orange peel, cut in strips, to decorate (optional)

Preheat the oven to 350°F. • Butter and flour a 9-inch springform pan. • Melt the chocolate in a double boiler over barely simmering water until smooth. Set aside to cool. • Sift the flour, cinnamon, baking powder, and salt into a large bowl. • Place the sugar, honey, and water in a large saucepan over medium-low heat, stirring until the sugar has dissolved. • Remove from the heat and gradually stir in the dry ingredients. • Stir in the chocolate, almonds, raisins, pine nuts, and orange peel. • Spoon the batter into the prepared pan. • Bake for 55–65 minutes, or until a toothpick inserted into the center comes out clean. • Cool the cake in the pan for 15 minutes. Loosen and remove the pan sides. Invert the cake onto a rack. Loosen and remove the pan bottom and let cool completely. • Decorate with the orange peel.

Makes one 9-inch cake · Prep: 35 min. · Cooking: 55–65 min. · Level: 1 · Keeps: 4–5 days

ROLLED OAT AND DATE SLICE

This delicious slice looks and tastes like one big granola bar.

- 1²/₃ cups old-fashioned rolled oats
- 1¹/₂ cups cornflakes
- 1 cup shredded coconut
- 1 cup firmly packed brown sugar
- 1 cup pitted dates, coarsely chopped
- ¹/₄ teaspoon salt
- ¹/₂ cup (1 stick) butter, melted
- 2 tablespoons honey

Preheat the oven to 350°F. • Butter an 11 x 7-inch baking pan. • Stir together the oats, cornflakes, coconut, brown sugar, dates, and salt in a large bowl. • Stir in the butter and honey. • Spoon the batter into the prepared pan and press down gently, using the back of the spoon. • Bake for 25–35

French honey cake

minutes, or until lightly browned. • Cool the cake completely in the pan on a rack.

Makes one 11 x 7-inch cake · Prep: 10 min. · Cooking: 25–35 min. · Level: 1 · Keeps: 5 days

MOIST DATE CAKE

- ¹/₃ cup butter, softened
- 4 oz cream cheese, softened
- 1¹/₄ cups firmly packed brown sugar
- 3 large eggs, at room temperature
- 1 cup all-purpose flour
- 1 teaspoon baking powder
- ¹/₄ teaspoon salt
- ¹/₄ cup brandy
- 2 cups pitted dates, coarsely chopped
- ¹/₂ cup mixed candied fruit peel, chopped
- 2 tablespoons rum
- 3 tablespoons confectioners' sugar, to dust

Preheat the oven to 300°F. • Butter a 9-inch round cake pan. • Beat the butter, cream cheese, and brown sugar in a large bowl with an electric mixer at medium speed until smooth. • Add the eggs, one at a time, until just blended after each addition. • With mixer at low speed, gradually beat in the flour, baking powder, and salt, alternating with the brandy. • Stir in the dates and candied fruit peel. • Spoon the batter into the prepared pan. • Bake for 70–80 minutes, or until a toothpick inserted into the center comes out clean. • Brush the cake with rum. • Cool the cake completely in the pan on a rack. • Dust with the confectioners' sugar.

Makes one 9-inch cake · Prep: 25 min. · Cooking: 70–80 min. · Level: 1 · Keeps: 2 weeks

LEMONY DATE CAKE

- 1¹/₂ cups all-purpose flour
- 1 cup granulated sugar
- ¹/₂ cup (1 stick) butter, softened
- 2 large eggs, at room temperature
- 2 teaspoons grated lemon zest
- ¹/₃ cup fresh lemon juice
- 1¹/₂ teaspoons baking powder
- ¹/₄ teaspoon salt
- 1 cup pitted dates, chopped

LEMON FROSTING

- ¹/₄ cup (¹/₂ stick) butter, softened
- 1 tablespoon grated lemon zest
- 1¹/₂ cups confectioners' sugar
  about 2 tablespoons lemon juice

Preheat the oven to 350°F. • Butter and flour a 10-inch tube pan. • Beat the flour, sugar, butter, eggs, lemon zest and juice, baking powder, and salt in a large bowl with an electric mixer at low speed until well blended. Increase the speed to medium, and beat for 2 minutes, or until the batter is smooth. Stir in the dates. • Spoon the batter into the prepared pan. • Bake for 40–50 minutes, or until a toothpick inserted into the center comes out clean. • Cool the cake in the pan for 5 minutes. Turn out onto a rack to cool completely. • *Lemon Frosting*: Beat the butter and lemon zest in a medium bowl until creamy. Gradually beat in the confectioners' sugar. Add enough lemon juice to obtain a thick, spreadable frosting. • Spread the frosting on the top of the cake.

Makes one 10-inch cake · Prep: 15 min. · Cooking: 40–50 min. · Level: 1 · Keeps: 2–3 days

TURKISH CAKE

The unusual inclusion of rose water is reminiscent of the famous gelatin candy, Turkish delight. If you are able to use a turban ring mold, this will add to the Eastern appeal of the cake.

- 1 quart milk
- 3/4 cup granulated sugar
- 1/4 teaspoon salt
- 1 1/2 cups uncooked short-grain rice
- 2 large eggs + 2 extra egg yolks
- 1/3 cup finely ground almonds
- 1/2 cup golden raisins
- 1/3 cup pine nuts
- 10 dates, preferably fresh, coarsely chopped
- 1 tablespoon rose water

Preheat the oven to 350°F. • Butter and flour a 9-inch ring mold. • Bring the milk to a boil in a large saucepan. • Stir in the sugar, rice, and salt. Cook, stirring constantly, for 10 minutes. Drain off any milk that has not been absorbed and transfer the rice to a large bowl. • Beat in the eggs, egg yolks, almonds, raisins, pine nuts, dates, and rose water with an electric mixer at low speed. • Spoon the batter into the prepared pan. Bake for 25–35 minutes, or until lightly browned. Cool the cake in the pan for 15 minutes. Invert onto a serving plate and serve warm.

Makes one 9-inch cake · Prep: 15 min. · Cooking: 25–35 min. · Level: 1 · Keeps: 1–2 days

FROSTED DATE AND NUT CAKE

This cake is also lovely with a simple dusting of confectioners' sugar.

- 1 1/2 cups all-purpose flour
- 1 1/2 teaspoons baking powder
- 1/2 teaspoon baking soda
- 1 teaspoon ground cinnamon
- 1 teaspoon ground ginger
- 1/4 teaspoon ground cloves
- 1/4 teaspoon salt
- 1/2 cup (1 stick) butter, softened
- 3/4 cup granulated sugar
- 1 teaspoon vanilla extract
- 2 large eggs, at room temperature
- 1 cup buttermilk
- 1 cup walnuts or pecans, coarsely chopped
- 1 cup pitted dates, coarsely chopped
- 1 cup old-fashioned rolled oats
- 1 cup Soft Lemon Frosting (see page 349)

Preheat the oven to 325°F. • Butter and flour a 9-inch tube pan. • Sift the flour, baking powder, baking soda, cinnamon, ginger, cloves, and salt into a medium bowl. • Beat the butter, sugar, and vanilla in a large bowl with an electric mixer at medium speed until creamy. • Add the eggs, one at a time, until just blended after each addition. • With mixer at low speed, gradually beat in the dry ingredients, alternating with the buttermilk. Stir in the nuts, dates, and oats. • Spoon the batter into the prepared pan. • Bake for 45–55 minutes, or until a toothpick inserted into the center comes out clean. • Cool the cake in the pan for 10 minutes. Turn out onto a rack to cool completely. • Spread the top and sides of the cake with the frosting.

Makes one 9-inch cake · Prep: 25 min. · Cooking: 45–55 min. · Level: 1 · Keeps: 3–4 days

GLAZED APPLE AND WALNUT CAKE

- 2 cups all-purpose flour
- 1 cup whole-wheat flour
- 2 teaspoons ground cinnamon
- 2 teaspoons baking powder
- 1 teaspoon baking soda
- 1 teaspoon ground ginger
- 1/2 teaspoon salt
- 1/4 teaspoon ground cloves
- 1 1/2 cups vegetable oil
- 2 cups firmly packed brown sugar
- 3 large eggs, at room temperature
- 1/4 cup apple brandy, such as Calvados
- 4 cups walnuts, coarsely chopped
- 2 large tart apples, (Granny Smiths are ideal), peeled, cored, and coarsely chopped

BRANDY AND CIDER GLAZE

- 1/4 cup (1/2 stick) butter
- 1/3 cup granulated sugar
- 2 tablespoons brown sugar
- 2 tablespoons apple brandy, such as Calvados
- 1/4 cup apple cider
- 2 tablespoons fresh orange juice
- 2 tablespoons heavy cream

Preheat the oven to 325°F. • Butter and flour a 13 x 9-inch baking pan. • Sift the flours, cinnamon, baking powder, baking soda, ginger, salt, and cloves into a large bowl. • Beat the oil and brown sugar in a large bowl with an electric mixer at medium speed. • Add the eggs, one at a time, until just blended after each addition. • With mixer at low speed, gradually beat in the dry ingredients, alternating with the brandy. Stir in the walnuts and apples. • Spoon the batter into the prepared pan. • Bake for 60–70 minutes, or until a toothpick inserted into the center comes out clean. • Cool the cake in the pan on a rack. • *Brandy and Cider Glaze*: Stir the butter in a medium saucepan over medium heat until melted. Stir in both sugars, followed by the brandy, cider, orange juice, and cream. Bring to a boil, reduce the heat, and boil for 3–4 minutes. Set aside to cool a little. • Place the cake on the rack on a jelly-roll pan. Poke holes in the cake with a skewer. Spoon the syrup over the cake. Scoop up any syrup from the pan and drizzle on the cake.

Makes one 13 x 9-inch cake · Prep: 40 min. · Cooking: 60–70 min. · Level: 1 · Keeps: 3–4 days

Turkish cake

Preheat the oven to 325°F. • Butter a 9-inch round cake pan. Line with waxed paper. Butter the paper. • Sift the flour, baking powder, baking soda, and salt into a medium bowl. • Beat the butter, brown sugar, cream cheese, and lemon zest in a large bowl with an electric mixer at medium speed until creamy. • Add the eggs, one at a time, until just blended after each addition. • With mixer at low speed, gradually beat in the dry ingredients, alternating with the sherry. Stir in the dates, raisins, mangoes, apricots, and ginger. • Spoon the batter into the prepared pan. • Bake for 50–60 minutes, or until the cake shrinks from the pan sides and a toothpick inserted into the center comes out clean. • Cool the cake completely in the pan. Turn out onto a rack and carefully remove the paper.

Makes one 9-inch cake · Prep: 25 min. · Cooking: 50–60 min. · Level: 1 · Keeps: 5–6 days

Poor man's cake

SHERRY FRUIT CAKE

3	cups golden raisins
2¼	cups dark raisins
1½	cups pitted prunes, coarsely chopped
1	cup currants
1	cup quartered candied red cherries
½	cup dry sherry + 2 tablespoons, to brush
⅓	cup honey
1	cup (2 sticks) butter, softened
1	cup firmly packed dark brown sugar
5	large eggs, at room temperature
1¼	cups all-purpose flour
1	teaspoon baking powder
¼	teaspoon salt

Mix the golden and dark raisins, prunes, currants, cherries, ½ cup sherry, and honey in a large bowl. Cover and let stand for 12 hours. • Preheat the oven to 300°F. • Butter an 8-inch square cake pan. Line with waxed paper. Butter the paper • Beat the butter and brown sugar in a large bowl with an electric mixer at medium speed until creamy. • Add the eggs, one at a time, until just blended after each addition. • With mixer at low speed, gradually beat in the flour, baking powder, and salt. Stir in the fruit mixture. • Spoon the batter into the prepared pan. • Bake for about 3 hours, or until a toothpick inserted into the center comes out clean. • Remove from the oven and brush with the sherry. Cool the cake in the pan for 15 minutes. Turn out onto a rack. Carefully remove the paper and let cool completely.

Makes one 8-inch cake · Prep: 20 min. + 12 hr. to stand · Cooking: 3 hr. · Level: 1 · Keeps: up to 12 months, wrapped tightly in foil

SHERRIED CREAM CHEESE FRUITCAKE

1¼	cups all-purpose flour
1	teaspoon baking powder
1	teaspoon baking soda
¼	teaspoon salt
½	cup (1 stick) butter, softened
¾	cup firmly packed brown sugar
1	package (3 oz) cream cheese, softened
2	tablespoons grated lemon zest
2	large eggs, at room temperature
¼	cup sweet sherry
1	cup pitted dates, chopped
¾	cup raisins
¾	cup candied mangoes, chopped
¾	cup candied apricots, chopped
¾	cup crystallized ginger. chopped

POOR MAN'S CAKE

This is an old Italian recipe. Like most Italian cooking, it originated in peasants' homes in the countryside where food was often scarce. Bread was a staple food, and therefore not to be wasted. This is just one of many ways of using up yesterday's bread.

1½	cups golden raisins
½	cup dark Jamaica rum
12	slices (12 oz) stale 2–3 day-old white sandwich bread, cut into small cubes
4	cups milk
1	cup granulated sugar
½	cup (1 stick) butter, cut up
5	large eggs, lightly beaten
1	tablespoon grated lemon zest

Plump the raisins in the rum in a medium bowl for 30 minutes. Drain well and pat dry with paper towels. • Place the bread in a large bowl. • Bring the milk to a boil, add the sugar and butter, and stir until the sugar has dissolved and the butter has melted. Pour over the bread. • Let stand until all the milk has been absorbed, about 30 minutes. • Preheat the oven to 350°F. •

Butter a 9-inch springform pan. • Stir the eggs, raisins, and lemon zest into the bread mixture until well blended. • Spoon the batter into the prepared pan, pressing the batter down with the back of the spoon. • Bake for 30–40 minutes, or until lightly browned and set. • Cool the cake in the pan on a rack for 15 minutes. Loosen and remove the pan sides and let cool completely. Serve warm or cool.

Makes one 9-inch cake · Prep: 15 min. + 30 min. · Cooking: 30–40 min.. · Level: 1 · Keeps: 1–2 days

PANFORTE

Siena, a town in central Italy, is the origin of this traditional cake that dates from the Middle Ages. The rice paper used for lining the pan is edible. It may be found in cake decorating stores or Asian markets.

- 1 cup candied orange peel, cut into small diamonds
- 2 tablespoons candied lemon peel, cut into small diamonds
- $1^2/_3$ cups unblanched, toasted almonds, coarsely chopped
- $^2/_3$ cup walnuts, coarsely chopped
- 1 cup all-purpose flour
- $^1/_2$ teaspoon each ground coriander, mace, cloves, and nutmeg
- 1 cup firmly packed brown sugar
- $^1/_2$ cup honey
- 1 tablespoon cold water

SPICE POWDER

- 3 tablespoons ground cardamom
- 1 tablespoon ground cinnamon
- $^1/_4$ cup confectioners' sugar, to dust

Preheat the oven to 350°F. • Line a baking sheet with rice paper. • Mix the candied peels, nuts, flour, and spices in a large bowl. • Heat the brown sugar, honey, and water in a medium saucepan over medium heat, stirring constantly, until the sugar has dissolved. • Wash down the sides of the pan with a pastry brush dipped in cold water to prevent sugar crystals from forming. Cook, without stirring, until small bubbles form on the surface and the syrup registers 230–234°F on a candy thermometer. • Remove from the heat and beat into the nut mixture. • Pour onto the prepared sheet. Shape the dough into a round about $^1/_2$-inch thick. • *Spice Powder*: Mix the cardamom and cinnamon. Sprinkle the spice powder over. • Bake for 25–35 minutes. • Cool the cake completely on the baking sheet. • Remove the excess

Panforte

rice paper from the edges before serving. Dust with the confectioners' sugar.

Makes one cake · Prep: 25 min. · Cooking: 25–35 min. · Level: 2 · Keeps: 1–2 weeks

FRUIT CAKE WITH BEER

- $1^1/_2$ cups dark raisins
- $1^1/_2$ cups pitted dates, chopped
- 1 cup golden raisins
- $^1/_2$ cup mixed candied fruit peel, chopped
- $^1/_2$ cup dried apricots, chopped
- $^1/_2$ cup halved candied cherries
- $^1/_4$ cup crystallized ginger, chopped
- 1 can or bottle (12 oz) beer
- $^1/_4$ cup water
- $1^1/_2$ cups whole-wheat flour
- $1^1/_2$ cups all-purpose flour
- 2 teaspoons baking powder
- 1 teaspoon ground nutmeg
- 1 teaspoon ground ginger
- 1 teaspoon ground cinnamon
- $^1/_2$ teaspoon salt
- 1 cup (2 sticks) butter, softened
- $^3/_4$ cup honey
- $^1/_2$ cup light corn syrup
- 3 large eggs, at room temperature
- $^1/_2$ cup slivered almonds

Place the dried and candied fruits in a large bowl and pour in the beer. Cover and let stand for 12 hours. • Preheat the oven to 300°F. • Butter a 13 x 9-inch baking pan. Line with waxed paper. Butter the paper. • Sift the flours, baking powder, nutmeg, ginger, cinnamon, and salt into a large bowl. • Beat the butter, honey, and corn syrup in a large bowl with an electric mixer at medium speed until creamy.• Add the eggs, one at a time, until just blended after each addition. • With mixer at low speed, gradually beat in the dry ingredients and the fruit mixture. • Spoon the batter into the prepared pan. Sprinkle with the almonds. • Bake for 2 hours and 20–30 minutes, or until dark brown at the edges and a toothpick inserted into the center comes out clean. • Cool the cake in the pan for 15 minutes. Turn out onto a rack. Carefully remove the paper and let cool completely.

Makes one 13 x 9-inch cake · Prep: 20 min. + 12 hr. to stand · Cooking: 2 hr. 20–30 min. · Level: 1 · Keeps: 1 month

LIGHT FRUIT CAKE

- 4 cups chopped mixed candied fruit
- 1½ cups white grape juice
- ⅔ cup firmly packed dark brown sugar
- 2½ cups all-purpose flour
- 1½ teaspoons baking powder
- 1 teaspoon baking soda
- 1 teaspoon ground cinnamon
- 1 teaspoon ground nutmeg
- ½ teaspoon salt
- 2 large egg whites, lightly beaten
- ¼ cup vegetable oil
- ⅓ cup 1% milk or reduced fat milk
- ¼ cup brandy

Stir together the candied fruit, grape juice, and brown sugar in a large bowl. Cover and set aside for 8 hours. • Preheat the oven to 300°F. • Butter and flour a 9-inch square baking pan. • Sift the flour, baking powder, baking soda, cinnamon, nutmeg, and salt into a large bowl. • Use a large rubber spatula to stir the egg whites, oil, milk, and 2 tablespoons brandy into the fruit mixture. Stir in the dry ingredients. • Spoon the batter into the prepared pan. • Bake for 1 hour and 30–40 minutes, or until a toothpick inserted into the center comes out clean. • Drizzle the hot cake with the remaining brandy. Cool the cake in the pan on a rack.

Makes one 9-inch cake · Prep: 15 min. + 8 hr. to soak · Cooking: 1 hr. 30–40 min. · Level: 1 · Keeps: 2–3 weeks

NUTTY FRUIT CAKE

- 3 cups all-purpose flour
- 2 teaspoons ground cinnamon
- 2 teaspoons baking powder
- ½ teaspoon baking soda
- ½ teaspoon salt
- ¼ cup (½ stick) butter, melted
- 1 can (14 oz) sweetened condensed milk
- 2 teaspoons vanilla extract
- 2 large eggs, at room temperature
- 1⅓ cups applesauce
- ½ cup dates, chopped
- ½ cup green candied cherries, chopped
- ½ cup red candied cherries, chopped
- 1 cup nuts, chopped
- 1 cup golden raisins
- ¼ cup confectioners' sugar, to dust

Preheat the oven to 325°F. • Butter and flour a 13 x 9-inch baking pan. • Sift the flour, cinnamon, baking powder, baking soda, and salt into a large bowl. • Beat the butter, condensed milk, and vanilla in a large bowl with an electric mixer at medium speed until creamy. • Add the eggs, one at a time, until just blended after each addition. • With mixer at low speed, gradually beat in the dry ingredients, alternating with the applesauce. Stir in the dates, cherries, nuts, and raisins. • Spoon the batter into the prepared pan. • Bake for 50–60 minutes, or until a toothpick inserted into the center comes out clean. • Cool the cake completely in the pan on a rack. • Dust with the confectioners' sugar.

Makes one 13 x 9-inch cake · Prep: 25 min. · Cooking: 50–60 min. · Level: 1 · Keeps: 4–5 days

TROPICAL FRUIT CAKE

The delicious tang of fresh passion fruit cannot be replaced in this recipe with packaged juice. Passion fruit can be found in the tropical fruit sections of many supermarkets or in specialty stores. To juice a fresh passion fruit, either squeeze it on a lemon juicer or cut the fruit in half, remove the pulp with a teaspoon, and press it through a small strainer.

- 1 lb mixed candied fruit, chopped, such as pineapple, mango, papaya, citrus peel, or cherries
- 1 cup firmly packed brown sugar
- ½ cup strained fresh passion fruit juice
- ½ cup (1 stick) butter, cut up
- 1 tablespoon grated lemon zest
- ¼ cup fresh lemon juice
- 1½ cups all-purpose flour
- 1 teaspoon baking powder
- ½ teaspoon baking soda
- 1 teaspoon ground ginger
- 1 teaspoon ground cinnamon
- 1 teaspoon ground nutmeg
- ½ teaspoon salt
- 3 large eggs, lightly beaten

Stir together the candied fruit, brown sugar, passion fruit juice, butter, and lemon zest and juice in a large saucepan over medium heat until the sugar has dissolved. Bring to a boil and simmer for 3 minutes. Remove from the heat and set aside to cool for 1 hour. • Preheat the oven to 325°F. • Butter a 9-inch square baking pan. Line with waxed paper. Butter the paper. • Sift the flour, baking powder, baking soda, ginger, cinnamon, nutmeg, and salt into a medium bowl. • Stir the eggs and dry ingredients into the fruit mixture. • Spoon the batter into the prepared pan. • Bake for 75–85 minutes, or until the cake shrinks from the pan sides and a toothpick inserted into the center comes out clean. • Cool the cake completely in the pan. Turn out onto a rack. Carefully remove the paper.

Makes one 9-inch cake · Prep: 25 min.+ 1 hr. to cool · Cooking: 75–85 min. · Level: 1 · Keeps: 5–6 days

RICH FRUIT CAKE

- 1 cup (2 sticks) butter, cut up
- 1 cup firmly packed brown sugar
- ½ cup rum
- ½ cup water
- 2 cups golden raisins
- 1 cup dark raisins
- 1 cup currants
- ½ cup mixed candied fruit peel, chopped
- ½ cup candied cherries, chopped
- ¼ cup candied pineapple, chopped
- ¼ cup crystallized ginger, chopped
- ¼ cup dried apricots, chopped
- 2¼ cups all-purpose flour
- 2 teaspoons baking powder
- 1 teaspoon baking soda
- ½ teaspoon salt
- 5 large eggs, lightly beaten
- 2 tablespoons grated lemon, orange, or lime zest

Stir the butter, brown sugar, rum, water, and all dried and candied fruit in a large saucepan over medium low heat until the sugar has dissolved. Bring to a boil, reduce the heat to low, and simmer for 5–6 minutes. • Remove from the heat and let cool for 1 hour. • Preheat the oven to 300°F. • Butter a 13 x 9-inch baking pan. Line with waxed paper. Butter the paper. • Sift the flour, baking powder, baking soda, and salt into a large bowl. • Beat in the eggs and citrus zest with an electric mixer at low speed. Gradually beat in the dry ingredients. Stir in the cooled fruit mixture. • Spoon the batter into the prepared pan. • Bake for 1 hour and 30–40 minutes, or until dark brown at the edges and a toothpick inserted into the center comes out clean. • Cool the cake completely in the pan. Turn out onto a rack. Carefully remove the paper.

Makes one 13 x 9-inch cake · Prep: 20 min. + 1 hr. to cool · Cooking: 1 hr. 30–40 min. · Level: 1 · Keeps: 2 months (wrapped in foil)

MIXED FRUIT CAKE

- 1⅓ cups all-purpose flour
- 2 teaspoons baking powder
- 1 teaspoon pumpkin pie spice
- ½ teaspoon baking soda
- ¼ teaspoon salt
- 3 large eggs, at room temperature
- ¾ cup granulated sugar
- ½ cup (1 stick) butter, melted
- ⅓ cup dry Marsala wine or dry sherry
- 2 large apples, peeled, cored, and cut into small pieces
- 1 cup stemmed dried figs, chopped
- ½ cup raisins
- ½ cup mixed candied fruit, chopped
- ⅓ cup almonds, coarsely chopped
- 2 tablespoons grated lemon zest

Preheat the oven to 350°F. • Butter and flour a 9-inch springform pan. • Sift the flour, baking powder, pumpkin pie spice, baking soda, and salt into a large bowl. • Beat the eggs and sugar in a large bowl with an electric mixer at medium speed until pale and thick. • With mixer at low speed, gradually beat in the butter and dry ingredients, alternating with the Marsala. • Stir in the apples, figs, raisins, candied fruit, almonds, and lemon zest. • Spoon the batter into the prepared pan. • Bake for 40–50 minutes, or until a toothpick inserted into the center comes out clean. • Cool the cake in the pan for 10 minutes. Loosen and remove the pan sides. Cool the cake completely on a rack.

Makes one 9-inch cake · Prep: 20 min. · Cooking: 40–50 min. · Level: 1 · Keeps: 5–7 days

Mixed fruit cake

Fruit and nut cake with crunchy topping

FRUIT AND NUT CAKE WITH CRUNCHY TOPPING

- 1½ cups mixed dried fruit, chopped
- 1½ cups ⅓ cup water
- ¾ cup raisins
- ¾ cup firmly packed dark brown sugar
- 2 tablespoons butter
- 1 teaspoon ground cinnamon
- 1 teaspoon ground nutmeg
- ½ teaspoon ground cloves
- 2 large eggs, lightly beaten
- ¾ cup walnuts, chopped
- ½ cup candied mangoes, chopped
- ½ cup unsalted sunflower seeds
- 2 cups whole-wheat flour
- 2 teaspoons baking powder
- ½ teaspoon baking soda
- ½ teaspoon salt

CRUNCHY TOPPING

- 2 tablespoons pumpkin seeds
- 2 tablespoons raw sunflower seeds

Stir the mixed fruit, ½ cup water, the raisins, brown sugar, butter, cinnamon, nutmeg, and cloves in a large saucepan over medium-low heat until the sugar has dissolved. Bring to a boil, reduce the heat to low, and simmer for 3 minutes, stirring constantly. • Set aside to cool for 1 hour. • Preheat the oven to 325°. • Butter a 9-inch square baking pan. Line with waxed paper. • Stir the eggs, walnuts, mangoes, sunflower seeds, and remaining ⅓ cup water into the fruit mixture. Stir in the flour, baking powder, baking soda, and salt. • Spoon the batter into the prepared pan. Sprinkle with the pumpkin seeds and sunflower seeds. • Bake for about 1 hour and 45 minutes. • Cool the cake completely in the pan. Turn out onto a rack. Carefully remove the paper before serving.

Makes one 9-inch cake · Prep: 20 min. + 1 hr. to cool · Cooking: 1 hr. 45 min. · Level: 1 · Keeps: 2 weeks

DUNDEE CAKE

- 1 cup all-purpose flour
- ½ teaspoon baking powder
- ½ teaspoon baking soda
- ¼ teaspoon salt
- ⅓ cup almonds, finely ground
- ⅔ cup butter, softened
- ¾ cup firmly packed brown sugar
- 1 teaspoon vanilla extract
- 2 large eggs, at room temperature, + 1 large egg white, lightly beaten
- 1½ cups raisins
- 1½ cups + 2 tablespoons currants
- ½ cup chopped mixed candied lemon and orange peel
- ¼ cup candied cherries, halved
- 1 tablespoon grated lemon zest
- 1½ tablespoons fresh lemon juice about 60 whole blanched almonds

Preheat the oven to 350°F. • Butter a 9-inch springform pan. • Sift the flour, baking powder, baking soda, and salt into a medium bowl. Stir in the ground almonds. • Beat the butter, brown sugar, and vanilla in a large bowl with an electric mixer at medium speed until creamy.• Add the eggs, one at a time, until just blended after each addition. • With mixer at low speed, gradually beat in the dry ingredients. Stir in the raisins, currants, candied fruit peel, candied cherries, and lemon zest and juice. • Spoon the batter into the prepared pan. Cover with the halved almonds and brush with the egg white. • Bake for 1 hour. Reduce the oven temperature to 300°F and bake for 1 hour more, or until a toothpick inserted into the center comes out clean. • Cool the cake in the pan for 30 minutes. Loosen and remove the pan sides. Invert the cake onto a rack. Loosen and remove the pan bottom. Turn the cake top-side up onto the rack and let cool completely.

Makes one 9-inch cake · Prep: 30 min. · Cooking: 2 hr. · Level: 1 · Keeps: 3–4 weeks

FRUIT AND NUT COCONUT CAKE

Sweetened cream of coconut can be found in the drink mixes section of your supermarket.

- 1½ cups shredded coconut
- 3 cups Rice Krispies
- ⅔ cup bran flakes
- 1½ cups candied apricots, chopped
- 1 cup candied pineapple, chopped
- 1¼ cups walnuts, chopped
- ½ cup (1 stick) butter
- ½ cup sweetened cream of coconut
- ½ cup honey
- ⅓ cup firmly packed dark brown sugar
- 1 teaspoon ground ginger

Butter a 9 x 13-inch baking pan. • Stir the coconut, rice cereal, bran flakes, apricots, pineapple, and walnuts in a large bowl until well mixed. • Mix the butter, cream of coconut, honey, brown sugar, and ginger in a large saucepan. Cook over low heat, stirring constantly, until the sugar has dissolved. Bring to a boil, reduce the heat, and simmer for about 5 minutes, or until syrupy. Use a large rubber spatula to stir the hot syrup into the dry ingredients until well blended. • Spoon the mixture into the prepared pan. • Refrigerate for at least 6 hours, or until firm.

Makes one 9 x 13-inch cake · Prep: 15 min. + 6 hr. to chill · Level: 1 · Keeps: 3–4 days

TWO-TONE FRUIT CAKE

DARK LAYER

- 1 cup candied mangoes, chopped
- 1 cup candied cherries, chopped
- 1 cup mixed candied peel, chopped
- 1 cup raisins
- $^1/_2$ cup pitted dates, chopped
- $^1/_2$ cup rum
- 1 cup all-purpose flour
- 1 teaspoon baking powder
- $^1/_2$ teaspoon baking soda
- 1 teaspoon ground ginger
- 1 teaspoon pumpkin pie spice
- $^1/_4$ teaspoon salt
- $^1/_4$ cup ($^1/_2$ stick) butter, softened
- $^3/_4$ cup firmly packed brown sugar
- 3 large eggs, at room temperature
- 3 oz bittersweet chocolate, coarsely chopped

LIGHT LAYER

- $1^1/_2$ cups all-purpose flour
- 1 teaspoon baking powder
- $^1/_2$ teaspoon baking soda
- $^1/_4$ teaspoon salt
- $^1/_2$ cup (1 stick) butter, softened
- 1 cup granulated sugar
- 3 large eggs, at room temperature
- $^1/_2$ cup dry sherry
- 1 cup candied cherries, chopped
- $^3/_4$ cup raisins
- $^3/_4$ cup slivered almonds
- $^1/_2$ cup pecans, chopped
- $^1/_2$ cup mixed candied fruit peel, chopped
- $^1/_4$ cup candied pineapple, chopped

Dark Layer: Place the candied and dried fruit in a medium bowl and pour the rum over. Cover and let stand for 12 hours. • Preheat the oven to 300°F. • Butter a 13 x 9-inch baking pan. Line with waxed paper. Butter the paper. • Sift the flour, baking powder, baking soda, ginger, pumpkin pie spice, and salt into a medium bowl. • Beat the butter and brown sugar in a large bowl with an electric mixer at medium speed until creamy. • Add the eggs, one at a time, until just blended after each addition. • With mixer at low speed, gradually beat in the chocolate and dry ingredients. Stir in the fruit mixture. • Spoon the batter into the prepared pan. • *Light Layer*: Sift the flour,

Polenta fruit cake

baking powder, baking soda, and salt into a medium bowl. • With mixer at high speed, beat the butter and sugar in a large bowl until creamy. • Add the eggs, one at a time, until just blended after each addition. • With mixer at low speed, gradually beat in the dry ingredients, alternating with the sherry. Stir in the fruits and nuts. • Spoon the batter over the dark layer. • Bake for about 2 hours, or until dark brown, and a toothpick inserted into the center comes out clean. • Cool the cake completely in the pan. Turn out onto a rack. Carefully remove the paper.

Makes one 13 x 9-inch cake · Prep: 30 min. + 12 hr. to stand · Cooking: 2 hr. · Level: 1 · Keeps: 1 month

POLENTA FRUIT CAKE

- $^1/_3$ cup coarsely chopped blanched almonds
- $^1/_3$ cup chopped candied peel and cherries
- $^1/_4$ cup grappa
- 3 tablespoons golden raisins
- 2 tablespoons chopped dried figs
- 1 teaspoon fennel seeds
- 1 quart milk
- $2^1/_2$ cups yellow cornmeal
- $^1/_3$ cup all-purpose flour
- $^1/_2$ cup granulated sugar
- $^1/_3$ cup cold butter, cut up
- $^1/_4$ cup + 2 tablespoons vegetable shortening or butter
- $^1/_4$ teaspoon salt

Preheat the oven to 350°F. • Butter and flour a 10-inch springform pan. • Stir together the almonds, grappa, candied peel and cherries, raisins, figs, and fennel seeds in a medium bowl. Stand for 15 minutes. • Bring the milk to a boil in a large saucepan over medium heat. Reduce the heat to low. Gradually beat in the cornmeal and flour, stirring constantly, for 15 minutes. Stir in the sugar, butter, shortening, and salt, and cook, stirring occasionally, for 10 minutes more. • Remove from the heat. Stir in the fruit and grappa mixture. • Spoon the batter into the prepared pan. • Bake for 50–60 minutes, or until lightly browned. After 30 minutes, cover the top of the cake loosely with a piece of foil to prevent the cake from drying out. • Cool the cake completely in the pan on a rack. Loosen and remove the pan sides to serve.

Makes one 10-inch round cake · Prep: 25 min. · Cooking: 50–60 min. · Level: 1 · Keeps: 2–3 days

WHOLE-WHEAT FRUIT CAKE WITH NUTTY TOPPING

1½ cups whole-wheat flour
½ cup all-purpose flour
1 teaspoon baking powder
½ teaspoon baking soda
1 teaspoon ground ginger
1 teaspoon ground cinnamon
1 teaspoon pumpkin pie spice
¼ teaspoon salt
¾ cup (1½ sticks) butter, softened
¾ cup firmly packed brown sugar
3 large eggs, at room temperature
½ cup peach nectar
1 cup walnuts, coarsely chopped
½ cup sunflower seeds
⅔ cup currants
½ cup dried figs, chopped
½ cup dried apricots, chopped
½ cup raisins

NUTTY TOPPING

¼ cup nuts, finely chopped
¼ cup raw sugar or light brown sugar
2 tablespoons sunflower seeds
½ teaspoon ground ginger
½ teaspoon ground cinnamon
½ teaspoon pumpkin pie spice

Preheat the oven to 300°F. • Butter a 13 x 9-inch baking pan. Line with waxed paper. Butter the paper. • Sift the flours, baking powder, baking soda, ginger, cinnamon, pumpkin pie spice, and salt into a large bowl. • Beat the butter and brown sugar in a large bowl with an electric mixer at medium speed until creamy.• Add the eggs, one at a time, until just blended after each addition. • With mixer at low speed, gradually beat in the dry ingredients, alternating with the peach nectar. Stir in the walnuts, sunflower seeds, currants, figs, apricots, and raisins. •

Tressian (Venetian polenta cake)

Spoon the batter into the prepared pan. • *Nutty Topping*: Mix the nuts, raw sugar, sunflower seeds, ginger, cinnamon, and pumpkin pie spice in a medium bowl. Sprinkle the topping over the batter. • Bake for 2 hours, or until a toothpick inserted into the center comes out clean. • Cool the cake completely in the pan. Turn out onto a rack. Carefully remove the paper before serving.

Makes one 13 x 9-inch cake · Prep: 30 min. · Cooking: 2 hr. · Level: 1 · Keeps: 2–3 weeks

SHREDDED WHEAT CAKE

Use large biscuits of shredded wheat and crush them with your fingers. This recipe makes two cakes, or they can be stacked to make a layer cake.

1½ cups all-purpose flour
¼ teaspoon baking soda
¼ teaspoon salt
⅔ cup butter, softened
1¼ cups granulated sugar
1 tablespoon grated lemon zest
1 teaspoon vanilla extract
4 large eggs, separated
⅔ cup buttermilk
1½ cups finely crumbled shredded wheat biscuits
⅔ cup dried sweetened cranberries, coarsely chopped
⅓ cup walnuts, coarsely chopped
¼ teaspoon cream of tartar

LEMON-CREAM CHEESE FROSTING

1 package (3 oz) cream cheese, softened
¼ cup (½ stick) butter, softened
3 cups confectioners' sugar
1 tablespoon grated lemon zest
1 tablespoon fresh lemon juice
walnut halves, to decorate (optional)

Preheat the oven to 350°F. • Butter two 9 x 2-inch round cake pans. Line with waxed paper. Butter the paper. • Sift the flour, baking soda, and salt into a medium bowl. •

Beat the butter, sugar, lemon zest, and vanilla in a large bowl with an electric mixer at medium speed until creamy.• Add the egg yolks, one at a time, until just blended after each addition. • With mixer at low speed, gradually beat in the dry ingredients, alternating with the buttermilk. Stir in the shredded wheat, cranberries, and walnuts. • With mixer at high speed, beat the egg whites and cream of tartar in a large bowl until stiff peaks form. Use a large rubber spatula to fold the beaten whites into the batter. • Spoon the batter evenly into the prepared pans. • Bake for 30–40 minutes, or until a toothpick inserted into the center comes out clean. • Cool the cakes in the pans for 10 minutes. Turn out onto racks. Carefully remove the paper and let cool completely. • *Lemon-Cream Cheese Frosting*: With mixer at medium speed, beat the cream cheese and butter in a medium bowl until smooth. Gradually beat in the confectioners' sugar, and lemon zest and juice until creamy. Spread the tops and sides of the cakes with the frosting. If desired, decorate the cakes with walnut halves.

Makes two 9-inch cakes · Prep: 35 min. · Cooking: 30–40 min. · Level: 1 · Keeps: 3–4 days

TRESSIAN (VENETIAN POLENTA CAKE)

Polenta is finely ground yellow cornmeal cooked with salt and water to make a nourishing dish that is somewhere between porridge and bread. It comes from northern Italy, where it is served in a variety of ways. Polenta is now widely available in supermarkets and stores outside Italy. Choose a precooked polenta that only requires 8–10 minutes stirring. To obtain 1 lb of ready-made polenta, you will need about 1½ cups of polenta cornmeal, prepared according to the instructions on the package.

1 lb ready-made polenta (not too firm), cooled
⅔ cup all-purpose flour
¾ cup granulated sugar
2 teaspoons baking powder
2 large eggs, at room temperature
¼ cup milk
1 large tart apple, (Granny Smiths are ideal), peeled, cored, and chopped
¾ cup candied fruit, chopped
½ cup raisins
¼ cup (½ stick) butter, softened

Preheat the oven to 350°F. • Butter a 10-inch springform pan. • Mash the polenta in a large bowl. Stir in the flour, sugar, baking powder, eggs, and milk. Mix in the apple, candied fruit, raisins, and butter until well blended. • Spoon the batter into the prepared pan. • Bake for 55–65 minutes, or until golden brown. • Loosen and remove the pan sides to serve. Serve hot or warm.

Makes one 10-inch cake · Prep: 25 min. · Cooking: 55–65 min. · Level: 1 · Keeps: 2–3 days

ALMOND-POLENTA CAKE

If possible, prepare this cake with coarsely ground cornmeal.

1²/₃   cups blanched almonds
 ³/₄   cup granulated sugar
1¹/₄   cups all-purpose flour
2¹/₂   cups yellow cornmeal
1¹/₂   teaspoons grated lemon zest
  1   teaspoon vanilla extract
 ¹/₄   teaspoon salt
 ¹/₂   cup (1 stick) cold butter, cut up
 ¹/₃   cup chopped lard
  2   egg yolks, lightly beaten
 ¹/₄   cup confectioners' sugar, to dust

Preheat the oven to 350°F. • Butter a 9-inch round cake pan. Line with waxed paper. Butter the paper. • Place the almonds and ¹/₂ cup sugar in a food processor and chop finely. • Transfer to a large bowl. Stir in the flour, cornmeal, lemon zest, remaining sugar, vanilla, and salt. Make a well in the center. • Use your fingers to work in the butter, lard, and egg yolks until smooth. • Spoon the batter in the prepared pan, pressing down lightly to make a dimpled surface. • Bake for 35–45 minutes, or until golden brown and a toothpick inserted into the center comes out clean. • Cool the cake completely in the pan on a rack. Dust with the confectioners' sugar.

Makes one 9-inch round cake · Prep: 25 min. · Cooking: 35–45 min.. · Level: 1 · Keeps: 2–3 days

POLENTA AND DATE CAKE

1³/₄   cups granulated sugar
  1   cup polenta or finely ground cornmeal
1³/₄   cups milk
1¹/₂   cups all-purpose flour
  2   teaspoons baking powder
 ¹/₄   teaspoon salt
1¹/₂   cups pitted dates, coarsely chopped
 ¹/₂   cup (1 stick) butter, softened
  1   tablespoon grated lemon zest
  2   large eggs, at room temperature
 ¹/₄   cup confectioners' sugar, to dust

Preheat the oven to 325°F. • Butter an 11 x 7-inch baking pan and a jelly-roll pan or 13 x 9-inch baking pan. • Stir together 1¹/₄ cups

Semolina heart

sugar and the polenta in a large saucepan. Gradually stir in the milk over medium heat. Bring to a boil, stirring constantly. Reduce the heat to low, and simmer, stirring constantly, for about 5 minutes, or until the polenta is thick. • Spread the polenta into the prepared jelly-roll pan or baking pan. Set aside to cool. • Sift the flour, baking powder, and salt into a medium bowl. Stir in the dates. • Beat the butter, lemon zest, and remaining ¹/₂ cup sugar in a large bowl with an electric mixer at medium speed until creamy. Add the eggs, one at a time, until just blended after each addition. • Stir in the cooled polenta and the dry ingredients. • Spoon the batter into the prepared 11 x 7-inch pan. Cover the pan loosely with foil. • Bake for 45 minutes. Remove the foil and bake for about 45 minutes more, or until a toothpick inserted into the center comes out clean. • Cool the cake completely in the pan on a rack. • Dust with the confectioners' sugar.

Makes one 11 x 7-inch cake · Prep: 15 min. · Cooking: 90 min. · Level: 1 · Keeps: 2–3 days

SEMOLINA HEART

  2   cups milk
 ³/₄   cup granulated sugar
  1   teaspoon vanilla extract
 ¹/₄   teaspoon salt
 ¹/₃   cup semolina
  2   large eggs, separated
 ²/₃   cup candied fruit, finely chopped, extra to decorate
  2   tablespoons fresh orange juice

  1   tablespoon finely grated orange zest
 ¹/₄   cup apricot preserves
 ¹/₃   cup cold water
  1   tablespoon fresh lemon juice

Preheat the oven to 400°F. • Butter a 9-inch heart-shaped pan. • Bring the milk, sugar, vanilla, and salt to a boil in a medium saucepan. Gradually add the semolina, stirring constantly to avoid lumps. Cook for 10 minutes over medium heat, stirring constantly. Remove from the heat and set aside to cool. • Stir the egg yolks, candied fruit, orange juice, and zest into the semolina. • Beat the egg whites in a medium bowl with an electric mixer at high speed until stiff peaks form. • Use a large rubber spatula to fold the beaten whites into the semolina. • Spoon the batter into the prepared pan. • Place the heart-shaped pan in a roasting pan and fill with enough cold water to come halfway up the sides of the heart-shaped pan. • Bake for 1 hour, or until firm to the touch. • Cool the cake completely in the pan on a rack. • Warm the apricot preserves, water, and lemon juice in a small saucepan. Pour the mixture into a serving pitcher. • Dip the pan in hot water for a few seconds. Turn out onto a serving plate. • Decorate the cake with the extra candied fruit. • Serve immediately, passing the sauce on the side.

Makes one 9-inch heart-shaped cake · Prep: 35 min. · Cooking: 1 hr. · Level: 1 · Keeps: 1–2 days

SPONGE CAKES & ROLLS

The classic sponge cake is light and always contains a high ratio of liquid to flour. Height is achieved through beaten egg whites, often used in combination with baking powder. The versatility of the sponge cake lies in its numerous forms—jelly rolls, angel food cakes, and chiffon cakes—all of which look and taste fabulous.

PORTUGUESE BABA CAKE

1	cup all-purpose flour
2	teaspoons baking powder
1/4	teaspoon salt
1 1/4	cups granulated sugar
4	large eggs, separated

ORANGE SYRUP

1	cup fresh orange juice
1/3	cup dry Marsala wine or sherry

Preheat the oven to 350°F. • Butter a 9 x 5-inch loaf pan. Line with parchment paper. • Sift the flour, baking powder, and salt into a medium bowl. • Beat the sugar and egg yolks in a large bowl with an electric mixer at high speed until pale and thick. • With mixer at low speed, gradually beat in the dry ingredients. • With mixer at high speed, beat the egg whites in a large bowl until stiff peaks form. Use a large rubber spatula to fold them into the batter. • Spoon the batter into the prepared pan. • Bake for 30–40 minutes, or until springy to the touch and a toothpick inserted into the center comes out clean. • Cool the cake in the pan for 10 minutes. Turn out onto a rack. Carefully remove the paper and let cool completely. • *Orange Syrup*: Mix the orange juice and Marsala in a small bowl. Place the cake on a serving plate. Poke holes all over the cake and drizzle with the syrup. Serve the remaining syrup on the side.

Makes one 9 x 5-inch cake · Prep: 25 min. · Cooking 30–40 min. · Level: 1 · Keeps: 2–3 days

< Raspberry hazelnut gâteau (see page 163)

> Portuguese baba cake

Rolling a Jelly Roll

Jelly rolls just require a gentle touch and a little patience. Rolled up with preserves or cream, a jelly roll makes an impressive presentation.

1 Lay out a large kitchen towel or cloth on a flat surface. Sprinkle with the required amount of sugar from the recipe directions.

2 Carefully remove the parchment paper from the cake and use a large sharp knife to cut away the crisp edges.

3 Use the cloth as a guide to roll up the cake. Stand seam-side down until cooled.

4 Unroll the cake and use a thin metal spatula to spread the filling over, leaving a border.

5 Reroll the cake and stand seam-side down.

Cooling an Angel Food Cake

1 As soon as the cake has baked, it must be inverted. If you are using a pan without feet, invert the pan over a heat-resistant pudding mold until just cooled, about 1½ hours.

2 If you have a pan complete with feet, invert the pan onto the feet until just cooled, about 1½ hours.

3 Use a long sharp knife to run around the outer pan sides and the central ring, easing the cake gently from the sides. Turn upside down and turn onto a rack or serving plate.

BASIC SPONGE CAKE

4 large eggs
³/₄ cup sugar
³/₄ cup cornstarch
2 tablespoons all-purpose flour
1 teaspoon cream of tartar
¹/₂ teaspoon baking soda

Preheat the oven to 350°F. • Butter two 9-inch or one 10-inch round cake pans. Line with parchment paper. • Beat the egg whites in a large bowl with an electric mixer at high speed until stiff peaks form. • Add the egg yolks and sugar and continue beating until pale and thick. Use a large rubber spatula to fold in the dry ingredients. • Bake for 15–20 minutes, or until a toothpick inserted into the center comes out clean. • Turn out onto racks and carefully remove the paper. Let cool completely.

Makes two cakes · Prep: 15 min. · Cooking: 15–20 min. · Level: 1 · Keeps: 2 days

ITALIAN SPONGE CAKE (PAN DI SPAGNA)

This classic Italian sponge cake contains no butter or oil, and the leavening comes entirely from the beaten egg whites. It is used as the basis for many different layer cakes and desserts. You may replace the lemon zest with vanilla extract or another flavoring of your choice, depending on how you intend to use it.

1 cup cake flour
¹/₄ teaspoon salt
6 large eggs, separated
1¹/₄ cups granulated sugar
¹/₂ tablespoon grated lemon zest

Preheat the oven to 350°F. • Butter a 9-inch springform pan. Line with parchment paper. • Sift the flour and salt into a medium bowl. • Beat the egg yolks, sugar, and lemon zest in a large bowl with an electric mixer at high speed until pale and

very thick. • Beat the egg whites in a large bowl until stiff peaks form. • Use a large rubber spatula to fold the dry ingredients into the egg yolk mixture. Carefully fold in the beaten whites. • Working quickly, spoon the batter into the prepared pan. • Bake for 35–45 minutes, or until springy to the touch and the cake shrinks from the pan sides. • Cool the cake in the pan for 5 minutes. Loosen and remove the pan sides. Invert the cake onto a rack. Loosen and remove the pan bottom. Carefully remove the paper. Turn the cake top-side up and let cool completely.

Makes one 9-inch cake · Prep: 20 min. · Cooking: 35–45 min. · Level: 2 · Keeps: 3–4 days

GÉNOISE

This is the classic French sponge cake. It is the backbone of many delicious gâteaux and a host of other French classics. It is made with whole eggs and butter but contains no baking powder. It is said to have been made first in the 19th century by the Parisian pastry cook, Chiboust, who also invented the delicious Saint Honoré Gâteau (see page 178). Two cakes may be sliced into two layers each. The larger cake may be sliced into three layers.

²/₃ cup cake flour
²/₃ cup cornstarch
6 large eggs
³/₄ cup superfine sugar
¹/₃ cup butter, melted and cooled slightly
1 teaspoon vanilla extract

Preheat the oven to 375°F. • Butter a 9-inch springform pan (or two 9 x 2-inch round cake pans). Line with parchment paper. • Sift the flour and cornstarch into a medium bowl. • Beat the eggs and superfine sugar in a large heatproof bowl. Fit the bowl into a large wide saucepan of barely simmering water over low heat. (Bottom of bowl should not touch the water.) Beat constantly until the sugar has dissolved, the mixture is hot to the touch, and it registers 110–120°F on an instant-read thermometer. Remove from the heat. Beat the eggs with an electric mixer at high speed until cooled, tripled in volume, and very thick. • Use a large rubber spatula to gradually fold the dry ingredients into the batter. • Place 2 cups of batter in a small bowl and fold in the melted butter and vanilla. Fold the butter mixture into the batter. • Working quickly, spoon the batter

into the prepared pans. • Bake for 20–30 minutes for two pans, and 30–40 minutes for one pan, or until golden brown, the cake shrinks from the pan sides, and a toothpick inserted into the center comes out clean. • Cool the cakes in the pans for 5 minutes. • For the springform: Loosen and remove the pan sides. Invert the cake onto a rack. Loosen and remove the pan bottom. Carefully remove the paper. Turn the cake top-side up and let cool completely. • For the cake pans: Loosen the edges of the cakes and turn out onto racks. Carefully remove the paper. Turn top-side up and let cool completely.

Makes one or two 9-inch cakes · Prep: 25 min. · Cooking: 20–40 min. · Level: 2 · Keeps: 3–4 days

BASIC CHOCOLATE SPONGE CAKE

³/₄ cup cornstarch
2 tablespoons all-purpose flour
¹/₄ cup unsweetened cocoa powder
1 teaspoon cream of tartar
¹/₂ teaspoon baking soda
4 large eggs, separated
³/₄ cup granulated sugar

Preheat the oven to 350°F. • Butter two 9-inch or 10-inch round cake pans. Line with parchment paper. • Sift the cornstarch, flour, cocoa, cream of tartar, and baking soda into a large bowl. • Beat the egg whites in a large bowl with an electric mixer at medium speed until stiff peaks form. • Add the egg yolks and sugar until pale and thick. Use a large rubber spatula to fold in the dry ingredients. • Bake for 15–20 minutes, or until a toothpick inserted into the center comes out clean. • Cool the cakes in the pans for 15 minutes. Turn out onto racks and carefully remove the paper. Let cool completely.

Makes two cakes · Prep: 15 min. · Cooking: 15–20 min. · Level: 1 · Keeps: 2 days

Beat the egg whites and salt in a medium bowl until stiff peaks form. • Use a large rubber spatula to fold the dry ingredients into the yolks. Fold in the beaten whites. • Spoon half the batter into each of the prepared pans. • Bake for 20–25 minutes, or until a toothpick inserted into the center comes out clean. • Cool the cakes in the pans for 5 minutes. Turn out onto racks. Carefully remove the paper and let cool completely. • *Lemon Filling*: With mixer at high speed, beat the cream in a medium bowl until stiff. Fold the lemon curd into the cream. • Place one cake on a serving plate. Spread with the filling. Top with the remaining cake. Dust with confectioners' sugar and decorate with lemon peel.

Makes one 9-inch cake · Prep: 10 min. · Cooking: 20–25 min. · Level: 2 · Keeps: 1 day

CREAMY ORANGE DELIGHT

    5   large eggs, at room temperature
  3/4   cup superfine sugar
        pinch of salt
1 1/4   cups all-purpose flour
    1   teaspoon vanilla extract
        grated zest of 1 orange
    2   teaspoons orange liqueur
1 1/2   cups heavy cream
    1   tablespoon confectioners' sugar
1 1/2   cups candied orange peel, finely chopped
  1/2   cup heavy cream, beaten until stiff
    1   orange, segmented

Preheat the oven to 325°F. • Butter and flour a 10-inch round cake pan. • Beat the eggs, superfine sugar, and salt in a large bowl with an electric mixer at high speed until pale and thick. Use a large rubber spatula to fold the flour, vanilla, and zest into the batter. • Spoon the batter into the prepared pan. • Bake for 30–35 minutes, or until a toothpick inserted into the center comes out clean. Cool the cake in the pan for 5 minutes. Turn out onto a rack and let cool completely. • Cut a circle into the cake 3/4-inch from the edge. Remove the circle and cut the removed cake into cubes. • Invert the cake ring onto a baking sheet. Drizzle with liqueur. Return to the oven until crisp, about 3 minutes. • With mixer at high speed, beat the cream in a large bowl until stiff. Fold in the confectioners' sugar, cake cubes, and orange peel. • Spoon the cream mixture into the cake. • Refrigerate

Lemon cream gâteau

DAFFODIL CAKE

  2/3   cup confectioners' sugar
  2/3   cup cake flour
  1/4   teaspoon salt
    8   large egg whites, at room temperature
1 1/2   teaspoons vanilla extract
    1   teaspoon cream of tartar
  1/2   cup granulated sugar
    6   large egg yolks, at room temperature
    2   teaspoons grated lemon zest
    2   cups Tangy Lemon Frosting (see page 349)
        finely shredded lemon zest, to decorate

Preheat the oven to 350°F. • Set out a 10-inch tube pan with a removable bottom. • Sift the confectioners' sugar, flour, and salt into a medium bowl. • Beat the egg whites, vanilla, and cream of tartar in a large bowl with an electric mixer at medium speed until frothy. • With mixer at high speed, beat in the granulated sugar, beating until stiff, glossy peaks form. • Use a large rubber spatula to fold in the dry ingredients. • Place half the batter in another bowl. • With mixer at high speed, beat the egg yolks in a large bowl until pale and thick. Add the lemon

zest. • Fold the beaten egg yolks into a bowl of beaten whites. • Place spoonfuls of the batters into the pan. • Bake for 40–50 minutes, or until springy to the touch. • Cool the cake following the instructions on page 156. • Spread with the frosting. Decorate with the lemon zest.

Makes one 10-inch cake · Prep: 20 min. · Cooking: 40–50 min. · Level: 1 · Keeps: 5 days

LEMON CREAM GÂTEAU

  1/2   cup cake flour, sifted
  1/2   teaspoon baking powder
    3   large eggs, separated
  1/3   cup granulated sugar
  1/4   teaspoon salt

LEMON FILLING

    1   cup heavy cream
  1/2   cup Lemon Curd (see page 345)
    2   tablespoons confectioners' sugar, to dust
        candied lemon peel, to decorate

Preheat the oven to 350°F. • Butter two 9-inch round cake pans. Line with parchment paper. • Sift the flour and baking powder into a medium bowl. • Beat the egg yolks and sugar in a large bowl with an electric mixer at high speed until pale and thick. •

for 90 minutes, or until firm. • Carefully transfer to a serving plate. Spoon the beaten cream into a pastry bag and pipe on top. Decorate with the orange.

Makes one 10-inch cake · Prep: 40 min. + 90 min. to chill · Cooking: 35 min. · Level: 2 · Keeps: 2 days

ORANGE SURPRISE

- 1   cup heavy cream
- 2   tablespoons granulated sugar
- 1   teaspoon vanilla extract
- 1   9-inch Basic Sponge cake (see page 157)
- 1   cup fresh orange juice
- 1/2   cup + 2 tablespoons orange marmalade
      mandarin orange segments, to decorate

Beat the cream, sugar, and vanilla in a medium bowl with an electric mixer at high speed until stiff. • Split the cake horizontally. Place one layer on a serving plate. Brush with half the orange juice. Spread with the cream. Top with the remaining layer and brush with the remaining orange juice. • Warm 1/2 cup marmalade in a small saucepan over low heat. Brush the cake with the marmalade. Cover with plastic wrap and refrigerate for 1 hour. • Decorate with the orange segments. Warm the remaining marmalade and brush over the fruit.

Makes one 9-inch cake · Prep: 20 min. + 1 hr. to chill · Level: 1 · Keeps: 1–2 days

ORANGE CREAM SPONGE

- 5   large egg yolks
- 2/3   cup confectioners' sugar
- 1   package (8 oz) cream cheese, softened
- 1/4   cup fresh orange juice
- 2   tablespoons finely grated orange zest
- 2   tablespoons unflavored gelatin
- 3   tablespoons orange liqueur
- 1   cup heavy cream
- 1   9-inch Basic Sponge cake (see page 157)
- 25   ladyfingers

FROSTING

- 1   cup heavy cream
- 1   tablespoon confectioners' sugar
- 1/2   teaspoon vanilla extract

Beat the egg yolks and confectioners' sugar in a large bowl with an electric mixer at medium speed until pale and thick. Add the cream cheese, and orange juice and zest. • Sprinkle the gelatin over the liqueur in a saucepan. Let stand 1 minute. Stir over low heat until the gelatin has completely dissolved. Stir the gelatin mixture into the cream cheese mixture. • With mixer at high

Orange cream sponge

speed, beat the cream in a medium bowl until stiff. • Use a large rubber spatula to fold the cream into the cream cheese mixture. • Place the cake in a 9-inch springform pan. • Spread with half the filling. Top with a layer of ladyfingers and spread with half of the remaining filling. Lightly press down and top with another layer of ladyfingers. Spread with the remaining filling. • Cover with plastic wrap and refrigerate for 3 hours. • *Frosting*: With mixer at high speed, beat the cream, confectioners' sugar, and vanilla in a bowl until stiff. • Loosen and remove the pan sides and place on a serving plate. Spoon the cream into a pastry bag and pipe a lattice on top.

Makes one 9-inch cake · Prep: 50 min. + 3 hr. to chill · Level: 2 · Keeps: 1–2 days in the refrigerator

LEMON LADYFINGERS

- 2   large eggs
- 1/3   cup superfine sugar + extra, to dust
      grated zest of 1 lemon
- 1/3   cup all-purpose flour

Preheat the oven to 375°F. • Line two baking sheets with parchment paper. • Beat the eggs, sugar, and lemon zest in a large bowl with an electric mixer at high speed until pale and very thick. • Use a large rubber spatula to gradually fold in the flour. • Spoon the batter into a pastry bag fitted with 1/2-inch nozzle. Pipe into 2-inch long lines, 3-inches apart on the prepared sheets. • Dust with superfine sugar. • Bake for 5–10 minutes, or until golden brown. Let cool completely.

Makes 20 ladyfingers · Prep: 15 min. · Cooking: 5–10 min. · Level: 1 · Keeps: 1–2 days

COFFEE LADYFINGERS

- 2   large eggs
- 1/3   cup superfine sugar + extra, to dust
- 1   tablespoon freeze-dried coffee granules, dissolved in 1/4 cup lukewarm water, cooled
- 1/3   cup all-purpose flour

Use the instructions for Lemon Ladyfingers (see recipe left), substituting the coffee for lemon zest.

Makes 20 ladyfingers · Prep: 15 min. · Cooking: 5–10 min. · Level: 1 · Keeps: 1–2 days

ALMOND AND CARROT SPONGE CAKE

- 1/2 cup all-purpose flour
- 3/4 teaspoon baking powder
- 1/4 teaspoon salt
- 2 cups almonds, finely ground
- 5 large eggs, separated
- 1 1/2 cups granulated sugar
- 1 tablespoon grated lemon zest
- 2 cups firmly packed finely grated carrots
- 1/4 cup confectioners' sugar, to dust

Preheat the oven to 350°F. • Butter and flour a 10-inch springform pan. • Sift the flour, baking powder, and salt into a large bowl. Stir in the almonds. • Beat the egg yolks, granulated sugar, and lemon zest in a large bowl with an electric mixer at high speed until pale and thick. • With mixer at low speed, gradually beat in the carrots and dry ingredients. • With mixer at high speed, beat the egg whites in a large bowl until stiff peaks form. Use a large rubber spatula to fold them into the batter. • Spoon the batter into the prepared pan. • Bake for 55–60 minutes, or until a toothpick inserted into the center comes out clean. • Cool the cake in the pan for 10 minutes. Loosen and remove the pan sides and let cool completely. • Dust with the confectioners' sugar.

Makes one 10-inch cake · Prep: 15 min. · Cooking: 55–60 min. · Level: 1 · Keeps: 2 days

ORANGE GÂTEAU

- 4 large eggs, separated
- 1/4 cup hot water
- 1 cup granulated sugar
  grated zest and juice of 1/2 lemon
- 1 1/3 cups all-purpose flour
- 1/2 teaspoon baking powder

FILLING

- 4 large egg yolks
  grated zest of 1 orange
- 1/2 cup 1 tablespoon granulated sugar
- 2 tablespoons unflavored gelatin
  juice of 3 oranges
- 1 tablespoon fresh lemon juice
- 3/4 cup 1 tablespoon heavy cream

TOPPING

- 2 tablespoons orange liqueur
- 3 tablespoons apricot preserves
- 3/4 cup flaked almonds
- 1/4 cup (1/2 stick) butter, softened
- 1/2 cup granulated sugar
- 3 oranges, thinly sliced
  sliced star fruit and candied cherries, to decorate

Orange gâteau

Preheat the oven to 350°F. • Line a 10-inch springform pan with parchment paper. • Beat the egg yolks and water in a large bowl with an electric mixer at high speed until pale and thick. Beat in 2/3 cup sugar and lemon zest and juice. • With mixer at medium speed, beat the egg whites in a large bowl until frothy. With mixer at high speed, gradually beat in the remaining 1/3 cup sugar, beating until stiff, glossy peaks form. Use a large rubber spatula to fold them into the egg yolk mixture. • Fold the flour and baking powder into the batter. • Spoon the batter into the prepared pan. • Bake for 35–40 minutes, or until a toothpick inserted into the center comes out clean. • Cool the cake in the pan for 15 minutes. Loosen and remove the pan sides. Invert onto the rack. Loosen and remove the pan bottom. Carefully remove the paper and let cool completely. • *Filling*: Beat the egg yolks, orange zest, and sugar in a saucepan until well blended. Cook over low heat, stirring constantly with a wooden spoon, until the mixture lightly coats a metal spoon or registers 160°F on an instant-read thermometer. Immediately plunge the pan into a bowl of ice water and stir until the egg mixture has cooled. • Sprinkle the gelatin over the orange and lemon juices in a saucepan. Let stand 1 minute. Stir over low heat until the gelatin has completely dissolved. • Heat the juice mixture over low heat until the mixture thickens. • Remove

from the heat. Gradually fold the egg mixture into the gelatin mixture. • With mixer at high speed, beat the cream in a large bowl until stiff. Use a large rubber spatula to fold the cream into the egg mixture. • Split the cake horizontally. Sprinkle the orange liqueur over the cake layers. • Place one layer on a serving plate and surround with the pan sides. Spread with the filling. Top with the remaining layer. • Refrigerate for 3 hours. • Remove the pan sides. • Warm the apricot preserves in a saucepan over low heat. Brush the cake with the preserves. Stick the almonds onto the sides. • Melt the butter and sugar in a saucepan over low heat. Add the orange slices and cook until the oranges begin to caramelize, about 10 minutes. Arrange the oranges in a circle around the edge of the cake. Decorate with slices of star fruit and candied cherries.

Makes one 10-inch cake · Prep: 60 min. + 3 hr. to chill · Cooking: 35–40 min. · Level: 2 · Keeps: 1–2 days in the refrigerator

GLAZED LEMON CHIFFON CAKE

- 2 cups cake flour
- 1 tablespoon baking powder
- 1/2 teaspoon salt
- 1 1/2 cups granulated sugar
- 1/2 cup vegetable oil
- 1 tablespoon finely grated lemon zest
- 1/4 cup fresh lemon juice
- 1/2 cup milk
- 6 large egg whites
- 3/4 cup Lemon Glaze (see page 348)
  shredded lemon zest, to decorate

Preheat the oven to 325°F. • Butter and flour a 10-inch Bundt or tube pan. • Sift the flour, baking powder, and salt into a large bowl. Stir in the sugar. Add the oil, lemon zest and juice and milk. • Beat the egg whites in a large bowl with an electric mixer at high speed until stiff peaks form. • Use a large rubber spatula to fold them into the batter. • Spoon the batter into the prepared pan. • Bake for 55–65 minutes, or until springy to the touch and a toothpick inserted into the center of the cake comes out clean. • Turn out onto a rack and let cool completely. • Turn top-side up and drizzle with the glaze. Decorate with the lemon zest.

Makes one 10-inch cake · Prep: 30 min. · Cooking: 55–65 min. · Level: 2 · Keeps: 2–3 days

PASSION FRUIT CREAM SPONGE

The passion fruit adds the perfect complement of sweet and tangy to this light-as-air cake.

- ³/₄ cup cornstarch
- 3 tablespoons all-purpose flour
- ¹/₂ teaspoon baking powder
- ¹/₄ teaspoon salt
- 4 large eggs, separated
- ³/₄ cup granulated sugar

FROSTING

- 1¹/₂ cups confectioners' sugar
- ¹/₃ cup passion fruit pulp
- 1 tablespoon butter, melted

- 1 cup Chantilly Cream (see page 345)

Preheat the oven to 375°F. • Butter two 8-inch round cake pans. Line with parchment paper. • Sift the cornstarch, flour, baking powder, and salt into a small bowl. • Beat the egg yolks and sugar in a large bowl with an electric mixer at high speed until pale and thick. • Use a large rubber spatula to fold in the dry ingredients. • With mixer at high speed, beat the egg whites in a large bowl until stiff peaks form. Use a large rubber spatula to fold them into the batter. • Spoon half the batter into each of the prepared pans. • Bake for 15–20 minutes, or until a toothpick inserted into the center comes out clean. • Cool the cakes in the pans for 5 minutes. Turn out onto racks. Carefully remove the paper and let cool completely. • *Frosting*: Beat the confectioners' sugar, passion fruit

pulp, and butter in a medium bowl. • Place one cake on a serving plate. Spread with the chantilly cream. Top with the remaining cake. Spread with the frosting.

Makes one 8-inch cake · Prep: 25 min. · Cooking: 15–20 min. · Level: 2 · Keeps: 1 day

FRENCH HAZELNUT SPONGE CAKE

A large, magnificent cake. Another of the endless variations on the sponge cake.

- 8 large eggs
- 1 cup + 1 tablespoon confectioners' sugar
- 1¹/₃ cups toasted hazelnuts, finely ground
- 1 cup cake flour

Preheat the oven to 400°F. • Butter a 9-inch springform pan. Line with parchment paper. • Beat the eggs and confectioners' sugar in a large heatproof bowl. Fit the bowl into a large saucepan of barely simmering water over low heat. (Bottom of pan should not touch the water.) Beat constantly until the mixture registers 110–120°F on an instant-read thermometer. Remove from the heat. Beat the eggs with an electric mixer at high

speed until tripled in volume, and thick. • Use a large rubber spatula to gradually fold the hazelnuts and flour into the batter. • Spoon the batter into the prepared pan. • Bake for 35–45 minutes, or until a toothpick inserted into the center comes out clean. • Cool the cake in the pan for 5 minutes. Loosen and remove the pan sides. Invert onto a rack. Loosen and remove the pan bottom. Carefully remove the paper. Turn top-side up and let cool completely.

Makes one 9-inch cake · Prep: 25 min. · Cooking: 35–45 min. · Level: 2 · Keeps: 3–4 days

FRENCH ALMOND SPONGE CAKE

- 8 large eggs
- 1 cup + 1 tablespoon confectioners' sugar
- 1¹/₃ cups toasted almonds, finely ground
- 1 cup cake flour

Use the instructions for French Hazelnut Sponge Cake (see recipe left), substituting the almonds for hazelnuts.

Makes one 9-inch cake · Prep: 25 min. · Cooking: 35–45 min. · Level: 2 · Keeps: 3–4 days

Glazed lemon chiffon cake

Viennese strawberry cream cake

VIENNESE STRAWBERRY CREAM CAKE

CHERRY SYRUP

- 1/3 cup water
- 3 tablespoons granulated sugar
- 1/3 cup kirsch

STRAWBERRY FILLING

- 1 tablespoon unflavored gelatin
- 1/3 cup cold water
- 4 cups fresh strawberries, hulled and sliced
- 3/4 cup granulated sugar
- 1 tablespoon fresh lemon juice
- 2 cups heavy cream, chilled

- 1 9-inch Basic Sponge cake (see page 157)
- 1/2 cup Chantilly Cream (see page 345)
- 8–10 perfect small strawberries, to decorate

Butter a 9-inch springform pan. • *Cherry Syrup*: Bring the water and sugar to a boil in a small saucepan. Boil until the sugar dissolves, stirring constantly. Remove from the heat and stir in the kirsch. Set aside to cool. • *Strawberry Filling*: Sprinkle the gelatin over the water in a medium saucepan. Let stand 5 minutes. • Puree half the strawberries in a food processor. Stir the pureed strawberries, sugar, and lemon juice into the gelatin. Stir over low heat, until the gelatin has dissolved. • Set aside, stirring often, until cool and thick. • Beat the cream in a large bowl with an electric mixer at high speed until stiff. Use a large rubber spatula to fold it into the cooled strawberry mixture. • Split the cake horizontally. Use an 8-inch cake pan as a guide to trim the sponge cake to 8 inches. Crumble the excess cake and set aside. • Place one layer in the prepared pan and brush with half the syrup. Spread half the filling over the cake. Arrange the remaining strawberries on the cake. Top with the remaining layer and drizzle with the remaining syrup. Spread with the remaining filling. Cover with plastic wrap and refrigerate for 4 hours. • Press the cake crumbs onto the sides of the cake. • Decorate with the chantilly cream and strawberries.

Makes one 8-inch cake · Prep: 45 min. + 4 hr. to chill · Cooking: 10 min. · Level: 3 · Keeps: 1–2 days

STRAWBERRY CREAM CAKE

- 4 large eggs, separated
- 2/3 cup superfine sugar
    pinch of salt
- 3/4 cup all-purpose flour

STRAWBERRY CREAM FILLING

- 3/4 cup whole ripe strawberries, hulled and sliced
- 1/4 cup confectioners' sugar
- 3/4 cup heavy cream
- 1/2 cup wild strawberries, or small ripe strawberries

Preheat the oven to 425°F. • Butter and flour a 13 x 9-inch baking pan. Line with parchment paper. • Beat the egg yolks and 1/3 cup superfine sugar in a large bowl with an electric mixer at medium speed until pale and thick. • With mixer at medium speed, beat the egg whites and salt in a large bowl until frothy. With mixer at high speed, gradually beat in the remaining 1/3 cup superfine sugar, beating until stiff, glossy peaks form. Use a large rubber spatula to fold them into the beaten yolks. • Sift the flour into the batter. • Spoon the batter into the prepared pan. • Bake for 5–10 minutes, or until lightly browned. • Turn out onto a rack. Carefully remove the paper and let cool completely. • *Strawberry Cream Filling*: Dust the sliced strawberries with the confectioners' sugar. With mixer at high speed, beat the cream in a medium bowl until stiff. Stir in the strawberry mixture. • Split the cake vertically. • Place one layer on a serving plate. Spread with half the filling and the wild strawberries. Top with the remaining layer. • Spoon the remaining filling into a pastry bag and decorate the cake. • Refrigerate until just before serving.

Makes one cake · Prep: 30 min. · Cooking: 5–10 min. · Level: 2 · Keeps: 2 days in the refrigerator

STRAWBERRY CREAM GÂTEAU

- 2 lb ripe strawberries, hulled and rinsed (reserve 12 berries for decoration)
- 1/2 cup orange liqueur
- 8 large egg yolks
- 1 1/4 cups dry white wine
- 1 cup granulated sugar
- 2 tablespoons unflavored gelatin
- 3 tablespoons fresh lemon juice
- 2 cups Chantilly Cream (see page 345)
- 1 9-inch Génoise (see page 157)
- 1/2 cup sliced almonds, toasted

Cut the strawberries in half. Place in a large bowl with the liqueur. Soak 1 hour. • Beat the egg yolks, wine, and sugar in a double boiler until well blended. Cook over low heat, stirring constantly with a wooden spoon, until the mixture lightly coats a metal spoon or registers 160°F on an instant-read thermometer. Remove from the heat. • Sprinkle the gelatin over the lemon juice. Let stand 1 minute. Stir the gelatin into the yolk mixture until the gelatin has completely dissolved. Immediately plunge the pan in a bowl of ice water and stir until the egg mixture has cooled. Transfer to a large bowl, cover, and refrigerate, stirring occasionally, until well chilled. • Stir ⅓ of the chantilly cream into the yolk mixture. (Keep remainder refrigerated). • Drain the strawberries, reserving the juice, and stir into the yolk mixture. • Split the cake horizontally. • Butter a 9-inch springform pan. Place one layer in the prepared pan. Drizzle with enough of the reserved strawberry juice to soak it well. Spread with the strawberry mixture and top with the remaining layer. Drizzle with strawberry juice. Cover and refrigerate for 6 hours. • Loosen and remove the pan sides. • Spread with the remaining cream. • Decorate with the almonds and strawberries.

Makes one 9-inch cake · Prep: 45 min. + 7 hr. to soak and chill · Level: 2 · Keeps: 1–2 days in the refrigerator

RASPBERRY AND APPLE CAKE

- 2 lb tart cooking apples (Granny Smiths are ideal), peeled, cored, and thinly sliced
- 2 cups raspberries
- ⅓ cup superfine sugar
- 1 recipe Basic Sponge cake batter (see page 157)

Preheat the oven to 375°F. • Butter and flour a 10-inch round cake pan. Line with parchment paper. • Spread the apples and raspberries in the prepared pan. Sprinkle with the superfine sugar. • Pour the batter over the fruit. • Bake for 30–40 minutes, or until a toothpick inserted into the center comes out clean. • Cool the cake in the pan for 15 minutes. Turn out onto a rack. Carefully remove the paper and let cool completely.

Makes one 10-inch cake · Prep: 15 min. · Cooking: 30–40 min. · Level: 2 · Keeps: 3–4 days

Strawberry cream gâteau

RASPBERRY HAZELNUT GÂTEAU

- 1 lb fresh raspberries, (reserve 12 for decoration)
- 1⅔ cups confectioners' sugar
- 1 cup kirsch
- 1 package (8 oz) cream cheese, softened
- 1 tablespoon finely grated lemon zest
- 1¼ cups heavy cream
- 2 tablespoons unflavored gelatin
- ¼ cup cold water
- 1 9-inch French Hazelnut Sponge Cake (see page 161)
- 1 cup raspberry jelly

Place the raspberries, 1 cup confectioners' sugar, and kirsch in a large bowl. Soak 1 hour. • Drain the raspberries, reserving the raspberries and syrup. • Beat the cream cheese, remaining confectioners' sugar, and lemon zest in a large bowl with an electric mixer at medium speed until creamy. With mixer at low speed, beat in the raspberries. • Sprinkle the gelatin over the water in a saucepan. Let stand 1 minute. Stir over low heat until the gelatin has dissolved. • With mixer at high speed, beat the cream in a medium bowl until stiff. Use a large rubber spatula to fold the cream and the gelatin mixture into the raspberry mixture. • Split the cake in three horizontally. Place one layer on a serving plate. Brush with the syrup. Spread with half the raspberry mixture. Top with a second layer and spread with the remaining raspberry mixture. Top with the remaining layer. • Brush with the remaining syrup. • Heat the raspberry jelly in a saucepan until liquid. Spread over the cake. • Decorate with the raspberries. • Refrigerate for 1 hour.

Makes one 9-inch cake · Prep: 45 min. + 2 hr. to soak and chill · Level: 2 · Keeps: 1–2 days

BAVARIAN FRUIT DELIGHT

- 1 lb frozen puff pastry, thawed
- 1/4 cup firmly packed brown sugar

BAVARIAN CREAM FILLING

- 1 1/4 cups milk
- 3 large eggs, separated
- 1/2 cup granulated sugar
- 2 tablespoons cornstarch
- 1 teaspoon vanilla extract
- 2 tablespoons unflavored gelatin
- 2 tablespoons cold water
- 1 9-inch Italian Sponge Cake (see page 157)
- 1/4 cup kirsch or other fruit liqueur
- 2 1/2 cups heavy cream
  fresh fruit, to decorate
- 1/4 cup confectioners' sugar, to dust

Preheat the oven to 400°F. • Butter two baking sheets. • Unroll or unfold the puff pastry and place on the baking sheets. Sprinkle with the brown sugar. Prick all over with a fork. • Bake for 10–12 minutes, or until golden brown. Set aside to cool. • *Bavarian Cream Filling*: Bring the milk to a boil in a saucepan over low heat. • Beat the egg yolks, sugar, cornstarch, vanilla, and milk in a double boiler until well blended. Cook over low heat, stirring constantly with a wooden spoon, until the mixture lightly coats a metal spoon or registers 160°F on an instant-read thermometer. Immediately plunge into a bowl of ice water and stir until the egg mixture has cooled. • Remove from the heat. • Sprinkle the gelatin over the water in a saucepan. Let stand 1 minute. Stir over low heat until the gelatin has completely dissolved. Stir the gelatin into the egg yolk mixture. Set aside to cool. • Trim the edges off the cake. Split the cake horizontally. Brush the cake layers with the kirsch. • Place a layer in a 9-inch springform pan. • When the Bavarian cream begins to thicken, beat 1 1/2 cups cream with mixer at high speed until stiff. Use a large rubber spatula to fold it into the Bavarian cream. • Spoon the beaten cream over the cake. Top with the remaining layer and refrigerate for at least 8 hours. • Cut two 9-inch rounds from the puff pastry. Place a pastry round on a serving plate. Loosen the pan sides and carefully place the cake on the pastry round. • With mixer at high speed, beat the remaining cream until stiff. Spread the

Bavarian fruit delight

RASPBERRY SPONGE ROLL

- 1 cup cake flour
- 1 1/2 teaspoons baking powder
- 1/4 teaspoon salt
- 3 large eggs, separated
- 3/4 cup granulated sugar
- 1 teaspoon vanilla extract
- 1/4 cup milk
- 1/4 teaspoon cream of tartar
- 1/4 cup confectioners' sugar

RASPBERRY FILLING

- 1 cup fresh or frozen unsweetened raspberries, thawed
- 1 1/2 cups heavy cream
- 1/4 cup granulated sugar
- 1/4 cup pistachios, chopped
  raspberries and chopped pistachios, to decorate (optional)

Preheat the oven to 400°F. • Butter and flour a 15 1/2 x 10 1/2-inch jelly-roll pan. Line with parchment paper. • Sift the flour, baking powder, and salt into a medium bowl. • Beat the egg yolks in a large bowl with an electric mixer at high speed until pale and thick. Beat in the granulated sugar and vanilla until very thick. • With mixer at low speed, gradually beat in the dry ingredients, alternating with the milk. • With mixer at high speed, beat the egg whites and cream of tartar in a large bowl until stiff peaks form. • Use a large rubber spatula to fold them into the batter. • Spread the batter into the prepared pan. • Bake for 10–15 minutes, or until lightly browned. • Roll up the cake, using the confectioners' sugar and following the instructions on page 156. • *Raspberry Filling*: Process the raspberries in a food processor until smooth. Strain out the seeds. • With mixer at high speed, beat the cream and sugar in a large bowl until stiff. Fold in the raspberries and pistachios. • Unroll the cake and spread with most of the filling, leaving a 1-inch border. Reroll the cake. Place on a serving dish and spoon the remaining filling on the top. Decorate with the raspberries and pistachios, if liked.

Makes one 10 1/2-inch roll · Prep: 45 min. · Cooking: 10–15 min. · Level: 2 · Keeps: 1–2 days

cream over and top with the remaining pastry round. Spread with the remaining cream. • Decorate with fresh fruit and dust with the confectioners' sugar.

Makes one 9-inch cake · Prep: 45 min. + 8 hr. to chill · Cooking: 10–12 min. · Level: 2 · Keeps: 1–2 days in the refrigerator

COLLARED RED CURRANT CAKE

CAKE BORDER
- 1/3 cup all-purpose flour
- 1/3 cup cornstarch
- 1/2 teaspoon baking powder
- 1/4 teaspoon salt
- 3 large eggs, separated
- 2/3 cup granulated sugar
- 2 tablespoons butter, melted
  green food coloring

- 3 cups Chantilly Cream (see page 345)
- 2 9-inch Basic Sponge cakes (see page 157)
- 1 cup fresh red currants

Preheat the oven to 350°F. • Line a baking sheet with parchment paper. Draw 3 parallel lines 11 inches long and 2 inches apart. • *Cake Border*: Sift the flour, cornstarch, baking powder, and salt into a medium bowl. • Beat the egg yolks and sugar in a large bowl with an electric mixer at high speed until pale and thick. • With mixer at low speed, gradually beat in the dry ingredients. • With mixer at high speed, beat the egg whites until stiff peaks form. Use a large rubber spatula to fold them into the batter. • Divide the mixture into two bowls. Mix the coloring into a bowl. • Spoon the plain batter into a pastry bag fitted with a 1/2-inch nozzle. Using the lines as a guide, pipe strips at 1/2-inch intervals between the lines. • Spoon the green batter into the cleaned pastry bag. Pipe between the plain lines. • Bake for 5–8 minutes, or until the white strips are pale. • Cool the cake in the pan for 5 minutes. Turn out onto a rack to cool completely. • Split the sponge cakes horizontally. Place one layer on a serving plate. Spread with the chantilly cream. Top with a second layer and spread with the cream. Repeat with a third layer. • Spread the top and sides of the cake with the cream. • Gently attach the borders around the cake. • Decorate with the red currants.

Makes one 9-inch cake · Prep: 30 min. · Cooking: 5–8 min. · Level: 2 · Keeps: 1 day

Collared red currant cake

LAMINGTONS

Lamingtons are an Australian cake named after Lord Lamington, Governor of Queensland, who on January 1, 1901, read the proclamation that made Western Australia part of the Commonwealth of Australia. You could also make Chocolate Lamingtons by adding 1/2 cup unsweetened cocoa powder to the dry ingredients.

- 1 cup all-purpose flour
- 1/3 cup cornstarch
- 1 teaspoon baking powder
- 1/4 teaspoon salt
- 6 large eggs, at room temperature
- 3/4 cup granulated sugar
- 1/3 cup hot water
- 2 tablespoons butter, melted

PINK FROSTING
- 4 cups confectioners' sugar
- 1/2 cup milk
- 1 tablespoon butter, melted
- 1–2 teaspoons red food coloring
- 3 cups shredded coconut

Preheat the oven to 350°F. • Butter a 13 x 9-inch baking pan. Line with parchment paper. • Sift the flour, cornstarch, baking powder, and salt into a medium bowl. Beat the eggs and sugar in a large bowl with an electric mixer at high speed until pale and thick. • Use a large rubber spatula to fold in the dry ingredients, alternating with the water and butter. • Spoon the batter into the prepared pan. • Bake for 30–35 minutes, or until a toothpick inserted into the center comes out clean. • Cool the cake in the pan for 15 minutes. Turn out onto a rack. Carefully remove the paper and let cool completely. • *Pink Frosting*: Mix the confectioners' sugar, milk, and butter in a large bowl. Stir in the food coloring to make a pink frosting. • Cut the cake into 25 squares. Place the coconut in a jelly-roll pan. Dip each cake in the frosting, then in the coconut.

Makes 25 lamingtons · Prep: 25 min. · Cooking: 30–35 min. · Level: 1 · Keeps: 2–3 days

CHERRY AND CREAM SPONGE

- 1 recipe Génoise batter (see page 157)
- 1 cup heavy cream
- 1/4 cup granulated sugar
- 8 oz frozen sour cherries, thawed
- 1 tablespoon kirsch

Preheat the oven to 350°F. • Butter and flour an 8 x 3-inch charlotte mold or straight-sided soufflé mold. Spoon the batter into the mold. • Bake for 30–40 minutes, or until a toothpick inserted into the center comes out clean. • Cool the cake in the pan for 15 minutes. Turn out onto a rack to cool completely. • Beat the cream and 2 tablespoons sugar in a medium bowl with an electric mixer at high speed until stiff. • Place the cherries (reserving a few to decorate) and their juices in a medium bowl. Sprinkle with the remaining 2 tablespoons sugar and drizzle with the kirsch. Soak 15 minutes. • Place the cake on a board. • Use a knife to carefully cut the center out of the cake, leaving a 3/4-inch shell at the bottom and around the sides. • Chop the removed cake into cubes and stir into the cherry mixture. • Fold 2 tablespoons of the cream into the cherry mixture. • Place the cake on a serving plate. Spoon the cherry mixture into the cake. • Spoon the remaining cream into a pastry bag and pipe on top in a decorative manner. Decorate with the cherries.

Makes one 8-inch cake · Prep: 40 min. · Cooking: 30–40 min. · Level: 2 · Keeps: 1 day in the refrigerator

CANDIED FRUIT SPONGE CAKE

Fondant may be purchased through mail-order sources, such as Maid of Scandinavia.

- 1/3 cup water
- 1/3 cup granulated sugar
- 1/2 cup kirsch
- 1 cup Vanilla Pastry Cream (see page 342), cooled
- 1 9-inch Génoise (see page 157)
- 1 cup mixed candied fruit, chopped
- 1 cup Fondant (see pages 348–9)

Stir the water and sugar in a small saucepan over medium heat until the sugar has dissolved. Bring to a boil and remove from the heat. Stir in 5 tablespoons kirsch. • Stir 2 tablespoons kirsch into the pastry cream. • Split the cake horizontally. • Place one layer on a serving plate. Drizzle with the syrup and spread with the pastry cream. Sprinkle with the candied fruit, reserving 2 tablespoons to decorate. Top with the remaining layer. • Heat the fondant and remaining 1 tablespoon kirsch in a small saucepan until spreadable. Spoon the fondant over the cake and spread it quickly in an even layer over the top and sides. • Sprinkle with the remaining candied fruit.

Makes one 9-inch cake · Prep: 50 min. · Level: 2 · Keeps: 2–3 days in the refrigerator

BASIC ANGEL FOOD CAKE

- 1 cup all-purpose flour
- 2 tablespoons cornstarch
- 1 1/2 cups superfine sugar
- 10 large egg whites
- 1 1/4 teaspoons cream of tartar
- 1/4 teaspoon salt
- 1 teaspoon vanilla extract
- 1/4 teaspoon almond extract
      confectioners' sugar, to dust

Preheat the oven to 325°F. • Set out a 10-inch tube pan with a removable bottom. • Sift the flour and cornstarch into a large bowl. Stir in 1/2 cup superfine sugar. • Beat the egg whites, cream of tartar, and salt in a large bowl with an electric mixer at medium speed until frothy. • With mixer at high speed, gradually beat in the remaining 1 cup sugar, beating until stiff peaks form. Add the vanilla and almond extracts. • Use a large rubber spatula to gradually fold in the dry ingredients. •

Spoon the batter into the pan. • Bake for 50–60 minutes, or until golden brown and springy to the touch. • Cool the cake following the instructions on page 156. • Dust with the confectioners' sugar.

Makes one 10-inch cake · Prep: 15 min. · Cooking: 50–60 min. · Level: 2 · Keeps: 2–3 days

ORANGE ANGEL FOOD CAKE

- 1 cup cake flour
- 1 1/2 cups confectioners' sugar
- 12 large egg whites
- 1 1/2 teaspoons cream of tartar
- 1/2 teaspoon salt
- 1 cup granulated sugar
- 2 tablespoons orange juice
      grated zest of 1 orange

Preheat the oven to 350ºF. • Set out a 10-inch tube pan with a removable bottom. • Sift the flour into a large bowl. Stir in the confectioners' sugar. • Beat the egg whites, cream of tartar, and salt in a large bowl with an electric mixer at medium speed until frothy. With mixer at high speed, gradually beat in the granulated sugar, beating until stiff peaks form. • Use a large rubber spatula to gradually fold in the dry ingredients, followed by the orange juice and zest. • Spoon the batter into the pan. • Bake for 45–50 minutes, or until golden brown and springy to the touch. • Cool the cake following the instructions on page 156.

Makes one 10-inch cake · Prep: 15 min. · Cooking: 40–45 min. · Level: 2 · Keeps: 2–3 days

Cherry and cream sponge

LAVENDER ROSE ANGEL FOOD CAKE

- 1 cup cake flour
- 1½ cups confectioners' sugar
- 12 large egg whites
- 1 cup granulated sugar
- 1½ teaspoons cream of tartar
- ¼ teaspoon salt
- 1 teaspoon vanilla extract
  petals of 2 roses, well washed and coarsely chopped
- 2 tablespoons dried lavender

Preheat the oven to 350°F. • Set out a 10-inch tube pan with a removable bottom. • Sift the flour and confectioners' sugar into a large bowl. • Beat the egg whites, cream of tartar, and salt in a large bowl with an electric mixer at medium speed until frothy. With mixer at high speed, gradually beat in the granulated sugar, beating until stiff, glossy peaks form. Add the vanilla. • Use a large rubber spatula to gradually fold in the dry ingredients, rose petals, and lavender. • Spoon the batter into the pan. • Bake for 30–40 minutes, or until golden brown and springy to the touch. • Cool the cake following the instructions on page 156.

Makes one 10-inch cake · Prep: 15 min. · Cooking: 30–40 min. · Level: 2 · Keeps: 2–3 days

POPPY SEED ANGEL FOOD CAKE

- 1 cup cake flour
- 1½ cups superfine sugar
- 12 large egg whites
- 2 tablespoons lukewarm water (105–115°F)
- 1¼ teaspoons cream of tartar
- ½ teaspoon salt
- 2 teaspoons vanilla extract
- 3 tablespoons poppy seeds
- 1½ cups Lemon Curd (see page 345)

Preheat the oven to 350°F. • Set out a 10-inch tube pan with a removable bottom. • Sift the flour into a large bowl. Stir in the ½ cup superfine sugar. • Beat the egg whites, water, cream of tartar, and salt in a large bowl with an electric mixer at medium speed until frothy. With mixer at high speed, gradually beat in the remaining 1 cup sugar, beating until stiff, glossy peaks form. Add the vanilla. • Use a large rubber spatula to gradually fold in the dry ingredients and poppy seeds. • Spoon the batter into the pan. • Bake for 40–45 minutes, or until golden brown and springy

to the touch. • Cool the cake following the instructions on page 156. • Serve with the Lemon Curd passed on the side.

Makes one 10-inch cake · Prep: 15 min. · Cooking: 40–45 min. · Level: 2 · Keeps: 2–3 days

MOCHA ANGEL FOOD CAKE

- ¾ cup cake flour
- ⅓ cup unsweetened cocoa powder
- 1 teaspoon freeze-dried coffee granules
- 1½ cups superfine sugar
- 12 large egg whites
- 1 teaspoon cream of tartar
- ¼ teaspoon salt
- 1 teaspoon vanilla extract

Preheat the oven to 325°F. • Set out a 10-inch tube pan with a removable bottom. • Sift the flour and cocoa into a large bowl. Stir in the coffee and ¾ cup superfine sugar. • Beat the egg whites, cream of tartar, and salt in a large bowl with an electric mixer at medium speed until frothy. • With mixer at high speed, gradually beat in the remaining ¾ cup superfine sugar, beating until stiff peaks form. Add the vanilla. • Use a large rubber spatula to gradually fold in the dry ingredients. • Spoon the batter into the pan. • Bake for 40–45 minutes, or until golden brown and springy to the

touch. • Cool the cake following the instructions on page 156.

Makes one 10-inch cake · Prep: 15 min. · Cooking: 40–45 min. · Level: 2 · Keeps: 2–3 days

GOLDEN ANGEL FOOD CAKE

- 1⅓ cups cake flour
- 2 cups firmly packed brown sugar
- 12 large egg whites, at room temperature
- 1½ teaspoons cream of tartar
- ½ teaspoon salt
- 2 teaspoons vanilla extract
- ⅓ cup confectioners' sugar, to dust

Preheat the oven to 350°F. • Set out a 10-inch tube pan with a removable bottom. • Stir the flour and 1 cup brown sugar in a medium bowl. • Beat the egg whites, cream of tartar, and salt in a large bowl with an electric mixer at medium speed until frothy. • With mixer at high speed, gradually beat in the remaining 1 cup brown sugar, beating until stiff peaks form. Add the vanilla. • With mixer at low speed, gradually beat in the dry ingredients. • Spoon the batter into the pan. • Bake for 40–50 minutes, or until golden brown and springy to the touch. • Cool the cake following the instructions on page 156. • Dust with the confectioners' sugar.

Makes one 10-inch cake · Prep: 30 min. · Cooking: 40–45 min. · Level: 2 · Keeps: 2–3 days

CHOCOLATE ANGEL FOOD CAKE

1½ cups confectioners' sugar
1 cup cake flour
¼ cup unsweetened cocoa powder, sifted if lumpy
¼ teaspoon salt
10 large egg whites, at room temperature
1½ teaspoons cream of tartar
1 cup granulated sugar
1 teaspoon vanilla extract
2 cups mixed fresh berries
1 cup Lower-Fat Chocolate Sauce (see page 353)

Preheat the oven to 350°F. • Set out a 10-inch tube pan with a removable bottom. • Sift the confectioners' sugar, flour, cocoa, and salt into a medium bowl. • Beat the egg whites and cream of tartar in a large bowl with an electric mixer at medium speed until frothy. • With mixer at high speed, beat in the granulated sugar, beating until stiff, glossy peaks form. Add the vanilla. • Use a large rubber spatula to fold in the dry ingredients. • Spoon the batter into the pan. • Bake for 40–50 minutes, or until springy to the touch and the cake shrinks from the pan sides. • Cool the cake following the instructions on page 156. • Serve slices with the fruit and chocolate sauce.

Makes one 10-inch cake · Prep: 20 min. · Cooking: 40–50 min. · Level: 2 · Keeps: 2–3 days

DOUBLE CHOCOLATE ANGEL FOOD CAKE

¾ cup cake flour
¼ cup unsweetened cocoa powder
1 cup superfine sugar
12 large egg whites
1 teaspoon cream of tartar
¼ teaspoon salt
1 teaspoon vanilla extract
¼ cup Chocolate Syrup (plastic squeeze bottle)

Preheat the oven to 325°F. • Set out a 10-inch tube pan with a removable bottom. • Sift the flour and cocoa powder into a large bowl. Stir in ½ cup superfine sugar. • Beat the egg whites, cream of tartar, and salt in a large bowl with an electric mixer at medium speed until frothy. • With mixer at high speed, gradually beat in the remaining ½ cup sugar, beating until stiff peaks form. Add the vanilla. • Use a large rubber spatula to gradually fold in the dry ingredients. • Spoon ⅓ of the batter into the pan. Drizzle with half the chocolate syrup. Use a spoon

Chocolate cherry sponge

to swirl the syrup and batter together. Spoon another ⅓ of the batter over and drizzle with the remaining syrup. Swirl the syrup and batter once more. Top with the remaining batter. • Bake for 50–60 minutes, or until golden brown and springy to the touch. • Cool the cake following the instructions on page 156.

Makes one 10-inch cake · Prep: 20 min. · Cooking: 50–60 min. · Level: 2 · Keeps: 2–3 days

CHOCOLATE CHERRY SPONGE

14 oz bittersweet chocolate, coarsely chopped
1 cup heavy cream
1¼ cups canned sour cherries, drained (reserve the juice)
1 tablespoon kirsch
1 9-inch Basic Chocolate Sponge cake (see page 157) grated chocolate, to decorate

Place the chocolate in a medium bowl. • Bring the cream to a boil in a small saucepan over medium heat. Pour the cream over the chocolate. Cover and let stand 3–4 minutes until it starts to melt. Stir vigorously and set aside to cool. • When the chocolate mixture has cooled, beat with an electric mixer at medium speed until glossy. Mix the reserved cherry juices and the kirsch in a small bowl. • Split the cake in three horizontally. Place one layer on a serving plate. • Drizzle with the kirsch mixture. Spread with ¼ of the chocolate cream and top with a layer of cherries. Top with another layer. Drizzle

with the kirsch mixture, spread with chocolate cream, and top with the remaining cherries. Place the remaining layer on top. Spread the cake with the remaining chocolate cream. • Decorate with the grated chocolate.

Makes one 9-inch cake · Prep: 25 min. · Level: 2 · Keeps: 1–2 days

CHOCOLATE CAKE WITH CHANTILLY CREAM

1 cup all-purpose flour
¼ cup unsweetened cocoa powder
1 teaspoon baking powder
¼ teaspoon salt
4 large eggs, separated
¾ cup granulated sugar
¼ cup milk
1 cup Chantilly Cream (see page 345)

FROSTING

2½ cups confectioners' sugar
¼ cup unsweetened cocoa powder
2 tablespoons butter, melted
1 tablespoon freeze-dried coffee granules dissolved in 2 tablespoons hot water, or more as needed

Preheat the oven to 375°F. • Butter two 8-inch round cake pans. Line with parchment paper. • Sift the flour, cocoa, baking powder, and salt onto a sheet of paper. • Beat the egg yolks and sugar in a large bowl with an electric mixer at high speed until pale and thick. • With mixer at low speed, gradually beat in the dry ingredients, alternating with the milk. • With mixer at high speed, beat the egg whites in a large bowl until stiff peaks form. Use a large rubber spatula to fold them into the batter. • Spoon half the batter into each of the prepared pans. • Bake for 25–35 minutes, or until springy to the touch and a toothpick inserted into the center comes out clean. • Cool the cakes in the pans for 5 minutes. Turn out onto racks. Carefully remove the paper and let cool completely. • *Frosting*: With mixer at medium speed, beat the confectioners' sugar, cocoa, butter, and coffee mixture in a medium bowl until smooth. Add extra coffee if needed to make a spreadable frosting. • Place one cake on a serving plate and spread with the chantilly cream. Top with the remaining cake. Spread with the frosting.

Makes one 8-inch cake · Prep: 25 min. · Cooking: 25–35 min. · Level: 2 · Keeps: 2–3 days

ALMOND COFFEE GÂTEAU

  1   9-inch French Hazelnut Sponge Cake (see page 161)

ALMOND BUTTER FILLING
  5   large egg yolks
 1/2 cup granulated sugar
  1   tablespoon cornstarch
  1   cup milk
 3/4 cup (1 1/2 sticks) butter, softened
  1   cup almonds, finely ground
 1–2 tablespoons cold strong coffee

FROSTING
 3–4 tablespoons cold strong coffee
  1   tablespoon kirsch
 1 2/3 cups confectioners' sugar

Preheat the oven to 350°F. • *Almond Butter Filling*: Beat the egg yolks and sugar in a double boiler until well blended. • Mix the cornstarch and milk in a small bowl. Stir in the yolk mixture. Place over barely simmering water and cook, stirring constantly with a wooden spoon, until the mixture lightly coats a metal spoon or registers 160°F on an instant-read thermometer. • With mixer at high speed, beat until the mixture thickens. Remove from the heat. • Gradually beat in the butter. Add the almonds and the coffee. • Split the cake horizontally. Place one layer on a serving plate. Spread with 2/3 of the filling. Top with the remaining layer. • *Frosting*: Heat the coffee, kirsch, and confectioners' sugar in a saucepan over low heat. • Spread the cake with the frosting. Set aside. • Spoon the remaining filling into a pastry bag. Pipe on top in a decorative manner.

Makes one 9-inch cake · Prep: 30 min. · Level: 2 · Keeps: 1–2 days in the refrigerator

CHILLED CHOCOLATE CITRUS CAKE

CITRUS CREAM FILLING
  2   large egg yolks
 3/4 cup granulated sugar
  3   cups heavy cream
  1   cup chopped candied orange and lemon peel
       extra peel, to decorate
 1/4 cup shredded coconut

  1   recipe Basic Chocolate Sponge cake (see page 157), baked in 2 rectangular baking pans
 1/4 cup fruit liqueur

Preheat the oven to 400°F. • *Citrus Cream Filling*: With mixer at high speed, beat the eggs and sugar in a large bowl until pale and thick. • Heat 2 cups cream in a saucepan over low heat until almost boiling. • Stir a few tablespoons of the hot cream into the egg mixture. Pour in the remaining hot cream, stirring constantly. • Stir in the candied peel and coconut. Transfer the mixture to a double boiler over barely simmering water. Cook over low heat, stirring constantly with a wooden spoon, until the mixture lightly coats a metal spoon, or registers 160°F on an instant-read thermometer. Immediately plunge the pan into a bowl of ice water and stir until the egg mixture has cooled. • Split the cake horizontally. • Line a 9 x 4 1/2-inch loaf pan with aluminum foil and place a layer in the pan. Drizzle with the fruit liqueur. • Spoon the filling over and top with the remaining layer. Drizzle with the remaining fruit liqueur. • Refrigerate for 4 hours. • With mixer at high speed, beat the remaining cream in a medium bowl until stiff. Place the cake on a serving plate. Decorate with the candied peel.

Makes one 4 1/2 x 9-inch cake · Prep: 30 min. + 4 hr. to chill · Cooking: 12–15 min. · Level: 1 · Keeps: 1–2 days

Chilled chocolate citrus cake

AMARETTO SPONGE

- 3 large eggs + 2 large egg yolks
- ³/₄ cup granulated sugar
- ¹/₄ teaspoon salt
- ²/₃ cup all-purpose flour
- ¹/₄ cup cornstarch
- 8 soft amaretto cookies, crumbled
- ¹/₄ cup (¹/₂ stick) butter, melted

TOPPING

- 1²/₃ cups heavy cream
- 3 oz hazelnut nougat, broken up, or hazelnuts, coarsely chopped
  amaretto cookies, to decorate
  confectioners' sugar, to dust
  unsweetened cocoa powder, to dust

Preheat the oven to 350°F. • Butter a 10-inch round cake pan. Line with parchment paper. • Beat the eggs, egg yolks, sugar, and salt in a large bowl with an electric mixer at high speed until pale and very thick. • Fold in the flour and cornstarch. Add the cookie crumbs and butter. • Spoon the batter into the prepared pan. • Bake for 30–35 minutes, or until a toothpick inserted into the center comes out clean. • Cool the cake in the pan for 15 minutes. Turn out onto a rack to cool completely. • Split the cake horizontally. Place one layer on a serving plate. • *Topping*: With mixer at high speed, beat the cream in a large bowl until stiff. Spread with half the cream and sprinkle with the nougat. Top with the remaining layer. • Spoon the remaining cream into a pastry bag and pipe in a decorative manner. Arrange the cookies on top and dust with the confectioners' sugar and cocoa.

Makes one 10-inch cake   Prep: 45 min.   Cooking: 30–35 min.   Level: 2   Keeps: 1 day in the refrigerator

CARAMEL SPONGE CAKE

FILLING

- 1 cup heavy cream
- ²/₃ cup granulated sugar
- 1 cup milk
- 6 3 x ¹/₂-inch strips lemon zest, removed with a vegetable peeler
- 3 large egg yolks
- ¹/₄ cup cornstarch dissolved in ¹/₄ cup water
- 1 teaspoon vanilla extract
- 1 9-inch Italian Sponge Cake (see page 157)

TOPPING

- 1 cup heavy cream
- 2 tablespoons granulated sugar
- 1 teaspoon vanilla extract

Filling: Place the cream and ¹/₃ cup sugar in a saucepan over medium heat. Cook, stirring often, until pale gold. Remove from the heat and set aside to cool. • Bring the milk and lemon zest to a boil in a small saucepan over medium heat. Remove from the heat. • Beat the egg yolks, remaining ¹/₃ cup sugar, and 2 tablespoons milk mixture in a double boiler until well blended. Cook over low heat, stirring constantly with a wooden spoon, until the mixture lightly coats a metal spoon or registers 160°F on an instant-read thermometer. Add the cornstarch mixture and vanilla. • Remove the lemon zest from the milk and gradually beat the remaining milk into the egg mixture until smooth. Immediately plunge the pan into a bowl of ice water and stir until the egg mixture has cooled. • Pour the mixture into a bowl and stir in the cream mixture. Place plastic wrap directly on the surface and refrigerate until chilled. • Split the cake horizontally. Place one layer in a 9-inch springform pan. Spread with the filling. Top with the remaining layer. Refrigerate for 1 hour. • *Topping*: Beat the cream, sugar, and vanilla in a medium bowl until stiff. • Loosen and remove the pan sides. Carefully lift the cake off the pan bottom and place on a serving plate. Spread with the cream. • Refrigerate until serving.

Makes one 9-inch cake · Prep: 45 min. + 1 hr. to chill · Level: 2 · Keeps: 1–2 days in the refrigerator

ALMOND ROLL WITH CARAMEL CRUNCH

CARAMEL CRUNCH

- 1¹/₂ cups granulated sugar
- ³/₄ cup blanched whole almonds

- 5 large eggs, separated
- ³/₄ cup granulated sugar
- ¹/₃ cup almonds, finely ground
- 1 teaspoon almond extract
- ¹/₄ teaspoon salt
- 3 tablespoons granulated sugar, to dust
- 1¹/₂ cups heavy cream

Preheat the oven to 350°F. • Butter a 10¹/₂ x 15¹/₂-inch jelly-roll pan. Line with parchment paper. • *Caramel Crunch*: Oil a baking sheet. Cook the sugar and almonds in a saucepan over low heat, stirring constantly, until the sugar melts. Continue cooking, stirring frequently, until deep golden brown. • Pour onto the prepared sheet and set aside to cool. • When cool, crush into small pieces. • Beat the egg yolks and sugar in a large bowl

Caramel sponge cake

with an electric mixer at high speed until pale and very thick. • Add the almonds and almond extract. • With mixer at high speed, beat the egg whites and salt in a large bowl until stiff peaks form. • Use a large rubber spatula to fold them into the almond mixture. • Spoon the batter into the prepared pan. • Bake for 15–20 minutes, or until a toothpick inserted into the center comes out clean. • Roll up the cake, using 3 tablespoons sugar, following the instructions on page 156. • With mixer at high speed, beat the cream in a large bowl until stiff. • Unroll the cake and spread evenly with the cream, leaving a 1-inch border. Reroll the cake. • Press the caramel pieces into the sides of the roll.

Almond roll with caramel crunch

Makes one 8-inch roll · Prep: 30 min. · Cooking: 15–20 min. · Level: 2 · Keeps: 1–2 days in the refrigerator

CHOCOLATE ROULADE

8   oz bittersweet chocolate, coarsely chopped
1¼ cups granulated sugar
8   large eggs, separated
¼   teaspoon salt
1   cup Orange Mascarpone Cream (see page 344)

Preheat the oven to 350°F. • Butter 15½ x 10½-inch jelly-roll pan. Line with parchment paper. • Melt the chocolate in a double boiler over barely simmering water. Set aside to cool. • Beat the sugar and egg yolks in a large bowl with an electric mixer at high speed until pale and thick. • With mixer at medium speed, gradually beat in the chocolate. • With mixer at high speed, beat the egg whites and salt in a large bowl until stiff peaks form. • Use a large rubber spatula to fold them into the chocolate mixture. • Spread the batter into the prepared pan. • Bake for 15–20 minutes, or until springy to the touch and a toothpick inserted into the center comes out clean. • Cool the cake in the pan for 5 minutes. • Roll up the cake, following the instructions on page 156. • Unroll the cake and spread with ¾ of the filling, leaving a 1-inch border. • Reroll the cake and decorate with the filling.

Makes one 10½-inch roll · Prep: 30 min. · Cooking: 15–20 min. · Level: 2 · Keeps: 1 day in the refrigerator

BASIC CHOCOLATE CREAM ROLL

8   oz semisweet chocolate
3   tablespoons water
2   tablespoons strong cold coffee
7   large eggs, separated
¾   cup superfine sugar
¼   teaspoon salt
1⅓ cups heavy cream
⅓   cup confectioners' sugar, to dust

Preheat the oven to 350°F • Butter and flour a 10½ x 15½-inch jelly-roll pan. Line with parchment paper. • Melt the chocolate with the water and coffee in a double boiler over barely simmering water. Set aside. • Beat the egg yolks and superfine sugar in a large bowl with an electric mixer at high speed until pale and thick. Use a large rubber spatula to fold in the chocolate mixture. • With mixer at high speed, beat the egg whites and salt in a large bowl until stiff peaks form. Fold them into the batter. • Pour the batter into the prepared pan. • Bake for 10–15 minutes, or until a toothpick inserted into the center comes out clean. • Roll up the cake, using 2 tablespoons confectioners' sugar, following the instructions on page 156. • With mixer at high speed, beat the cream in a large bowl until stiff. • Unroll the cake and spread evenly with the cream, leaving a 1-inch border. Reroll the cake. • Dust with the remaining confectioners' sugar.

Makes one 10-inch cake · Prep: 15 min. · Cooking: 10–15 min. · Level: 2 · Keeps: 2–3 days in the refrigerator

CHOCOLATE COFFEE CREAM ROLL

½   cup all-purpose flour
⅓   cup + 2 tablespoons unsweetened cocoa powder
½   teaspoon baking powder
5   large eggs, separated
¾   cup granulated sugar
2   tablespoons butter, melted
1   teaspoon vanilla extract
½   teaspoon salt
1   cup Liqueur Pastry Cream, flavored with Irish coffee liqueur (see page 346)

Preheat the oven to 400°F. • Butter and flour a 17 x 12½-inch jelly-roll pan. Line with parchment paper. • Sift the flour, ⅓ cup cocoa, and baking powder into a large bowl. • Beat the egg yolks, ¼ cup sugar, and butter in a large bowl with an electric mixer at high speed until pale and thick. Add the vanilla. Use a large rubber spatula to fold in the dry ingredients. • With mixer at medium speed, beat the egg whites and salt in a large bowl until frothy. With mixer at high speed, gradually beat in the remaining ½ cup sugar, beating until stiff, glossy peaks form. Fold them into the batter. • Spoon into the prepared pan. • Bake for 10–12 minutes, or until springy to the touch. • Roll up the cake, using 2 tablespoons cocoa, following the instructions on page 156. • Unroll the cake and spread evenly with the cream, leaving a 1-inch border. Reroll the cake.

Makes one 12½-inch roll · Prep: 15 min. · Cooking: 10–12 min. · Level: 2 · Keeps: 2–3 days in the refrigerator

Preheat the oven to 400°F. • Oil a 15 x 10-inch parchment paper and place on a baking sheet. • Beat the egg whites in a large bowl with an electric mixer at medium speed until frothy. With mixer at high speed, beat in the sugar, beating until stiff, glossy peaks form. Use a large rubber spatula to fold in the egg yolks, followed by the cocoa and flour. • Spread the batter into a 9-inch rectangle on the paper. • Bake for 12–15 minutes, or until a toothpick inserted into the center comes out clean. • Roll up the cake, using 2 tablespoons confectioners' sugar, following the instructions on page 156. • With mixer at high speed, beat the cream in a medium bowl until stiff. • Unroll the cake and spread evenly with the cream, leaving a 1-inch border. Reroll the cake and place on a serving plate. • *Frosting*: With mixer at high speed, beat the butter and sugar in a medium bowl until creamy. Add the cocoa. • Spread with the frosting. Decorate with the walnuts.

Makes one 9-inch roll · Prep: 25 min. · Cooking: 12–18 min. · Level: 2 · Keeps: 1 day

CRISPY NOUGAT TILE

CRISPY NOUGAT

1	cup superfine sugar
2	tablespoons water
1	tablespoon butter
1	cup toasted whole almonds

SPONGE BASE

4	large eggs, separated
1¼	cups granulated sugar
	pinch of salt
¾	cup all-purpose flour
	grated zest of ½ lemon
2	cups Vanilla Custard (see page 344)
	confectioners' sugar, to dust

Crispy Nougat: Butter a baking sheet. • Heat the superfine sugar, water, and butter in a medium saucepan over medium heat, stirring constantly, until pale gold. • Stir in the almonds. • Pour the mixture onto the prepared sheet and spread with a large rubber spatula. Set aside to cool completely. • *Sponge Base*: Preheat the oven to 350°F. • Butter a baking sheet. Line with aluminum foil. Butter the foil. • Beat the egg yolks and ¾ cup sugar in a large bowl with an electric mixer at medium speed until pale and thick. • Beat the egg whites and salt in a large bowl

---

Franz Joseph chocolate cream roll

COFFEE CREAM ROLL

1	cup all-purpose flour
1	teaspoon baking powder
¼	teaspoon salt
5	large eggs, at room temperature
1	cup + 2 tablespoons granulated sugar
⅓	cup butter, melted
2	tablespoons freeze-dried coffee granules dissolved in 1 tablespoon boiling water
1	cup Liqueur Pastry Cream, flavored with Irish coffee liqueur (see page 346)

Preheat the oven to 400°F. • Butter a 15½ x 10½-inch jelly-roll pan. Line with parchment paper. • Sift the flour, baking powder, and salt into a large bowl. • Beat the eggs in a large bowl with an electric mixer at high speed until pale and thick. Gradually beat in 1 cup sugar. • With mixer at low speed, gradually beat in the dry ingredients, alternating with the butter and coffee mixture. • Spoon the batter into the prepared pan. • Bake for 15–20 minutes, or until set. • Roll up the cake, using 2 tablespoons sugar, following the instructions on page 156. • Unroll the cake and spread evenly with the liqueur cream, leaving a 1-inch border. Reroll the cake.

Makes one 10½-inch roll · Prep: 20 min. · Cooking: 16–20 min. · Level: 2 · Keeps: 1 day in the refrigerator

FRANZ JOSEPH CHOCOLATE CREAM ROLL

Franz Joseph was crowned emperor of Austria in 1848 at the age of 18. He later became king of Hungary and ruled the Austro-Hungarian Empire until his death in 1916. Franz Joseph was married to the beautiful Empress Elizabeth (Sissi). They ruled from Vienna at a time when the city was a major center of the civilized world. Music, art, architecture, and café society flourished. This recipe is said to date from that time.

6	large egg whites, at room temperature
¼	cup granulated sugar
2	large egg yolks, lightly beaten
½	cup unsweetened cocoa powder
1	tablespoon all-purpose flour
2	tablespoons confectioners' sugar
1	cup heavy cream

FROSTING

¾	cup (1½ sticks) butter, softened
½	cup granulated sugar
½	cup unsweetened cocoa powder
¾	cup walnuts, coarsely chopped

until frothy. With mixer at high speed, gradually beat in the remaining $^1/_2$ cup sugar, beating until stiff, glossy peaks form. Use a large rubber spatula to fold them into the batter. Gradually fold in the flour and lemon zest. • Use a metal spatula to spread the batter into three 4 x 10-inch rectangles on the prepared sheet. • Bake for 15–20 minutes, or until browned. • Turn the rectangles out onto a rack. Carefully remove the foil. Cool completely on the rack. • Wrap the nougat up in a kitchen towel and break it up into small pieces with a wooden mallet. • Mix the nougat pieces into the custard. • Place one layer on a serving plate. Spread with half the custard. Top with a second layer and spread with the remaining custard. Top with the remaining layer. • Refrigerate for 30 minutes, or until set. • Dust with the confectioners' sugar.

Makes one 10-inch cake · Prep: 90 min. · Cooking: 15–20 min. · Level: 2 · Keeps: 2 days in the refrigerator

CHOCOLATE RASPBERRY ROLL

3	oz bittersweet chocolate, coarsely chopped
$^1/_2$	cup all-purpose flour
$^1/_2$	teaspoon baking powder
$^1/_2$	teaspoon baking soda
$^1/_4$	teaspoon salt
4	large eggs, at room temperature
$^3/_4$	cup granulated sugar
1	teaspoon vanilla extract
2	tablespoons cold water
2	tablespoons confectioners' sugar
2	cups Chantilly Cream (see page 345)
2	cups fresh raspberries

Preheat the oven to 375°F. • Butter a 15$^1/_2$ x 10$^1/_2$-inch jelly-roll pan. Line with parchment paper. • Melt the chocolate in a double boiler over barely simmering water. Set aside to cool. • Sift the flour, baking powder, baking soda, and salt into a medium bowl. • Beat the eggs and granulated sugar in a large bowl with an electric mixer at high speed until pale and thick. Add the vanilla. Use a large rubber spatula to fold the dry ingredients into the egg mixture, alternating

Fruit jelly roll cake

with the water. Add the chocolate. • Spread the batter into the prepared pan. • Bake for 15–20 minutes, or until springy to the touch. • Roll up the cake, using the confectioners' sugar, following the instructions on page 156. Unroll the cake and spread evenly with the chantilly cream, leaving a 1-inch border. Sprinkle with the raspberries. • Reroll the cake.

Makes one 10$^1/_2$-inch roll · Prep: 20 min. · Cooking: 15–20 min. · Level: 1 · Keeps: 1–2 days in the refrigerator

FRUIT JELLY ROLL CAKE

1	Basic Jelly Roll (see page 174), before filling

FRUIT FILLING

1	tablespoon unflavored gelatin
3$^1/_4$	cups cold water
2	cups strawberries, hulled
1$^1/_2$	cups granulated sugar
$^1/_4$	cup orange liqueur
$^3/_4$	cup fresh orange juice
2	bananas, peeled and thinly sliced
1–2	tablespoons fresh lemon juice
11	strawberries, 6 halved + 5 whole, to decorate

Prepare the jelly roll to the stage where it is cooled completely. • *Fruit Filling*: Sprinkle the gelatin over $^1/_4$ cup cold water in a saucepan. Let stand 1 minute. Stir over low heat until the gelatin has completely dissolved . • Puree the $^1/_2$ cup strawberries, $^1/_4$ cup sugar, and liqueur in a food processor. • Unroll the cake and spread evenly with the strawberry mixture, leaving a 1-inch border. Reroll the cake. • Stir the remaining 3 cups water and remaining 1$^1/_4$ cups sugar in a medium saucepan over medium heat until the sugar has dissolved. Stir in the gelatin mixture and orange juice. Set aside to cool. • Slice the remaining 1$^1/_2$ cups strawberries. • Slice the cake into 10 pieces and arrange the slices in a 9-inch springform pan. • Slice the bananas and drizzle with the lemon juice. Arrange around the pan sides. Fill with the fruit jelly mixture. • Refrigerate for 6 hours. • Decorate with the strawberries.

Makes one 9-inch cake · Prep: 30 min. + 6 hr. to chill · Cooking: 12–15 min. · Level: 2 · Keeps: 1–2 days

Best-ever lemon roll

SPECKLED SPONGE ROLL

- $^1/_2$ cup all-purpose flour
- $^1/_2$ teaspoon baking powder
- $^1/_4$ teaspoon salt
- 4 large eggs, separated
- $^2/_3$ cup + 2 tablespoons granulated sugar
- 2 tablespoons hot water
- 3 oz semisweet chocolate, grated
- 1 cup heavy cream
- $^1/_4$ cup confectioners' sugar
- 1 teaspoon vanilla extract

Preheat the oven to 350°F. • Butter a 15$^1/_2$ x 10$^1/_2$-inch jelly-roll pan. Line with parchment paper. • Sift the flour, baking powder, and salt into a medium bowl. • Beat the egg yolks and $^2/_3$ cup granulated sugar in a large bowl with an electric mixer at high speed until pale and thick. • Use a large rubber spatula to fold in the hot water and chocolate. Fold in the dry ingredients. • With mixer at high speed, beat the egg whites in a large bowl until stiff peaks form. Fold them into the batter. • Spoon the batter into the prepared pan. • Bake for 15–20 minutes, or until lightly browned and springy to the touch. • Roll up the cake, using 2 tablespoons granulated sugar, following the instructions on page 156. • With mixer at high speed, beat the cream, 1 tablespoon confectioners' sugar, and vanilla in a medium bowl until stiff. • Unroll the cake and spread evenly with the cream. Reroll the cake. Dust with the remaining confectioners' sugar.

Makes one 10$^1/_2$-inch roll · Prep: 15 min. · Cooking: 15–20 min. · Level: 2 · Keeps: 1 day in the refrigerator

BASIC JELLY ROLL

Raspberry or strawberry are the classic preserves used for this simple but delicious jelly roll. But feel free to experiment with other jam flavors, including apricot, gooseberry, or ginger. If you like, serve with a bowl of freshly whipped cream.

- 3 large eggs, separated
- $^1/_2$ cup + 1$^1/_2$ teaspoons granulated sugar
- $^3/_4$ cup cake flour, sifted twice
- 2 tablespoons warm milk
- 1 cup jam or preserves, warmed

Preheat the oven to 350°F. • Butter a 15$^1/_2$ x 10$^1/_2$-inch jelly-roll pan. Line with parchment paper. • Beat the egg whites in a large bowl with an electric mixer at medium speed until frothy. • With mixer at high speed, gradually beat in the sugar, beating until stiff, glossy peaks form. • Add the egg yolks, one at a time, until just blended after each addition. Continue beating until the batter is very thick and creamy, about 10 minutes. • Use a large rubber spatula to fold the flour into the batter, alternating with the milk. • Spoon the batter into the prepared pan. • Bake for 15–20 minutes, or until a toothpick inserted into the center comes out clean. • Roll up the cake, using 1$^1/_2$ teaspoons sugar, following the instructions on page 156. • Unroll the cake and spread with the preserves, leaving a 1-inch border. Reroll the cake.

Makes one 10$^1/_2$-inch jelly roll · Prep: 20 min. · Cooking: 15–20 min. · Level: 2 · Keeps: 1–2 days

BEST-EVER LEMON ROLL

This is not an easy cake to make, but it is so good that you will be tempted to make it again.

- 2 large eggs
- $^1/_3$ cup granulated sugar
- $^1/_4$ teaspoon salt
- $^2/_3$ cup all-purpose flour
- 2 tablespoons confectioners' sugar
- $^1/_2$ cup apricot jam or preserves
- 1 cup slivered almonds

LEMON CREAM

- 1 large egg + 5 egg yolks
- $^2/_3$ cup + 2 tablespoons granulated sugar
- 2 tablespoons fresh lemon juice
- $^1/_4$ cup ($^1/_2$ stick) butter, melted

SYRUP

- zest of 1 lemon, cut into very thin strips
- $^1/_4$ cup granulated sugar
- $^1/_2$ cup water
- $^1/_4$ cup rum

Preheat the oven to 400°F. • Butter a 15$^1/_2$ x 10$^1/_2$-inch jelly-roll pan. Line with parchment paper. • Beat the eggs, granulated sugar, and salt in a medium bowl with an electric mixer at high speed until pale and very thick. • Use a large rubber spatula to fold in the flour. • Spread the batter into the prepared pan. • Bake for 8–10 minutes, or until springy to the touch. •Roll up the cake, using 2 tablespoons confectioners' sugar, following the instructions on page 156. • *Lemon Cream*: Beat the egg and egg yolks, $^1/_2$ cup sugar, and lemon juice in a double boiler until well blended. Cook over low heat, stirring constantly with a wooden spoon, until the mixture lightly coats a metal spoon or registers 160°F on an instant-read thermometer. Add the butter. Immediately plunge the pan into a bowl of ice water and stir until the egg mixture has cooled. • *Syrup*: Cook the lemon zest, sugar, and $^1/_4$ cup water in a saucepan over medium heat. Cook for 3–4 minutes, until the water is slightly reduced. • Strain the liquid and discard the zest. Stir the remaining $^1/_4$ cup water and the rum into the syrup. • Unroll the cake and brush with the syrup. Spread the cake evenly with the lemon cream, leaving a 1-inch border. •Reroll the cake and refrigerate for 2 hours. •Unroll the cake, remove the kitchen towel, and spread the roll with the apricot preserves. Sprinkle with the almonds. Reroll the cake.

Makes one 10$^1/_2$-inch roll · Prep: 45 min. + 2 hr. to chill · Cooking: 8–10 min. · Level: 3 · Keeps: 1–2 days

SPONGE ROLL WITH APPLE FILLING

- 1 cup cake flour
- 1 teaspoon baking powder
- 1 teaspoon ground cinnamon
- 1 teaspoon ground ginger
- 3 large eggs, separated
- $1/2$ cup granulated sugar
- $1/4$ teaspoon salt
- 6 tablespoons confectioners' sugar

APPLE FILLING

- 2 large tart green apples, peeled, cored, and chopped
- $1/4$ cup water
- 2 tablespoons granulated sugar
- 1 tablespoon fresh lemon juice
- 1 cup heavy cream

Preheat the oven to 375°F. • Butter a $15^1/2$ x $10^1/2$-inch jelly-roll pan. Line with parchment paper. • Sift the flour, baking powder, cinnamon, and ginger into a medium bowl. • Beat the egg yolks and sugar in a large bowl with an electric mixer at high speed until pale and very thick. • With mixer at high speed, beat the egg whites and salt in a large bowl until stiff peaks form. Use a large rubber spatula to fold them into the egg yolk mixture. Gradually fold the dry ingredients into the batter. • Spread the batter into the prepared pan. • Bake for 12–15 minutes, or until springy to the touch. • Roll up the cake, using 3 tablespoons confectioners' sugar, following the instructions on page 156. • *Apple Filling*: Bring the apples and water to a boil in a saucepan over medium heat. Cover and simmer until tender, 5–8 minutes. Stir in the sugar and lemon juice. Set aside to cool. Drain. • With mixer at high speed, beat the cream in a large bowl until stiff. • Unroll the cake and spread

Pistachio roll

evenly with the cream, leaving a 1-inch border. Spoon the apples over the cream. Reroll the cake. Dust with the remaining 3 tablespoons confectioners' sugar.

Makes one $10^1/2$-inch roll · Prep: 20 min. · Cooking: 12–15 min. · Level: 2 · Keeps: 1 day in the refrigerator

SPONGE ROLL WITH PEACH FILLING

PEACH FILLING

- 1 lb peaches, peeled, pitted, and chopped
- 1 cup granulated sugar
- $1^1/2$ teaspoons finely grated lemon zest

SPONGE ROLL

- $1/3$ cup granulated sugar
- 2 large eggs
- $1/4$ teaspoon salt
- $1/2$ cup cake flour
- $1/2$ teaspoon vanilla extract
- 3 tablespoons dark rum
- 1 large fresh peach, peeled and finely chopped, to decorate
- $1/4$ cup confectioners' sugar, to dust

Peach Filling: Cook the peaches, sugar, and lemon zest in a large saucepan over medium heat, stirring frequently, for about 20 minutes, or until the peaches are tender and the syrup has reduced. Set aside to cool. • *Sponge Roll*: Preheat the oven to 350°F. • Butter a 13 x 9-inch baking pan. Line with parchment paper. • Beat the eggs, sugar, and salt in a large bowl with an electric mixer at

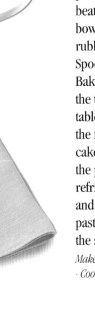

high speed until pale and very thick, about 20 minutes. • Use a large rubber spatula to fold the flour and vanilla into the beaten eggs. • Spoon the batter into the prepared pan. • Bake for 10–15 minutes, or until golden brown. • Roll up the cake, using 2 tablespoons confectioners' sugar, following the instructions on page 156. • Unroll the cake and brush with the rum. Spread evenly with the peach filling, leaving a 1-inch border. • Reroll the cake, wrap in plastic wrap, and refrigerate for 1 hour. Just before serving, decorate with the chopped peach and dust with the confectioners' sugar.

Makes one 9-inch roll · Prep: 35 min. · Cooking 10–15 min. · Level: 2 · Keeps: 1–2 days

PISTACHIO ROLL

- $1/2$ cup shelled and peeled pistachios
- $1/2$ cup granulated sugar
- $1/2$ teaspoon vanilla extract
- 2 large eggs, separated
- $1/2$ cup all-purpose flour
- $1/4$ teaspoon salt
- $3/4$ cup confectioners' sugar
- 2 tablespoons rum
- $3/4$ cup fruit preserves
- 2 cups Vanilla Pastry Cream (see page 342)
- $1/4$ cup slivered almonds

Preheat the oven to 350°F. • Butter and flour a $15^1/2$ x $10^1/2$-inch jelly-roll pan. Line with parchment paper. • Process the pistachios and 2 tablespoons sugar in a food processor until finely chopped. • Beat the egg yolks, remaining 6 tablespoons sugar, and vanilla in a medium bowl with an electric mixer at high speed until pale and thick. • With mixer at low speed, gradually beat in the flour and pistachio mixture. • With mixer at high speed, beat the egg whites and salt in a medium bowl until stiff peaks form. • Use a large rubber spatula to fold them into the batter. • Spoon the batter into the prepared pan. • Bake for 10–12 minutes, or until springy to the touch. • Roll up the cake, using 2 tablespoons confectioners' sugar, following the instructions on page 156. • Unroll the cake and drizzle with the rum. Spread with the preserves. • Reroll the cake and refrigerate for 1 hour. • Remove the towel and cut into $1/2$-inch slices. • Spread the pastry cream on a serving plate and arrange the slices over. Sprinkle with the almonds.

Makes one $10^1/2$-inch roll · Prep: 30 min. + 1 hr. to chill · Cooking: 10–12 min. · Level: 2 · Keeps: 1–2 days

FESTIVE CAKES

A child's birthday. A wedding anniversary. Or even a more unusual holiday such as April Fool's Day. Special celebrations such as these can be made more festive with a cake made especially for the occasion.

APRIL FOOL'S DAY FISH

- 1   cup all-purpose flour
- 1   teaspoon baking powder
- 1/4   teaspoon salt
- 2   large eggs, at room temperature
- 1   cup granulated sugar
- 1/2   teaspoon vanilla extract
- 1/4   cup (1/2 stick) butter, melted
- 1/2   cup flaked almonds
- 2   tablespoons confectioners' sugar, to dust

Preheat the oven to 350°F. • Butter and flour a 10-inch fish-shaped baking pan. • Sift the flour, baking powder, and salt into a medium bowl. • Beat the eggs, sugar, and vanilla in a large bowl with an electric mixer at high speed until pale and very thick. • Use a large rubber spatula to fold in the butter, followed by the dry ingredients. Fold in the 1/4 cup almonds. • Spoon the batter into the prepared pan. • Bake for 25–30 minutes, or until a toothpick inserted into the center comes out clean. • Cool the cake in the pan for 10 minutes. Turn out onto a rack to cool completely. • Transfer to a serving plate. Decorate with the remaining almonds and dust with the confectioners' sugar.

Makes one 12-inch fish-shaped cake · Prep: 30 min. · Cooking: 25–30 min. · Level: 1 · Keeps: 3–4 days

◄ Children's birthday cat cake (see page 186)

➤ April fool's day fish

Apricot gâteau

APRICOT GÂTEAU

1²/₃ cups all-purpose flour
2 teaspoons baking powder
¹/₄ teaspoon salt
1 cup (2 sticks) butter, softened
1¹/₄ cups granulated sugar
1 teaspoon vanilla extract
4 large eggs, at room temperature

FILLING AND TOPPING
1 can (15¹/₄ oz) apricots in syrup, drained (reserve the syrup)
2 tablespoons granulated sugar
¹/₄ teaspoon almond extract
1¹/₂ tablespoons unflavored gelatin
5 tablespoons kirsch
¹/₄ cup apricot preserves or jam
¹/₂ cup flaked almonds, toasted

Preheat the oven to 400°F. • Butter and flour a 10-inch springform pan. • Sift the flour, baking powder, and salt into a large bowl. • Beat the butter, sugar, and vanilla in a large bowl with an electric mixer at medium speed until creamy. • Add the eggs, one at a time, until just blended after each addition. • With mixer at low speed, gradually beat in the dry ingredients. • Spoon the batter into the

prepared pan. • Bake for 30–40 minutes, or until a toothpick inserted into the center comes out clean. • Cool the cake in the pan for 10 minutes. Loosen and remove the pan sides. Invert onto a rack. Loosen and remove the pan bottom and let cool completely. • *Filling and Topping*: Mash the apricots, sugar, and almond extract in a medium bowl with a fork until smooth. • Place ¹/₄ of the apricot syrup in a saucepan. Sprinkle the gelatin over. Let stand 1 minute. Stir over low heat until the gelatin has completely dissolved. Stir into the apricot mixture. Refrigerate until set but still malleable. • Split the cake horizontally. Place one layer in the cleaned springform pan. • Add ¹/₄ cup kirsch to the remaining syrup and drizzle over. Spread with the apricot mixture and top with the remaining layer. Refrigerate for 4 hours • Heat the preserves and remaining 1 tablespoon kirsch in a saucepan over low heat. • Remove the pan sides. • Brush with the preserves. Sprinkle with the almonds.

Makes one 10-inch cake · Prep: 30 min. · Cooking: 30–40 min. + 4 hr. to set · Level: 2 · Keeps: 2–3 days

SAINT-HONORÉ GÂTEAU
1¹/₃ cups all-purpose flour
1 tablespoon granulated sugar
¹/₃ cup + 1 tablespoon cold butter
1 large egg yolk + 1 large egg, lightly beaten
2 cups Choux Pastry (see page 308)
1 large egg, lightly beaten

FILLING
2 cups milk
4 large egg yolks
³/₄ cup granulated sugar
¹/₂ cup all-purpose flour
1 tablespoon dark rum
1 teaspoon vanilla extract

CARAMEL GLAZE
1 cup granulated sugar
2 tablespoons water

FROSTING
²/₃ cup confectioners' sugar
2 tablespoons water
1 tablespoon unsweetened cocoa powder

Preheat the oven to 400°F. • Stir together the flour and sugar in a medium bowl. Use a pastry blender to cut in the butter until the mixture resembles coarse crumbs. Stir in the egg yolk until a smooth dough is formed. • Roll the dough out on a lightly floured surface to form a 10-inch round. Prick all over with a fork and place on a baking sheet. Brush a little beaten egg around the edge. • Prepare the Choux Pastry. Fit a pastry bag with a plain ³/₄-inch tip and fill half-full with pastry. • Pipe the pastry around the edge of the pastry round. • Set aside the remaining pastry. • Brush some beaten egg over the top. • Bake for 20–25 minutes, or until golden. • Cool the pastry completely on a rack. • Line a baking sheet with waxed paper. • Fill a pastry bag with the remaining choux pastry. Pipe heaps the size of small nuts on the prepared sheet. Brush the remaining beaten egg over. • Bake for 15–20 minutes, or until golden. Cool the pastry puffs completely on racks. • *Filling*: Warm the milk in a saucepan over low heat. • Beat the egg yolks and sugar in a large bowl with an electric mixer at high speed until pale and thick. Use a large rubber spatula to fold in the flour. Gradually stir in the hot milk. • Transfer the mixture to a medium saucepan. Bring to a boil, stirring constantly. Remove from the heat and stir in the rum and vanilla. Set aside to cool completely. • *Caramel Glaze*: Warm the sugar and water in a saucepan over medium heat until the sugar has dissolved. Continue cooking, without stirring, until pale gold in color. Remove from the heat. • Spread the cooled filling into the pastry base. • Dip the tops of the choux puffs in the caramel to glaze. Dip the bases of the puffs in the caramel and stick on the crown, pressing down lightly. • *Frosting*: Mix the confectioners' sugar and enough water to make a smooth frosting. Spoon half the frosting over the filling. • Trace crossing diagonal lines on the frosting with a small knife. Stir the cocoa into the remaining frosting. Spoon the frosting into a pastry bag. Use the lines as a guide to pipe thin lines over.

Makes one 10-inch cake · Prep: 1 hr. 45 min. · Cooking: 35–45 min. · Level: 3 · Keeps: 1 day in the refrigerator

BRIDE'S ALMOND CAKE

Delicious served with a glass of champagne to toast a soon-to-be bride at a shower.

- 3 cups cake flour
- 1 tablespoon baking powder
- 1/2 teaspoon salt
- 3/4 cup (1 1/2 sticks) unsalted butter, softened
- 2 cups granulated sugar
- 1 teaspoon vanilla extract
- 1 teaspoon almond extract
- 1 cup milk
- 5 large egg whites, at room temperature
- 4 cups Almond Butter Frosting (see page 350)
- 3/4 cup flaked almonds, toasted

Preheat the oven to 350°F. • Butter and flour two 9-inch round cake pans. Line with waxed paper. Butter and flour the paper. • Sift the flour, baking powder, and salt into a large bowl. • Beat the butter, sugar, vanilla, and almond extract in a large bowl with an electric mixer at high speed until creamy. • With mixer at low speed, gradually beat in the dry ingredients, alternating with the milk. • With mixer at high speed, beat the egg whites in a large bowl until stiff peaks form. Use a large rubber spatula to fold them into the batter. • Spoon half the batter into each of the prepared pans. • Bake for 25–30 minutes, or until a toothpick inserted into the center comes out clean. • Cool the cakes in the pans for 10 minutes. Turn out onto racks. Carefully remove the paper and let cool completely.

Saint-Honoré gâteau

• Place one cake on a serving plate and spread with 1/3 of the frosting. Place the remaining cake on top. Spread with the remaining frosting. Press the almonds into the sides of the cake.

Makes one 9-inch cake · Prep: 25 min. · Cooking: 25–30 min. · Level: 1 · Keeps: 2–3 days

CELEBRATION CAKE WITH FLOWERS

- 2 cups milk
- 3 coffee beans
  zest of 1 lemon, in one piece
- 1 teaspoon vanilla extract
- 4 large egg yolks
- 3/4 cup superfine sugar
- 1/3 cup all-purpose flour
- 1 Italian Sponge Cake (see page 157)
- 1 teaspoon amaretto

TOPPING

- 2 cups egg whites
- 1/4 cup confectioners' sugar
- 1 teaspoon Alchermes liqueur or Marsala wine
  marzipan flowers, to decorate

Preheat the oven to 325°F. • Set out a baking sheet. • Bring the milk, coffee beans, and lemon zest to a boil in a saucepan over medium heat. • Remove from the heat and add the vanilla. • Beat the egg yolks and superfine sugar in a large bowl with an electric mixer at high speed until pale and thick. • Use a large rubber spatula to fold in the flour. • Gradually add the milk mixture. Return the mixture to the saucepan and cook over a low heat, stirring constantly with a wooden spoon, until the mixture lightly coats a metal spoon or registers 160°F on an instant-read thermometer. Discard the coffee beans and lemon zest. • Split the cake horizontally. Drizzle with the amaretto. Place one layer on the baking sheet. Spread with the milk mixture. Top with the remaining layer. • *Topping*: With mixer at high speed, beat the egg whites in a large bowl until stiff peaks form. Add the liqueur. • Spread with the frosting. Bake for 25–30 minutes, or until lightly browned. • Decorate with marzipan flowers.

Makes one cake · Prep: 30 min. · Cooking: 25–30 min. Level: 2 · Keeps: 2 days in the refrigerator

SÉNATEUR

This is a classic French cake. It can be served as a dessert, but it is also delicious with afternoon tea or coffee. Be sure to assemble the cake just before serving so that the puff pastry doesn't get soggy.

1½ lb frozen puff pastry, thawed
1 tablespoon kirsch or other fruit liqueur
2 cups Vanilla Pastry Cream (see page 342)
1 cup red currant jelly
1 cup toasted flaked almonds

Preheat the oven to 450°F. • Line 3 baking sheets with parchment paper. • Unroll or unfold the pastry on a lightly floured surface. • Roll out, if necessary, to measure ⅛-inch thick. Cut into three rounds, each measuring 10 inches across. Prick all over with a fork. Place the pastry on the prepared baking sheets. • Bake for 10–15 minutes, or until golden brown. You may have to bake the pastry in 2 or 3 batches depending on the size of your oven. • Cool the pastry on racks. • Stir the kirsch into the pastry cream. • Place one pastry round on a serving plate and spread with half the pastry cream. Cover with another layer of cream and top with the remaining pastry round. • Heat the jelly in a small saucepan over low heat until liquid. Pour onto the cake. Spread over the top and sides of the cake. Press the almonds into the sides and sprinkle over the top.

Makes one 10-inch cake · Prep: 45 min. · Cooking: 15 min. · Level: 2 · Keeps: 1 day

WALNUT LAYER CAKE

1½ cups all-purpose flour
1½ teaspoons baking powder
1 teaspoon ground cinnamon
1 teaspoon ground nutmeg
1 teaspoon ground ginger
¼ teaspoon salt
¾ cup (1½ sticks) butter, softened
¾ cup granulated sugar
¼ cup + 2 tablespoons pure maple syrup
1 teaspoon vanilla extract
2 large eggs, at room temperature
2 tablespoons milk
¾ cup walnuts, coarsely chopped
1 cup Mock Cream (see page 344)
1 cup Lemon Butter Frosting (see page 350)
    walnut halves, to decorate

Preheat the oven to 350°F. • Butter two 9-inch round cake pans. Line with waxed paper. Butter the paper. • Sift the flour, baking powder, cinnamon, nutmeg, ginger, and salt into a medium bowl. • Beat the butter, sugar, maple syrup, and vanilla in a large bowl with an electric mixer at medium speed until creamy. • Add the eggs, one at a time, until just blended after each addition. • With mixer at low speed, gradually beat in the dry ingredients, alternating with the milk. Stir in the walnuts. • Spoon half the batter into each of the prepared pans. • Bake for 20–25 minutes, or until a toothpick inserted into the center comes out clean. • Cool the

Sénateur

cakes in the pans for 10 minutes. Turn out onto racks. Carefully remove the paper and let cool completely. • Place one cake on a serving plate. Spread with the mock cream. Top with the remaining cake. Spread with the frosting. • Decorate with walnut halves.

Makes one 9-inch cake · Prep: 25 min. · Cooking: 20–25 min. · Level: 1 · Keeps: 2–3 days

COCONUT LAYER CAKE

This cake is best with unsweetened coconut, which is often found in the natural foods section of your supermarket. If it's not available, you may use shredded sweetened coconut instead.

2½ cups all-purpose flour
2½ teaspoons baking powder
½ teaspoon salt
1 cup (2 sticks) butter, softened
2 cups granulated sugar
1 teaspoon vanilla extract
1 teaspoon coconut extract
4 large eggs, at room temperature
1 cup milk
½ cup macadamia nuts or almonds, chopped

FILLING
1 package (8 oz) cream cheese, softened
2 tablespoons butter, softened
2 teaspoons vanilla extract
2 cups confectioners' sugar
1 cup shredded unsweetened coconut

TOPPING
1 cup heavy cream
¼ cup confectioners' sugar
1 teaspoon vanilla extract
½ cup shredded unsweetened coconut

Preheat the oven to 350°F. • Butter two 9-inch round cake pans. Line with waxed paper. Butter the paper. • Sift the flour, baking powder, and salt into a large bowl. • Beat the butter, sugar, vanilla, and coconut extract in a large bowl with an electric mixer at medium speed until creamy. • Add the eggs, one at a time, until just blended after each addition. • With mixer at low speed, gradually beat in the dry ingredients, alternating with the milk. Stir in the nuts. • Spoon half the batter into each of the prepared pans. • Bake for 25–30 minutes, or until a toothpick inserted into the center comes out clean. • Cool the cakes in the pans for 10 minutes. Turn out onto racks. Carefully remove the paper and let cool completely. • *Filling*: With mixer at medium speed, beat the cream cheese, butter, and vanilla in a large

bowl until smooth. Add the confectioners' sugar and coconut. • *Topping*: With mixer at high speed, beat the cream, confectioners' sugar, and vanilla in a medium bowl until stiff. • Split each cake horizontally. Place one layer on a serving plate. Spread with ¹/₃ of the filling. Repeat with two more layers. Place the remaining layer on top. Spread with the topping and sprinkle with the coconut. • Refrigerate for 30 minutes before serving.

Makes one 9-inch cake · Prep: 30 min. + 30 min. to chill · Cooking: 25–30 min. · Level: 2 · Keeps: 1–2 days

OPERA

This is another classic French pâtisserie cake. It was invented by the famous French chef Gaston Lenôtre.

    5   large eggs + 5 large egg whites
    1   cup granulated sugar
1¹/₃   cups finely ground almonds
   ¹/₃   cup all-purpose flour
   ¹/₄   teaspoon salt
   ¹/₄   cup (¹/₂ stick) butter, melted

    2   cups Chocolate Ganache (see page 350)
    1   tablespoon rum
   ¹/₂   recipe Coffee Buttercream (see page 346)

Syrup
   ¹/₂   cup granulated sugar
   ¹/₂   cup water
   ¹/₄   cup + 1 tablespoon rum

    2   tablespoons unsweetened cocoa powder, to dust

Preheat the oven to 350°F. • Butter a 9-inch cake pan. Line with waxed paper. Butter the paper. • Beat the whole eggs and sugar in a large bowl with an electric mixer at high speed until pale and thick. • With mixer at high speed, beat the egg whites in a large bowl until stiff peaks form. • Stir together the almonds, flour, and salt in a large bowl. • Use a large rubber spatula to fold the dry ingredients into the batter. Add the melted butter. Fold in the beaten whites. • Spoon the batter into the prepared pan. • Bake for 25–30 minutes, or until a toothpick inserted into the center comes out clean. • Cool the cake in the pan for 5 minutes. Invert onto a rack. Carefully remove the paper and let cool completely. • Prepare

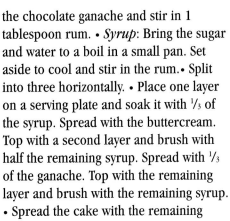

Opera

the chocolate ganache and stir in 1 tablespoon rum. • *Syrup*: Bring the sugar and water to a boil in a small pan. Set aside to cool and stir in the rum. • Split into three horizontally. • Place one layer on a serving plate and soak it with ¹/₃ of the syrup. Spread with the buttercream. Top with a second layer and brush with half the remaining syrup. Spread with ¹/₃ of the ganache. Top with the remaining layer and brush with the remaining syrup. • Spread the cake with the remaining ganache. Dust with the cocoa before the ganache has set. Refrigerate for 1 hour before serving.

Makes one 9-inch cake · Prep: 1 hr. 15 min. + 1 hr. to chill · Cooking: 25–30 min. · Level: 2 · Keeps: 1–2 days in the refrigerator

VIENNESE WALNUT TORTE

Elegant with a dense, nutty texture.

2¹/₄   cups walnuts, finely ground
   ¹/₃   cup all-purpose flour
   ¹/₂   teaspoon baking powder
   ¹/₄   teaspoon salt
    1   cup (2 sticks) butter, softened
1¹/₄   cups granulated sugar
    5   large eggs, separated
    1   teaspoon vanilla extract

Chocolate Glaze
    5   oz semisweet chocolate, coarsely chopped
   ¹/₂   cup (1 stick) butter, softened
    2   tablespoons heavy cream (optional)
   ¹/₂   cup orange marmalade

Preheat the oven to 350°F. • Butter and flour a 9-inch springform pan. • Stir together the walnuts, flour, baking powder, and salt in a medium bowl. • Beat the butter, 10 tablespoons sugar, and vanilla in a large bowl with an electric mixer at medium speed until creamy. • Add the egg yolks, one at a time, until just blended after each addition. • With mixer at medium speed, beat the egg whites in a large bowl until frothy. With mixer at high speed, gradually beat in the remaining 10 tablespoons sugar until stiff, glossy peaks form. • Use a large rubber spatula to fold them into the batter. Fold in the dry ingredients. • Spoon the batter into the prepared pan. • Bake for 50–60 minutes, or until a toothpick inserted into the center comes out clean. • Cool the cake in the pan for 10 minutes. Loosen and remove the pan sides. Invert onto a rack. Loosen and remove the pan bottom and let cool completely. • *Chocolate Glaze*: Melt the chocolate in a double boiler over barely simmering water. Remove from the heat and gradually stir in the butter until glossy. If needed, stir in the cream. • Split the cake horizontally. Place one layer on a serving plate. Spread with the marmalade. Top with the remaining layer. Drizzle with the glaze.

Makes one 9-inch cake · Prep: 35 min. · Cooking: 50–60 min. · Level: 1 · Keeps: 2–3 days

Dobos torte

DOBOS TORTE

This famous Hungarian cake was created by master chef Jósef Dobos in the second half of the 19th century. He presented it officially at a national show in 1885. No one quite got it right until 1906, when chef Dobos finally released the recipe.

- 1 cup cake flour
- 1/4 teaspoon salt
- 6 large eggs, separated
- 1 1/2 cups confectioners' sugar
- 1 teaspoon vanilla extract

CHOCOLATE BUTTERCREAM

- 5 oz bittersweet chocolate, coarsely chopped
- 1 3/4 cups (3 1/2 sticks) unsalted butter, softened
- 1 1/2 cups confectioners' sugar
- 2 tablespoons unsweetened cocoa powder
- 1 teaspoon vanilla extract

GLAZE

- 1 cup granulated sugar
- 3 tablespoons water
- 1 tablespoon unsalted butter
- 2 teaspoons fresh lemon juice
- 10 whole, toasted and peeled hazelnuts

Preheat the oven to 350°F. • Butter two 9-inch round cake pans. Line with parchment paper. • Sift the flour and salt into a medium bowl. Beat the egg yolks, 3/4 cup confectioners' sugar, and vanilla in a large bowl with an electric mixer at high speed until pale and very thick. • With mixer at medium speed, beat the egg whites in a large bowl until frothy. With mixer at high speed, gradually beat in the remaining 3/4 cup confectioners' sugar, beating until stiff, glossy peaks form. Use a large rubber spatula to fold them into the batter. Fold in the dry ingredients. • Spoon 2/3 cup batter into each of the prepared pans. • Bake for 5–8 minutes, or until golden brown and springy to the touch. • Cool the cakes in the pans for 5 minutes. Turn out onto racks. Carefully remove the paper and let cool completely. Cool and clean the pans, butter and flour them, and reline with parchment paper. Repeat until all the batter is used up, making 6 or 7 layers. • *Chocolate Buttercream*: Melt the chocolate in a double boiler over barely simmering water. Set aside to cool. • With mixer at medium speed, beat the butter in a large bowl until creamy. Add the confectioners' sugar and cocoa, followed by the chocolate and vanilla. • Place one layer on a serving plate and spread with some buttercream. Repeat with all but the top layer. Place this layer on a large plate. Spread the cake with the remaining buttercream. • *Glaze*: Bring the sugar, water, butter, and lemon juice to a boil in a saucepan over medium heat, until the sugar has dissolved. Boil until the mixture is amber colored. • Spread the caramel over the reserved cake layer. Set for about 30 seconds. Use a sharp knife to cut the layer into 10 equal, wedge-shaped portions. Let cool completely. • Using the whole hazelnuts as props, arrange the wedges of cake on top of the cake overlapping, and each on an angle, to resemble the photograph.

Makes one 9-inch cake · Prep: 1 hr. 15 min. · Cooking: 15–32 min. · Level: 3 · Keeps: 1–2 days

PECAN WEDDING CAKE

- 1/2 cup buttermilk
- 1 teaspoon baking soda
- 1 teaspoon salt
- 1/2 cup vegetable shortening
- 1/2 cup (1 stick) butter, softened
- 2 cups granulated sugar
- 1 teaspoon vanilla extract
- 1/2 teaspoon almond extract
- 5 large eggs, separated
- 2 cups all-purpose flour
- 1/2 cup crushed pineapple, drained
- 1/2 cup flaked coconut
- 1 cup pecans, chopped

CREAM CHEESE FROSTING

- 3/4 cup (1 1/2 sticks) butter, softened
- 1 package (8 oz) cream cheese, softened
- 4 cups confectioners' sugar
- 2 teaspoons vanilla extract
- 1/2 cup pecans, chopped

Preheat the oven to 350°F. • Butter three 8-inch round cake pans. Line with waxed paper. Butter the paper. • Mix the buttermilk, baking soda, and salt in a bowl and set aside. • Beat the shortening, butter, sugar, vanilla, and almond extract in a large bowl with an electric mixer at medium speed until creamy. • Add the egg yolks, one at a time, until just blended after each addition. • With mixer at low speed, gradually beat in the flour, alternating with the buttermilk mixture. • Stir in the pineapple, coconut, and pecans. • With mixer at high speed, beat the egg whites in a large bowl until stiff peaks form. Use a large rubber spatula to fold them into the batter. • Spoon the batter into the prepared pans. • Bake for 25–35 minutes, or until a toothpick inserted into the center comes out clean. • Cool the cakes in the pans for 5 minutes. Turn out onto racks. Carefully remove the paper and let cool completely. • *Cream Cheese Frosting*: With mixer at low speed, beat the butter, cream cheese, confectioners' sugar, and vanilla in a large bowl until it has a spreading consistency. • Place one layer on a serving dish and spread with $1/4$ of the frosting. Place a layer on top and spread with $1/4$ of the frosting. Top with the remaining layer. Spread with the remaining frosting. Sprinkle with pecans.

Makes one 8-inch cake · Prep: 30 min. · Cooking: 25–35 min. · Level: 1 · Keeps: 2–3 days

ALMOND BERRY SUPREME

3	cups all-purpose flour
2	teaspoons baking powder
$1/2$	teaspoon baking soda
$1/2$	teaspoon salt
2	cups finely ground almonds
2	cups (4 sticks) butter, softened
4	cups granulated sugar
12	large eggs, at room temperature
$1^1/4$	cups sour cream
$1^1/4$	cups fresh or frozen and thawed raspberries
$1^1/4$	cups fresh or frozen and thawed blackberries
2	recipes White Chocolate Ganache (see page 350)
5	oz white chocolate, coarsely chopped
10	oz dark chocolate, coarsely chopped
$2^2/3$	cups mixed fresh berries, grapes, and fresh currants

Preheat the oven to 350°F. • Butter one 10 x 3-inch and one 7 x 3-inch round cake pans. Line with waxed paper. Butter the paper. • Sift the flour, baking powder, baking soda, and salt into a large bowl. Stir in the almonds. • Beat the butter and sugar in a large bowl with an electric mixer at medium speed until creamy. • Add the eggs, one at a time, until just blended after each addition. • With mixer at low speed, gradually beat in the dry ingredients, alternating with the sour cream, raspberries, and blackberries. • Spoon $3/4$ of the batter into the prepared 10-inch pan. Spoon the remaining batter into the 7-inch pan. • Bake the 10-inch cake for about 1 hour and 30–40 minutes, or until a toothpick inserted into the center comes out clean. Bake the 7-inch cake for 50–60

Almond berry supreme

minutes, or until a toothpick inserted into the center comes out clean. • Cool the cakes in the pans for 5 minutes. Turn out onto racks and carefully remove the paper. Let cool completely. • Place the large cake on a serving plate. Spread with $2/3$ of the white chocolate ganache. Center the smaller cake on top. Spread with the remaining ganache. • Melt the white chocolate in a double boiler over barely simmering water. Set aside. • Melt the dark chocolate in a double boiler over barely simmering water. Set aside. • Cut 1 strip of parchment paper to measure $2^1/2$ x $27^1/2$ inches. Cut another strip to measure $3^1/2$ x 40 inches. Cut a wave pattern $1/2$-inch from the top. Spread the short strip with the white chocolate. Spread the long strip with the dark chocolate. Wrap the smaller strip around the top layer of cake. Wrap the larger strip around the bottom layer. Set aside. Carefully remove the paper. • Decorate with the fruit.

Makes 1 cake · Prep: 1 hr. · Cooking: 1 hr. 30–40 min. · Level: 2 · Keeps: 2–3 days

HAWAIIAN WEDDING CAKE

2	cups all-purpose flour
2	cups granulated sugar
2	teaspoons baking powder
2	large eggs, lightly beaten
1	cup mixed nuts, finely chopped
1	cup shredded coconut
1	(20 oz) can crushed pineapple
1	cup cream cheese, softened
$1/4$	cup ($1/2$ stick) butter, softened
1	teaspoon vanilla extract
$1^1/2$	cups confectioners' sugar

Preheat the oven to 350°F. • Butter and flour a 13 x 9-inch baking pan. • Stir together the flour, sugar, and baking powder in a large bowl. Use a large rubber spatula to fold in the eggs, nuts, coconut, and pineapple and juice. • Pour the batter into the prepared pan. • Bake for 35–40 minutes, or until a toothpick inserted into the center comes out clean. • Cool the cake completely in the pan on a rack. • *Frosting*: Beat the cream cheese, butter, vanilla, and confectioners' sugar in a large bowl with an electric mixer at high speed until creamy. Spread over the cake

Makes one 13-inch cake · Prep: 15 min. · Cooking: 35–40 min. · Level: 1 · Keeps: 2–3 days

White chocolate mousse cake with lemon and kiwi

WHITE CHOCOLATE MOUSSE CAKE WITH LEMON AND KIWI

MOUSSE

- 6 oz white chocolate, coarsely chopped
- 2 packages (3 oz each) cream cheese, softened
- 1/4 cup granulated sugar
- 4 teaspoons unflavored gelatin
- 1/3 cup fresh orange juice
- 1 1/2 cups heavy cream

- 1 9-inch Basic Butter Cake (see page 14)

LEMON TOPPING

- 1/2 cup fresh lemon juice
- 1/4 cup granulated sugar
- 1 teaspoon unflavored gelatin
- 3–4 medium kiwifruit, peeled and sliced

Mousse: Melt the white chocolate in a double boiler over barely simmering water. Set aside to cool. • Beat the cream cheese and sugar in a large bowl with an electric mixer at medium speed until smooth. • Add the white chocolate. • Sprinkle the gelatin over the orange juice in a saucepan. Let stand 1 minute. Stir over low heat until the gelatin has completely dissolved. Set aside to cool for 30 minutes. • Beat the cooled orange juice into the cream cheese mixture. • With mixer at high speed, beat the cream in a medium bowl until stiff. • Use a rubber spatula to fold the cream into the cream cheese mixture. • Trim the rounded top off the cake. • Place the cake in a 9-inch springform pan. Pour the mousse over the cake and refrigerate for 6 hours. • Lemon Topping: Stir the lemon juice and sugar in a saucepan over low heat until the sugar has

dissolved. Remove from the heat and stir in the gelatin until dissolved. Set aside to cool. • Pour the topping over and refrigerate for 6 hours, or until set. • Loosen and remove the pan sides. Decorate with the kiwi.

Makes one 9-inch cake · Prep: 1 hr. + 12 hr. to chill · Level: 2 · Keeps: 1–2 days

CHOCOLATE CANTALOUPE CAKE

The combination of the delicious flavor of a cantaloupe melon and the richness of chocolate make this cake unusual.

- 4 oz bittersweet chocolate, coarsely chopped
- 1 1/3 cups all-purpose flour
- 1/4 cup unsweetened cocoa powder
- 1 teaspoon baking powder
- 1/4 teaspoon salt
- 1/2 cup (1 stick) butter, softened
- 3/4 cup granulated sugar
- 3 large eggs, separated

FILLING

- 1/2 ripe cantaloupe, seeded (about 1 1/4 lb)
- 1 tablespoon unflavored gelatin
- 1/4 cup water
- 3 large egg yolks
- 1/3 cup milk
- 1/2 cup granulated sugar
- 2 cups heavy cream, whipped
- 2 tablespoons coarsely grated bittersweet chocolate

Preheat the oven to 350°F. • Butter a 9-inch round cake pan. Dust with cocoa. • Melt the chocolate in a double boiler over barely simmering water. Set aside to cool. • Sift the flour, cocoa, baking powder, and salt into a medium bowl. • Beat the butter and sugar in a large bowl with an electric mixer at medium speed until creamy. • Add the egg

yolks, one at a time, until just blended after each addition. • With mixer at low speed, gradually beat in the chocolate, followed by the dry ingredients. • With mixer at high speed, beat the egg whites in a medium bowl until stiff peaks form. Use a large rubber spatula to fold them into the batter. • Spoon the batter into the prepared pan. • Bake for 35–40 minutes, or until a toothpick inserted into the center comes out clean. • Cool the cake in the pan for 10 minutes. Turn out onto a rack to cool completely. • *Filling*: Cut the cantaloupe half into 2 pieces. Peel one piece with a knife and cut into chunks. Puree the melon chunks in a food processor until smooth. Use a melon baller to scoop the remaining melon into balls, reserving any juice. Refrigerate the puree, melon balls and juice. • Sprinkle the gelatin over the water in a saucepan. • Beat the egg yolks, milk, and sugar in a medium saucepan. Place over low heat and cook, stirring constantly with a wooden spoon, until the mixture lightly coats a metal spoon or registers 160°F on an instant-read thermometer. Immediately plunge the pan into a bowl of ice water and stir until cooled. Beat the egg yolk mixture with a mixer at high speed until thick. Place the gelatin over low heat and stir until completely dissolved. • Stir the gelatin and pureed cantaloupe into the egg mixture. Use a large rubber spatula to fold in the whipped cream. • Split the cake horizontally. Place one layer in a 10-inch springform pan. • Drizzle with some reserved juice and spread with half the cantaloupe filling. Place the remaining layer on top. Drizzle with the cantaloupe juice and spread the remaining filling over the top and down onto the sides. • Decorate with the cantaloupe balls and the grated chocolate. • Refrigerate for 3 hours. Loosen and remove the pan sides.

Makes one 9-inch cake · Prep: 40 min. + 3 hr. to chill · Cooking: 35–40 min. · Level: 2 · Keeps: 1 day

CHERRY MILLE-FEUILLE

- 1 lb fresh or frozen puff pastry, thawed if frozen
- 6 (14 oz) cans Morello or sour cherries, drained (reserve 2 cups syrup)
- 2 tablespoons cornstarch
- 1 8-inch Basic Coconut Cake (see page 32)
- 2 recipes Vanilla Pastry Cream (see page 342)
- 9 tablespoons kirsch
  confectioners' sugar, to dust

Preheat the oven to 425°F. • Line a baking sheet with parchment paper. • Unfold or unroll the pastry. Roll, if necessary, to measure about $\frac{1}{8}$-inch thick. Fit the pastry into the prepared baking sheet. Prick all over with a fork. • Bake for 10–15 minutes, or until crisp. • Cool completely on racks. • Mix $\frac{1}{4}$ cup of the reserved cherry syrup and cornstarch in a saucepan. Stir in the remaining juice and cherries. Bring to a boil over medium heat, stirring constantly, and continue cooking until the mixture thickens. • Pour the cherry mixture into a large bowl and set aside to cool completely. • Split the cake into three horizontally. • Spread a pastry layer with $\frac{1}{3}$ of the cherry mixture. Top with a cake layer. Drizzle with 3 tablespoons kirsch. Spread with $\frac{1}{3}$ of the pastry cream. • Repeat these layers until the ingredients are used up, finishing with a pastry layer. • Use a serrated knife

to trim the cake to ensure that the sides are even. • Transfer the cake to a serving plate. Dust with confectioners' sugar.

Makes one 9-inch cake · Prep: 90 min. · Cooking: 10–15 min. · Level: 2 · Keeps: 1 day in the refrigerator

CHOCOLATE RICOTTA CAKE

- 1$\frac{1}{2}$ cups almonds, finely ground
- $\frac{2}{3}$ cup cake flour
- $\frac{2}{3}$ cup unsweetened cocoa powder
- 1$\frac{1}{2}$ teaspoons baking powder
- $\frac{1}{4}$ teaspoon salt
- 8 large eggs, separated
- 1$\frac{1}{2}$ cups granulated sugar
- 2 teaspoons vanilla extract
- $\frac{1}{2}$ teaspoon almond extract
- $\frac{1}{2}$ cup milk
  shavings of bittersweet chocolate, to decorate (optional)

RICOTTA FILLING

- 1 cup heavy cream
- 1 container (15–16 oz) ricotta cheese
- $\frac{1}{2}$ cup confectioners' sugar
- $\frac{1}{2}$ cup chopped candied orange peel

CHOCOLATE CREAM TOPPING

- 2 cups heavy cream
- $\frac{2}{3}$ cup confectioners' sugar
- $\frac{1}{3}$ cup unsweetened cocoa powder, sifted
- 2 teaspoons vanilla extract

Preheat the oven to 375°F. • Butter two 9-inch round cake pans. Line with parchment paper. • Stir together the almonds, flour, cocoa, baking powder, and salt in a large bowl. • Beat the egg yolks, 1 cup sugar, vanilla, and almond extract in a large bowl

with an electric mixer at high speed until pale and very thick. • With mixer at low speed, gradually beat in the dry ingredients, alternating with the milk. • With mixer at medium speed, beat the egg whites in a large bowl until frothy. • With mixer at high speed, gradually beat in the remaining $\frac{1}{2}$ cup sugar, beating until stiff, glossy peaks form. • Use a large rubber spatula to fold them into the batter. • Spoon half the batter into each of the prepared pans. • Bake for 20–25 minutes, or until a toothpick inserted into the center comes out clean. • Cool the cakes in the pans for 10 minutes. Turn out onto racks. Carefully remove the paper and let cool completely. • *Ricotta Filling*: With mixer at high speed, beat the cream in a medium bowl until stiff. • Process the ricotta, confectioners' sugar, and orange peel in a food processor until smooth. Transfer to a large bowl. • Use a large rubber spatula to fold the cream into the ricotta mixture. • *Chocolate Cream Topping*: With mixer at high speed, beat the cream, confectioners' sugar, cocoa, and vanilla in a large bowl until stiff. • Split the cakes horizontally. Place one layer on a serving plate. Spread with $\frac{1}{3}$ of the filling. Repeat with two more layers. Place the remaining layer on top. • Spread with the topping. Decorate with the chocolate, if desired.

Makes one 9-inch cake · Prep: 50 min. · Cooking: 20–25 min. · Level: 2 · Keeps: 1–2 days

Cherry mille-feuille

M&M CAKE

1⅓ cups all-purpose flour
1½ teaspoons baking powder
¼ teaspoon salt
⅔ cup shredded coconut
½ cup (1 stick) butter, softened
½ cup granulated sugar
2 teaspoons vanilla extract
3 large eggs, at room temperature
3 tablespoons milk
    scant 1 cup plain M & M's

Preheat the oven to 325°F. • Butter and flour a 9-inch square pan. • Sift the flour, baking powder, and salt into a medium bowl. Stir in the coconut. • Beat the butter, sugar, and vanilla in a large bowl with an electric mixer at medium speed until creamy. • Add the eggs, one at a time, until just blended after each addition. • With mixer at low speed, gradually beat in the dry ingredients, alternating with the milk. • Stir in ¾ of the M & M's. • Spoon the batter into the prepared pan. Sprinkle with the remaining M & M's. • Bake for 30–35 minutes, or until a toothpick inserted into the center comes out clean. • Cool the cake completely in the pan.

Makes one 9-inch cake · Prep: 20 min. · Cooking: 30–35 min. · Level: 1 · Keeps: 2–3 days

CLOWN PARTY CAKE

3 large eggs, separated
½ cup granulated sugar
1 cup finely ground almonds
⅔ cup all-purpose flour
¼ teaspoon salt

ALMOND ICE CREAM

3 large eggs, separated
½ cup granulated sugar
1 teaspoon vanilla extract
½ teaspoon almond extract
2 cups heavy cream

TOPPING

4 ice cream sugar cones
    brightly colored candy to make eyes, noses, and mouths on the clowns

Preheat the oven to 350°F. • Butter and flour a 9-inch springform pan. • Beat the egg yolks and sugar in a large bowl with an electric mixer at high speed until pale and thick. • With mixer at medium speed, gradually beat in the almonds and flour. • Beat the egg whites and salt with an electric mixer at high speed until stiff peaks form. Use a large rubber spatula to fold them into the batter. • Spoon the batter into the prepared pan. • Bake for 30–40 minutes, or until a toothpick inserted into the center comes out clean. • Cool the cake in the pan on a rack. • *Almond Ice Cream*: Beat the egg yolks, sugar, vanilla, and almond extract in a large bowl with an electric mixer at high speed until pale and thick. • Transfer to a double boiler. Cook over low heat until the mixture lightly coats a metal spoon or registers 160°F on an instant-read thermometer. Plunge the pan into a bowl of ice water and stir until the egg mixture has cooled. • With mixer at high speed, beat the cream in a medium bowl until stiff. • Fold the cream into the cooled egg mixture. • Place in a freezer-proof bowl and freeze for 2 hours, stirring at frequent intervals to prevent ice crystals forming. • Use a small ice cream scoop to make four 1½-inch balls. Set aside on a plate in the freezer. • Spread the remaining ice cream on the cake and return to the freezer for 1 hour. • Loosen and remove the pan sides and place the cake on a serving plate. • Place the balls of ice cream on top and top each with an upside-down ice cream cone to make a clown hat. • Use the candy to give each clown eyes, a nose, and a mouth.

Makes one 9-inch cake · Prep: 45 min. + 3 hr. to freeze · Cooking: 30–40 min. · Level: 2 · Keeps: 1 day in the freezer

CHILDREN'S BIRTHDAY CAT CAKE

8 oz bittersweet chocolate, coarsely chopped
1⅓ cups all-purpose flour
1 teaspoon baking powder
¼ teaspoon salt
¾ cup (1½ sticks) butter, softened
1 cup granulated sugar
8 large eggs, separated
½ cup apricot preserves or jam
2 cups Rich Chocolate Frosting (see page 349)
    candy pieces, for the eyes, mouth, and whiskers

Preheat the oven to 350°F. • Butter a 9 x 3-inch round cake pan. Line with waxed paper. Butter the paper. • Melt the chocolate in a double boiler over barely simmering water. Set aside to cool. • Sift the flour, baking powder, and salt into a large bowl. • Beat the butter and sugar in a large bowl with an electric mixer at medium speed until creamy. • Add the egg yolks, one at a time, until just blended after each addition. • With mixer at low speed, gradually beat in the dry ingredients, alternating with the chocolate. • With mixer at high speed, beat the egg whites in a large bowl until stiff peaks form. Use a large rubber spatula to fold them into the batter. • Spoon the batter into the prepared pan. • Bake for 50–60 minutes, or until a toothpick inserted into the center comes out clean. • Cool the cake in the pan for 10 minutes. Turn out onto a rack. Carefully remove the paper and let cool completely. • Split the cake horizontally. Place one layer on a serving plate. Spread with half the preserves. Top with the remaining layer. Spread with the remaining preserves. • Spread with the frosting. • Form the eyes, mouth, and whiskers with the candy.

Makes one 9-inch cake · Prep: 45 min. · Cooking: 50–60 min. · Level: 2 · Keeps: 2–3 days

LADYBUG BIRTHDAY CAKE

2 10-inch store-bought round sponge cakes
¾ recipe Rich Chocolate Frosting (see page 349)
1½ recipes Vanilla Frosting (see page 347)
1 teaspoon red food coloring
    brown and red M & M's, to decorate

Place one cake on a serving plate. Spread the top and sides of the cake with the chocolate frosting. • Slice the remaining cake in half vertically. • Mix the vanilla frosting and the red food coloring in a medium bowl until well blended. Spread the top and sides of the cake with the red frosting. Place the two halves of cake on top of the chocolate-frosted cake to resemble wings. • Decorate with the M & M's, adding spots, eyes, and a mouth.

Makes one 10-inch cake · Prep: 15 min. · Level: 1 ·Keeps: 2 days

PIG BIRTHDAY CAKE

1 recipe Basic Butter Cake, baked in an 8-inch round cake pan and a small ramekin (see page 14)
⅓ recipe Chocolate Buttercream (see page 346)
1 teaspoon red food coloring
1 cup Fondant (see pages 348–9)
    candies, to decorate

Split the large cake horizontally. • Place a layer on a serving plate. Spread with the buttercream. Top with the remaining large layer. • Center the small cake on top. • Stir the red food coloring into the fondant and spread over the top and sides of the cake. Set aside to dry completely. • Place the candies on top of the cake to form a snout and eyes.

Makes one 8-inch cake · Prep: 15 min. · Level: 2 · Keeps: 2–3 days in the refrigerator

Clown party cake

Birthday fruit box

BIRTHDAY FRUIT BOX

This eye-catching cake makes a wonderful birthday surprise for children and adults alike. Be sure to make it using the birthday boy or girl's favorite fruit and ice-cream.

2 recipes 9-inch square Basic Butter Cake or Coconut Cake, each batch baked in a 9-inch square pan (see pages 14, 32)
2 quarts favorite flavor ice cream
1/4 cup jam or preserves (raspberry, strawberry, or apricot are good choices), stirred until liquid
1 cup Apricot Glaze (see page 348), warm
1 lb strawberries, hulled and cut in half
3–4 kiwifruit, peeled and thinly sliced
1/2 cup blueberries and red currants, to decorate

Leave the ice cream at room temperature for 10 minutes to soften. • Wrap two pieces of cardboard with foil and place a cake on each. Slice the domed tops off the cakes. Cut around the inside of each cake leaving a 1/2-inch shell on the sides and bottom. Scoop out the insides of the cake. • Fill the hollow centers of the cakes with the ice cream, packing it down firmly. Brush the cake with the jam and place one cake over the other,

open-side down, to create a closed box. Press together firmly and wrap in plastic wrap or aluminum foil and freeze overnight. • Still on the cardboard, place the cake on a serving plate. Brush with a layer of glaze. Working quickly, stick strawberry halves and slices of kiwi all over the surface of the cake. Brush the fruit with more fruit glaze. Decorate with the fruit. Serve immediately or return to the freezer.

Makes one 9-inch cake · Prep: 1 hr. · Level: 2 · Keeps: 1 day

CHANTILLY FRESH FRUIT DELIGHT

2 cups all-purpose flour
1 1/2 teaspoons baking powder
3/4 teaspoon baking soda
1/4 teaspoon salt
1 1/2 cups granulated sugar
1 cup mashed ripe bananas (about 3 medium)
1/2 cup banana yogurt
1/2 cup (1 stick) butter, softened
2 large eggs, at room temperature
1 teaspoon vanilla extract

FILLING

2 cups Chantilly Cream (see page 345)
1 cup fresh raspberries

3/4 cup well-drained crushed canned pineapple
2 1/2 cups Chocolate-Sour Cream Frosting (see page 349)
1 cup walnuts or pecans, coarsely chopped

Preheat the oven to 350°F. • Butter two 9-inch round cake pans. Line with waxed paper. Butter the paper. • Sift the flour, baking powder, baking soda, and salt into a large bowl. Stir in the sugar. • Beat in the bananas, yogurt, butter, eggs, and vanilla with an electric mixer at medium speed. • Spoon half the batter into each of the prepared pans. • Bake for 20–30 minutes, or until a toothpick inserted into the center comes out clean. • Cool the cakes in the pans for 10 minutes. Turn out onto racks. Carefully remove the paper and let cool completely. • *Filling*: Divide the Chantilly cream in two equal portions. Fold the raspberries into one half and the pineapple into the other. • Split each cake horizontally. Place one layer on a serving plate. Spread with the raspberry cream. Top with another layer. Spread with some of the frosting. Sprinkle with half the nuts. Top with another layer. Spread with the pineapple cream. Place the remaining layer on top. • Spread with the remaining frosting. Press the remaining nuts into the sides of the cake.

Makes one 9-inch cake · Prep: 40 min. · Cooking: 20–30 min. · Level: 2 · Keeps: 1–2 days

CHILDREN'S PARTY CAKE

2 cups cake flour
2 teaspoons baking powder
1/4 teaspoon salt
4 large eggs, at room temperature
2 cups granulated sugar
1 cup boiling milk
2 teaspoons vanilla extract
2 cups Seven-Minute Frosting (see page 348)
1/2 cup M & M's

Preheat the oven to 350°F. • Butter three 8-inch round cake pans. Line with waxed paper. Butter the paper. • Sift the flour, baking powder, and salt into a large bowl. • Beat the eggs and sugar in a medium bowl with an electric mixer at medium speed until pale and thick. • With mixer at low speed, gradually beat in the dry ingredients, alternating with the milk and vanilla. • Spoon the batter evenly into the prepared pans. • Bake for 25–30 minutes, or until a toothpick inserted into the center comes out clean. • Cool the cakes in the pans for 10 minutes. Turn out onto racks. Carefully remove the paper and let cool completely. • Place one cake on a serving dish and spread with some frosting. Top with another cake and spread with some frosting. Place the remaining layer on top. Spread with the remaining frosting and sprinkle with the M & M's, pressing them into the frosting. Refrigerate for 1 hour before serving.

Makes one 8-inch cake · Prep: 30 min. + 1 hr. to chill · Cooking: 25–30 min. · Level: 1 · Keeps: 1–2 days

THAI BIRTHDAY CAKE

This recipe is a special celebration cake from Thailand.

- 1   cup jasmine rice
- 1   quart milk
- ³/₄ cup granulated sugar
- 4   cardamom pods, crushed
- 2   bay leaves
- 6   large eggs, separated
- 1¹/₄ cups heavy cream

FROSTING

- 1¹/₄ cups heavy cream
- 1   package (8 oz) cream cheese, softened
- 1   teaspoon vanilla extract
    grated zest of 1 lemon
- ¹/₄ cup confectioners' sugar

    fresh berries and star fruit or peeled and sliced kiwifruit, to decorate

Preheat the oven to 350°F. • Butter a 10 x 3-inch round cake pan. Line with waxed paper. Butter the paper. • Place the rice and enough water to cover in a medium saucepan over medium heat and bring to a boil. Cook for 3 minutes. Remove from the heat and drain well. • Return the rice to the pan and add the milk, sugar, cardamom, and bay leaves. Bring to a boil and reduce the heat to low. Simmer, stirring occasionally, for 20 minutes. Remove from heat and set aside to cool. Discard the bay leaves and cardamon husks. • Transfer the mixture to a large bowl. Add the egg yolks one at a time, until just blended after each addition. Beat in the cream with an electric mixer at high speed. • Beat the egg whites in a large bowl until stiff peaks form. Use a large rubber spatula to fold them into the rice mixture. • Spoon the batter into the prepared pan. • Bake for 40–50 minutes, or until golden brown. Refrigerate overnight. • Turn out onto a serving plate. •

Thai birthday cake

Frosting: With mixer at high speed, beat the cream in a large bowl until stiff. Beat in the cream cheese, vanilla, lemon zest, and confectioners' sugar. • Spread with the frosting. Decorate with the fruit.

Makes one 10-inch cake · Prep: 45 min. · Cooking: 40–50 min. · Level: 2 · Keeps: 1–2 days

NEW ZEALAND PAVLOVA

This is a classic dessert cake in New Zealand, where it is served at family lunches, on birthdays or anniversaries, or any number of other special occasions. It was created in New Zealand in the early 1930s in honor of the brilliant Russian ballet dancer Anna Pavlova, who toured the country at that time.

- 4   large egg whites, at room temperature
- ¹/₈ teaspoon salt
- 1¹/₄ cups granulated sugar
- 2   tablespoons water
- 1   tablespoon cornstarch
- 2   teaspoons vanilla extract
- 1   teaspoon white vinegar
- 1   cup heavy cream
- 2   tablespoons confectioners' sugar
    sliced seasonal fresh fruit, to decorate

Preheat the oven to 275°F. • Butter a baking sheet. Line with waxed paper. Drizzle a little water over the paper. • Beat the egg whites and salt in a large bowl with an electric mixer at medium speed until frothy. • With mixer at high speed, gradually beat in the sugar, beating until stiff, glossy peaks form. • With mixer at medium speed, beat in the water, cornstarch, 1 teaspoon vanilla, and vinegar. • Spoon the meringue mixture onto the prepared sheet. Do not spread much; the meringue will spread as it bakes. • Bake for 45–55 minutes, or until crisp and pale gold. Turn the oven off and leave the meringue in the oven until cold. Invert onto a rack and carefully remove the paper. Transfer to a serving plate. • With mixer at high speed, beat the cream, confectioners' sugar, and the remaining 1 teaspoon vanilla in a medium bowl until stiff. • Spread with the cream and decorate with the fruit.

Makes one cake · Prep: 25 min. · Cooking: 45–55 min. · Level: 1 · Keeps: 1 day

Filled panettone

FRUIT-FILLED PANETTONE

Panettone is a light, sweet Italian cake that is full of candied fruit and served at Christmastime. It is ubiquitous in Italy from October to January, then disappears again for 8 months. It is now widely available overseas. If you can't buy panettone, there is a recipe for one on page 322.

- 1 tall round panettone, weighing about 2 lb
- 2 tablespoons butter, melted
- 2 tablespoons slivered almonds
- 1/4 cup confectioners' sugar
- 1 cup heavy cream
- 1/4 cup rum
- 1 cup fresh sliced strawberries
- 6 slices canned pineapple, chopped

Preheat the oven to 400°F. • Butter a baking sheet. • Use a knife to slice off the top third of the panettone horizontally. Use the knife to hollow out the base of the panettone, leaving a shell about 1/2-inch thick. • Brush the top 1/3 slice of the panettone with the butter and place on the baking sheet. Sprinkle with the almonds and dust with 2 tablespoons of confectioners' sugar. • Bake for 5–7 minutes, or until crisp and golden brown. • Beat the cream and remaining 2 tablespoons confectioners' sugar in a medium bowl with an electric mixer at high speed until stiff. • Brush the bottom and sides of the hollowed-out panettone with the rum. • Spread 1/3 of the cream inside the panettone. Cover with half the strawberries and pineapple. Repeat, then finish with cream. • Cut the lid into 8–10 triangular pieces and arrange over the top. • Refrigerate for 12 hours before serving.

Makes one filled panettone · Prep: 25 min. + 12 hr. to rest · Cooking: 5–7 min. · Level: 1 · Keeps: 1 day

CHAMPAGNE PANETTONE

- 1 tablespoon unflavored gelatin
- 1/4 cup water
- 6 large eggs, at room temperature
- 1 cup superfine sugar
- 1 teaspoon vanilla extract
- 1 2/3 cups Champagne
- 1 panettone, weighing about 2 lb

Sprinkle the gelatin over the water in a small saucepan. Let stand 1 minute. Cook over low heat until completely dissolved. • Beat the egg yolks and sugar in a saucepan until well blended. Cook over low heat, stirring constantly with a wooden spoon, until the mixture lightly coats a metal spoon or registers 160°F on an instant-read thermometer. • Add the vanilla and Champagne and continue cooking, beating constantly until thick. • Stir in the gelatin mixture until completely dissolved. Set aside to cool. Make sure it does not set. • Invert the panettone. Cut a round into the bottom 3/4-inch from the edge. Remove the cake round and set aside. Remove the interior of the panettone, leaving the edge intact. • Spoon the egg mixture into the panettone. • Replace the cake round. • Transfer to a large bowl, bottom-side up, wrap with plastic wrap, and refrigerate for 6 hours, or until set. • Turn out onto a serving plate.

Makes one filled panettone · Prep: 40 min. + 6 hr. to chill · Level: 2 · Keeps: 2 days in the refrigerator

FILLED PANETTONE

This dessert is a good way to use up any panettone still left in January, when it begins to dry out.

- 1 panettone, weighing about 1 1/2 lb
- 2 cups heavy cream
- 1 1/2 cups Zabaglione (see page 348)
- 1/3 cup dry Marsala wine or dry sherry
- 1/4 cup brandy
- 2 1/2 cups Chocolate Pastry Cream (see page 346)
- 1 cup Vanilla Frosting (see page 347)
  candied cherries, to decorate

Cut the rounded top off the panettone and set aside. Use a knife to cut out the center of the cake, leaving a 1-inch shell open at both ends. Carefully lift out the interior of the cake and slice it horizontally in 5 or 6 slices. • Beat the cream in a large bowl with an electric mixer at high speed until stiff. Fold the cream into the zabaglione. • Mix the Marsala and brandy in a small bowl. Drizzle one layer with the Marsala and place on a serving plate. Spread with a thick layer of the zabaglione. Drizzle another layer with the Marsala mixture and place over the filled layer. Spread with a thick layer of pastry cream. Repeat layers, until all the ingredients are used up. • Slip the external cake round over the top (you may need to cut it down one side, and wrap it around the cake). Cover with the rounded top. • Spread with the frosting and decorate with cherries.

Makes one round cake · Prep: 30 min. · Level: 1 · Keeps: 1–2 days

CHOCOLATE LOG

MERINGUE
- 5 large egg whites
- ¾ cup superfine sugar
- ½ cup confectioners' sugar
- ¾ cup finely ground hazelnuts

VANILLA FILLING
- 1 tablespoon unflavored gelatin
- ¼ cup cold water
- 1 cup heavy cream
- ½ teaspoon vanilla extract
- ½ cup Vanilla Pastry Cream (see page 342)

HAZELNUT FILLING
- 3 oz milk chocolate
- ½ cup butter, melted
- 3 large eggs, separated
- ¾ cup chocolate hazelnut cream (Nutella)
- ¼ cup granulated sugar
- ½ teaspoon cream of tartar
- 2 cups Chocolate Ganache (see page 350)
- almond biscuits, to decorate

Preheat the oven to 250°F. • *Meringue*: Line a baking sheet with parchment paper. • Beat the egg whites in a large bowl with an electric mixer at medium speed until frothy. With mixer at high speed, gradually beat in the superfine sugar, beating until stiff, glossy peaks form. • Use a large rubber spatula to fold in the confectioners' sugar and hazelnuts. • Spoon the meringue into a pastry bag fitted with a plain nozzle and pipe two 14 x 6-inch long bands of meringue onto the prepared sheet. • Bake for 80–90 minutes, or until crisp and set. • *Vanilla Filling*: Sprinkle the gelatin over the cold water in a saucepan. Let stand 1 minute. Cook over low heat until completely dissolved. • With mixer at high speed, beat the cream in a large bowl until stiff. Mix the cream, gelatin mixture, and vanilla into the pastry cream. • With mixer at high speed, beat the cream in a large bowl until stiff. Fold the cream into the pastry cream mixture. • *Hazelnut Filling*: Melt the chocolate in a double boiler over barely simmering water. • With mixer at medium speed, beat the melted butter, egg yolks, chocolate hazelnut cream, and melted chocolate in a saucepan until well blended. Cook over low heat, stirring constantly with a wooden spoon until the mixture lightly coats a metal spoon or registers 160°F on an instant-read thermometer. Immediately plunge the pan

Chocolate log

into a bowl of ice water and stir until the egg mixture has cooled. • Stir the whites, sugar, and cream of tartar in a heavy saucepan until blended. Cook over low heat, beating constantly with an electric mixer at low speed until the whites register 160°F on an instant-read thermometer. Transfer to a bowl and beat at high speed until the whites form stiff peaks. Use a large rubber spatula to fold in the chocolate mixture. • Line a 14-inch Bûche de Nöel mold with plastic wrap. Spoon in the vanilla filling until half full. Top with a band of meringue. Spoon the hazelnut filling over and top with the remaining meringue band. • Refrigerate for at least 4 hours, or until firmly set. • Turn out onto a rack and remove the plastic wrap. • Use a thin metal spatula to spread the cake with the chocolate ganache. Decorate with the almond cookies.

Makes one log · Prep: 40 min. · Cooking: 80–90 min. · Level: 2 · Keeps: 3 days in the refrigerator

CHOUX TREE

- ⅓ cup butter, softened
- pinch of salt
- 1 cup water
- 1 cup all-purpose flour
- 4 large eggs, at room temperature
- 4 oz candied cherries, coarsely chopped
- ⅔ cup candied lemon peel, coarsely chopped
- ⅔ cup almonds, finely chopped
- confectioners' sugar, to dust

Preheat the oven to 375°F. • Butter and flour a 1½-quart Christmas tree pan. • Bring the butter, salt, and water to a boil in a saucepan over a medium heat. Beat in the flour until the mixture leaves the pan sides. Remove from the heat and add the eggs, one at a time, until just blended after each addition. Stir in the cherries, lemon peel, and almonds. Use a teaspoon to place spoonfuls of the mixture in the prepared pan. • Bake for 30–35 minutes, or until golden brown. Cool the cake in the pan for 5 minutes. Turn out onto a serving plate. Dust with confectioners' sugar.

Makes 1 dessert · Prep: 40 min. · Cooking: 30–35 min. · Level: 2 · Keeps: 2 days

CARAMELIZED VENETIAN CHRISTMAS CAKE

Venetian Christmas cake, known in Italy as pandoro or "bread of gold," can be bought in specialty stores or supermarkets. Finishing the cake in this way will lend an extra special touch to your Christmas.

1½ cups heavy cream
1 one pandoro (Venetian Christmas cake), about 1½ lb
1 cup crushed pineapple, drained
2 teaspoons ground cinnamon
1 cup granulated sugar
¼ cup water
2 tablespoons butter

Beat the cream in a large bowl with an electric mixer at high speed until stiff. • Cut the pandoro horizontally into 7 equal slices. • Place one layer on a serving plate. Spread with about ¹⁄₇ of the cream, a layer of pineapple, and a sprinkling of cinnamon. Top with another layer, turned slightly so that the pointed edges make a pretty pattern (see photo). Repeat until all the cake, cream, pineapple, and cinnamon have been layered to make a tall cake. • Stir the sugar, water, and butter in a medium saucepan over low heat until golden brown and caramelized. Remove from the heat. Continue stirring until the mixture forms a thread when dropped from a teaspoon. • Use a tablespoon to drizzle a long golden thread of the caramelized sugar around and around the cake.

Makes one 7-layered cake · Prep: 30 min. + 6 hr. to chill · Level: 2 · Keeps: 1 day in the refrigerator

Caramelized Venetian Christmas cake

CHRISTMAS CAKE

- 1½ cups all-purpose flour
- ½ cup self-rising flour
- 2 teaspoons allspice
- 1¼ cups butter, softened
- 1¼ cups firmly packed brown sugar
- 4 large eggs
- 2 tablespoons orange marmalade
- 7¾ cups mixed dried fruit
- ½ cup + 2 tablespoons sweet sherry
- ¼ cup whole almonds

Preheat the oven to 300°F. • Butter and flour an 8-inch square baking pan. • Sift both flours and allspice into a large bowl. • Beat the butter and brown sugar in a large bowl with an electric mixer at medium speed until creamy. • Add the eggs, one at a time, until just blended after each addition. Stir in the marmalade and fruit. • Use a large rubber spatula to fold in the dry ingredients. Stir in ½ cup sherry. • Spoon the batter into the prepared pan. Sprinkle with the almonds. • Bake for about 3 hours, or until a toothpick inserted into the center comes out clean. • Cool the cake in the pan on a rack for 15 minutes. Brush with the remaining 2 tablespoons sherry. Cover with aluminum foil and let cool completely.

Makes one 8-inch cake · Prep: 25 min. · Cooking: 3 hr. · Level: 1 · Keeps: 3 days in the refrigerator

CHRISTMAS STAR CAKE

- 2⅔ cups milk
- 10 coffee beans
- 5 large eggs, at room temperature
- 1 cup granulated sugar
- ¼ teaspoon salt
- 2 tablespoons freeze-dried coffee granules
- ⅓ cup all-purpose flour
- 35 ladyfingers
- ½ cup strong cold coffee
- 1⅔ cups egg whites
- 5 teaspoons water
- ¼ teaspoon cream of tartar
- 1 cup heavy cream
  candied cherries, to decorate

Line a 1½-quart star-shaped baking pan with waxed paper. Butter the paper. • Warm the milk and coffee beans in a small saucepan over low heat until lukewarm (105–115°F). • Beat the egg yolks, ½ cup sugar, and salt in a large bowl with an electric mixer at medium speed until frothy. Mix in the coffee granules and flour. Strain the milk, discarding the coffee beans. Add the milk to the egg yolk mixture. • Transfer the mixture to a large saucepan and bring to a boil over low heat. Cook for 3–4 minutes, or until thick. Set aside to cool. • Briefly dip the ladyfingers into the coffee. Arrange half the ladyfingers in the prepared pan. • Stir the egg whites, ¼ cup sugar, water, and cream of tartar in a saucepan until blended. Cook over low heat, beating constantly with a mixer at low speed until the whites register 160°F on an instant-read thermometer. Transfer to a bowl and beat at high speed until the whites form soft peaks. Beat in the remaining sugar until stiff peaks form. Use the spatula to fold them into the batter. • Pour the batter into the prepared pan. Cover with ladyfingers. Freeze for 3 hours, or until set. • Dip the mold in hot water for 5 seconds. Turn out onto a serving plate. Carefully remove the paper. • With mixer at high speed, beat the cream until stiff. Spoon into a pastry bag and pipe over the cake in a decorative manner. Decorate with the cherries.

Makes one 9-inch star cake · Prep: 1 hr. + 3 hr. to freeze · Level: 2 · Keeps: 1–2 days in the refrigerator

OLD-FASHIONED CHRISTMAS CAKE

If you prefer the cake to have a finer texture, chop the raisins and currants with a heavy knife.

- 1 box (15 oz) raisins
- 2 cups pitted prunes, chopped
- 1½ cups currants
- 8 oz candied cherries, chopped
- 8 oz mixed candied citrus peel, chopped
- 2 cups dry sherry
- 2 cups dark rum
- 3¾ cups firmly packed dark brown sugar
- ¾ cup water
- 3¼ cups all-purpose flour
- 1 tablespoon baking powder
- 1 teaspoon baking soda
- 1 teaspoon ground nutmeg
- 1 teaspoon ground cinnamon
- ½ teaspoon ground cloves
- ½ teaspoon salt
- 1½ cups (3 sticks) butter, softened
- 2 teaspoons vanilla extract
- 7 large eggs, at room temperature
- 1½ rolls (7 oz each) soft almond paste
- 3 cups Sherry Butter Christmas Cake Frosting (see page 349)

Mix the raisins, prunes, currants, candied cherries, candied peel, sherry, and rum in a large bowl. Soak at room temperature for 1 week. • Stir 1¾ cups brown sugar and water in a skillet over medium heat until the sugar has dissolved and the syrup boils. Reduce the heat and gently boil the syrup until reduced to about 1 cup, about 10 minutes. Set aside to cool. • Preheat the oven to 350°F. • Butter two 8-inch springform pans. Line with waxed paper. Butter the paper. • Sift the flour, baking powder, baking soda, nutmeg, cinnamon, cloves, and salt into a large bowl. • Beat the butter, remaining 2 cups brown sugar, and vanilla in a large bowl with an electric mixer at medium speed until creamy. • Add the eggs, one at a time, until just blended after each addition. • With mixer at low speed, gradually beat in the dry ingredients, alternating with the syrup. Stir in the fruit mixture. • Spoon half the batter into each of the prepared pans. • Bake for about 2 hours, or until dark brown and the cakes shrink from the pan sides. • Cool the cakes completely in the pans on racks. Loosen and remove the pan sides. Invert onto the racks. Loosen and remove the pan bottoms. Carefully remove the paper. Wrap in foil and store until ready to serve, up to 4 months. • Form the almond paste into 2 equal balls. Dust a surface lightly with confectioners' sugar. Roll out one ball of almond paste to a 8-inch round. Fit the almond paste over one of the cakes, trimming the edges if needed. Repeat with the remaining paste. • Spread with the frosting.

Makes two 8-inch cakes · Prep: 45 min. + 1 week to soak · Cooking: 2 hr. · Level: 2 · Keeps: 3–4 months

CHRISTMAS WREATH CAKE

- 1 10-inch Basic Pound Cake (see page 40)
- 1 cup Apricot Glaze (see page 348)
- 2 recipes Fondant (see pages 348–9)
- 1 cup Vanilla Frosting (see page 347)
- 2 cups red currants
- 1 bunch holly leaves, washed

Place the cake on a serving plate. Brush with the glaze. • Roll out the fondant on a surface lightly dusted with confectioners' sugar to a 10-inch round. Place the fondant circle on top of the cake and cut out the center, trimming the edges to fit. • Spread the Vanilla Frosting over the top of the fondant. • Refrigerate for at least 3 hours, or until almost set. • Arrange the red currants and holly leaves on top to resemble a wreath.

Makes one 10-inch cake · Prep: 15 min. + 3 hr. to chill · Level: 1 · Keeps: 2–3 days

Fathers' Day cake

ST. BASIL'S CAKE

Traditionally served on January 1 as a New Year's cake, this dessert normally contains a coin. The person who receives the slice of cake with the coin is said to have good luck for the year.

8   large eggs, separated
1   cup butter, softened
3   cups granulated sugar
2   tablespoons vanilla sugar
$^{1}/_{4}$ cup brandy (optional)
     juice and grated zest of 4 oranges
4   cups all-purpose flour
2   teaspoons baking powder
$^{1}/_{2}$ cup walnuts or sesame seeds

Preheat the oven to 350°F. • Butter and flour a 10-inch springform pan. • Beat the egg whites in a large bowl with an electric mixer at medium speed until stiff peaks form. • Beat the butter and sugar in a large bowl until creamy. Add the egg yolks and vanilla sugar. Add the brandy, if desired, and orange juice and zest. • With mixer at low speed, gradually beat in the flour and baking powder. • Spoon the batter into the prepared pan. Sprinkle with the walnuts. • Bake for

50–60 minutes, or until a toothpick inserted into the center comes out clean. • Cool the cake completely in the pan on a rack. Loosen and remove the pan sides.

Makes one 10-inch cake · Prep: 15 min. · Cooking: 50–60 min. · Level: 1 · Keeps: 2 days

THREE KINGS CAKE

This cake is served traditionally for the Epiphany celebrations in France.

$^{1}/_{2}$ cup butter, softened
$^{3}/_{4}$ cup sugar
3   large eggs, at room temperature
$1^{1}/_{3}$ cups finely ground almonds
1   lb frozen puff pastry, thawed

Preheat the oven to 400°F. • Butter and flour a 10-inch springform pan. • Beat the butter and sugar in a large bowl with an electric mixer at medium speed until creamy. • Add 2 eggs, one at a time, until just blended after each addition. With mixer at low speed, gradually beat in the ground almonds. • Unfold or unroll the pastry out on a lightly floured surface. Cut out two 9$^{1}/_{2}$-inch rounds. Fit one pastry round into the prepared pan. Spoon the almond mixture over. • Beat the

remaining egg in a small bowl. Brush with some of the beaten egg. Place the remaining pastry round on top and seal the edges well. Use a knife to score patterns in the pastry and brush with the remaining beaten egg. • Bake for 25–30 minutes, or until golden brown. Cool the cake in the pan on a rack for 15 minutes. Loosen and remove the pan sides and serve warm.

Makes one 10-inch cake · Prep: 20 min. · Cooking: 25–35 min.· Level: 1 · Keeps: 3 days in the refrigerator

FATHERS' DAY CAKE

The triangle shape of this cake means that you will have some cake left over to use for a trifle or to create small tasty cakes.

ALMOND BASE

$1^{1}/_{2}$ cups finely ground almonds
1   cup confectioners' sugar
6   large egg whites
$^{1}/_{4}$ cup superfine sugar
1   teaspoon vanilla extract

FROSTING

1   teaspoon unflavored gelatin
$^{1}/_{4}$ cup + 1 tablespoon cold water
$^{3}/_{4}$ cup superfine sugar
$^{1}/_{3}$ cup unsweetened cocoa powder
2   teaspoons light cream
1   teaspoon black food coloring
$^{1}/_{3}$ recipe Chocolate Mousse (see page 343)
7   oz rolled white fondant (see pages 348–9)
     pink M & M's, to decorate
$^{1}/_{2}$ teaspoon red food coloring

Almond Base: Preheat the oven to 400°F. • Line a 11 x 7-inch baking pan with waxed paper. • Stir together the almonds and confectioners' sugar in a large bowl. • Beat the egg whites in a large bowl with an electric mixer at medium speed until frothy. With mixer at high speed, gradually beat in the superfine sugar, beating until stiff, glossy peaks form. Add the vanilla. • Use a large rubber spatula to fold in the dry ingredients. • Spoon the batter into the prepared pan. • Bake for 12–15 minutes, or until a toothpick inserted into the center comes out clean. • Cool the cake completely in the pan. Turn out onto a rack and carefully remove the paper. Refrigerate overnight. • *Frosting*: Sprinkle the gelatin over the $^{1}/_{4}$ cup water in a small bowl. Let stand 3 minutes. • Bring the remaining 1 tablespoon water, superfine sugar, cocoa, and cream to a boil in a saucepan over medium heat, stirring constantly. Remove from the heat and stir in the gelatin mixture. Continue stirring until the frosting has cooled. Stir in the black food coloring. • Place the cake on a clean surface. Cut the cake into a triangle to resemble a tuxedo shape (see photo). Spread the top of the cake with the chocolate mousse and smooth the top. Freeze for 2 hours, or until set. • Spread the top and sides of the cake with the frosting. Refrigerate for 2 hours, or until the frosting has set. • Roll ³/₄ of the fondant out on a surface sprinkled with confectioners' sugar to ¹/₈-inch thick. Cut into a triangle to fit on top of the cake, leaving a 1-inch border on the long sides. Carefully place the fondant triangle on top of the cake. • Press the M & M's into the fondant triangle to resemble buttons. • Knead the red food coloring into the remaining fondant. Roll out the fondant on a surface and shape into 2 rectangles, one much smaller than the other. Place the smaller rectangle across the large rectangle and form into a bow. Place the bow on the cake.

Makes one triangle cake · Prep: 40 min. + 14 hr. to chill + 2 hr. to freeze · Cooking: 12–15 min. · Level: 2 · Keeps: 3 days in the refrigerator

HOLIDAY PECAN CAKE

    2   cups pecans, coarsely chopped
 1¹/₄   cups butter, softened
    3   cups all-purpose flour
    2   teaspoons baking powder
  ¹/₂   teaspoon salt
    2   cups granulated sugar
    4   large eggs
    1   cup milk
    2   teaspoons vanilla extract
    1   cup heavy cream

Preheat the oven to 350°F. • Butter and flour three 9-inch round cake pans. • Sauté the pecans in ¹/₄ cup butter in a large skillet over low heat for 20 minutes. • Sift the flour, baking powder, and salt into a large bowl. • Beat the remaining 1 cup butter and sugar in a large bowl with an electric mixer at medium speed until creamy. Add the eggs, until just blended after each addition. • With mixer at low speed, gradually beat in the dry ingredients, alternating with the milk. Add the vanilla. • Use a large rubber spatula to fold in the pecans. • Spoon the batter evenly into the prepared pans. • Bake for 20–25 minutes, or until a toothpick inserted into the center comes out clean. • Cool the cakes completely in the pans on a rack. • With

St. Valentine's cake

mixer at high speed, beat the cream in a small bowl until stiff. Place a cake on a serving plate and spread with the cream. Continue until all the cream and cakes are used up, finishing with a cake.

Makes one 9-inch cake · Prep: 15 min. · Cooking: 20–25 min. · Level: 1 · Keeps: 2–3 days

ST. VALENTINE'S CAKE

ORANGE BUTTERCREAM
  ¹/₄   cup (¹/₂ stick) butter, softened
  ³/₄   cup confectioners' sugar
    1   tablespoon orange liqueur
    1   9-inch Basic Butter Cake (see page 14), baked in a 9-inch heart-shaped cake pan
    1   lb rolled white fondant (see pages 348–9)
  ¹/₄   teaspoon green food coloring
    1   teaspoon red food coloring
    1   tablespoon confectioners' sugar
    1   teaspoon water

Orange Buttercream: Beat the butter in a large bowl with an electric mixer at medium speed until creamy. Beat in the confectioners' sugar. Add the liqueur. • Split the cake horizontally. • Place a layer

on a serving plate. • Spread with half the buttercream. Top with the remaining layer. Spread with the remaining buttercream. • Dust a surface lightly with confectioners' sugar. Knead the fondant until malleable. Break off a small piece of fondant. • Work a few drops of red food coloring into the larger part of fondant until light pink in color. • Break off a piece of the pink fondant and work in the remaining red food coloring until dark pink in color. • Roll out the larger piece of fondant to ¹/₄-inch thick. Fit the pink fondant over the cake, trimming the edges. Set aside the excess. • Shape each colored fondant into a ball. • Roll out the remaining pink and white fondant balls to ¹/₄-inch thick. Use a mini heart-shaped cutter to stamp out small heart shapes. • Mix together the remaining confectioners' sugar and water to make a smooth frosting. • Dot each heart with a little of the frosting and arrange on the cake in a decorative manner.

Makes one heart-shaped cake · Prep: 90 min. · Level: 2 · Keeps: 2–3 days

CAPPUCCINO SWEETHEART

This cake makes a wonderful Valentine's Day gift.

- 1 9-inch Basic Butter Cake (see page 14), baked in a 9-inch heart-shaped cake pan

COFFEE LIQUEUR TRUFFLES

- 4 oz bittersweet chocolate, coarsely chopped
- 3 tablespoons heavy cream
- 2 teaspoons freeze-dried coffee granules
- 1/2 tablespoon coffee liqueur

COFFEE BUTTERCREAM

- 10 oz white chocolate, coarsely chopped
- 2/3 cup heavy cream
- 1 3/4 cups (3 1/2 sticks) unsalted butter, softened
- 1 cup confectioners' sugar
- 1 tablespoon freeze-dried coffee granules dissolved in 1 tablespoon boiling water, cooled
- 1 cup hazelnuts, toasted and coarsely chopped
- 1/4 cup unsweetened cocoa powder, to dust

Truffles: Melt the chocolate with the cream in a double boiler over barely simmering water. Set aside to cool. • Dissolve the coffee in the liqueur and stir into the chocolate mixture. Refrigerate for 1 hour, or until thick and malleable. • Roll teaspoonfuls of the chocolate mixture into round truffles and place on a dish lined with waxed paper. This should yield about 12 truffles. Cover and refrigerate until firm. • *Coffee Buttercream*: Melt the white chocolate with the cream in a double boiler over barely simmering water. Set aside to cool. • Beat the butter in a large bowl with an electric mixer at high speed until creamy. Gradually beat in the confectioners' sugar. • Beat in the chocolate mixture and dissolved coffee. • Split the cake horizontally. Place one layer on a serving plate and spread with 1/4 of the buttercream. Place the remaining layer on top. Spread with the buttercream. • Press the hazelnuts into the sides of the cake and arrange the truffles on top. Dust with the cocoa.

Makes one heart-shaped cake · Prep: 1 hr. · Cooking: 15 min. · Level: 2 · Keeps: 2–3 days

STRAWBERRY HEART

- 8 oz frozen puff pastry, thawed
- 1 1/2 lb fresh strawberries (preferably all about the same size), hulled and cut in half
- 3/4 cup red currant jelly
- 2 tablespoons kirsch or other fruit liqueur
- 1/2 cup heavy cream
- 1 tablespoon granulated sugar

Preheat the oven to 400°F. • Butter and flour a 9-inch heart-shaped cake pan. • Unfold or unroll the pastry on a lightly floured surface. Roll the pastry into a 12-inch square. Trim to a 13-inch round. Fit the pastry into the prepared pan. Fold over and crimp the edges. Prick all over with a fork. • Line the pastry shell with foil and fill the foil with dried beans or pie weights. Bake for 10 minutes, then remove the foil with the beans and bake until crisp and golden brown. • Cool the pastry on a rack for 10 minutes. Carefully remove from the pan and place on a rack to cool completely. • Arrange the strawberries on the cooled pastry, packing them closely together, rounded side up. • Warm the red currant jelly and kirsch in a small saucepan over medium heat. Brush over the strawberries. • Beat the cream and sugar in a medium bowl with an electric mixer at high speed until stiff. Spoon over the cake.

Makes one 9-inch heart-shaped cake · Prep: 20 min. · Cooking: 20 min. · Level: 1 · Keeps: 1 day in the refrigerator

RED VELVET CAKE

- 2 cups all-purpose flour
- 1/2 cup unsweetened cocoa powder
- 1 teaspoon baking powder
- 1/2 teaspoon baking soda
- 1/4 teaspoon salt
- 1/2 cup (1 stick) butter, softened
- 1 1/2 cups granulated sugar
- 1 teaspoon vanilla extract
- 3 large eggs, at room temperature
- 1 cup buttermilk
- 2 tablespoons red food coloring
- 1 tablespoon white vinegar

CREAM CHEESE FROSTING

- 1 package (8 oz each) cream cheese, softened
- 1/2 cup (1 stick) butter, softened
- 1 teaspoon vanilla extract
- 3 cups confectioners' sugar

Preheat the oven to 350°F. • Butter two 9-inch round cake pans. Line with waxed paper. Butter the paper. • Sift the flour, cocoa, baking powder, baking soda, and salt into a large bowl. • Beat the butter, sugar, and vanilla in a large bowl with an electric mixer at medium speed until creamy. • Add the eggs, one at a time, until just blended after each addition. • With mixer at low speed, gradually beat in the dry ingredients, alternating with the buttermilk, food coloring, and vinegar. • Spoon half the batter into each of the prepared pans. • Bake for

Cappuccino sweetheart

Simnel cake

25–30 minutes, or until a toothpick inserted into the center comes out clean. • Cool the cakes in the pans for 10 minutes. Turn out onto racks. Carefully remove the paper and let cool completely. • *Cream Cheese Frosting*: With mixer at medium speed, beat the cream cheese, butter, and vanilla in a large bowl until creamy. Gradually beat in the confectioners' sugar until fluffy. • Place one cake on a serving plate. Spread with $^1/_3$ of the frosting. Place the other cake on top. Spread with the remaining frosting.

Makes one 9-inch cake · Prep: 35 min. · Cooking: 25–35 min. · Level: 1 · Keeps: 2–3 days

SPRING CAKE

$^1/_2$ cup water
$1^1/_2$ cups granulated sugar
12   large eggs, separated

1   teaspoon salt
1   teaspoon cream of tartar
2   cups cake flour
1   teaspoon almond extract
1   teaspoon orange flower water
2   cups Seven-Minute Frosting (see page 348)
1   teaspoon yellow food coloring

Preheat the oven to 350ºF. • Set out a 9 x 4-inch tube pan with a removable bottom. • Mix the water and sugar in a saucepan over medium heat. Wash down the sides of the pan with a pastry brush dipped in cold water to prevent sugar crystals from forming. Cook, without stirring, until the mixture reaches 238ºF, or the soft-ball stage. • Beat the egg whites, salt, and cream of tartar until

soft peaks form. Slowly beat the hot syrup into the egg whites until stiff, glossy peaks form. • With mixer at high speed, beat the egg yolks until pale and thick. • Use a large rubber spatula to fold $^1/_3$ of the beaten whites into the egg yolk mixture. • Gradually fold 1 cup flour into the beaten whites. Add the almond extract. • Fold the remaining flour into the egg yolk mixture. Add the orange flower water. • Spoon the egg yolk and egg white batters alternately into the pan. • Bake for 50–60 minutes, or until a toothpick inserted into the center comes out clean. • Cool the cake following the instructions on page 156. • Prepare the Seven-Minute Frosting, stirring in the yellow food coloring. Spread the frosting over.

Makes one 9-inch cake · Prep: 20 min. · Cooking: 50–60 min. · Level: 1 · Keeps: 2–3 days

SIMNEL CAKE

According to tradition, this rich British fruit and marzipan cake was given by servant girls to their mothers on the fourth Sunday of Lent. On that day, they were allowed a day off to visit their families. It is now usually prepared at Easter.

2   cups all-purpose flour
1   teaspoon ground nutmeg
1   teaspoon ground allspice
1   teaspoon baking powder
$^1/_2$ teaspoon baking soda
$^1/_4$ teaspoon salt
$^3/_4$ cup ($1^1/_2$ sticks) butter, softened
1   cup granulated sugar
4   large eggs, at room temperature
3   cups chopped mixed dried fruit
$^1/_4$ cup dry sherry

2   tablespoons grated orange zest
2   tablespoons grated lemon zest
1   lb marzipan
    ribbons, sugar eggs, and marzipan animals to decorate

Preheat the oven to 325°F. • Butter a 9-inch springform pan. Line with waxed paper. Butter the paper. • Sift the flour, nutmeg, allspice, baking powder, baking soda, and salt into a large bowl. • Beat the butter and sugar in a large bowl with an electric mixer at medium speed until creamy. • Add the eggs, one at a time, until just blended after each addition. • With mixer at low speed, gradually beat in the dried fruit, 3 tablespoons sherry, and the orange and lemon zests. Gradually beat in the dry ingredients. • Roll out half the marzipan on a board dusted with confectioners' sugar to a 9-inch round. Spoon half the batter into the prepared pan. Place the marzipan on top. Spoon the remaining batter over. • Bake for about 2 hours, or until golden brown and a toothpick inserted into the center comes out clean. • Cool the cake in the pan for 1 hour. Loosen and remove the pan sides. Invert onto a rack. Loosen and remove the pan bottom. • Turn top-side up and let cool completely. • Roll out the remaining marzipan to a 9-inch round. Trim around the marzipan with a fluted pastry cutter to make a decorative edge. Brush with the remaining sherry and cover with the marzipan. Use a fork to make patterns on the top.

Makes one 9-inch cake · Prep: 40 min. · Cooking: 2 hr. · Level: 2 · Keeps: 2–3 weeks

Chocolate Easter egg cake

CHOCOLATE EASTER EGG CAKE

To make this scrumptious Easter egg, you will need to temper the chocolate, a tricky process unless you have a thermometer to measure the temperature of the chocolate. This cake will not keep longer than one day, so serve it as soon as possible after it has set in the refrigerator.

1 lb bittersweet chocolate
2¹/₂ cups heavy cream
30 ladyfingers, broken in half
1 cup orange liqueur
¹/₂ cup slivered almonds
1 (13 oz) jar chocolate hazelnut cream (Nutella)

Butter a 9-inch oval (half egg-shaped) mold. • Melt the chocolate in a double boiler over barely simmering water. Heat to 113–122°F, then remove from the heat. Pour ²/₃ of the melted chocolate onto a marble surface and cool to 84°F. Return to the double boiler over barely simmering water and heat to 87°F. • Spread about ³/₄ of the melted chocolate in the mold in an even layer about ¹/₂-inch thick. Refrigerate until set. • Beat 1³/₄ cups of the cream in a large bowl with an electric mixer at medium

speed until stiff. • Dip the ladyfingers briefly in the liqueur. • Fill the egg with a layer of cream, followed by a layer of ladyfingers and almonds. Repeat until all the ingredients are in the egg, finishing with a layer of ladyfingers. Spread the remaining ³/₄ cup chocolate over the ladyfingers to seal the egg. Refrigerate for 6 hours. • Beat the remaining cream in a large bowl with an electric mixer at high speed until stiff. • Turn the egg out onto a serving plate. Spoon the whipped cream into a pastry bag and pipe around the edges of the cake. Place the hazelnut cream in a pastry bag and pipe around the edge.

Makes one 9-inch cake · Prep: 2 hr. + 6 hr. to chill · Level: 2 · Keeps: 1 day in the refrigerator

EASTER EGG CAKE

This recipe requires an egg-shaped mold, which can be located in a specialty cake store.

1 9-inch Italian Sponge Cake (see page 157), cut into ¹/₂-inch thick slices
¹/₃ cup rum or fruit liqueur
¹/₄ cup water
2 cups heavy cream
1 teaspoon almond extract
2 oz bittersweet chocolate, coarsely chopped
²/₃ cup candied fruit, chopped

FROSTING
1 cup Fondant (see pages 348–9)
1 teaspoon purple or pink food coloring

Cut the cake slices in half diagonally to make long triangular pieces. • Brush a 10-inch long egg-shaped mold with 2 tablespoons of the rum. Line with the cake pieces, pointed ends facing inward to the center of the mold. • Mix the remaining rum and water and drizzle over the cake. • Beat the cream and almond extract in a large bowl with an electric mixer at high speed until stiff. Fold in the chocolate and candied fruit. • Spoon the filling into the mold and top with a layer of cake slices. Drizzle with the remaining rum mixture. • Refrigerate for 4 hours. • *Frosting*: Knead the fondant on a surface sprinkled with confectioners' sugar and knead in the food coloring. Roll out thinly and cut into strips. Place the strips in a crisscross pattern over the cake.

Makes one 10-inch egg-shaped cake · Prep: 45 min. + 4 hrs. to chill · Level: 2 · Keeps: 1–2 days

EASTER HAZELNUT CAKE

Top this delicious Easter Cake with chocolate eggs or rabbits.

1 cup mixed fresh or frozen blackberries, blueberries, and raspberries
¹/₄ cup dark rum
1 9-inch Italian Sponge Cake (see page 157)
2 cups Vanilla Pastry Cream (see page 342)
2 cups skinned hazelnuts, chopped
4 tablespoons confectioners' sugar, to dust

Mix the berries and 3 tablespoons rum in a small bowl. Soak 10 minutes. • Split the cake horizontally. Place one layer on a serving plate. Drizzle with the remaining rum. Spread with 1 cup pastry cream and spread over the fruit mixture. Top with the remaining layer. • Spread with the remaining pastry cream. Sprinkle with the hazelnuts. • Dust with the confectioners' sugar.

Makes one 9-inch cake · Prep: 20 min. · Level: 1 · Keeps: 3 days in the refrigerator

ORANGE AND NUT PASSOVER CAKE

6 large eggs, separated
1¹/₂ cups granulated sugar
³/₄ cup finely ground almonds
grated zest and juice of 1 orange
1¹/₂ cups walnuts, coarsely chopped

Preheat the oven to 325°F. • Butter a 9-inch springform pan. Dust with matzo meal. • Beat the egg yolks and sugar in a large bowl with an electric mixer at high speed until pale and thick. • With mixer at low speed, beat in the almonds, orange zest and juice, and walnuts. • With mixer at high speed, beat the egg whites in a large bowl until stiff peaks form. • Use a large rubber spatula to fold them into the nut mixture. • Pour the batter into the prepared pan. • Bake for 80–90 minutes, or until a toothpick inserted into the center comes out clean. • Cool the cake completely in the pan on a rack. • Loosen and remove the pan sides to serve.

Makes one 9-inch cake · Prep: 15 min. · Cooking: 80–90 min. · Level: 1 · Keeps: 2–3 days

FLOURLESS COCONUT CAKE

1¹/₂	cups shredded coconut
¹/₄	cup finely ground almonds
2	tablespoons matzo meal
¹/₂	teaspoon grated lemon zest
4	large egg whites
¹/₈	teaspoon salt
¹/₂	cup granulated sugar
3	tablespoons light rum
	fresh fruit, to decorate (optional)

Preheat the oven to 350°F. • Butter a 9-inch round cake pan. Dust with matzo meal. • Stir together the coconut, almonds, matzo meal, and lemon zest in a large bowl. • Beat the egg whites and salt in a large bowl with an electric mixer at medium speed until frothy. With mixer at high speed, gradually beat in the sugar, beating until stiff, glossy peaks form. Add the rum. • Use a large rubber spatula to fold the beaten whites into the nut mixture. • Spread the batter into the prepared pan. • Bake for 15–20 minutes, or until light browned. • Cool the cake completely in the pan on a rack. • Turn out onto a serving plate. Serve with fresh fruit, if liked.

Makes one 9-inch cake · Prep: 15 min. · Cooking: 15–20 min. · Level: 1 · Keeps: 2–3 days

PASSOVER BANANA CAKE

7	large eggs, separated
1	cup granulated sugar
¹/₄	teaspoon salt
1	cup very ripe mashed bananas
³/₄	cup potato starch

Easter egg cake

1	cup walnuts, coarsely chopped
1	cup heavy cream
1	banana, peeled and finely sliced

Preheat the oven to 350°F. • Butter two 9-inch round cake pans. Dust with matzo meal. • Beat the egg yolks, sugar, and salt in a large bowl with an electric mixer at high speed until pale and thick. Use a large rubber spatula to fold in the banana, potato starch, and walnuts. • With mixer at high speed, beat the egg whites in a large bowl until stiff peaks form. Fold them into the batter. • Spoon half the batter into each of the prepared pans. • Bake for 25–30 minutes, or until a toothpick inserted into the center comes out clean. • Cool the cakes completely in the pans on racks. Turn out onto racks. • With mixer at high speed, beat the cream in a large bowl until stiff. • Place one cake on a serving plate. Spread with the cream and the banana slices. Top with the remaining layer.

Makes one 9-inch cake · Prep: 20 min. · Cooking: 25–30 min. · Level: 1 · Keeps: 2–3 days in the refrigerator

LEMON PASSOVER SPONGE CAKE

Potato starch, sometimes referred to as potato flour, is found in health food stores.

9	large eggs, separated
1¹/₃	cups confectioners' sugar
	juice of 1¹/₂ lemons
¹/₂	cup potato starch
¹/₂	cup matzo meal

Preheat the oven to 375°F. • Set out a 9-inch tube pan with a removable bottom. • Beat the egg whites in a large bowl with an electric mixer at medium speed until frothy. With mixer at high speed, add the confectioners' sugar, beating until stiff, glossy peaks form. • With mixer at high speed, beat the egg yolks and lemon juice in a large bowl until pale and thick. • Use a large rubber spatula to fold the yolk mixture into the beaten whites, followed by the potato starch and matzo meal. • Pour into the pan. • Bake for 50–60 minutes, or until a toothpick inserted into the pan comes out clean. • Cool the cake following the instructions on page 156.

Makes one 9-inch cake · Prep: 15 min. · Cooking: 50–60 min. · Level: 1 · Keeps: 2–3 days

Sicilian Easter cake

SICILIAN EASTER CAKE

    3   large eggs, at room temperature + 1 large egg,
        lightly beaten
    1   cup + 1 tablespoon superfine sugar
    1   teaspoon vanilla extract
    5   cups all-purpose flour
  $^1/_3$ cup + 1 tablespoon milk
    2   teaspoons baking soda
  $^1/_3$ cup + 1 tablespoon olive oil
    4   large eggs, to decorate

Preheat the oven to 400°F. • Butter and flour
a rectangular baking sheet. • Beat the eggs,
superfine sugar, and vanilla in a large bowl
with an electric mixer at high speed until
pale and thick. Sift the flour in a large bowl
and make a well in the center. Stir in the egg
mixture. • Warm the milk and baking soda
in a saucepan until the soda has dissolved.
Add enough of the milk mixture and oil to
the flour mixture to make a smooth dough.
• Use the instructions on page 316 to knead
the dough. • Break off a piece slightly larger
than an egg and set aside. • Divide the
remaining dough into 3 pieces. Use your

hands to roll the dough into three ropes
about 10 inches long. • Press the ends of the
ropes together and braid the dough. •
Transfer to the prepared baking sheet. Press
the ends of the braid together to form a ring.
• Roll the remaining dough into strips. •
Carefully press the 4 eggs reserved for
decoration securely into the braid and cross
the dough strips over each egg. • Brush with
the beaten egg. • Bake for 30–35 minutes,
or until golden. Cool the cake completely on
the sheet. Transfer to a serving plate.

*Makes one 10-inch cake · Prep: 60 min. · Cooking:
30–35 min. · Level: 2 · Keeps: 3–4 days*

RUSSIAN EASTER CAKE

    1   cup (2 sticks) butter, softened
    1   cup superfine sugar
    2   packages (8 oz each) cream cheese, softened
    2   large egg yolks
  $^1/_2$ cup heavy cream
  $^1/_2$ teaspoon vanilla extract
  $^2/_3$ cup raisins
  $^2/_3$ cup mixed candied peel, finely chopped + 1 cup to
        decorate
    1   tablespoon pistachios, finely chopped
    1   cup almonds, finely chopped

Set out a deep pudding mold and line with
moist muslin. • Beat the butter and $^3/_4$ cup
sugar in a large bowl with an electric mixer
at medium speed until creamy. Beat in the
cream cheese. • Beat the egg yolks, the
remaining $^1/_4$ cup sugar, and $^1/_4$ cup cream in
a double boiler until well blended. Cook
over low heat, stirring constantly with a
wooden spoon, until the mixture lightly coats
a metal spoon or registers 160°F on an
instant-read thermometer. Immediately
plunge the pan into a bowl of ice water and
stir until the egg mixture has cooled. • With
mixer at low speed, beat the egg yolk mixture
into the cream cheese mixture, followed by
the remaining cream, vanilla, $^2/_3$ cup candied
peel, pistachios, and almonds. • Spoon the
mixture into the prepared mold. • Refrigerate
for at least 12 hours, or until firmly set. •
Invert onto a serving plate, removing the
muslin. • Decorate with the remaining
candied peel in the form of a cross.

*Makes one Easter cake · Prep: 20 min. + 12 hr. to
chill · Level: 1 · Keeps: 1 day in the freezer*

STRAWBERRY ANGEL CAKE

This makes a big, festive cake—perfect for a
4th of July celebration. Add some blueberries to
the strawberries if they're in season.

    1   10-inch Basic Angel Food Cake (see page 166)
    4   pints vanilla ice cream, softened
    2   quarts fresh strawberries, hulled and sliced
  2–4   tablespoons granulated sugar
    1   tablespoon fresh lemon juice

Set out a 13 x 9-inch baking pan. • Cut the
cake into about 24 thin slices. Arrange half
the slices in the bottom of the pan. • Spread
the ice cream over, pressing down to
smooth it. Tear the remaining cake slices
and arrange on top. • Freeze for 2 hours. •
Mix the strawberries, sugar to taste, and
lemon juice in a large bowl. Cover and soak
while the cake is freezing. • To serve, cut
the cake into squares and spoon some of
the strawberries over each.

*Makes one 13 x 9-inch cake · Prep 20 min. + 2 hr to
freeze · Level: 1 · Keeps: 2–3 days*

GRAPE CLAFOUTIS

This cake was originally served in France after the grape harvest.

- 2 cups green seedless grapes + extra, halved, for decoration
- 2 cups black or red seedless grapes + extra, halved, for decoration
- 1¹/₂ cups all-purpose flour
- 1¹/₂ teaspoons baking powder
- ¹/₄ teaspoon salt
- ¹/₂ cup (1 stick) butter, softened
- ³/₄ cup granulated sugar
- 1 teaspoon vanilla extract
- 3 large eggs, at room temperature
- 1 tablespoon fresh lemon juice
- ¹/₂ cup apricot preserves or jam
- 1 tablespoon apricot brandy (or other fruit liqueur)

Preheat the oven to 375°F. • Butter and flour a 9-inch springform pan. • Rinse the grapes under cold running water and dry each one carefully. Cut each grape in half. • Sift the flour, baking powder, and salt into a medium bowl. • Beat the butter, sugar, and vanilla in a large bowl with an electric mixer at medium speed until creamy. • Add the eggs, one at a time, until just blended after each addition. • With mixer at low speed, gradually beat in the dry ingredients and the lemon juice. • Stir in the grape halves. • Spoon the batter into the prepared pan. • Bake for 35–45 minutes, or until a toothpick inserted into the center comes out clean. • Cool the cake in the pan for 10 minutes. Loosen and remove the pan sides and let cool completely. • Heat the apricot preserves and brandy in a small saucepan over low heat. Set aside to cool for 10 minutes. • Brush the cake with some preserves and decorate with the grape halves. Brush with the remaining preserves.

Makes one 9-inch cake · Prep: 45 min. · Cooking: 35–45 min. · Level: 1 · Keeps: 1–2 days

PERUVIAN FRUIT NOUGAT CAKE

A popular Peruvian dessert. Its origins are with Doña Pepa, a slave who is believed to have received the recipe from the saints in her dreams. It is served throughout October when thousands of Limeños wear purple robes and parade the streets for the feast of El Señor de los Milagros.

- 4 cups all-purpose flour
- 1¹/₂ teaspoons salt
- 5 large eggs, lightly beaten
- 2 cups vegetable shortening
- ¹/₄ cup granulated sugar
- 2 tablespoons ground toasted aniseed

Peruvian fruit nougat cake

- 1 tablespoon ground toasted sesame seeds
- ¹/₄ cup candy sprinkles

FRUIT SYRUP
- 1 lb fresh peaches, peeled and coarsely chopped
- 4 oz dried figs
- 1 lb apples, peeled, cored, and coarsely chopped
- 1 lb oranges, peeled and coarsely chopped
- ¹/₂ small pineapple, peeled and coarsely chopped
- 1 banana, peeled and coarsely chopped
- 1 lime, peeled and coarsely chopped
- 6 cups granulated sugar

Preheat the oven to 275°F. • Butter and flour two large baking sheets. • Sift the flour and salt into a large bowl. Mix in the eggs, shortening, sugar, aniseed, and sesame seeds to form a smooth dough. • Divide the dough into portions about the size of a golf ball. Roll each portion into a length 12 inches long and about ³/₄ inch thick. • Place the dough on the prepared sheets, leaving ¹/₂ inch between each. • Bake for 10–15 minutes, or until pale golden. Cool the cookies in the pan on a rack. • *Fruit Syrup*: Place the peaches, figs, apples, oranges, pineapple, banana, and lime in a large saucepan with enough water to cover and bring to a boil. Reduce the heat to low and simmer until reduced by half and the fruit has begun to break down, about 20 minutes. Set aside to cool. • Strain the fruit and reserve the juice. You should have about 8 cups. Mix the juice and sugar in a large saucepan and simmer over very low heat, or until it starts to bubble halfway up the pan and registers 240°F on a candy thermometer, about 2 hours. • Remove from the heat and cool for 20 minutes. • Line a 13 x 9-inch baking pan with waxed paper. Place the cookies in rows, so that they line the base, touching each other. Break off into smaller pieces to fit the dish, if necessary. • Spoon some of the syrup over the cookies, coating well. Place more cookies crosswise on top. Coat again with the syrup and top with another crosswise layer of cookies. Spoon the remaining syrup over. • Sprinkle with the candy sprinkles. Let set for several hours before serving.

Makes one 13 x 9-inch cake · Prep: 45 min. · Cooking: 2¹/₂ hr · Level: 2 · Keeps: 4–5 days

Meringues are decadent yet light desserts — a perfect finish following a heavy feast. Served with whipped cream and the freshest fruit, meringue desserts melt exquisitely in the mouth. The piped spiral of the French dacquoise, an airy confection of nut-flavored meringues stacked and filled with sweetened whipped cream or buttercream, is served chilled, often with fruit.

MERINGUES & DACQUOISES

CHOCOLATE DACQUOISE

8	oz bittersweet chocolate, coarsely chopped
1½	cups (3 sticks) unsalted butter, softened
6	large egg yolks, at room temperature
1	cup granulated sugar
½	cup water
2	teaspoons vanilla extract
3	Basic Dacquoise rounds (see page 215)
	toasted hazelnuts, to decorate
	ground hazelnuts, to decorate

Melt the chocolate in a double boiler over barely simmering water. Set aside to cool. • Beat the butter in a medium bowl with an electric mixer at medium speed until creamy. • With mixer at high speed, beat the egg yolks in a large bowl until pale and thick. • Stir the sugar and water in a saucepan over medium heat until the sugar has dissolved and the syrup boils. Wash down the sides of the pan with a

pastry brush dipped in cold water to prevent sugar crystals from forming. Cook, without stirring, until the mixture reaches 238°F, or the soft-ball stage. • Remove from the heat and slowly beat the syrup into the egg yolks. Continue beating until the mixture is cool. Gradually beat in the butter, followed by the chocolate and vanilla. • Place one meringue layer on a serving plate and spread with ⅓ of the filling. Top with another meringue layer and spread with ⅓ of the filling. Place the remaining

meringue layer on top. Spread with the remaining filling. • Sprinkle the top of the cake with the toasted hazelnuts. Press the ground hazelnuts around the sides.

Makes one 8-inch cake · Prep: 30 min. · Cooking: · Level: 2 · Keeps: 1 day in the refrigerator

◄ Raspberry meringue cake (see page 206)

⋏ Chocolate dacquoise

Italian marengo torta

ITALIAN MARENGO TORTA

This traditional Italian dessert cake comes from Tuscany, where it is served in the winter.

PASTRY
1²/₃ cups all-purpose flour
²/₃ cup confectioners' sugar
¹/₄ teaspoon salt
¹/₃ cup cold butter, cut up
2 tablespoons chopped lard or vegetable shortening
1 large egg 1 large egg yolk
1–2 tablespoons ice water

FILLING
3 large eggs, separated
¹/₃ cup granulated sugar
¹/₄ cup all-purpose flour
1 teaspoon vanilla extract
1²/₃ cups milk
¹/₂ recipe Italian Sponge Cake (see page 157)
3 tablespoons orange liqueur
1 cup confectioners' sugar

Pastry: Stir together the flour, confectioners' sugar, and salt in a large bowl. • Use a pastry blender to cut in the butter and lard until the mixture resembles fine crumbs. • Stir in the egg and egg yolk and water until a smooth dough is formed, adding more water if it is too dry. • Press into a disk, wrap in plastic wrap, and refrigerate for 1 hour. • *Filling*: Beat the egg yolks and sugar in a medium saucepan until pale and thick. Add the flour and vanilla. Gradually pour in the milk. • Cook over medium heat, beating constantly, until the mixture comes to a boil. Lower the heat and cook, stirring constantly, until thick. Spoon into a bowl. Press plastic wrap directly onto the surface and refrigerate until chilled. • Preheat the oven to 350°F. • Butter a 10-inch springform pan. • Roll half the dough out on a lightly floured surface to a 10-inch round. Place the round in the pan. Roll out the remaining dough and fit, lining the pan sides. Prick all over with a fork. • Cut the cake into thin slices vertically and place half in a layer over the pastry dough. Drizzle with half the liqueur. Spread with the custard. Top with the remaining cake slices. Drizzle with the remaining liqueur. • Beat the egg whites in a large bowl with an electric mixer at medium speed until frothy. With mixer at high speed, gradually beat in the confectioners' sugar, beating until stiff, glossy peaks form. Spread over the cake. • Bake for 35–45 minutes, or until pale gold. If the meringue starts to become too darkly browned, cover loosely with a piece of aluminum foil. • Cool the cake in the pan for 15 minutes. Loosen and remove the pan sides. Place the cake top-side up on a rack and let cool completely.

Makes one 9-inch cake · Prep: 1 hr. · Cooking: 35–45 min. · Level: 2 · Keeps: 1–2 days

MERINGUE SPONGE DELIGHT

²/₃ cup all-purpose flour
¹/₂ teaspoon baking powder
¹/₄ teaspoon salt
3 large eggs + 3 large egg yolks
¹/₂ cup granulated sugar
1 teaspoon vanilla extract
¹/₂ cup flaked almonds, to decorate
¹/₄ cup confectioners' sugar, to dust

MERINGUE
8 large egg whites, at room temperature
1 cup granulated sugar

RED CURRANT FILLING
1¹/₂ cups red currant jelly
1 tablespoon rum

Preheat the oven to 300°F. • Butter and flour two 9-inch springform pans. • Sift the flour, baking powder, and salt into a medium bowl. • Beat the eggs, egg yolks, granulated sugar, and vanilla in a large bowl with an electric mixer at high speed until pale and thick. • Use a large rubber spatula to fold in the dry ingredients. • *Meringue*: With mixer at medium speed, beat the egg whites in a large bowl until soft peaks form. With mixer at high speed, gradually beat in the sugar, beating until stiff, glossy peaks form. • Drop spoonfuls of the meringue, alternating with the batter into the prepared pans. • Bake for 20–25 minutes, or until springy to the touch. • Cool the cakes in the pans for 10 minutes. Loosen and remove the pan sides. Transfer onto racks and let cool completely. • *Red Currant Filling*: Stir the jelly and rum together in a bowl. • Place a cake layer on a serving plate and spread with half the filling. Top with the remaining layer and spread with the remaining filling. Sprinkle with the almonds and dust with the confectioners' sugar. • Refrigerate for 1–2 hours.

Makes one 9-inch cake · Prep: 45 min. + 1–2 hr. to chill · Cooking: 20–25 min. · Level: 2 · Keeps: 1–2 days

CHRISTMAS MERINGUE STAR

This recipe comes from France, where the cake is prepared at Christmas time. Its shape commemorates the star that is reported to have led the Three Wise Men to the stable in Bethlehem where the baby Jesus had just been born.

- 4 large egg whites, at room temperature
- 1¼ cups superfine sugar
- 1 pint vanilla ice cream
- 1 pint strawberry ice cream
- 2 cups Chantilly Cream (see page 345)
- ½ cup fresh strawberries, hulled and sliced, to decorate

Preheat the oven to 200°F. • Butter two shallow star-shaped 8- or 9-inch pans. Line with parchment paper. • Beat the egg whites in a large bowl with an electric mixer at medium speed until frothy. With mixer at high speed, gradually beat in the superfine sugar, beating until stiff, glossy peaks form. • Spoon the meringue evenly into the prepared pans. • Bake for 60–70 minutes, or until crisp. • Cool the meringues in the pans for 15 minutes. Turn out of the pans. Carefully remove the paper and let cool completely. • Leave the ice cream at room temperature to soften for 10–15 minutes. • Place one meringue on a serving plate. Spread with the vanilla ice cream, followed by the strawberry ice cream. Top with the remaining meringue. Freeze for 30 minutes. • Spoon the chantilly cream into a pastry bag fitted with a star tip. Pipe the cream all over in a decorative manner. • Decorate with the strawberries.

Makes one star-shaped cake · Prep: 30 min. + 30 min. to freeze · Cooking 60–70 min. · Level: 2 · Keeps: 1 day in the freezer

MERINGUE DELIGHT

- 6 large egg whites, at room temperature
- 1¼ cups granulated sugar
- 1 pint vanilla ice cream
- ⅓ cup mixed candied fruit, chopped
- 2 tablespoons brandy
- ½ cup heavy cream
  sliced fresh fruit, to decorate

Preheat the oven to 200°F. • Cut out three 8-inch parchment paper rounds. Place the parchment paper on one or two baking sheets. • Beat the egg whites in a large bowl with an electric mixer at medium speed until frothy. With mixer at high speed, gradually beat in the sugar, beating

Christmas meringue star

until stiff, glossy peaks form. • Spread the meringue evenly on the three parchment rounds. • Bake for 1 hour and 30–40 minutes, or until lightly browned and crisp. • Cool the meringues on the sheet for 15 minutes. Carefully remove the paper and let cool completely. • Soften the ice cream at room temperature for 10 minutes. Place the ice cream in a large bowl and stir in the candied fruit and brandy. • Place a meringue layer on a serving plate. Spread with the ice cream mixture. Top with a second meringue layer. Cover with foil and freeze for 1 hour. • Crumble the remaining meringue in a small bowl. • With mixer at high speed beat the cream in a medium bowl until stiff. • Remove the cake from the freezer. Spread with the cream and sprinkle with the meringue. Decorate with sliced fruit, if desired.

Makes one 9-inch cake · Prep: 45 min. + 1 hr. to freeze · Cooking: 1 hr. 30–40 min. · Level: 1 · Keeps: 1 day in the freezer

BROWN SUGAR MERINGUES

Use these delicious caramel-flavored meringues to top a nutty meringue cake or dacquoise. You may double the recipe and sandwich them together with cream and serve them on their own.

- 2 large egg whites, at room temperature
- ¼ cup granulated sugar
- ¼ cup firmly packed light brown sugar

Preheat the oven to 250°F. • Line a baking sheet with parchment paper. • Beat the egg whites in a large bowl with an electric mixer at medium speed until frothy. • With mixer at high speed, gradually beat in the sugars, beating until stiff peaks form. • Spoon the meringue into a pastry bag fitted with a ½-inch nozzle and pipe 20 small rounded meringues onto the prepared sheet. • Bake for 50–60 minutes, or until the meringues can be lifted off the parchment paper with a metal spatula without sticking. Turn off the oven and leave the door ajar until the meringues are completely cool.

Makes 20 small meringues · Prep: 20 min. · Cooking: 50–60 min. · Level: 1 · Keeps: 5–6 days in an airtight container

RASPBERRY MERINGUE CAKE

- 9 large egg whites, at room temperature
- 1/8 teaspoon salt
- 3 cups superfine sugar
- 3 cups heavy cream
- 1/3 cup confectioners' sugar
- 1 teaspoon vanilla extract
- 3 cups fresh raspberries

Preheat the oven to 200°F. • Cut three 9-inch rounds of parchment paper and place on two baking sheets. Cut one 8 x 12-inch rectangle of parchment paper and place on one of the baking sheets. • Beat the egg whites and salt in a large bowl with an electric mixer at medium speed until frothy. • With mixer at high speed, gradually beat in the superfine sugar, beating until stiff, glossy peaks form. • Spread 1/4 of the meringue onto each parchment round. • Use the remaining 1/4 of the meringue to make 6–8 small meringues to decorate the cake. • Bake with the oven door ajar for 50–60 minutes so that the meringue does not turn brown. Remove the small meringues and continue baking for 10–15 minutes, or until crisp. Turn the oven off and let the meringues cool in the oven with the door ajar. Remove from the oven and carefully remove the paper. • With mixer at high speed, beat the cream, confectioners'

sugar, and vanilla in a large bowl until stiff. • Place one meringue round on a serving plate. Spread with 1/3 of the cream and sprinkle with 1/3 of the raspberries. Top with another meringue round. Spread with 1/3 of the cream and sprinkle with 1/3 of the raspberries. Top with another round and spread with the cream. Decorate with the raspberries and meringues.

Makes one 9-inch cake · Prep: 1 hr. · Cooking: 60–75 min. · Level: 1 · Keeps: 1 day in the refrigerator

BAKED FLORENTINE CAKE

- 1 cup all-purpose flour
- 1 teaspoon baking powder
- 1/4 teaspoon salt
- 4 large eggs, at room temperature
- 3/4 cup granulated sugar
- 1/2 teaspoon vanilla extract

RASPBERRY FILLING
- 1 cup fresh or frozen raspberries
- 3/4 cup granulated sugar
- 2 tablespoons orange liqueur
- 1/2 cup heavy cream

TOPPING
- 3 large egg whites, at room temperature
- 3/4 cup granulated sugar
  fresh raspberries, to decorate

Preheat the oven to 350°F. • Butter and flour an 8-inch oval or round pan. • Sift the flour, baking powder, and salt into a medium bowl. • Beat the eggs, sugar, and

vanilla in a large bowl with an electric mixer at high speed until the batter falls from the beater in ribbons, about 20 minutes. • Use a large rubber spatula to fold in the dry ingredients. • Spoon the batter into the prepared pan. • Bake for 40–45 minutes, or until a toothpick inserted into the center comes out clean. • Turn out onto a rack to cool completely. • *Raspberry Filling*: Mash the raspberries in a large bowl. Stir in the sugar and liqueur. With mixer at high speed, beat the cream in a medium bowl until stiff. Fold into the raspberry mixture. • Split the cake into four horizontally. • Place the largest layer on a serving plate and spread with 1/3 of the raspberry mixture. Top with a second layer and spread with 1/3 of the raspberry mixture. Repeat and top with the remaining layer of cake. Cover with plastic wrap and refrigerate for 3 hours. • *Topping*: With mixer at high speed, beat the egg whites and sugar in a large bowl until stiff peaks form. • Turn out onto a baking sheet lined with waxed paper . Spread all over with the meringue. • Turn on the broiler. Broil the cake 6–8 inches from the heat source for 4–5 minutes, or until lightly browned. Decorate with the raspberries.

Makes one 8-inch dome-shaped cake · Prep: 1 hr. + 3 hr. to freeze · Cooking: 44–50 min. · Level: 2 · Keeps: 1–2 days

STRAWBERRY MERINGUE DESSERT

- 5 oz strawberries, hulled (reserve 8 for decoration)
- 1/4 cup confectioners' sugar
- 3 tablespoons orange liqueur
- 3/4 cup heavy cream
- 1 9-inch Italian Sponge Cake (see page 157)
- 2 tablespoons strawberry jelly
- 1 6-inch and 1 7-inch meringue round (see page 212)
- 20 meringue rosettes (see page 212)

Process the strawberries, confectioners' sugar, and 1 tablespoon liqueur until pureed. Strain the mixture into a large bowl. • Beat the cream in a large bowl with an electric mixer at high speed until stiff. • Use a large rubber spatula to gradually fold the cream into the strawberry mixture. • Place the cake on a serving plate. Drizzle with the remaining liqueur. Spread the top of the cake with the jelly. • Top with the larger meringue round and spread with 2 tablespoons strawberry

Baked Florentine cake

mixture. Top with the remaining meringue round. Spread the remaining strawberry mixture over the top and sides to form a mound. • Slice the remaining strawberries thinly. • Stick the meringues rosettes and sliced strawberries all over the mound in circles. • Refrigerate until before serving.

Makes 1 dessert · Prep: 45 min. · Level: 2 · Keeps: 2 days in the refrigerator

APRICOT MERINGUE CAKE

1	9-inch Italian Sponge Cake (see page 157)
1	can (15¼ oz) apricot halves, drained (reserve 2 halves, for decoration, and the juice)
4	large egg whites, at room temperature
1¼	cups superfine sugar
¼	cup firmly packed light brown sugar, to dust

Preheat the oven to 250°F. • Split the cake horizontally. • Place one layer on a serving plate and brush with the reserved syrup. • Slice the apricots and arrange on the cake. Top with the remaining layer. • Beat the egg whites in a large bowl with an electric mixer at medium speed until frothy. With mixer at high speed, gradually beat in the superfine sugar, beating until stiff, glossy peaks form. • Use a thin metal spatula to spread the meringue over the top and sides of the cake, swirling it in a decorative manner. • Bake for 45–55 minutes, or until crispy. Cool the cake completely on a rack. • Decorate with the apricot halves, cut into slices, and dust with the brown sugar.

Makes one 9-inch cake · Prep: 45 min. · Cooking: 45–55 min. · Level: 2 · Keeps: 1–2 days

PINEAPPLE MERINGUE CAKE

1⅓	cups all-purpose flour
1½	teaspoons baking powder
¼	teaspoon salt
⅓	cup butter, softened
¾	cup granulated sugar
1	teaspoon vanilla extract
3	large egg yolks
½	cup milk

TOPPING

3	large egg whites, at room temperature
1	teaspoon vanilla extract
½	teaspoon rum extract
½	cup granulated sugar
½	cup macadamia nuts, chopped

PINEAPPLE CREAM FILLING

1	cup heavy cream, chilled
2	tablespoons confectioners' sugar
1	teaspoon vanilla extract
1	can (8 oz) crushed pineapple, drained

Apricot meringue cake

Preheat the oven to 350°F. • Butter and flour two 8-inch springform pans. • Sift the flour, baking powder, and salt into a medium bowl. • Beat the butter, sugar, and vanilla in a large bowl with an electric mixer at medium speed until creamy. • Add the egg yolks, one at a time, until just blended after each addition. • With mixer at low speed, gradually beat in the dry ingredients, alternating with the milk. • Spoon the batter into the prepared pans. • *Topping*: With mixer at medium speed, beat the egg whites, vanilla, and rum extract in a large bowl until soft peaks form. With mixer at high speed, gradually beat in the sugar, beating until stiff, glossy peaks form. Stir in the macadamia nuts. • Drop spoonfuls of the meringue over the unbaked batter in the pans, spreading it out. • Bake for 25–30 minutes, or until a toothpick inserted into the center comes out clean. • Cool the cakes in the pans for 10 minutes. Loosen and remove the pan sides. Transfer onto racks, meringue-side up, and let cool completely. • *Pineapple Cream Filling*: With mixer at high speed, beat the cream, confectioners' sugar, and vanilla in a large bowl until stiff. Fold in the pineapple. • Place one cake, meringue-side up, on a serving plate. Spread with half the filling and top with the remaining cake. Spread with the remaining filling. • Refrigerate for 1 hour before serving.

Makes one 8-inch cake · Prep: 40 min. + 1 hr. to chill · Cooking: 25–30 min. · Level: 2 · Keeps: 1–2 days

PARTY PINK MERINGUE DESSERT

2	large egg whites, at room temperature
	pinch of salt
1	cup confectioners' sugar
½	teaspoon red food coloring
1	pint vanilla ice cream
1	pint pistachio ice cream

Preheat the oven to 275°F. • Line a baking sheet with parchment paper and mark an 11-inch circle on the paper. • Beat the egg whites and salt in a large bowl with an electric mixer at medium speed until frothy. With mixer at high speed, gradually beat in ¾ cup confectioners' sugar and red food coloring, beating until stiff, glossy peaks form. • Spoon the mixture into a pastry bag with a ½-inch nozzle and pipe the mixture into a spiral disk, starting at the center and filling the circle. • Dust with the remaining ¼ cup confectioners' sugar. • Bake for 30 minutes. Lower the oven temperature to 250°F and bake for 50–60 minutes, or until the meringue is crisp. • Turn off the oven and leave the door ajar until the meringue is completely cool. • Carefully remove the paper. • Soften the ice cream at room temperature for 10 minutes. • Place the meringue on a serving plate. Scoop the vanilla and pistachio ice cream into balls and serve on top of the meringue.

Makes one dessert · Prep: 45 min. · Cooking: 50–60 min. · Level: 2 · Keeps: 1 day in the freezer

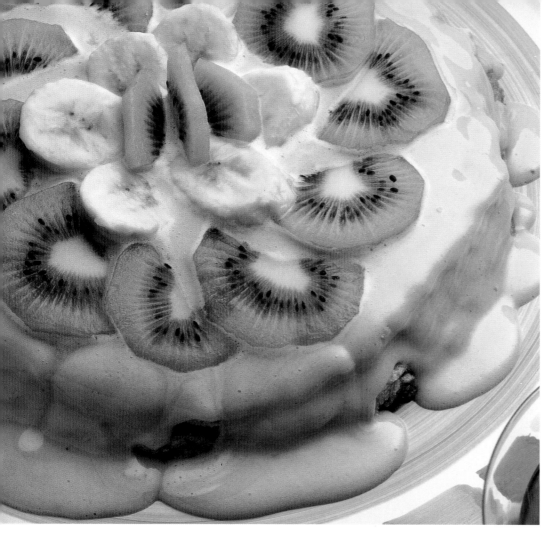

Meringue with zabaglione and fruit

MERINGUE WITH ZABAGLIONE AND FRUIT

  6   large egg whites
1½   cups confectioners' sugar
       pinch of salt
  1   teaspoon vanilla extract
1½   cups Zabaglione (see page 348)
  2   large bananas, peeled and sliced
  4   kiwifruit, peeled and thinly sliced
  2   tablespoons superfine sugar, to sprinkle

Butter a 9-inch springform pan. • Preheat the oven to 350°F. • Beat the egg whites in a large bowl with an electric mixer at medium speed until frothy. With mixer at high speed, gradually beat in the confectioners' sugar, salt, and vanilla, beating until stiff peaks form. • Spoon the batter into the prepared pan. • Bake for 80–90 minutes, or until lightly browned. • Carefully turn out onto a rack and let cool completely. • Sprinkle the bananas and kiwifruit with the sugar. • Pour the zabaglione over. • Arrange the fruit on top.

Makes one 9-inch cake · Prep: 10 min. · Cooking: 90 min. · Level: 1 · Keeps: 1 day in the refrigerator

NUTTY MERINGUE CAKE

  1   (18 oz) package white cake mix, baked in two 9-inch cake pans

NUTTY FILLING
  4   large egg yolks
  2   tablespoons all-purpose flour
  1   cup granulated sugar
½   cup (1 stick) butter, cut into small pieces
  2   cups mixed nuts, chopped
  1   cup raisins

TOPPING
  2   large egg whites, at room temperature
  1   cup granulated sugar
½   cup hot water

Bake the white cake mix, following the directions on the package. Cool the cakes in the pans for 30 minutes. Turn out onto racks to cool completely. • *Nutty Filling*: Beat the egg yolks, flour, sugar, and butter in a double boiler until well blended. Cook over low heat, stirring constantly with a wooden spoon, until the mixture lightly coats a metal spoon or registers 160°F on an instant-read thermometer. Immediately plunge the pan into a bowl of ice water and stir until the egg mixture has cooled. • Stir in the nuts and raisins. •

Place a cake layer on a serving plate and spread with half the filling. Top with the remaining layer and spread with the remaining filling. • *Topping*: Stir the egg whites, ¼ cup sugar, and 2 teaspoons water in a saucepan until blended. Cook over low heat, beating constantly with an electric mixer at low speed until the whites register 160°F on an instant-read thermometer. • Transfer to a bowl and beat at high speed until the whites form stiff peaks. • Place the remaining sugar and water in a saucepan over medium heat and bring to a boil. Boil gently without stirring, until the mixture will spin a long thread when dropped from a spoon, or reaches 230°–234°F. • Pour the hot syrup slowly over the egg whites, beating constantly. Continue beating until mixture is fluffy and will hold its shape. • Spread the cake with the meringue.

Makes one 9-inch cake · Prep: 40 min. · Cooking: 20–25 min. · Level: 2 · Keeps: 2–3 days in the refrigerator

LEMON MERINGUE GÂTEAU

  5   large egg whites, at room temperature
1¼   cups granulated sugar
  2   9-inch Italian Sponge Cakes (see page 157)
½   cup sweet lemon liqueur (Italian Limoncello)
  2   recipes Lemon Curd (see page 345)
  1   cup heavy cream
  1   tablespoon confectioners' sugar
¼   cup flaked almonds

Preheat the oven to 275°F. • Line two baking sheets with parchment paper and mark three 9-inch circles on the paper. • Beat the egg whites in a large bowl with mixer at medium speed until frothy. • With mixer at high speed, gradually beat in the granulated sugar, beating until stiff, glossy peaks form. • Spoon the mixture into a pastry bag with a ½-inch nozzle and pipe the mixture into three spiral disks, starting at the center and filling each 9-inch circle. • Bake for 60–70 minutes, or until crisp. • Turn off the oven and leave the door ajar until the meringues are completely cool. • Remove from the oven and carefully remove the paper. • Split the cakes horizontally. • Place one layer on a serving plate. Brush with the liqueur, spread with lemon curd, and top with meringue. Spread with lemon curd and top with another cake layer. Repeat until all the cake, lemon curd, liqueur, and meringue have been used, finishing with a cake layer. • With mixer at high speed, beat the cream and confectioners' sugar in a medium bowl until stiff. • Spread the top of the cake with the cream. Refrigerate for 1–2 hours to soften the meringue a little so that it can be cut. • Sprinkle with the almonds.

Makes one 9-inch cake · Prep: 50 min. + 1–2 hr. in refrigerator · Cooking: 60–70 min. · Level: 2 · Keeps: 1 day in the refrigerator

LEMON MERINGUE LAYER CAKE

- 4 large egg whites, at room temperature
- ¼ teaspoon salt
- 1 cup confectioners' sugar
- ½ cup granulated sugar

LEMON FILLING

- 3 large egg yolks
- ½ cup granulated sugar
- 1 tablespoon cornstarch
- ⅓ cup fresh lemon juice
- 1¼ cups heavy cream, whipped

Preheat the oven to 250°F. • Cut out three 8-inch rounds of parchment paper and place on two baking sheets. • Beat the egg whites and salt in a large bowl with an electric mixer at medium speed until frothy. • With mixer at high speed, gradually beat in both sugars, beating until stiff, glossy peaks form. • Spread ⅓ of the meringue onto each parchment round. • Bake for 35–45 minutes, or until crisp. Turn the oven off and leave the meringues in the oven with the door ajar until cool. Remove from the oven and carefully remove the paper. • *Lemon Filling*: Beat the egg yolks, sugar, cornstarch, and lemon juice in a double boiler until well blended. Cook over low heat, stirring constantly with a wooden spoon, until the mixture lightly coats a metal spoon or registers 160°F on an instant-read thermometer. Immediately plunge the pan into a bowl of ice water and stir until the filling has cooled. • With mixer at high speed, beat the cream in a large bowl until stiff. Fold the cream into the filling. • Spread the filling on two of the meringue rounds. Place the rounds on top of one another and place the third meringue round on top.

Makes one 8-inch cake · Prep: 20 min. · Cooking: 35–45 min. · Level: 2 · Keeps: 1 day

Lemon meringue sponge

LEMON MERINGUE SPONGE

MERINGUE

- 4 large egg whites, at room temperature
- 1 cup superfine sugar

- 2 9-inch Génoises, baked in four 9-inch cake pans (see page 157)

LEMON SYRUP

- ½ cup granulated sugar
- ¼ cup fresh lemon juice
- 2 tablespoons water

- ½ cup heavy cream
- 2 tablespoons confectioners' sugar
- ½ teaspoon vanilla extract
- 2 recipes Lemon Curd (see page 345)
- ½ cup sliced almonds

Preheat the oven to 250°F. • *Meringue*: Cut out three 9-inch rounds of parchment paper and place on two baking sheets. • Beat the egg whites in a large bowl with an electric mixer at medium speed until frothy. • With mixer at high speed, gradually beat in the superfine sugar, beating until stiff, glossy peaks form. • Spread ⅓ of the meringue onto each parchment round. • Bake for

50–60 minutes, or until crisp. Turn the oven off and leave the meringues in the oven with door ajar until cool. Remove from the oven and carefully remove the paper. • *Lemon Syrup*: Stir the sugar, lemon juice, and water in a saucepan over medium heat until the sugar has dissolved. Set aside to cool. • With mixer at high speed, beat the cream, confectioners' sugar, and vanilla in a medium bowl until stiff. • Place one cake on a serving plate. Drizzle with the syrup and spread with lemon curd. Top with a meringue round, trimming the edges if needed. Spread the meringue with lemon curd and top with another cake layer. Repeat, using all the lemon curd and lemon syrup. Place the remaining layer on top. • Spread the top of the cake with the cream. Sprinkle with the almonds.

Makes one 9-inch cake · Prep: 1 hr. · Cooking: 1 hr. · Level: 2 · Keeps: 1–2 days in the refrigerator

NORTHERN LIGHTS ICE CREAM CAKE

- 3 pints vanilla ice cream
- 8 oz candied fruit peel, finely chopped
- 1/2 cup orange liqueur
- 2 tablespoons finely grated orange zest
- 1/3 cup toasted almonds, finely chopped
- 3 oz semisweet chocolate, coarsely chopped
- 1 9-inch Italian Sponge Cake, cut into 1-inch slices (see page 157)
- 3 large egg whites
- 1 cup granulated sugar
- 1 tablespoon water
- 1/8 teaspoon cream of tartar

Line a 2-quart ice-cream mold with a moist muslin cloth. • Place half the ice cream in a large bowl and leave at room temperature to soften, 15 minutes. Mix in the candied fruit, 2 tablespoons liqueur, and 1 tablespoon orange zest. • Spoon the mixture into the mold, spreading it evenly on the bottom and sides of the mold. Freeze for 30 minutes. • Soften the remaining ice cream and mix in the almonds, chocolate, and the remaining liqueur and orange zest. • Spoon the almond mixture into the mold and smooth the top. • Place a layer of cake slices over the ice cream, working quickly so that the ice cream does not melt. Cover with aluminum foil and freeze for 3 hours. • Preheat the oven to 425°F. • Stir the egg whites, 6 tablespoon sugar, water, and cream of tartar in a saucepan until blended. Cook over low heat,

beating constantly, until the whites register 160°F on an instant-read thermometer. Trasnfer to a large bowl. With an electric mixer at high speed, gradually beat in the remaining sugar, beating until stiff, glossy peaks form. • Soak the mold in hot water for 10 seconds. Turn out onto an baking tray and remove the muslin. • Spread with the meringue. • Bake for 7–10 minutes, or until crispy to the touch.

Makes one 2-quart cake · Prep: 40 min. + 3 hr. to freeze · Cooking: 7–10 min. · Level: 1

HAZELNUT MERINGUE CAKE

MERINGUE ROUNDS
- 1/2 cup superfine sugar
- 1/4 cup water
- 2 large egg whites
  pinch of salt
- 2/3 cup confectioners' sugar

FILLING
- 1/2 cup + 1 teaspoon superfine sugar
- 1/4 cup water
- 1 large egg white
  pinch of salt
  scant 1 cup chocolate hazelnut cream (Nutella), melted
- 1 cup hazelnuts, finely chopped
- 1 tablespoon orange liqueur
- 2 cups heavy cream
  confectioners' sugar, to dust

Preheat the oven to 250°F. • Line a baking sheet with parchment paper and mark two 9-inch circles on the paper. • *Meringue Rounds*: Cook the superfine sugar and water in a saucepan over medium heat until the

Northern lights ice cream cake

sugar has dissolved. • Beat the egg whites and salt in a large bowl with an electric mixer at high speed until frothy. With mixer at high speed, beat in the hot sugar mixture and confectioners' sugar, beating until stiff, glossy peaks form. • Spoon the mixture into a pastry bag with a 1/2-inch nozzle and pipe the mixture into a spiral disk, starting at the center and filling the circle. • Bake for about 2 hours, or until crisp. • Turn off the oven and leave the meringues in the oven with the oven door slightly ajar, until the meringues are completely cool. • Remove from the oven and carefully remove the paper. • *Filling*: Cook 1/2 cup superfine sugar and water in a saucepan over medium heat until the sugar has dissolved. • With mixer at medium speed, beat the egg white and salt in a large bowl until frothy. With mixer at high speed, gradually beat in the hot sugar mixture and chocolate hazelnut cream until stiff. Set aside to cool. Drizzle with the liqueur. Use a large rubber spatula to fold in the hazelnuts and the remaining sugar. • With mixer at high speed, beat 1 1/4 cups cream in a medium bowl until stiff. Fold the cream into the chocolate mixture. • Place a meringue round on a freezerproof serving plate and spread with the filling. Top with the remaining meringue. • Freeze for 3 hours, or until set. • With mixer at high speed, beat the remaining 3/4 cup cream until stiff. Spoon the remaining cream into a pastry bag. Pipe on top of the meringue in a decorative manner. Dust with the confectioners' sugar. Serve immediately.

Makes one 9-inch cake · Prep: 1 hr. + 3 hr. to freeze · Cooking: 2 hr. · Level: 2 · Keeps:1 day in the freezer

WALNUT MERINGUE CAKE

Try with Black Currant Coulis (see page 351)

- 5 large egg whites
- 1 1/2 cups granulated sugar
- 1 cup walnuts, finely ground
- 1 teaspoon white wine vinegar
- 1 teaspoon vanilla extract
- 1 1/2 cups heavy cream
- 1 1/2 cups strawberries, hulled and sliced a few small whole ones, to decorate
- 2 tablespoons confectioners' sugar

Preheat the oven to 350°F. • Butter two 9-inch round cake pans. Line with waxed paper. Butter the paper. • Beat the egg whites in a large bowl with an electric mixer at medium speed until frothy. • With mixer at

high speed, gradually beat in the sugar, beating until stiff, glossy peaks form. • Use a large rubber spatula to fold in the ground walnuts, vinegar, and vanilla. • Spoon the mixture evenly into the prepared pans and smooth the tops with a thin metal spatula. • Bake for 25–30 minutes, or until crisp. • Cool the cakes in the pans for 20 minutes. Turn out onto racks. Carefully remove the paper and let cool completely. • About 1 hour before serving, beat the cream in a large bowl with mixer at high speed, until stiff. • Place a meringue layer on a serving plate. Spread with ²/₃ of the cream. Cover with the sliced strawberries. Top with the remaining meringue layer and spread with the remaining cream. Decorate with the strawberries and dust with the confectioners' sugar. • Refrigerate until serving. This will allow the cream to soften the meringue so that it doesn't splinter when you slice it.

Makes one 9-inch cake · Prep: 30 min. · Cooking: 25–30 min. · Level: 1 · Keeps: 1 day in the refrigerator

PORTUGUESE MERINGUE CAKE

This is a traditional recipe from Portugal, where it is served in the fall after the annual walnut harvest. The caramel flavoring may be found in specialty baking stores or through a mail-order source.

- 1¼ cups all-purpose flour
- ¼ teaspoon salt
- 3 large eggs + 5 large egg yolks
- ¾ cup granulated sugar

SYRUP
- 1½ cups granulated sugar
- 1 cup water
- 1 cup walnuts, coarsely chopped
- 3 tablespoons caramel flavoring

MERINGUE
- 5 large egg whites, at room temperature
- ¼ cup granulated sugar
- 5 teaspoons water
- ¼ teaspoon cream of tartar

Preheat the oven to 325°F. • Butter a 9-inch springform pan. Line with waxed paper. Butter the paper. • Sift the flour and salt into a medium bowl. • Beat the eggs, egg yolks, and sugar in a large bowl with an electric mixer at high speed until pale and very thick. • Gradually fold the dry ingredients into the batter. • Spoon the batter into the prepared pan. • Bake for 40–50 minutes, or until a toothpick inserted into the center comes out clean. • Cool the cake in the pan for 5

Portuguese meringue cake

minutes. Loosen and remove the pan sides. Invert onto a rack. Loosen and remove the pan bottom. Carefully remove the paper and let cool completely. • *Syrup*: Bring the sugar and water to a boil in a saucepan over medium heat. Boil for 5 minutes, stirring constantly. Remove from the heat and stir in the walnuts and caramel flavoring. • Preheat the oven to 350°F. • Slice the cake into three horizontally. Place one layer in the bottom of a dish, preferably with tall sides and only slightly larger than the cake itself. • Spoon ⅓ of the syrup over the cake. Repeat with the remaining 2 layers and the syrup. • *Meringue*: Stir the egg whites, sugar, water, and cream of tartar in a saucepan until blended. Cook over low heat, beating constantly, until the whites register 160°F on an instant-read thermometer. Transfer to a large bowl. With an electric mixer at high speed, beat until stiff, glossy peaks form. • Spread the meringue over. • Bake for 8–10 minutes, or until lightly browned. • Cool the cake completely in the pan on a rack.

Makes one 9-inch cake · Prep: 35 min. · Cooking: 50–60 min. · Level: 2 · Keeps: 1–2 days

CHOCOLATE AND SPICE MERINGUE SLICE

- 1½ cups all-purpose flour
- 1½ teaspoons baking powder
- 1 teaspoon pumpkin pie spice
- ¼ teaspoon salt
- ½ cup (1 stick) butter, at room temperature

- ²/₃ cup granulated sugar
- 3 large eggs, at room temperature
- 4 oz bittersweet chocolate, coarsely grated
- ²/₃ cup milk

MERINGUE
- 2 large egg whites, at room temperature
- ½ cup granulated sugar

SPICE TOPPING
- ½ cup slivered almonds
- 2 tablespoons shredded coconut
- 1 tablespoon granulated sugar
- 1 teaspoon ground cinnamon

Preheat the oven to 325°F. • Butter and flour a 13 x 9-inch baking pan. • Sift the flour, baking powder, pumpkin pie spice, and salt into a medium bowl. • Beat the butter and sugar in a large bowl with an electric mixer at medium speed until creamy. • Add the eggs, one at a time, until just blended after each addition. • Beat in the chocolate. With mixer at low speed, gradually beat in the dry ingredients, alternating with the milk. • Spoon the batter into the prepared pan. • *Meringue*: With mixer at high speed, beat the egg whites and sugar in a medium bowl until stiff peaks form. Gently spread the meringue over the batter. • *Spice Topping*: Mix all the ingredients in a small bowl. Sprinkle over the meringue. • Bake for 60–75 minutes, or until golden and a toothpick inserted into the center comes out clean. • Cool the cake completely in the pan on a rack.

Makes one 13 x 9-inch cake · Prep: 30 min. · Cooking: 60–75 min. · Level: 2 · Keeps: 1 day

BASIC MERINGUES

    3 large egg whites
       pinch of salt
    3 tablespoons cold water
  1½   cups granulated sugar
    3 teaspoons cornstarch
    1 teaspoon vinegar
   ½   teaspoon vanilla extract

Preheat the oven to 300°F. • Beat the egg whites and salt in a large bowl with an electric mixer at high speed until stiff peaks form. • With mixer at low speed, gradually beat in the water, sugar, and cornstarch. Add the vinegar and vanilla. • Spread spoon the meringue into a pastry bag fitted with ½-inch plain tip. • *Meringue Round*: Cut out a 9-inch round of parchment paper and place on a baking sheet. Pipe the meringue in a spiral to fill the round, leaving a ½-inch border around the edge. • Bake for 70–75 minutes, or until crisp. • *Meringue Rosettes*: Line a baking sheet with parchment paper. • Pipe the meringue in 1½-inch rosettes on the paper. • Bake for 20–25 minutes, or until crisp. • Invert onto racks and let cool completely.

Makes one 9-inch meringue or 20 small meringues · Prep: 15 min. · Cooking: 70–75 min. · Level: 1 · Keeps: 1 day in the refrigerator

CHOCOLATE MINT MERINGUES

> The mint syrup used here can be found in your supermarket with imported items.

MERINGUE

  1¼   cups superfine sugar
   ¼   cup water
   ¾   cup egg white, at room temperature
       pinch of salt

CHOCOLATE MINT SAUCE

    4 large egg yolks
   ⅓   cup superfine sugar
    1 teaspoon vanilla extract
    1 teaspoon cornstarch
    1 cup milk
    1 cup chocolate ice cream
    2 teaspoons mint syrup
       unsweetened cocoa powder, to dust

Preheat the oven to 250°F. • Line a baking sheet with parchment paper and mark eight 5-inch circles on the paper. • *Meringue*: Cook 1 cup sugar and water in a saucepan over medium heat until the sugar has dissolved. • Beat the egg whites and salt in a large bowl with an electric mixer at medium speed until frothy. With mixer at high speed,

beat in the remaining sugar, beating until stiff, glossy peaks form. Add the hot sugar syrup. • Spoon the mixture into a pastry bag with a ½-inch nozzle and pipe the mixture into spiral disks, starting at the centers and filling the circles. • Bake for about 2 hours, or until crisp. • Turn off the oven and leave the meringues in the oven with the oven door slightly ajar until the meringues are completely cool. • Carefully remove the paper. • *Chocolate Mint Sauce*: Mix the egg yolks, sugar, vanilla, cornstarch, and milk in a medium saucepan until well blended. Cook over low heat, stirring constantly with a wooden spoon, until the mixture lightly coats a metal spoon or registers 160°F on an instant-read thermometer. Immediately plunge the pan into a bowl of ice water and stir until the egg mixture has cooled. • Leave the ice cream at room temperature to soften, 15 minutes. • Stir the mint syrup into the sauce and pour onto the plates. • Place a meringue on each plate. Spread with chocolate ice cream. Top with a second meringue. • Dust with the cocoa.

Makes one dessert · Prep: 60 min. · Cooking: 2 hr. · Level: 2 · Keeps: 1 day in the freezer

CHERRY CHOCOLATE MERINGUE CAKE

   ⅔   cup self-rising flour
    1 teaspoon baking powder
   ⅓   cup butter, softened
   ½   cup superfine sugar
    2 large eggs
    3 tablespoons unsweetened cocoa powder dissolved in 3 tablespoons hot water
   ½   cup walnuts, coarsely chopped
   12 sour cherries, coarsely chopped

TOPPING

    2 large egg whites, at room temperature
    6 tablespoons superfine sugar
    2 teaspoons water
   ⅛   teaspoon cream of tartar
       pinch of salt

Preheat the oven to 325°F. • Butter and flour an 8-inch round cake pan. Line with waxed paper. Butter the paper. • Sift the flour and baking powder into a large bowl. • Beat the butter, superfine sugar, and eggs in a large bowl with an electric mixer at high speed until creamy. Add the cocoa mixture. • With mixer at low speed, gradually beat the dry ingredients into the batter. Stir in the walnuts and cherries. • Spoon the batter into the

prepared pan. • Bake for 25–30 minutes, or until a toothpick inserted into the center comes out clean. • Cool the cake in the pan for 15 minutes. Invert onto a rack and carefully remove the paper. • *Topping:* Stir the egg whites, ¼ cup superfine sugar, water, cream of tartar, and salt in a saucepan until blended. Cook over low heat, beating constantly, until the whites register 160°F on an instant-read thermometer. Transfer to a large bowl. With mixer at high speed, gradually beat in the remaining 2 tablespoons sugar, beating until stiff, glossy peaks form. • Spread the meringue over the cake. • Bake for 10–15 minutes more, or until golden.

Makes one 8-inch cake · Prep: 25 min. · Cooking: 35–45 min. · Level: 1 · Keeps: 1 day in the refrigerator

CHOCOLATE MERINGUE CAKE

- 1 cup all-purpose flour
- ½ cup unsweetened cocoa powder
- 1 teaspoon baking powder
- ¼ teaspoon salt
- ½ cup (1 stick) butter, softened
- 1¼ cups granulated sugar
- 4 large eggs, separated
- ½ cup buttermilk
- ½ cup sour cream
- ¼ cup sliced almonds

TOPPING

- 1 cup heavy cream
- 2 tablespoons granulated sugar
- 1 cup strawberries, hulled and thickly sliced

Preheat the oven to 350°F. • Butter two 9-inch round cake pans. Line with waxed paper. Butter the paper. • Sift the flour, cocoa, baking powder, and salt into a medium bowl. • Beat the butter and ½ cup sugar in a large bowl with an electric mixer at medium speed until creamy. • Add the egg yolks, one at a time, until just blended after each addition. • Use a large rubber spatula to fold in the dry ingredients, followed by the buttermilk and sour cream. • Spoon half the batter into each of the prepared pans. • With mixer at medium speed, beat the egg whites in a large bowl until frothy. With mixer at high speed, gradually beat in the remaining ¾ cup sugar, beating until stiff, glossy peaks form. • Spoon the meringue over the batter.

Sprinkle the almonds over one of the cakes. • Bake for 10 minutes. Cover loosely with foil and bake for 25 minutes more. • Remove the foil and cool the cakes in the pans for 5 minutes. Turn out onto racks and carefully remove the paper. Turn meringue-side up and let cool completely. • *Topping:* With mixer at high speed, beat the cream and sugar until stiff. Place the cake without almonds on a serving plate. Spread with the cream and arrange the strawberries on the cream. Top with the remaining cake.

Makes one 9-inch round cake · Prep: 25 min. · Cooking: 35 min. · Level: 2 · Keeps: 1 day

BAKED MERINGUE WITH CHOCOLATE FILLING

Meringue made with confectioners' sugar tends to be drier and crisper. It is just right for this recipe with its moist creamy chocolate filling. If you like, decorate the top of the cake with small meringues.

- 5 large egg whites, at room temperature
- 1½ cups confectioners' sugar
- ¾ cup heavy cream
- 1 tablespoon granulated sugar
- ½ teaspoon vanilla extract
- 2 cups Chocolate Pastry Cream (see page 346), chilled
- 8 Brown Sugar Meringues (see page 205)
- 5 ripe strawberries, washed

Preheat the oven to 250°F. • Line a baking sheet with parchment paper and mark two 9-inch circles on the paper. • Beat the egg whites in a large bowl with an electric mixer at medium speed until frothy. • With mixer at high speed, gradually beat in the confectioners' sugar until stiff, glossy peaks form. • Spoon the mixture into a pastry bag with a plain ½-inch nozzle and pipe into two spiral disks, starting at the center and filling each 9-inch circle. • Bake for 60–70 minutes, or until crisp and dry. Turn off the oven and leave the door ajar until the meringues are completely cool. • With mixer at high speed, beat the cream, sugar, and vanilla in a small bowl until stiff. • Carefully transfer one meringue layer from the paper and place on a serving plate. Spread with the pastry cream. Top with the remaining meringue layer. • Spread with the cream and decorate with the brown sugar meringues and strawberries.

Makes one 9-inch cake · Prep: 30 min. · Cooking: 60–70 min. · Level: 1 · Keeps: 1 day

Baked meringue with chocolate filling

Whole-wheat apple tart
with meringue topping

WHOLE-WHEAT APPLE TART WITH MERINGUE TOPPING

APPLE FILLING
- 2 lb large tart apples (Granny Smiths are ideal), peeled, cored, and grated
- 4 large whole-wheat cookies (digestive), crushed
- $2/3$ cup plain yogurt
- 3 large egg yolks
- 1 tablespoon fresh lemon juice
- 1 teaspoon ground cinnamon

CRUST
- $3/4$ cup ($1\frac{1}{2}$ sticks) butter, softened
- 3 tablespoons honey
- 1 large egg, at room temperature
- $1\frac{1}{2}$ cups whole-wheat flour
- $1/4$ teaspoon salt
- $1/3$ cup apple juice

TOPPING
- 3 large egg whites, at room temperature
- $1/4$ teaspoon salt
- $1/2$ teaspoon fresh lemon juice
- 1 tablespoon honey

- 1 large red apple, to decorate

Preheat the oven to 400°F. • Butter and flour a 9-inch springform pan. • *Apple Filling*: Stir together the apples, crumbs, yogurt, egg yolks, lemon juice, and cinnamon in a large bowl. • *Crust*: Beat the butter, honey, and egg in a medium bowl with an electric mixer at high speed until creamy. • With mixer at low speed, gradually beat in the flour and salt, alternating with the apple juice. • Press into the bottom and halfway up the sides of the prepared pan. • Spoon the filling into the crust. • Bake for 20–25 minutes, or until golden brown. • *Topping*: With mixer at high speed, beat the egg whites, salt, lemon juice,

and honey until stiff peaks form. • Remove from the oven. Use a metal spatula to spread the meringue evenly over the tart. Bake for 5 minutes more, or until the meringue is golden. • Cool the tart in the pan for 5 minutes. • Loosen and remove the pan sides. Transfer onto a serving plate. • Slice the red apple thinly and arrange on top of the meringue in a fan shape.

Makes one 9-inch tart · Prep: 45 min. · Cooking: 30 min. · Level: 1 · Keeps: 1–2 days

COFFEE VACHERIN

- 5 large egg whites, at room temperature
- $1\frac{1}{2}$ cups granulated sugar
- 3 tablespoons coffee liqueur
- $1\frac{1}{2}$ cups heavy cream
- 2 tablespoons confectioners' sugar
- 8–10 whole coffee beans

Preheat the oven to 275°F. • Line a baking sheet with parchment paper and mark two 9-inch circles on the paper. • Beat the egg whites in a large bowl with an electric mixer at medium speed until frothy. With mixer at high speed, gradually beat in the sugar, beating until stiff, glossy peaks form. Add 1 tablespoon coffee liqueur. • Spoon the mixture into a pastry bag fitted with a $1/2$-inch nozzle and pipe the mixture into two spiral disks, starting at the center of the drawn circles and filling each circle. • Bake for 50–60 minutes, or until crisp. Turn off the oven and leave the door ajar until the meringues are completely cool. • Carefully remove the paper. • About 1 hour before

serving, beat the cream, confectioners' sugar, and remaining coffee liqueur in a large bowl with mixer at high speed until stiff. • Place a meringue layer on a serving plate. Spread with $3/4$ of the cream. Top with the remaining meringue layer. Spoon the remaining cream into a pastry bag and decorate the top of the vacherin with 8–10 rosettes. Top each with a coffee bean.

Makes one 9-inch cake · Prep: 30 min. · Cooking: 50–60 min. · Level: 1 · Keeps: 1 day in the refrigerator

CHOCOLATE VACHERIN

- 5 large egg whites, at room temperature
- $1\frac{1}{2}$ cups granulated sugar
- $1/3$ cup unsweetened cocoa powder
- 1 teaspoon vanilla extract
- 2 cups Chocolate Ganache (see page 350)
- $3/4$ cup heavy cream
- 2 oz bittersweet chocolate, grated

Preheat the oven to 275°F. • Line a baking sheet with parchment paper and mark two 9-inch circles on the paper. • Beat the egg whites in a large bowl with an electric mixer at medium speed until frothy. • With mixer at high speed, gradually beat in the sugar, beating until stiff, glossy peaks form. • Use a large rubber spatula to fold in the cocoa and vanilla. • Spoon the mixture into a pastry bag fitted with a $1/2$-inch nozzle and pipe the mixture into two spiral disks, starting at the center of the drawn circles and filling each circle. • Bake for 50–60 minutes, or until crisp. Turn off the oven and leave the door ajar until the meringues are completely cool. • Carefully remove the paper. • About 1 hour before serving, place a meringue layer on a serving plate. Spread with the ganache. Top with the remaining meringue layer. • With mixer at high speed, beat the cream in a large bowl until stiff. Spread over the top of the cake. Sprinkle with chocolate.

Makes one 9-inch cake · Prep: 30 min. · Cooking: 50–60 min. · Level: 1 · Keeps: 1 day in the refrigerator

CARAMEL VACHERIN

- 5 large egg whites, at room temperature
- $3/4$ cup granulated sugar
- $3/4$ cup firmly packed light brown sugar
- 1 teaspoon vanilla extract
- $1\frac{1}{2}$ cups heavy cream
- 2 tablespoons confectioners' sugar
  caramel ice cream topping (plastic squeeze bottle)

Preheat the oven to 275°F. • Line a baking sheet with parchment paper and mark two 9-inch circles on the paper. • Beat the egg whites in a large bowl with an electric mixer at medium speed until frothy. • With mixer at high speed, gradually beat in both sugars, beating until stiff, glossy peaks form. • Add the vanilla. • Spoon the mixture into a pastry bag fitted with a $^1/_2$-inch nozzle and pipe the mixture into two spiral disks, starting at the center of the drawn circles and filling each circle. • Bake for 50–60 minutes, or until crisp. Turn off the oven and leave the door ajar until the meringues are completely cool. • Carefully remove the paper. • About 1 hour before serving, beat the cream and confectioners' sugar in a large bowl with mixer at high speed until stiff. • Place a meringue layer on a serving plate. Spread with $^3/_4$ of the cream. Top with the remaining meringue layer and spread with the remaining cream. • Gently squeeze the plastic container with the caramel sauce and make a decorative crisscross pattern over.

Makes one 9-inch cake · Prep: 30 min. · Cooking: 60–70 min. · Level: 1 · Keeps: 1 day in the refrigerator

BANANA VACHERIN

Serve this with Sweet Wine Kiwi Coulis (see page 351) for a special treat.

- 5 large egg whites, at room temperature
- 1$^1/_2$ cups firmly packed light brown sugar
- 1 teaspoon vanilla extract
- 1$^1/_2$ cups heavy cream
- 2 tablespoons confectioners' sugar
- 2 medium very ripe (but not brown) bananas, peeled and very thinly sliced

Preheat the oven to 275°F. • Line a baking sheet with parchment paper and mark two 9-inch circles on the paper. • Beat the egg whites in a large bowl with an electric mixer at medium speed until frothy. • With mixer at high speed, gradually beat in the brown sugar, beating until stiff, glossy peaks form. • Add the vanilla. • Spoon the mixture into a pastry bag fitted with a $^1/_2$-inch nozzle and pipe the mixture into two spiral disks, starting at the center of the drawn circles and filling each circle. • Bake for 50–60 minutes, or until crisp. Turn off the oven and leave the door

ajar until the meringues are completely cool. • Carefully remove the paper. • About 1 hour before serving, beat the cream and confectioners' sugar in a large bowl with mixer at high speed until stiff. • Place $^2/_3$ of the cream in a separate bowl and fold in the bananas (reserve a few slices to decorate). • Place a meringue layer on a serving plate. Spread with the cream. Top with the remaining layer and spread with the remaining cream. • Decorate with the banana slices.

Makes one 9-inch cake · Prep: 30 min. · Cooking: 50–60 min. · Level: 1 · Keeps: 1 day in the refrigerator

BASIC DACQUOISE

- 6 large egg whites, at room temperature
- $^1/_8$ teaspoon salt
- 1$^1/_2$ cups granulated sugar
- 1$^1/_2$ cups almonds, finely ground
- 1 tablespoon cornstarch

Preheat the oven to 300°F. • Cut out three 9-inch rounds of parchment paper and place the rounds on the baking sheets. • Beat the egg whites and salt in a large bowl with an electric mixer at medium speed until frothy. With mixer at high speed, gradually beat in the sugar, beating until stiff, glossy peaks form. • Use a large rubber spatula to fold in the almonds and cornstarch. • Spoon the meringue into a pastry bag fitted with a $^1/_2$-inch plain tip. Pipe the meringue in a spiral to fill the rounds, leaving a $^1/_2$-inch border around the edge. Repeat to fill the other rounds. •

Coffee cream dacquoise

Bake for 80–90 minutes, or until crisp. • Cool the meringues for 10 minutes. Transfer onto racks. Carefully remove the paper and let cool completely.

Makes 3 dacquoise rounds · Prep: 30 min. · Cooking: 80–90 min. · Level: 2 · Keeps: 1 day in the refrigerator

COFFEE CREAM DACQUOISE

- 2 Basic Dacquoise rounds (see recipe left)
- 2 cups Coffee Buttercream (see page 346)
- $^1/_3$ cup confectioners' sugar
- $^3/_4$ cup flaked toasted almonds

Place one round of dacquoise on a serving plate. Spread with the buttercream. Cover with the other round. • Dust with the confectioners' sugar and stick the almonds all around the sides. • Refrigerate for 30 minutes before serving.

Makes one 9-inch dacquoise · Prep: 15 min. + 30 min to chill · Level: 2 · Keeps: 1–2 days in the refrigerator

CHOCOLATE CREAM DACQUOISE

- 2 Basic Dacquoise rounds (see recipe left)
- $^2/_3$ recipe Chocolate Buttercream (see page 346)
- $^1/_3$ cup confectioners' sugar
- $^3/_4$ cup flaked toasted almonds

Place one dacquoise round on a serving plate. Spread with the buttercream. Cover with the other round. • Dust with the confectioners' sugar and stick the almonds all around the sides. • Refrigerate for 30 minutes before serving.

Makes one 9-inch cake · Prep: 15 min. + 30 min to chill · Level: 1 · Keeps: 1–2 days in the refrigerator

Red fruit dacquoise

RED FRUIT DACQUOISE

- ¹/₂ recipe Choux Pastry (see page 308)
- 2 Basic Dacquoise rounds (see page 215)

RED FRUIT FILLING

- 2 cups cream cheese, softened
- ¹/₂ cup granulated sugar
  grated zest and juice of 1 lemon
- 2 tablespoons unflavored gelatin
- ¹/₄ cup cold water
- 1 cup heavy cream
- 3 cups mixed red fruit, such as raspberries or red currants

FROSTING

- ¹/₂ cup heavy cream
- 1 tablespoon granulated sugar
- ¹/₂ cup slivered almonds
  confectioners' sugar, to dust
  red currants, to decorate

Preheat the oven to 425°F. • Line a baking sheet with parchment paper and draw a 9-inch circle on the paper. • Spoon the choux pastry into a pastry bag fitted with a plain ¹/₂-inch nozzle and pipe the mixture into a spiral disk, starting at the center of the drawn circle and filling it. • Bake for 15–20 minutes, or until set. Cool the pastry

completely in the pan on a rack. • *Red Fruit Filling*: Beat the cream cheese, sugar, and lemon zest and juice in a large bowl with an electric mixer at high speed. • Sprinkle the gelatin over the water in a small saucepan. Let stand 1 minute. Cook over low heat until the gelatin has completely dissolved. • With mixer at high speed, beat the cream in a large bowl until stiff peaks form. • Fold the gelatin mixture, cream, and the fruit into the cream cheese mixture. • Place one dacquoise on a serving plate. Surround with springform sides. Spoon in half the filling and place the remaining dacquoise on top. Spoon in the remaining filling and top with the pastry circle. Refrigerate for 1 hour, or until set. • *Frosting*: With mixer at high speed, beat the cream and granulated sugar in a large bowl until stiff peaks form. • Remove the pan sides. Spread the sides with the cream and press in the almonds. Dust with the confectioners' sugar and decorate with the red currants.

Makes one 9-inch cake · Prep: 30 min. + 1 hr. to chill · Cooking: 15–20 min. · Level: 2 · Keeps: 3 days in the refrigerator

CHOCOLATE SPONGE DACQUOISE

- 2 9-inch Basic Chocolate Sponge Cakes (see page 157)
- 4 large egg whites, at room temperature
- 1 cup granulated sugar
- ³/₄ cup almonds, finely ground
- 1 teaspoon almond extract
- ¹/₂ cup rum
- 2 cups Chocolate Cream Frosting (see page 347)

Preheat the oven to 300°F. • Butter three 9-inch round cake pans. Line with parchment paper. • Beat the egg whites in a large bowl with an electric mixer at medium speed until frothy. • With mixer at high speed, gradually beat in the sugar, beating until stiff, glossy peaks form. • Use a large rubber spatula to fold the almonds and almond extract into the mixture. • Spoon the batter evenly into the prepared pans. • Bake for 60–70 minutes, or until pale gold and crisp. • Cool the meringues in the pans for 10 minutes. Invert onto racks. Carefully remove the paper and let cool completely. • Split the cakes horizontally. Place one layer on a serving plate. Brush with the rum and spread with some of the frosting. Top with a meringue layer and spread with frosting. Top with a cake layer. Repeat until all the cake, frosting, rum, and meringue have been used, finishing with a layer of frosted cake. • Refrigerate for 1–2 hours to soften the meringue a little so that the cake can be cut.

Makes one 9-inch cake · Prep: 45 min. + 1–2 hr. in refrigerator · Cooking: 60–70 min. · Level: 2 · Keeps: 1–2 days in the refrigerator

CHOCOLATE ALMOND DACQUOISE

- 1 9-inch Basic Chocolate Sponge cakes (see page 157)
- 3 large egg whites, at room temperature
- ¹/₂ cup superfine sugar
- ³/₄ cup almonds, finely ground
- 2 teaspoons almond extract
- 2 cups Rich Chocolate Frosting (see page 349)

Preheat the oven to 300°F. • Butter three 8-inch round cake pans. Line with parchment paper. • Beat the egg whites in a large bowl with an electric mixer at medium speed until frothy. With mixer at high speed, gradually beat in the superfine sugar, beating until stiff, glossy peaks form. • Use a large rubber spatula to fold the almonds and almond extract into the batter. • Spoon the batter evenly into the prepared pans. • Bake for 60–70 minutes, or until pale gold and crisp. • Cool the meringues in the pans for 10 minutes. Turn out onto racks. Carefully remove the paper and let cool completely. • Split the cake into three horizontally. Place a layer on a serving plate. Spread with $^1/_3$ of the frosting. Top with a meringue layer, followed by a cake layer. Spread with half the remaining frosting. Top with another meringue layer and the remaining cake layer, finishing with a layer of frosting.

Makes one 9-inch cake · Prep: 45 min. · Cooking: 60–70 min. · Level: 2 · Keeps: 1–2 days

COFFEE ALMOND DACQUOISE

5	large egg yolks, at room temperature
$^1/_2$	cup granulated sugar
$^1/_2$	cup milk
$1^1/_4$	cups ($2^1/_2$ sticks) unsalted butter, softened
2	tablespoons coffee extract
2	cans ($15^1/_4$ oz) apricot halves, drained
3	Basic Dacquoise rounds (see page 215)
$^3/_4$	cup flaked almonds
2	tablespoons confectioners' sugar

Beat the egg yolks and sugar in a large bowl with an electric mixer at high speed until pale and very thick. • Bring the milk to a boil in a large saucepan over medium heat. Remove from the heat. Slowly beat the hot milk into the egg mixture. • Transfer the mixture to the saucepan. Cook over low heat, stirring constantly with a wooden spoon, until the mixture lightly coats a metal spoon or registers 160°F on an instant-read thermometer. Immediately plunge the pan into a bowl of ice water and stir until the egg mixture has cooled. • Gradually add the butter and the coffee extract. Transfer to a bowl. Press plastic wrap directly on the surface, and refrigerate until chilled. • Reserve 3–4 apricot halves to decorate and chop the rest coarsely. • Spoon half the filling into another bowl and fold in the apricots. • Place one dacquoise round on a serving plate and spread with half the apricot filling. Top with another dacquoise round and spread with the remaining apricot filling. Place the remaining dacquoise on top. Spread with the plain filling. • Sprinkle with the almonds and decorate with the reserved apricots. Dust with the confectioners' sugar.

Makes one 9-inch cake · Prep: 30 min. · Cooking: 1 hr 20–30 min. · Level: 2 · Keeps: 1 day

Coffee almond dacquoise

STRAWBERRY CREAM DACQUOISE

2	Basic Dacquoises rounds (see page 215)
$^3/_4$	cup strawberries, hulled and finely chopped
2	cups Italian Buttercream (see page 346)
$^1/_3$	cup confectioners' sugar
$^3/_4$	cup slivered toasted almonds

Place one dacquoise on a serving plate. • Stir the strawberries into the buttercream. Spread the dacquoise with the buttercream. Cover with the other round. • Dust with the confectioners' sugar and press the almonds into the buttercream all around the sides. • Refrigerate for 30 minutes before serving.

Makes one 9-inch cake · Prep: 15 min. + 30 min to chill · Level: 1 · Keeps: 1–2 days in the refrigerator

RASPBERRY CREAM DACQUOISE

2	Basic Dacquoises rounds (see page 215)
$^3/_4$	cup raspberries, hulled and finely chopped
2	cups Italian Buttercream (see page 346)
$^1/_3$	cup confectioners' sugar
$^3/_4$	cup slivered toasted almonds

Place one dacquoise on a serving plate. • Stir the raspberries into the buttercream.

Spread the dacquoise with the buttercream. Cover with the other round. • Dust with the confectioners' sugar and press the almonds into the buttercream all around the sides. • Refrigerate for 30 minutes before serving.

Makes one 9-inch cake · Prep: 15 min. + 30 min to chill · Level: 1 · Keeps: 1–2 days in the refrigerator

ORANGE CREAM DACQUOISE

2	Basic Dacquoise rounds (see page 215)
2	cups Orange Liqueur Buttercream (see page 347)
$^1/_3$	cup confectioners' sugar
$^3/_4$	cup flaked toasted almonds

Place one dacquoise round on a serving plate. Spread with the buttercream. Cover with the other round. • Dust with the confectioners' sugar and stick the almonds all around the sides. • Refrigerate for 30 minutes before serving.

Makes one 9-inch cake · Prep: 15 min. + 30 min to chill · Level: 1 · Keeps: 1–2 days in the refrigerator

Strudels have German origins, delighting everyone with their crispy buttery pastry and scrumptious fruity fillings. Perfect for a winter evening served with creamy custards, whipped cream, or ice cream, a strudel can easily become the family favorite.

STRUDELS

APRICOT STRUDEL

1¹/₂	lb fresh apricots, pitted and thinly sliced
¹/₄	cup brandy
1	recipe Basic Strudel Dough (see page 220)
¹/₂	cup pistachios, shelled and finely chopped
1	tablespoon butter, melted
2	tablespoons confectioners' sugar, to dust

Place the apricots in a medium bowl with the brandy and soak 30 minutes. • Roll out the dough on a lightly floured surface into a large rectangle about ¹/₄- inch thick. • Preheat the oven to 400°F. • Line a large baking sheet with parchment paper. • Drain the apricots well and stir in the pistachios. • Use the instructions on page 220 to fill and roll up the strudel, filling the strudel with the apricot mixture. • Transfer the strudel to the baking sheet. • Bake for 25–30 minutes, or until golden brown. • Brush the strudel with the melted butter and dust with the confectioners' sugar. • Serve hot or warm.

Makes one strudel · Prep: 15 min. · Cooking: 25–30 min. · Level: 2 · Keeps: 1–2 days

◄ Dried fruit and nut strudel (see page 226)

➤ Apricot strudel

STRUDEL

The secret to making a perfect strudel lies in the pastry. Thinly rolled, its unique crispy texture gives the strudel its essential character.

Preparing a strudel

BASIC STRUDEL DOUGH

- ¼ cup (½ stick) butter
- ½ cup lukewarm water (105°–115°F), or more as needed
- 1⅔ cups all-purpose flour, or more as needed
- ⅛ teaspoon salt
- 1 large egg, lightly beaten

Melt the butter in the water. • Sift the flour and salt into a large bowl and make a well in the center. Mix in the egg and the butter mixture. The dough should be soft enough to knead, but not sticky. Add more flour or water as needed. • Knead the dough on a lightly floured surface until smooth and elastic, about 5–7 minutes. • Shape into a ball, wrap in plastic wrap, and let rest in a warm place, 25 minutes.

Makes dough for one strudel · Prep: 20 min. + 25 min. to rest · Level: 1 · Keeps: 1–2 days

1 Sift the flour and salt into a bowl and make a well in the center. Stir in the wet ingredients until a smooth dough is formed.

2 Cover a surface with a large clean cloth. Roll the dough out thinly. Stretch the dough out thinly, placing your fists underneath with your knuckles upward and pulling gently outward from the center. The dough should be as thin as a sheet of paper.

3 Brush the butter all over the dough.

4. Sprinkle or spoon the filling onto half the dough, leaving a wide border all around.

5 Carefully fold the end over the filling and prepare to roll.

6 Use the cloth underneath as a guide to carefully roll the strudel over until the filling is all contained. Fold the two short ends over and seal.

7 Brush with butter and slide onto a baking sheet lined with parchment paper to bake.

EASY JAM STRUDEL

2 cups all-purpose flour
1 cup sour cream
1 cup (2 sticks) butter
1/2 cup cherry jam
1/2 cup apricot preserves or jam
1/3 cup sweetened coconut
1/2 cup mixed nuts, finely chopped
1/2 cup maraschino cherries, chopped
1/2 cup confectioners' sugar

Stir together the flour, sour cream, and butter in a large bowl until a smooth dough is formed. Divide into 3 equal parts and roll into balls. • Wrap in waxed paper and chill overnight. • Preheat the oven to 350°F. • Roll the dough out on a lightly floured surface to a rectangle. Use your hands to stretch it out on a clean kitchen towel until it becomes very thin. • Spread with the cherry and apricot jams, leaving a border. Sprinkle with the coconut, nuts, and cherries. • Use the instructions on page 220 to roll up the strudel. Transfer to the baking sheet. • Bake for 15–20 minutes, or until lightly browned. • Dust with confectioners' sugar and serve.

Makes one strudel · Prep: 30 min. + 12 hr. to chill · Cooking: 15–20 min. · Level: 1 · Keeps: 1–2 days

PINEAPPLE STRUDEL

6 sheets phyllo dough, thawed if frozen
2 teaspoons butter, melted
3 apples, peeled, cored, and thinly sliced
8 oz crushed pineapple, drained
1 tablespoon cornstarch
2 teaspoons pumpkin pie spice
1 teaspoon vanilla extract
3 tablespoons honey

Preheat the oven to 400°F. • Butter a large baking sheet. Lay the sheets of dough out flat and cover with waxed paper and a damp kitchen towel. (This will stop them from drying out.) Brush the first sheet with butter. Top with a second sheet and brush with butter. Repeat with three more sheets. • Mix the apples, pineapple, cornstarch, pumpkin pie spice, vanilla, and honey in a large bowl. • Spread with the pineapple mixture, leaving a border. • Cover with the remaining sheet of dough. Brush with butter. Use the instructions on page 220 to roll up the strudel. Transfer to the baking sheet. • Bake for 10–15 minutes, or until lightly browned. • Serve warm.

Makes one strudel · Prep: 30 min. · Cooking: 20–30 min. · Level: 2 · Keeps: 1–2 days

RHUBARB STRUDEL

1 lb rhubarb, washed and cut into 1/2-inch pieces
1/2 cup granulated sugar
1 1/2 teaspoons ground ginger
1 recipe Basic Strudel Dough (see page 220)
3 tablespoons butter, melted
superfine sugar, to dust

Preheat the oven to 400°F. • Mix the rhubarb, granulated sugar, and ginger in a large bowl. • Roll out the dough on a lightly floured surface into a rectangle. Use your hands to stretch it out on a clean kitchen towel. Brush all over with the butter. Use the instructions on page 220 to fill and roll up the strudel, using the rhubarb mixture to fill. • Transfer to the baking sheet. • Bake for 40–50 minutes, or until crisp. • Dust with the superfine sugar and serve warm.

Makes one strudel · Prep: 30 min. · Cooking: 40–50 min. · Level: 2 · Keeps 3 days

GINGER PEAR STRUDEL

1 quart water
1 cup granulated sugar
1 1/2 inches fresh ginger, peeled and sliced 1/2-inch thick
2 firm-ripe pears, peeled

ALMOND CREAM
3/4 cup flaked almonds
1 cup confectioners' sugar
1/2 cup (1 stick) butter, softened
1/3 cup all-purpose flour
2 large eggs
1 tablespoon dark rum

12 sheets phyllo dough, thawed if frozen
1/2 cup (1 stick) butter, melted

Butter a large baking sheet. • Stir the water, sugar, and ginger in a pan large enough to hold all the pears. Stir over low heat until the sugar has dissolved. Increase the heat so that the liquid simmers. Add the pears and poach for 15–20 minutes, or until the pears can be easily pierced with a toothpick. Cool and then refrigerate. • Preheat the oven to 400°F. • *Almond Cream*: Process the almonds and confectioners' sugar until smooth. • Beat the butter in a large bowl with an electric mixer

at medium speed until creamy. With mixer at low speed, gradually beat in the almond mixture and flour. Add the eggs, one at a time, until just blended after each addition. Add the rum. • Halve the poached pears and scoop out the cores. Slice each half pear thinly lengthwise and set aside. • Lay the sheets of dough out flat and cover with waxed paper and a damp kitchen towel. (This will stop them from drying out.) Brush the first sheet with melted butter. Top with another sheet and brush with butter. Repeat with 4 more sheets. • Spoon half the almond cream 1/4-inch thick on the top layer, leaving a border. Fan out a pear half on one end of the dough. Use the instructions on page 220 to roll up the strudel.• Transfer to the baking sheet. Brush with butter. Repeat with the remaining dough, almond cream, and pear halves. • Bake for 10–15 minutes, or until lightly browned. • Serve warm.

Makes two strudels · Prep: 30 min. · Cooking: 10–15 min. · Level: 2 · Keeps: 1–2 days

MANGO STRUDEL WITH CITRUS SAUCE

6 sheets phyllo dough, thawed if frozen
2/3 cup butter, melted
6 tablespoons dry bread crumbs
3 mangoes (1 lb each), peeled and cut into 1-inch chunks
2–3 tablespoons granulated sugar
grated zest of 1/2 lime
1/2 cup macadamia nuts, finely chopped
2 cups Citrus Sauce (see page 353)

Preheat the oven to 400°F. • Butter a large baking sheet. • Lay the sheets of dough out flat and cover with waxed paper and a damp kitchen towel. (This will stop them from drying out.) Brush the first sheet with melted butter. Sprinkle with 2 teaspoons bread crumbs. Top with a second sheet and brush with melted butter. Sprinkle with bread crumbs. Repeat until all the phyllo sheets are used up. • Mix the mangoes, sugar, lime zest, remaining bread crumbs, and macadamias in a large bowl. • Spread with the mango filling, leaving a border. Use the instructions on page 220 to roll up the strudel. • Transfer to the sheet. Brush with the remaining butter. • Bake for 20–25 minutes, or until golden brown. • Cool for 30 minutes before serving. • Serve with the sauce passed on the side.

Makes one strudel · Prep: 30 min. · Cooking: 20–25 min. · Level: 2 · Keeps: 1–2 days

BLACKBERRY-APRICOT STRUDEL

- 6 sheets phyllo dough, thawed if frozen
- 1/2 cup (1 stick) 2 tablespoons butter, melted
- 1/4 cup fine dry bread crumbs
- 2 tart cooking apples (Granny Smiths are ideal), peeled, cored, and thinly sliced
- 1 1/2 cups fresh blackberries
- 3/4 cup granulated sugar
- 1/2 cup dried apricots, finely chopped
- 1 cup pecans, toasted and coarsely chopped
- 1 teaspoon ground cinnamon

Preheat the oven to 425°F. • Butter a large baking sheet. • Lay the sheets of dough out flat and cover with waxed paper and a damp kitchen towel. (This will stop them from drying out.) • Brush the first sheet with melted butter. Sprinkle with some bread crumbs. Top with another sheet and brush with butter. Repeat with 4 more sheets, finishing with a phyllo layer. • Sauté the apples in 2 tablespoons butter in a large skillet over medium heat for 5 minutes. Stir in the blackberries and sugar and cook, stirring, for 8–10 minutes. Stir in the apricots, pecans, and cinnamon. Drain any juice and set aside to cool. • Use the instructions on page 220 to fill and roll up the strudel, using the blackberry mixture. • Transfer to the baking sheet. Brush with the remaining butter. • Bake for 20–25 minutes, or until lightly browned. • Serve warm.

Makes one strudel · Prep: 30 min. · Cooking: 20–25 min. · Level: 2 · Keeps: 1–2 days

PEACH-RASPBERRY STRUDEL

- 1/2 cup whole almonds, toasted
- 3/4 cup old-fashioned rolled oats
- 1/2 cup firmly packed light brown sugar
- 1/4 cup granulated sugar
- 2 teaspoons ground cinnamon
- 3 medium peaches, peeled, pitted, and diced
- 1 cup raspberries
- 1/2 teaspoon vanilla extract
- 6 sheets phyllo dough
- 1/3 cup butter, melted

Preheat the oven to 375°F. • Butter a large baking sheet. • Chop the almonds and oats finely in a food processor. Add the sugars and 1 teaspoon cinnamon. • Mix the peaches, raspberries, remaining cinnamon and vanilla in a large bowl. • Lay the sheets of dough out flat and cover with waxed paper and a damp kitchen towel. (This will stop them from drying out.) Brush the first sheet with melted butter. Top with another sheet and brush with butter. • Spoon 1/4 of the almond mixture over half the pastry, leaving a section uncovered. Top with a sheet of dough and brush with butter. Spoon over some more almond mixture. Repeat until almond mixture and phyllo are used up, finishing with almond mixture. • Use the instructions on page 220 to fill and roll up the strudel, using the peach mixture to fill. • Transfer to the baking sheet. • Bake for 20–25 minutes, or until crisp. • Serve warm.

Makes one strudel · Prep: 30 min. · Cooking: 20–25 min. · Level: 2 · Keeps 3 days

AUSTRIAN GRAPE STRUDEL

- 1/2 cup (1 stick) butter, melted
- 1 cup fresh bread crumbs
- 3/4 cup hazelnuts, toasted and peeled
- 1/4 cup granulated sugar
- 1 teaspoon ground cinnamon
- 1/4 teaspoon ground ginger
- 1/4 teaspoon ground nutmeg
- 1 recipe Basic Strudel Dough (see page 220), rolled
- 1 1/4 lb seedless green grapes
- 2 cups Fruit and Wine Egg Cream (see page 345)

Preheat the oven to 400°F. • Line a baking sheet with parchment paper. • Pour 1/4 cup of the butter into a large skillet over medium heat. Stir in the crumbs until golden, about 3 minutes. Set aside to cool. • Very finely chop the hazelnuts with the sugar, cinnamon, ginger, and nutmeg in a food processor. • Fit the strudel dough into the baking sheet, trimming the edges as needed. Brush 3 tablespoons of the remaining butter over the dough and sprinkle with the crumbs. Spread the hazelnuts in a 6-inch wide strip about 3 inches from the short side of the dough. Spread the grapes over the hazelnuts. • Use the instructions on page 220 to roll up the strudel. • Carefully transfer to the prepared sheet. Gently pull into a horseshoe shape. Brush the top with the remaining butter. • Bake for 30–40 minutes, or until golden brown. • Serve hot, passing the cream on the side.

Makes one strudel · Prep: 30 min. · Cooking: 30–40 min. · Level: 2 · Keeps: 1–2 days

RICOTTA CHEESE STRUDEL

- 1 2/3 cups all-purpose flour
- 1/4 teaspoon salt
- 1/4 cup butter, melted
- 1/4 cup milk

FILLING

- 1 1/2 cups ricotta cheese
- 1/3 cup granulated sugar
- 1/4 cup (1/2 stick) butter, melted
- 2 tablespoons vodka or brandy
- 1 tablespoon grated lemon zest
- 1 cup raisins
- 1/3 cup walnuts, coarsely chopped (optional)
- 1/2 cup graham cracker crumbs

GLAZE

- 1 large egg
- 2 tablespoons granulated sugar

Sift the flour and salt into a medium bowl. Stir in the butter and milk until well blended. • Knead the dough on a lightly floured

Austrian grape strudel

Ricotta cheese strudel

surface until smooth and elastic, about 10 minutes. Shape into a ball, place in a clean bowl, and cover with a tea towel. Set aside to rest for 30 minutes. • *Filling*: Beat the ricotta, sugar, butter, vodka, and lemon zest in a large bowl with an electric mixer at low speed until well blended. Beat in the raisins and nuts. • Preheat the oven to 375°F. • Line a large baking sheet with parchment paper. • Roll the pastry out on a lightly floured surface into an oval shape, as thin as possible. Sprinkle with the graham cracker crumbs. Use the instructions on page 220 to fill and roll up the strudel, using the ricotta mixture to fill.• Carefully transfer the strudel onto the prepared sheet. Gently pull it into a horseshoe shape. • *Glaze*: Mix the egg and sugar in a small bowl. Brush over the strudel. • Bake for 50–60 minutes, or until golden brown. Slide onto a rack to cool. • Serve warm or at room temperature.

Makes one strudel · Prep: 1 hr. · Cooking: 50–60 min. · Level: 2 · Keeps: 2–3 days

APPLE AND ROSEMARY STRUDEL

4 apples, peeled, cored, and finely grated
1 tablespoon fresh rosemary
2 tablespoons firmly packed soft brown sugar
2 tablespoons fresh bread crumbs
1 teaspoon ground cinnamon
1 teaspoon ground nutmeg
3 tablespoons golden raisins
1 recipe Basic Strudel Dough (see page 220)
2 tablespoons butter, melted

Preheat the oven to 400°F. • Butter a large baking sheet. • Mix the apples, rosemary, brown sugar, bread crumbs, cinnamon, nutmeg, and raisins in a large bowl. • Roll out the dough on a lightly floured surface into a rectangle. Use your hands to stretch it out on a clean tea towel until it becomes very thin. Spread all over with butter. Use the instructions on page 220 to fill and roll up the strudel, using the apple mixture to fill. Transfer to the baking sheet. Brush with the butter. • Bake for 35–40 minutes. or until lightly browned. • Serve warm.

Makes one strudel · Prep: 30 min. · Cooking: 35–40 min. · Level: 2 · Keeps: 1–2 days

APPLE-WALNUT STRUDEL

8 sheets phyllo dough, thawed if frozen
2 apples, peeled, cored, and finely sliced
1/3 cup walnuts, coarsely chopped
1/4 teaspoon lemon juice
1/4 cup butter, melted
1 cup fine dry bread crumbs

Preheat the oven to 350°F. • Butter a large baking sheet. • Lay the sheets of dough out flat and cover with waxed paper and a damp kitchen towel. (This will stop them from drying out.) • Brush the first sheet with butter. Top with another sheet and brush with butter. Repeat until half of the sheets are used up. • Mix the apples, walnuts, and lemon juice in a large bowl. • Use the instructions on page 220 to fill and roll up the strudel, using the apple mixture. •

Transfer to the baking sheet. Repeat with the remaining sheets of dough and the remaining apple mixture. • Bake for 20–25 minutes, or until browned. • Serve warm.

Makes one strudel · Prep: 30 min. · Cooking: 20–25 min. · Level: 2 · Keeps: 1–2 days

RAISIN-APPLE STRUDEL

6 sheets phyllo dough, thawed if frozen
1/4 cup (1/2 stick) butter, melted
1/4 cup finely ground almonds
6 medium apples, peeled, cored, and diced
1/2 cup golden raisins
1/2 cup granulated sugar
1 teaspoon ground cinnamon
2 tablespoons all-purpose flour

Preheat the oven to 375°F. • Butter a large baking sheet. • Lay the sheets of dough out flat and cover with waxed paper and a damp kitchen towel. (This will stop them from drying out.) • Brush the first sheet with melted butter. Sprinkle with some almonds. Top with another sheet and brush with butter. Repeat with the third sheet. • Mix the apples, raisins, sugar, cinnamon, and flour in a large bowl. • Use the instructions on page 220 to fill and roll up the strudel, using the apple mixture to fill. • Transfer to the baking sheet. Brush with the remaining butter. • Repeat with the remaining 3 sheets of dough and remaining apple mixture. • Bake for 30–35 minutes, or until golden brown. • Serve warm.

Makes two strudels · Prep: 30 min. · Cooking: 30–35 min. · Level: 2 · Keeps: 1–2 days

Apple strudel

APPLE STRUDEL

Apple strudel is best when it is served hot,
topped with vanilla ice cream or cream.

1 cup raisins
8 large tart apples (Granny Smiths are ideal),
peeled, cored, and thinly sliced
$^1/_2$ cup granulated sugar
$1^1/_2$ teaspoons grated lemon zest
1 teaspoon ground cinnamon
1 cup fine dry bread crumbs
$^1/_3$ cup butter, melted
1 recipe Basic Strudel Dough (see page 220)
$^1/_2$ cup apricot preserves or jam
$^1/_4$ cup confectioners' sugar, to dust

Plump the raisins in warm water to cover
for 10 minutes. Drain well and pat dry with
paper towels. • Mix the raisins, apples,
sugar, lemon zest, and cinnamon in a small
bowl. • Sauté the bread crumbs in 3
tablespoons butter in a medium skillet over
medium heat, stirring, until golden. Set
aside. • Preheat the oven to 350°F. • Line a
baking sheet with parchment paper. Roll out
the dough on a lightly floured surface.
Stretch the dough out thinly, placing your

fists underneath with your knuckles upward
and pulling gently outward from the center.
The dough should be as thin as a sheet of
paper. Brush with the remaining 3
tablespoons melted butter. • Sprinkle half
the dough with the bread crumbs. Spread
with the apple mixture. Brush with the
apricot preserves. • Use the instructions on
page 220 to roll up the strudel. • Brush with
the remaining butter. • Bake for 50-60
minutes, or until golden brown. • Dust with
the confectioners' sugar and serve hot.

*Makes one strudel · Prep: 40 min. · Cooking: 50–60
min. · Level: 2 · Keeps: 3 days*

APPLE-GINGER STRUDEL

8 sheets phyllo dough, thawed if frozen
3 tablespoons butter, melted
4 cups peeled, cored, and thinly sliced apples
1 tablespoon fresh lemon juice
$^1/_2$ cup golden raisins
$^1/_3$ cup ground almonds
3 tablespoons honey
3 tablespoons maple syrup
1 teaspoon grated lemon zest
1 teaspoon ground ginger
confectioners' sugar, to dust

Preheat the oven to 375°F. • Butter a large
baking sheet. • Lay the sheets of dough out
flat and cover with waxed paper and a
damp kitchen towel. (This will stop them
from drying out.) • Brush the first sheet
with melted butter. Top with another sheet
and brush with butter. Repeat with 2 more
layers. • Toss the apples with the lemon
juice in a large bowl. Mix in the raisins,
almonds, honey, maple syrup, lemon zest,
and ginger. Use the instructions on page
220 to fill and roll up the strudel, using
half the apple mixture to fill. • Transfer to
the baking sheet. Brush with a little melted
butter. Repeat with the 4 sheets of dough
and the remaining apple mixture. Brush
with the remaining melted butter. • Bake
for 15–20 minutes, or until lightly
browned. • Dust with the confectioners'
sugar. • Serve warm.

*Makes two strudels · Prep: 30 min. · Cooking: 15–20
min. · Level: 2 · Keeps: 1–2 days*

APPLE AND APRICOT STRUDEL

4 sheets phyllo dough, thawed if frozen
$^1/_4$ cup ($^1/_2$ stick) butter, melted
$^1/_3$ cup fine dry bread crumbs
3 cups apple chunks
$^1/_2$ cup granulated sugar
$^1/_4$ cup raisins
$^1/_2$ cup dried apricots, coarsely chopped
$^1/_4$ cup almonds, coarsely chopped
$^1/_4$ teaspoon grated lemon zest
$^1/_2$ teaspoon lemon juice
1 tablespoon granulated sugar
$^1/_2$ teaspoon ground cinnamon

Preheat the oven to 375°F. • Butter a large
baking sheet. • Lay the 2 sheets of dough
out flat and cover with waxed paper and a
damp kitchen towel. (This will stop them
from drying out.) • Brush the first sheet
with melted butter. Top with another sheet
and brush with butter. Sprinkle with bread
crumbs. • Mix the apples, sugar, raisins,
almonds, and lemon zest and juice in a
large bowl. • Use the instructions on page
220 to fill and roll up the strudel, using half
the filling. • Transfer to the sheet. Brush
with the remaining melted butter. Sprinkle
with the sugar and cinnamon. • Repeat with
the remaining two sheets of dough and the
remaining apple mixture. • Bake for 30–40
minutes, or until lightly browned.

*Makes two strudels · Prep: 30 min. · Cooking: 30–40
min. · Level: 2 · Keeps: 1–2 days*

APPLE STRUDEL
WITH CINNAMON SAUCE

- 6 sheets phyllo dough, thawed if frozen
- 1/4 cup (1/2 stick) butter, melted
- 8 medium Granny Smith apples, peeled, cored, and thinly sliced
- 1/2 cup raisins
- 2 tablespoons honey
- 1/2 teaspoon ground cinnamon
- 1/2 teaspoon ground nutmeg

CINNAMON SAUCE
- 2 cups apple cider
- 1 tablespoon cornstarch
- 1/2 teaspoon ground cinnamon
- 1/2 teaspoon ground nutmeg

Preheat the oven to 400°F. • Butter a large baking sheet. • Lay the sheets of dough out flat and cover with waxed paper and a damp kitchen towel. (This will stop them from drying out.) • Brush the first sheet with melted butter. Top with another sheet and brush with butter. Repeat with a third layer. • Mix the apples, raisins, honey, cinnamon, and nutmeg in a large bowl. • Use the instructions on page 220 to fill and roll up the strudel, using half the apple mixture to fill. • Transfer to the baking sheet. Repeat with the remaining 3 sheets of dough and the remaining apple mixture. • Bake for 25–30 minutes, or until lightly browned. • *Cinnamon Sauce*: Stir the cider, cornstarch, cinnamon, and nutmeg in a small saucepan. Bring to a boil and serve passed on the side.

Makes two strudels · Prep: 35 min. · Cooking: 25–30 min. · Level: 2 · Keeps: 1–2 days

APPLE AND STILTON STRUDEL

- 1 lb apples, peeled, cored, and coarsely chopped
  grated zest and juice of 1 lemon
- 8 oz Stilton cheese, crumbled
- 1/4 cup walnuts, coarsely chopped
- 10 sprigs fresh thyme
  freshly grated nutmeg
  freshly ground black pepper
- 10 sheets phyllo dough, thawed if frozen
- 1/2 cup (1 stick) butter, melted
- 1/2 cup dry bread crumbs

Preheat the oven to 350°F. • Butter a large baking sheet. • Sprinkle the apples with the lemon juice in a large bowl. Add the lemon zest, stilton, walnuts, thyme, nutmeg, and black pepper. • Lay the sheets of dough out flat and cover with waxed paper and a damp kitchen towel. (This will stop them from drying out.) Carefully fold two sheets

Nut and raisin strudel

of dough to fit on the baking sheet. Brush with some melted butter and sprinkle with bread crumbs. Top with another two sheets and repeat until all the phyllo is used up, finishing with a little butter and some bread crumbs. Use the instructions on page 220 to fill and roll up the strudel, using the apple mixture to fill. Transfer to the sheet. Brush with the remaining butter and sprinkle with the remaining bread crumbs. • Bake for 30–35 minutes, or until lightly browned. • Serve warm.

Makes one strudel · Prep: 30 min. · Cooking: 30–35 min. · Level: 2 · Keeps: 1–2 days

NUT AND RAISIN STRUDEL

- 4 cups mixed nuts, finely chopped
- 1 1/2 cups almonds, coarsely chopped
- 1 cup pine nuts
- 2 1/4 cups golden raisins
- 3 oz semisweet chocolate, grated
- 1 cup granulated sugar
- 1/2 cup candied lemon peel
  juice of 2 oranges
- 1/4 cup dark rum
- 1 teaspoon vanilla extract
- 1/4 teaspoon salt
- 2 recipes Basic Strudel Dough (see page 220)
- 2 tablespoons butter, melted
- 1 large egg, lightly beaten
- 2 tablespoons granulated sugar
- 1 teaspoon milk

Preheat the oven to 375°F. • Line 2 baking sheets with parchment paper. • Mix the nuts, almonds, pine nuts, raisins, chocolate, sugar, candied peel, orange juice, rum, vanilla, and salt in a large bowl. • Roll out half the dough on a lightly floured surface into a rectangle. Use your hands to stretch it out on a clean kitchen towel until it becomes very thin. Brush with 1 tablespoon butter. Spoon half the mixture evenly onto the rectangle, leaving a border. • Use the instructions on page 220 to fill and roll up the strudel, using half the nut filling. Transfer to the baking sheet. • Repeat with remaining dough and filling. • Mix the egg, sugar, and milk in a small bowl. • Brush the strudels with the milk mixture. • Bake for 30–40 minutes, or until browned.

Makes two strudels · Prep: 2 hr. + 40 min. to rest · Cooking: 30–40 min. · Level: 2 · Keeps: 2–3 days

CHERRY-APPLE STRUDEL

- 6 sheets frozen phyllo dough, thawed
- 1/4 cup (1/2 stick) butter, melted
- 4 tart cooking apples (Granny Smiths are ideal), peeled and thinly sliced
- 1 cup superfine sugar
- 1 cup sour cherries, pitted
- 1/8 teaspoon ground cinnamon
- 1/3 cup golden raisins
- 3/4 tablespoons apricot preserves or jam
- 1/2 cup fresh bread crumbs
- 1/2 tablespoon flaked almonds
- 1 large egg, lightly beaten

Chocolate nut strudel

Preheat the oven to 350°F. • Butter a large baking sheet. • Lay the sheets of dough out flat and cover with waxed paper and a damp kitchen towel. (This will stop them from drying out.) • Brush the first sheet with butter. Top with another sheet and brush with butter. Repeat with three more sheets. • Sauté the apples in the remaining 2 tablespoons butter in a large skillet until just softened. Mix the apples, superfine sugar, cherries, cinnamon, raisins, apricot preserves, bread crumbs, and almonds in a large bowl. • Spread with the cherry filling, leaving a border. Use the instructions on page 220 to roll up the strudel. • Brush with a little beaten egg and transfer to the baking sheet. • Bake for 25–30 minutes, or until lightly browned. • Serve warm.

Makes one strudel · Prep: 30 min. · Cooking: 25–30 min. · Level: 2 · Keeps: 1–2 days

APPLE-DATE STRUDEL

- 1/3 cup fine dry bread crumbs
- 2 tablespoons butter
- 1/2 cup walnuts, coarsely chopped
- 4 cups peeled, cored, and coarsely chopped tart cooking apples (Granny Smiths are ideal),
- 8 oz pitted dates, finely chopped
- 1/2 cup granulated sugar
- 1/4 cup fresh lemon juice
- 1 recipe Basic Strudel Dough (see page 220)
- 1 teaspoon ground cinnamon

Preheat the oven to 400°F. • Line a large baking sheet with parchment paper. • Sauté the bread crumbs in 2 tablespoons butter until lightly toasted. Stir in the walnuts and set aside. • Mix the apples, dates, sugar, and lemon juice in a large bowl. Roll out the dough on a lightly floured surface into a 24 x 16-inch rectangle. Use your hands to stretch it out on a clean kitchen towel until it becomes very thin. Brush with 2 tablespoons melted butter. Sprinkle with the crumb mixture. • Use the instructions on page 220 to fill and roll up the strudel, using the apple mixture to fill. • Transfer to the baking sheet. Seal the ends and shape into a horseshoe. Brush with the remaining butter. • Bake for 35–40 minutes, or until lightly browned. • Serve warm.

Makes one strudel · Prep: 30 min. · Cooking: 35–40 min. · Level: 2 · Keeps: 1–2 days

DRIED FRUIT AND NUT STRUDEL

This is an excellent way to use up any leftover dried fruit and nuts after Christmas.

- 1 recipe Basic Strudel Pastry (see page 220)
- 2 cups mixed dried fruit and nuts, coarsely chopped.
- 3/4 cup granulated sugar
- 1/4 cup brandy
- 1/4 cup shredded coconut (optional)
- 1 tablespoon grated lemon zest
- 1 tablespoon grated orange zest
- 1 teaspoon ground cinnamon
- 1/4 teaspoon freshly ground black pepper
- 1/2 cup vanilla wafer crumbs
- 2 tablespoons cold butter, cut up

Place the fruit and nuts in a large bowl. Stir in the sugar, brandy, coconut, if using, lemon and orange zests, cinnamon, and pepper. Cover and let stand 1 hour. • Preheat the oven to 375°F. • Line a large baking sheet with parchment paper. • Roll the strudel pastry out on a lightly floured surface into an oval shape, as thin as possible. Sprinkle with the cookie crumbs. Use the instructions on page 220 to fill and roll up the strudel, using the fruit and nut mixture to fill. • Carefully transfer the strudel to the prepared sheet. Gently pull it into a horseshoe shape. If the dough breaks while you are moving it, take a little dough from the end to make a patch. • Bake for 50–60 minutes, or until golden brown. • Slide onto a rack to cool. Serve warm or at room temperature.

Makes one strudel · Prep: 1 hr. · Cooking: 50–60 min. · Level: 2 · Keeps: 2–3 days

CHOCOLATE NUT STRUDEL

- 2 cups all-purpose flour
- 1/4 cup granulated sugar
- 1/4 teaspoon salt
- 1/4 cup (1/2 stick) butter, melted
- 2 large eggs, lightly beaten
- 2 tablespoons milk

FILLING

- 1 cup walnuts, coarsely chopped
- 2/3 cup raisins
- 1/3 cup flaked almonds
- 6 dried figs, coarsely chopped
- 5 canned pineapple rings, well drained and chopped
- 2 1/2 oz semisweet chocolate, coarsely chopped
- 1/3 cup unsweetened cocoa powder
- 3/4 cup granulated sugar
- 1 large egg
- 1/4 cup (1/2 stick) butter

GLAZE

- 1 large egg yolk
- 2 tablespoons granulated sugar
- 1 tablespoon milk

Stir together the flour, sugar, and salt in a large bowl. Stir in the butter, eggs, and milk until well blended. • Knead the dough on a lightly floured surface until smooth and elastic, about 10 minutes. Set aside to rest for 15 minutes. • *Filling*: Mix the walnuts, raisins, almonds, figs, pineapple, chocolate, and cocoa in a large bowl. • Beat the sugar, egg, and butter in a medium bowl with an electric mixer at medium speed until creamy. • Preheat the oven to 375°F. • Line a large baking sheet with parchment paper. •Roll the dough out on a lightly floured surface into an oval shape, as thin as possible. • Spread the sugar mixture over the pastry, leaving a ½ inch border at all sides. Gently spread with the fruit mixture, leaving a ½ inch border. From a long side, carefully roll the strudel up, pinching the ends together. • Carefully transfer the strudel to the prepared sheet. Gently pull it into a horseshoe shape. If the dough breaks while you are moving it, take a little dough from the end to make a patch. • *Glaze*: Mix the egg yolk, sugar, and milk in a small bowl and brush over the strudel. • Bake for 50–60 minutes, or until golden brown. Slide onto a rack to cool. • Serve warm or at room temperature.

Makes one strudel · Prep: 1 hr. · Cooking: 50–60 min. · Level: 2 · Keeps: 2–3 days

FRUIT AND CHOCOLATE RING

2⅔ cups all-purpose flour
⅔ cup butter, softened
½ cup granulated sugar
1 large egg. lightly beaten 1 large egg yolk, lightly beaten
¼ teaspoon salt
⅓ cup dry Marsala wine
1 cup dried figs, coarsely chopped
⅔ cup toasted almonds, coarsely chopped
3½ oz semisweet chocolate, coarsely chopped
⅓ cup pistachios, coarsely chopped
⅓ cup walnuts, coarsely chopped
2 tablespoons grated lemon zest
1 teaspoon ground cinnamon

Use a wooden spoon to mix the flour, butter, sugar, egg, salt, and half the Marsala in a large bowl until a firm dough is formed. • Cover the bowl with a kitchen towel and set aside to rest for about 2 hours. • Stir together the figs, almonds, chocolate, pistachios, and walnuts in a medium saucepan. Add the lemon zest,

cinnamon, and the remaining Marsala. • Cook over low heat for about 10 minutes, stirring frequently. Set aside to cool. • Preheat the oven to 400°F. • Line a baking sheet with parchment paper. • Roll the dough out on a lightly floured surface into a ½-inch thick rectangle. • Use the instructions on page 220 to fill and roll up the strudel, using the fruit and nut mixture to fill. Form a ring. • Carefully transfer the ring to the prepared sheet. • Bake for 25–30 minutes. • Remove the ring from the oven and brush with the egg yolk. Return to the oven and bake for 5 minutes more. • Turn the oven off and leave the ring in the oven until the ring has cooled. • Serve at room temperature.

Makes one ring. · Prep: 30 min. + 2 hr. to rest · Cooking: 35 min. · Level: 2 · Keeps: 2–3 days

CHOCOLATE WALNUT STRUDEL

12 oz semisweet chocolate, coarsely chopped
2 tablespoons milk
1 tablespoon butter
18   oz frozen puff pastry sheets, thawed
½ cup walnuts, coarsely chopped
1 large egg. lightly beaten with 1 tablespoon water confectioners' sugar, to dust

Preheat the oven to 375ºF. • Line a large baking sheet with parchment paper. • Melt the chocolate with the milk and butter in a double boiler over barely simmering water. • Unfold or unroll the pastry on a lightly floured surface. Roll into a 16 x 12-inch rectangle. • Spoon the chocolate mixture

onto the rectangle, leaving a border around the edges. Sprinkle with the walnuts. Use the instructions on page 220 to roll up the strudel. • Transfer to the baking sheet. Brush with a little beaten egg. • Bake for 30–35 minutes, or until lightly browned. • Dust with confectioners' sugar.

Makes one strudel · Prep: 30 min. · Cooking: 30–35 min. · Level: 2 · Keeps: 1–2 days

BANANA CHOCOLATE STRUDEL

4 sheets phyllo dough, thawed if frozen
3 tablespoons butter, melted
2 firm-ripe bananas, thickly sliced
2 oz semisweet chocolate, finely chopped
1 large egg, beaten with 1 teaspoon water confectioners' sugar, to dust

Preheat the oven to 425ºF. • Lay the sheets of dough out flat and cover with waxed paper and a damp kitchen towel. (This will stop them from drying out.) • Brush the first sheet with butter. Top with another sheet and brush with butter. Repeat with 2 more sheets. Arrange the bananas, horizontally, in overlapping rows on lower third of phyllo, leaving a 1-inch border on both sides. Sprinkle the chocolate over the bananas. Use the instructions on page 220 to roll up the strudel. • Transfer to a large baking sheet. Brush with a little beaten egg. • Bake for 12–15 minutes, or until golden. • Dust with confectioners' sugar.

Makes one strudel · Prep: 30 min. · Cooking: 12–15 min. · Level: 2 · Keeps: 1–2 days

Fruit and chocolate ring

CHARLOTTES

This classy dessert was created in France in the 19th century. Charlottes combine sponge cake, cream, and fruit to form either a hot or cold delicacy. Dreamy, attractive, and smooth on the palate, charlottes are ideal on a summer's evening, served with a sparkling wine.

APPLE SORBET CHARLOTTE

- 30   pirouette cookies
- 2   pints apple sorbet, softened
- 14   ladyfingers

APPLE LIQUEUR SAUCE

- 4   large egg yolks
- ½   cup granulated sugar
- ¼   cup apple liqueur
- ¼   cup caramel ice cream topping

Butter a 7-inch charlotte mold. Line the pan sides with the pirouettes standing on their ends. Freeze for 1 hour. • Spoon 2 cups sorbet into the mold and cover with a layer of ladyfingers. Spread the remaining sorbet over. Top with the remaining ladyfingers. • Cover and freeze for 1 hour. • *Apple Liqueur Sauce*: Beat the egg yolks and sugar in a double boiler over barely simmering water until well blended. Cook, stirring constantly with a wooden spoon, until the mixture lightly coats a metal spoon or registers 160°F on an instant-read thermometer. Beat with an electric mixer at high speed until pale and creamy. Add the liqueur. • Soak the mold in hot water for 10 seconds, then turn out onto a serving dish, with the sorbet layer facing up. • Spoon the caramel topping over the charlotte. • Serve immediately with the liqueur sauce passed on the side.

Makes one 7-inch charlotte · Prep: 35 min. + 2 hr. to freeze · Level: 1 · Keeps: 1–2 days in the freezer

◄ Raspberry mousse cake (see page 235)

⌃ Apple sorbet charlotte

Rosita charlotte

CREAMY COFFEE CHARLOTTE

- 4 tablespoons apricot preserves or jam, melted
  about 24 ladyfingers
- 4 large egg yolks
- 1 cup confectioners' sugar
- 4 teaspoons coffee extract
- 3 tablespoons dark rum
- 3 cups heavy cream
- 4 oz semisweet chocolate, coarsely grated

Brush the sides of a 9-inch springform pan with the apricot preserves. Trim the ends off the ladyfingers and stand them around the sides. • Beat the egg yolks, confectioners' sugar, coffee extract, and rum in a saucepan until blended. Cook over low heat, beating constantly with a wooden spoon, until the mixture lightly coats a metal spoon or registers 160°F on an instant-read thermometer. Immediately plunge the pan into a bowl of ice water and stir until the egg mixture has cooled. • Beat the cream in a large bowl with an electric mixer at high speed until stiff. • Use a large rubber spatula to fold the cream into the egg yolk mixture. • Spoon the mixture into the prepared pan. • Freeze for 8 hours, or until set. • Loosen and remove the pan sides and turn out onto a serving plate. Decorate with chocolate.

Makes one 9-inch charlotte · Prep: 20 min. + 8 hr. to freeze · Level: 2 · Keeps: 1–2 days in the freezer

FRESH FRUIT CHARLOTTE

- 1¹/₂ tablespoons unflavored gelatin
- ¹/₄ cup cold water
- 2 large egg yolks
- ³/₄ cup granulated sugar
- 1 cup fresh orange juice
- 5 tablespoons orange liqueur
- 2 tablespoons fresh lemon juice
- 1¹/₄ cups heavy cream
- 7 oz ladyfingers
- ¹/₂ cup apricot preserves or jam
- 1¹/₂ cups mixed sliced fresh fruit

Sprinkle the gelatin over the water in a saucepan. Let stand 1 minute. Stir over low heat until the gelatin has completely dissolved. • Beat the egg yolks, sugar, and orange juice in a medium saucepan. Cook over low heat, stirring constantly with a wooden spoon, until the mixture lightly coats a metal spoon or registers 160°F on an instant-read thermometer. Immediately plunge the pan into a bowl of ice water and stir until the egg mixture has cooled. • Add the gelatin mixture, 2 tablespoons liqueur,

GRANDMA'S CHARLOTTE CAKE

- 7 oz ladyfingers
- ¹/₄ cup amaretto
- 1 cup strawberries, hulled
- 2 large eggs + 1 large egg yolk
- ¹/₂ cup superfine sugar
- 1 teaspoon vanilla extract
  pinch of salt
- ¹/₂ cup milk
- ¹/₄ cup (¹/₂ stick) cold butter, cut up
  whipped cream, to serve
  halved strawberries, to decorate

Preheat the oven to 350°F. • Butter and flour an 11 x 7-inch baking pan. • Arrange half the ladyfingers in the pan. Drizzle with 2 tablespoons liqueur and top with the strawberries. Cover with ladyfingers and drizzle with the liqueur. • Beat the eggs and egg yolk, superfine sugar, vanilla, and salt in a large bowl with an electric mixer at medium speed until pale and thick. Add the milk. • Pour over the ladyfingers. Set aside for 5 minutes. • Dot with butter. • Bake for 35 minutes. Remove from the oven and cover with aluminum foil. Return to the oven and bake for 15 minutes more, or until lightly browned. • Cool completely in the pan. Serve with whipped cream and arrange the strawberries on top.

Makes one charlotte · Prep: 30 min. · Cooking: 50 min. · Level: 1 · Keeps: 5 days in the refrigerator

ROSITA CHARLOTTE

This recipe calls for a jelly roll filled with raspberry jelly. Roll the cake up tightly, wrap in waxed paper, and store in the refrigerator for at least an hour to make for easy slicing.

- 1 Basic Jelly Roll, filled with 1¹/₄ cups
  raspberry jelly, jam, or preserves (see page 174)
- ¹/₂ recipe Classic Bavarian Cream (see page 341)

Rinse a 1¹/₂-quart charlotte mold or soufflé dish with cold water. Without drying, line the mold with plastic wrap. • Cut the jelly roll into ¹/₂-inch thick slices. Line the mold with the slices, fitting them tightly. Spoon the Bavarian cream over. Cover and refrigerate for 4 hours, or until set. • Place a serving plate over the mold and invert. Carefully remove the wrap.

Makes 1 charlotte · Prep: 45 min. + 4 hr. to chill · Level: 3 · Keeps: 1–2 days in the refrigerator

and the lemon juice. Transfer to a large bowl. Cover and refrigerate until thick. • Beat the cream in a large bowl with an electric mixer at high speed until stiff. • Use a large rubber spatula to fold the cream into the orange mixture. • Butter a 9-inch springform pan. Line with some of the ladyfingers, fitting them tightly. Fill any gaps with ladyfinger pieces. Drizzle with 2 tablespoons liqueur. • Spoon the orange cream over, cover, and refrigerate for 3 hours, or until set. • Loosen and remove the pan sides. Transfer to a serving plate. • Stir the jam and the remaining 1 tablespoon liqueur in a saucepan and heat over low heat. Trim the ladyfingers to just taller than the mousse. Brush each ladyfinger with a little jam and press against the mousse, making a border. • Decorate with the fruit and brush jam over the top.

Makes one 10-inch cake · Prep: 50 min. + 4 hr. to chill · Level: 2 · Keeps: 1–2 days in the refrigerator

FRESH FRUIT AND CREAM CHARLOTTE

1²/₃ cups heavy cream
²/₃ cup kirsch
²/₃ cup water
   about 30 ladyfingers
1¹/₂ cups thinly sliced strawberries
1¹/₂ cups peeled and thinly sliced peaches

Butter an 8-inch springform pan. • Beat the cream and 1 tablespoon kirsch in a large bowl with an electric mixer at medium speed until stiff. • Mix the remaining liqueur and water. • Trim the ladyfingers so that 15 can be placed in a spokelike pattern to cover the pan bottom. Arrange strawberry slices around the pan sides. • Reserve a few slices to decorate. • Dip the ladyfinger trimmings in the liqueur mixture. Mix ³/₄ of the cream, remaining fruit, and ladyfinger trimmings. • Spoon the mixture over the ladyfingers. Arrange the remaining ladyfingers in a spokelike pattern to cover the top. • Refrigerate for 4 hours, or until set. • Loosen and remove the pan sides. Transfer onto a serving dish. Decorate with the cream and fruit.

Makes one 8-inch charlotte · Prep: 30 min. + 4 hr. to chill · Level: 1 · Keeps: 1–2 days in the refrigerator

APRICOT CHARLOTTE

   about 30 ladyfingers
2 cups dried apricots
¹/₃ cup granulated sugar

Fresh fruit and cream charlotte

1¹/₄ cups water
2 tablespoons unflavored gelatin
2 cups heavy cream
¹/₂ cup confectioners' sugar

Line a 9-inch springform pan with ladyfingers. • Place the apricots in a bowl with hot water to cover. Microwave at medium heat for 8 minutes. • Drain. Mix in the granulated sugar and 1 cup water. Microwave for 15 minutes. • Sprinkle the gelatin over ¹/₄ cup water in a small saucepan. Let stand 1 minute. Stir over low heat until completely dissolved. • Process the apricot mixture until pureed. Add the gelatin mixture. Refrigerate until thickened. • Beat the cream and confectioners' sugar in a large bowl with an electric mixer at high speed until stiff. Use a large rubber spatula to fold into apricot mixture. • Pour half the mixture into the pan and top with ladyfingers. Pour in the remaining mixture. Refrigerate for 4 hours. Invert onto a serving plate.

Makes one 9-inch charlotte · Prep: 30 min. + 4 hr. to chill · Level: 2 · Keeps: 1–2 days

PEAR MOLDS WITH CITRUS SAUCE

4 large ripe pears, peeled, cored, and thinly sliced
¹/₂ cup + 2 tablespoons butter, melted
¹/₄ cup granulated sugar
10 slices white sandwich bread, crusts removed
¹/₂ recipe Citrus Sauce (see page 353)

Preheat the oven to 400°F. • Butter four ¹/₂-cup charlotte molds. Dip 4 bread slices in ¹/₃ the butter. Line each mold with bread. • Sauté the pears in the remaining 2 tablespoons butter in a skillet over medium heat until golden. Sprinkle with sugar and cook, stirring, until caramelized. • Process the pears until smooth and transfer to a bowl. • Process 2 slices bread until finely chopped. Add the crumbs to the pear mixture. • Spoon the pear mixture into the molds. Brush the remaining bread slices with remaining butter and top the molds with them, pressing down gently. • Bake for 20–25 minutes, or until golden brown. • Pour a little citrus sauce onto 4 serving plates. Carefully invert onto the plates.

Makes four ¹/₂ cup charlottes · Prep: 35 min. · Cooking: 20–25 min. · Level: 2 · Keeps: 1–2 days

CHOCOLATE MOUSSE CHARLOTTE

- 1 lb bittersweet chocolate
- 8 oz granulated sugar
- ³/₄ cup water
- 2 large eggs
- 8 large egg yolks
- 1 tablespoon unflavored gelatin
- 1¹/₂ cups heavy cream
- 36 ladyfingers

Set out the sides only of a 10-inch springform pan. Place on a serving plate lined with a 10-inch disk of parchment paper. • Melt the chocolate in a double boiler over barely simmering water. Set aside to cool. • Dissolve the sugar in ¹/₂ cup water in a saucepan over medium heat. Wash down the pan sides with a pastry brush dipped in cold water to prevent sugar crystals from forming. Cook, without stirring, until the mixture reaches 238°F, or the soft-ball stage. • Beat the eggs and egg yolks in a large bowl with an electric mixer at medium speed until frothy. With mixer at high speed, gradually beat in the sugar mixture, beating until stiff. • Sprinkle the gelatin over the remaining ¹/₄ cup water in a small saucepan. Let stand 1 minute. Cook over low heat until completely dissolved. • Add the gelatin mixture to the egg mixture. • With mixer at high speed, beat the cream in a large bowl until stiff. • Use a large rubber spatula to fold in the chocolate, followed by the cream. • Cover the parchment paper with ladyfingers, flat side down, then position all around the edge, curved-side outward. • Spoon the mousse into the mold and refrigerate for 6 hours, or until set. Carefully remove the pan sides before serving.

Makes one 10-inch cake · Prep: 30 min. + 6 hr. to chill · Level: 2 · Keeps: 1–2 days in the refrigerator

MAPLE SYRUP CHARLOTTE

- 1 tablespoon unflavored gelatin
- ¹/₄ cup water
- 1 cup maple syrup + extra to drizzle
- 3¹/₂ cups heavy cream
- 1 cup walnuts, coarsely chopped
  about 30 ladyfingers

Lightly oil a 1¹/₂-quart charlotte mold. Line with waxed paper. • Sprinkle the gelatin over the water in a small saucepan. Let stand 1 minute. Warm the maple syrup and stir into the gelatin mixture until the gelatin has completely dissolved. Refrigerate until

thickened, 20 minutes. • Beat the cream in a large bowl with an electric mixer at high speed until stiff. Use a large rubber spatula to fold 2 cups of cream into the maple syrup mixture. Stir in ³/₄ cup walnuts. • Line the prepared mold with the ladyfingers. • Spoon the filling into the mold. • Refrigerate for 4 hours, or until set. • Invert onto a serving plate and drizzle with a little maple syrup. Sprinkle with the remaining nuts. Serve with remaining cream.

Makes one 1¹/₂-quart charlotte · Prep: 40 min. + 4 hr. to chill · Level: 2 · Keeps: 1–2 days in the refrigerator

CHESTNUT CHARLOTTE

- ¹/₄ cup dark rum
- ¹/₂ cup water
  about 30 ladyfingers
- 2 cups heavy cream
- ¹/₂ cup granulated sugar
- 14 oz candied chestnuts, crumbled

Mix the rum and water in a large bowl. Dip the ladyfingers in the rum mixture. • Line a 1 quart charlotte mold with ladyfingers. • Beat the cream and sugar in a large bowl with an electric mixer at high speed until stiff. • Use a large rubber spatula to fold the chestnuts into the cream. Repeat layers of chestnut cream and ladyfingers in the mold until all the ingredients have been used up, finishing with ladyfingers. • Refrigerate overnight. • Invert onto a serving plate.

Makes one 1-quart charlotte · Prep: 20 min. + 12 hr. to chill · Level: 2 · Keeps: 1–2 days in the refrigerator

MARBLED MASCARPONE CHARLOTTE

- 4 oz white chocolate, chopped
- 4 oz semisweet chocolate, chopped
- 3 large egg yolks
- ²/₃ cup granulated sugar
- ¹/₄ cup brandy
- 3 tablespoons white wine
- 1¹/₂ cups mascarpone cheese
- 1 9-inch Basic Sponge Cake (see page 157)

Butter a 9-inch springform pan. • Melt the white chocolate in a double boiler over barely simmering water. Set aside to cool. Repeat with the semisweet chocolate and set aside to cool. • Beat the egg yolks, sugar, brandy, and white wine in a double boiler with an electric mixer at medium speed over barely simmering water until the mixture falls in ribbons, about 20 minutes. • Fold half the egg mixture into each of the cooled

chocolate mixtures. • Stir half the mascarpone into each mixture until well blended. • Cut the cake horizontally and place one layer in the prepared pan. • Spoon in the white and dark mixtures alternately and swirl with a knife to create a marbled pattern. Refrigerate for 6 hours. Loosen and remove the pan sides. Remove the paper.

Makes one 9-inch cake · Prep: 40 min. + 6 hr. to chill · Level: 2 · Keeps: 1–2 days in the refrigerator

HAZELNUT-PUMPKIN CHARLOTTE

	about 30 ladyfingers
2	tablespoons unflavored gelatin
2/3	cup milk
1/3	cup dark rum
4	large eggs, separated
2/3	cup firmly packed brown sugar
2	cups mashed pumpkin
2	teaspoons grated orange zest
1	teaspoon ground cinnamon
1	teaspoon ground nutmeg
1	teaspoon ground ginger
1 1/2	cups heavy cream
4	teaspoons water
1/4	teaspoon cream of tartar
1/2	cup toasted hazelnuts, coarsely chopped

Butter a 9-inch springform pan. • Trim the ends off the ladyfingers. Arrange the ladyfingers in the pan, curved-side outward. • Stir the gelatin, milk, rum, egg yolks, and 1/3 cup brown sugar in a large saucepan over low heat until the mixture coats a metal spoon or reaches 160°F on an instant-read thermometer. Remove from the heat and stir in the pumpkin, orange zest, and spices. • Beat the cream in a large bowl with an electric mixer at high speed until stiff. • Stir the egg whites, remaining 1/3 cup brown sugar, water, and cream of tartar in a saucepan until blended. Cook over low heat, beating constantly, until the whites register 160°F on an instant-read thermometer. Transfer to a large bowl. With an electric mixer at high speed, beat until stiff, glossy peaks form. Use a large rubber spatula to fold them and the cream into the pumpkin mixture. Add the hazelnuts. • Spoon the mixture into the prepared pan. • Refrigerate for 6 hours, or until set. • Loosen and remove the pan sides.

Makes one 9-inch cake · Prep: 20 min. + 6 hr. to chill · Level: 2 · Keeps: 1–2 days in the refrigerator

Strawberry charlotte

STRAWBERRY CHARLOTTE

1/2	cup dry white wine
1/4	cup kirsch
1	Basic Pound Cake (see page 40), cut into 1/2-inch thick slices
3	packed cups vanilla ice cream, softened
1	lb strawberries, hulled and halved (reserve 10 to decorate)

Mix the wine and kirsch and drizzle a little on each cake slice. Use the slices to line a 2-quart straight-sided soufflé dish. • Spoon 1/3 of the ice cream over the cake. Top with 1/3 of the strawberries. Cover with cake slices. Repeat with the ice cream, strawberries, and cake slices until they have all been used, finishing with a layer of ice cream. • Freeze for 1 hour. • Soak the mold in hot water for 10 seconds. Turn out onto a serving dish, ice cream-side facing up. Decorate with the strawberries, cut in half.

Makes 1 charlotte · Prep: 30 min. + 1 hr. to freeze · Level: 1 · Keeps: 2–3 days in the freezer

BANANA CHARLOTTE

2	tablespoons unflavored gelatin
1/2	cup cold + 1/2 cup hot water
	about 20 ladyfingers
7	ripe bananas, peeled
2	tablespoons fresh lemon juice
1/4	cup granulated sugar
1/2	cup walnuts, coarsely chopped
1 1/2	cups heavy cream

Lightly oil a 1 1/2-quart charlotte mold. • Sprinkle the gelatin over 1/4 cup cold water. Add 1/2 cup hot water and stir until completely dissolved. Pour a thin layer of gelatin into the mold. When set, cut several slices of banana and sprinkle over the gelatin. Pour over more of the gelatin mixture, enough to cover the bananas, and let set. • Line the mold with ladyfingers. • Process the remaining bananas until pureed. Add the lemon juice, sugar, and nuts. • Beat the cream in a large bowl with an electric mixer at high speed until stiff. • Sprinkle the remaining gelatin over the remaining 1/4 cup cold water in a small saucepan. Let stand 1 minute. Stir over low heat until completely dissolved. • Fold the cream and gelatin mixture into the banana mixture. Pour the mixture into the mold. Refrigerate for 4 hours, or until set. Invert onto a serving plate.

Makes one 1 1/2-quart charlotte · Prep: 20 min. + 4 hr. to chill · Level: 2 · Keeps: 1–2 days

³/₄ cup firmly packed brown sugar
1   teaspoon ground cinnamon
1   teaspoon ground nutmeg
    about 24 ladyfingers
2   cups Caramel Sauce (see page 353)

Line a 1-quart charlotte mold with plastic wrap. Sprinkle the apples with lemon zest and juice in a large bowl. Soak 1 hour. • Heat the apple juice and water in a saucepan. Add the brown sugar, cinnamon, and nutmeg and cook over medium heat until the sugar has dissolved. Simmer 5 minutes. Add the apples and juices, stirring often, and cook until tender. Transfer the apples onto a plate. • Dip the ladyfingers briefly in the apple syrup. • Line the mold with half the ladyfingers. Spoon in the apples and top with the ladyfingers. Drizzle with syrup. Place a plate on top and let stand 30 minutes. • Turn out onto the serving plate. • Serve with the sauce passed on the side.

Makes one 1-quart charlotte · Prep: 20 min. + 30 min. to stand · Level: 2 · Keeps: 1–2 days

LEMON CHARLOTTE

    about 30 ladyfingers
1   cup granulated sugar
3   tablespoons cornstarch
1   tablespoon grated lemon zest
¹/₂ cup fresh lemon juice
¹/₂ cup cold water
4   large eggs, lightly beaten
¹/₄ teaspoon salt
¹/₂ cup butter, softened
1¹/₂ cups flaked almonds

Line a 1¹/₂-quart charlotte mold with waxed paper. Butter the paper. • Line with ¹/₃ of the ladyfingers. • Beat the sugar, cornstarch, lemon zest and juice, water, eggs, and salt in a saucepan until blended. Cook over low heat, beating constantly with a wooden spoon, until the mixture lightly coats a metal spoon or registers 160°F on an instant-read thermometer. Immediately plunge the pan into a bowl of ice water and stir until the egg mixture has cooled. • With mixer at medium speed, beat the butter in a medium bowl until creamy. Gradually add the lemon mixture and almonds. • Spoon the mixture into the prepared pan. Top with another ¹/₃ of the ladyfingers. Spoon in the remaining mixture and top with ladyfingers. • Refrigerate for 4 hours. • Invert onto a serving plate.

Makes one 1¹/₂-quart charlotte · Prep: 30 min. + 4 hr. to chill · Level: 2 · Keeps: 1–2 days in the refrigerator

Spicy mini apple charlottes

SPICY MINI APPLE CHARLOTTES

¹/₄ cup (¹/₂ stick) butter
6   large tart apples, peeled, cored, and thinly sliced
¹/₄ cup granulated sugar
1   teaspoon ground nutmeg
¹/₂ teaspoon ground ginger
¹/₄ teaspoon ground cloves
12 slices white sandwich bread, crusts removed
1¹/₂ cups mixed nuts, coarsely chopped
20 prunes, pitted and chopped
¹/₄ cup dry white wine

Preheat the oven to 400°F. • Butter six 3-inch charlotte molds. • Melt 2 tablespoons butter in a skillet and sauté the apples, sugar, nutmeg, ginger, and cloves. • Line the molds with bread. Fill with the apple mixture. Sprinkle with nuts. Repeat until the ingredients are all in the molds. • Bake for 12–15 minutes, or until golden brown. • Melt the remaining butter in the skillet and sauté the prunes for 10 minutes. Add the wine and cook until tender. • Unmold the charlottes onto serving plates. • Spoon the prunes on top and serve with the sauce on the side.

Makes 6 mini charlottes · Prep: 40 min. · Cooking: 15 min. · Level: 1 · Keeps: 1–2 days

BAKED APPLE CHARLOTTE

6   slices white sandwich bread, crusts removed
¹/₂ cup (1 stick) butter, melted
1¹/₂ lb apples, peeled, cored, and thinly sliced
¹/₂ cup golden raisins
3   tablespoons water
¹/₂ cup granulated sugar
1   tablespoon grated lemon zest

Preheat the oven to 375°F. • Set out a 1¹/₂-quart charlotte mold. • Dip the bread in the butter and line the mold, reserving bread to cover the top. • Cook the apples, raisins, water, sugar, and lemon zest in a saucepan until slightly softened, about 7 minutes. • Spoon the mixture into the prepared mold. Dip the remaining bread in butter and cover. • Bake for 50–60 minutes, or until golden. Cool in the mold for 5 minutes. Turn out onto a serving plate and serve warm.

Makes one 9-inch cake · Prep: 20 min. + 6 hr. to chill · Level: 2 · Keeps: 1–2 days

APPLE CHARLOTTE IN CARAMEL SAUCE

    grated zest and juice of 1 lemon
3   lb Granny Smith apples, peeled, cored, and thinly sliced
³/₄ cup apple juice
¹/₂ cup water

RASPBERRY MOUSSE CAKE

- ³/₄ cup all-purpose flour
- 1 teaspoon baking powder
- ¹/₄ teaspoon salt
- ¹/₄ cup shredded coconut
- 4 large eggs, separated
- ¹/₄ cup granulated sugar
- 1 teaspoon vanilla extract

RASPBERRY MOUSSE

- 1 tablespoon unflavored gelatin
- ¹/₄ cup fresh lemon juice
- 1 lb fresh raspberries
- ¹/₂ cup granulated sugar
- 1¹/₃ cups heavy cream
- 2 large eggs, separated
- ¹/₄ teaspoon salt

- 1 tablespoon fresh lemon juice
- ¹/₂ cup raspberry or red currant jelly
- 8 oz ladyfingers
- 1¹/₂ cups raspberries, to decorate

Preheat the oven to 350°F. • Butter an 8-inch springform pan. Line with waxed paper. Butter the paper. • Sift the flour, baking powder, and salt into a medium bowl. Stir in the coconut. • Beat the egg whites in a medium bowl with an electric mixer at medium speed until frothy. With mixer at high speed, gradually beat in the sugar, beating until stiff, glossy peaks form. • Beat the yolks in a medium bowl. • With mixer at low speed, add the yolks to the beaten whites. • Use a large rubber spatula to fold in the dry ingredients and vanilla. • Spoon the batter into the prepared pan. • Bake for 15–20 minutes, or until a toothpick inserted into the center comes out clean. • Cool the cake in the pan for 10 minutes. Loosen and remove the pan sides. Invert onto a rack. Loosen and remove the pan bottom. Carefully remove the paper and let cool completely. • Reline the pan with waxed paper and return the cake to the pan. • *Raspberry Mousse*: Sprinkle the gelatin over 2 tablespoons lemon juice in a small bowl and stir until completely dissolved. • Beat the egg yolks and the remaining lemon juice in a double boiler until well blended. Cook over low heat, stirring constantly with a wooden spoon, until the mixture lightly coats a metal spoon or registers 160°F on an instant-read thermometer. Immediately plunge the pan into a bowl of ice water and stir until the egg mixture has cooled. • Place the gelatin mixture, half the raspberries, 1/4 cup sugar, and egg yolk mixture in a food processor and process until smooth. • Beat the cream in a large bowl with an electric mixer at high speed until stiff. • Stir the egg whites, the remaining sugar, water, and cream of tartar in a saucepan until blended.

Mini fruit charlottes

Cook over low heat, beating constantly, until the whites register 160°F on an instant-read thermometer. Transfer to a bowl. With an electric mixer at high speed, beat in the remaining sugar, beating until stiff, glossy peaks form. • Use a large metal spatula to fold the beaten whites and cream into the raspberry mixture until well blended. Refrigerate for 4 hours, or until set. Spread the mousse over. • Refrigerate for 4 hours, or until set. Remove from the pan and place on a serving plate. • Stir the lemon juice into the jelly and spread over the top. Use some jelly to stick the ladyfingers to the sides. • Decorate with the raspberries.

Makes one 8-inch round cake · Prep: 45 min. + 4 hr. to chill · Cooking: 15–20 min. · Level: 2 · Keeps: 1–2 days

MINI FRUIT CHARLOTTES

You may prefer to buy a sponge cake and slice it up to line the molds.

- 1¹/₄ cups granulated sugar
- 1 9-inch Basic Sponge Cake (see page 157), sliced
- 2 cups fresh fruit salad, chopped into ¹/₄-inch cubes
- ¹/₄ cup (¹/₂ stick) butter
- 2 cups milk
- ¹/₄ teaspoon salt
- ²/₃ cup semolina

- 3 large egg yolks, lightly beaten
- 1 cup heavy cream
- 1 teaspoon vanilla extract
- 2 tablespoons rum
- ¹/₂ cup fresh raspberries

Preheat the oven to 400°F. • Butter 6 individual crème brûlée dishes or ramekins. Sprinkle with 1¹/₂ teaspoons of the sugar and line with cake slices . • Sauté the fruit salad in 2 tablespoons butter in a skillet over medium heat for 3–4 minutes. Set aside to cool. • Bring the milk, ¹/₄ cup sugar, and salt to a boil in a saucepan. Slowly add the semolina and, stirring frequently, cook for 10 minutes, or until thick. • Remove from the heat and stir in the remaining butter, fruit salad, egg yolks, 3 tablespoons cream, vanilla, rum, and raspberries until well blended. • Spoon the filling evenly into the molds. • Bake for 25–30 minutes. • Just before the mini charlottes are cooked, melt the remaining sugar in a small pan over medium heat. Cook until the syrup is pale gold. Remove from the heat and add the remaining cream. • Turn the hot charlottes out onto individual serving dishes and spoon the sauce over.

Makes 6 mini charlottes · Prep: 30 min. · Cooking: 25–30 min. · Level: 2 · Keeps: 1–2 days

CHEESECAKES

Rich in flavor and smooth in texture, cheesecakes are well worth the indulgence. They melt in the mouth and are easily flavored by citrus fruit, coffee, and chocolate. By varying ingredients slightly, or by arranging dramatic presentations, you'll be able to create cheesecakes to suit every occasion.

KEY LIME CHEESECAKE

1½ cups graham cracker crumbs
¾   cup granulated sugar
⅔   cup butter, melted

FILLING

2   tablespoons unflavored gelatin
1   cup fresh lime juice
¼   cup water
1½ cups granulated sugar
5   large eggs
2   teaspoons freshly grated lime zest
½   cup (1 stick) butter, softened
2   packages (8 oz each) cream cheese, softened
½   cup heavy cream
    fresh lime slices, to decorate

Set out a 9-inch springform pan. • Mix the crumbs, sugar, and butter in a medium bowl. Press into the bottom and partway up the sides of the pan. • *Filling*: Sprinkle the gelatin over the lime juice and water in a saucepan. Let stand 1 minute. • Beat the sugar, eggs, and lime zest into the lime juice. Cook over low heat, stirring constantly with a wooden spoon, until the mixture lightly coats a metal spoon or registers 160°F on an instant-read thermometer. Immediately plunge the pan into a bowl of ice water and stir until the egg mixture has cooled. • Beat the butter and cream cheese in a large bowl with an electric mixer at medium speed until creamy. • With mixer at low speed, add the lime mixture. • Refrigerate for 45 minutes. • With mixer at high speed, beat the cream in a large bowl until stiff. Use a large rubber spatula to fold the cream into the lime mixture. • Spoon the filling into the crust. Refrigerate for 3 hours before serving. Loosen and remove the pan sides to serve. Decorate with the lime slices.

Makes one 9-inch cheesecake · Prep: 20 min. + 3 hr. 45 min. to chill · Level: 2 · Keeps: 1–2 days in the refrigerator

◄ Rice and berry cake (see page 256)

➤ Key lime cheesecake

NEW YORK–STYLE CHEESECAKE

- 1 cup graham cracker crumbs
- ¼ cup (½ stick) butter, melted
- ¼ cup granulated sugar

FILLING

- 4 packages (8 oz) cream cheese, softened
- 1 cup granulated sugar
- 3 tablespoons all-purpose flour
- 4 large eggs, at room temperature
- 1 cup sour cream
- 2 teaspoons vanilla extract
  fresh fruit, to decorate (optional)

Preheat the oven to 350°F. • Butter a 9-inch springform pan. • Mix the crumbs, butter, and sugar in a medium bowl. Press into the bottom of the prepared pan. • Bake for 8–10 minutes. Cool completely in the pan on a rack. • *Filling*: Beat the cream cheese, sugar, and flour in a large bowl with an electric mixer at medium speed until creamy. Add the eggs, one at a time, until just blended after each addition. Add the sour cream and vanilla. • Spoon the filling into the crust. • Bake for 50–60 minutes, or until set. Cool the cake in the pan on a rack. • Loosen and remove the pan sides. Refrigerate for 6 hours. • Serve with fresh fruit, if desired.

Makes one 9-inch round cake · Prep: 25 min. + 6 hr. to chill · Cooking: 50–60 min. · Level: 1 · Keeps: 1 day

FAMILY FAVORITE CHEESECAKE

If you want to dress this up, arrange strawberries on the top. Brush with melted jelly and they'll glisten like jewels.

- 1½ cups graham cracker crumbs
- ¼ cup granulated sugar
- ¼ cup (½ stick) butter, melted
- 1½ teaspoons ground cinnamon

FILLING

- 3 packages (8 oz each) cream cheese, softened
- 1½ cups granulated sugar
- 2 tablespoons grated lemon or orange zest
- 2 teaspoons vanilla extract
- 4 large eggs, at room temperature
- 2 cups sour cream

Butter a 9-inch springform pan. • Mix the crumbs, sugar, butter, cinnamon in a medium bowl. • Press into the bottom and partway up the sides of the prepared pan. Refrigerate for 30 minutes. • *Filling*: Preheat the oven to 350°F. • Beat the cream cheese, sugar, lemon zest, and vanilla in a large bowl with an electric mixer at medium speed until

smooth. • Add the eggs, one at a time, until just blended after each addition. • With mixer at low speed, add the sour cream. • Spoon the filling into the crust. • Bake for 50–60 minutes, or until set. • Cool the cake in the pan on a rack. Refrigerate for 6 hours. Loosen and remove the pan sides to serve.

Makes one 9-inch cake · Prep: 25 min. + 6 hr. to chill · Cooking: 50–60 min. · Level: 1 · Keeps: 1–2 days in the refrigerator

KIDS' FAVORITE CHEESECAKE

It tastes just like a peanut butter and jelly sandwich!

- 1½ cups graham cracker crumbs
- ¼ cup granulated sugar
- ¼ cup (½ stick) butter, melted

FILLING

- 3 packages (8 oz each) cream cheese, softened
- 1 cup granulated sugar
- ½ cup crunchy peanut butter
- 3 tablespoons cornstarch
- 4 large eggs, at room temperature
- ½ cup milk

TOPPING

- ¾ cup strawberry or red currant jelly
- 2 teaspoons fresh lemon juice

Preheat the oven to 325°F. • Butter a 9-inch springform pan. • Mix the crumbs, sugar, and butter in a medium bowl. • Press into the bottom and partway up the sides of the prepared pan. • Bake for 8–10 minutes. Cool the cake in the pan on a rack. • *Filling*: Beat the cream cheese, sugar, peanut butter, and cornstarch in a large bowl with an electric mixer at medium speed until smooth. • Add the eggs, one at a time, until

just blended after each addition. • With mixer at low speed, add the milk. • Spoon the filling into the crust. • Bake for 50–60 minutes, or until set. • Cool in the pan on a rack. Refrigerate for 6 hours. • *Topping*: Heat the jelly and lemon juice in a saucepan over medium heat until liquid. Set aside to cool a little. Loosen and remove the pan sides. Spread with the jelly.

Makes one 9-inch cake · Prep: 35 min. + 6 hr. to chill · Cooking: 50–60 min. · Level: 1 · Keeps: 1–2 days in the refrigerator

VANILLA CRUMBLE CHEESECAKE

- 1½ cups graham cracker crumbs
- ¼ cup (½ stick) butter, melted
- 2 tablespoons brown sugar
- 1 teaspoon ground cinnamon

FILLING

- 2 tablespoons unflavored gelatin
- 1¼ cups milk
- 2 packages (8 oz each) cream cheese, softened
- ½ cup granulated sugar
- 1 teaspoon vanilla extract
- ½ cup white chocolate chips

Preheat the oven to 350°F. • Butter a 9-inch springform pan. • Mix the crumbs, butter, sugar, and cinnamon in a medium bowl. • Press into bottom and partway up the sides of the prepared pan. • Bake for 8–10 minutes, or until lightly browned. Cool the crust completely in the pan on a rack. • *Filling*: Sprinkle the gelatin over ¼ cup milk in a food processor. Let stand 2 minutes. • Heat the remaining milk in a saucepan over medium heat until almost boiling. Pour the milk into the processor. Process until the

New York-style cheesecake

gelatin has completely dissolved. • Add the cream cheese, sugar, and vanilla and process until smooth. Add the chocolate chips. • Spoon the filling into the crust. • Sprinkle with the crumbs. Cover and refrigerate for 6 hours, or until set. Loosen and remove the pan sides to serve.

Makes one 9-inch round cake · Prep: 25 min. + 6 hr. to chill· Cooking: 10 min. · Level: 1 · Keeps: 1–2 days in the refrigerator

EASY MINI-CHEESECAKES

18   round Keebler Sandies shortbread cookies
2   packages (8 oz each) cream cheese, softened
1/2   cup granulated sugar
1   teaspoon vanilla extract
2   large eggs, at room temperature

TOPPING

1/2   cup red currant jelly or orange marmalade
2   teaspoons cornstarch dissolved in 1 tablespoon water

Preheat the oven to 325°F. • Line 18 muffin-pan cups with paper baking cups. • Fit a cookie into each cup. • Beat the cream cheese, sugar, and vanilla in a large bowl with an electric mixer at medium speed until smooth. • Add the eggs, one at a time, until just blended after each addition. • Spoon the filling evenly into the prepared cups, filling each ³/₄ full. • Bake for 20–25 minutes, or until set. • Cool the cakes in the pans on racks. Refrigerate for 2 hours. • *Topping*: Stir the jelly in a small saucepan until liquid. Remove from the heat and let cool slightly. Drizzle some jelly over each cheesecake. • Refrigerate for 30 minutes more.

Makes 18 small cheesecakes Prep: 15 min. + 2 hr. 30 min. to chill · Cooking: 20–25 min. · Level: 1 · Keeps: 1–2 days in the refrigerator

LEMON-VANILLA CHEESECAKE

1¹/₂   cups graham cracker crumbs
¹/₄   cup (¹/₂ stick) butter, melted
2   tablespoons brown sugar
1   teaspoon ground cinnamon
1   teaspoon ground nutmeg

FILLING

2   packages (8 oz each) cream cheese, softened
³/₄   cup granulated sugar
1   tablespoon vanilla extract
1   teaspoon lemon extract
1   cup heavy cream

Preheat the oven to 350°F. • Butter a 9-inch springform pan. • Mix the crumbs, butter, brown sugar, cinnamon, and nutmeg in a medium bowl. • Press into the bottom and partway up the sides of the prepared pan. • Bake for 8–10 minutes, or until lightly browned. • Cool the crust completely in the pan on a rack. • *Filling*: Beat the cream cheese, sugar, vanilla, and lemon extract in a large bowl with an electric mixer at medium speed until smooth. • With mixer at high speed, beat the cream in a large bowl until stiff. Use a large rubber spatula to fold the cream into the cheese mixture. • Spoon the filling into the crust. Refrigerate for 6 hours. Loosen and remove the pan sides to serve.

Makes one 9-inch cake · Prep: 15 min. + 6 hr. to chill · Cooking: 8–10 min. · Level: 1 · Keeps: 1–2 days in the refrigerator

VANILLA CHEESECAKE WITH CHANTILLY AND RASPBERRIES

1³/₄   cups graham cracker crumbs
¹/₂   cup firmly packed brown sugar
¹/₄   cup (¹/₂ stick) butter, melted
1   teaspoon ground cinnamon

FILLING

3   packages (8 oz each) cream cheese, softened
1³/₄   cups granulated sugar
1   tablespoon vanilla extract
4   large eggs, at room temperature
¹/₄   cup heavy cream
2   tablespoons all-purpose flour

2   cups Chantilly Cream (see page 345)
1–2   cups fresh raspberries

Preheat the oven to 400°F. • Butter a 10-inch springform pan. • Mix the crumbs, brown sugar, butter, and cinnamon in a medium bowl. • Press into the bottom and partway up the sides of the prepared pan. • Bake for 8–10 minutes, or until lightly browned. • Cool the crust completely in the pan on the rack. • *Filling*: Beat the cream cheese, sugar, and vanilla in a large bowl with an electric mixer at medium speed until smooth. • Add the eggs, one at a time, until just blended after each addition. • With mixer at low speed, add the cream and flour. • Spoon the filling into the crust. • Bake for 10 minutes, then lower the oven to 200°F and bake for 50–60 minutes more, or until set. • Cool the cake in the pan on a rack. Refrigerate for 6 hours. • Loosen and remove the pan sides. Spread the top with the chantilly cream and sprinkle with raspberries.

Makes one 10-inch cake · Prep: 25 min. + 6 hr. to chill · Cooking: 60–70 min. · Level: 1 · Keeps: 1–2 days in the refrigerator

SPICY SWEET CHEESECAKE

A delicious and unique cheesecake. One of our favorites.

1¹/₂   cups graham cracker crumbs
¹/₄   cup (¹/₂ stick) butter, melted
¹/₃   cup firmly packed brown sugar
1¹/₂   teaspoons ground cinnamon
1   teaspoon ground ginger
¹/₂   teaspoon ground nutmeg

FILLING

3   packages (8 oz each) cream cheese, softened
1   cup granulated sugar
2   teaspoons vanilla extract
1   teaspoon almond extract
3   large eggs, at room temperature
1   teaspoon ground cinnamon
1   teaspoon ground ginger
1   teaspoon ground nutmeg

TOPPING

1   container (16 oz) sour cream
1   tablespoon granulated sugar
1   teaspoon vanilla extract

Butter a 9-inch springform pan. • Mix the crumbs, butter, sugar, cinnamon, ginger, and nutmeg in a medium bowl. • Press into the bottom and partway up the sides of the prepared pan. Refrigerate for 30 minutes. • *Filling*: Preheat the oven to 375°F. • Beat the cream cheese, sugar, vanilla, and almond extract in a large bowl with an electric mixer at medium speed until smooth. • Add the eggs, one at a time, until just blended after each addition. • With mixer at low speed, add the cinnamon, ginger, and nutmeg. • Spoon the filling into the crust. • Bake for 50–60 minutes, or until set. • Cool the cake in the pan for 10 minutes. • *Topping*: Beat together the sour cream, sugar, and vanilla in a medium bowl. Spread over the cheesecake. • Bake for 10–15 more minutes, or until set. • Cool in the pan on a rack. Refrigerate for 6 hours. Loosen and remove the pan sides to serve.

Makes one 9-inch cake · Prep: 30 min. + 6 hr. to chill · Cooking: 60–75 min. · Level: 1 · Keeps: 1–2 days in the refrigerator

Neapolitan ricotta cheesecake

PEANUT-CHOCOLATE CHEESECAKE

1¹/₂   cups graham cracker crumbs
¹/₄   cup granulated sugar
3   tablespoons creamy peanut butter
1   tablespoon butter, melted
1   teaspoon ground cinnamon

FILLING
8   oz semisweet chocolate, coarsely chopped
3   packages (8 oz each) cream cheese, softened
1   cup granulated sugar
5   large eggs, at room temperature
¹/₄   cup milk
¹/₄   cup all-purpose flour
²/₃   cup creamy peanut butter
1   teaspoon vanilla extract

Butter a 10-inch springform pan. • Mix the crumbs, sugar, peanut butter, butter, and cinnamon in a medium bowl. • Press into the bottom and partway up the sides of the prepared pan. • Refrigerate for 30 minutes. • Preheat the oven to 375°F. • *Filling*: Melt the chocolate in a double boiler over barely simmering water. Let cool. Beat the cream cheese and sugar in a large bowl with electric mixer at medium speed until creamy. • Add the eggs, one at a time, until just blended after each addition. • With mixer at low speed, gradually beat in the flour, alternating with the milk. • Place ¹/₃ of the batter in a small bowl and add the peanut butter. Place another ¹/₃ of the batter in small bowl and add the chocolate. Stir the vanilla into the remaining filling. • Spoon alternate dollops of the three different fillings into the crust . Use a knife to swirl them attractively. • Bake for 55–65 minutes, or until set. • Cool the cake in the pan on a rack. Refrigerate for 6 hours. Loosen and remove the pan sides to serve.

Makes one 10-inch cake · Prep: 35 min. + 6 hr. to chill · Cooking: 55–65 min. · Level: 1 · Keeps: 1–2 days

NEAPOLITAN RICOTTA CHEESECAKE

³/₄   cup granulated sugar
1¹/₂   tablespoons cold water
1   container (15–16 oz) ricotta cheese, pressed through a sieve
3   tablespoons Galliano liqueur or brandy
1   teaspoon vanilla extract
1¹/₂   recipes Italian Sponge Cake (see page 157), baked in a rectangular baking pan
¹/₄   cup rum
5   oz bittersweet chocolate, grated

Stir the sugar and water in a saucepan over low heat until the mixture begins to boil. Continue cooking, without stirring, until the syrup is pale gold. Remove from the heat. • Place the ricotta in a large bowl and add the syrup, liqueur, and vanilla. • Split the cake horizontally. Place one layer on a serving plate. Drizzle with 2 tablespoons rum. Spread with half the ricotta cream and sprinkle with half the chocolate. Top with the remaining layer. Drizzle with the remaining rum. Spread with the ricotta cream and sprinkle with the remaining chocolate. • Refrigerate for 2 hours.

Makes one cake · Prep: 20 min. · Level: 1 · Keeps: 1–2 days in the refrigerator

PEANUT-CHOCOLATE CHEESECAKE

1¹/₂   cups graham cracker crumbs
¹/₂   cup (1 stick) butter, melted
¹/₂   cup peanuts, finely chopped
¹/₄   cup firmly packed brown sugar
1   teaspoon ground nutmeg

FILLING
3   packages (8 oz each) cream cheese, softened
1   cup granulated sugar
³/₄   cup smooth peanut butter
2   tablespoons cornstarch
2   teaspoons vanilla extract
3   large eggs, at room temperature
¹/₄   cup sour cream
1   cup semisweet chocolate chips

Preheat the oven to 375°F . • Butter a 9-inch springform pan. • Mix the crumbs, butter, peanuts, sugar, and nutmeg in a medium bowl. • Press into the bottom and partway up the sides of the prepared pan. • Bake for 8–10 minutes, or until lightly browned. • Cool completely in the pan on a rack. • *Filling*: Reduce the oven temperature to 350°F . • Beat the cream cheese, sugar, peanut butter, cornstarch, and vanilla in a large bowl with an electric mixer at medium speed until smooth. • Add the eggs, one at a time, until just blended after each addition. • With mixer at low speed, beat in the sour cream. Add the chocolate chips. • Spoon the filling into the crust. • Bake for 45–55 minutes, or until set. • Cool in the pan on a rack. Refrigerate for 6 hours. Loosen and remove the pan sides to serve.

Makes one 9-inch cake · Prep: 25 min. + 6 hr. to chill · Cooking: 55–65 min. · Level: 1 · Keeps: 1–2 days

CHOCOLATE-MASCARPONE CAKE

CHOCOLATE MOUSSE
- 7 oz dark chocolate, coarsely chopped
- 4 large eggs, separated
- 1/3 cup + 1 tablespoon butter, melted
- 1/4 cup granulated sugar
- 4 teaspoons water
- 1/4 teaspoon cream of tartar

MASCARPONE MOUSSE
- 1 tablespoon unflavored gelatin
- 1/4 cup cold water + 4 teaspoons water
- 4 large eggs, separated
- 1/2 cup granulated sugar
- 1 cup mascarpone cheese
- 1/4 teaspoon cream of tartar
- 1 teaspoon almond extract
- 1 French Hazelnut Sponge Cake (see page 161) chocolate shavings, to decorate (see page 55)

Chocolate Mousse: Melt the chocolate in a double boiler over barely simmering water. • With mixer at medium speed, beat in the egg yolks. Cook over low heat, stirring constantly with a wooden spoon, until the mixture lightly coats a metal spoon or registers 160°F on an instant-read thermometer. Add the melted butter. Immediately plunge the pan into a bowl of ice water and stir until the chocolate mixture has cooled. • Stir the egg whites, 2 tablespoons sugar, water, and cream of tartar in a double boiler until blended. Cook over low heat, beating constantly with a hand-held mixer at low speed until the whites register 160°F on an instant-read thermometer. Transfer to a bowl and beat at high speed until frothy. With mixer at high speed, gradually beat in the remaining sugar, beating until stiff, glossy peaks form. • Use a large rubber spatula to fold them into the chocolate mixture. Set aside to cool completely. • Refrigerate for 3 hours, or until set. • *Mascarpone Mousse*: Sprinkle the gelatin over the water in a small saucepan. Let stand 1 minute. Stir over low heat until the gelatin has completely dissolved. Set aside. • Beat the egg yolks and 1/4 cup sugar in a double boiler until well blended. Cook the yolk mixture to 160°F as for the Chocolate Mousse, folding in the mascarpone when cooled. • Stir the egg whites, water, remaining 1/4 cup sugar, and cream of tartar in a double boiler until blended. Cook and beat the whites mixture as for the Chocolate Mousse until soft peaks form. Use a large rubber spatula to fold them into the

Chocolate-mascarpone cake

mascarpone mixture. Add the gelatin mixture and almond extract. • Place the cake in a 9-inch springform pan. Spoon the chocolate mousse on top. Spread with the mascarpone mousse. • Refrigerate for 6 hours. • Loosen and remove the pan sides to serve. Decorate with the chocolate shavings.

Makes one 9-inch cake · Prep: 50 min. + 9 hr. to chill · Level: 3 · Keeps: 1 day in the refrigerator

FUDGE BROWNIE CHEESECAKE

- 4 oz bittersweet chocolate, coarsely chopped
- 1/2 cup (1 stick) cold butter, cut up
- 1 1/2 cups granulated sugar
- 2 large eggs, at room temperature
- 1 cup all-purpose flour
- 1/4 teaspoon salt
- 1/4 cup milk
- 1 teaspoon vanilla extract
- 1/2 cup walnuts, coarsely chopped

FILLING
- 3 packages (8 oz each) cream cheese, softened
- 1/2 cup granulated sugar
- 2 teaspoons vanilla extract
- 1/2 cup sour cream
- 4 large eggs, at room temperature

Preheat the oven to 350°F. • Butter and flour a 10-inch springform pan. • Melt the chocolate and butter in a double boiler over barely simmering water. Set aside to cool for 15 minutes. • Transfer to a bowl. Beat in the sugar with an electric mixer at medium speed. • Add the eggs, one at a time, until just blended after each addition. • .With mixer at low speed, gradually beat in the flour and salt, alternating with the milk and vanilla extract. Stir in the walnuts. • Spoon the batter into the prepared pan. • Bake for 35–40 minutes, or until set. • Cool completely in the pan on a rack. • *Filling*: With mixer at medium speed, beat the cream cheese, sugar, and vanilla in a large bowl until smooth. Add the sour cream. and the eggs, one at a time, until just blended after each addition. • Spoon the filling over the brownie. • Bake for 55–65 minutes, or until set. • Cool the cake in the pan on a rack. Refrigerate for 6 hours. Let stand for 30 minutes. Loosen and remove the pan sides to serve.

Makes one 10-inch cake · Prep: 1 hr. + 6 hr. to chill · Cooking: 90–100 min. · Level: 2 · Keeps: 1–2 days in the refrigerator

ALMOND CHEESECAKE

1½ cups graham cracker crumbs
½ cup almonds, finely chopped
¼ cup (½ stick) butter, melted
2 tablespoons brown sugar

FILLING

3 packages (8 oz each) cream cheese, softened
¾ cup granulated sugar
2 teaspoons vanilla extract
2 teaspoons almond extract
3 large eggs, at room temperature

Butter a 9-inch springform pan. • Mix the crumbs, almonds, butter, and sugar in a medium bowl. • Press into the bottom and partway up the sides of the prepared pan. • Refrigerate for 30 minutes. • *Filling*: Preheat the oven to 350°F. • Beat the cream cheese, sugar, vanilla, and almond extract in a large bowl with an electric mixer at medium speed until smooth. • Add the eggs, one at a time, until just blended after each addition. • Spoon the filling into the crust. • Bake for 40–50 minutes, or until set. • Cool the cake in the pan on a rack. Refrigerate for 6 hours. • Loosen and remove the pan sides to serve.

Makes one 9-inch cake · Prep: 25 min. + 6 hr. 30 min. to chill · Cooking: 40–50 min. · Level: 1 · Keeps: 1–2 days in the refrigerator

CHOCOLATE-ALMOND CHEESECAKE

1 cup graham cracker crumbs
½ cup toasted almonds, coarsely ground
½ cup granulated sugar
2 tablespoons butter, melted
½ teaspoon almond extract

FILLING

6 oz bittersweet chocolate, coarsely chopped
3 packages (8 oz each) cream cheese, softened
1 cup granulated sugar
1 teaspoon almond extract
½ teaspoon vanilla extract
4 large eggs, at room temperature

TOPPING

1 cup heavy cream
2 tablespoons confectioners' sugar
1 oz bittersweet chocolate, coarsely grated

Butter a 9-inch springform pan. • Mix the crumbs, almonds, sugar, butter, and almond extract in a medium bowl. • Press into the bottom and partway up the side of the prepared pan. Refrigerate for 30 minutes. • *Filling*: Melt the chocolate in a double boiler over barely simmering water. Set aside to cool. • Preheat the oven to 350°F. • Beat the cream cheese, sugar, almond extract, and vanilla in a large bowl with an

electric mixer at medium speed until smooth. • Add the eggs, one at a time, until just blended after each addition. • With mixer at low speed, beat in the chocolate. • Spoon the filling into the crust. • Bake for 55–65 minutes, or until set. • Cool the cake in the pan on a rack. Refrigerate for 6 hours. • *Topping*: With mixer at high speed, beat the cream and confectioners' sugar in a small bowl until stiff. • Loosen and remove the pan sides. Spread with cream and sprinkle with the chocolate.

Makes one 9-inch cake · Prep: 30 min. + 6 hr. 30 min. to chill · Cooking: 55–65 min. · Level: 1 · Keeps: 1–2 days in the refrigerator

LIGHT CHOCOLATE ALMOND CAKE

8 chocolate wafer cookies, finely crushed
2 packages (8 oz each) light cream cheese, softened
1 cup granulated sugar
1 cup part-skim ricotta cheese
2 large eggs, at room temperature
⅓ cup unsweetened cocoa powder
¼ cup all-purpose flour
2 teaspoons almond extract
1 teaspoon vanilla extract
2 tablespoons miniature semisweet chocolate chips

Preheat the oven to 350°F. • Butter a 9-inch springform pan. • Sprinkle the crumbs into the pan. • Beat the cream cheese, sugar, and ricotta in a large bowl with an electric mixer at medium speed until smooth. • Add the eggs, one at a time, until just blended after each addition. With mixer at low speed, gradually beat in the cocoa, flour, almond extract, and vanilla. Stir in the chocolate chips. • Spoon the filling into the crust. • Bake for 45–55 minutes, or until set. • Cool in the pan on a rack. Refrigerate for 6 hours. Loosen and remove the pan sides to serve.

Makes one 9-inch cake · Prep: 30 min. + 6 hr. to chill · Cooking: 45–55 min. · Level: 1 · Keeps: 1–2 days in the refrigerator

CHOCOLATE HAZELNUT CHEESECAKE

2 cups shortbread cookies or vanilla wafers
½ cup hazelnuts, toasted and peeled
¼ cup granulated sugar
½ teaspoon vanilla extract
⅓ cup butter, softened

FILLING

3 packages (8 oz each) cream cheese, softened
1 cup chocolate hazelnut cream (Nutella)
½ cup granulated sugar
1 tablespoon hazelnut liqueur
2 teaspoons vanilla extract

4 large eggs, at room temperature
1 cup sour cream

TOPPING

1 cup heavy cream
2 tablespoons granulated sugar
½ cup hazelnuts, toasted and peeled, coarsely chopped

Butter a 10-inch springform pan. • Process the cookies, hazelnuts, sugar, and vanilla until finely chopped. • Add the butter and process until moist lumps form. • Press into the bottom and partway up the sides of the prepared pan. • Refrigerate for 30 minutes. • *Filling*: Preheat the oven to 350°F. • Beat the cream cheese, chocolate hazelnut cream, liqueur, sugar, and vanilla in a large bowl with an electric mixer at medium speed until smooth. • Add the eggs, one at a time, until just blended after each addition. • Add the sour cream until smooth. • Spoon the filling into the crust. • Bake for 60–70 minutes, or until set. • Cool the cake in the pan on a rack. Refrigerate for 6 hours. • *Topping*: With mixer at high speed, beat the cream and sugar in a medium bowl until stiff. Loosen and remove the pan sides. Spread the top with the cream. Sprinkle with the hazelnuts.

Makes one 10-inch cake · Prep: 30 min. + 6 hr. 30 min. to chill · Cooking: 60–70 min. · Level: 1 · Keeps: 1–2 days in the refrigerator

CHOCOLATE-COFFEE CHEESECAKE

2 cups chocolate cookie crumbs
⅓ cup confectioners' sugar
⅓ cup unsweetened cocoa powder
¼ cup (½ stick) butter, melted

FILLING

3 packages (8 oz each) cream cheese, softened
1¼ cups granulated sugar
⅓ cup unsweetened cocoa powder
3 tablespoons cornstarch
1 teaspoon vanilla extract
3 large eggs, at room temperature
½ cup sour cream
¼ cup coffee liqueur

TOPPING

1 cup heavy cream
2 tablespoons confectioners' sugar
2 teaspoons coffee liqueur
1 tablespoon whole coffee beans, to decorate

Preheat the oven to 350°F. • Butter a 9-inch springform pan. • Mix the crumbs, confectioners' sugar, cocoa, and butter in a medium bowl. • Press into the bottom and partway up the sides of the prepared pan. Bake for 10 minutes, or until lightly browned. Cool the crust completely in the pan on a rack. • *Filling*: Beat the cream cheese, sugar, cocoa, cornstarch, and vanilla in a large bowl with an electric mixer at medium speed until smooth. • Add the eggs, one at a time, until just blended after each addition. • With mixer at low speed, beat in the sour cream and liqueur. • Spoon the filling into the crust. • Bake for 50–60 minutes, or until set. • Cool in the pan on a rack. Refrigerate for 6 hours. • *Topping*: With mixer at high speed, beat the cream, confectioners' sugar, and liqueur in a medium bowl until stiff. Spoon into a pastry bag. Loosen and remove the pan sides. Pipe the cream in a decorative manner over the cheesecake. Decorate with coffee beans.

Makes one 9-inch cake · Prep: 35 min.+ 6 hr. to chill · Cooking: 60–70 min. · Level: 1 · Keeps: 1–2 days in the refrigerator

MOCHA CHEESECAKE

A creamy, light cheesecake with mocha flavor.

1³/₄ cups chocolate wafer crumbs
¹/₄ cup (¹/₂ stick) butter, melted
2 tablespoons granulated sugar
1 teaspoon ground cinnamon

FILLING
8 oz semisweet chocolate, coarsely chopped
2 tablespoons heavy cream
3 packages (8 oz each) cream cheese, softened
1 cup granulated sugar
3 large eggs, at room temperature
1 cup sour cream
¹/₄ cup coffee liqueur
2 teaspoons freeze-dried coffee granules, dissolved in ¹/₄ cup strong hot coffee
2 teaspoons vanilla extract

TOPPING
1 cup heavy cream
2 tablespoons confectioners' sugar
2 tablespoons coffee liqueur
2 oz semisweet chocolate, coarsely grated

Preheat the oven to 350°F. • Butter a 10-inch springform pan. • Mix the crumbs, butter, sugar, and cinnamon in a medium bowl. • Press into the bottom and partway up the sides of the prepared pan. • *Filling*: Melt the chocolate in a double boiler over barely simmering water. Stir in the cream and set aside to cool. • Beat the cream cheese and sugar in a large bowl with an electric mixer at high speed until creamy. • With mixer at medium speed, add the eggs, one at a time, until just blended after each addition. •

With mixer at low speed, beat in the chocolate mixture. • Add the sour cream, coffee liqueur, coffee mixture, and vanilla. • Spoon the filling into the crust. • Bake for 55–65 minutes, or until set. • Cool the cake in the pan on a rack. Refrigerate for 6 hours. • *Topping*: With mixer at high speed, beat the cream, confectioners' sugar, and coffee liqueur in a medium bowl until stiff. Loosen and remove the pan sides. Spread with the cream and sprinkle with chocolate.

Makes one 10-inch cake · Prep: 30 min. + 6 hr. to chill · Cooking: 55–65 min. · Level: 1 · Keeps: 1–2 days in the refrigerator

IRISH CREAM CHEESECAKE

2 cups graham cracker crumbs
¹/₃ cup butter, melted
¹/₄ cup firmly packed brown sugar

FILLING
4 packages (8 oz each) cream cheese, softened
1¹/₂ cups granulated sugar
1 tablespoon vanilla extract
5 large eggs, at room temperature
1 cup Irish cream liqueur
³/₄ cup semisweet chocolate chips

TOPPING
1 cup heavy cream
2 tablespoons confectioners' sugar
2 teaspoons freeze-dried coffee granules
2 tablespoons whole coffee beans, to decorate

Preheat the oven to 350°F. • Butter a 10-inch springform pan. • Mix the crumbs, butter, and brown sugar in a medium bowl. • Press into the bottom and partway up the sides of the prepared pan. • Bake for 8–10 minutes, or until lightly browned. • Cool the crust completely in the pan on a rack. • *Filling*: Beat the cream cheese, sugar, and vanilla in

Mocha cheesecake

a large bowl with an electric mixer at medium speed until creamy. • Add the eggs, one at a time, until just blended after each addition. • With mixer at low speed, beat in the liqueur and chocolate chips. • Spoon the filling into the crust. • Bake for 65–70 minutes, or until set. • Cool completely in the pan on a rack. Refrigerate for 6 hours. • *Topping*: With mixer at high speed, beat the cream, confectioners' sugar, and coffee granules in a medium bowl until stiff. Loosen and remove the pan sides. Spread with the cream. Sprinkle with coffee beans.

Makes one 10-inch cake · Prep: 30 min. + 6 hr. to chill · Cooking: 65–70 min. · Level: 1 · Keeps: 1–2 days in the refrigerator

ORANGE CREAM CHEESECAKE

2 cups graham cracker crumbs
¹/₃ cup butter, melted
¹/₄ cup firmly packed brown sugar

FILLING
4 packages (8 oz each) cream cheese, softened
1¹/₂ cups granulated sugar
1 tablespoon vanilla extract
5 large eggs, at room temperature
1 cup orange liqueur
³/₄ cup semisweet chocolate chips

TOPPING
1 cup heavy cream
2 tablespoons confectioners' sugar
2 teaspoons orange liqueur

Prepare this cake following the instructions for Irish Cream Cheesecake, substituting the orange liqueur for the Irish cream liqueur and for the coffee granules in the topping.

Makes one 10-inch cake · Prep: 30 min. + 4 hr. to chill · Cooking: 65–70 min. · Level: 1 · Keeps: 1–2 days in the refrigerator

CHOCOLATE LIQUEUR SUICIDE CAKE

This fabulous cheesecake is even better when served with Raspberry Coulis (see page 350).

1 1/2 cups graham cracker crumbs
3/4 cup toasted almonds or hazelnuts, finely chopped
7 tablespoons butter, melted
1/4 cup granulated sugar
6 oz semisweet chocolate, coarsely chopped

FILLING

1 lb bittersweet chocolate, coarsely chopped
1 1/2 cups heavy cream
1/4 cup unsweetened cocoa powder
3/4 cup Irish cream liqueur
4 packages (8 oz each) cream cheese, softened
1 cup granulated sugar
1 teaspoon vanilla extract
4 large eggs, at room temperature

TOPPING

1 cup heavy cream
2 tablespoons granulated sugar
1/2 teaspoon vanilla extract

Preheat the oven to 350°F. • Butter a 10-inch springform pan. • Mix the crumbs, nuts, butter, and sugar in a medium bowl. • Press into the bottom and partway up the sides of the prepared pan. • Bake for 8–10 minutes, or until lightly browned. • Cool the crust completely in the pan on a rack. • Melt the semisweet chocolate in a double boiler over barely simmering water. Set aside to cool. Pour the chocolate into the crust. Freeze for 15 minutes. • *Filling*: Melt the chocolate in a double boiler over barely simmering water. Set aside to cool. • Warm 1/2 cup cream in a saucepan over low heat. Add the cocoa. Cook, stirring constantly, until the cream begins to thicken. Remove

Rum raisin cheesecake

from the heat. Add the liqueur and remaining 1 cup cream and set aside to cool. • Beat the cream cheese, sugar, and vanilla in a large bowl with an electric mixer at medium speed until smooth. • Add the eggs, one at a time, until just blended after each addition. • With mixer at low speed, beat in the cocoa mixture and chocolate. • Spoon the filling into the crust. • Bake for 50–60 minutes, or until set. • Cool in the pan on the rack. Refrigerate for 6 hours. • *Topping*: With mixer at high speed, beat the cream, sugar, and vanilla until stiff. Spoon the cream into a pastry bag. Loosen and remove the pan sides. Pipe the cream in a decorative manner over the cake.

Makes one 10-inch cake · Prep: 45 min. + 6 hr. to chill · Cooking: 60–70 min. · Level: 2 · Keeps: 1–2 days in the refrigerator

RUM-RAISIN CHEESECAKE

2 cups old-fashioned rolled oats
1/2 cup firmly packed brown sugar
1/4 cup (1/2 stick) tablespoons butter, melted

FILLING

1 lb cream cheese, softened
1/2 cup granulated sugar
2 tablespoons all-purpose flour
2 large eggs, at room temperature
1/2 cup sour cream
3 tablespoons dark rum

TOPPING

3 tablespoons cold butter, cut up
2 tablespoons all-purpose flour
1/2 cup firmly packed brown sugar
1/2 cup raisins
1/2 cup chopped nuts
2 tablespoons old-fashioned rolled oats

Preheat the oven to 350°F • Butter a 9-inch springform pan. • Mix the oats, brown sugar, and butter in a medium bowl. Press into the bottom and partway up the sides of the prepared pan. Bake for 15 minutes. Cool completely in the pan on a rack. • *Filling*: Beat the cream cheese, sugar, and flour in a large bowl with an electric mixer at medium speed. • Add the eggs, one at a time, until just blended after each addition. • With mixer at low speed, beat in the sour cream and rum. • Spoon the filling into the crust. • *Topping*: Use a pastry blender to cut the butter into the flour and brown sugar until the mixture resembles coarse crumbs. • Stir in the raisins, nuts, and oats. • Sprinkle the cake with the topping. Bake for 40–50 minutes, or until set. • Cool the cake in the pan on a rack. Refrigerate for 6 hours. Loosen and remove the pan sides to serve.

Makes one 9-inch round cake · Prep: 35 min. + 6 hr to chill · Cooking: 40–50 min. · Level: 1 · Keeps: 1–2 days

CHRISTMAS EGGNOG CHEESECAKE

2 cups graham cracker crumbs
1/3 cup butter, melted
1/4 cup firmly packed brown sugar
1 teaspoon ground cinnamon

FILLING

2 tablespoons unflavored gelatin
1 1/4 cups prepared eggnog
3 large eggs, separated
1/2 cup granulated sugar
1 container (15-16 oz) ricotta cheese
2 packages (8 oz each) cream cheese, softened
1 tablespoon water
1/4 teaspoon cream of tartar
1 cup heavy cream
2 teaspoons vanilla extract

Preheat the oven to 350°F. • Butter a 10-inch springform pan. • Mix the crumbs, butter, brown sugar, and cinnamon in a medium bowl. • Press into the bottom and partway up the sides of the prepared pan. • Bake for 8–10 minutes, or until lightly browned. • Cool completely in the pan on a rack. • *Filling*: Sprinkle the gelatin over 1/4 cup eggnog in a small saucepan. Let stand 1 minute. Stir over low heat until completely dissolved. • Beat the egg yolks and 1/4 cup sugar in a double boiler until the sugar has dissolved. Add the remaining eggnog.

Chocolate chip–amaretto cake

Place over barely simmering water and cook gently, beating constantly, until the mixture lightly coats a metal spoon or registers 160°F on an instant-read thermometer. Immediately plunge the pan into a bowl of ice water and stir until the egg mixture has cooled. • Add the gelatin mixture. • Beat the ricotta and cream cheese in a large bowl with an electric mixer at medium speed until creamy. Add the eggnog mixture. • Stir the egg whites, remaining $\frac{1}{4}$ cup sugar, water, and cream of tartar in a saucepan until blended. Cook over low heat until the whites register 160°F on an instant-read thermometer. Transfer to a large bowl and beat until stiff peaks form. Use a large rubber spatula to fold them into the ricotta mixture. • With mixer at high speed, beat the cream and vanilla until stiff. Use the spatula to fold the cream into the ricotta mixture. • Spoon the filling into the crust. Refrigerate for 6 hours. • Loosen and remove the pan sides.

Makes one 10-inch cake · Prep: 50 min. + 6 hr. to chill · Cooking: 10 min. · Level: 2 · Keeps: 1–2 days in the refrigerator

CHOCOLATE CHEESECAKE

- 2 cups graham cracker crumbs
- $\frac{1}{3}$ cup butter, melted
- 1 teaspoon ground cinnamon

FILLING
- 10 oz semisweet chocolate, coarsely chopped
- $\frac{3}{4}$ cup sour cream
- 2 tablespoons unsweetened cocoa powder
- 1 tablespoon chocolate or coffee liqueur
- 4 packages (8 oz each) cream cheese, softened

- 1 cup granulated sugar
- 4 large eggs, at room temperature

Preheat the oven to 350°F. • Butter a 10-inch springform pan. • Mix the crumbs, butter, and cinnamon in a medium bowl. Press into the bottom and partway up the sides of the prepared pan. • *Filling*: Melt the chocolate in a double boiler over barely simmering water. Set aside to cool. • Mix the sour cream, cocoa, and liqueur in a small bowl. • Beat the cream cheese and sugar with an electric mixer at medium speed until creamy. Add the eggs, one at a time, until just blended after each addition. • Stir in the sour cream mixture, followed by the melted chocolate. • Spoon the filling into the crust. • Bake for 50–60 minutes, or until set. • Cool the cake in the pan on a rack. • Refrigerate for 6 hours. Loosen and remove the pan sides to serve.

Makes one 10-inch cheesecake · Prep: 25 min. + 6 hr. to chill· Cooking: 50–60 min. · Level: 1 · Keeps: 1–2 days in the refrigerator

CHOCOLATE CHIP–AMARETTO CAKE

- 2 cups crushed amaretti cookies
- $\frac{1}{2}$ cup almonds, finely chopped
- $\frac{1}{2}$ cup (1 stick) butter, melted

FILLING
- 3 packages (8 oz each) cream cheese, softened
- 1 cup granulated sugar
- 2 tablespoons cornstarch
- 3 large eggs, at room temperature
- 3 tablespoons amaretto
- 1 tablespoon vanilla extract
- $\frac{3}{4}$ cup semisweet chocolate chips

Preheat the oven to 400°F. • Butter a 10-inch springform pan. • Mix the crumbs,

almonds, and butter in a medium bowl. • Press into the bottom and partway up the sides of the prepared pan. • Bake for 8–10 minutes, or until lightly browned. Cool the crust completely in the pan on a rack. • *Filling*: Beat the cream cheese, sugar, and cornstarch in a large bowl with an electric mixer at medium speed until smooth. • Add the eggs, one at a time, until just blended after each addition. • With mixer at low speed, beat in the amaretto and vanilla. Stir in the chocolate chips. • Spoon the filling into the crust. • Bake for 50–60 minutes, or until set. • Cool the cake in the pan on a rack. Refrigerate for 6 hours. Loosen and remove the pan sides to serve.

Makes one 10-inch cake · Prep: 2 min. + 6 hr. to chill · Cooking: 50–60 min. · Level: 1 · Keeps: 1–2 days in the refrigerator

AMARETTO CHEESECAKE

This would be great served with tiny cups of espresso laced with a shot of amaretto.

- $1\frac{3}{4}$ cups finely crushed amaretti cookies
- $\frac{1}{2}$ cup toasted almonds, finely chopped
- $\frac{1}{3}$ cup butter, melted

FILLING
- 2 packages (8 oz each) cream cheese, softened
- $\frac{3}{4}$ cup granulated sugar
- 3 large eggs, at room temperature
- $\frac{3}{4}$ cup sour cream
- 2 tablespoons amaretto
- 1 teaspoon vanilla extract

Preheat the oven to 350°F. • Butter a 9-inch springform pan. • Mix the crumbs, almonds, and butter in a medium bowl. • Press into the bottom and partway up the sides of the prepared pan. • Bake for 8–10 minutes, or until lightly browned. Cool the crust completely in the pan on the rack. • *Filling*: Beat the cream cheese and sugar in a large bowl with an electric mixer at medium speed until creamy. • Add the eggs, one at a time, until just blended after each addition. • With mixer at low speed, beat in the sour cream, amaretto, and vanilla. • Spoon the filling into the crust. • Bake for 50–60 minutes, or until set. • Cool the cake in the pan on a rack. Refrigerate for 6 hours. Loosen and remove the pan sides to serve.

Makes one 9-inch cake · Prep: 25 min. + 4 hr. to chill · Cooking: 50–60 min. · Level: 1 · Keeps: 1–2 days

White chocolate and raspberry cheesecake

WHITE CHOCOLATE AND RASPBERRY CHEESECAKE

    2   cups graham cracker crumbs
  1/3   cup butter, melted
  1/4   cup granulated sugar

FILLING

    8   oz white chocolate, coarsely chopped
    1   lb cream cheese, softened
  3/4   cup granulated sugar
    2   large eggs, at room temperature
  1/2   cup raspberry jelly or preserves, warmed
    3   tablespoons raspberry liqueur
  1/2   teaspoon red food coloring

TOPPING

   13   oz white chocolate, coarsely chopped
   12   oz cream cheese, softened
    2   tablespoons fresh lemon juice
    1   cup raspberry jelly or preserves

Butter a 9-inch springform pan. • Mix the crumbs, butter, and sugar in a medium bowl. Press into the bottom and partway up the sides of the prepared pan. • *Filling*: Preheat the oven to 350°F. • Melt the chocolate in a double boiler over barely simmering water. Set aside to cool. • Beat the cream cheese and sugar in a large bowl with an electric mixer at medium speed until fluffy. Add the eggs, one at a time, until just blended after each addition. Add the chocolate. • Reserve 1/4 cup of the filling. Spoon the remaining filling into the crust. • Stir the jelly, raspberry liqueur, and food coloring into the reserved filling. Use a metal spatula to spread the jelly mixture over the filling. • Bake for 50–60 minutes, or until set. • Cool the cake in the pan on a rack. Refrigerate overnight. • *Topping*: Melt the white chocolate in a double boiler over barely simmering water. Set aside to cool. • Transfer the chocolate to a large bowl. With mixer at low speed, add the cream cheese and lemon juice. • Loosen and remove the pan sides. • Use a metal spatula to spread the topping over. • Refrigerate for 1 hour. • Melt the jelly in a saucepan over low heat. Spread over the topping. • Refrigerate for 30 minutes, or until set.

Makes one 9-inch cake · Prep: 1 hr. + 13 hr. to chill · Cooking: 50–60 min. · Level: 3 · Keeps: 1–2 days in the refrigerator

CHOCOLATE CREAM CHEESECAKE

    1   cup chocolate wafer crumbs
  1/2   cup toasted pecans or hazelnuts, coarsely ground
  1/3   cup granulated sugar
    2   tablespoons butter, melted
  1/2   teaspoon vanilla extract

FILLING

    8   oz bittersweet chocolate, coarsely chopped
    2   packages (8 oz each) cream cheese, softened
  3/4   cup granulated sugar
    1   teaspoon vanilla extract
    4   large eggs, at room temperature
 1 1/2 cups sour cream

TOPPING

  1/2   cup heavy cream
  1/4   cup sour cream
    1   tablespoon granulated sugar
    1   tablespoon coffee liqueur
        chocolate leaves, (see page 55), to decorate

Butter a 9-inch springform pan. • Mix the crumbs, nuts, sugar, butter, and vanilla in a large bowl. • Press into the bottom and partway up the sides of the prepared pan. Refrigerate for 30 minutes. • *Filling*: Melt the chocolate in a double boiler over barely simmering water. Set aside to cool. • Preheat the oven to 350°F. • Beat the cream cheese, sugar, and vanilla in a large bowl with an electric mixer at medium speed until smooth. • Add the eggs, one at a time, until just blended after each addition. • With mixer at low speed, beat in the chocolate and sour cream. • Spoon the filling into the crust. • Bake for 50–60 minutes, or until set. • Cool the cake in the pan on a rack. Refrigerate for 6 hours. • *Topping*: With mixer at high speed, beat the cream, sour cream, sugar, and liqueur in a medium bowl until stiff. • Loosen and remove the pan sides. Spread the top with the cream. Decorate with the chocolate leaves.

Makes one 9-inch cake · Prep: 30 min. + 6 hr. 30 min. to chill · Cooking: 50–60 min. · Level: 1 · Keeps: 1–2 days in the refrigerator

CRÈME DE CASSIS AND WHITE CHOCOLATE CHEESECAKE

    2   cups shortbread or butter cookie crumbs
  1/4   cup granulated sugar
  1/4   cup (1/2 stick) butter, melted

FILLING

    4   packages (8 oz each) cream cheese, softened
    1   cup granulated sugar
    4   large eggs, at room temperature
    4   oz white chocolate, grated
    2   tablespoons crème de cassis

Mascarpone mold

- 1 cup sour cream
- 1/4 cup granulated sugar
- 1 teaspoon crème de cassis
- 1/2 cup fresh black currants or raspberries
- 2 oz white chocolate, grated

Butter a 10-inch springform pan. • Mix the crumbs, sugar, and butter in a medium bowl. • Press into the bottom and partway up the sides of the prepared pan. Refrigerate for 30 minutes. • *Filling*: Preheat the oven to 350°F. • Beat the cream cheese and sugar in a large bowl with an electric mixer at medium speed until creamy. • Add the eggs, one at a time, until just blended after each addition. • With mixer at low speed, beat in the white chocolate and liqueur. • Spoon the filling into the crust. • Bake for 50–60 minutes, or until set. Cool the cake in the pan for 15 minutes. • *Topping*: With mixer at medium speed, beat the sour cream, sugar, and liqueur in a small bowl. Spread the topping over. • Bake for 10 minutes more. • Cool in the pan on a rack. Refrigerate for 6 hours. Loosen and remove the pan sides. • Top with the black currants and sprinkle with the chocolate.

Makes one 10-inch cake · Prep: 30 min. + 6 hr. and 30 min. to chill · Cooking: 60–70 min. · Level: 1 · Keeps: 1–2 days in the refrigerator

MASCARPONE MOLD

- 2 cups mascarpone cheese
- 1 cup heavy cream
- 1 cup confectioners' sugar
- 1/2 teaspoon ground cinnamon
- 14 oz ladyfingers
- 2 tablespoons Alchermes liqueur, or Marsala wine
- 2 cups Zabaglione (see page 348)

Line an 8-inch mold with waxed paper. • Use a large rubber spatula to mix the mascarpone, cream, confectioners' sugar, and cinnamon in a large bowl. Line with 1/3 of the ladyfingers and drizzle with 1/3 of the liqueur. • Spread with half the mascarpone mixture. • Repeat until the mold is packed, finishing with ladyfingers. • Refrigerate for 4 hours, or until set. • Dip the mold into a cold water. Invert onto a serving plate. Serve with the zabaglione passed on the side.

Makes one 8-inch mold · Prep: 25 min. + 4 hr. to chill · Level: 1 · Keeps: 3–4 days in the refrigerator

MARBLED CHOCOLATE AND RASPBERRY CHEESECAKE

- 1 1/2 cups all-purpose flour
- 1/4 cup granulated sugar
- 1/4 teaspoon salt
- 1/3 cup cold unsalted butter, cut up about 2 tablespoons ice water

FILLING

- 8 oz semisweet chocolate, coarsely chopped
- 4 packages (8 oz each) cream cheese, softened
- 1 cup granulated sugar
- 6 large eggs, at room temperature
- 1/4 cup all-purpose flour
- 2 tablespoons raspberry liqueur

Mix the flour, sugar, and salt in a large bowl. Use a pastry blender to cut in the butter until the mixture resembles coarse crumbs. Gradually drizzle in the ice water until a smooth dough is formed. Press into a disk, wrap in plastic wrap, and refrigerate for 30 minutes. • Preheat the oven to 350°F. • Roll the dough out on a lightly floured surface into an 11-inch round. Press into the bottom and partway up the sides of a 10-inch springform pan. Prick all over with a fork. • Bake for 15 minutes, or until golden. Cool the crust in the pan on a rack. • *Filling*: Melt the chocolate in a double boiler over barely simmering water. Let cool. • Beat the cream cheese and sugar with an electric mixer at medium speed until creamy. Add the eggs, one at a time, until just blended after each addition. With mixer at low speed, gradually beat in the flour and raspberry liqueur. • Spoon 2/3 of the filling into the crust. • Mash 1 1/2 cups of the raspberries with a fork. Stir the mashed raspberries and chocolate into the remaining filling. • Drop spoonfuls of the chocolate batter into the filling at regular intervals. Use a knife to swirl the batter to create a marbled effect. Place the pan on a baking sheet. • Bake for 75–85 minutes, or until set and golden brown. • Cool the cake in the pan on a rack. • Refrigerate for 6 hours. • Loosen and remove the pan sides.

Makes one 10-inch cheesecake · Prep: 1 hr. + 6 hr. 30 min. to chill · Cooking: 75–85 min. · Level: 2 · Keeps: 1–2 days in the refrigerator

CHOCOLATE-BOTTOM CHEESECAKES

These delightful little cheesecakes are ideal for a party or open house.

2 cups chocolate wafer crumbs
1/3 cup butter, melted
3 tablespoons granulated sugar
1 teaspoon vanilla extract

FILLING
2 packages (8 oz each) cream cheese, softened
1 1/4 cups sweetened condensed milk
2 tablespoons butter, softened
1 1/2 teaspoons vanilla extract
2 large eggs, at room temperature

GLAZE
6 oz semisweet chocolate, coarsely chopped
1/2 cup heavy cream
1/2 teaspoon vanilla extract

Line two 12-cup muffin pans with paper baking cups. • Mix the crumbs, butter, sugar, and vanilla in a medium bowl. • Press about 1 tablespoon mixture into each prepared cup. • *Filling*: Preheat the oven to 300°F. • Beat the cream cheese, condensed milk, butter, and vanilla in a large bowl with an electric mixer at medium speed until smooth. • Add the eggs, one at a time, until just blended after each addition. • Spoon the filling evenly into the cups, filling each almost to the top. • Bake for 30–40 minutes, or until set. • Cool the cakes in the cups on racks. Refrigerate for 4 hours. • *Glaze*: Melt the chocolate with the cream, and vanilla in a double boiler over barely simmering water. Set aside to cool until warm. Drizzle the glaze over each cake. • Freeze for 15 minutes.

Makes 24 cakes · Prep: 30 min. + 4 hr. 15 min. to chill · Cooking: 30–40 min. · Level: 1 · Keeps: 1–2 days in the refrigerator

CARAMEL CHOCOLATE-CHIP CAKE

1 cup old-fashioned rolled oats
1 cup pecans, coarsely chopped
1 cup firmly packed brown sugar
1/3 cup butter, melted
1 teaspoon ground cinnamon

FILLING
3 packages (8 oz each) cream cheese, softened
1/2 cup firmly packed brown sugar
1/3 cup corn syrup
2 tablespoons cornstarch
2 teaspoons vanilla extract
4 large eggs, at room temperature
1 cup miniature semisweet chocolate chips

Preheat the oven to 350°F. • Butter a 10-inch springform pan. • Mix the oats, pecans, nuts, brown sugar, butter, and cinnamon in a medium bowl. • Press into the bottom and partway up the sides of the prepared pan. • Bake for 15–20 minutes, or until lightly browned. • Cool completely in the pan on the rack. • *Filling*: Beat the cream cheese, brown sugar, corn syrup, cornstarch, and vanilla in a large bowl with an electric mixer at medium speed until creamy. • Add the eggs, one at a time, until just blended after each addition. Stir in the chocolate chips. • Spoon the filling into the crust. • Bake for 15 minutes. Lower the oven temperature to 250°F and bake for 40–50 minutes more, or until set. • Cool the cake in the pan on a rack. Refrigerate for 6 hours. Loosen and remove the pan sides to serve.

Makes one 10-inch cake · Prep: 30 min. + 6 hr. to chill · Cooking: 75–85 min. · Level: 1 · Keeps: 1–2 days in the refrigerator

NUTTY CARAMEL CHEESECAKE

1 1/2 cups graham cracker crumbs
1/2 cup toasted nuts, such as walnuts, pecans, or macadamia nuts, finely chopped
1/4 cup firmly packed brown sugar
1/4 cup (1/2 stick) butter, melted
1 teaspoon ground cinnamon
1 teaspoon ground nutmeg

FILLING
2 packages (8 oz each) cream cheese, softened
1/2 cup granulated sugar
1 teaspoon vanilla extract
2 large eggs, at room temperature

TOPPING
1/3 cup caramel ice cream topping
1 cup mixed toasted nuts, finely chopped

Preheat the oven to 350°F. • Butter a 9-inch springform pan. • Mix the crumbs, nuts, brown sugar, butter, cinnamon, and nutmeg in a medium bowl. • Press into the bottom and partway up the sides of the prepared pan. • Bake for 8–10 minutes, or until lightly browned. • Cool completely in the pan on a rack. • *Filling*: Beat the cream cheese, sugar, and vanilla in a large bowl with an electric mixer at medium speed until creamy. • Add the eggs, one at a time, until just blended after each addition. • Spoon the filling into the crust. • Bake for 40–50 minutes, or until set. • Cool the cake in the pan on a rack. • *Topping*: Mix the caramel topping and nuts in a small bowl. Spread the topping over. Refrigerate for 6 hours. Loosen and remove the pan sides to serve.

Makes one 9-inch cake · Prep: 30 min. + 6 hr. to chill · Cooking: 50–60 min. · Level: 1 · Keeps: 1–2 days in the refrigerator

CARAMEL CHEESECAKE

Butterscotch extract can be obtained from various sources found on the Internet.

1 cup graham cracker crumbs
1/4 cup firmly packed brown sugar
1/4 cup (1/2 stick) butter, melted
1 teaspoon vanilla extract

FILLING
3 packages (8 oz each) cream cheese, softened
1 cup firmly packed brown sugar
1 teaspoon vanilla extract
1 teaspoon butterscotch extract (optional)
3 large eggs, at room temperature
1/2 cup sour cream
1/2 cup toasted macadamia nuts, coarsely chopped

TOPPING
1 1/2 cups sour cream
1/4 cup firmly packed brown sugar
1 teaspoon butterscotch or vanilla extract

Preheat the oven to 350°F. • Butter a 9-inch springform pan. • Mix the crumbs, brown sugar, butter, and vanilla in a large bowl. • Press into the bottom and partway up the sides of the prepared pan. • Bake for 8–10 minutes, or until lightly browned. • Cool completely in the pan on a rack. • *Filling*: Beat the cream cheese, brown sugar, vanilla and butterscotch extracts in a large bowl with an electric mixer at medium speed until creamy. • Add the eggs, one at a time, until just blended after each addition. • With mixer at low speed, add the sour cream. Add the nuts. • Spoon into the crust. • Bake for 35–45 minutes, or until set. • *Topping*: With mixer at medium speed, beat the sour cream, sugar, and butterscotch extract in a medium bowl. Spread the topping over. • Bake for 10 minutes, or until set. • Cool the cake in the pan on a rack. Refrigerate for 6 hours.

Makes one 9-inch cake · Prep: 25 min. + 6 hr. to chill · Cooking: 55–65 min. · Level: 1 · Keeps: 1–2 days in the refrigerator

TOFFEE-TOPPED CHEESECAKE

- 1½ cups graham cracker crumbs
- ¼ cup granulated sugar
- ¼ cup (½ stick) butter, melted
- 1 teaspoon ground cinnamon

FILLING

- 3 packages (8 oz each) cream cheese, softened
- 1 cup granulated sugar
- 2 teaspoons vanilla extract
- 4 large eggs, at room temperature
- ½ cup sour cream
- 8 oz toffee candies (such as Werther's Original), crushed in a food processor

Preheat the oven to 325°F. • Butter a 9-inch springform pan. • Mix the crumbs, sugar, butter, and cinnamon in a large bowl. • Press into the bottom and partway up the sides of the prepared pan. • Bake for 8–10 minutes, or until lightly browned. Cool completely in the pan on a rack. • *Filling*: Beat the cream cheese, sugar, and vanilla in a large bowl with an electric mixer at medium speed until creamy. • Add the eggs, one at a time, until just blended after each addition. • With mixer at low speed, beat in the sour cream. Stir in half the toffee. • Spoon the filling into the crust. Sprinkle with the remaining toffee. • Bake for 50–60 minutes, or until set. • Cool the cake in the pan on a rack. Refrigerate for 6 hours. Loosen and remove the pan sides to serve.

Makes one 9-inch cake · Prep: 25 min. 6 hr. to chill · Cooking: 60–70 min. · Level: 1 · Keeps: 1–2 days in the refrigerator

LIGHT COFFEE CHEESECAKE

You'll never miss the extra calories.

- 1¼ cups graham cracker crumbs
- 1 tablespoon granulated sugar
- 1 large egg white

FILLING

- ½ cup granulated sugar
- ¼ cup all-purpose flour
- 2 teaspoons cornstarch
- 1 cup part-skim ricotta cheese
- 1 package (8 oz) light cream cheese, softened
- 1 large egg + 3 large egg whites, at room temperature
- 2 tablespoons freeze-dried coffee granules dissolved in ⅓ cup skim milk
- ¼ cup reduced-fat sour cream
- 1 teaspoon vanilla extract
- 3 tablespoons granulated sugar

Preheat the oven to 375°F. • Butter a 10-inch springform pan. • Mix the crumbs, sugar, and egg white in a large bowl. • Press into the bottom and partway up the sides of the prepared pan. • Bake for 8–10 minutes, or until lightly golden. Cool completely in the pan on a rack. • *Filling*: Reduce the oven temperature to 300°F. • Stir together the sugar, flour, and cornstarch in a small bowl. • Process the ricotta in a food processor until smooth. Transfer to a large bowl. • Beat in the cream cheese, whole egg, and 1 egg white with an electric mixer at medium speed until smooth. • With mixer at low speed, gradually beat in the dry ingredients. • With mixer at low speed, beat in the coffee mixture, sour cream, and vanilla. • With mixer at medium speed, beat the remaining 2 egg whites in a medium bowl until frothy. • With mixer at high speed, beat in the 3 tablespoons sugar, beating until stiff, glossy peaks form. • Use a large rubber spatula to fold them into the cheese mixture. • Spoon the filling into the crust. • Bake for 60–70 minutes, or until set. • Cool the cake in the pan on a rack. • Refrigerate for 6 hours. Loosen and remove the pan sides to serve.

Makes one 10-inch cake · Prep: 30 min. + 6 hr. to chill · Cooking: 70–80 min. · Level: 1 · Keeps: 1–2 days in the refrigerator

CAPPUCCINO CHEESECAKE

This cake tastes just like a frothy cappuccino.

- 1½ cups graham cracker crumbs
- ½ cup walnuts or pecans, finely chopped
- 5 tablespoons butter, melted
- ¼ cup firmly packed brown sugar

FILLING

- 1 tablespoon freeze-dried coffee granules
- 1 teaspoon ground cinnamon
- ¼ cup strong hot coffee

Cappuccino cheesecake

- 4 packages (8 oz each) cream cheese, softened
- 1 cup granulated sugar
- 1 cup sour cream
- 3 tablespoons all-purpose flour
- 1 teaspoon vanilla extract
- 4 large eggs, at room temperature

TOPPING

- 1 cup heavy cream
- 2 tablespoons confectioners' sugar
- 1 tablespoon coffee liqueur
  whole coffee beans, to decorate (optional)

Preheat the oven to 350°F. • Butter a 10-inch springform pan. • Mix the crumbs, walnuts, butter, and brown sugar in a medium bowl. • Press into the bottom and partway up the sides of the prepared pan. • Bake for 8–10 minutes, or until lightly browned. Cool completely in the pan on a rack. • *Filling*: Dissolve the coffee granules and cinnamon in the coffee in a small bowl. Set aside to cool. • Beat the cream cheese, sugar, sour cream, flour, and vanilla in a large bowl with an electric mixer at medium speed until creamy. • Add the eggs, one at a time, until just blended after each addition. • With mixer at low speed, beat in the coffee mixture. • Spoon the filling into the crust. • Bake for 60–70 minutes, or until set. • Cool the cake in the pan on a rack. Refrigerate for 6 hours. • *Topping*: With mixer at high speed, beat the cream, confectioners' sugar, and liqueur in a medium bowl until stiff. • Loosen and remove the pan sides. Spread with the cream. Decorate with coffee beans, if liked.

Makes one 10-inch cake · Prep: 30 min. + 6 hr. to chill · Cooking: 70–80 min. · Level: 1 · Keeps: 1–2 days in the refrigerator

Tiramisu cheesecake

TIRAMISU CHEESECAKE

This cake is made with ladyfingers, coffee, and chocolate, like its Italian namesake.

- 2 packages (8 oz each) cream cheese, softened
- 1/2 cup granulated sugar
- 2 teaspoons vanilla extract
- 2 large eggs, at room temperature
- 12 ladyfingers, each cut in half lengthwise
- 1/3 cup strong cold coffee
- 1/4 cup kirsch
- 1 cup heavy cream
- 2 oz semisweet chocolate, grated

Preheat the oven to 350°F. • Butter a 9-inch springform pan. • Beat the cream cheese, sugar, and vanilla in a large bowl with an electric mixer at medium speed until creamy. • Add the eggs, one at a time, until just blended after each addition. • Arrange the ladyfingers in the prepared pan, fitting them together tightly, and using small pieces to fill in any gaps. Cut the remaining ladyfingers in half crosswise. Arrange with the flat sides against the pan sides. Mix the coffee and kirsch and drizzle over. • Spoon the cheese mixture into the pan. • Bake for 35–40 minutes, or until set. • Cool the cake completely in the pan on a rack. • Refrigerate for 6 hours. • With mixer at high speed, beat the cream in a medium bowl until stiff . Loosen and remove the pan sides. Spread with cream. Sprinkle with chocolate.

Makes one 9-inch cake · Prep: 20 min. + 6 hr. to chill · Cooking: 35–40 min. · Level: 1 · Keeps: 1–2 days in the refrigerator

CHOCOLATE-CHERRY CHEESECAKE

Chocolate and cherry is always a winning combination.

- 1/2 cups graham cracker crumbs
- 1/4 cup (1/2 stick) butter, melted
- 2 tablespoons brown sugar
- 1/2 teaspoon ground nutmeg

FILLING

- 4 oz semisweet chocolate, coarsely chopped
- 2 packages (8 oz each) cream cheese, softened
- 3/4 cup granulated sugar
- 1/2 teaspoon vanilla extract
- 2 large eggs, at room temperature

CHERRY TOPPING

- 1 cup heavy cream
- 2 tablespoons confectioners' sugar
- 1/2 teaspoon vanilla extract
- 1/2 cups cherry pie filling

Preheat the oven to 350°F. • Butter a 9-inch springform pan. • Mix the crumbs, butter, brown sugar, and nutmeg in a medium bowl. • Press into the bottom and partway up the sides of the prepared pan. • Bake for 8–10 minutes, or until lightly browned. • Cool completely in the pan on a rack. • *Filling*: Melt the chocolate in a double boiler over barely simmering water. Set aside to cool. • Beat the cream cheese, sugar, and vanilla in a large bowl with an electric mixer at medium speed until creamy. • Add the eggs, one at a time, until just blended after each addition. • With mixer at low speed, beat in the chocolate. • Spoon the filling into the crust. • Bake for 35–45 minutes, or until set. • Cool the cake in the pan on a rack.

Refrigerate for 6 hours. • *Cherry Topping*: With mixer at high speed, beat the cream, confectioners' sugar, and vanilla in a medium bowl until stiff. • Loosen and remove the pan sides. Spread with the cherry pie filling and decorate with the cream.

Makes one 9-inch cake · Prep: 25 min. + 6 hr. to chill · Cooking: 45–55 min. · Level: 1 · Keeps: 1–2 days in the refrigerator

BLACK FOREST CHEESECAKE

- 1/2 cups chocolate wafer crumbs
- 1/4 cup (1/2 stick) butter, melted
- 2 tablespoons granulated sugar
- 1 teaspoon ground cinnamon

FILLING

- 3 packages (8 oz each) cream cheese, softened
- 1/2 cups granulated sugar
- 4 large eggs, at room temperature
- 1/3 cup kirsch

TOPPING

- 6 oz bittersweet chocolate, coarsely chopped
- 1/2 cup sour cream
- 1/2 cup maraschino cherries

Preheat the oven to 350°F. • Butter a 10-inch springform pan. • Mix the crumbs, butter, sugar, and cinnamon in a medium bowl. • Press into the bottom and partway up the sides of the prepared pan. • *Filling*: Beat the cream cheese and sugar in a large bowl with an electric mixer at medium speed until creamy. • Add the eggs, one at a time, until just blended after each addition. • Add the kirsch. • Spoon the filling into the crust. • Bake for 50–60 minutes, or until set. • Cool the cake in the pan on a rack. • *Topping*: Melt the chocolate in a double boiler over barely simmering water. Set aside to cool. Add the sour cream. • Loosen and remove the pan sides. • Spread with the topping. Arrange the cherries around the edge of the cake in a decorative manner. Refrigerate for 6 hours.

Makes one 10-inch cake · Prep: 30 min. + 6 hr. to chill · Cooking: 50–60 min. · Level: 1 · Keeps: 1–2 days in the refrigerator

CHOCOLATE AND LEMON CHEESECAKE

- 1/2 cups chocolate wafer crumbs
- 1/3 cup butter, melted
- 1 teaspoon pumpkin pie spice

FILLING

- 7 oz white chocolate, coarsely chopped
- 1/2 cup heavy cream
- 2 packages (8 oz) cream cheese, softened
- 3/4 cup granulated sugar

3 large eggs, at room temperature
2 tablespoons grated lemon zest
1/4 cup fresh lemon juice
1 cup Lemon Glaze (see page 348)

Butter a 9-inch springform pan. • Mix the crumbs, butter, and pumpkin pie spice in a medium bowl. Press into the bottom and partway up the sides of the prepared pan. Refrigerate for 30 minutes. • Preheat the oven to 350°F. *Filling*: Melt the chocolate and cream in a double boiler over barely simmering water. Set aside to cool. • Beat the cream cheese and sugar in a large bowl with an electric mixer at low speed until creamy. • With mixer at medium speed, add the eggs, one at a time, until just blended after each addition. With mixer at low speed, beat in the lemon zest and juice, and the chocolate mixture. • Spoon the filling into the crust. • Bake for 45–55 minutes, or until set. • Cool the cake in the pan on a rack. • Spread with the glaze. • Refrigerate for 6 hours. Loosen and remove the pan sides to serve.

Makes one 9-inch cake · Prep: 30 min. + 6 hr. to chill · Cooking: 45–55 min. · Level: 1 · Keeps: 1–2 days in the refrigerator

CANDIED ORANGE AND WHITE CHOCOLATE CHEESECAKE

1 1/2 cups graham cracker crumbs
1/2 cup pecans, finely ground
1/4 cup firmly packed brown sugar
1/4 cup (1/2 stick) butter, melted
2 teaspoons ground cinnamon

FILLING

6 oz white chocolate, coarsely chopped
2-inch long piece orange zest, removed with a vegetable peeler
1 1/2 cups fresh orange juice
4 packages (8 oz each) cream cheese, softened
3/4 cup granulated sugar
2 tablespoons orange liqueur
1 tablespoon finely grated orange zest
4 large eggs, at room temperature

TOPPING

1 quart water
2 cups granulated sugar
3 oranges, cut into paper-thin slices

Preheat the oven to 350°F . • Butter a 10-inch springform pan. • Mix the crumbs, pecans, brown sugar, butter, and cinnamon in a medium bowl. • Press into the bottom and partway up the sides of the prepared pan. • Bake for 8–10 minutes, or until lightly browned. • Cool in the pan on a rack. • *Filling*: Melt the white chocolate in a double

boiler over barely simmering water. Set aside to cool. • Boil the strip of orange zest and orange juice in a saucepan until reduced to about 1/4 cup. Discard the orange zest and set aside to cool. • Beat the cream cheese, sugar, grated orange zest, liqueur, and reduced juice in a large bowl with an electric mixer at medium speed until smooth. • Add the eggs, one at a time, until just blended after each addition. • With mixer at low speed, beat in the white chocolate. • Spoon the filling into the crust. • Bake for 50–60 minutes, or until set. • Cool the cake in the pan on a rack. Refrigerate for 6 hours. • *Topping*: Cover two racks with waxed paper. • Stir the water and sugar in a skillet over medium heat until the sugar has dissolved. Bring to a boil and simmer 5 minutes. • Add the orange slices, one at a time, and reduce the heat so that the syrup bubbles only around the edges of the pan. Simmer for 60 minutes. • Turn the oranges over and cook for 60 minutes more, or until the slices are translucent and the peel is tender. Lift out of the syrup, letting excess syrup drip off. • Arrange in a single layer on the prepared racks. Set aside to cool. • Boil the syrup until thick, about 5 minutes. • Loosen and remove the pan sides. Transfer to a serving plate. Decorate with the candied orange slices. Drizzle with the syrup.

Makes one 10-inch cake · Prep: 30 min. + 6 hr. to chill · Cooking: 3 hr. 20–30 min. · Level: 3 · Keeps: 1–2 days in the refrigerator

ORANGE CHOCOLATE-CHIP CHEESECAKE

1 3/4 cups graham cracker crumbs
1 cup + 3 tablespoons granulated sugar
3 tablespoons unsweetened cocoa powder
1 teaspoon ground cinnamon
1/4 cup (1/2 stick) butter, melted
8 oz bittersweet chocolate, coarsely chopped
2 packages (8 oz each) cream cheese, softened
1/2 cup sour cream
1 tablespoon grated orange zest
5 large eggs, at room temperature
1 cup heavy cream
2 tablespoons grated orange zest, to decorate

Preheat the oven to 350°F. • Butter a 9-inch springform pan. • Mix the crumbs, 3 tablespoons sugar, 1 tablespoon cocoa, cinnamon, and butter in a medium bowl. • Press into the bottom and halfway up the pan sides. • Refrigerate for 30 minutes. • Melt the chocolate in a double boiler over

barely simmering water. • Beat the cream cheese in a large bowl with an electric mixer at high speed until creamy. • Beat in the sour cream, orange zest, remaining 1 cup sugar, and the melted chocolate. With mixer at medium speed, add the eggs, one at a time, until just blended after each addition. • Spoon the filling into the crust. • Bake for 60–70 minutes, or until set. • Cool the cake in the pan on a rack. • Refrigerate for 6 hours. Loosen and remove the pan sides. Transfer to a serving plate. • With mixer at high speed, beat the cream in a medium bowl until stiff. Spread with cream and sprinkle with orange zest.

Makes one 9-inch cake · Prep: 30 min. + 6 hr. 30 min. to chill · Cooking: 60–70 min. · Level: 2 · Keeps: 1–2 days in the refrigerator

BITTER ORANGE CHEESECAKE

1 1/2 cups graham cracker crumbs
1/4 cup brown sugar
1/4 cup (1/2 stick) butter, melted
1 teaspoon ground nutmeg

FILLING

3 packages (8 oz each) cream cheese, softened
1/2 cup granulated sugar
2 teaspoons vanilla extract
2 large eggs, at room temperature

TOPPING

1 cup heavy cream
1 tablespoon granulated sugar
1/4 cup orange marmalade

Preheat the oven to 325°F. • Butter and flour a 9-inch springform pan. • Mix the crumbs, brown sugar, butter, and nutmeg in a large bowl. • Press into the bottom and partway up the sides of the prepared pan. • Bake for 8–10 minutes, or until lightly browned. • Cool in the pan on a rack. • *Filling*: Beat the cream cheese, sugar, and vanilla in a large bowl with an electric mixer at medium speed until creamy. • Add the eggs, one at a time, until just blended after each addition. • Spoon the filling into the crust. • Bake for 35–45 minutes, or until set. • Cool the cake completely in the pan on a rack. Refrigerate for 6 hours. • *Topping*: With mixer at high speed, beat the cream and sugar in a medium bowl until stiff. Fold the marmalade into the cream and spread over the cake. Refrigerate for 2 hours. Loosen and remove the pan sides to serve.

Makes one 9-inch cake · Prep: 25 min. + 8 hr. to chill · Cooking: 45–55 min. · Level: 1 · Keeps: 1–2 days

CITRUS FRUIT GÂTEAU

CITRUS MOUSSE

- 3 pink grapefruit, peeled and cut into segments (reserve the juice)
- 1 orange, peeled and cut into segments (reserve the juice)
- 1 grapefruit, peeled and cut into segments (reserve the juice)
- 1½ teaspoons unflavored gelatin
- ¼ cup cornstarch
- 1 cup white wine
- ¾ cup granulated sugar

CREAMY CHEESE FILLING

- 2 tablespoons unflavored gelatin
- ¼ cup cold water
- ⅔ cup ricotta cheese
- ⅔ cup plain yogurt
- ¾ cup granulated sugar
  grated zest and juice of ½ lemon
- 1⅔ cups heavy cream

- 1 Basic Chocolate Sponge Cake (see page 157)

GLAZE

- ¼ cup milk
- 2 tablespoons heavy cream
- 1 tablespoon granulated sugar
- 2 tablespoons water
- 2 tablespoons honey
- 7 oz semisweet chocolate, coarsely chopped

CANDIED ORANGES

- ¼ cup (½ stick) butter, softened
- ½ cup granulated sugar
- 2 oranges, thinly sliced

Citrus Mousse: Measure the reserved citrus juices. You should have about 2 cups. • Sprinkle the gelatin over 1¾ cups of the reserved juice in a medium saucepan. Let stand 1 minute. • Mix together the cornstarch and the remaining juice in a small bowl. • Bring the wine and sugar to a boil over medium heat. Stir in the cornstarch mixture and continue boiling until the mixture thickens. Add the grapefruit and orange segments. Remove from the heat and add the gelatin mixture. • *Creamy Cheese Filling*: Sprinkle the gelatin over the water in a small saucepan. Let stand 1 minute. Stir over low heat until the gelatin has completely dissolved. • Beat the ricotta, yogurt, and sugar in a large bowl with an electric mixer at medium speed until creamy. Beat in the lemon zest and juice. Stir in the gelatin mixture. With mixer at high speed, beat the cream in a large bowl until stiff. Use a large rubber spatula to fold the cream into the lemon mixture. • Place the cake on a serving plate and

Citrus fruit gâteau

surround with springform pan sides. Spread with the citrus mousse. Spread the filling on top. • Refrigerate for 3 hours, or until set. • *Glaze*: Bring the milk, cream, sugar, water, and honey to a boil in a small saucepan over low heat, stirring constantly. Remove from the heat and stir in the chocolate until melted. • Remove the pan sides. Spoon the glaze over the top. Refrigerate for 1 hour. • *Candied Oranges*: Melt the butter and sugar in a medium saucepan over low heat. Add the orange slices and cook until the oranges begin to caramelize. Arrange the oranges in a circle around the edge of the cake.

Makes one 9-inch cake · Prep: 60 min. + 4 hr. to chill · Level: 3 · Keeps: 1–2 days in the refrigerator

MANDARIN CHOCOLATE CHEESECAKE

- 1½ cups graham cracker crumbs
- ¼ cup (½ stick) butter, melted
- 2 tablespoons brown sugar
- 1 teaspoon ground nutmeg

FILLING

- 2 packages (8 oz each) cream cheese, softened
- ¾ cup granulated sugar
- 1 teaspoon orange extract
- 3 large eggs, at room temperature
- 2 tablespoons all-purpose flour
- ½ cup semisweet chocolate chips

TOPPING

- 1 cup sour cream
- 2 tablespoons granulated sugar
- 1 teaspoon vanilla extract
- 1 can (11 oz) mandarin oranges, drained
- ½ cup semisweet chocolate chips

Preheat the oven to 375°F. • Butter a 9-inch springform pan. • Stir the crumbs, butter, brown sugar, and nutmeg in a medium bowl. • Press into the bottom and partway up the sides of the prepared pan. • Bake for 8–10 minutes, or until lightly browned. • Cool completely in the pan on a rack. • *Filling*: Beat the cream cheese, sugar, and orange extract in a large bowl with electric mixer at medium speed. • Add the eggs, one at a time, until just blended after each addition. • With mixer at low speed, gradually beat in the flour. Stir in the chocolate chips. • Spoon the filling into the crust. • Bake for 35–45 minutes, or until set. Cool the cake in the pan for 15 minutes. • *Topping*: With mixer at medium speed, beat the sour cream, sugar, and vanilla. Spread with the topping. • Bake for 10 minutes more, or until set. • Cool the cake in the pan on a rack.

Refrigerate for 6 hours. • Loosen and remove the pan sides. Decorate with the oranges and chocolate chips.

Makes one 9-inch cake · Prep: 25 min. + 6 hr. to chill · Cooking: 55–65 min. · Level: 1 · Keeps: 1–2 days in the refrigerator

LEMON AND LIME CHEESECAKE

- 1⅓ cups all-purpose flour
- ½ cup granulated sugar
- 1 tablespoon grated lemon zest
- ¼ cup (½ stick) butter, melted
- 1 large egg, lightly beaten
- 1 tablespoon water

FILLING

- 2 packages (8 oz each) cream cheese, softened
- 1 cup granulated sugar
- ½ cup honey
- 2 tablespoons cornstarch
- 1 tablespoon freshly grated lime zest
- 1 tablespoon freshly grated lemon zest
- 2 teaspoons lemon extract
- 1 teaspoon vanilla extract
- 3 large eggs, at room temperature
- 1 cup sour cream

TOPPING

- ¾ cup lemon preserves or fine-cut lemon marmalade
- 1 tablespoon fresh lime juice

Preheat the oven to 400°F. • Butter a 10-inch springform pan. • Mix the flour, sugar, and lemon zest in a medium bowl. Stir in the butter, egg, and water until the mixture resembles coarse crumbs. • Press into the bottom and partway up the sides of the prepared pan. • Bake for 10–15 minutes, or until golden brown. • Cool completely in the pan on a rack. • *Filling*: Reduce the oven temperature to 350°F. • Beat the cream cheese, sugar, honey, cornstarch, lemon and lime zest, lemon extract, and vanilla in a large bowl with an electric mixer at medium speed until creamy. • Add the eggs, one at a time, until just blended after each addition. • With mixer at low speed, beat in the sour cream. • Spoon the filling into the crust. • Bake for 50–60 minutes, or until set. • Cool the cake in the pan on a rack. Refrigerate for 6 hours. • *Topping*: Bring the lemon preserves and lime juice to a boil in a saucepan over medium heat. Set aside to cool for 15 minutes. Loosen and remove the pan sides. Spread with the preserves. • Refrigerate for 30 minutes.

Makes one 10-inch cake · Prep: 25 min. + 6 hr. 30 min. to chill · Cooking: 60–75 min. · Level: 1 · Keeps: 1–2 days in the refrigerator

NO-BAKE LIME CHEESECAKE

This cheesecake is equally good if made using lemons.

- ³/₄ cup graham cracker crumbs
- 2 tablespoons brown sugar
- ¹/₄ cup (¹/₂ stick) butter, melted

LIME FILLING
- 1 can (14 oz) sweetened condensed milk
- 1 package (8 oz) reduced-fat cream cheese, softened
- ¹/₂ cup light cream
- 2 tablespoons grated lime zest
- ¹/₄ cup fresh lime juice

TOPPING
- ³/₄ cup heavy cream
  sliced ripe fresh fruit, to decorate

Butter a 9-inch springform pan. • Mix the crumbs, sugar, and butter in a small bowl. • Press into the bottom of the prepared pan. Refrigerate for 1 hour. • *Lime Filling*: Beat the condensed milk, cream cheese, cream, and lime zest in a large bowl with an electric mixer at low speed until creamy. Beat in the lime juice. • Spoon the filling into the crust. • Refrigerate for 4 hours. Loosen and remove the pan sides. • *Topping*: With mixer at high speed, beat the cream in a medium bowl until stiff. Spread with the cream. Decorate with the fruit.

Makes one 9-inch cake · Prep: 25 min. + 5 hr. to chill · Level: 1 · Keeps: 2 days

PASSION FRUIT CHEESECAKE

- 1¹/₂ cups graham cracker crumbs
- ¹/₃ cup butter, melted
- ¹/₄ cup granulated sugar

FILLING
- 2 packages (8 oz each) cream cheese, softened
- ¹/₂ cup granulated sugar
- 3 large eggs, separated
- ¹/₃ cup all-purpose flour
- 1 teaspoon grated lemon zest
- 1 tablespoon fresh lemon juice
- 1 teaspoon vanilla extract
- ¹/₂ cup heavy cream
- ¹/₄ cup strained fresh passion fruit pulp

Preheat the oven to 350°F. • Butter a 9-inch springform pan. • Mix the crumbs, butter, and sugar in a medium bowl. • Press into the bottom and partway up the sides of the prepared pan. • Bake for 8–10 minutes, or until lightly browned. • Cool completely in the pan on a rack. • *Filling*: Lower the oven temperature to 300°F. • Beat the cream cheese and sugar in a large

No-bake lime cheesecake

bowl with an electric mixer at low speed until smooth • Add the egg yolks, one at a time, until just blended after each addition. • Add the flour, lemon zest and juice, and vanilla. • With mixer at high speed, beat the cream in a small bowl until stiff. • With mixer at high speed, beat the egg whites in a medium bowl until stiff peaks form. • Stir the passion fruit pulp into the cream cheese mixture. • Use a large rubber spatula to fold the cream and whites into the batter. • Spoon the filling into the crust. • Bake for 50–60 minutes, or until set. • Cool in the pan on a rack. Refrigerate for 6 hours. Loosen and remove the pan sides to serve.

Makes one 9-inch cheesecake · Prep: 35 min. + 6 hr. to chill · Cooking 60–70 min. · Level: 1 · Keeps: 1–2 days in the refrigerator

TREASURE ISLAND CHEESECAKE

This cheesecake is perfect for hot summer nights. For a lighter version, serve with just the sliced fruit and omit the cream.

- 1¹/₂ cups graham cracker crumbs
- 3 tablespoons firmly packed brown sugar
- 3 tablespoons butter, melted
- 1 tablespoon rum
- 1 teaspoon ground cinnamon
- 1 teaspoon ground nutmeg

FILLING
- 3 packages (8 oz each) cream cheese, softened
- ¹/₂ cup granulated sugar
- 2 tablespoons rum
- 3 large eggs, at room temperature

- 1 can (8 oz) crushed pineapple, drained
- ¹/₂ cup toasted macadamia nuts, chopped

TOPPING
- 1 cup heavy cream
- 2 tablespoons confectioners' sugar
- 1 tablespoon rum
- 2 kiwifruit, peeled and sliced
- 1 mango, peeled and sliced

Preheat the oven to 350°F. • Butter a 10-inch springform pan. • Mix the crumbs, brown sugar, butter, rum, cinnamon, and nutmeg in a large bowl. • Press into the bottom and partway up the sides of the prepared pan. • Bake for 8–10 minutes, or until lightly browned. • Cool completely in the pan on a rack. • *Filling*: Beat the cream cheese, sugar, and rum in a large bowl with an electric mixer at medium speed until creamy. • Add the eggs, one at a time, until just blended after each addition. • Stir in the pineapple and macadamia nuts. • Spoon the filling into the crust. • Bake for 45–55 minutes, or until set. • Cool the cake completely in the pan on a rack. Refrigerate for 6 hours. • *Topping*: With mixer at high speed, beat the cream, confectioners' sugar, and rum in a medium bowl until stiff. Loosen and remove the pan sides. • Arrange the sliced fruit on top and decorate with the cream.

Makes one 10-inch cake · Prep: 25 min. 6 hr. to chill · Cooking: 55–65 min. · Level: 1 · Keeps: 1–2 days in the refrigerator

QUICK PINEAPPLE CHEESECAKE

- 28 ladyfingers
- 2 packages (8 oz each) cream cheese, softened
- 1/3 cup granulated sugar
- 1 can (20 oz) crushed pineapple in its own juice, undrained
- 2 cups heavy cream
- 1/4 cup confectioners' sugar
- 2 teaspoons vanilla extract

Arrange a layer of ladyfingers in the bottom of a 10-inch springform pan, fitting them together tightly, and using small pieces to fill in any gaps. Cut the remaining ladyfingers in half crosswise. Arrange them with the flat sides against the pan sides. • Beat the cream cheese, sugar, and half the pineapple in a large bowl with an electric mixer at medium speed. • With mixer at low speed, beat in the remaining pineapple. • With mixer at high speed, beat the cream, confectioners' sugar, and vanilla in a large bowl until stiff. • Use a large rubber spatula to fold the cream into the pineapple mixture. • Spoon the batter over the ladyfingers. Refrigerate for 6 hours. Loosen and remove the pan sides to serve.

Makes one 10-inch cake · Prep: 15 min. + 6 hr. to chill · Level: 2 · Keeps: 1–2 days in the refrigerator

TUTTI-FRUTTI CHEESECAKE

If using bananas to top the cheesecake, be sure to sprinkle them with a little fresh lime juice so they stay fresh-looking.

- 1 1/2 cups shredded coconut
- 1/4 cup almonds, finely chopped
- 3 tablespoons butter, melted
- 1 tablespoon grated lemon or lime zest

FILLING
- 3 packages (8 oz each) cream cheese, softened
- 1/2 cup granulated sugar
- 1/4 cup all-purpose flour
- 1 tablespoon grated orange zest
- 1 teaspoon vanilla extract
- 1/2 cup apricot nectar
- 1/2 cup unsweetened coconut milk
- 4 large eggs, at room temperature
- 1 can (8 oz) crushed pineapple, drained

TOPPING
- 1/3 cup white chocolate chips
- 1 tablespoon butter
- 1/3 cup semisweet chocolate chips
- 2 cups sliced fresh fruit

Preheat the oven to 350°F. • Butter a 10-inch springform pan. • Mix the coconut, almonds, butter, and lemon zest in a medium bowl. • Press into the bottom and partway up the sides of the prepared pan. • Bake for 10–15 minutes, or until lightly browned. • Cool completely in the pan on a rack. • *Filling*: Beat the cream cheese, sugar, flour, orange zest, and vanilla in a large bowl with an electric mixer at medium speed until creamy. Add the apricot nectar and coconut milk. • Add the eggs, one at a time, until just blended after each addition. • Add the pineapple. Spoon the filling into the crust. • Bake for 60–70 minutes, or until set. • Cool the cake completely in the pan on a rack. Refrigerate for 6 hours. • *Topping*: Melt the white chocolate and 1 1/2 teaspoons butter in a double boiler over barely simmering water. Transfer to a small bowl and set aside to cool. • Melt the semisweet chocolate and remaining 1 1/2 teaspoons butter in a double boiler over barely simmering water. Set aside to cool. Arrange the fruit over the top. • Spoon the chocolates into two pastry bags and pipe over the cake in a decorative manner.

Makes one 10-inch cake · Prep: 25 min. + 6 hr. to chill · Cooking: 70–85 min. · Level: 1 · Keeps: 1–2 days in the refrigerator

COCONUT CHEESECAKE

- 1 3/4 cups graham cracker crumbs
- 1/3 cup granulated sugar
- 1/4 cup (1/2 stick) butter, melted

FILLING
- 3 packages (8 oz each) cream cheese, softened
- 1 cup granulated sugar
- 1 teaspoon coconut extract
- 4 large eggs, at room temperature
- 1 cup sour cream
- 1 cup unsweetened coconut milk or heavy cream

TOPPING
- 1 1/4 cups sour cream
- 1/3 cup shredded coconut, toasted
- 2 tablespoons granulated sugar

Butter a 10-inch springform pan. • Preheat the oven to 350°F. • Mix the crumbs, sugar, and butter in a medium bowl. • Press into the bottom and partway up the sides of the prepared pan. • Bake for 8–10 minutes, or until lightly browned. • Cool completely in the pan on a rack. • *Filling*: Beat the cream cheese, sugar, and coconut extract in a large bowl with an electric mixer at medium speed until smooth. • Add the eggs, one at a time, until just blended after each addition. Add the sour cream and coconut milk. • Spoon the filling into the crust. • Bake for 60–70 minutes, or until set. • Cool the cake in the pan for 15 minutes. • *Topping*: Mix the sour cream, coconut, and sugar in a medium bowl. • Spread with the topping. • Bake for 8–10 minutes more, or until set. • Cool the cake in the pan on a rack. Refrigerate for 6 hours. Loosen and remove the pan sides to serve.

Makes one 10-inch cake · Prep: 35 min. + 6 hr. to chill · Cooking: 80–90 min. · Level: 1 · Keeps: 1–2 days in the refrigerator

COCONUT-MANGO CHEESECAKE

- 1 1/2 cups graham cracker crumbs
- 1 1/2 cups shredded coconut, toasted
- 1/2 cup (1 stick) butter, melted
- 1/4 cup granulated sugar
- 1 teaspoon ground ginger

FILLING
- 3 packages (8 oz each) cream cheese, softened
- 3/4 cup granulated sugar
- 2 teaspoons vanilla extract
- 3 large eggs, at room temperature
- 1 can (15 oz) cream of coconut
- 1 cup heavy cream
- 1 cup shredded coconut
- 1 large ripe mango, peeled and sliced

Preheat the oven to 325°F. • Butter a 9-inch springform pan. • Mix the crumbs, coconut, butter, sugar, and ginger in a medium bowl. • Press into the bottom and partway up the sides of the prepared pan. • Bake for 8–10 minutes, or until lightly browned. • Cool completely in the pan on a rack. • *Filling*: Beat the cream cheese, sugar, and vanilla in a large bowl with an electric mixer at medium speed until smooth. • Add the eggs, one at a time, until just blended after each addition. • With mixer at low speed, beat in the cream of coconut, cream, and shredded coconut. • Spoon the filling into the crust. • Bake for 60–70 minutes, or until set. • Cool the cake in the pan on a rack. Refrigerate for 6 hours. • Loosen and remove the pan sides. Decorate with mango.

Makes one 9-inch cake · Prep: 35 min. + 6 hr. to chill · Cooking: 80–90 min. · Level: 1 · Keeps: 1–2 days in the refrigerator

Cornflake cheesecake with Champagne filling

CORNFLAKE CHEESECAKE WITH CHAMPAGNE FILLING

- 1 cup granulated sugar
- $^1/_2$ cup (1 stick) cold butter, cut up
- $^1/_3$ cup heavy cream
- 2 cups cornflakes
    scant 1 cup toasted flaked almonds

FILLING

- $2^1/_2$ tablespoons unflavored gelatin
- $^1/_4$ cup + $1^1/_2$ tablespoons cold water
- 4 packages (8 oz each) cream cheese, softened
- $^1/_3$ cup granulated sugar
- 1 cup Champagne
- 2 tablespoons fresh lemon juice
- $^3/_4$ cup heavy cream
- 1 teaspoon gum arabic
- 1 cup green seedless grapes, to decorate
- 2 tablespoons granulated sugar, to sprinkle

Line a 9-inch springform pan with waxed paper. • Cook the sugar in a saucepan over medium heat until melted. Cook, without stirring, until golden. Remove from the heat and add the butter and cream. Return to the heat and bring to a boil. Set aside. • Add the cornflakes and almonds. • Press into the

bottom and partway up the sides of the prepared pan. Refrigerate for 1 hour. • *Filling*: Sprinkle the gelatin over the water in a saucepan. Let stand 1 minute. Stir over low heat until the gelatin has completely dissolved. • Beat the cream cheese and sugar in a large bowl with an electric mixer at medium speed until creamy. • With mixer at low speed, add the Champagne, lemon juice, and gelatin mixture. • With mixer at high speed, beat the cream in a large bowl until stiff. • Use a large rubber spatula to fold the cream into the cream cheese mixture. • Spoon the filling into the prepared pan. • Refrigerate for 4 hours. • Loosen and remove the pan sides. • Dissolve the gum arabic in the remaining $1^1/_2$ tablespoons water. Brush each grape with the gum arabic mixture and sprinkle with sugar. Arrange on top.

Makes one 9-inch cake · Prep: 45 min. + 5 hr. to chill · Level: 2 · Keeps: 1–2 days

SPICY BLUEBERRY CHEESECAKE

- $1^1/_2$ cups graham cracker crumbs
- $^1/_4$ cup firmly packed brown sugar

- $^1/_4$ cup ($^1/_2$ stick) butter, melted
- 1 teaspoon ground cinnamon
- 1 teaspoon ground ginger
- $^1/_2$ teaspoon ground allspice

FILLING

- 3 packages (8 oz each) cream cheese, softened
- $^1/_2$ cup granulated sugar
- 2 teaspoons vanilla extract
- 4 large eggs, at room temperature
- 1 can (21 oz) blueberry pie filling

Preheat the oven to 350°F. • Butter a 9-inch springform pan. • Mix the crumbs, brown sugar, butter, cinnamon, ginger, and allspice in a medium bowl. • Press into the bottom and partway up the sides of the prepared pan. • Bake for 8–10 minutes, or until lightly browned. Cool completely in the pan on a rack. • *Filling*: Beat the cream cheese, sugar, and vanilla in a large bowl with an electric mixer at medium speed until creamy. • Add the eggs, one at a time, until just blended after each addition. • Spoon the filling into the crust. • Bake for 50–60 minutes, or until set. • Cool the cake completely in the pan on a rack. • Spread with the pie filling. Refrigerate for 6 hours. Loosen and remove the pan sides to serve.

Makes one 9-inch cake · Prep: 30 min. + 6 hr. to chill · Cooking: 50–60 min. · Level: 1 · Keeps: 1–2 days in the refrigerator

RICE AND BERRY CAKE

- 1 cup all-purpose flour
- $^1/_4$ cup granulated sugar
- $^1/_2$ teaspoon baking powder
- $^1/_4$ teaspoon salt
- $^1/_4$ cup ($^1/_2$ stick) butter, melted
- 1 large egg, at room temperature
- 2 tablespoons water

CREAMY RICE FILLING

- 2 cups milk
- 2 tablespoons finely grated lemon zest
- $^1/_4$ teaspoon salt
- 1 cup short-grain rice
- $^1/_4$ cup granulated sugar
- 1 tablespoon unflavored gelatin
- $^1/_4$ cup cold water
- 1 cup heavy cream
- 1 cup mascarpone cheese
- 1 teaspoon vanilla extract

- $1^2/_3$ cups mixed red berries
- $^1/_2$ cup apricot preserves or jam

Mix the flour, sugar, baking powder, and salt in a medium bowl. Add the butter, egg, and water until well blended. Press into a disk, wrap in plastic wrap, and refrigerate for 30 minutes. • Preheat the oven to 350°F. • Butter and flour a 10-inch springform pan. • Roll the dough out on a lightly floured surface into a 10-inch round. Fit into the prepared pan, trimming the edges if needed. Prick with a fork. • Bake for 20–25 minutes, or until lightly browned. • Loosen and remove the pan sides. Cool completely on a rack. • *Creamy Rice Filling*: Bring the milk, lemon zest, and salt to a boil in a saucepan over medium heat. Stir in the rice and sugar and simmer for 25–30 minutes, or until the rice is tender, stirring occasionally. Remove from the heat. • Sprinkle the gelatin over the water in a saucepan. Let stand 1 minute. Stir over low heat until completely dissolved. Stir the gelatin into the rice mixture and refrigerate for 15 minutes. • Beat the cream in a large bowl with an electric mixer at high speed until stiff. •Stir the mascarpone, vanilla, and cream into the rice mixture. • Transfer the base to a serving plate. Place the springform pan around the crust. Spoon the filling into the prepared crust. Refrigerate for 1 hour, or until set. • Decorate with the berries. • Warm the preserves in a saucepan over low heat. Brush over the fruit. Refrigerate for 15 minutes. Loosen and remove the pan sides to serve.

Makes one 10-inch cake · Prep: 30 min. + 75 min. to chill · Cooking: 20–25 min. · Level: 1 · Keeps: 1–2 days in the refrigerator

CRANBERRY CHEESECAKE

A dessert for a Thanksgiving dessert table.

1³/₄ cups graham cracker crumbs
¹/₄ cup (¹/₂ stick) butter, melted
2 tablespoons brown sugar
1 teaspoon ground cinnamon
¹/₂ teaspoon ground nutmeg

FILLING
3 packages (8 oz each) cream cheese, softened
³/₄ cup granulated sugar
¹/₄ cup all-purpose flour
2 teaspoons vanilla extract
3 large eggs, at room temperature
1 cup sour cream
1 can (16 oz) whole berry cranberry sauce

Preheat the oven to 350°F. • Butter a 10-inch springform pan. • Mix the crumbs, butter, sugar, cinnamon, and nutmeg in a medium bowl. • Press into the bottom and partway up the sides of the prepared pan. • Bake for 8–10 minutes, or until lightly browned. • Cool completely in the pan on a rack. •

Berry cheesecake with white wine

Filling: Reduce the oven temperature to 300°F. • Beat the cream cheese, sugar, flour, and vanilla in a large bowl with an electric mixer at medium speed until creamy. • Add the eggs, one at a time, until just blended after each addition. Add the sour cream. • Spoon the filling into the crust. • Bake for 50–60 minutes, or until set. • Cool the cake in the pan on a rack. • Spread with the cranberry sauce. Refrigerate for 6 hours. Loosen and remove the pan sides to serve.

Makes one 10-inch cake · Prep: 25 min. + 6 hr. to chill · Cooking: 60–70 min. · Level: 1 · Keeps: 1–2 days in the refrigerator

BERRY CHEESECAKE WITH WINE

1¹/₂ cups graham cracker crumbs
¹/₂ cup toasted walnuts or pecans, finely chopped
3 tablespoons butter, melted
2 tablespoons firmly packed brown sugar
2 tablespoons rum

FILLING
1¹/₂ tablespoons unflavored gelatin
²/₃ cup dry white wine
1 package (8 oz) cream cheese, softened

³/₄ cup granulated sugar
¹/₄ cup fresh lemon juice
1¹/₂ cups heavy cream
²/₃ cup drained, sliced canned apricots
1 cup fresh raspberries, strawberries, and blueberries

Butter a 9-inch springform pan. • Mix the crumbs, nuts, butter, brown sugar, and rum in a large bowl. • Press into the prepared pan. • Refrigerate for 30 minutes. • Sprinkle the gelatin over ¹/₄ cup wine in a saucepan. Let stand 1 minute. Stir over low heat until gelatin has completely dissolved. • Beat the cream cheese, sugar, lemon juice, and remaining wine in a large bowl with an electric mixer at medium speed until creamy. Stir in the gelatin mixture. • With mixer at high speed, beat the cream in a medium bowl until stiff. • Use a large rubber spatula to fold the cream into the cheese mixture. • Spoon ¹/₃ of the filling into the crust. Top with the apricots and ²/₃ of the berries. Spread with the remaining filling. Refrigerate for 4 hours, or until set. • Loosen and remove the pan sides. Decorate with the remaining berries.

Makes one 9-inch cake · Prep: 25 min. + 4 hr. to chill · Level: 2 · Keeps: 1–2 days in the refrigerator

Fruits of the forest tofu cake

filling into the crust. Refrigerate for 6 hours. • Loosen and remove the pan sides. Arrange the fruit in a decorative manner on the top. • Heat the preserves and water in a saucepan over medium heat until boiling. Spoon the sauce over or serve on the side.

Makes one 9-inch cake · Prep: 25 min. + 6 hr. 30 min. to chill · Level: 1 · Keeps: 2–3 days in the refrigerator

BLACKBERRY CHEESECAKE

1¼ cups graham cracker crumbs
½ cup granulated sugar
½ cup (1 stick) butter, melted
1 teaspoon ground cinnamon
½ teaspoon ground nutmeg

FILLING
1 cup cottage cheese
2 packages (8 oz each) cream cheese, softened
¾ cup granulated sugar
2 tablespoons cornstarch
2 teaspoons vanilla extract
3 large eggs, at room temperature
¼ cup kirsch
1 cup fresh blackberries

BLACKBERRY TOPPING
2 cups fresh blackberries
1 tablespoon granulated sugar
1 tablespoon kirsch

Preheat the oven to 350°F. • Butter a 9-inch springform pan. • Mix the crumbs, sugar, butter, cinnamon, and nutmeg in a medium bowl. • Press into the bottom and partway up the sides of the prepared pan. • Bake for 8–10 minutes, or until lightly browned. Cool completely in the pan on a rack. • *Filling*: Process the cream cheese in a food processor until smooth. • Beat the cream cheese, sugar, cornstarch, and vanilla in a large bowl with an electric mixer at medium speed until creamy. • Add the eggs, one at a time, until just blended after each addition. • With mixer at low speed, beat in the cottage cheese and kirsch. • Spoon half the filling into the crust. Sprinkle with the blackberries. Spoon the remaining filling over. • Bake for 45–55 minutes, or until set. • Cool the cake in the pan on a rack. Refrigerate for 6 hours. • *Blackberry Topping*: Stir the blackberries, sugar, and kirsch. Set aside 2 hours. Loosen and remove the pan sides. Spoon the berries over the cake.

Makes one 9-inch cake · Prep: 25 min. + 6 hr. to chill · Cooking: 55–65 min. · Level: 1 · Keeps: 1–2 days in the refrigerator

ITALIAN BLACK CURRANT CAKE

1½ cups all-purpose flour
4 teaspoons granulated sugar
¼ teaspoon salt
½ cup (1 stick) cold butter, cut up
1 tablespoon ice water

FILLING
¼ cup (½ stick) butter, softened
½ cup granulated sugar
1 container (15–16 oz) ricotta cheese
1 tablespoon grated lemon zest
2 tablespoons fresh lemon juice
3 large eggs, at room temperature
½ cup currants

¼ cup confectioners' sugar, to dust
1 teaspoon ground nutmeg

Butter and flour a 10-inch springform pan. • Mix the flour, sugar, and salt in a medium bowl. Use a pastry blender to cut in the butter until the mixture resembles fine crumbs. Sprinkle in the ice water, a little at a time, until a smooth dough is formed. Press the dough into a disk, wrap in plastic wrap, and refrigerate for 30 minutes.• Roll ⅔ of the dough out on a lightly floured surface into a 10-inch round. Fit into the prepared pan. Roll the remaining dough into a sausage, about 10-inches long. Press the dough onto the pan sides to form an edge about 1½-inches high. • Refrigerate for 30 minutes. • Preheat the oven to 400°F. • Line the pastry shell with foil and fill with dried beans or pie weights. Bake for 10 minutes. Remove the foil with the beans and bake for 15 minutes more until crisp. Cool completely in the pan on a rack. • *Filling*: Lower the oven temperature to 350°F. • Beat the butter and sugar in a large bowl with an electric mixer at high speed until creamy. • With mixer at medium speed, beat in the ricotta and lemon zest and juice. Add the eggs, one at a time, until just blended after each addition. • Stir in the currants. • Spoon the filling into the crust. • Bake for 60–70 minutes, or until lightly browned. • Cool the cake completely in the pan on a rack. Loosen and remove the pan sides. • Transfer to a serving plate. Dust with the confectioners' sugar and nutmeg.

Makes one 10-inch cake · Prep: 30 min. + 1 hr. to chill · Cooking: 85–95 min. · Level: 2 · Keeps: 1–2 days in the refrigerator

FRUITS OF THE FOREST TOFU CAKE

1½ cups crushed bran flakes
5 tablespoons butter, melted
3 tablespoons apple juice
½ teaspoon ground cinnamon
½ teaspoon ground nutmeg

FILLING
1 tablespoon unflavored gelatin
¼ cup apple juice
1¾ cups soft, silken tofu (about 14 oz)
1 cup plain yogurt
1 teaspoon vanilla extract

1¾ cups mixed blueberries and red currants or raspberries
¼ cup blueberry preserves or jam
¼ cup boiling water

Butter a 9-inch springform pan. • Mix the bran flakes, butter, apple juice, cinnamon, and nutmeg in a medium bowl. • Press into the prepared pan. • Refrigerate for 30 minutes. • *Filling*: Sprinkle the gelatin over the apple juice in a small saucepan. Let stand 1 minute. Stir over low heat until gelatin has completely dissolved. • Beat the tofu and yogurt in a large bowl with an electric mixer at low speed until smooth. • Stir in the gelatin mixture and vanilla. • Spoon the

RICOTTA CAKE WITH BERRIES

- 1 cup plain yogurt
- 1 container (15–16 oz) ricotta cheese, drained and pressed through a strainer
- 1¼ cups granulated sugar
- 1¾ cups heavy cream
- 1 lb mixed fresh berries
- 1 9-inch Basic Sponge Cake (see page 157)
- 1 tablespoon fresh lemon juice

Set out a 9-inch springform pan. • Beat the ricotta, yogurt, and ¾ cup sugar in a large bowl with an electric mixer at low speed. • With mixer at high speed, beat the cream in a large bowl until stiff. Use a large rubber spatula to fold the cream into the ricotta. • Stir in 3 tablespoons berries. • Split the cake horizontally. Place a layer in the pan. Spoon the ricotta mixture over. Top with the remaining layer. • Cook the remaining berries, remaining ½ cup sugar, and the lemon juice in a large saucepan over medium heat until the juices are released. • Spoon the fruit over the cake. Refrigerate for 3 hours. • Loosen and remove the pan sides. Transfer to a serving plate.

Makes one 9-inch cake · Prep: 20 min. · Level: 1 · Keeps: 1–2 days in the refrigerator

LIGHT RICOTTA CHEESECAKE

- 1 cup graham cracker crumbs
- ¼ cup vegetable oil
- 3 tablespoons granulated sugar
- 1 teaspoon ground cinnamon
- ½ teaspoon ground nutmeg

FILLING

- 1 container (15–16 oz) part-skim ricotta cheese
- ¾ cup nonfat sour cream
- ¾ cup granulated sugar
- 2 large eggs, separated
- 2 tablespoons all-purpose flour
- 2 tablespoons grated lemon zest
- 1 teaspoon vanilla extract

TOPPING

- 1 cup nonfat sour cream
- ½ cup plain nonfat yogurt
- ¼ cup granulated sugar
- 1 teaspoon vanilla extract

Preheat the oven to 350°F. • Butter a 9-inch springform pan. • Mix the crumbs, oil, sugar, cinnamon, and nutmeg in a medium bowl. • Press into the bottom and partway up the sides of the prepared pan. • Bake for 8–10 minutes, or until lightly browned. • Cool completely in the pan on a rack. • *Filling*: Beat the ricotta cheese and sour cream in a large bowl with an electric mixer at medium speed until creamy. With mixer at low speed, gradually beat in the sugar, egg yolks, flour, lemon zest, and vanilla. • With mixer at high speed, beat the egg whites in a medium bowl until stiff peaks form. • Use a large rubber spatula to fold them into the ricotta mixture. • Spoon the filling into the crust. • Bake for 40–50 minutes, or until set. • Cool the cake completely in the pan on a rack. • *Topping*: Increase the oven temperature to 400°F. • Beat the sour cream, yogurt, sugar, and vanilla in a medium bowl. Spread the cake with the topping. • Bake for 10 minutes more, or until set. • Cool the cake in the pan on a rack. Refrigerate for 6 hours. Loosen and remove the pan sides to serve.

Makes one 9-inch cake · Prep: 30 min. + 6 hr. to chill · Cooking: 60–70 min. · Level: 1 · Keeps: 1–2 days in the refrigerator

RICOTTA PEACH CAKE

- ⅔ cup cake flour
- ⅓ cup cornstarch
- 1 teaspoon baking powder
- 3 large eggs, separated
- ½ cup granulated sugar
- 1 tablespoon grated lemon zest
- 1 teaspoon vanilla extract
- ¼ teaspoon salt

FILLING

- 1 lb ricotta cheese
- ¼ cup + 2 tablespoons peach liqueur or kirsch
- 1 tablespoon grated lemon zest
- 3 tablespoons fresh lemon juice
- 1 cup granulated sugar
- 1 cup heavy cream
- 1 lb fresh peaches, peeled and thinly sliced
- 2 tablespoons confectioners' sugar

Preheat the oven to 350°F. • Butter a 9-inch round cake pan. Line with waxed paper. Butter the paper. • Mix the flour, cornstarch, and baking powder in a medium bowl. • Beat the egg yolks and sugar in a large bowl with an electric mixer at high speed until pale and thick. • With mixer at low speed, gradually beat in the dry ingredients, lemon zest, and vanilla. • With mixer at high speed, beat the egg whites and salt in a large bowl until stiff peaks form. Use a large rubber spatula to fold them into the batter. • Spoon the batter into the prepared pan. • Bake for 30–40 minutes, or until a toothpick inserted into the center comes out clean. • Cool the cake in the pan for 15 minutes. Turn out onto a rack. Carefully remove the paper and let cool completely. • *Filling*: Place the peaches and ¼ cup liqueur in a bowl. Soak 30 minutes. • Press ricotta cheese twice through a sieve and place in a large bowl. Beat in the sugar, remaining liqueur, and the lemon zest and juice. • With mixer at high speed, beat the cream in a medium bowl until stiff. Use a large rubber spatula to fold the cream into the ricotta mixture. • Split the cake horizontally. Place one layer on a serving plate. Brush with the liquid from the peaches. Spread with half the filling and top with the peaches. Carefully spread with the remaining filling. Top with the remaining layer. • Cover the cake and refrigerate for 2 hours. Dust with the confectioners' sugar.

Makes one 9-inch cake · Prep: 30 min. + 2 hr. to chill · Cooking: 30–40 min. · Level: 2 · Keeps: 1–2 days in the refrigerator

Ricotta peach cake

Autumn cheesecake

AUTUMN CHEESECAKE

Make this delicious cheesecake in the fall, when the apples are at their tastiest. Butterscotch extract can be obtained from various sources found on the Internet.

1 cup graham cracker crumbs
$^1/_2$ cup toasted walnuts, finely chopped
$^1/_4$ cup granulated sugar
$^1/_4$ cup ($^1/_2$ stick) unsalted butter, melted
$^1/_2$ teaspoon ground cinnamon

FILLING

2 packages (8 oz each) cream cheese, softened
$^1/_2$ cup granulated sugar
2 teaspoons vanilla extract
1 teaspoon butterscotch extract (optional)
2 large eggs, at room temperature

TOPPING

$^1/_2$ cup granulated sugar
1 teaspoon ground cinnamon
1 teaspoon ground ginger
1 large Golden Delicious apple, peeled, cored, and thinly sliced
$^1/_2$ cup walnuts, coarsely chopped

Preheat the oven to 350°F. • Butter a 9-inch springform pan. • Mix the crumbs, walnuts, sugar, butter, and cinnamon in a medium bowl. • Press into the bottom and partway up the sides of the prepared pan. • Bake for 8–10 minutes, or until lightly browned. • Cool completely in the pan on a rack. • *Filling*: Beat the cream cheese, sugar, vanilla, and butterscotch extracts in a large bowl with an electric mixer at medium speed until creamy. • Add the eggs, one at a time, until just blended after each addition. • Spoon the filling into the crust. • *Topping*: Stir together the sugar, cinnamon, and ginger in a medium bowl. Toss the apple in the sugar mixture. Arrange the apple slices on top and sprinkle with walnuts. Sprinkle with any remaining sugar mixture. • Bake for 65–75 minutes, or until set. • Cool the cake in the pan on a rack. Refrigerate for 6 hours. Loosen and remove the pan sides to serve.

Makes one 9-inch cake · Prep: 30 min. + 6 hr. to chill · Cooking: 75–85 min. · Level: 1 · Keeps: 1–2 days in the refrigerator

APPLE STREUSEL CHEESECAKE

$1^1/_2$ cups graham cracker crumbs
$^1/_4$ cup firmly packed brown sugar
$^1/_4$ cup ($^1/_2$ stick) butter, melted
1 teaspoon ground cinnamon
1 teaspoon ground nutmeg

TOPPING

$^1/_3$ cup all-purpose flour
$^1/_4$ cup firmly packed brown sugar
1 teaspoon ground cinnamon
$^1/_2$ teaspoon ground nutmeg
$^1/_4$ cup ($^1/_2$ stick) cold butter, cut up
$^1/_2$ cup walnuts, hazelnuts, almonds, or pecans, chopped

FILLING

3 packages (8 oz each) cream cheese, softened
1 cup granulated sugar
$^3/_4$ cup sour cream
2 teaspoons vanilla extract
1 teaspoon ground cinnamon
1 teaspoon ground nutmeg
1 teaspoon ground ginger
4 large eggs, at room temperature
2 cups peeled, cored, and diced apples

Preheat the oven to 350°F. • Butter a 10-inch springform pan. • Mix the crumbs, brown sugar, butter, cinnamon, and nutmeg in a medium bowl. • Press into the bottom and partway up the sides of the prepared pan. • Bake for 8–10 minutes, or until lightly browned. • Cool completely in the pan on a rack. • *Topping*: Mix the flour, sugar, cinnamon, and nutmeg in a large bowl. Use a pastry blender to cut in the butter until the mixture resembles fine crumbs. Stir in the nuts. • *Filling*: Beat the cream cheese and sugar in a large bowl with an electric mixer at medium speed until creamy. • Beat in the sour cream, vanilla, cinnamon, nutmeg, and ginger. Add the eggs, one at a time, until just blended after each addition. • Stir in the apples. • Spoon the filling into the crust. • Sprinkle the topping over the filling. • Bake for 80–90 minutes, or until set. • Cool in the pan on a rack. • Refrigerate for 6 hours. Loosen and remove the pan sides to serve.

Makes one 10-inch cake · Prep: 30 min. + 6 hr. to chill · Cooking: 90–100 min. · Level: 1 · Keeps: 1–2 days in the refrigerator

CARROT CHEESECAKE

Use very sweet carrots to prepare this colorful cheesecake.

$1^1/_4$ cups graham cracker crumbs
$^1/_2$ cup walnuts, coarsely chopped
$^1/_2$ cup firmly packed brown sugar
$^1/_4$ cup ($^1/_2$ stick) butter, melted
1 teaspoon ground cinnamon

FILLING

$2^1/_2$ packages (8 oz each) cream cheese, softened
$^1/_2$ cup granulated sugar
$^1/_2$ cup cornstarch

1   teaspoon vanilla extract
4   large eggs, at room temperature
1   cup finely shredded carrots
1/2 cup raisins
1   tablespoon grated orange zest
1/4 cup fresh orange juice
1   teaspoon ground nutmeg
1   teaspoon ground ginger
1   teaspoon ground cinnamon

TOPPING

1/2 package (8 oz) cream cheese, softened
1   cup confectioners' sugar
1/4 cup sour cream
1   tablespoon fresh orange juice
    finely shredded orange zest, to decorate

Preheat the oven to 350°F. • Butter a 10-inch springform pan. • Mix the crumbs, walnuts, brown sugar, butter, and cinnamon in a large bowl. • Press into the bottom and partway up the sides of the prepared pan. • Bake for 8–10 minutes, or until lightly browned. • Cool completely in the pan on a rack. • *Filling*: Beat the cream cheese, sugar, cornstarch, and vanilla in a large bowl with an electric mixer at medium speed until creamy. • Add the eggs, one at a time, until just blended after each addition. • With mixer at low speed, beat in the carrots, raisins, orange zest and juice, nutmeg, ginger, and cinnamon. • Spoon the filling into the crust. • Bake for 55–65 minutes, or until set. • Cool the cake in the pan on a rack. Refrigerate for 6 hours. • *Topping*: With mixer at medium speed, beat the cream cheese, confectioners' sugar, sour cream, and orange juice in a medium bowl until smooth. Loosen and remove the pan sides. Spread the topping over. Decorate with the orange zest.

Makes one 10-inch cake · Prep: 25 min. + 6 hr. to chill · Cooking: 65–75 min. · Level: 1 · Keeps: 1–2 days in the refrigerator

GINGER ALMOND CHEESECAKE

1½ cups graham cracker crumbs
1/4 cup (½ stick) butter, melted
2   tablespoons brown sugar
1   teaspoon ground ginger

FILLING

2   packages (8 oz each) cream cheese, softened
1/2 cup granulated sugar
1/2 cup honey
1½ teaspoons vanilla extract
3   large eggs, at room temperature
1   cup sour cream
3   tablespoons crystallized ginger, finely chopped
2/3 cup flaked almonds

Carrot cheesecake

Butter a 9-inch springform pan. • Mix the crumbs, butter, sugar, and ginger in a large bowl. • Press into the bottom and partway up the sides of the prepared pan. • Refrigerate for 30 minutes. • Preheat the oven to 350°F. • *Filling*: Beat the cream cheese, sugar, honey, and vanilla in a large bowl with an electric mixer at medium speed until creamy. • Add the eggs, one at a time, until just blended after each addition. • With mixer at low speed, beat in the sour cream and ginger. • Spoon the filling into the crust. Sprinkle with the almonds. • Bake for 50–60 minutes, or until set. • Cool the cake in the pan on a rack. Refrigerate for 6 hours. Loosen and remove the pan sides to serve.

Makes one 9-inch cake · Prep: 25 min. + 6 hr. 30 min. to chill · Cooking: 50–60 min. · Level: 1 · Keeps: 1–2 days in the refrigerator

CRYSTALLIZED GINGER CHEESECAKE

1¾ cups graham cracker crumbs
1/4 cup (½ stick) butter, melted
2   tablespoons brown sugar

FILLING

3   packages (8 oz each) cream cheese, softened
1¼ cups granulated sugar
1½ teaspoons vanilla extract
3   large eggs, at room temperature
1/2 cup sour cream
1/4 cup crystallized ginger, finely chopped

Preheat the oven to 350°F. • Butter a 10-inch springform pan. • Mix the crumbs, butter, and sugar in a medium bowl. • Press into the bottom and partway up the sides of the prepared pan. • Bake for 8–10 minutes, or until lightly browned. • Cool completely in the pan on a rack. • *Filling*: Reduce the oven temperature to 325°F. • Beat the cream cheese, sugar, and vanilla in a large bowl with an electric mixer at medium speed until creamy. • Add the eggs, one at a time, until just blended after each addition. • Stir in the sour cream and crystallized ginger. • Spoon the filling into the crust. • Bake for 50–60 minutes, or until set. • Cool the cake in the pan on a rack. Refrigerate for 6 hours. Loosen and remove the pan sides to serve.

Makes one 10-inch cake · Prep: 30 min. + 6 hr. to chill · Cooking: 60–70 min. · Level: 1 · Keeps: 1–2 days in the refrigerator

GINGER-APPLE CHEESECAKE

- 1 cup all-purpose flour
- 1/2 cup granulated sugar
- 1 teaspoon ground ginger
- 1/2 cup (1 stick) cold butter, cut up

FILLING

- 2 packages (8 oz each) cream cheese, softened
- 1 cup granulated sugar
- 1 teaspoon vanilla extract
- 1 teaspoon lemon extract
- 2 large eggs, at room temperature
- 3 medium Golden Delicious apples, peeled, cored, and thinly sliced
- 1/4 cup crystallized ginger, finely chopped
- 1 tablespoon grated lemon zest
- 1/2 cup Apricot Glaze (see page 348), warmed

Preheat the oven to 350°F. • Butter a 9-inch springform pan. • Mix the flour, sugar, and ginger in a medium bowl. Use a pastry blender to cut in the butter until the mixture resembles coarse crumbs. • Press into the bottom and partway up the sides of the prepared pan. Prick all over with a fork. • Bake for 8–10 minutes, or until lightly browned. • Cool completely in the pan on a rack. • *Filling*: Beat the cream cheese, 1/2 cup sugar, vanilla, and lemon extract in a large bowl with an electric mixer at medium speed until creamy. • Add the eggs, one at a time, until just blended after each addition. • Spoon the filling into the crust. • Arrange the apple slices on top. • Mix the remaining 1/2 cup sugar, ginger, and lemon zest in a small bowl. Sprinkle over the apples. • Bake for 40–50 minutes, or until set. • Cool the cake completely in the pan on a rack. Refrigerate for 6 hours. • Brush the glaze over. • Refrigerate for 30 more minutes. Loosen and remove the pan sides to serve.

Makes one 9-inch cheesecake · Prep: 25 min. + 6 hr. 30 min. to chill · Cooking: 50–60 min. · Level: 1 · Keeps: 1–2 days in the refrigerator

GINGER-PUMPKIN CHEESECAKE

- 1 1/4 cups gingersnap cookie crumbs
- 3/4 cup pecans, finely ground
- 1/3 cup firmly packed brown sugar
- 1/3 cup butter, melted
- 1/2 teaspoon ground allspice

FILLING

- 3 packages (8 oz each) cream cheese, softened
- 1 cup firmly packed brown sugar
- 2 teaspoons vanilla extract
- 4 large eggs, at room temperature
- 1 1/2 cups plain canned pumpkin
- 1/2 cup heavy cream
- 1/4 cup pure maple syrup

- 1 teaspoon ground cinnamon
- 1 teaspoon ground ginger
- 1/2 teaspoon ground allspice

Preheat the oven to 325°F. • Butter a 9-inch springform pan. • Mix the crumbs, pecans, brown sugar, butter, and allspice in a medium bowl. • Press into the bottom and partway up the sides of the prepared pan. • Refrigerate for 30 minutes. • *Filling*: Beat the cream cheese, brown sugar, and vanilla in a large bowl with an electric mixer at medium speed until creamy. • Add the eggs, one at a time, until just blended after each addition. • With mixer at low speed, beat in the pumpkin, cream, maple syrup, cinnamon, ginger, and allspice. • Spoon the filling into the crust. • Bake for 65–75 minutes, or until set. • Cool the cake completely in the pan on a rack. Refrigerate for 6 hours. Loosen and remove the pan sides to serve.

Makes one 9-inch cake · Prep: 25 min. + 6 hr. 30 min. to chill · Cooking: 65–75 min. · Level: 1 · Keeps: 2–3 days

SPICY PUMPKIN CHEESECAKE

- 1 1/2 cups graham cracker crumbs
- 1/4 cup (1/2 stick) butter, melted
- 2 tablespoons brown sugar
- 1 teaspoon ground cinnamon
- 1/2 teaspoon ground nutmeg

FILLING

- 2 packages (8 oz each) cream cheese, softened
- 3/4 cup granulated sugar
- 1 teaspoon vanilla extract
- 2 large eggs, at room temperature
- 1/2 cup plain canned pumpkin
- 1 teaspoon ground cinnamon
- 1/2 teaspoon ground cloves
- 1/2 teaspoon ground nutmeg

Preheat the oven to 350°F. • Butter a 9-inch springform pan. • Mix the crumbs, butter, brown sugar, cinnamon, and nutmeg in a medium bowl. • Press into the bottom and partway up the sides of the prepared pan. • Bake for 8–10 minutes, or until lightly browned. • Cool completely in the pan on a rack. • *Filling*: Beat the cream cheese, sugar, and vanilla in a large bowl with an electric mixer at medium speed until creamy. • Add the eggs, one at a time, until just blended after each addition. • Mix the pumpkin, cinnamon, cloves, and nutmeg in a large bowl. Stir the pumpkin mixture into the cheese mixture. • Spoon the batter into the crust. • Bake for 35–45 minutes, or until set. • Cool the cake in the pan on a rack.

Refrigerate for 6 hours. Loosen and remove the pan sides to serve.

Makes one 9-inch cake · Prep: 25 min. + 6 hr. to chill · Cooking: 45–55 min. · Level: 1 · Keeps: 1–2 days in the refrigerator

SWEET POTATO CHEESECAKE

Bake the sweet potatoes at least 2 hours before starting this cake. Baking will take about 1 hour in a 350°F oven.

- 1 1/2 cups graham cracker crumbs
- 1/4 cup granulated sugar
- 1/4 cup (1/2 stick) butter, melted
- 1 teaspoon ground cinnamon

FILLING

- 1 1/2 lb sweet potatoes, scrubbed, baked, and cooled
- 3 packages (8 oz each) cream cheese, softened
- 3/4 cup granulated sugar
- 1 teaspoon vanilla extract
- 3 large eggs, at room temperature
- 1/3 cup sour cream
- 1/4 cup heavy cream

BROWN-SUGAR TOPPING

- 3/4 cup firmly packed brown sugar
- 1/4 cup (1/2 stick) cold butter, cut up
- 1 cup pecans or walnuts, coarsely chopped
- 1/4 cup heavy cream

Preheat the oven to 350°F. • Butter and flour a 9-inch springform pan. • Mix the crumbs, sugar, butter, and cinnamon in a medium bowl. • Press into the bottom and partway up the sides of the prepared pan. • Bake for 6–8 minutes, or until lightly browned. Cool completely in the pan on a rack. • *Filling*: Halve the sweet potatoes and spoon the insides into a medium bowl. Mash to a smooth puree. You should get about 1 1/2 cups sweet potato puree. • Beat the cream cheese, sugar, and vanilla in a large bowl with an electric mixer at medium speed until creamy. • Beat in the sweet potatoes. Add the eggs, one at a time, until just blended after each addition. • With mixer at low speed, beat in the sour cream and cream. • Spoon the filling into the crust. • Bake for 50–60 minutes, or until set. • Cool the cake in the pan on a rack. • *Brown-Sugar Topping*: Stir the brown sugar and butter in a saucepan over low heat until the sugar has dissolved. • Increase the heat and bring to a boil. Remove from the heat and stir in the nuts and cream. Spread with the topping. Refrigerate for 6 hours. Loosen and remove the pan sides to serve.

Makes one 9-inch cake · Prep: 30 min. + 6 hr. to chill · Cooking: 60–70 min. · Level: 1 · Keeps: 1–2 days in the refrigerator

APPLE CRUNCH CHEESECAKE

- 1½ cups graham cracker crumbs
- ¼ cup (½ stick) butter, melted
- 2 tablespoons brown sugar
- 1 teaspoon ground cinnamon

FILLING

- 2 tablespoons unflavored gelatin
- ⅓ cup cold water
- 1¾ cups apple juice
- ½ cup granulated sugar
- 3 large egg yolks
- 3 packages (8 oz each) cream cheese, softened
- 1 teaspoon ground cinnamon
- ½ teaspoon ground nutmeg
- 1 cup heavy cream

TOPPING

- ¾ cup walnuts, coarsely chopped
- 2 tablespoons butter
- 1 cup applesauce
- ⅓ cup firmly packed brown sugar
- 2 teaspoons ground cinnamon

Preheat the oven to 350°F. • Butter a 9-inch springform pan. • Mix the crumbs, butter, brown sugar, and cinnamon in a medium bowl. • Press into the bottom and partway up the sides of the prepared pan. • Bake for 8–10 minutes, or until lightly browned. Cool completely in the pan on a rack. • *Filling*: Sprinkle the gelatin over the water in a small saucepan. Let stand 1 minute. Stir over low heat until completely dissolved. • Beat the apple juice, sugar, and egg yolks in a medium saucepan over low heat. Cook, beating constantly, until the mixture lightly coats a metal spoon or registers 160°F on an instant-read thermometer. Immediately plunge the pan into a bowl of ice water and stir until the egg mixture has cooled. • Beat the cream cheese, cinnamon, and nutmeg in a large bowl with an electric mixer at medium speed until smooth. Stir in the gelatin mixture and

Italian ricotta cake

the egg yolk mixture. Refrigerate until slightly thickened, 20 minutes. • With mixer at high speed, beat the cream in a medium bowl until stiff. Use a large rubber spatula to fold the cream into the cream cheese. • Spoon the filling into the crust. • Refrigerate for 4 hours. • *Topping*: Sauté the walnuts in the butter in a saucepan for 2 minutes. • Stir in the applesauce, brown sugar, and cinnamon. Cook for 5 minutes. Loosen and remove the pan sides. • Spread the topping over the cake.

Makes one 9-inch cake · Prep: 25 min. + 4 hr. 20 min. to chill · Cooking: 10 min. · Level: 1 · Keeps: 1–2 days in the refrigerator

SPICY CARROT CHEESECAKE

- 1¾ cups graham cracker crumbs
- ¼ cup firmly packed brown sugar
- ¼ cup (½ stick) butter, melted
- 1 teaspoon ground cinnamon
- 1 teaspoon ground ginger

FILLING

- 2½ packages (8 oz each) cream cheese, softened
- ¾ cup granulated sugar
- 4 large eggs, at room temperature
- 1 cup finely grated carrots
- ½ cup all-purpose flour
- ½ cup raisins
- ¼ cup fresh lemon juice
- 1 teaspoon ground nutmeg
- 1 teaspoon ground cinnamon
- 1 teaspoon ground ginger

TOPPING

- 1 cup confectioners' sugar
- ½ package (8 oz) cream cheese, softened
- 1 tablespoon fresh lemon juice
- 1–2 tablespoons raisins, to decorate

Preheat the oven to 325°F. • Butter a 10-inch springform pan. • Mix the crumbs, brown sugar, butter, cinnamon, and ginger in a medium bowl. • Press into the bottom and partway up the

sides of the prepared pan. • Bake for 8–10 minutes, or until lightly browned. • Cool completely in the pan on a rack. • *Filling*: Beat the cream cheese and sugar in a large bowl with an electric mixer at medium speed until creamy. • Add the eggs, one at a time, until just blended after each addition. • With mixer at low speed, beat in the carrots, flour, raisins, lemon juice, nutmeg, cinnamon, and ginger. • Spoon the filling into the crust. • Bake for 45–55 minutes, or until set. • Cool the cake completely in the pan on a rack. Refrigerate for 6 hours. Loosen and remove the pan sides. • *Topping*: With mixer at high speed, beat the confectioners' sugar, cream cheese, and lemon juice in a medium bowl. Spread the topping. Decorate with raisins.

Makes one 10-inch cake · Prep: 30 min. + 4 hr. to chill · Cooking: 55–65 min. · Level: 1 · Keeps: 1–2 days in the refrigerator

ITALIAN RICOTTA CAKE

- 1½ cups ricotta cheese
- ⅓ cup milk
- 3 large eggs, separated
- 1⅔ cups all-purpose flour
- 1 cup granulated sugar
- 2 tablespoons grated lemon zest
- 2 teaspoons baking powder
- ¼ teaspoon salt

WALNUT CREAM

- 1 cup heavy cream
- 2 teaspoons sweet sherry
- 2 tablespoons granulated sugar
- ½ cup walnuts, coarsely chopped

Preheat the oven to 350°F. • Butter a 9-inch springform pan. • Mix the ricotta and milk in a large bowl. • Add the egg yolks, flour, sugar, lemon zest, baking powder, and salt. • Beat the egg whites in a medium bowl with an electric mixer at high speed until stiff. Use a large rubber spatula to fold them into the batter. • Spoon the batter into the prepared pan. • Bake for 35–45 minutes, or until a toothpick inserted into the center comes out clean. • Cool the cake in the pan for 10 minutes. Loosen and remove the pan sides. • *Walnut Cream*: With mixer at high speed, beat the cream, sherry, and sugar in a large bowl until stiff. Stir in the walnuts. • Split the cake horizontally. Place a layer on a serving plate. Spread with cream. Top with the remaining layer.

Makes one 9-inch cake · Prep: 30 min. · Cooking: 35–45 min. · Level: 1 · Keeps: 1 day in the refrigerator

NO-BAKE CAKES

The no-bake cake provides an alternative for those with limited cooking facilities or for those who do not wish to heat up the kitchen. Chilled, frozen, or simply made at room temperature, these cakes taste just as delightful as their oven-baked counterparts. Simple and delicious, no-bake cakes will become part of your cooking repertoire!

CHOCOLATE ICE CREAM CAKE

This no-bake cake is a snap to prepare. It is especially ideal for young cooks, who will also enjoy its simple flavors.

1½   cups vanilla wafer crumbs
⅓   cup butter, melted
1   tablespoon coffee liqueur or chocolate syrup

FILLING

4½   cups packed chocolate ice cream
7   oz bittersweet chocolate, coarsely grated

Mix the crumbs, butter, and liqueur in a medium bowl until well blended. Press into the bottom of a 9-inch springform pan. Refrigerate for 30 minutes. • *Filling*: Leave the ice cream at room temperature to soften, 10 minutes. • Beat the ice cream in a large bowl with an electric mixer at low speed until fluffy. • Spread the ice cream evenly into the crust. Freeze for 2 hours. · Loosen and remove the pan sides. Place the cake on a serving plate and sprinkle with the chocolate. Let stand at room temperature for 10 minutes.

Makes one 9-inch cake · Prep: 20 min. + 30 min. to chill + 2 hr. to freeze · Level: 1 · Keeps: 5–6 days in the freezer

◀ Rainbow sorbet delight (see page 274)

➢ Chocolate ice cream cake

Coffee ice cream cake

PEPPERMINT ICE CREAM CAKE

- 1 cup hard peppermint-flavored candies
- 1/4 cup water
- 1 1/2 cups heavy cream
- 1/3 cup confectioners' sugar
- 1 teaspoon vanilla extract
- 1 8-inch angel food cake, store-bought
- 2 cups vanilla ice cream

Coarsely chop 1/2 cup candies in a food processor. Set aside. Repeat with the remaining candies, but leave in the food processor. Add the water and process until syrupy. • Beat the cream, confectioners' sugar, and vanilla in a medium bowl with an electric mixer at high speed until stiff. • Split the cake into three horizontally. • Place one layer on a serving plate. Drizzle with 2 tablespoons syrup. Spread with 1/2 cup cream and sprinkle with 1 tablespoon of chopped candy. Top with the second layer, drizzle with syrup, and spread with 1/2 cup cream. Sprinkle with the candy. Invert the remaining layer and drizzle the cut side with the remaining syrup. Place top-side up on the cake. • Spread the remaining cream over the cake. Sprinkle with the chopped candies. • Scoop up about 10 small ice cream balls and arrange on top. Sprinkle with the remaining chopped candies. • Freeze for 2 hours.

Makes one 8-inch cake · Prep: 35 min. + 2 hr. to freeze · Level: 1 · Keeps: 2–3 days in the freezer

ICE CREAM-COOKIE CAKE

- 1 cup heavy cream
- 1/3 cup granulated sugar
- 2 tablespoons orange liqueur
- 2 cups vanilla ice cream, softened
- 1 cup graham cracker crumbs, crushed
- 3/4 cup miniature semisweet chocolate chips
- 1/2 cup raisins
- 1 cup heavy cream
- 2 tablespoons confectioners' sugar
- 1 teaspoon vanilla extract

Line a 2-quart metal bowl with plastic wrap. • Beat the cream, sugar, and orange liqueur in a large bowl with an electric mixer at high speed until stiff. Use a large rubber spatula to fold in the ice cream, crumbs, 1/2 cup chocolate chips, and raisins. Spoon the mixture into the prepared bowl, pressing down firmly. Freeze for 3 hours. • With mixer at high speed, beat the cream, confectioners' sugar, and vanilla in a medium bowl until stiff. • Turn out onto a serving plate. Remove the wrap. Pipe the cream on top in a decorative manner. Sprinkle with the remaining 1/4 cup chocolate chips.

Makes one 2-quart ice cream cake · Prep: 20 min. + 3 hr. to freeze · Level: 1 · Keeps: 3–4 days in the freezer

COFFEE ICE CREAM CAKE

You'll need an ice cream maker to prepare this cake.

ICE CREAM

- 2 cups milk
- 1/2 cup heavy cream
- 4 large egg yolks
- 1/3 cup granulated sugar
- 2 teaspoons vanilla extract
- 1/4 cup confectioners' sugar
- 4 oz bittersweet chocolate, coarsely chopped
- 1/2 cup strong coffee

TOPPING

- 2 cups heavy cream
- 2 tablespoons brandy
- 2 tablespoons confectioners' sugar
- 1 tablespoon whole coffee beans

Ice Cream: Bring the milk and cream to a boil in a saucepan over medium heat. Remove from the heat. • Beat the egg yolks, sugar, and hot milk mixture in a double boiler until well blended. Cook over low heat, stirring constantly with a wooden spoon, until the mixture lightly coats a metal spoon or registers 160°F on an instant-read thermometer. Add the vanilla. Immediately plunge the pan into a bowl of ice water and stir until the egg mixture has cooled. • Press plastic wrap directly onto the surface and refrigerate until chilled. Freeze in an ice cream maker according to manufacturer's directions. • Pack into a freezer-proof container dusted with confectioners' sugar. Freeze the ice cream for 1 hour. • Divide the ice cream into two equal portions. Stir the chocolate into one portion and the coffee into the other. • Spoon the mixture into a 9-inch ring mold in layers. Freeze for 1 hour. • *Topping*: Beat the cream, brandy, and confectioners' sugar in a medium bowl with an electric mixer at high speed until stiff. • Unmold onto a serving plate. Pipe the cream over the cake in a decorative manner. Decorate with the coffee beans.

Makes one 9-inch cake · Prep: 30 min. + 2 hr. to freeze · Level: 1 · Keeps: 1 week in the freezer

STRAWBERRY VANILLA CAKE

Assemble this cake just 10 minutes before serving. If you're really short of time, buy a 9-inch round sponge cake, 2–2¹⁄₂ inches deep, instead of making the cake at home.

- 1 Génoise (see page 157)
- 2 pints vanilla ice cream, softened
- 1¹⁄₂ cups fresh medium-sized strawberries, hulled
- ¹⁄₄ cup confectioners' sugar

Cut the cake horizontally. • Place one layer on a serving plate and cover with small scoops of ice cream alternating with strawberries. • Cover with the top layer and sprinkle with the confectioners' sugar.

Makes one 9-inch cake · Prep: 10 min. · Level: 1 · Keeps: 1 day in the freezer

ROCKY ROAD-STRAWBERRY CAKE

- 3 pints rocky road ice cream, softened
- 3 pints strawberry ice cream, softened
- 1 cup heavy cream
- ¹⁄₂ cup candied cherries, coarsely chopped

Use the instructions for Pistachio and Cherry Cake (see recipe below), substituting the rocky road ice cream for the pistachio.

Makes one 2¹⁄₂ quart cake · Prep: 15 min. + 2 hr. 30 min. to freeze · Level: 1 · Keeps: 3 days in the freezer

CHOCOLATE ICE CREAM CAKE WITH FIGS AND RASPBERRIES

- 1 cup unsweetened cocoa powder
- 1¹⁄₄ cups milk
- 1 cup heavy cream
- 4 large egg yolks
- ¹⁄₂ cup granulated sugar
- 4 fresh figs, sliced
- 1 cup fresh raspberries

Beat the cocoa and ³⁄₄ cup milk in a large saucepan until smooth. Beat in the remaining ¹⁄₂ cup milk and the cream. Bring to a boil over medium heat, stirring constantly. Remove from the heat. • Beat the egg yolks, sugar, and 2 tablespoons milk mixture in a saucepan until well blended. Cook over low heat, stirring constantly with a wooden spoon, until the mixture lightly coats a metal spoon or registers 160°F on an instant-read thermometer. Add the remaining milk mixture. Immediately plunge the pan into a bowl of ice water and stir until the egg mixture has cooled. Transfer to a large bowl. Press plastic wrap directly onto the surface. Refrigerate until chilled. Freeze in an ice cream maker according to manufacturer's

Strawberry vanilla cake

directions. • Oil an 8-inch round cake pan. Spoon the ice cream into the prepared pan. Freeze for 3 hours. • Turn out onto a serving dish. Decorate with figs and strawberries.

Makes one 8-inch cake · Prep: 25 min. + 3 hr. to freeze · Level: 1 · Keeps: 3–4 days in freezer

COOKIES AND CREAM CAKE

- 3 pints cookies and cream ice cream, softened
- 2 pints strawberry ice cream, softened
- 1 cup heavy cream
- 1 cup raspberries

Use the instructions for Pistachio and Cherry Cake (see recipe below), substituting the cookies and cream ice cream for the pistachio. Decorate with the raspberries.

Makes one 2¹⁄₂ quart cake · Prep: 15 min. + 2 hr. 30 min. to freeze · Level: 1 · Keeps: 3 days in the freezer

PISTACHIO AND CHERRY CAKE

- 3 pints pistachio ice cream, softened
- 2 pints strawberry ice cream, softened
- 1 cup heavy cream
- ¹⁄₂ cup candied cherries, coarsely chopped

Line a 2¹⁄₂ quart metal bowl with plastic wrap. • Beat the pistachio ice cream in a large bowl with an electric mixer at low speed until smooth. Spread pistachio ice cream in the prepared bowl. Freeze for 1 hour. • With mixer at low speed, beat the strawberry ice cream in a large bowl until smooth. Spread strawberry ice cream over the pistachio layer. Freeze for 1 hour. • With mixer at high speed, beat the cream in a large bowl until stiff. Use a large rubber spatula to fold in the cherries. Spread the cream over. Freeze for 30 minutes. Dip the mold in warm water and unmold.

Makes one 2¹⁄₂ quart cake · Prep: 15 min. + 2 hr. 30 min. to freeze · Level: 1 · Keeps: 3 days in the freezer

ALMOND ICE CREAM CAKE

- 3 pints almond ice cream, softened
- 2 pints chocolate chip ice cream, softened
- 1 cup heavy cream
- ¹⁄₂ cup candied cherries, coarsely chopped

Use the instructions for Pistachio and Cherry Cake (see left), substituting the ice creams.

Makes one 2¹⁄₂ quart cake · Prep: 15 min. + 2 hr. 30 min. to freeze · Level: 1 · Keeps: 3 days in the freezer

EASY ICE CREAM CAKE

- 1 pint maple-walnut ice cream, softened
- 1 pint cherry ice cream, softened
- 2 cups heavy cream
- 2 tablespoons confectioners' sugar
- 1 teaspoon vanilla extract
- 15 strawberries, hulled
- 3 kiwifruit, peeled and thickly sliced

Line a 9-inch round cake pan with muslin. • Spoon maple-walnut ice cream into the prepared pan, followed by the cherry ice cream. Cover with plastic wrap and freeze for 2 hours. • Beat the cream, confectioners' sugar, and vanilla in a large bowl with an electric mixer at high speed until stiff. • Turn out onto a serving plate. Spread with cream. Spoon the remaining cream into a pastry bag and decorate the top. Decorate with fruit and serve.

Makes one 9-inch cake · Prep: 25 min. + 2 hr. to chill · Level: 1 · Keeps: 1–2 days in the freezer

BANANA SPLIT CAKE

- 4 cups vanilla wafer crumbs
- 1 cup (2 sticks) butter, melted
- 1 package (8 oz) cream cheese, softened
- 1²/₃ cups + 2 tablespoons confectioners' sugar
- 1 can (20 oz) crushed pineapple, drained
- 6 bananas, peeled and sliced
- 1¹/₂ cups heavy cream
- 1 teaspoon vanilla extract
- ¹/₄ cup nuts, coarsely chopped

Butter a 9 x 13-inch baking pan. • Mix the crumbs and butter in a large bowl. • Press into the prepared pan. • Beat the cream cheese and 1²/₃ cups confectioners' sugar with an electric mixer at high speed until creamy. • Spread the cheese mixture over the crust. • Spoon the pineapple over the cream cheese and top with bananas. • With mixer at high speed, beat the cream, the remaining confectioners' sugar, and vanilla in a large bowl until stiff. • Spread the cream over and sprinkle with nuts. • Refrigerate for 1 hour.

Makes 9 x 13-inch cake · Prep: 30 min. + 1 hr to chill · Level: 1 · Keeps: 2–3 days in the refrigerator

POUND CAKE WITH FRUIT AND ZABAGLIONE

- 1 pineapple, peeled and sliced
- 1 kiwifruit, peeled and sliced
- 1 banana, peeled and sliced
- 4 small strawberries, hulled
  juice of 1 lemon
- 1 10-inch Basic Pound Cake (see page 40)
- 1 tablespoon kirsch
  confectioners' sugar, to dust
- 2 cups Zabaglione (see page 348)

Mix the fruit and lemon juice in a large bowl. • Drizzle the cake with the liqueur. • Place the cake on a serving plate. Dust with the confectioners' sugar. Arrange the fruit salad on top in a decorative manner. • Serve with the zabaglione passed on the side.

Makes 1 dessert · Prep: 30 min. · Level: 2 · Keeps: 2 days in the refrigerator

HAZELNUT LADYFINGER CAKE

- 1 quart milk
- 6 large egg yolks, at room temperature
- 1 cup granulated sugar
- 1 teaspoon vanilla extract
- ¹/₃ cup + 2 tablespoons cornstarch
- 28 ladyfingers
- 6 tablespoons chocolate hazelnut cream (Nutella)
- 1 cup heavy cream
- ¹/₂ cup sliced fresh fruit, such as strawberries, kiwifruit, bananas, or pineapple, to decorate

Set out a 9-inch springform pan. • Bring the milk to a boil in a small saucepan over low heat. Remove from the heat. • Beat the egg yolks, sugar, and vanilla in a large bowl with an electric mixer at high speed until pale and thick. • With mixer at low speed, gradually add the cornstarch. Pour the hot milk into the egg mixture. Return the mixture to the saucepan over low heat and cook, stirring constantly, with a wooden spoon, until the mixture lightly coats a metal spoon or registers 160°F on an instant-read thermometer. Immediately plunge the pan in a bowl of ice water and stir until the egg mixture has cooled. • Spoon half the custard into the pan. Arrange 14 ladyfingers on top in a spokelike pattern. • Stir the chocolate hazelnut cream into the remaining custard. Spread on top of the ladyfingers. Arrange the remaining ladyfingers on top in a spokelike pattern. Refrigerate for 8 hours. • Loosen and remove the pan sides. Transfer onto a serving plate. • With mixer at high speed, beat the cream in a large bowl until stiff. Spoon the cream into a pastry bag and pipe it onto the top and sides of the cake. Decorate with the fruit.

Makes one 9-inch cake · Prep: 30 min. + 8 hr. to chill · Level: 1 · Keeps: 1–2 days in the refrigerator

Easy ice cream cake

STRAWBERRY LADYFINGER CAKE

1¼ cups mascarpone cheese
6–7 oz ladyfingers
1 cup sweet white wine
1½ cups thinly sliced strawberries
1 cup heavy cream

Set out a deep serving dish. • Drizzle the ladyfingers with the wine. Soak 20 minutes. • Spread half the mascarpone in the dish. Top with ladyfingers. • Arrange the strawberries on top. Spread with the remaining mascarpone. • Beat the cream in a large bowl with an electric mixer at high speed until stiff. Spoon into a pastry bag and pipe on top in a decorative manner. Arrange the remaining strawberries on top. • Refrigerate for 2 hours.

Makes 8–10-inch cake · Prep: 30 min. + 2 hr. to chill · Level: 2 · Keeps: 2 days in the refrigerator

RASPBERRY LADYFINGER CAKE

1¼ cups mascarpone cheese
6–7 oz ladyfingers
1 cup sweet white wine
1½ cups thinly sliced raspberries
1 cup heavy cream

Use the instructions for Strawberry Ladyfinger Cake (see recipe above), substituting the raspberries for the strawberries.

Makes one 8–10-inch cake · Prep: 30 min. + 2 hr. to chill · Level: 2 · Keeps: 2 days in the refrigerator

BLUEBERRY LADYFINGER CAKE

1¼ cups mascarpone cheese
6–7 oz ladyfingers
1 cup sweet white wine
1½ cups blueberries, washed, hulled, and thinly sliced
1 cup heavy cream

Use the instructions for Strawberry Ladyfinger Cake (see recipe above), substituting the blueberries for the strawberries.

Makes one 8–10-inch cake · Prep: 30 min. + 2 hr. to chill · Level: 2 · Keeps: 2 days in the refrigerator

MOCHA LADYFINGER CAKE

5 large eggs, separated
⅔ cup + 2 tablespoons granulated sugar
2 cups mascarpone cheese
5 teaspoons water
¼ teaspoon cream of tartar
30 ladyfingers
1 cup strong cold coffee
7 oz dark chocolate, grated
1 tablespoon unsweetened cocoa powder

Bombe surprise

Set out a deep serving dish. • Beat the egg yolks and sugar in a double boiler until well blended. Cook over low heat, stirring constantly with a wooden spoon, until the mixture lightly coats a metal spoon or registers 160°F on an instant-read thermometer. Immediately plunge the pan into a bowl of ice water and stir until the egg mixture has cooled. • Use a large rubber spatula to fold in the mascarpone. • Stir the whites, remaining sugar, water, and cream of tartar in a saucepan until blended. Cook over low heat, beating constantly with an electric mixer at low speed until the whites register 160°F on an instant-read thermometer. Transfer to a bowl. With mixer at high speed, beat the whites until stiff peaks form. Fold them into the mascarpone mixture. • Dip the ladyfingers briefly into the coffee. • Spread a layer of mascarpone mixture in the dish. Top with a layer of ladyfingers. Cover with a mascarpone layer and sprinkle with some chocolate. Repeat until all the ingredients are used up, finishing with chocolate. • Refrigerate for 2 hours. Dust with the cocoa.

Makes one cake · Prep: 30 min. + 2 hr. to chill · Level: 2 · Keeps: 2 days in the refrigerator

BOMBE SURPRISE

BERRY SAUCE

1½ teaspoons unflavored gelatin
juice of 1 orange
3 tablespoons granulated sugar
1¼ cups mixed berries

FILLING

juice of 2 oranges
⅔ cup strawberries, hulled
½ cup raspberries
¼ cup orange liqueur
2 tablespoons granulated sugar
8 slices white sandwich bread
1⅔ cups vanilla ice cream
1¼ cups whipped cream

Set out six 2-inch individual domed molds. • *Berry Sauce*: Sprinkle the gelatin over the orange juice in a saucepan. Let stand 1 minute. Stir in the sugar. Warm over low heat until the gelatin has completely dissolved. Bring to a boil, stirring constantly. Add the berries and stir until completely covered. • Remove from the heat. Pour into a medium bowl and set aside to cool. • Freeze for 1 hour, then refrigerate for 30 minutes. • *Filling*: Drizzle ¼ cup orange juice over the strawberries and raspberries in a large bowl. Let soak 15 minutes. • Mix the remaining orange juice, orange liqueur, and sugar in a large bowl. • Soak the bread in the orange mixture. • Leave the ice cream out at room temperature to soften, 10 minutes. • Mix the ice cream, cream, and fruit and juices in a large bowl. • Line the prepared molds with the bread slices. Spoon in the ice cream mixture. • Cover with aluminum foil and freeze for 2 hours. • Dip the molds briefly into cold water. Invert each onto a dessert plate. • Spoon the berry sauce over, pressing down.

Makes six molds · Prep: 30 min. + 3 hr. to freeze · Level: 1 · Keeps: 2–3 days in the freezer

Neapolitan ice cream cake

CHOCOLATE COOKIE CHILL

A rich, fudgy cake, a little goes a long way.

7   oz semisweet chocolate, coarsely chopped
1/2 cup (1 stick) butter, cut up
1/4 cup eggnog
3/4 cup pitted dates and prunes, coarsely chopped
1/2 cup walnuts, coarsely chopped
30 vanilla wafers, broken into small pieces
1/2 recipe Rich Chocolate Frosting (see page 349)

Butter a 9-inch springform pan. Line with aluminum foil. Butter the foil. • Melt the butter and chocolate in a double boiler over barely simmering water. • Remove from the heat and add the eggnog. • Stir in the fruit, walnuts (reserving some to decorate), and cookie pieces until well blended. • Spoon into the prepared pan, pressing it into the edges. Refrigerate for 5 hours. • Loosen and remove the pan sides. Turn out onto a serving plate. Remove the foil and turn top-side up. • Spread the frosting over the cake. Decorate with the walnut pieces.

Makes one 9-inch cake · Prep: 15 min. + 5 hr. to chill · Level: 1 · Keeps: 2–3 days

PEPPERMINT CHILL

A playful treat – perfect for a children's party.

1 1/2 cups vanilla wafer crumbs
3   tablespoons butter, melted
2   cups heavy cream
1   cup crushed peppermint hard candies or candy canes
25 pink and white marshmallows, chopped
1   cup walnuts or pecans, chopped

Mix the crumbs and butter in a medium bowl. Press half the mixture into a 9-inch springform pan. • Beat the cream in a medium bowl with an electric mixer at high speed until stiff. Use a large rubber spatula to fold in the peppermints, marshmallows, and nuts. • Spoon the mixture over the crust. Top with the remaining cookies and press down lightly. • Refrigerate for 12 hours.

Makes one 9-inch cake · Prep: 30 min. + 12 hr. to chill · Level: 1 · Keeps: 2–3 days in the refrigerator

NO-BAKE CHOCOLATE MINT CAKE

2   cups Rice Krispies cereal
1/4 cup (1/2 stick) butter, melted
3   packed cups mint-chocolate-chip ice cream, softened
1/2 cup bittersweet or semisweet chocolate shavings, to decorate

Butter an 8-inch round cake pan. Line with 2 sheets of aluminum foil, placing one across the other, letting the edges overhang. • Place the cereal in the prepared pan and drizzle with butter. Spread the cereal up the pan sides. • Carefully spoon the ice cream over, taking care not to knock the cereal off the sides. Cover with the overhanging foil and freeze for 2 hours. • Invert onto a serving dish. Carefully remove the foil. Sprinkle with the chocolate shavings.

Makes one 8-inch cake · Prep: 15 min. + 2 hr. to freeze · Level: 1 · Keeps: 5–6 days in freezer

NEAPOLITAN ICE CREAM CAKE

1 1/2 cups candied cherries, finely chopped
2   cups kirsch
1   Italian Sponge Cake (see page 157)
2   cups pistachio ice cream, softened
2   cups chocolate ice cream, softened
1/4 cup confectioners' sugar, to dust
11 candied cherries, to decorate

Line a 9-inch round cake pan with waxed paper. • Soak the cherries in the kirsch, 1 hour. • Place the cake in the prepared pan. Freeze for 30 minutes. • Drain the cherries, reserving the liqueur. Drizzle over the cake. Spread with the pistachio ice cream. Arrange the cherries on top of the ice cream and spread with the chocolate ice cream. • Freeze for 4 hours. • Dip the pan briefly into cold water. Invert onto a serving plate. • Dust with the confectioners' sugar and decorate with the candied cherries.

Makes one 9-inch cake · Prep: 15 min. + 4 hr. 30 min. to freeze · Level: 1 · Keeps: 1–2 days in the freezer

CHOCOLATE SALAMI

The sausage shape give this delicacy the appearance of an Italian salami sausage!

11 oz semisweet chocolate, chopped
2/3 cup sweetened condensed milk
2   tablespoons butter
2   tablespoons orange liqueur
1/2 cup raisins
1/3 cup hazelnuts, chopped and toasted
1/3 cup walnuts, coarsely chopped
2   tablespoons candied fruit, coarsely chopped, such as apricots, pineapple, or mango

Melt the chocolate with the condensed milk, butter, and liqueur in a double boiler over barely simmering water. Remove from the heat. • Transfer to a large bowl. Stir in the raisins, hazelnuts, walnuts, and candied fruit. • Set aside to cool slightly. Transfer to a sheet of waxed paper and shape and roll into a log about 12 inches long and 3 inches around. Wrap the log in aluminum foil and freeze for 2 hours. • Remove the foil and waxed paper and slice thinly, as though you were serving salami.

Makes one 12-inch long sweetmeat · Prep: 15 min. + 2 hr. to freeze · Level: 1 · Keeps: 2–3 days in the freezer

NO-BAKE CHOCOLATE SLICE

- ½ cup (1 stick) butter, cut up
- 60 vanilla wafers, crushed (heaping 2 cups)
- ½ cup granulated sugar
- ¼ cup unsweetened cocoa powder
- 1 large egg
- 2 cups Chocolate Walnut Frosting (see page 347)
- ¼ cup walnuts, coarsely chopped

Butter a 13 x 9-inch baking pan. • Melt ⅔ of the butter in a saucepan over low heat. • Stir in the sugar, cocoa, and egg. Cook, stirring constantly, until the mixture lightly coats a metal spoon or registers 160°F on an instant-read thermometer. Remove from the heat. • Stir in the crumbs. • Spoon into the prepared pan. • Refrigerate for 2 hours. • Spread with frosting. Decorate with walnuts.

Makes one 13 x 9-inch cake · Prep: 20 min. · Level: 1 · Keeps: 2–3 days

NO-BAKE CHOCOLATE MARSHMALLOW CAKE

This cake is just like a big chocolate marshmallow cookie. Children will love it and they will also enjoy helping to make it.

- ½ cup (1 stick) butter, cut up
- 4 oz semisweet chocolate, coarsely chopped
- ¼ cup firmly packed brown sugar
- 1½ cups coarsely crumbled vanilla wafers
- ½ cup raisins
- ½ cup snipped marshmallows or mini marshmallows

Butter an 8-inch round cake pan. • Melt the butter, chocolate, and brown sugar in a saucepan over low heat. • Remove from the heat. Stir in the cookie crumbs, raisins, and marshmallows. • Press into the prepared pan. Place a sheet of waxed paper on top and press down evenly with your hands. Refrigerate for 8 hours. Turn out onto a serving plate.

Makes one 8-inch cake · Prep: 15 min. · Level: 1 · Keeps: 2–3 days

Bavarian zabaglione cake

CHOCOLATE CREAM DESSERT

CHOCOLATE FILLING

- 6 oz semisweet chocolate, coarsely chopped
- ⅔ cup heavy cream
- 2 tablespoons mixed nuts, finely chopped
- 1 tablespoon rum

- 1 unfilled Basic Chocolate Cream Roll (see page 171)
- ½ cup hazelnuts, finely chopped
- 2 cups Classic Bavarian Cream (see page 341)

Preheat the oven to 375°F. • *Chocolate Filling*: Melt the chocolate in the cream in a double boiler over barely simmering water. • Stir in the nuts and rum. Set aside to cool. • Prepare the roll to the stage where it is has been cooled on a rack. • Spread with the chocolate filling. Roll up the cake. • Line a baking tray with waxed paper. Sprinkle with the hazelnuts and pour in half of the Bavarian cream. Place the jelly roll on top of the cream and lightly press down. Repeat with the remaining nuts and cream. Refrigerate for 4 hours.

Makes one jelly roll · Prep: 45 min. + 4 hr. to chill · Level: 2 · Keeps: 1–2 days in the refrigerator

BAVARIAN ZABAGLIONE CAKE

- 2 cups heavy cream
- 1½ recipes Classic Bavarian Cream (see page 341)
- 1½ cups Zabaglione (see page 348)
- 20 ladyfingers
  semisweet chocolate, grated, to decorate
  crumbled meringues, to decorate

Set out 9-inch springform pan. • Beat the cream in a medium bowl with an electric mixer at high speed until stiff. • Mix the Bavarian cream and zabaglione in a large bowl. Use a large rubber spatula to fold ¾ of the cream into the bowl. • Trim the bottom off one end of each ladyfinger and stand them around the pan sides, curved-side outward. • Spoon half the cream mixture into the pan. Top with ladyfingers. Spoon in remaining cream mixture. Refrigerate for 8 hours. • Loosen and remove the pan sides. Transfer onto a serving plate. • Spoon the remaining cream into a pastry bag and pipe onto the cake. Sprinkle with chocolate and meringues.

Makes one 9-inch cake · Prep: 30 min. + 8 hr. to chill · Level: 2 · Keeps: 1 day in the refrigerator

NO-BAKE CHOCOLATE YOGURT LOAF

1½ cups heavy cream
½ cup granulated sugar
½ cup plain yogurt
7 oz milk chocolate, coarsely grated
1½ teaspoons vanilla extract

Line an 8½ x 4½-inch loaf pan with aluminum foil, letting the edges overhang. • Beat the cream and sugar in a large bowl with an electric mixer at high speed until stiff. • Use a large rubber spatula to fold in the yogurt, chocolate, and vanilla. • Spoon into the prepared pan. Freeze for 3 hours. • Turn out onto a serving dish. Carefully remove the foil. Cut into slices.

Makes one 8½ x 4½-inch cake · Prep: 15 min. + 3 hr. to freeze · Level: 1 · Keeps: 5–6 days in freezer

CHOCOLATE SNOWSTORM CAKE

4 pints vanilla ice cream, softened
2 cups crumbled chocolate wafers
½ cup raisins, chopped
½ cup almonds, chopped
¼ cup chocolate or coffee liqueur
1 cup heavy cream
1 tablespoon confectioners' sugar

Set out a 10-inch springform pan. • Mix the ice cream, crumbs, raisins, nuts, and liqueur in a large bowl. Pack into the pan. Freeze for 4 hours. Loosen and remove the pan sides. • Beat the cream and confectioners' sugar in a small bowl with an electric mixer at high speed until stiff. Decorate with cream.

Makes one 10-inch cake · Prep: 15 min. + 4 hr. to freeze · Level: 1 · Keeps: 3–4 days in the freezer

PEAR-MARSALA ICE CREAM DOME

6 large egg yolks
¾ cup superfine sugar
½ cup Marsala wine
¾ cup milk
¾ cup light cream
4 large pears, peeled, thinly sliced, and drained
1 teaspoon butter
2 teaspoons firmly packed brown sugar
1 teaspoon light rum
1 Italian Sponge Cake (see page 157), thinly sliced unsweetened cocoa powder, to dust

Mix the egg yolks, superfine sugar, and Marsala in a saucepan until well blended. Cook over low heat, stirring constantly with a wooden spoon, until the mixture lightly coats a metal spoon or registers 160°F on an instant-read thermometer. Immediately plunge the pan into a bowl of ice water and

stir until the egg mixture has cooled. • Gradually stir in the milk and cream. • Freeze in an ice cream maker, according to manufacturer's directions. • Sauté the pears in the butter in a large skillet over medium heat until softened. Sprinkle with the brown sugar. Drizzle with the rum. • Line a domed 2-quart mold or a stainless steel bowl with half the cake slices. Arrange the pears over the cake slices and along the sides of the mold. Spoon in the ice cream to fill the mold. Top with the remaining cake slices. Place a serving plate on top. • Freeze for 2 hours, or until firmly set. • Refrigerate for 15 minutes before serving. • Dip the mold briefly into cold water, then invert onto a serving plate. • Dust with the cocoa.

Makes one dessert · Prep: 1 hr. + 2 hr. to freeze · Level: 2 · Keeps: 5 days in the freezer

RICOTTA AND STRAWBERRY DOME

2 large limes, peeled and very thinly sliced
¾ cup granulated sugar
½ cup lemon liqueur
4 large egg yolks
1 teaspoon vanilla extract
1 container (15–16 oz) ricotta cheese
2 tablespoons finely grated orange zest
1½ cups finely chopped fresh strawberries
1 tablespoon unflavored gelatin
1 cup heavy cream

Sprinkle the limes with ¼ cup sugar and the lemon liqueur in a large bowl. Soak 2 hours. • Beat the egg yolks, remaining sugar, and vanilla in a large bowl with an electric mixer at high speed until pale and thick. • Transfer to a double boiler over barely simmering water. Cook over low heat, stirring constantly with a wooden spoon, until the mixture lightly coats a metal spoon or registers 160°F on an instant-read thermometer. Immediately plunge the pan in a bowl of ice water and stir until the egg mixture has cooled. • Mix the ricotta, orange zest and strawberries in a large bowl. • Sprinkle the gelatin over ¼ cup cream in a saucepan. Let soften 1 minute. Stir over low heat until the gelatin has completely dissolved. • With mixer at high speed, beat the remaining ¾ cup cream in a medium bowl until stiff. • Stir the gelatin mixture into the ricotta mixture. • Use a large rubber spatula to fold in the whipped cream. • Rinse a 2-quart bowl with cold

water, tipping out the excess water. Line with the limes, overlapping them as if you were laying roofing tiles. • Carefully spoon in the ricotta mixture, taking care not to disturb the limes. • Refrigerate for 4 hours. • Top with a serving plate and invert the mold.

Makes one 2-quart mold · Prep: 30 min. + 6 hr. to soak + chill · Level: 1 · Keeps: 2–3 days in the refrigerator

RICOTTA ICE CREAM LOAF

This lovely no-bake cake reminds us of the flavorful filling used for cannolis, the Italian pastries.

1 container (15–16 oz) ricotta cheese
½ cup walnuts, chopped
½ cup pistachios, chopped
½ cup hazelnuts, chopped
½ cup mixed candied fruit, chopped
½ cup raisins
½ cup granulated sugar
2 tablespoons kirsch (or other fruit liqueur)
1 tablespoon grated lemon zest
1 tablespoon grated orange zest
1 teaspoon vanilla extract

Line an 8½ x 4½-inch loaf pan with aluminum foil, letting the edges overhang. • Mix the ricotta, walnuts, pistachios, hazelnuts, candied fruit, raisins, sugar, liqueur, lemon and orange zest, and vanilla in a large bowl. • Spoon the mixture into the prepared pan. Freeze for 3 hours. • Turn out onto a serving dish. Carefully remove the foil. Cut into ½-inch thick slices to serve.

Makes one 8½ x 4½-inch cake · Prep: 20 min. + 3 hr. to freeze · Level: 1 · Keeps: 5–6 days in freezer

MIMOSA CAKE

1½ Basic Sponge Cakes or Italian Sponge Cakes (see page 157)
¾ cup water
½ cup orange liqueur
½ cup granulated sugar
2 cups Vanilla Pastry Cream (see page 342)

Split the cake horizontally. Rub the half cake into coarse crumbs. • Mix the water, liqueur, and sugar in a small bowl. • Place a cake layer on a serving plate. Drizzle with the liqueur mixture. Spread with ⅓ of the pastry cream, mounding it up slightly in the middle. • Top with the remaining layer. Spread with the remaining pastry cream. • Sprinkle with cake cubes.

Makes one 9-inch cake · Prep: 15 min. · Level: 2 · Keeps: 3 days in the refrigerator

Ricotta and strawberry dome

RAINBOW SORBET DELIGHT

1¹/₂ cups finely crushed vanilla wafers
¹/₄ cup (¹/₂ stick) butter, melted
1¹/₄ cups lime sorbet, softened
1¹/₄ cups raspberry sorbet, softened
1¹/₄ cups orange sorbet, softened
    raspberries, to decorate

Mix the crumbs and butter in a large bowl. • Press into the bottom of a 9-inch springform pan. • Spread the sorbets in alternate layers. • Freeze for 30 minutes. • Loosen and remove the pan sides. Decorate with the raspberries.

Makes one 9-inch cake · Prep: 25 min. + 30 min. to freeze · Level: 1 · Keeps: 1 week in the freezer

Fresh and fruity bombe

FRUITY FROZEN YOGURT CAKES

1   cup heavy cream
¹/₃ cup confectioners' sugar
1   cup plain whole-milk yogurt
2   cups mixed fresh fruit, chopped into bite-sized pieces, if needed

Line 12 muffin-pan cups with foil or paper baking cups. • Beat the cream and confectioners' sugar in a large bowl with an electric mixer at high speed until stiff. • Use a large rubber spatula to fold in the yogurt and 1¹/₂ cups fruit. • Spoon the mixture into the prepared cups. Decorate with some fruit. • Freeze for 3 hours. • Transfer to a serving dish and let soften 10 minutes.

Makes 12 frozen cupcakes · Prep: 15 min. + 3 hr. to freeze · Level: 1 · Keeps: 3–4 days in the freezer

MARBLED ICE CREAM BOMBE

4   oz bittersweet chocolate, coarsely chopped
9   tablespoons butter
4   oz milk chocolate, coarsely chopped
4   oz white chocolate, coarsely chopped
³/₄ cup raisins
¹/₄ cup dark rum
4   pints vanilla ice cream, softened
1   cup pistachios, chopped

Lightly oil a 2-quart stainless steel bowl. Line with aluminum foil. Freeze. • Place the bittersweet chocolate and 3 tablespoons butter in a medium microwave-safe bowl. Microwave on high for 1¹/₂–2¹/₂ minutes, stirring once. Remove from microwave and stir until melted. Repeat with the milk and white chocolates, and the remaining butter. Let each cool to warm. • Drop spoonfuls of the three chocolates into the bowl, swirling

them together to create a marbled effect. Freeze until the chocolate is set, 30 minutes. • Cook the raisins and rum in a saucepan over medium heat for 3–4 minutes. Set aside to cool. • Mix the ice cream, raisins, and pistachios in a large bowl. • Spoon into the chocolate shell, cover with plastic wrap, and freeze 8 hours. • Turn out onto a serving dish. Remove the foil.

Makes one 2-quart cake · Prep: 30 min. + 8 hr. 30 min. to freeze · Level: 1 · Keeps: 1 month in freezer

FRESH AND FRUITY BOMBE

1   cup fresh raspberries
¹/₂ cup fresh red currants (or additional raspberries)
2   apricots, pitted and chopped
1   large peach, peeled, pitted and chopped
2   kiwifruit, peeled and chopped
¹/₂ cup granulated sugar
2   tablespoons fresh lemon juice
¹/₂ pint coconut or peach ice cream, softened
1   pint strawberry ice cream
¹/₃ cup flaked almonds

Line a 2-quart metal bowl with plastic wrap. Mix the fruit, sugar, and lemon juice in a medium bowl, dissolving the sugar as much as possible. • Stir in the coconut ice cream. • Pack the ice cream mixture into the prepared bowl. Freeze for 12 hours. • Soften the strawberry ice cream at room temperature, 10 minutes. Turn the bombe out onto a serving dish. Remove the wrap. Spread with the strawberry ice cream. Freeze for 1 hour. • Sprinkle with almonds.

Makes one 2-quart bombe · Prep: 15 min. + 13 hr. to freeze · Level: 1 · Keeps: 3–4 days in the freezer

NO-BAKE CHERRY CAKE

2   packages (8 oz each) cream cheese, softened
1   cup granulated sugar
2   teaspoons vanilla extract
1¹/₂ cups heavy cream
1   Italian Sponge Cake (see page 157), thinly sliced
2   cans (21 oz each) cherry pie filling or cherry jam

Beat the cream cheese, sugar, and vanilla in a large bowl with an electric mixer at high speed until smooth • With mixer at high speed, beat the cream in a large bowl until stiff. • Use a large rubber spatula to fold the cream into the cheese mixture. • Line a 9 x 12-inch serving plate with cake slices. Spoon half the cheese mixture and half the cherry filling over the top. Cover with cake slices, followed by the cheese mixture and cherry filling. • Refrigerate for 5 hours.

Makes 9 x 12-inch cake · Prep: 25 min. + 5 hr. to chill · Level: 1 · Keeps: 2–3 days in the refrigerator

TOFFEE CREAM ANGEL CAKE

1   Basic Angel Food Cake (see page 166)
1¹/₃ cups heavy cream
1¹/₂ cups crushed toffee candy bars

Split the cake horizontally. • Beat the cream in a large bowl with an electric mixer at high speed until stiff. • Use a large rubber spatula to fold the candy into the cream. • Place a cake layer on a serving plate. Spread with the toffee cream. Top with the remaining layer. Spread the remaining cream over the top. • Refrigerate for 1 hour.

Makes one 10-inch cake · Prep: 15 min. + 1 hr. to chill · Level: 1 · Keeps: 2 days in the refrigerator

ITALIAN TRIFLE MOLD

2 cups milk
  zest of $1/2$ lemon, in one piece
4 large egg yolks, at room temperature
1 cup superfine sugar
1 tablespoon all-purpose flour
1 teaspoon vanilla extract
5 oz semisweet chocolate, coarsely chopped
$1/4$ cup water
$2/3$ cup Alchermes liqueur or Marsala wine
1 Italian Sponge Cake (see page 157), cut into $1/4$-inch thick slices

Set out a domed 2-quart mold or a stainless steel bowl. • Warm the milk and lemon zest in a saucepan over medium heat. • Beat the egg yolks and $3/4$ cup superfine sugar in a large bowl with an electric mixer at high speed until pale and thick. Stir in the flour and warm milk. • Discard the lemon zest. • Return the mixture to the saucepan and bring to a boil, stirring constantly, over medium heat. Simmer for 5 minutes until thick and creamy. • Add the vanilla. • Transfer half of the mixture to a medium bowl. • Melt the chocolate in a double boiler over barely simmering water. • Stir the chocolate into one of the bowls. • Cook the remaining $1/4$ cup sugar and water in a saucepan over medium heat until the sugar has dissolved. • Remove from the heat and add the liqueur. • Line the mold with half the cake slices. Drizzle with the liqueur mixture. Spoon the vanilla filling into the mold. Top with the half the remaining cake slices. Spoon the chocolate mixture over. Top with the remaining cake slices. • Refrigerate for 3 hours. • Dip the mold briefly into cold water. Invert onto a serving plate.

Makes one 2-quart cake · Prep: 1 hr. + 3 hr. to chill · Level: 2 · Keeps: 2 days in the refrigerator

CHOCOLATE TRIFLE CAKE

$1/2$ cup granulated sugar
3 large egg yolks
$1/2$ cup all-purpose flour
3 cups warm milk
5 oz bittersweet chocolate, coarsely grated
1 Basic Sponge Cake (see page 157), thinly sliced
$1/2$ cup Alchermes liqueur or Jamaica rum
$3/4$ cup cherry or plum preserves, warmed

Beat the sugar, egg yolks, and 2 tablespoons milk in a double boiler until well blended. Cook over low heat, stirring constantly with a wooden spoon, until the mixture lightly coats a metal spoon or registers 160°F on an instant-read thermometer. Immediately plunge the pan into a bowl of ice water and stir until the egg mixture has cooled. • Gradually beat in the flour with an electric mixer at low speed. Add the remaining milk. • Fit the bowl into a saucepan of gently simmering water, without letting the bowl touch the water. Cook, stirring, until the mixture thickens. • Remove from the heat and pour half the mixture into another bowl. • Stir the chocolate into the mixture remaining in the first bowl over barely simmering water until the chocolate is melted. Remove from the heat. Press plastic wrap directly on the surface of each bowl. Refrigerate for 30 minutes until cooled. • Butter a 9-inch springform pan. Line with cake slices. Brush with half the liqueur to moisten. • Brush with the preserves. • Spread with the plain custard. Top with the chocolate custard. Top with the remaining cake slices and brush with the remaining liqueur. Refrigerate for 3–4 hours. Loosen and remove the pan sides to serve.

Makes one 9-inch cake · Prep: 30 min. · Level: 1 · Keeps: 1–2 days in the refrigerator

FLORENTINE ICE CREAM CAKE

This cake is called Zuccotto in its hometown of Florence. It takes its name (the Italian word "zuccotto" means skullcap) from the traditional head coverings worn by church dignitaries.

1 cup granulated sugar
1 cup water
3 tablespoons brandy
3 tablespoons rum
1 Italian Sponge Cake (see page 157), cut into $1/4$-inch-thick slices
$1/3$ cup confectioners' sugar
$1/3$ cup almonds, finely ground
$1/3$ cup hazelnuts, finely ground
$1/4$ cup mixed candied fruit, chopped
6 oz semisweet chocolate, grated
4 cups prepared whipped cream

Mix the sugar and water in a saucepan over medium heat until the sugar has dissolved and it comes to a boil. Boil for 5 minutes. Remove from the heat. Add the brandy and rum and let cool. • Moisten the edges of a domed 2-quart mold or a stainless steel bowl with a little syrup and line with half the cake slices. Brush with the remaining syrup. • Gently fold the confectioners' sugar, nuts, candied fruit, and 5 oz grated chocolate into the cream. Spoon the cream into the mold and top with the remaining cake slices. • Refrigerate for 5 hours. • Dip the mold briefly into cold water. Invert onto a serving plate. Sprinkle with the remaining grated chocolate.

Makes one 2-quart cake · Prep: 45 min. + 5 hr. to chill · Level: 2 · Keeps: 1 week in the refrigerator

CHOCOLATE REFRIGERATOR CAKE

2 cups heavy cream
$1/4$ cup Chocolate Syrup (plastic squeeze bottle)
$1 1/2$ cups graham cracker crumbs

Set out a deep serving dish. • Beat the cream and chocolate syrup in a large bowl with an electric mixer at high speed until stiff. • Spread a layer of crumbs, followed by a layer of chocolate cream. Repeat until the ingredients have all been used up, finishing with a layer of chocolate cream. • Refrigerate for 3 hours.

Makes one 8–10-inch cake · Prep: 15 min. + 3 hr. to chill · Level: 1 · Keeps: 2 days in the refrigerator

Florentine ice cream cake

Frosted Sicilian ricotta cake

FROSTED SICILIAN RICOTTA CAKE

Orange-flower water may be found at fancy food stores or at pharmacies.

- 1   Italian Sponge Cake (see page 157), thinly sliced
- 1¼ cups granulated sugar
- ½   cup water
- 1   whole vanilla bean
- 1   container (15–16 oz) ricotta cheese, drained and pressed through a strainer
- 5   oz bittersweet chocolate, finely chopped
- 1½ cups mixed candied fruit, chopped + whole pieces, to decorate
- 2   tablespoons pistachios
- 2   tablespoons kirsch
- 6   tablespoons apricot preserves or jam, warmed
- 2   tablespoons orange-flower water
- 1   tablespoon confectioners' sugar
- 2   cups Fondant (see pages 348–9), prepared with green food coloring
- 1   cup confectioners' sugar
- ¼   cup lukewarm water (110°–115°F)

Bring the sugar, water, and vanilla bean to a boil in a saucepan over medium heat. Cook, stirring frequently, until the sugar has completely dissolved. Set aside to cool, then discard the vanilla bean. • Beat the ricotta in a large bowl with an electric mixer at high speed until smooth. Gradually stir in the syrup. • Stir in the chocolate, candied fruit, pistachios, and kirsch. • Line a 9-inch springform pan with half the cake slices. Warm 2 tablespoons apricot preserves and brush over the cake slices. • Spread with a layer of the ricotta mixture. • Top with the remaining cake slices. Refrigerate for 2 hours. • Loosen and remove the pan sides. Invert onto a serving plate and remove the pan bottom. • Warm the apricot preserves, orange-flower water, and the confectioners' sugar, in a saucepan over low heat until syrupy. • Drizzle the glaze over. Spread the green fondant over the cake. • Mix the confectioners' sugar and water in a small bowl until a slightly liquid frosting is formed. Spoon into a plastic pastry bag. Cut off the end to create a tiny opening. Pipe over the cake in swirling patterns. • Decorate with the reserved candied fruit.

Makes one 9-inch cake · Prep: 15 min. + 2 hr. to chill · Level: 2 · Keeps: 1–2 days

RICOTTA CASSATAS WITH RASPBERRY SAUCE

- ⅓ cup + 2 teaspoons granulated sugar
- 2   tablespoons water
- 1   tablespoon unflavored gelatin
- 1   container (15–16 oz) ricotta cheese
- ⅓ cup chopped mixed candied fruit
- 2   oz semisweet chocolate, grated
- 2   teaspoons kirsch
- 1   cup raspberries

Preheat the oven to 375°F. • Set out six individual terrine dishes or ramekins. • Cook ¼ cup sugar and water in a medium saucepan over medium heat until the sugar has dissolved. • Sprinkle the gelatin over the sugar mixture. Let stand 1 minute. Place over low heat and stir until the gelatin has completely dissolved. • Place the ricotta in a large bowl. Stir in the sugar mixture. Mix in the candied fruit, chocolate, and kirsch. • Spoon into the dishes. • Refrigerate for 2 hours. • Process the raspberries and the remaining 2 teaspoons sugar in a food processor until pureed. • Turn out onto individual serving plates. • Serve with the raspberry sauce passed on the side.

Makes 6 cassatas · Prep: 30 min. + 2 hr. to chill · Level: 2 · Keeps: 2 days in the refrigerator

SICILIAN CASSATA

- 1   Italian sponge cake (see page 157), cut into ½-inch thick slices
- ¼   cup apricot preserves or jam
- 2   teaspoons water

FILLING

- 1¼ cups granulated sugar
- 1   tablespoon water
- ½   teaspoon vanilla extract
- 2   cups ricotta cheese
- 3   cups mixed candied fruit peel, finely chopped
- 2   tablespoons pistachios, coarsely chopped
- 2   teaspoons kirsch

ORANGE GLAZE

- 1⅓ cups confectioners' sugar
- ½   cup apricot preserves or jam
- 2   teaspoons orange-flower water
- 1   cup mixed candied fruit peel, to decorate

Line a 9-inch round cake pan with waxed paper. Line with the cake slices. • Warm the preserves and water in a small saucepan over low heat until liquid. Fill the spaces in the pan with the preserves. • *Filling*: Warm the sugar, water, and vanilla in a saucepan over medium heat, stirring constantly, until the sugar has dissolved. • Place the ricotta in a large bowl and gradually beat in the sugar mixture with an electric mixer at high speed until stiff. • Use a large rubber spatula to stir in the candied fruit peel and pistachios. Add the liqueur. • Pour over the cake slices. • Top with the remaining cake slices. • Refrigerate for 2 hours. • Dip the pan briefly into cold water. Invert onto a serving plate. • *Orange Glaze*: Stir the confectioners' sugar, preserves, and orange-flower water in a saucepan over medium heat until smooth. Drizzle over the cake. • Arrange the candied peel on top in a decorative manner.

Makes one 9-inch cake · Prep: 60 min. + 2 hr. to chill · Level: 2 · Keeps: 2–3 days in the refrigerator

NO-BAKE FRUIT AND NUT CAKE

1¹/₂ cups vanilla wafer crumbs
2 cups pecans, chopped
2 cups walnuts, chopped
1¹/₂ cups raisins, chopped, if desired
1 can (14 oz) sweetened condensed milk
1 can (13–14 oz) unsweetened coconut milk
1 cup shredded coconut
4 oz figs or pitted prunes, coarsely chopped
2 oz candied fruit peel, chopped
¹/₄ cup halved candied cherries
1 teaspoon vanilla extract

Butter a 10-inch springform pan. • Mix the crumbs, pecans, walnuts, raisins, condensed milk, coconut milk, coconut, figs, candied peel and cherries, and vanilla in a large bowl. • Press into the prepared pan. Refrigerate for 2 hours. Loosen and remove the pan sides and cut into small wedges.

Makes one 10-inch cake · Prep: 25 min. + 2 hr. to chill · Level: 1 · Keeps: 3–4 days

FROZEN RASPBERRY LIQUEUR CAKE

1 large egg + 3 large egg yolks
³/₄ cup granulated sugar
¹/₂ cup all-purpose flour
1 teaspoon vanilla extract
¹/₄ teaspoon salt
1²/₃ cups milk
1 tablespoon unflavored gelatin
¹/₄ cup water
about 14 oz plain butter cake, sponge cake, or pound cake (homemade or store-bought), cut into ¹/₂-inch thick slices
²/₃ cup raspberry liqueur
¹/₂ cup raspberry jam or preserves, stirred
1 cup heavy cream
2 tablespoons confectioners' sugar
1 cup fresh raspberries
¹/₄ cup slivered almonds

Sicilian cassata

Beat the egg and egg yolks, sugar, flour, vanilla, and salt in a large bowl with an electric mixer at high speed until well blended. • Add the milk. Transfer to a large saucepan. Cook over low heat, stirring constantly with a wooden spoon, until the mixture lightly coats a metal spoon or registers 160°F on an instant-read thermometer. • Sprinkle the gelatin over the water in a saucepan. Let soften 1 minute. Stir in the gelatin over low heat until it has completely dissolved. Immediately plunge the pan into a bowl of ice water and stir until the egg mixture has cooled. Stir in the gelatin mixture. • Line a 2-quart bowl with some cake slices. Brush with the liqueur and press the cake against the sides of the bowl. Spread with jam, followed by cream. Cover with cake slices. Repeat until all the ingredients are in the bowl, finishing with cake slices. Press down lightly. • Freeze for 2 hours. • With mixer at high speed, beat the cream and

confectioners' sugar in a medium bowl until stiff. • Turn the cake out onto a serving dish. Spread with the cream and decorate with raspberries and almonds.

Makes one 2-quart cake · Prep: 30 min. + 2 hr. to freeze · Level: 1 · Keeps: 3–4 days in the freezer

PINEAPPLE VANILLA CAKE

4 cups vanilla wafer cookies, crushed
2 cups crushed pineapple, drained
3 tablespoons butter, melted
¹/₃ cup walnuts, coarsely chopped
¹/₃ cup granulated sugar
¹/₂ package (8 oz) cream cheese, softened
1 teaspoon vanilla extract

Set out a 1-quart serving dish. Sprinkle with ¹/₃ of the crumbs. • Miix the pineapple, butter, walnuts, sugar, cream cheese, and vanilla in a large bowl. • Spread half the mixture over the crumbs, followed by ¹/₃ of the remaining crumbs. Repeat until all the ingredients are used up, finishing with crumbs. • Refrigerate for 3 hours.

Makes one 1-quart cake · Prep: 15 min. + 3 hr. to chill · Level: 1 · Keeps: 2 days in the refrigerator

The French tart and the Italian crostata are classic desserts made with a pastry base and filled with beautiful fruits and velvety custards. These desserts always look impressive, yet they are surprisingly easy to make.

TARTS

APPLE CROSTATA

PASTRY
1½ cups all-purpose flour
⅓ cup granulated sugar
⅓ cup cold butter, cut up
3 large egg yolks
¼ teaspoon salt

TOPPING
4 medium apples, peeled, cored, and grated
⅓ cup granulated sugar
2–3 tablespoons fresh lemon juice
2–3 tablespoons brandy (optional)

Set out a 9-inch springform pan. • Prepare a dough using the pastry ingredients and following the Short-Crust Pastry instructions on page 280, beating the egg yolks with the butter into the dry ingredients. • Set ¼ of the dough aside and fit the rest into the bottom and up the pan sides of the pan. Refrigerate for 30 minutes. • Preheat the oven to 375°F. • *Topping*: Drizzle the apples with the lemon juice. Soak 3 minutes. • Squeeze out most of the lemon juice and spread a layer over the pastry. Sprinkle with sugar. Cover with more apple. Repeat until all of the apple is in the pan, reserving 1 tablespoon of sugar. Drizzle with the brandy, if desired. • Use your hands to roll the remaining dough into long, thin sausage shapes. Place in a lattice pattern over the top. Roll down the top of the pastry to meet the ends of the lattice strips and form an edging around the tart. • Bake for 50–60 minutes, or until lightly browned. After 40 minutes, sprinkle the apple (not the pastry sides) with the reserved sugar. • Cool the crostata in the pan. Loosen and remove the pan sides. Serve warm.

Makes one 9-inch cake · Prep: 20 min. + 30 min to chill · Level: 2 · Cooking: 50–60 min. · Keeps: 1–2 days

◄ Fresh fruit crostata (see page 282)

➤ Apple crostata

Honey and nut crostata

SHORT-CRUST PASTRY

- 2 cups all-purpose flour
- 1¹/₂ teaspoons salt
- ¹/₄ cup (¹/₂ stick) butter, at room temperature, cut up
- 5–6 tablespoons cold water

Sift the flour and salt into a large bowl and make a well in the center. • Stir in the butter and enough water to form a smooth dough. • Knead the dough on a lightly floured surface until smooth and elastic, about 7 minutes. • Shape into a rectangle and fold the short sides over. Roll into a rectangle once more, working in the opposite direction. • Fold the short side over once more. Repeat once more. • Shape into a disk, wrap in plastic wrap, and refrigerate until ready to use.

Makes 1 lb or enough to cover a 9-inch pan · Prep: 20 min. · Level: 2

HAZELNUT CROSTATA

- 1²/₃ cups all-purpose flour
- 1¹/₄ cups superfine sugar
- 1 tablespoon unsweetened cocoa powder
- 1 teaspoon baking powder
  pinch of salt
- 1 large egg + 1 egg yolk, lightly beaten
- ¹/₂ cup butter, softened

HAZELNUT FILLING

- 2 large egg yolks
- 1²/₃ cups milk
- ¹/₃ cup superfine sugar
- ¹/₃ cup all-purpose flour
  pinch of salt
- 1 cup hazelnuts, finely chopped

Preheat the oven to 375°F. • Stir together the flour, superfine sugar, cocoa, baking powder, and salt in a large bowl and make a well in the center. Stir in the egg, egg yolk and butter to form a smooth dough. • Roll the dough out on a lightly floured surface to a 12-inch round. Fit into a 10-inch round cake pan, trimming the edges if needed. Prick all over with a fork. • Line the pastry shell with foil and fill the foil with dried beans or pie weights. • Bake for 15 minutes, then remove the foil with the beans. Bake for 5 minutes more. • Cool completely in the pan on a rack. • Lower the oven temperature to 300°F. • *Hazelnut Filling*: Beat the egg yolks, 1 tablespoon milk, sugar, flour, and salt with an electric mixer at high speed in a saucepan until well blended. Add the remaining milk and warm over medium heat, beating constantly, until thick. Stir in the hazelnuts. Remove from the heat and set aside to cool. • Spoon the filling into the pastry shell. • Bake for 10–15 minutes, or until set. • Cool completely in the pan on a rack.

Makes one 10-inch tart · Prep: 1 hr. · Cooking: 30–45 min. · Level: 2 · Keeps: 2 days

HONEY AND NUT CROSTATA

- 1 cup all-purpose flour
- ¹/₄ cup granulated sugar
- ¹/₄ teaspoon salt
- 1 large egg
- 2 tablespoons extra-virgin olive oil

FILLING

- ¹/₄ cup honey
- ¹/₂ cup crushed amaretti cookies
- ¹/₃ cup almonds, coarsely chopped
- 2 tablespoons pine nuts
- 1 tablespoon finely grated lemon zest
- ¹/₄ cup (¹/₂ stick) butter

Stir together the flour, sugar, and salt in a large bowl. Stir in the egg and oil. Use your hands to work the dough until soft and non-sticky. Refrigerate for 30 minutes. • *Filling*: Stir the honey, crumbs, almonds, pine nuts, lemon zest, and butter in a saucepan over low heat. • Roll the dough out on a lightly floured surface to a 12-inch round. • Preheat the oven to 400°F. • Fit the dough into a 8-inch springform pan, leaving the long edges draped over the sides. Spoon the filling into the pastry and fold the edges over to form uneven folds. • Bake for 25–35 minutes, or until golden brown. • Loosen and remove the pan sides. Serve warm.

Makes one 8-inch tart · Prep: 25 min. + 30 min. to chill · Cooking: 25–35 min. · Level: 2 · Keeps: 1–2 days

CHESTNUT CROSTATA

- 1¹/₂ cups candied chestnuts, lightly crushed, + a few extra. to decorate
- 2 tablespoons dark rum
- 1 lb short-crust pastry (see recipe left)
- 2 large eggs + 2 large egg yolks
- ¹/₃ cup granulated sugar
- ¹/₃ cup chestnut flour or fine whole-wheat flour
- ¹/₃ cup all-purpose flour
- ¹/₃ cup butter, melted
  unsweetened cocoa powder, to dust

Preheat the oven to 375°F. • Mix the chestnuts and rum in a large bowl. Soak 10 minutes. • Roll the pastry out on a lightly floured surface to an 11-inch round. • Fit into a 9-inch round cake pan, trimming the edges if needed. Prick all over with a fork. • Beat the eggs, egg yolks, and sugar in a large bowl with an electric mixer at medium speed until pale and thick. • Use a large rubber spatula to fold in the flours and butter. • Spoon the chestnut mixture over the pastry. Spoon the batter over the chestnuts. • Bake for 50–60 minutes, or until lightly browned. • Cool the crostata completely in the pan. • Decorate with candied chestnuts. Dust with the cocoa.

Makes one 9-inch tart · Prep: 30 min. · Cooking: 1 hr. · Level: 2 · Keeps: 3 days

LEMON CROSTATA

- 1 lb short-crust pastry (see recipe left)
- 1 cup almonds, finely ground
- 1/2 cup superfine sugar
  grated zest and juice of 2 lemons
- 1 tablespoon flaked almonds

Preheat the oven to 325°F. • Roll the pastry out on a lightly floured surface to a 12-inch round. • Fit into a 10-inch round cake pan, trimming the edges if needed. Prick all over with a fork. Line the pastry shell with foil and fill the foil with dried beans or pie weights. • Bake for 25 minutes, then remove the foil with the beans. Bake for 5 minutes more. • Cool completely in the pan on a rack.• Mix the almonds, superfine sugar, and lemon zest and juice in a large bowl. • Spoon the lemon mixture into the pastry. Sprinkle with almonds. • Bake for 35–40 minutes, or until a toothpick inserted into the center comes out clean. • Cool in the pan on a rack for 15 minutes. Transfer to a serving plate.

Makes one 10-inch tart · Prep: 30 min. · Cooking: 65–70 min. · Level: 2 · Keeps: 2 days

MARMALADE CROSTATA

- 1 1/2 cups all-purpose flour
- 1 teaspoon baking powder
- 1/4 teaspoon salt
- 1/3 cup butter, softened
- 1/2 cup granulated sugar
- 1 tablespoon grated lime zest
- 2 large eggs, at room temperature
- 1 cup chunky orange marmalade
- 1 tablespoon fresh lime juice

Preheat the oven to 350°F. • Stir together the flour, baking powder, and salt in a large bowl. • Beat the butter, sugar, and lime zest in a medium bowl with an electric mixer at medium speed until creamy. • Add the eggs, one at a time, until just blended after each addition. • With mixer at low speed, gradually beat in the dry ingredients. • Press into a 10-inch tart pan with a removable bottom. Mix the marmalade and lime juice. Spread over the dough, leaving a 1/2-inch border. • Bake for 30–40 minutes, or until golden brown and the marmalade is bubbly. • Cool the crostata completely in the pan on a rack.

Makes one 10-inch tart · Prep: 25 min. · Cooking: 35–40 min. · Level: 1 · Keeps: 2–3 days

COCONUT CROSTATA

Orange-flower water may be found in gourmet food stores.

TOPPING
- 1 cup shredded coconut
- 1 2/3 cups water
- 1/4 cup granulated sugar
- 1 tablespoon fresh lemon juice

PASTRY
- 1 1/2 cups all-purpose flour
- 1/3 cup granulated sugar
- 1/2 cup (1 stick) cold butter, cut up
- 2 large egg yolks
- 1/4 teaspoon salt

FILLING
- 3 large egg yolks
- 1 1/4 oz all-purpose flour
- 1/3 cup granulated sugar
- 1 1/4 cups milk
- 2 tablespoons orange-flower water
- 1/4 teaspoon salt

Place the coconut and 1/4 cup water in a medium bowl. Set aside 12 hours. • *Pastry*: Prepare a dough using the pastry ingredients following the Short-Crust Pastry instructions on page 280, beating the egg yolks with the butter into the dry ingredients. • Press into a 9-inch springform pan. Prick with a fork. Refrigerate for 30 minutes. • Preheat the oven to 375°F. • Bake, covered with aluminum foil, for 20 minutes. Remove the foil and cool completely in the pan. • *Filling*: Beat the egg yolks, flour, sugar, and salt in a saucepan. • Bring the milk to a boil in a pan over medium heat. Gradually pour it into the egg mixture. Place the saucepan over low heat and stir until thick. Add the orange-flower water. • Pour into the pastry shell. • *Topping*: Boil the remaining water and

Coconut crostata

sugar in a saucepan for 2 minutes. Add the prepared coconut and lemon juice and cook for 2 minutes, stirring often • Spread over the filling. Bake for 10–15 minutes, or until browned. • Cool the tart completely in the pan. Loosen and remove the pan sides to serve.

Makes one 9-inch tart · Prep: 30 min. + 12 hr. to soak · Level: 2 · Cooking: 30–35 min. · Keeps: 1–2 days in the refrigerator

FRUIT CROSTATA

- 1 lb short-crust pastry (see page 280)
- 10 lightly crushed Italian biscotti
- 2 cups Vanilla Custard (see page 344)
- 8 small red plums, halved and pitted
- 8 small yellow plums, halved and pitted
- 6 medium large apricots, pitted and thinly sliced
- 1 banana, peeled, thinly sliced, and brushed with lemon juice
- 1/3 cup apricot preserves or jam, warmed

Preheat the oven to 375°F. • Roll the pastry out on a lightly floured surface to a 14-inch rectangle. • Fit into a 13 x 4-inch tart pan, trimming the edges, if needed. • Line the pastry shell with foil and fill the foil with dried beans or pie weights. • Bake for 25 minutes, then remove the foil with the beans. Bake for 5 minutes more. • Cool completely in the pan on a rack. • Refrigerate for 2 hours, or until well chilled. • Transfer to a serving plate. • Sprinkle with the crumbs. Spoon the cooled custard into the pastry. Arrange the fruit in alternating rows on top. Brush with the preserves. • Refrigerate for 2 hours.

Makes one 13-inch tart · Prep: 25 min. + 4 hr. to chill · Cooking: 30 min. · Level: 2 · Keeps: 2 days in the refrigerator

BAKED CUSTARD CROSTATA

- 1 lb short-crust pastry (see page 280)
- 1 large egg, lightly beaten
- 2 cups Vanilla Custard (see page 344)

Preheat the oven to 350°F. • Roll half the dough out on a lightly floured surface to a 13-inch round. Fit into a 10-inch pie plate. Prick all over with a fork. Brush with some beaten egg. • Spoon the custard into the pastry shell. Roll out the remaining pastry, cut into strips, and arrange in a lattice pattern over the cream filling. Brush with a little beaten egg. • Bake for 35–40 minutes, or until golden brown. • Serve warm.

Makes one 10-inch tart · Prep: 30 min. · Cooking: 35–40 min. · Level: 1 · Keeps: 1–2 days in the refrigerator

CREAMY FRUIT CROSTATA

- 1½ cups all-purpose flour
- ⅓ cup granulated sugar
- ⅓ cup butter
- 1 large egg yolk
- ¼ teaspoon salt

- 2 cups Vanilla Custard (see page 344)

TOPPING

- 1 large banana, peeled and sliced
- 2 medium peaches, peeled and sliced
- 2 tablespoons all-purpose flour
- 1 tablespoon butter
- 2 tablespoons granulated sugar
- ½ teaspoon ground cinnamon

Pineapple and plum crostata

Prepare the dough using the ingredients and following the Short-Crust Pastry instructions on page 280, beating the egg yolks with the butter into the dry ingredients. • Press into a 9-inch springform pan. Refrigerate for 30 minutes. • Preheat the oven to 400°F. • Spoon the custard into the pastry. Top with the banana and peaches. • Mix the flour, butter, sugar, and cinnamon in a small bowl. Sprinkle over the fruit. • Bake for 35–45 minutes, or until set. • Cool the tart in the pan on a rack. Loosen and remove the pan sides. Serve warm.

Makes one 9-inch tart · Prep: 25 min. + 30 min to chill · Cooking: 35–45 min. · Level: 1 · Keeps: 1–2 days in the refrigerator

FRESH FRUIT CROSTATA

This eye-catching crostata must be made with the best quality fruit. If you are using bananas, brush with lemon juice to prevent discoloring.

- 1 cup all-purpose flour
- 2 tablespoons granulated sugar
- ⅛ teaspoon salt
- ⅓ cup cold butter, cut up
- 1 egg yolk, at room temperature
- 1 tablespoon ice water

TOPPING

- 2 cups Vanilla Custard (see page 344)
- 1–2 cups sliced fresh fruit or whole berries
- ¼ cup apricot preserves

Stir together the flour, sugar, and salt in a large bowl. Use a pastry blender to cut in the butter until the mixture resembles coarse crumbs. Add the egg yolk and water and, working quickly, using your hands, work the pastry until smooth. Shape into a disk, wrap in plastic wrap, and refrigerate for 30 minutes. • Roll the dough out on a lightly floured surface to a 14-inch rectangle. Fit into a 13 x 4-inch rectangular tart pan, trimming the edges if needed. • Preheat the oven to 375°F. • Line the pastry shell with foil and fill the foil with dried beans or pie weights. Bake for 15 minutes. Remove the foil with the beans and bake for 15–20 minutes more, or until crisp. Cool completely in the pan on a rack. • *Topping*: Spread with custard and arrange the fruit on top. Warm the preserves in a saucepan over low heat. Brush with preserves.

Makes one 13 x 4-inch tart · Prep: 40 min. · Cooking: 30–35 min. · Level: 2 · Keeps: 1 day in the refrigerator

PINEAPPLE AND PLUM CROSTATA

- 1⅔ cups all-purpose flour
- ⅓ cup granulated sugar
- ½ cup (1 stick) butter
- 1 large egg
- 1 tablespoon brandy or dry Marsala wine
- ¼ teaspoon salt

TOPPING

- 4 rings of pineapple (fresh or canned), finely chopped
- 6 oz fresh dark red Italian-style plums, pitted and coarsely chopped
- ¼ cup brandy or dry Marsala wine
- ¼ cup pineapple jelly

Place the pineapple and plums in a bowl with the brandy. Soak 1 hour. • Butter and flour a 9-inch springform pan. • Prepare a dough using the ingredients and following the Short-Crust Pastry instructions on page 280, beating the egg yolks and Marsala with the butter into the dry ingredients. • Set ¼ of the dough aside and press the rest into the bottom and halfway up the sides of the prepared pan. Refrigerate for 30 minutes. • Preheat the oven to 375°F. • *Topping*: Spread the jelly, warmed, over the pastry and top with the pineapple and plum mixture. Drizzle any remaining liquid in the bowl over the fruit. • Use your hands to roll the remaining dough into long, thin sausage shapes. Place in a lattice pattern over the fruit. • Bake for 30–40 minutes, or until lightly browned. • Cool the tart in the pan on a rack. Loosen and remove the pan sides. Serve warm or at room temperature.

Makes one 9-inch tart · Prep: 25 min. + 30 min to chill · Level: 1 · Cooking: 30–40 min. · Keeps: 1–2 days

APRICOT AND PRUNE CROSTATA

1 9-inch unbaked pie shell, thawed if frozen
3 large egg yolks
2 cups Lemon Pastry Cream (see page 346)
1 cup dried apricots
1 cup pitted prunes
1/4 cup granulated sugar

Preheat the oven to 400°F. • Fit the dough into a 9-inch pie plate, trimming the edges if needed. • Beat the egg yolks into the Lemon Pastry Cream and spread over the pastry. • Arrange the apricots and prunes in a decorative manner over the cream. Sprinkle with sugar. • Bake for 30–35 minutes, or until lightly browned. • Serve warm.

Makes one 9-inch tart · Prep: 30 min. · Cooking: 30–35 min. · Level: 1 · Keeps: 2–3 days in the refrigerator

APRICOT SPONGE CROSTATA

1 lb short-crust pastry (see page 280)
1 Italian Sponge Cake (see page 157), thinly sliced
2 tablespoons raisin wine or sweet dessert wine
1 1/4 lb apricots, peeled, pitted, and thinly sliced
4 large egg yolks
1/4 cup superfine sugar
    confectioners' sugar, to dust

Use the instructions for Peach Sponge Crostata (see recipe below), substituting the apricots for the peaches.

Makes one 10-inch tart · Prep: 45 min. · Cooking: 35–40 min. · Level: 2 · Keeps: 2 days in the refrigerator

PEACH SPONGE CROSTATA

1 lb short-crust pastry (see page 280)
1 Italian Sponge Cake (see page 157), thinly sliced
2 tablespoons raisin wine or sweet dessert wine
1 1/4 lb peaches, peeled, pitted, and thinly sliced
4 large egg yolks
1/4 cup superfine sugar
    confectioners' sugar, to dust

Preheat the oven to 375°F. • Roll the pastry out on a lightly floured surface to a 12-inch round. • Fit into a 10-inch round cake pan, trimming the edges if needed. • Line the pastry shell with foil and fill the foil with dried beans or pie weights. • Bake for 20 minutes, then remove the foil with the beans. Cool completely in the pan. • Refrigerate until chilled. • Arrange the cake slices in the pastry shell. Drizzle with 1 tablespoon wine. Arrange the peach slices on top. • Beat the egg yolks, superfine sugar, and remaining 1 tablespoon wine with an electric mixer at medium speed until pale and thick. • Spoon over the peaches. • Dust with the

Apricot and prune crostata

confectioners' sugar. • Bake for 15–20 minutes more, until lightly browned. • Cool the tart in the pan for 15 minutes. • Transfer onto a serving plate. • Serve warm.

Makes one 10-inch tart · Prep: 45 min. · Cooking: 35–40 min. · Level: 2 · Keeps: 2 days in the refrigerator

PEACH CROSTATA

2 cups all-purpose flour
1/4 teaspoon salt
1/2 cup (1 stick) butter, melted
1 large egg
1/4 cup milk
2/3 cup granulated sugar
4 large yellow peaches, peeled and thinly sliced
3/4 cup heavy cream
1 tablespoon confectioners' sugar
1/2 teaspoon vanilla extract

Preheat the oven to 400°F. • Sift the flour and salt into a large bowl and make a well in the center. Beat in the butter, egg, milk, and 7 tablespoons sugar with an electric mixer at medium speed. Shape into a disk and set aside. • Arrange the peaches in a 9-inch pie plate and sprinkle with sugar. • Roll the dough out on a lightly floured surface into a 9-inch round. • Place over the peaches and press to seal the edges. Prick all over with a fork. • Bake for 35–45 minutes, or until lightly browned. • Cool the tart in the pan for 10 minutes. • With mixer at high speed, beat the cream, confectioners' sugar, and vanilla in a medium bowl until stiff. • Spoon the

cream into a pastry bag and decorate over the top. • Serve warm or at room temperature.

Makes one 9-inch tart · Prep: 30 min. · Cooking 35–45 min. · Level: 1 · Keeps: 1–2 days in the refrigerator

UPSIDE-DOWN CHERRY CROSTATA

1 cup all-purpose flour
1/4 cup granulated sugar
1 tablespoon finely grated lemon zest
1/4 teaspoon salt
1/2 cup (1 stick) cold butter, cut up
1/3 cup confectioners' sugar
2 cups ripe fresh sweet cherries, pitted

Stir together the flour, sugar, lemon zest, and salt in a large bowl. Use a pastry blender to cut in the butter. Use your hands to work the dough into a disk. Wrap with plastic wrap and refrigerate for 30 minutes. • Dust a 9-inch pie plate with the confectioners' sugar. • Preheat the oven to 400°F. • Place the cherries in the plate with their bottoms upward. • Roll the dough out on a lightly floured surface to a 9-inch round. Place over the cherries, pressing down to seal. • Bake for 25–30 minutes, or until lightly browned. • Cool the tart completely in the pan.

Makes one 9-inch tart · Prep: 30 min. + 30 min. to chill · Cooking: 25–30 min. · Level: 2 · Keeps: 1–2 days

Creamy apple crostata

FRUITS OF THE FALL CROSTATA

PASTRY

1 1/2	cups all-purpose flour
1/4	cup (1/2 stick) butter
1/4	cup lard or vegetable shortening
1/2	teaspoon salt
2	tablespoons water

FILLING

1/2	cup graham cracker crumbs
1/3	cup granulated sugar
1/3	cup raisins
2/3	cup almonds, coarsely chopped
1/3	cup chopped candied peel
1	teaspoon ground cinnamon
1/2	teaspoon ground nutmeg
1/4	teaspoon cloves
3	tablespoons orange liqueur or brandy
1	small apple, peeled, cored, and thinly sliced
1	small pear, peeled, cored, and thinly sliced

Prepare the dough using the pastry ingredients and following the Short-Crust Pastry instructions on page 280, beating the lard with the butter and mixing the water into the dry ingredients. • Set 1/4 of the dough aside and roll the remainder out into a disk large enough to line an 8-inch springform pan, trimming the edges if needed. Refrigerate for 30 minutes. • Preheat the oven to 375°F. • *Filling*: Mix the crumbs, sugar, raisins, almonds, peel, cinnamon, nutmeg, cloves, and liqueur in a large bowl. • Spread 2/3 of the crumb mixture over the pastry shell. Cover with the apple and pear. Top with the remaining crumbs. • Roll the reserved dough out into a disk large enough to cover the top. Fit into the pan and seal the edges. Use a sharp knife to make five long openings in a star shape in the top. • Bake for 50–60 minutes, or until lightly browned. • Cool in the pan on a rack. Loosen and remove the pan sides. Serve warm.

Makes one 8-inch cake · Prep: 30 min. + 30 min to chill · Level: 2 · Cooking: 50–60 min. · Keeps: 1–2 days

CREAMY APPLE CROSTATA

PASTRY

1 2/3	cups all-purpose flour
1/3	cup granulated sugar
1/2	cup (1 stick) butter
1	large egg
1	tablespoon brandy (or water)
1/4	teaspoon salt

TOPPING

2	medium apples, peeled, cored, and cut into wedges
1	large egg + 1 large egg yolk
1/3	cup granulated sugar
2	teaspoons cornstarch
1	teaspoon vanilla extract
1/4	teaspoon salt
2/3	cup milk

Prepare the dough using the pastry ingredients and following the Short-Crust Pastry instructions on page 280, beating the egg with the butter and brandy with the water into the dry ingredients. • Press into the bottom and halfway up the sides of a 9-inch springform pan. Refrigerate for 30 minutes. • Preheat the oven to 400°F. • *Topping*: Arrange the apple slices in circles on the pastry. Bake for 25–30 minutes, or until lightly browned. • Beat the egg, egg yolk, sugar, cornstarch, vanilla, and salt in a medium saucepan. Gradually pour in the milk. Place over medium heat and stir until the mixture thickens. • Spoon the cream over the apples in the pastry. • Bake for 10–15 minutes more, or until golden brown. • Cool in the pan on a rack. Loosen and remove the pan sides. Serve warm or at room temperature.

Makes one 9-inch tart · Prep: 25 min. + 30 min to chill · Cooking: 35–45 min. · Level: 1 · Keeps: 1–2 days in the refrigerator

CHOCOLATE CROSTATA

1	lb short-crust pastry (see page 280)
2–3	tablespoons vanilla wafer crumbs

CREAMY CHOCOLATE FILLING

1/2	cup (1 stick) butter
1	cup granulated sugar
6	oz bittersweet chocolate, coarsely chopped
1/4	cup cornstarch
1	teaspoon vanilla extract
1/4	cup milk
4	large eggs, separated
1	cup heavy cream
1/4	cup unsweetened cocoa powder, to dust

Preheat the oven to 375°F. • Butter a 9-inch springform pan. Sprinkle with the crumbs. • Roll the dough out on a lightly floured surface to a 9-inch round. Fit into the prepared pan. Refrigerate for 30 minutes, or until firm. • *Creamy Chocolate Filling*: Melt the butter in a saucepan over low heat. Stir in the sugar, chocolate, cornstarch, and vanilla. Add the milk and egg yolks and continue cooking, stirring constantly, for about 10 minutes, or until the filling thickens. Remove from the heat and set aside to cool. • Beat the egg whites in a large bowl with an electric mixer at medium speed until stiff peaks form. • Use a large rubber spatula to fold the beaten whites into the chocolate filling. • Spoon into the pastry shell. • Bake for 50–60 minutes, or until set. • Cool completely in the pan on a rack. • Loosen and remove the pan sides. Transfer to a serving plate. Dust with the cocoa.

Makes one 9-inch tart · Prep: 30 min. + 30 min. to chill · Cooking: 50–60 min. · Level: 2 · Keeps: 2–3 days in the refrigerator

CHOCOLATE-BERRY CROSTATA

1½ cups finely crushed vanilla wafers
⅔ cup almonds, finely ground
¾ cup (1½ sticks) butter, melted
2 cups Chocolate Pastry Cream (see page 346)
1¼ cups mixed berries
¼ cup apricot preserves or jam

Mix the crumbs, almonds, and butter in a large bowl. • Press into the bottom and partway up the sides of a 9-inch pie plate. • Refrigerate for 2 hours, or until set. • Spoon the pastry cream into the pastry and refrigerate for 2 hours. • Decorate with the fruit. • Heat the apricot preserves in a small pan until liquid. Brush with the preserves.

Makes one 9-inch tart · Prep: 30 min. + 4 hr. to chill · Level: 1 · Keeps: 1 day in the refrigerator

STRAWBERRY-ALMOND CROSTATA

1⅓ cups all-purpose flour
⅔ cup confectioners' sugar
½ teaspoon baking powder
¼ teaspoon salt
½ cup (1 stick) butter, melted
2 tablespoons dry white wine
1 large egg yolk + 1 large egg
1 tablespoon finely grated lemon zest
½ teaspoon vanilla extract
⅔ cup milk
1 tablespoon orange liqueur or other fruit liqueur
½ cup amaretti cookies, crushed
⅓ cup amaretto
20 medium strawberries, hulled and quartered
½ cup strawberry preserves

Stir together 1 cup flour, ⅓ cup confectioners' sugar, baking powder, and salt in a large bowl. Add the butter, wine, egg yolk, and lemon zest. Work the dough into a ball. Wrap in plastic wrap and refrigerate for 30 minutes. • Preheat the oven to 400°F. • Beat the egg, remaining ⅓ cup confectioners' sugar, remaining flour, and vanilla in a saucepan. Gradually add the

Chocolate berry crostata

milk, whisking constantly. Bring to a boil over medium heat, stirring constantly. The cream should thicken a little. • Remove from the heat and add the liqueur. • Roll out the dough on a lightly floured surface to a 11-inch rectangle. Fit into a 9½ x 6-inch rectangular tart pan, trimming the edges to fit. Prick all over with a fork. • Sprinkle with the crumbs, drizzle with the amaretto, and spread with the cream. • Arrange the strawberries, cut-side up, in the cream. • Bake for 35–45 minutes, or until lightly browned. • Cool in the pan on a rack. • Warm the strawberry preserves in a saucepan over low heat until liquid. Brush over the strawberries. • Serve warm or at room temperature.

Makes one 9½-inch tart · Prep: 30 min. + 30 min. to chill · Cooking: 35–45 min. · Level: 2 · Keeps: 1–2 days in the refrigerator

STRAWBERRY CROSTATA

1 lb short-crust pastry (see page 280)
½ cup milk
½ cup light cream
2 large eggs + 1 large egg yolk, lightly beaten
¼ cup superfine sugar
1 lb strawberries, hulled and sliced

Preheat the oven to 375°F. • Roll the pastry out on a lightly floured surface to a 12-inch round. • Fit into a 10-inch round cake pan, trimming the edges if needed. Prick all over with a fork. • Line the pastry shell with foil and fill the foil with dried beans or pie weights. • Bake for 25 minutes, then remove the foil with the beans. Lower the oven temperature to 300°F and bake for 20 minutes more, or until crisp. • Arrange the strawberries in the pastry shell. Mix the milk, cream, eggs and egg yolk, and superfine sugar in a large bowl. • Spoon over the strawberries. • Bake for 30–40 minutes, or until set. • Cool the crostata in the pan on a rack for 15 minutes. Transfer onto a serving plate. • Serve warm.

Makes one 10-inch tart · Prep: 30 min. · Cooking: 75–85 min. · Level: 2 · Keeps: 2 days in the refrigerator

RASPBERRY CROSTATA

This crostata is equally good when made with small or sliced strawberries. Use the same weight of fruit and replace the strawberry jelly with red or black currant jelly.

PASTRY

1²/₃ cups all-purpose flour
¹/₃ cup granulated sugar
¹/₂ cup (1 stick) butter, softened
1 large egg
3–5 tablespoons water
¹/₄ teaspoon salt

TOPPING

1 lb fresh raspberries
³/₄ cup strawberry jelly
¹/₄ cup confectioners' sugar (optional)

Raspberry crostata

Prepare the dough using the pastry ingredients and following the Short-Crust Pastry instructions on page 280, beating the egg with the butter. • Press into a 9-inch springform pan, forming a ¹/₂-inch thick rim at the top. Prick all over with a fork. Refrigerate for 30 minutes. • Preheat the oven to 375°F. • Bake, covered with aluminum foil, for 20 minutes. Remove the foil and bake for 7–8 minutes more, or until lightly browned. Set aside on a rack to cool. • Heat the jelly in a small saucepan over low heat until liquid. • Loosen and remove the pan sides. Place the pastry on a serving plate. • *Topping*: Arrange the raspberries over the top and drizzle with the warm jelly. • Dust with the confectioners' sugar, if desired.

Makes one 9-inch tart · Prep: 30 min. + 30 min to chill · Level: 1 · Cooking: 25–30 min. · Keeps: 1–2 days

CHOCOLATE-ALMOND CROSTATA

4 oz bittersweet chocolate, coarsely chopped
1¹/₃ cups all-purpose flour
1¹/₃ cups finely ground almonds
¹/₂ cup granulated sugar
¹/₂ teaspoon salt
³/₄ cup (1¹/₂ sticks) butter, softened
3 large egg yolks, at room temperature
2 cups Chocolate Pastry Cream, chilled (see page 346)
1 cup heavy cream

Melt the chocolate in a double boiler over barely simmering water. Set aside to cool. • Stir together the flour, almonds, sugar, and salt in a large bowl. Beat in the butter and egg yolks with an electric mixer at medium speed. • With mixer at low speed, beat in the chocolate. • Shape into a smooth ball. Wrap in plastic wrap and refrigerate for 1 hour. • Preheat the oven to 350°F. • Roll the dough

out on a lightly floured surface into a 10-inch round. Fit into a 9-inch pie plate. Prick all over with a fork. • Bake for 20–30 minutes, or until firm. • Cool the crust completely in the pan on a rack. • Fill with with the pastry cream. • With mixer at high speed, beat the cream in a medium bowl until stiff. • Spread with the cream.

Makes one 9-inch tart · Prep: 30 min. + 1 hr to chill · Cooking: 20–30 min. · Level: 2 · Keeps: 1–2 days

STRAWBERRY TART

PASTRY

1¹/₂ cups all-purpose flour
4 tablespoons granulated sugar
¹/₂ cup (1 stick) butter
3 tablespoons milk
¹/₄ teaspoon salt

FILLING

2 large eggs
¹/₃ cup granulated sugar
¹/₃ cup light cream
²/₃ cup almonds, finely ground
2 tablespoons all-purpose flour
1 teaspoon baking powder
2 cups small strawberries, hulled

Preheat the oven to 350°F. • *Pastry*: Prepare the dough using the pastry ingredients and following the Short-Crust Pastry instructions on page 280, replacing the milk for the water. Roll the pastry out on a lightly floured surface to a 10-inch round. Fit into a 9-inch cake pan, trimming the edges if needed. Line the pastry shell with foil and fill the foil with dried beans or pie weights. • Bake for 20 minutes, then remove the foil with the beans. • *Filling*: Beat the eggs and sugar in a large bowl with

an electric mixer at high speed until pale and thick. • With mixer at low speed, gradually beat in the cream, almonds, flour, and baking powder. • Top the pastry with strawberries. Spoon the batter over. • Bake for 30–35 minutes more, or until a toothpick inserted into the center comes out clean. • Cool completely in the pan on a rack.

Makes one 9-inch tart · Prep: 15 min. · Cooking: 50-55 min. · Level: 2 · Keeps: 3 days in the refrigerator

STRAWBERRY-LEMON TART

3 large eggs, at room temperature
³/₄ cup superfine sugar
1¹/₃ cups all-purpose flour
1 tablespoon baking powder
2 tablespoons sunflower oil
¹/₄ cup milk
   grated zest of 1 lemon
1¹/₂ cups strawberries, hulled
   confectioners' sugar, to dust
   whipped cream, to serve (optional)

Preheat the oven to 375°F. • Butter a 10-inch round cake pan. Dust with fine bread crumbs. • Beat the eggs and superfine sugar in a large bowl with an electric mixer at high speed until pale and thick. • Use a large rubber spatula to fold the flour and baking powder into the batter. • Mix the oil and milk in a small bowl. Add the lemon zest. Stir the oil mixture into the batter. • Spoon half the batter into the prepared pan. Arrange half the strawberries on top. • Spoon in the remaining batter. Arrange the remaining strawberries on top. • Bake for 30–40 minutes, or until a toothpick inserted into the center comes out clean. • Cool the tart in the pan for 5 minutes. Transfer to a serving plate and let cool completely. • Dust with the confectioners' sugar. Serve with whipped cream, if desired.

Makes one 10-inch tart · Prep: 30 min. · Cooking: 40 min. · Level: 2 · Keeps: 2 days

MIXED BERRY TART

 1⅓ cups all-purpose flour
 1 teaspoon baking powder
 ⅔ cup butter, softened
 1 cup granulated sugar
 8 large eggs, separated
 ¼ teaspoon salt
 3½ cups mixed berries (reserve some to decorate)
 ⅓ cup confectioners' sugar, to dust

Preheat the oven to 375°F. • Butter and flour a 9-inch springform pan. • Stir in the flour and baking powder in a large bowl. Beat the butter and sugar in a large bowl with an electric mixer at medium speed until creamy. • Add the egg yolks, one at a time, until just blended after each addition. • With mixer at high speed, beat the egg whites and salt in a large bowl until stiff peaks form. Use a large rubber spatula to fold them into the batter, followed by the dry ingredients. • Spoon the batter into the prepared pan. Sprinkle the berries over. • Bake for 50–60 minutes, or until a toothpick inserted into the center comes out clean. • Cool the cake completely in the pan on a rack. • Loosen and remove the pan sides. Dust with the confectioners' sugar and decorate with berries.

Makes one 9-inch tart · Prep: 25 min. · Cooking: 50–60 min. · Level: 1 · Keeps: 1–2 days

CHERRY JELLY TART

 1 large egg + 2 large egg yolks, at room temperature
 ½ cup granulated sugar
 ⅔ cup butter, melted
 2 cups all-purpose flour
 1 tablespoon kirsch
 1 tablespoon finely grated lemon zest
 1 teaspoon baking powder
 1 cup cherry jelly or preserves

Beat the egg, egg yolks, and sugar in a large bowl with an electric mixer at high speed until pale and thick. Add the butter. • With mixer at low speed, gradually beat in the flour, kirsch, lemon zest, and baking powder. Divide the dough into ⅔ and ⅓ portions and shape into disks. Cover with a clean kitchen towel and set aside for 30 minutes. • Preheat the oven to 350°F. • Line a 9-inch springform pan with ⅔ of the pastry, pressing it down gently. Prick all over with a fork. Spread the jelly over the pastry. • Roll out the remaining pastry and cut into strips long enough to fit on the tart. Arrange in a lattice pattern on top. Roll down the top of the pastry to meet the ends of the lattice strips and form an edging around the tart. • Bake for 25–35 minutes, or until lightly browned. • Cool the tart completely in the pan on a rack. Loosen and remove the pan sides to serve.

Makes one 9-inch tart · Prep: 25 min. · Cooking: 25–35 min. · Level: 1 · Keeps: 2 days

OLD-FASHIONED PLUM TART

 1 cup all-purpose flour
 ¼ cup granulated sugar
 ¼ teaspoon salt
 1 large egg yolk, at room temperature
 ½ teaspoon vanilla extract
 ½ cup (1 stick) cold butter, softened

Yogurt Cream

 1½ teaspoons unflavored gelatin
 2 tablespoons cold water
 ¼ cup plain yogurt

Filling

 ¾ cup granulated sugar
 2 cups water
   juice of 1 lemon
 1¾ lb plums, greengages are preferred, pitted
 2 tablespoons raspberry jelly

 ¼ cup apricot preserves or jam
 1 tablespoon fruit liqueur
 ⅔ cup heavy cream
 1 tablespoon confectioners' sugar

Stir together the flour, sugar, salt, egg yolk, and vanilla in a large bowl. Beat in the butter until a smooth dough is formed. Press into a disk, wrap in plastic wrap, and refrigerate for 1 hour. • Preheat the oven to 400°F. • Roll the dough out on a lightly floured surface to a thin 12-inch round. Fit into a 10-inch pie plate. Line the prepared pan with the pastry. Prick all over with a fork. • Line the pastry shell with foil and fill the foil with dried beans or pie weights. Bake for 15 minutes. Remove the foil with the beans and bake for 5 minutes more, or until crisp. Cool the pastry completely in the pan on a rack. • *Yogurt Cream*: Sprinkle the gelatin over the water in a saucepan. Let stand 1 minute. Stir over low heat until the gelatin has completely dissolved. • Mix the yogurt and gelatin in a large bowl until thickened. • *Filling*: Bring the sugar, water, and lemon juice to a boil over medium heat in a large saucepan. Reduce the heat to low, add the plums, and continue cooking for 10 minutes, or until softened. • Drain the plums. • Warm the preserves in a small saucepan over low heat until liquid. Brush the preserves over the pastry. • Spoon the yogurt cream over the top. Spoon the plums over. • Warm the apricot preserves and liqueur in a saucepan over low heat until liquid. Brush over the plums. • Beat the cream and confectioners' sugar with an electric mixer at high speed until stiff. Spoon into a pastry bag and decorate the top.

Makes 10-inch tart · Prep: 90 min. + 1 hr. to chill. · Cooking: 25 min. · Level: 2 · Keeps: 1–2 days in the refrigerator

Chocolate-almond crostata

CHERRY TART

1³/₄ lb dark sweet cherries, pitted
1 cup granulated sugar
3 tablespoons fresh lemon juice
4 whole cloves
1 cinnamon stick
2 cups all-purpose flour
1 tablespoon grated lemon zest
¹/₂ cup granulated sugar
³/₄ cup (1¹/₂ sticks) + 2 tablespoons cold butter, cut up
3 large egg yolks
1¹/₂ cups cherry jam or preserves
2 tablespoons kirsch

Mix the cherries, ¹/₂ cup sugar, lemon juice, cloves, and cinnamon stick in a large bowl. Let stand for 2 hours. Drain well. • Stir together the flour, lemon zest, and the remaining ¹/₂ cup sugar in a large bowl. Use a pastry blender to cut in ³/₄ cup butter until the mixture resembles fine crumbs. • Add the egg yolks until a smooth dough is formed. Divide the dough into ²/₃ and ¹/₃ portions. Press each into a disk, wrap in plastic wrap, and refrigerate for 1 hour. • Mix the jelly, kirsch, and the remaining 2 tablespoons butter in a saucepan. Simmer over low heat for 5 minutes. Set aside to cool. • Preheat the oven to 375°F. • Roll the larger portion of dough out on a lightly floured surface. Fit into a 10-inch springform pan, letting the edges overhang the sides. • Spread the jelly mixture over the pastry. Top with the cherries. • Roll the remaining pastry out into a rectangle. Cut into ¹/₂-inch wide strips with a pastry cutter. Arrange the strips in a lattice pattern on top. Fold the overhanging pastry over the ends of the lattice to form a rolled edging. • Bake for

Linzertorte

35–45 minutes, or until lightly browned. Cool the cake in the pan on a rack. Loosen and remove the pan sides. • Serve warm or at room temperature.

Makes one 10-inch cake · Prep: 30 min. · Cooking: 35–45 min. · Level: 1 · Keeps: 1–2 days

WILD CHERRY TART

1 lb short-crust pastry (see page 280)
2 large eggs + 2 large egg yolks, lightly beaten
1 tablespoon all-purpose flour
²/₃ cup milk
²/₃ cup light cream
¹/₂ cup granulated sugar
1¹/₂ cups wild black or sour cherries, stoned
    confectioners' sugar, to dust

Preheat the oven to 400°F. • Roll the dough out on a lightly floured surface to a 12-inch round. Fit into a 9-inch pie plate, trimming the edges if needed. Line the pastry with foil and fill the foil with dried beans or pie weights. • Bake for 15 minutes. Remove the foil with the beans. • Bake for 5 minutes more, or until crisp. Set aside to cool completely. • Lower the oven temperature to 350°F. • Beat together the eggs, egg yolks, flour, milk, cream, and sugar in a large bowl. Add the cherries. • Spoon into the pastry shell. • Bake for 40–45 minutes, or until set. • Cool the tart in the pan on a rack. Dust with the confectioners' sugar. Serve warm.

Makes one 9-inch tart · Prep: 30 min. · Cooking: 60–65 min. · Level: 2 · Keeps: 2–3 days

LINZERTORTE

1¹/₂ cups all-purpose flour
³/₄ cup granulated sugar
¹/₂ cup finely ground almonds
¹/₂ teaspoon ground cinnamon
¹/₂ teaspoon ground nutmeg
¹/₄ teaspoon salt
    yolks of 3 hard-boiled eggs, mashed
3 tablespoons rum
1 tablespoon grated lemon zest
¹/₂ cup (1 stick) cold butter, cut up
²/₃ cup raspberry preserves
¹/₄ cup confectioners' sugar (optional)

Stir together the flour, sugar, almonds, cinnamon, nutmeg, and salt in a large bowl. Stir in the egg yolks, rum, and lemon zest. Use a pastry blender to cut in the butter until the mixture resembles coarse crumbs. • Divide the dough into ³/₄ and ¹/₄ portions and shape each into a disk. Roll the larger disk of dough out on a lightly floured surface to a 10-inch round. Fit into a 9-inch springform pan, forming a ¹/₂ inch rim at the top. • Spread the preserves over the bottom of the pastry. • Use your hands to roll the remaining dough into long, thin sausage shapes. Arrange in a lattice pattern over the top, sealing well. • Preheat the oven to 375°F. • Bake for 35–40 minutes, or until lightly browned. • Cool the tart completely in the pan on a rack. Loosen and remove the pan sides. Dust with confectioners' sugar, if desired.

Makes one 9-inch tart · Prep: 20 min. · Level: 1 · Cooking: 35–40 min. · Keeps: 2–3 days

GRAPE TART

1 lb short-crust pastry (see page 280)
1 cup almonds, finely ground
1¹/₂ lb seedless green grapes, halved
1 tablespoon butter
1 tablespoon firmly packed brown sugar
1 tablespoon dark rum
5 amaretti cookies, crushed

Prepare the pastry, adding ¹/₂ cup ground almonds to the dough. Set aside to rest for 30 minutes. • Roll the dough out on a lightly floured surface to a 12-inch round. Fit the dough into a 9-inch pie plate, trimming the edges if needed. • Preheat the oven to 350°F. • Sauté the grapes in the butter in a skillet over medium heat for 5 minutes. • Increase the heat to high and add the brown sugar and rum. Stir well and remove from the heat. • Sprinkle the cookies over the pastry. Add

Almond chocolate tart

the grapes and juice. Sprinkle with the remaining $^1/_2$ cup almonds. • Bake for 25–30 minutes, or until lightly browned. Cool completely in the pan on a rack.

Makes one 9-inch tart · Prep: 20 min. · Cooking: 25–30 min. · Level: 2 · Keeps: 1 day

PEAR TART

2   lb firm-ripe pears, peeled, cored, and thinly sliced
$1^1/_4$ cups very good-quality dry red wine
$^1/_3$ cup granulated sugar
$^1/_2$ teaspoon ground cinnamon
2   tablespoons unsweetened cocoa powder

$1^1/_2$ cups all-purpose flour
1   cup yellow cornmeal
$^3/_4$ cup granulated sugar
$^1/_4$ teaspoon salt
$^2/_3$ cup butter, slivered, slightly softened
3   large egg yolks
10   amaretti cookies, coarsely crushed

Place the pears in a saucepan. Add the wine, sugar, and cinnamon, and, stirring occasionally, cook gently over medium heat, 10 minutes. • Drain the pears. Sprinkle with cocoa. Set aside to cool. • Stir together the flour, cornmeal, sugar, and salt in a large bowl. • Add the butter and egg yolks, mixing together until the mixture resembles fine crumbs. • Divide the dough into $^2/_3$ and $^1/_3$ portions. Shape each into a ball. • Press the larger portion into a 9-inch springform pan. Refrigerate for 1 hour. • Wrap the remaining dough in plastic wrap and set aside in a cool place. • Preheat the oven to 400°F. • Sprinkle with the tart shell with the cookies and arrange the pears on top. • On a lightly floured surface, roll out the remaining pastry dough into a round slightly larger than the

pan. Place over the pears, pinching the pastry edges together to seal. Prick all over with a fork. • Bake for 35–40 minutes, or until lightly browned. • Cool the tart in the pan for 5 minutes. Loosen and remove the pan sides. Transfer onto a serving plate and let cool completely.

Makes one 9-inch tart · Prep: 30 min. + 1 hr. to chill · Cooking: 35–40 min. · Level: 2 · Keeps: 2–3 days

CARAMEL-WALNUT TART

$^1/_2$ cup toasted walnuts
$^1/_2$ cup granulated sugar
$^2/_3$ cup butter, softened
$^2/_3$ cup confectioners' sugar
2   large eggs
$2^2/_3$ cups all-purpose flour
$^1/_4$ teaspoon salt

CARAMEL FILLING
$^1/_4$ cup cold water
1   cup granulated sugar
2   tablespoons light corn syrup
$^1/_4$ cup ($^1/_2$ stick) butter, softened
$^1/_3$ cup heavy cream
$^3/_4$ cup toasted walnuts, finely chopped
$^1/_2$ teaspoon vanilla extract

2   cups Chocolate Ganache (see page 350)

Chop the walnuts and granulated sugar in a food processor until finely chopped. • Beat the butter, confectioners' sugar, and walnut mixture in a large bowl with an electric mixer at medium speed until creamy. • Add the eggs, one at a time, until just blended after each addition. • With mixer at low speed, gradually beat in the flour and salt. • Shape into a disk, wrap in plastic wrap, and refrigerate overnight. • Roll out the dough on a lightly floured surface to a 12-inch round. Fit into a 10-inch pie plate, trimming the edges if needed. Refrigerate for 1 hour. • Preheat the oven to 350°F. • Line the dough

with foil and fill the foil with dried beans or pie weights. • Bake for 15 minutes. Remove from the oven, remove the foil with the beans, and let cool. • *Caramel Filling*: Stir the water, sugar, and corn syrup in a saucepan over medium heat until the sugar has dissolved. Wash down the pan sides with a pastry brush dipped in cold water to prevent sugar crystals from forming. Cook, without stirring, until the mixture reaches 238°F, or the soft-ball stage. • Remove from the heat and beat in the butter and cream. Fold in the walnuts and vanilla. Pour into the pastry shell. Cool to room temperature. • Refrigerate for 2 hours before serving. • Spread with the chocolate ganache.

Makes one 10-inch tart · Prep: 45 min. + 2 hr. to chill · Level: 2 · Keeps: 2–3 days

ALMOND-CHOCOLATE TART

1   cup all-purpose flour
$^1/_4$ teaspoon salt
1   large egg yolk
2   tablespoons butter, softened
$^1/_4$ cup water

FILLING
$^1/_4$ cup ($^1/_2$ stick) butter
$^1/_3$ cup cornstarch
$1^1/_4$ cups milk
$^3/_4$ cup + 1 tablespoon granulated sugar
3   oz semisweet chocolate, coarsely chopped
1   cup almonds, finely chopped
$^1/_2$ teaspoon vanilla extract
4   large eggs, at room temperature

Preheat the oven to 325°F. • Sift the flour and salt into a large bowl and make a well in the center. Mix in the egg yolk, butter, and enough water to make a smooth dough. • Roll the dough out on a lightly floured surface to a 10-inch round. Fit into a 9-inch pie plate. • *Filling*: Melt the butter in a saucepan over low heat. Gradually stir in the cornstarch, milk, sugar, and chocolate. Add the almonds and vanilla. • Remove from the heat and set aside to cool. • Add the eggs, one at a time, with an electric mixer at high speed, until just blended after each addition. • Pour the batter into the pastry shell. • Bake for 40–45 minutes, until a toothpick inserted into the center comes out clean. • Cool the tart completely in the pan. • Refrigerate for 2 hours before serving.

Makes one 9-inch tart · Prep: 30 min. + 2 hr. to chill · Cooking: 40–45 min. · Level: 1 · Keeps: 1–2 days in the refrigerator

COCOA-ALMOND TART

1²/₃ cups all-purpose flour
¹/₃ cup granulated sugar
2 teaspoons baking powder
¹/₄ teaspoon salt
¹/₂ cup (1 stick) cold butter, cut up
2 large egg yolks
2 tablespoons dark rum

FILLING

1 cup toasted almonds, finely chopped
³/₄ cup granulated sugar
¹/₂ cup unsweetened cocoa powder, sifted
2 large egg yolks
5 tablespoons strong coffee, cooled

Preheat the oven to 350°F. • Sift together the flour, sugar, baking powder, and salt into a large bowl. Use a pastry blender to cut in the butter until the mixture resembles crumbs. • Add the egg yolks and rum. Use your fingertips to work the dough until a smooth dough is formed. Refrigerate for 30 minutes. • *Filling*: Mix the almonds, sugar and cocoa powder in a large bowl. • Stir in the egg yolks and coffee. • Roll out the pastry on a lightly floured surface to a 12-inch round. Fit into a 10-inch tart pan. • Fill the pastry with the filling. • Bake for 30–40 minutes, or until lightly browned. • Serve warm.

Makes one 10-inch tart · Prep: 45 min. + 30 min. to chill · Cooking: 30–40 min. · Level: 2 · Keeps: 2–3 days

PEACH-NUT PUFF

1¹/₄ lb peaches, peeled, pitted, and cut into cubes
1 cup slivered almonds
¹/₂ cup pistachios, chopped
3 lightly crushed amaretti cookies
1 teaspoon superfine sugar
1 teaspoon vanilla extract
1 lb fresh or frozen puff pastry, thawed if frozen
1 large egg, lightly beaten
confectioners' sugar, to dust

Preheat the oven to 400°F. • Set out a baking sheet. • Stir together the peaches, almonds, pistachios, crumbs, sugar, and vanilla in a large bowl. • Roll the pastry out on a lightly floured surface to a ¹/₈-inch thick rectangle or square. Prick all over with a fork. Place the pastry on the prepared sheet. • Spoon the peach mixture into the center. Fold the pastry over. • Cut slashes into the top of the pastry and seal the edges with a fork. • Brush with the beaten egg. Dust with the confectioners' sugar. • Bake for 40–45 minutes, or until golden. • Serve warm.

Makes one tart · Prep: 30 min. · Cooking: 40–45 min. · Level: 1 · Keeps: 2 days

PEAR AND HAZELNUT PUFF

4 firm ripe pears, peeled, cored, and halved
2 tablespoons fresh lemon juice
1¹/₂ cups granulated sugar
¹/₄ cup white wine
¹/₂ lb fresh or frozen puff pastry, thawed if frozen
1 large egg, lightly beaten
40 hazelnuts, coarsely chopped

Preheat the oven to 350°F. • Butter a 9 x 13-inch baking pan. • Drizzle the pears with the lemon juice. Use a sharp knife to make deep cuts in the pears lengthwise. Place in the baking pan, curved-side up and sprinkle with ³/₄ cup sugar. • Bake for 10–12 minutes, and drizzle with the wine. Bake for

Pineapple puff

12 minutes more. • Roll out the pastry to fit a 10-inch pie plate. Use the extra pastry to make a twisted rope-like border and place it around the edge of the pastry, pressing to seal. • Brush the pastry with the egg and sprinkle with the remaining sugar and the nuts. • Bake for 20–25 minutes, or until golden brown. • Scoop a few of the nuts off the pastry with a spoon and arrange the pears on the pastry, curved-sides up. Sprinkle with the nuts. • Serve warm or at room temperature.

Makes one 10-inch tart · Prep: 35 min. · Cooking 45–50 min. · Level: 1 · Keeps: 1–2 days

PINEAPPLE PUFF

If you do not have a pastry cutting wheel to cut a spider's web pattern onto a piece of pastry, cut the rolled pastry into thin strips and place them over the pineapple in a crisscross pattern.

1 tablespoon butter
¹/₃ cup granulated sugar
2 tablespoons fresh lemon juice
1 fresh pineapple, weighing about 2 lb, peeled and finely chopped
1 lb fresh or frozen frozen puff pastry, thawed if frozen
³/₄ cup pistachios
3 ladyfingers
1 large egg, lightly beaten
2 tablespoons confectioners' sugar, to dust

Preheat the oven to 400°F. • Set out a round pizza pan. • Cook the butter, ¹/₄ cup sugar and lemon juice in a saucepan over medium heat until golden brown. • Add the pineapple and cook until the mixture is dry, about 10 minutes. Set aside to cool. • Unroll or unfold the pastry on a lightly floured surface and roll out to form two 10-inch rounds. Use one to line the pan, folding the edges over the form a raised rim. Prick all over with a fork. • Finely chop the pistachios, ladyfingers, and remaining ¹/₄ cup sugar in a food processor. • Sprinkle the pistachio mixture over the pastry. Spread with the pineapple mixture. • Run a pastry cutting wheel over the remaining round of pastry to create an open spider's web pattern and drape the pastry over the pineapple. • Brush the pastry with the egg. • Dust with the confectioners' sugar. • Bake for 20–25 minutes, or until golden brown. • Serve warm or at room temperature.

Makes one 10-inch tart · Prep: 40 min. · Cooking: 20–25 min. · Level: 2 · Keeps: 1–2 days

LATTICED APPLE PUFF

- 1 lb puff pastry, thawed if frozen
- 1 jar (16 oz) unsweetened applesauce
- 1/3 cup granulated sugar
- 1 tablespoon grated lemon zest
- 1 teaspoon ground cinnamon
- 1 large egg yolk, lightly beaten
- 1/4 cup confectioners' sugar

Preheat the oven to 400°F. • Set aside 1/4 of the pastry and roll the remainder out on a lightly floured surface, piecing pieces together as needed to form a 13-inch square. Fit into a 12-inch square tart pan, pressing up the sides. Prick all over with a fork. • Stir the applesauce, sugar, lemon zest, and cinnamon in a large bowl. Spread evenly over the pastry, leaving a 1/2-inch border. • Roll out the remaining dough and cut into long strips. Arrange the strips over the apple filling in a lattice pattern, sealing them to the pastry sides. Brush the egg yolk onto the pastry. • Bake for 30–35 minutes, or until golden brown. Cool the tart in the pan on a rack. • Dust with confectioners' sugar.

Makes one 12-inch tart · Prep: 20 min. · Cooking: 30–35 min. · Level: 1 · Keeps: 1–2 days

ORANGE PUFF

- 1/4 cup (1/2 stick) butter
- 1/4 cup firmly packed brown sugar
- 1 large orange, very thinly sliced
- 1 lb frozen puff pastry, thawed

Line a 9- or 10-inch pie plate with parchment paper. Dampen the paper. • Beat the butter and brown sugar in a small bowl with an electric mixer at high speed until creamy. Spread in the prepared pie plate. Refrigerate for 30 minutes. • Arrange the orange slices on the prepared base, overlapping slightly them. • Preheat the oven to 350°F. • Roll the pastry out on a lightly floured surface to a 9- or 10-inch round (depending on your pie plate). Place the pastry over the oranges. Prick all over with a fork. • Bake for 20–30 minutes, or until crisp. • Invert onto a serving plate. Carefully remove the paper and serve. • If the surface is not caramelized, place under the broiler for a few minutes.

Makes one 9- or 10-inch tart · Prep: 15 min. · Cooking: 20–30 min. · Level: 1 · Keeps: 2–3 days

Latticed apple puff

SMALL CAKES

Minute in size but full in flavor, these miniature cakes are perfect for children's birthday parties or to satisfy smaller appetites. Tangy muffins served with freshly squeezed fruit juice are great to begin the day for breakfast. Fuller–flavored chocolate cupcakes, filled with buttercreams and frostings, are devilishly tempting.

FAIRY CAKES

- 2 cups all-purpose flour
- 2 teaspoons baking powder
- 1/4 teaspoon salt
- 2/3 cup butter, softened
- 3/4 cup granulated sugar
- 1 teaspoon vanilla extract
- 2 large eggs, at room temperature
- 1/2 cup milk
- 1 tablespoon fresh lemon juice
- 1/2 cup strawberry jam
- 1 cup heavy cream

Preheat the oven to 350°F. • Arrange 20–24 foil baking cups on baking sheets. • Sift the flour, baking powder, and salt into a medium bowl. • Beat the butter, sugar, and vanilla in a large bowl with an electric mixer at medium speed until creamy. • Add the eggs, one at a time, until just blended after each addition. • With mixer at low speed, gradually beat in the dry ingredients, alternating with the milk and lemon juice. • Spoon the batter into the baking cups, filling them half full. • Bake for 10–15 minutes, or until golden brown. • Cool the cakes on racks. • With mixer at high speed, beat the cream in a medium bowl until stiff. • Cut a small circle about 1/2-inch deep from the top of each cake. Fill with 1/2 teaspoon of jam and 1 teaspoon of whipped cream. Cut the tops in half and arrange like butterfly wings.

Makes 20–24 fairy cakes · Prep: 15 min. · Cooking: 10–15 min. · Level: 1 · Keeps: 1-2 days

◄ Coffee-almond mini mousses (see page 310)

➤ Fairy cakes

BASIC MUFFINS

For vanilla muffins, add 1 teaspoon vanilla extract.

- 2   cups all-purpose flour
- 1   tablespoon baking powder
- 1/4   teaspoon salt
- 1/2   cup granulated sugar
- 2   large eggs, lightly beaten
- 1/2   cup milk
- 1/2   cup (1 stick) butter, melted

Preheat the oven to 375°F. • Butter and flour a 12-cup muffin pan, or line with foil or paper baking cups. • Sift the flour, baking powder, and salt into a large bowl. Add the sugar. Make a well in the center and stir in the eggs, milk, and butter. • Spoon the batter into the prepared cups. • Bake for 15–25 minutes, or until springy to the touch. Cool the muffins on racks.

Makes about 12 muffins · Prep: 10 min. · Cooking: 15–25 min. · Level: 1 · Keeps: 2 days

OATMEAL MUFFINS

- 1   cup old-fashioned rolled oats
- 1   cup sour cream
- 1 1/3   cups all-purpose flour
- 1   teaspoon baking powder
- 1   teaspoon ground cinnamon
- 1/2   teaspoon ground nutmeg
- 1/2   teaspoon baking soda
- 1/4   teaspoon salt
- 1   large egg, at room temperature
- 1/2   cup firmly packed brown sugar
- 1/2   cup vegetable oil

VANILLA FROSTING (OPTIONAL)
- 1 1/4   cups confectioners' sugar
- 2   tablespoons butter, melted
- 1   teaspoon vanilla extract

Mix the oats and sour cream in a medium bowl. Cover and let stand for 1 hour. • Preheat the oven to 400°F. • Butter and flour a 12-cup muffin pan, or line with foil or paper baking cups. • Sift the flour, baking powder, cinnamon, nutmeg, baking soda, and salt into a large bowl. Add the egg, beating until just blended. • Beat in the brown sugar and oil. Stir in the oatmeal mixture. • Spoon the batter into the prepared cups, filling each 2/3 full. • Bake for 15–20 minutes, or until a toothpick inserted into the center comes out clean. • Cool the muffins on racks. • *Vanilla Frosting*: Beat the confectioners' sugar, butter, and vanilla in a medium bowl. Spread the frosting over.

Makes about 12 muffins · Prep: 20 min. + 1 hr to soak · Cooking: 15–20 min · Level: 1 · Keeps: 2–3 days

CORNMEAL MUFFINS

A not-too-sweet muffin that's perfect for breakfast or brunch.

- 1   cup all-purpose flour
- 1/4   teaspoon salt
- 4   teaspoons baking powder
- 1   cup yellow cornmeal
- 1/4   cup granulated sugar
- 3/4   cup milk
- 1/2   cup (1 stick) butter, melted and cooled slightly
- 2   large eggs, lightly beaten

Preheat the oven to 400°F. • Butter and flour a 12-cup muffin pan, or line with foil or paper baking cups. • Sift the flour, baking powder, and salt into a large bowl. Add the cornmeal and sugar. Make a well in the center. • Stir in the milk, butter, and eggs. • Spoon the batter into the prepared cups. • Bake for 20–25 minutes, or until a toothpick inserted into the center comes out clean. Cool the muffins on racks.

Makes about 12 muffins · Prep: 10 min. · Cooking: 20–25 min. · Level: 1 · Keeps: 4 days

GLUTEN-FREE MUFFINS

Your friends who have gluten allergies will appreciate these muffins. Most of the ingredients can be found in the natural-foods section of a good supermarket.

- 1 1/3   cups brown rice flour
- 1   cup rice bran
- 2   teaspoons baking powder
- 1   teaspoon ground ginger
- 1   teaspoon ground nutmeg

Basic muffins

- 1/4   teaspoon salt
- 1   large egg, at room temperature
- 1/2   cup firmly packed brown sugar
- 1/4   cup vegetable oil
- 1   cup mashed ripe bananas
- 3/4   cup milk
- 1/2   cup finely chopped dried apricots
- 1/2   cup raisins

Preheat the oven to 375°F. • Arrange about 14 foil baking cups on a baking sheet. • Stir together the flour, bran, baking powder, ginger, nutmeg, and salt in a large bowl. • Beat the egg, brown sugar, and oil in a medium bowl. Beat in the bananas, milk, apricots, and raisins. Stir the banana mixture into the dry ingredients. • Spoon the batter into the cups, filling each 3/4 full. • Bake for 20–25 minutes, or until a toothpick inserted into the center comes out clean. • Cool the muffins on racks.

Makes about 14 muffins · Prep: 15 min. · Cooking: 20–25 min. · Level: 1 · Keeps: 2–3 days

BRAN MUFFINS

- 1 1/2   cups all-purpose flour
- 2   teaspoons baking powder
- 1   teaspoon baking soda
- 1   cup wheat bran
- 1/4   cup (1/2 stick) butter
- 1   tablespoon light molasses
- 1/2   cup firmly packed brown sugar
- 1   large egg
- 3/4   cup milk
- 1/2   cup raisins

Preheat the oven to 400°F. • Butter and flour a 12-cup muffin pan, or line with foil or paper baking cups. • Sift the flour, baking powder, baking soda, and salt into a large bowl. Stir in the bran. • Melt the butter and the molasses in a medium saucepan over low heat. Beat in the brown sugar, egg, milk, and raisins. • Stir the butter mixture into the dry ingredients. • Spoon the batter into the prepared cups, filling each ¾ full. • Bake for 12–15 minutes, or until a toothpick inserted into the center comes out clean. • Cool the muffins on racks.

Makes 12 muffins · Prep 15 min. · Cooking: 12–15 min. · Level: 1 · Keeps: 2–3 days

Bran muffins

WHOLE-WHEAT STRAWBERRY MUFFINS

These are best fresh accompanied with a bowl of sweet berries or some strawberry jam.

- 1½ cups all-purpose flour
- ⅔ cup whole-wheat flour
- 2 teaspoons baking powder
- ½ teaspoon baking soda
- ¼ teaspoon salt
- ½ cup firmly packed brown sugar
- 1 cup milk
- 2 large eggs, lightly beaten
- ¼ cup (½ stick) butter, melted
- 1 cup fresh strawberries, hulled and chopped

Preheat the oven to 400°F. • Butter and flour a 12-cup muffin pan, or line with foil or paper baking cups. • Sift both flours, baking powder, baking soda, and salt into a large bowl. Stir in the brown sugar and make a well in the center. Beat in the milk, eggs, and butter with an electric mixer at low speed. • Stir in the strawberries. • Spoon the batter into the prepared cups, filling each ¾ full. • Bake for 20–25 minutes, or until a toothpick inserted into the center comes out clean. • Cool the muffins on racks.

Makes 12 muffins · Prep: 10 min. · Cooking: 20–25 min. · Level: 1 · Keeps: 1 day

WHOLE-WHEAT BANANA MUFFINS

- 1½ cups whole-wheat flour
- 1 teaspoon baking powder
- ½ teaspoon baking soda
- ½ teaspoon pumpkin pie spice
- ¼ teaspoon salt
- 2 large eggs, at room temperature
- ½ cup firmly packed brown sugar
- ½ cup vegetable oil
- 1½ cups mashed ripe banana, (about 4 large bananas)
- ¾ cup milk

Preheat the oven to 375°F. • Butter and flour a 12-cup muffin pan, or line with foil or paper baking cups. • Sift the flour, baking powder, baking soda, pumpkin pie spice, and salt into a large bowl. • Beat the eggs, brown sugar, and oil in a medium bowl. Beat in the mashed banana and milk. Stir the banana mixture into the dry ingredients. • Spoon the batter into the prepared cups. • Bake for 20–25 minutes, or until springy to the touch. • Cool the muffins on racks.

Makes about 12 muffins · Prep: 10 min. · Cooking: 20–25 min. · Level: 1 · Keeps: 3 days

BLUEBERRY MUFFINS

- 3 cups all-purpose flour
- 1 tablespoon baking powder
- ¼ teaspoon ground cinnamon
- ½ teaspoon ground nutmeg
- ¾ teaspoon salt
- ¾ cup (1½ sticks) butter, softened
- 1½ cups granulated sugar
- 3 large eggs
- 1½ cups milk
- 1 teaspoon vanilla extract
- 1½ cups blueberries

Preheat the oven to 350°F. • Butter and flour a 12-cup muffin pan, or line with foil or paper baking cups. • Stir together the flour, baking powder, cinnamon, nutmeg, and salt in a large bowl. • Beat the butter and sugar in a large bowl with an electric mixer at medium speed until creamy. Add the eggs, one at a time until just blended after each addition. • With mixer at low speed, gradually beat in the dry ingredients. Add

the milk and vanilla. • Use a large rubber spatula to fold in the blueberries. • Spoon the batter evenly into the prepared cups. • Bake for 20–30 minutes, or until a toothpick inserted into the center comes out clean. • Cool the muffins on racks for 15 minutes. • Serve warm.

Makes 12 muffins. · Prep: 15 min. · Cooking: 20–30 min. · Level: 1 · Keeps: 2 days

STRAWBERRY MUFFINS

Serve these muffins with Chantilly Cream (see page 345) and fresh strawberries.

- 2 cups all-purpose flour
- 2 teaspoons baking powder
- ½ teaspoon salt
- ½ cup granulated sugar
- 1 large egg, at room temperature
- 1 cup milk
- ½ cup (1 stick) butter, melted
- 1 cup fresh strawberries, hulled and chopped

Preheat the oven to 375°F. • Butter and flour a 12-cup muffin pan, or line with foil or paper baking cups. • Sift the flour, baking powder, and salt into a large bowl. Stir in the sugar. • Beat the egg, milk, and butter in a large bowl with an electric mixer at medium speed. • With mixer at low speed, gradually beat in the dry ingredients. • Stir in the strawberries. • Spoon the batter into the prepared cups, filling each ¾ full. • Bake for 20–25 minutes, or until a toothpick inserted into the center comes out clean. • Cool the muffins on racks.

Makes about 12 muffins · Prep: 20 min. · Cooking: 20–25 min. · Level: 1 · Keeps: 2–3 days

Apricot muffins

APRICOT MUFFINS

- 2 cups all-purpose flour
- 1 tablespoon baking powder
- 1/4 teaspoon salt
- 2/3 cup chopped dried apricots
- 3/4 cup cold water
- 1/2 cup (1 stick) butter, cut up
- 3/4 cup firmly packed brown sugar
- 1/2 cup milk
- 1 large egg, lightly beaten
- 2 teaspoons vanilla extract

Preheat the oven to 350°F. • Butter and flour a 12-cup muffin pan, or line with foil or paper baking cups. • Sift the flour, baking powder, and salt into a large bowl. • Bring the apricots and water in a saucepan over medium heat to a boil. Reduce the heat and simmer for 5 minutes. Remove from the heat and beat in the butter and sugar until the sugar has dissolved. Stir in the milk, eggs, and vanilla. Stir the apricot mixture into the dry ingredients. • Spoon the batter into the prepared cups, filling each 2/3 full. • Bake for 15–20 minutes, or until a toothpick inserted into the center comes out clean. • Cool the muffins on racks.

Makes about 12 muffins · Prep: 10 min. · Cooking: 15–20 min. · Level: 1 · Keeps: 3–4 days

PEACH MUFFINS

- 3 cups all-purpose flour
- 1 tablespoon baking powder
- 1 teaspoon ground allspice
- 1 teaspoon ground nutmeg
- 1 teaspoon ground cinnamon
- 1/2 teaspoon salt

- 1 1/2 cups firmly packed dark brown sugar
- 3/4 cup milk
- 2 large eggs, lightly beaten
- 1/2 cup vegetable oil
- 3 large peaches, diced
- 1/4 cup granulated sugar

Preheat the oven to 400°F. • Arrange about 16 foil baking cups on baking sheets. • Sift the flour, baking powder, allspice, nutmeg, cinnamon, and salt into a large bowl. Stir in the brown sugar and make a well in the center. • Stir in the milk, eggs, oil, and peaches. • Spoon the batter into the cups, filling each 3/4 full. Sprinkle with sugar. • Bake for 30–40 minutes, or until a toothpick inserted into the center comes out clean. • Cool the muffins on racks.

Makes about 16 muffins · Prep: 20 min. · Cooking: 30–40 min. · Level: 1 · Keeps: 1 day

RASPBERRY-CREAM CHEESE MUFFINS

- 3 large eggs, at room temperature
- 3/4 cup granulated sugar
- 1/3 cup vegetable oil
- 1/3 cup raspberry yogurt
- 3 tablespoons raspberry jelly or preserves + 1/2 cup for filling
- 2 1/2 cups all-purpose flour
- 1 tablespoon baking powder
- 2 oz cream cheese, cut into 12 pieces
- 2 tablespoons confectioners' sugar

Preheat the oven to 375°F. • Butter 18 muffin-pan cups, or line with foil or paper baking cups. • Beat the eggs, sugar, oil, yogurt, and 3 tablespoons jelly in a large bowl with an electric mixer at medium

speed. • With a mixer at low speed, gradually beat in the flour and baking powder. • Spoon 2–3 tablespoons of batter into each prepared cup. • Place a piece of cream cheese in the center and top each with 2 teaspoons jelly. • Spoon the remaining batter on top. • Bake for 25–30 minutes, or until golden brown at the edges. • Cool the muffins in the pans for 10 minutes. Turn out onto racks to cool completely. • Dust with the confectioners' sugar.

Makes about 18 muffins · Prep: 15 min. · Cooking: 30 min. · Level: 1 · Keeps: 2 days

HONEY-CREAM CHEESE MUFFINS

- 2 cups all-purpose flour
- 1 tablespoon baking powder
- 1/2 teaspoon ground nutmeg
- 1/2 teaspoon salt
- 1/8 teaspoon ground cloves
- 1 cup peeled, cored, and shredded apple
- 1/2 cup walnuts, chopped
- 2 large eggs, at room temperature
- 2/3 cup firmly packed brown sugar
- 2/3 cup apple juice
- 1/4 cup (1/2 stick) butter, melted
- 1 cup wheat bran

HONEY–CREAM CHEESE FROSTING

- 1 package (3 oz) cream cheese, softened
- 1 cup confectioners' sugar
- 1 tablespoon honey
- 1–2 tablespoons milk

Preheat the oven to 400°F. • Butter and flour a 12-cup muffin pan, or line with foil or paper baking cups. • Sift the flour, baking powder, nutmeg, salt, and cloves into a large bowl. Make a well in the center. • Stir in the apple and walnuts. • Beat the eggs, brown sugar, apple juice, and butter in a large bowl. Stir the egg mixture into the dry ingredients. Stir in the bran. • Spoon the batter into the prepared cups, filling each 3/4 full. • Bake for 20–25 minutes, or until a toothpick inserted into the center comes out clean. • Cool the muffins on racks. • *Honey–Cream Cheese Frosting*: Beat the cream cheese, confectioners' sugar, and honey in a medium bowl with an electric mixer at medium speed until smooth. Beat in enough milk to make a thick, spreadable frosting. • Spread the frosting over.

Makes about 12 muffins · Prep: 20 min. · Cooking: 20–25 min. · Level: 1 · Keeps: 2–3 days

TROPICAL MORNING MUFFINS

- 2 cups all-purpose flour
- 2 teaspoons baking powder
- 1/2 teaspoon baking soda
- 1/4 teaspoon salt
- 1/2 cup (1 stick) butter, softened
- 2/3 cup granulated sugar
- 2 large eggs, at room temperature
- 1/2 cup heavy cream
- 1/2 cup finely chopped candied mango
- 1/4 cup fresh passion fruit pulp

YOGURT CREAM FILLING

- 1/2 cup heavy cream
- 1/2 cup plain yogurt
- 2 teaspoons grated lemon zest
- 1 tablespoon fresh passion fruit pulp

Preheat the oven to 350°F. • Butter and flour a 12-cup muffin-pan, or line with foil or paper baking cups. • Sift the flour, baking powder, baking soda, and salt into a large bowl. • Beat the butter and sugar in a large bowl with an electric mixer at medium speed until creamy. • Add the eggs, one at a time, until just blended after each addition. • With mixer at low speed, gradually beat in the dry ingredients, alternating with the cream. • Stir in the mango and passion fruit pulp. • Spoon the batter into the prepared cups, filling each 2/3 full. • Bake for 15–20 minutes, or until a toothpick inserted into the center comes out clean. • Cool the muffins on racks. • *Yogurt Cream Filling*: With mixer at high speed, beat the cream and yogurt in a medium bowl until stiff. Fold in the lemon zest and passion fruit pulp. • Cut a small 1/2-inch deep hole in the top of each muffin. Fill with the cream and cover with the removed piece from each muffin.

Makes about 12 muffins · Prep: 15 min. · Cooking: 15–20 min. · Level: 1 · Keeps: 1–2 days

CHRISTMAS MORNING MUFFINS

Serve these muffins warm for breakfast on Christmas morning. They are great with Sherry Butter Christmas Cake Frosting (see page 349).

- 1 cup mixed dried fruit, chopped
- 1/2 cup dry sherry
- 1/2 cup water
- 3 cups all-purpose flour
- 2 teaspoons baking powder
- 1 teaspoon baking soda
- 1/4 teaspoon salt
- 1/2 cup (1 stick) butter, softened
- 1 cup granulated sugar
- 2 teaspoons vanilla extract
- 2 large eggs, at room temperature
- 1/2 cup milk

Mix the dried fruit, sherry, and water in a small bowl. Cover and let soak overnight. • Preheat the oven to 375°F. • Arrange about 17 foil baking cups on baking sheets. • Sift the flour, baking powder, baking soda, and salt into a large bowl. • Beat the butter, sugar, and vanilla in a large bowl with an electric mixer at medium speed until creamy. • Add the eggs, one at a time, until just blended after each addition. • With mixer at low speed, gradually beat in the dry ingredients, alternating with the milk. • Drain the dried fruit, if needed. • Stir the fruit into the batter. • Spoon the batter into the prepared cups, filling each 3/4 full. • Bake for 20–25 minutes, or until a toothpick inserted into the center comes out clean. • Cool the muffins on racks.

Makes about 17 muffins · Prep: 15 min. · Cooking: 20–25 min. · Level: 1 · Keeps: 2–3 days

COCONUT-APRICOT MUFFINS

- 2 cups all-purpose flour
- 1 tablespoon baking powder
- 1/2 cup butter, softened
- 3/4 cup superfine sugar
- 1 cup chopped dried apricots
- 3/4 cup shredded coconut
- 3/4 cup milk
- 2 large eggs, at room temperature

Preheat the oven to 350°F. • Butter and flour a 12-cup muffin pan, or line with foil or paper baking cups. • Sift the flour and baking powder into a large bowl. Use your fingertips to rub in the butter. Stir in the

sugar, apricots, coconut, milk, and eggs until well blended. • Spoon the batter into the prepared cups, filling each 1/2 full. • Bake for 15–20 minutes, or until a toothpick inserted into the center comes out clean. • Cool the muffins in the pan for 15 minutes. Transfer to racks and let cool completely.

Makes about 12 muffins · Prep: 15 min. · Cooking: 15–20 min. · Level: 1 · Keeps: 1 day

HEALTHY BREAKFAST MUFFINS

- 1 cup whole-wheat flour
- 2 teaspoons baking powder
- 1 1/2 teaspoons ground cinnamon
- 1/2 teaspoon baking soda
- 1 1/2 cups wheat bran
- 3/4 cup milk
- 3/4 cup apple juice
- 1 large egg, lightly beaten
- 2 tablespoons honey
- 1 tablespoon vegetable oil
- 3/4 cup raisins
- 2 tablespoons coarsely chopped crystallized ginger

Preheat the oven to 375°F. • Butter and flour a 12-cup muffin pan, or line with foil or paper baking cups. • Sift the flour, baking powder, cinnamon, and baking soda into a large bowl. Stir in the bran. • Beat in the milk, juice, egg, honey, and oil. Stir in the raisins and crystallized ginger. • Spoon the batter into the prepared cups. • Bake for 15–20 minutes, or until springy to the touch. • Cool the muffins on racks.

Makes about 12 muffins · Prep: 10 min. · Cooking: 15–20 min. · Level: 1 · Keeps: 3 days

Tropical morning muffins

GINGER MUFFINS

Very appropriate served at holiday time, perhaps with a mug of hot ginger tea or eggnog.

1½ cups all-purpose flour
1½ teaspoons ground ginger
1 teaspoon baking powder
¼ teaspoon salt
½ cup (1 stick) butter, softened
¾ cup granulated sugar
1 tablespoon honey
1 teaspoon vanilla extract
1 large egg, at room temperature
⅓ cup milk
3 tablespoons finely chopped crystallized ginger
1 cup Mock Cream (see page 344)

Preheat the oven to 375°F. • Butter and flour a 12-cup muffin pan, or line with foil or paper baking cups. • Sift the flour, ground ginger, baking powder, and salt into a medium bowl. • Beat the butter, sugar, honey, and vanilla in a large bowl with an electric mixer at medium speed until creamy. Add the egg, beating until just blended. • With mixer at low speed, gradually beat in the dry ingredients, alternating with the milk. Stir in 2 tablespoons of the crystallized ginger. • Spoon the batter into the prepared cups. • Bake for 15–20 minutes, or until a toothpick inserted into the center comes out clean. • Cool the muffins on racks. • Spread with the Mock Cream and sprinkle with the remaining 1 tablespoon ginger.

Makes 12 muffins · Prep: 20 min. · Cooking: 15–20 min. · Level: 1 · Keeps: 3–4 days

GINGER MUFFINS WITH CARAMEL SAUCE

2½ cups all-purpose flour
1 cup firmly packed brown sugar
1 tablespoon baking powder
2 teaspoons ground ginger
¼ teaspoon salt
¾ cup walnuts, chopped
¼ cup finely chopped crystallized ginger
1 cup milk
¼ cup vegetable oil
1 large egg, lightly beaten

2 cups Caramel Sauce (see page 353)

Preheat the oven to 400°F. • Butter and flour 18 muffin pan cups. • Stir together the flour, brown sugar, baking powder, ground ginger, and salt in a large bowl. Stir in the walnuts and crystallized ginger. Make a well in the center and stir in the milk, oil, and egg. • Spoon the batter into the prepared cups. • Bake for 15–20 minutes, or until a toothpick inserted into the center comes out clean. Cool the cakes on racks. • Serve the muffins warm, with the caramel sauce spooned over the top.

Makes 18 muffins · Prep: 15 min. · Cooking: 20 min. · Level: 1 · Keeps: 1 day

GINGER MUFFINS WITH CITRUS SAUCE

2½ cups all-purpose flour
1 cup firmly packed brown sugar
1 tablespoon baking powder
2 teaspoons ground ginger
¼ teaspoon salt
¼ cup finely chopped crystallized ginger
¾ cup walnuts, chopped
1 cup milk
¼ cup vegetable oil
1 large egg, lightly beaten

2 cups Citrus Sauce (see page 353)

Use the instructions for Ginger Muffins with Caramel Sauce (see recipe left), substituting the citrus sauce for the caramel sauce. • Serve the muffins warm, with the citrus sauce spooned over the top.

Makes 18 muffins · Prep: 15 min. · Cooking: 20 min. · Level: 1 · Keeps: 1 day

PUMPKIN-GINGER MUFFINS

2 cups all-purpose flour
2 teaspoons baking powder
½ teaspoon baking soda
1 teaspoon ground ginger
½ teaspoon ground cinnamon
½ teaspoon ground nutmeg
¼ teaspoon salt
⅓ cup butter, softened
1 cup granulated sugar
2 large eggs, at room temperature
1 cup plain canned pumpkin
¾ cup milk

GINGER FROSTING
¼ cup (½ stick) butter, cut up
1 tablespoon honey
1½ cups confectioners' sugar
⅓ cup firmly packed brown sugar
1 teaspoon ground ginger
2 tablespoons milk
2 tablespoons coarsely chopped crystallized ginger

Preheat the oven to 375°F. • Arrange 20 foil baking cups on baking sheets. • Sift the flour, baking powder, baking soda, ginger, cinnamon, nutmeg, and salt into a medium bowl. • Beat the butter and sugar in a large bowl with an electric mixer at medium speed until creamy. • Add the eggs, one at a time, until just blended after each addition. • With mixer at low speed, gradually beat in the pumpkin, followed by the dry ingredients, alternating with the milk. • Spoon the batter into the cups, filling each ¾ full. • Bake for 20–25 minutes, or until a toothpick inserted into the center comes out clean. • Cool the muffins on racks. • *Ginger Frosting*: Melt the butter and honey in a saucepan over low heat. Remove from the heat and stir in the confectioners' sugar, brown sugar, ground ginger, and 1 tablespoon milk, adding the additional milk, if needed, to make the frosting smooth and spreadable. Spread the frosting over. Sprinkle with the ginger.

Makes about 20 muffins · Prep: 20 min. · Cooking: 20–25 min. · Level: 1 · Keeps: 2–3 days

PUMPKIN MUFFINS

1⅓ cups all-purpose flour
1 teaspoon baking powder
1 teaspoon baking soda
1 teaspoon ground ginger
1 teaspoon ground nutmeg
1 teaspoon ground cinnamon
¼ teaspoon salt
⅔ cup butter, softened
¾ cup firmly packed brown sugar
½ teaspoon vanilla extract
2 large eggs, at room temperature
1 cup plain canned pumpkin
⅓ cup dark corn syrup
½ cup raisins

Preheat the oven to 400°F. • Butter and flour a 12-cup muffin pan, or line with foil or paper baking cups. • Sift the flour, baking powder, baking soda, ginger, nutmeg, cinnamon, and salt into a medium bowl. • Beat the butter, brown sugar, and vanilla with an electric mixer at medium speed until creamy. • Add the eggs, one at a time, until just blended after each addition. Beat in the pumpkin and corn syrup. • With mixer at low speed, gradually beat in dry ingredients. • Stir in the raisins. • Spoon the batter into the prepared cups, filling each ¾ full. • Bake for 20–25 minutes, or until a toothpick inserted into the center comes out clean. • Cool the muffins on racks.

Makes 12 muffins · Prep: 10 min. · Cooking: 20–25 min. · Level: 1 · Keeps: 2–3 days

Ginger muffins with caramel sauce

LEMON-MARMALADE MUFFINS

- 2 cups all-purpose flour
- 1 tablespoon baking powder
- 1/4 teaspoon salt
- 1/3 cup granulated sugar
- 1 cup milk
- 1/2 cup lemon marmalade
- 2 large eggs, lightly beaten
- 1/4 cup (1/2 stick) butter, melted

Preheat the oven to 375°F. • Arrange 18 foil baking cups on a baking sheet. • Sift the flour, baking powder, and salt into a large bowl. Stir in the sugar and make a well in the center. • Stir in the milk, marmalade, eggs, and butter. • Spoon the batter into the cups, filling each 3/4 full. • Bake for 12–15 minutes, or until springy to the touch. Cool the muffins on racks.

Makes 18 muffins · Prep: 15 min. · Cooking: 12–15 min. · Level: 1 · Keeps: 2 days

LEMON-YOGURT MUFFINS

- 2 cups all-purpose flour
- 2 1/2 teaspoons baking powder
- 1/4 teaspoon salt
- 3/4 cup granulated sugar
- 2 large eggs, at room temperature
- 1 cup plain yogurt
- 1/3 cup butter, melted
- 2 tablespoons grated lemon zest
- 1/2 cup fresh lemon juice

Preheat the oven to 400°F. • Butter a 12-cup muffin pan, or line with foil or paper baking cups. • Sift the flour, baking powder, and salt into a large bowl. Stir in the sugar and make a well in the center. • Beat the eggs, yogurt, butter, and lemon zest and juice in a medium bowl. Stir the yogurt mixture into the dry ingredients. • Spoon the batter into the prepared cups, filling each 3/4 full. • Bake for 12–15 minutes, or until springy to the touch. Cool the muffins on racks.

Makes about 12 muffins · Prep: 15 min. · Cooking: 12–15 min. · Level: 1 · Keeps: 2 days

LEMON AND RAISIN ROCK CAKES

- 1 1/2 cups all-purpose flour
- 1/3 cup butter, melted
- 1 tablespoon grated lemon zest
- 2 teaspoons baking powder
- 1 large egg, lightly beaten
- 1/3 cup granulated sugar
- 2 tablespoons fresh lemon juice
- 2/3 cup raisins
- 2 tablespoons raw or coarse sugar

Preheat the oven to 375°F. • Butter a baking sheet. • Beat the flour, butter, lemon zest, and baking powder in a large bowl with an electric mixer at medium speed until well blended. • Add the egg, sugar, lemon juice, and raisins. • Drop heaping tablespoons of the batter onto the prepared sheet, spacing them 2 inches apart. Sprinkle with the sugar. • Bake for 15–20 minutes, or until golden brown. • Cool the cakes on racks.

Makes about 12–15 cakes · Prep: 10 min. · Cooking: 15–20 min. · Level: 1 · Keeps: 3 days

Lemon and raisin rock cakes

LEMON-COCONUT MUFFINS

- 2 1/4 cups all-purpose flour
- 1 tablespoon baking powder
- 1/4 teaspoon salt
- 1 1/4 cups shredded coconut
- 3/4 cup granulated sugar
- 2 tablespoons grated lemon zest
- 1 cup milk
- 1/2 cup (1 stick) butter, melted
- 2 large eggs, lightly beaten

- 3/4 cup Lemon Glaze (see page 348)

Preheat the oven to 400°F. • Butter and flour 20 muffin-pan cups. • Sift the flour, baking powder, and salt into a large bowl. Stir in the coconut, sugar, and lemon zest. Make a well in the center. Stir in the milk, butter, and eggs. • Spoon the batter into the prepared cups. • Bake for 15–18 minutes, or until a toothpick inserted into the center comes out clean. • Cool the muffins on racks. • Poke holes all over the muffins while still hot, then dip them into the glaze. Return to the racks. Place the muffins on racks in a jelly-roll pan. Spoon any remaining glaze over the top.

Makes about 20 muffins · Prep: 20 min. · Cooking: 15–18 min. · Level: 1 · Keeps: 1 day

KIWIFRUIT AND COCONUT MUFFINS

- 2 cups all-purpose flour
- 2 1/2 teaspoons baking powder
- 1/2 teaspoon baking soda
- 1/4 teaspoon salt
- 1/2 cup shredded coconut
- 1/3 cup butter, softened
- 3/4 cup granulated sugar
- 1/2 teaspoon vanilla extract
- 1 large egg
- 1 cup plain yogurt
- 2–3 fresh kiwifruit, peeled and sliced, to decorate

COCONUT FROSTING
- 1 cup mascarpone cheese
- 1/3 cup confectioners' sugar
- 3/4 cup shredded coconut

Preheat the oven to 350°F. • Butter and flour a 12-cup muffin pan. • Sift the flour, baking powder, baking soda, and salt in a large bowl. Stir in the coconut. • Beat the butter, sugar, and vanilla in a large bowl with an electric mixer at medium speed until creamy. • Add the egg, beating until just blended. • With mixer at low speed, gradually beat in the dry ingredients, alternating with the yogurt. • Spoon the batter into the prepared cups, filling each 3/4 full. • Bake for 20–25 minutes, or until a toothpick inserted into a center comes out clean. • Cool the muffins on racks. • *Coconut Frosting*: With mixer at medium speed, beat the mascarpone, confectioners' sugar, and coconut in a medium bowl until creamy. • Spread with the frosting and decorate with the kiwifruit.

Makes about 12 muffins · Prep: 20 min. · Cooking: 20–25 min. · Level: 1 · Keeps: 1–2 days

CARROT MUFFINS WITH LEMON FROSTING

- 2 cups all-purpose flour
- 1/2 cup whole-wheat flour
- 1 tablespoon baking powder
- 1/4 teaspoon salt
- 2/3 cup firmly packed brown sugar
- 1/2 cup (1 stick) butter, melted
- 2 large eggs, lightly beaten
- 1 1/2 cups firmly packed finely grated carrots
- 1/2 cup milk
- 1/4 cup fresh lemon juice

LEMON FROSTING

- 1 package (8 oz) cream cheese, softened
- 1/2 cup confectioners' sugar
- 1 tablespoon grated lemon zest

Preheat the oven to 350°F. • Butter and flour a 12-cup muffin pan, or line with foil or paper baking cups. • Sift both flours, baking powder, and salt into a large bowl. Stir in the brown sugar. • Add the butter, eggs, carrots, milk, and lemon juice. • Spoon the batter into the prepared cups, filling each 2/3 full. • Bake for 20–25 minutes, or until a toothpick inserted into the center comes out clean. • Cool the muffins on racks. • *Lemon Frosting*: Beat the cream cheese, confectioners' sugar, and lemon zest in a medium bowl with an electric mixer at high speed until creamy. • Spread the frosting over.

Makes about 12 muffins · Prep: 10 min. · Cooking: 20–25 min. · Level: 1 · Keeps: 1-2 days

PINEAPPLE MUFFINS

- 1 cup all-purpose flour
- 2 1/2 teaspoons baking powder
- 1/2 teaspoon baking soda
- 1/4 teaspoon salt
- 1 cup old-fashioned rolled oats
- 1/3 cup butter, softened
- 1/2 cup granulated sugar
- 1/2 teaspoon vanilla extract
- 1 large egg, at room temperature
- 1/2 cup canned crushed pineapple, drained
- 3/4 cup milk

Carrot muffins with lemon frosting

CREAM CHEESE FROSTING (OPTIONAL)

- 1 package (8 oz) cream cheese, softened
- 2 tablespoons finely grated orange zest
- 2 tablespoons fresh orange juice
- 1/2 cup confectioners' sugar
- 2–3 fresh kiwifruit, peeled and sliced, to decorate

Preheat the oven to 350°F. • Butter and flour a 12-cup muffin pan. • Sift the flour, baking powder, baking soda, and salt in a large bowl. Stir in the oats. • Beat the butter, sugar, and vanilla in a large bowl with an electric mixer at medium speed until creamy. • Add the egg, beating until just blended. • With mixer at low speed, gradually beat in the dry ingredients, alternating with the pineapple and milk. • Spoon the batter into the prepared cups, filling each 3/4 full. • Bake for 20–25 minutes, or until a toothpick inserted into a center comes out clean. • Cool the muffins on racks. • *Cream Cheese Frosting*: With mixer at medium speed, beat the cream cheese, confectioners' sugar, orange zest and juice in a medium bowl until creamy. • Spread the frosting over and decorate with the kiwifruit.

Makes about 12 muffins · Prep: 20 min. · Cooking: 20–25 min. · Level: 1 · Keeps: 1–2 days

ZUCCHINI-LEMON AND LIME MUFFINS

- 2 cups all-purpose flour
- 2 teaspoons baking powder
- 1 teaspoon baking soda
- 1/2 teaspoon salt
- 1/2 cup firmly packed brown sugar

- 1 tablespoon grated lemon zest
- 3/4 cup walnuts, coarsely chopped
- 1/2 cup raisins
- 2 large eggs, at room temperature
- 1/3 cup vegetable oil
- 1/4 cup fresh lime juice
- 1/4 cup milk
- 1 packed cup shredded zucchini

CITRUS-CREAM CHEESE FROSTING

- 3 oz cream cheese, softened
- 1 cup confectioners' sugar
- 1 tablespoon grated lemon or lime zest
- 1 tablespoon fresh lemon or lime juice

Preheat the oven to 400°F. • Butter and flour a 12-cup muffin pan, or line with paper or foil baking cups. • Sift the flour, baking powder, baking soda, and salt into a large bowl. Stir in the brown sugar, lemon zest, walnuts, and raisins. • Beat the eggs, oil, lime juice, and milk in a large bowl. Stir the egg mixture into the dry ingredients. Use a large rubber spatula to fold in the zucchini. • Spoon the batter into the prepared cups, filling each 3/4 full. • Bake for 20–25 minutes, or until a toothpick inserted into the center comes out clean. • Cool the muffins on racks. • *Citrus-Cream Cheese Frosting*: Beat the cream cheese and confectioners' sugar in a medium bowl with an electric mixer at medium speed until creamy. Beat in the citrus zest and enough citrus juice to make a thick, spreadable frosting. • Spread the frosting over.

Makes about 12 muffins · Prep: 20 min. · Cooking: 20–25 min. · Level: 1 · Keeps: 2–3 days

CRANBERRY-NUT MUFFINS

 2   cups all-purpose flour
 2   teaspoons baking powder
 1   teaspoon ground cinnamon
 1/2 teaspoon ground nutmeg
 1/4 teaspoon salt
 1   cup dried cranberries
 1/2 cup toasted walnuts, chopped
 1   cup buttermilk
 1/2 cup firmly packed brown sugar
 2   large eggs, at room temperature
 1/4 cup (1/2 stick) butter, melted

Preheat the oven to 400°F. • Butter and flour a 12-cup muffin pan, or line with foil or paper baking cups. • Sift the flour, baking powder, cinnamon, nutmeg, and salt into a large bowl. • Stir in the cranberries and walnuts. • Beat the buttermilk, brown sugar, eggs, and butter in a medium bowl with an electric mixer at medium speed. • Stir the egg mixture into the dry ingredients. • Spoon the batter into the prepared cups, filling each 2/3 full. • Bake for 20–25 minutes, or until a toothpick inserted into the center comes out clean. • Cool the muffins on racks.

Makes about 12 muffins · Prep: 20 min. · Cooking: 20–25 min. · Level: 1 · Keeps: 2–3 days

ALMOND–RASPBERRY JAM MUFFINS

 2 1/2 cups all-purpose flour
 1   tablespoon baking powder
 1/4 teaspoon salt
 1/2 cup (1 stick) butter, softened
 1   cup granulated sugar
 1   teaspoon almond extract
 2   large eggs, at room temperature
 1   cup milk
 1   cup sliced unblanched almonds
     about 1/2 cup raspberry jam

Preheat the oven to 375°F. • Arrange 15 foil baking cups on a baking sheet. • Sift the flour, baking powder, and salt into a large bowl. • Beat the butter, sugar, and almond extract in a large bowl with an electric mixer at medium speed until creamy. • Add the eggs, one at a time, until just blended after each addition. • With mixer at low speed, gradually beat in the dry ingredients, alternating with the milk. • Stir in the almonds. • Spoon the batter into the cups, filling each 3/4 full. Top each muffin with a heaping teaspoon of raspberry jam. • Bake for 25–30 minutes, or until golden brown. • Cool the muffins on racks.

Makes about 15 muffins · Prep: 15 min. · Cooking: 25–30 min. · Level: 1 · Keeps: 1–2 days

ALMOND AND RASPBERRY MUFFINS

 6   large egg whites
 1 3/4 cups + 3 tablespoons confectioners' sugar
 1   cup almonds, finely ground
 3/4 cup (1 1/2 sticks) butter, melted
 1/2 cup all-purpose flour
 1   cup small raspberries

Preheat the oven to 400°F. • Butter and flour a 12-cup muffin pan, or line with foil or paper baking cups. • Use a fork to beat the egg whites in a large bowl until frothy. Stir in the 1 3/4 cups confectioners' sugar, almonds, butter, and flour. • Spoon the batter into the prepared cups. Sprinkle with raspberries. • Bake for 20–25 minutes, or until golden brown. • Cool the muffins in the pan for 10 minutes. Turn out onto racks to cool. • Serve warm. Dust with the remaining 3 tablespoons confectioners' sugar.

Makes about 12 muffins · Prep: 15 min. · Cooking: 20–25 min. · Level: 2 · Keeps: 1 day

PEAR AND NUT MUFFINS

 1 1/2 cups all-purpose flour
 2   teaspoons baking powder
 1   teaspoon ground cinnamon
 1/2 teaspoon ground ginger
 1/4 teaspoon salt
 1/2 cup + 1/4 cup firmly packed brown sugar
 1   large egg, at room temperature
 1/2 cup vegetable oil
 1/2 cup plain low-fat yogurt
 1   teaspoon vanilla extract
 1   large ripe pear, peeled, cored, and finely chopped
 1/2 cup nuts, coarsely chopped

Preheat the oven to 400°F. • Butter and flour a 12-cup muffin pan, or line with foil or paper baking cups. • Sift the flour, baking powder, cinnamon, ginger, and salt into a large bowl. Stir in 1/2 cup brown sugar. • Beat the egg, oil, yogurt, and vanilla in a large bowl. Stir the yogurt mixture into the dry ingredients. Add the pear. • Spoon the batter into the prepared cups, filling each 3/4 full. • Mix the nuts and remaining 1/4 cup brown sugar in a small bowl. Sprinkle over the muffins. • Bake for 20–25 minutes, or until a toothpick inserted into the center comes out clean. • Cool the muffins on racks. Serve warm.

Makes about 12 muffins · Prep: 20 min. · Cooking: 20–25 min. · Level: 1 · Keeps: 2–3 days

CHERRY-ALMOND MUFFINS

 2   cups all-purpose flour
 2   teaspoons baking powder
 1/4 teaspoon salt
 1/2 cup (1 stick) butter, softened
 1 1/4 cups granulated sugar
 1   teaspoon almond extract
 2   large eggs, at room temperature
 1/2 cup milk
 2   cups dark sweet cherries, pitted, coarsely chopped, and drained
 3/4 cup sliced almonds, lightly toasted

Preheat the oven to 375°F. • Arrange 18 foil baking cups on baking sheets. Sift the flour, baking powder, and baking soda into a large bowl. • Beat the butter, 1 cup sugar, and almond extract in a large bowl with an electric mixer at medium speed until creamy. • Add the eggs, one at a time, until just blended after each addition. • With mixer at low speed, gradually beat in the dry ingredients, alternating with the milk. • Stir in the cherries and almonds. • Spoon the batter into the cups, filling each 2/3 full. Dust with the remaining 1/4 cup sugar. • Bake for 25–30 minutes, or until a toothpick inserted into the center comes out clean. • Cool the muffins on racks.

Makes about 18 muffins · Prep: 20 min. · Cooking: 25–30 min. · Level: 1 · Keeps: 2–3 days

CINNAMON-APPLE MUFFINS

CINNAMON CRUMBLE
 1/2 cup all-purpose flour
 1/4 cup firmly packed brown sugar
 1 1/2 teaspoons ground cinnamon
 1/3 cup cold butter, cut up

 2   large apples, peeled, cored, and chopped
 2   tablespoons water
 2 1/4 cups all-purpose flour
 1   tablespoon baking powder
 2   teaspoons ground cinnamon
 1/4 teaspoon salt
 3/4 cup firmly packed brown sugar
 2/3 cup milk
 1/3 cup vegetable oil
 1   large egg, lightly beaten
 1/2 cup walnuts, coarsely chopped

Cinnamon Crumble: Stir together the flour, brown sugar, and cinnamon in a medium bowl. Use a pastry blender to cut in the butter until the mixture resembles coarse crumbs. • Place the apples and water in a saucepan over medium heat. Cover and cook until tender, about 5 minutes. Mash until smooth and set aside to cool. • Preheat the oven to 400°F. • Arrange 20 foil baking cups on baking sheets. • Sift the flour, baking powder, cinnamon, and salt into a large bowl. Stir in the sugar and make a well in the center. • Stir in the milk, oil, and egg, followed by the applesauce and walnuts. • Spoon the batter into the cups. • Sprinkle the crumble over the muffins. • Bake for 20–25 minutes, or until springy to the touch. • Cool the muffins on racks.

Makes about 20 muffins · Prep: 20 min. · Cooking: 20–25 min. · Level: 1 · Keeps: 2 days

RHUBARB MUFFINS

   1   cup all-purpose flour
   1   cup whole-wheat flour
   2   teaspoons baking powder
   1   teaspoon ground cinnamon
  1/4   teaspoon ground nutmeg
  1/4   teaspoon salt
  1/2   cup firmly packed brown sugar
   2   large eggs, separated
  3/4   cup milk
   3   tablespoons raspberry jam
   2   tablespoons butter, melted
   1   teaspoon vanilla extract
  1 1/2 cups fresh rhubarb, finely chopped
   1   cup frozen unsweetened raspberries, thawed

STREUSEL
  1/2   cup all-purpose flour
  1/2   cup firmly packed brown sugar
  1/2   cup old-fashioned rolled oats
   1   teaspoon ground cinnamon
  1/4   cup (1/2 stick) cold butter, cut up

Preheat the oven to 375°F. • Arrange about 16 foil baking cups on baking sheets. • Sift both flours, baking powder, cinnamon, nutmeg, and salt into a large bowl. Make a well in the center. • Beat the brown sugar, egg yolks, milk, jam, butter, and vanilla in a large bowl with an electric mixer at medium speed until smooth. Stir in the rhubarb and raspberries. • Stir the rhubarb mixture into the dry ingredients. • With mixer at high speed, beat the egg whites in a medium bowl until stiff peaks form. Use a large rubber spatula to fold them into the batter. • Spoon the batter into the cups, filling each 2/3 full. • *Streusel*: Mix the flour, brown sugar, oats, and cinnamon in a medium bowl. Use a pastry blender to cut in the butter until the mixture resembles coarse crumbs. Sprinkle over the muffins. • Bake for 20–25 minutes, or until a toothpick inserted into the center comes out clean. • Cool the muffins on racks.

Makes about 16 muffins · Prep: 20 min. · Cooking: 20–25 min · Level: 1 · Keeps: 2–3 days

BANANA-CHOCOLATE CHIP MUFFINS

   1   cup whole-wheat flour
   1   cup all-purpose flour
   2   teaspoons baking powder
  1/2   teaspoon baking soda
  1/4   teaspoon salt
  1/2   cup (1 stick) unsalted butter, softened
   1   cup granulated sugar
   3   large eggs, at room temperature
   2   large very ripe bananas, mashed
  1/4   cup milk
   1   cup semisweet chocolate chips
   1   cup walnuts, chopped

Preheat the oven to 375°F. • Arrange 20 foil baking cups on baking sheets. • Sift both flours, baking powder, baking soda, and salt into a large bowl. • Beat the butter and sugar in a large bowl with an electric mixer at medium speed until creamy. • Add the eggs, one at a time, until just blended after each addition. • With mixer at low speed, beat in the bananas, followed by the dry ingredients, alternating with the milk. •

Chocolate muffins

Stir in the chocolate chips and walnuts. • Spoon the batter into the cups, filling each 3/4 full. • Bake for 20–30 minutes, or until a toothpick inserted into the center comes out clean. • Cool the muffins on racks.

Makes about 20 muffins · Prep: 20 min. · Cooking: 20–30 min. · Level: 1 · Keeps: 2–3 days

CHOCOLATE MUFFINS

   2   cups all-purpose flour
  1/2   cup unsweetened cocoa powder
   2   teaspoons baking powder
  1/4   teaspoon salt
  3/4   cup milk
  1/2   cup (1 stick) butter, softened
  1 1/4 cups granulated sugar
   1   tablespoon honey
   2   large eggs, at room temperature
   2   oz semisweet chocolate chips

Preheat the oven to 350°F. • Butter 16 muffin-pan cups, or line with foil or paper baking cups. • Sift the flour, cocoa, baking powder, and salt into a large bowl. • Beat the butter, sugar, and honey in a large bowl with an electric mixer at medium speed until creamy. • Add the eggs, one at a time, until just blended after each addition. • With mixer at low speed, gradually beat in the dry ingredients, alternating with the milk. Stir in the chocolate chips. • Spoon the batter into the prepared cups. • Bake for 20–25 minutes, or until a toothpick inserted into the centers comes out clean. Cool the muffins on racks.

Makes 16 muffins · Prep: 15 min. · Cooking: 20–25 min. · Level: 1 · Keeps: 2–3 days

FROSTED CHOCOLATE MUFFINS

    4   oz semisweet chocolate, coarsely chopped
    1   tablespoon heavy cream
    2   cups all-purpose flour
    2   teaspoons baking powder
 $^1/_4$ teaspoon salt
 $^3/_4$ cup (1$^1/_2$ sticks) butter, softened
 1$^1/_2$ cups granulated sugar
    3   large eggs, at room temperature
 $^2/_3$ cup milk
    2   teaspoons vanilla extract
    1   cup Rich Chocolate Frosting (see page 349)

Preheat the oven to 350°F. • Line 20 muffin-pan cups with foil or paper baking cups. • Melt the chocolate with the cream in a double boiler over barely simmering water. Set aside to cool. • Sift the flour, baking powder, and salt into a large bowl. • Beat the butter and sugar in a large bowl with an electric mixer at medium speed until creamy. • Add the eggs, one at a time, until just blended after each addition. • With mixer at low speed, gradually beat in the chocolate, followed by the dry ingredients, alternating with the milk and vanilla. • Spoon the batter into the prepared pans, filling each $^2/_3$ full. • Bake for 20–25 minutes, or until a toothpick inserted into the center comes out clean. • Cool the muffins on racks. • Spread the frosting over.

Makes about 20 muffins · Prep: 20 min. · Cooking: 20–25 min. · Level: 1 · Keeps: 2–3 days

WHITE CHOCOLATE MUFFINS

    2   cups all-purpose flour
 2$^1/_2$ teaspoons baking powder
 $^1/_4$ teaspoon salt
 $^1/_4$ cup granulated sugar
 1$^1/_2$ cups white chocolate chips
    1   cup milk
 $^1/_4$ cup ($^1/_2$ stick) butter, melted
    1   large egg, lightly beaten
    2   tablespoons honey
    2   teaspoons vanilla extract

Preheat the oven to 400°F. • Arrange 20 foil baking cups on baking sheets. • Sift the flour, baking powder, and salt in a large bowl. Stir in the sugar and chocolate chips. Make a well in the center. • Stir in the milk, butter, egg, honey, and vanilla. • Spoon the batter into the cups, filling each $^3/_4$ full. • Bake for 15–20 minutes, or until a toothpick inserted into the center comes out clean. Cool the muffins on racks.

Makes about 20 muffins · Prep: 10 min. · Cooking: 15–20 min. · Level: 1 · Keeps: 2 days

Chocolate Easter muffins

CHOCOLATE-CHERRY MUFFINS

 1$^1/_2$ cups all-purpose flour
 $^1/_3$ cup unsweetened cocoa powder
    2   teaspoons baking powder
 $^1/_4$ teaspoon salt
    2   large eggs, at room temperature
 $^1/_2$ cup firmly packed brown sugar
 $^1/_2$ cup (1 stick) butter, melted
 $^3/_4$ cup milk
   24   red candied cherries, halved

Preheat the oven to 375°F. • Butter and flour a 12-cup muffin pan, or line with foil or paper baking cups. • Sift the flour, cocoa, baking powder, and salt into a large bowl. Beat the eggs, brown sugar, and butter in a medium bowl until creamy. Add the milk. • Stir into the dry ingredients. • Spoon the batter into the prepared cups, filling each $^3/_4$ full. Press four pieces of candied cherry into each muffin, leaving 1 or 2 pieces visible on top. • Bake for 15–20 minutes, or until springy to the touch. Cool the muffins on racks.

Makes about 12 muffins · Prep: 15 min. · Cooking: 20 min. · Level: 1 · Keeps: 2 days

CHOCOLATE EASTER MUFFINS

Children will love these muffins at Eastertime. Throughout the rest of the year, replace the Easter egg with a small square of semisweet chocolate.

 1$^1/_2$ cups all-purpose flour
 $^1/_2$ cup granulated sugar
 $^1/_2$ cup unsweetened cocoa powder
    2   large eggs, lightly beaten
 $^1/_3$ cup butter, melted
    2   teaspoons vanilla extract
    1   tablespoon baking powder
   20   small solid chocolate Easter eggs
    2   tablespoons miniature chocolate chips (optional)

Preheat the oven to 350°F. • Butter and flour a 12-cup muffin pan, or line with foil or paper baking cups. • Beat the flour, sugar, cocoa, eggs, butter, vanilla, and baking powder in a large bowl with an electric mixer at medium speed until well blended. • Spoon half the batter into the cups. Place a chocolate egg in each. Top each with some of the remaining batter. • Sprinkle each with a few chocolate chips, if using. Bake for 15–20 minutes, or until springy to the touch. Cool the muffins on racks.

Makes about 12 muffins · Prep: 10 min. · Cooking: 15–20 min. · Level: 1 · Keeps: 2 days

WHITE CHOCO-STRAWBERRY MUFFINS

1 1/2 cups all-purpose flour
2 teaspoons baking powder
1/4 teaspoon salt
1/2 cup granulated sugar
1/2 cup (1 stick) butter, melted
1/2 cup milk
1 large egg, at room temperature
1/2 teaspoon vanilla extract
1 1/2 cups white chocolate chips
1/2 cup strawberry jam

Preheat the oven to 350°F. • Line a 12-cup muffin pan with foil or paper baking cups. • Sift the flour, baking powder, and salt into a large bowl. Stir in the sugar. • Beat the butter, milk, egg, and vanilla in a medium bowl. Stir the milk mixture into the dry ingredients, followed by the chocolate chips. • Spoon 3/4 of the batter into the prepared cups. Spoon a heaping 1 teaspoon strawberry jam into each muffin, making a hole in the batter. Top with the remaining batter. • Bake for 25–30 minutes, or until a toothpick inserted into the center comes out clean. • Cool the cakes on racks.

Makes 12 muffins · Prep 15 min. · Cooking: 25–30 min. · Level: 1 · Keeps: 2–3 days

Cappuccino muffins

ORANGE-CHOCOLATE MUFFINS

2 cups all-purpose flour
2 teaspoons baking powder
1/2 teaspoon baking soda
1/4 teaspoon salt
1 cup granulated sugar
1 large egg
3/4 cup milk
1/2 cup vegetable oil
2 tablespoons grated orange zest
2 teaspoons vanilla extract
1 cup semisweet chocolate chips

Preheat the oven to 375°F. • Butter and flour a 12-cup muffin pan, or line with foil or paper baking cups. • Sift the flour, baking powder, baking soda, and salt into a large bowl. • Beat the sugar, egg, milk, oil, orange zest, and vanilla in a medium bowl. Stir the orange mixture into the dry ingredients. • Use a large rubber spatula to fold in the chocolate chips. • Spoon the batter into the prepared cups, filling each 3/4 full. • Bake for 20–25 minutes, or until a toothpick inserted into the center comes out clean. • Cool the muffins on racks.

Makes about 12 muffins · Prep: 15 min. · Cooking: 20–25 min. · Level: 1 · Keeps: 2–3 days

CAPPUCCINO MUFFINS

2 cups all-purpose flour
1 tablespoon baking powder
1/4 teaspoon salt
1/2 cup firmly packed brown sugar
1 large egg, at room temperature
1/4 cup heavy cream
1 cup very strong cold black coffee
1/4 cup confectioners' sugar, to dust

Preheat the oven to 375°F. • Butter and flour a 12-cup muffin pan, or line with foil or paper baking cups. • Sift the flour, baking powder, and salt into a large bowl. Stir in the sugar and make a well in the center. • Beat the egg and cream in a small bowl. • Beat the cream mixture and coffee into the dry ingredients with an electric mixer at low speed. • Spoon the batter into the prepared cups, filling each 2/3 full. • Bake for 15–20 minutes, or until a toothpick inserted into the center comes out clean. • Cool the muffins on racks. • Dust with the confectioners' sugar.

Makes about 12 muffins · Prep: 15 min. · Cooking: 15–20 min. · Level: 1 · Keeps: 2–3 days

CHOCOLATE RUM-RAISIN MUFFINS

1 1/4 cups raisins
1/3 cup rum
2 1/2 cups all-purpose flour
1/2 cup unsweetened cocoa powder
1 tablespoon baking powder
1/4 teaspoon salt
1 cup granulated sugar
1 cup light cream or half-and-half
2 eggs, lightly beaten
1/3 cup butter, melted
1 cup semisweet chocolate chips

Plump the raisins in the rum in a small bowl for 30 minutes. • Preheat the oven to 400°F. • Butter and flour two 12-cup muffin pans, or line with foil or paper baking cups. • Sift the flour, cocoa, baking powder, and salt into a large bowl. Stir in the sugar and make a well in the center. • Stir in the raisin mixture, cream, eggs, and butter. Stir in the chocolate chips. • Spoon the batter into the prepared cups. • Bake for 20–25 minutes, or until a toothpick inserted into the center comes out clean. Cool the muffins on racks.

Makes about 24 muffins · Prep: 10 min. + 30 min. to soak · Cooking: 20–25 min. · Level: 1 · Keeps: 2 days

SICILIAN PISTACHIO CAKES

1¼ cups pistachio nuts, blanched and finely ground
1 cup granulated sugar
4 large eggs, separated
2 tablespoons grated orange zest
½ cup cornstarch, sifted

Preheat the oven to 325°F. • Butter and flour 10–12 little cake molds (or a muffin tray). • Stir together the ground pistachios and sugar in a large bowl. • Beat the egg whites in a large bowl with an electric mixer at high speed until stiff peaks form. • Stir the egg yolks and orange zest into the pistachio mixture. • Use a large rubber spatula to gradually fold the pistachio mixture into the beaten whites, alternating with the cornstarch. • Spoon the batter into the prepared molds, filling each ¾ full. • Bake for 20–25 minutes, or until a toothpick inserted into the center comes out clean. • Cool the cakes on racks.

Makes 10–12 small cakes · Prep: 45 min. · Cooking: 20–25 min. · Level: 1 · Keeps: 2–3 days

CHOCOLATE-NUT CUPCAKES

1¾ cups all-purpose flour
2 teaspoons baking powder
½ teaspoon baking soda
¼ teaspoon salt
½ cup (1 stick) butter, softened
½ cup granulated sugar
1 teaspoon rum or butterscotch extract
2 large eggs, at room temperature
1 cup heavy cream
4 oz nut chocolate, coarsely chopped
6 oz milk chocolate, coarsely chopped

Preheat the oven to 350°F. • Butter and flour a 12-cup muffin pan, or line with foil or paper baking cups. • Sift the flour, baking powder, baking soda, and salt into a medium bowl. • Beat the butter, sugar, and rum extract in a large bowl with an electric mixer at medium speed until creamy. • Add the eggs, one at a time, until just blended after each addition. • With mixer at low speed, gradually beat in the dry ingredients, alternating with the cream. Stir in the nut chocolate. • Spoon the batter into the prepared cups, filling each ¾ full. • Bake for 20–30 minutes, or until a toothpick inserted into the

center comes out clean. • Cool the cakes on racks. • Melt the milk chocolate in a double boiler over barely simmering water. Set aside to cool. Spread over each cupcake.

Makes 12 cupcakes · Prep: 20 min. · Cooking: 20–30 min. · Level: 1 · Keeps: 2–3 days

CHOCOLATE-MINT CUPCAKES

Tastes like a chocolatey after-dinner mint. Refreshing and addictive.

2 cups all-purpose flour
½ cup unsweetened cocoa powder
1 teaspoon baking powder
½ teaspoon baking soda
¼ teaspoon salt
⅔ cup butter, softened
1½ cups granulated sugar
3 large eggs, at room temperature
¾ cup milk
1 teaspoon peppermint extract
12 chocolate cream after-dinner mints (After Eights), chopped

CHOCOLATE GLAZE

6 oz semisweet chocolate, coarsely chopped
½ cup (1 stick) butter, cut up
1 teaspoon peppermint extract

Preheat the oven to 350°F. • Line 18 muffin-pan cups with foil or paper baking cups. • Sift the flour, cocoa, baking powder, baking soda, and salt into a large bowl. • Beat the butter and sugar in a large bowl with an electric mixer at medium speed until creamy. • Add the eggs, one at a time, until just blended after each addition. • With mixer at low speed, beat in the dry ingredients, alternating with the milk and

peppermint extract. Stir in the chopped chocolate mints. • Spoon the batter into the prepared cups, filling each ¾ full. • Bake for 20–30 minutes, or until a toothpick inserted into the center comes out clean. • Cool the cakes on racks. • *Chocolate Glaze*: Melt the chocolate and butter in a double boiler over barely simmering water. Add the peppermint extract. Set aside to cool to warm. • Drizzle the glaze over.

Makes about 18 cupcakes · Prep: 20 min. · Cooking: 20–30 min. · Level: 1 · Keeps: 2–3 days

PEANUT BUTTER-RAISIN CUPCAKES

1⅓ cups all-purpose flour
¾ cup raisins
¾ cup granulated sugar
¾ cup milk
⅓ cup smooth peanut butter
1 large egg, at room temperature
2 tablespoons oil
2 teaspoons baking powder
1 teaspoon vanilla extract

Preheat the oven to 375°F. • Line a 12-cup muffin pan with foil or paper baking cups. • Process all the ingredients in a food processor until smooth. • Or, place all the ingredients in a large bowl and beat with an electric mixer at low speed until blended. • Spoon the batter into the prepared cups, filling each ⅔ full. • Bake for 25–30 minutes, or until a toothpick inserted into the center comes out clean. • Cool the cakes on racks.

Makes 12 cupcakes · Prep: 10 min. · Cooking: 25–30 min. · Level: 1 · Keeps: 2–3 days

Sicilian pistachio cakes

SWEETHEART CUPCAKES

Lovely cupcakes to bake for your sweetheart.
They're so easy, why wait for a special occasion?

1³/₄ cups all-purpose flour
2 teaspoons baking powder
¹/₂ teaspoon baking soda
¹/₄ teaspoon salt
¹/₂ cup (1 stick) butter, softened
¹/₂ cup granulated sugar
1 teaspoon vanilla extract
2 large eggs, at room temperature
1 cup heavy cream
4 oz milk chocolate, finely chopped
12 small heart-shaped milk chocolates

Preheat the oven to 350°F. • Butter
and flour a 12-cup muffin pan, or line with
foil or paper baking cups. • Sift the flour,
baking powder, baking soda, and salt into
a medium bowl. • Beat the butter, sugar,
and vanilla in a large bowl with an electric
mixer at medium speed until creamy. • Add
the eggs, one at a time, until just blended
after each addition. • With mixer at low
speed, gradually beat in the dry ingredients,
alternating with the cream. Stir in the
chopped chocolate. • Spoon the batter into
the prepared cups, filling each ³/₄ full. •
Bake for 20–25 minutes, or until a
toothpick inserted into the center comes out
clean. • Cool the cakes on racks. • When the
cupcakes are still warm, press a chocolate
into the top of each. Let cool completely.

*Makes 12 cupcakes · Prep: 20 min. · Cooking: 20–25
min. · Level: 1 · Keeps: 2–3 days*

RASPBERRY TARTLETS

12 store-bought tartlet shells
1 cup raspberries + about 24 extra, to decorate
²/₃ cup confectioners' sugar
¹/₂ cup raspberry (or other berry fruit) liqueur
     grated zest and juice of 1 lemon
²/₃ cup fresh ricotta cheese
1 cup plain yogurt
1¹/₂ tablespoons unflavored gelatin
¹/₄ cup cold water
1¹/₂ cups heavy cream

Set out the tartlet shells. • Process 1 cup
raspberries in a food processor until
pureed. • Transfer the raspberries to a large
bowl and stir in the confectioners' sugar,
liqueur, lemon zest and juice, ricotta, and
yogurt. • Sprinkle the gelatin over the water
in a saucepan. Let stand 1 minute. Stir over
low heat until the gelatin has completely
dissolved. • Stir the gelatin into the
raspberry mixture and refrigerate until

Raspberry tartlets

thickened. • Beat the cream in a medium
bowl with an electric mixer at medium
speed until stiff. Fold the cream into the
raspberry mixture. • Spoon the raspberry
mixture into a pastry bag with a ¹/₄-inch
plain tip. Pipe into the tartlets. Decorate with
the raspberries. Refrigerate for 1 hour.

*Makes 12 tartlets · Prep: 50 min. + 1 hr. to chill ·
Level: 1 · Keeps: 1–2 days in the refrigerator*

PINEAPPLE TARTLETS

20 store-bought tartlet shells
¹/₂ cup apricot preserves or jam
2 cups Vanilla Pastry Cream (see page 342)
20 pieces canned pineapple chunks
10 large fresh strawberries, cut in halves
¹/₄ cup confectioners' sugar, to dust

Set out the tartlet shells. • Spread each
tartlet with ¹/₂ tablespoon apricot
preserves. • Fill each with 1–2
tablespoons of the pastry cream. Place a
pineapple chunk and a piece of
strawberry in each tartlet. • Dust with the
confectioners' sugar.

*Makes 20 tartlets · Prep: 30 min. · Level: 1 · Keeps:
1–2 days*

CHERRY TARTLETS

20 store-bought tartlet shells
¹/₂ cup apricot preserves or jam
2 cups Vanilla Pastry Cream (see page 342)
20 pieces canned cherries
10 large fresh strawberries, cut in halves
¹/₄ cup confectioners' sugar

Set out the tartlet shells. • Spread each
tartlet with ¹/₂ tablespoon apricot preserves.
• Fill each with 1–2 tablespoons of the
pastry cream. Place a cherry and a piece of
strawberry in each tartlet. • Dust with the
confectioners' sugar.

*Makes 20 tartlets · Prep: 30 min. · Level: 1 · Keeps:
1–2 days*

RAISIN AND CREAM CAKES

1¹/₂ cups all-purpose flour
2 teaspoons baking powder
¹/₈ teaspoon salt
¹/₂ cup granulated sugar
³/₄ cup raisins
1 large egg, lightly beaten
¹/₄ cup heavy cream
¹/₄ cup (¹/₂ stick) butter, melted
1 teaspoon vanilla extract
¹/₄ cup confectioners' sugar, to dust

Preheat the oven to 350°F. • Arrange 18–20
foil baking cups on a baking sheet. • Sift the
flour, baking powder, and salt into a large
bowl. Stir in the sugar and raisins. Stir in the
egg, cream, butter, and vanilla. • Spoon a
generous tablespoon of batter into each
cup. • Bake for 15–17 minutes, or until
golden. • Cool the cakes on racks. • Dust
with the confectioners' sugar.

*Makes 18–20 small cakes · Prep: 10 min. · Cooking:
15–17 min. · Level: 1 · Keeps: 2 days*

CHOUX PASTRY

- 2 cups water
- ⅔ cup butter, cut up
- 1 tablespoon granulated sugar
- ¼ teaspoon salt
- 1⅔ cups all-purpose flour
- 5–6 large eggs

Line a baking sheet with parchment paper. • Place the water, butter, sugar, and salt in a large pan over medium-low heat. When the mixture boils, remove from the heat and add the flour all at once. Use a wooden spoon to stir vigorously until a smooth paste forms. Return to medium heat and stir constantly until the mixture pulls away from the pan sides. Remove from the heat and let cool for 5 minutes. • Add the eggs, one at a time, until just blended after each addition. The batter should be shiny and stiff enough to hold its shape if dropped onto a baking sheet. Add another egg if required.

Makes 1 recipe · Prep: 15 min. · Level: 3 · Keeps: 1 day

INDIVIDUAL CHRISTMAS CAKES

- 1 recipe Light Fruit Cake batter (see page 148)

HOLLY DECORATIONS
- 2 oz marzipan
- ¼ teaspoon green food coloring

WHITE FROSTING
- ⅓ cup apricot preserves
- 3 lb rolled white fondant
- 1 tablespoon confectioners' sugar
- 1 teaspoon water
  red currants, to decorate

Preheat the oven to 300°F. • Butter a 12-cup muffin pan and line with paper baking cups. • Spoon the batter evenly into the cups. • Bake for 75–80 minutes, or until a toothpick inserted into the center comes out clean. • Cool the cakes completely in the pan. Turn out onto racks to decorate. • *Holly Decorations*: Dust a surface lightly with confectioners' sugar. • Knead the marzipan until malleable. Roll out to ⅛-inch thick. Use a leaf-shaped cutter to stamp out 24 small holly shapes. • Lightly brush green coloring over each leaf. Dry the leaves on waxed paper. • *White Frosting*: Warm the preserves in a saucepan over low heat. • Brush each cake with a thin layer of preserves. • Knead the fondant until malleable. Divide into 12 equal pieces. Roll out one piece at a time to ⅛-inch thick. Fit the fondant over each cake, trimming the edges if needed. • Mix together the confectioners' sugar and water to make a smooth paste. Dot the leaves and 2 red currants with a little frosting and arrange on each cake in a decorative manner. • Wrap each cake bottom with a narrow red or green narrow ribbon, if desired.

Makes 12 individual cakes · Prep: 60 min. · Cooking: 75–80 min. · Level: 2 · Keeps: 1 month

MADELEINES

- ½ recipe Basic Sponge Cake batter (see page 157)
- 1 cup Lemon Curd (see page 345)
- 1 cup shredded coconut
- 8 candied cherries, to decorate

Preheat the oven to 400°F. • Butter and flour 8 baba molds. • Spoon the batter into the prepared molds, filling each half full. • Bake for 8–10 minutes, or until a toothpick inserted into the center comes out clean. • Cool the cakes in the molds for 15 minutes. Turn out onto racks and let cool completely. • Brush each cake with a thin layer of lemon curd. Place the coconut on a plate and roll each cake until well coated. Decorate with the candied cherries.

Makes 8 cakes · Prep: 15 min. · Cooking: 8–10 min. · Level: 1 · Keeps: 1 day

MINI BERRY MERINGUES

- 1 recipe Brown Sugar Meringues (see page 205)
- 3 cups mixed berry fruit
- ½ package (4 oz) cream cheese, softened
- ⅓ cup currants or golden raisins
- 1 tablespoon confectioners' sugar, to dust

Prepare the meringues and let cool completely. • Heat the berry fruit in a large saucepan over medium heat until the fruit starts to break down, about 8 minutes. • Spoon some cream cheese into each meringue, heaping slightly. Top with the berry fruit and dust with the confectioners' sugar.

Makes 20 meringues · Prep: 20 min. · Level: 1 · Keeps: 1 day in the refrigerator

JAM TARTS

- ¼ recipe Short-Crust Pastry (see page 280)
- ½ cup raspberry preserves

Preheat the oven to 400°F. • Set out twelve 2½-inch tartlet molds. • Roll the pastry out on a lightly floured surface to 2½-inch disks to line the tartlet molds. Prick all over with a fork. Line the pastry shells with foil and fill the foil with dried beans or pie weights. Bake for 5 minutes, then remove the foil with the beans and bake for 10–15 minutes, or until crisp. Cool on racks. • Use a teaspoon to spoon a little preserves into the tarts. • Bake for 10–15 minutes, or until the pastry is crisp and the preserves begin to bubble. • Cool the tarts completely in the molds on racks.

Makes 12 tarts · Prep: 15 min. · Cooking: 15–20 min. · Level: 2 · Keeps: 3 days

LEMON CURD TARTS

¼   recipe Short-Crust Pastry (see page 280)
½   cup Lemon Curd (see page 345)

Preheat the oven to 400°F. • Set out twelve 2½-inch tartlet molds. • Roll the pastry out on a lightly floured surface to 2½-inch disks to line the tartlet molds. Prick all over with a fork. Line the pastry shells with foil and fill the foil with dried beans or pie weights. Bake for 5 minutes. Remove from the oven and remove the foil. Cool on racks. • Use a teaspoon to spoon a little lemon curd into the tarts. • Bake for 10–15 minutes, or until the pastry is crisp and the curd begins to bubble. • Cool the tarts completely in the molds on racks.

Makes 12 tarts · Prep: 15 min. · Cooking: 15–20 min. · Level: 2 · Keeps: 3 days

FONDANT FANCY CAKES

2   large eggs, at room temperature
¼   cup superfine sugar
½   cup all-purpose flour
2   tablespoons butter, melted
½   cup Italian Buttercream (see page 346)
1   cup Fondant (see pages 348–9)
1   teaspoon pink food coloring

Preheat the oven to 375°F. • Line an 8-inch square baking pan with parchment paper. • Beat the eggs and sugar in a large bowl with an electric mixer at high speed until pale and thick. • Use a large rubber spatula to fold in the flour, followed by the

Individual Christmas cakes

butter. • Pour the batter into the prepared pan. • Bake for 20–25 minutes, or until a toothpick inserted into the center comes out clean. • Turn out onto a rack and carefully remove the paper. Cut into 16 squares and let cool completely. • Spoon the buttercream into a pastry bag fitted with a plain ½-inch tip. • Pipe a small amount on the center of each square. • Set aside 4 tablespoons fondant in a small bowl. • Heat the remaining fondant until liquid and stir in the coloring until deep pink. • Use a thin metal spatula to spread the pink fondant over the top and sides of each square. • Heat the plain fondant in a small saucepan until liquid. Spoon into a pastry bag and pipe in a decorative manner over the squares. Set aside.

Makes 16 small cakes · Prep: 25 min. · Cooking: 20–25 min. · Level: 2 · Keeps: 2 days

ORANGE DROPS

⅔   cup all-purpose flour
3   tablespoons cornstarch
1½ teaspoons baking powder
¼   teaspoon salt
⅓   cup butter, softened
¾   cup granulated sugar
2   tablespoons grated orange zest
2   large eggs, at room temperature
1   tablespoon freshly orange juice
1   cup Orange Liqueur Buttercream (see page 347), (optional)
1–2 clementines, peeled and divided into sections, to decorate (optional)

Preheat the oven to 375°F. • Butter and flour a 12-cup muffin pan, or line with foil or paper baking cups. • Sift the flour, cornstarch, baking powder, and salt into a medium bowl. • Beat the butter, sugar, and orange zest in a large bowl with an electric mixer at medium speed until creamy. • Add the eggs, one at a time, until just blended after each addition. • With mixer at low speed, beat in the dry ingredients, alternating with the orange juice. • Spoon the batter into the prepared cups, filling each ½ full. • Bake for 20–25 minutes, or until a toothpick inserted into the center comes out clean. • Cool the cakes on racks. If desired, spread with the frosting. Top each with a piece of clementine, if desired.

Makes 12 small cakes · Prep: 20 min. · Cooking: 20–25 min. · Level: 1 · Keeps: 3–4 days

Chocolate éclairs

COFFEE-ALMOND MINI MOUSSES

You'll need 8 metal rings about 3 inches in diameter and 1½ inches tall.

- 1 cup almonds, finely ground
- ¾ cup granulated sugar
- 3 large eggs + 3 large egg whites
- ⅓ cup all-purpose flour
- ¼ teaspoon salt

COFFEE MOUSSE

- 3 large egg yolks
- ¼ cup granulated sugar
- ½ cup cold strong coffee
- 1½ teaspoons unflavored gelatin
- 1 cup heavy cream
- 2 tablespoons unsweetened cocoa powder
- ½ cup heavy cream
  raspberries, to decorate

Preheat the oven to 375°F. • Butter a baking sheet. Line with waxed paper. Butter the paper. • Stir together the almonds and ½ cup sugar in a large bowl. Add the eggs, one at a time, until just blended after each addition. Stir in the flour and salt. • Beat the egg whites in a large bowl with an electric mixer at medium speed until frothy. With mixer at high speed, gradually beat in the remaining sugar, beating until stiff, glossy peaks form. • Use a large rubber spatula to fold them into the almond mixture. • Spoon the batter onto the prepared sheet, spreading it to about ¼-inch thick. • Bake for 10–15 minutes, or until lightly browned. Cool the cake on the sheet for 10 minutes. • Use one of the metal rings to cut out eight 3-inch disks. Carefully remove the paper from each disk and set on a rack to cool. • *Coffee Mousse*: Beat the egg yolks, sugar, and 1 tablespoon coffee in a double

boiler until well blended. Cook over barely simmering water, stirring constantly with a wooden spoon, until the mixture lightly coats a metal spoon or registers 160°F on an instant-read thermometer. Immediately plunge the pan into a bowl of ice water and stir until the egg mixture has cooled. Transfer to a large bowl. Set aside to cool. • Sprinkle the gelatin over 2 tablespoons coffee in a saucepan. Let stand 1 minute. Stir over low heat until the gelatin has completely dissolved. Stir into the egg and sugar mixture. • With mixer at high speed, beat the cream in a large bowl until stiff. Fold the cream into the cooled egg mixture. Refrigerate until the mousse begins to set. • Dip the bases quickly into the remaining coffee. • Set them out on one or two serving plates and place a metal ring around each one. Spoon the mousse over each of the bases. Refrigerate for 12 hours, or until firm. • Remove the metal rings and dust with the cocoa. • With mixer at high speed, beat the cream in a large bowl until stiff. • Spoon into a pastry bag and pipe onto each mousse. Decorate with the raspberries.

Makes eight 3-inch cakes · Prep: 1 hr. + 12 hr. to chill · Cooking: 10–15 min. · Level: 2 · Keeps: 1–2 days in the refrigerator

CHOCOLATE ÉCLAIRS

- 1 recipe Choux Pastry (see page 308)
- 1 large egg
- 1 teaspoon water
- ½ cup heavy cream
- 2 cups Vanilla Pastry Cream (see page 342), cooled
- 1½ cups Rich Chocolate Frosting (see page 349)

Preheat the oven to 425°F. • Line a baking sheet with parchment paper. • Place the choux pastry in a pastry bag fitted with a ¾-inch tip and pipe ten 4-inch strips of pastry onto the baking sheet. • Lightly beat the egg with the water and brush over the pastry. Score the top of the pastry with a fork to keep the pastry flat during baking. • Bake for 15 minutes. Reduce the oven temperature to 400°F and bake for 15 minutes more. Remove from the oven and turn off the heat. Use the point of a sharp knife to make a few small cuts along the sides of the éclairs to release steam. Return the éclairs to the oven and leave the door slightly ajar for 10 minutes. • Transfer to racks to cool. • Beat the cream with an electric mixer at high speed until stiff. Fold it into the pastry cream. • Just before serving, place the cream filling in a pastry bag fitted with a ¼-inch tip. Make a hole in one end of each éclair and fill with 3 tablespoons of the filling. • Spread the top of each éclair with the frosting. Refrigerate for 15 minutes.

Makes 10 éclairs · Prep: 45 min. + 15 min. to chill · Cooking: 30 min. · Level: 3 · Keeps: 1 day

COFFEE ÉCLAIRS

- 1 recipe Choux Pastry (see page 308)
- 1 large egg
- 1 teaspoon water

COFFEE CREAM FILLING

- 2½ cups heavy cream
- ⅓ cup granulated sugar
- 1 tablespoon freeze-dried coffee granules

COFFEE FROSTING

- 1½ cups confectioners' sugar
- 1 tablespoon freeze-dried coffee granules, dissolved in 1 tablespoon boiling water
  chocolate-covered coffee beans, to decorate

Use the instructions for Chocolate Éclairs (see recipe above) to prepare the éclairs to the stage when the éclairs have cooled. • Using a sharp knife, carefully cut each éclair in half lengthwise. • *Coffee Cream Filling*: Beat the cream, sugar, and coffee granules in a large bowl with an electric mixer at high speed until stiff. • *Coffee Frosting*: Place the confectioners' sugar in a small bowl and stir in the dissolved coffee. • Just before serving, place the filling in a pastry bag fitted with a ¼-inch tip and cover the bottom half of each éclair with about 3 tablespoons filling. Cover with the top half of the éclair. • Spread the top of each éclair with some frosting. Refrigerate for 15 minutes. Decorate with the coffee beans.

Makes 10 éclairs · Prep: 45 min. + 15 min. to chill · Cooking: 30 min. · Level: 3 · Keeps: 1 day

MOLTEN CHOCOLATE CAKES

14	oz bittersweet chocolate, coarsely chopped
$^1/_2$	cup all-purpose flour
$^1/_2$	teaspoon baking soda
$^1/_4$	teaspoon salt
$^1/_4$	cup ($^1/_2$ stick) butter, softened
$^1/_2$	cup + 2 tablespoons granulated sugar
4	large eggs, at room temperature
1	teaspoon vanilla extract
1	cup heavy cream

Preheat the oven to 400°F. • Butter six 6-oz custard cups. • Melt the chocolate in a double boiler over barely simmering water. Set aside to cool. • Sift the flour, baking soda, and salt into a small bowl. Beat the butter and $^1/_2$ cup sugar in a large bowl with an electric mixer at medium speed until creamy. • Add the eggs, one at a time, until just blended after each addition. • With mixer at low speed, gradually beat in the dry ingredients, chocolate, and vanilla. • Spoon the batter into the prepared dishes and place them on a baking sheet. • Bake for 10–12 minutes, or until springy to the touch at the edges and the center is molten but "set." • While the cakes are baking, beat the cream and the remaining 2 tablespoons sugar with mixer at high speed until stiff. • Invert onto dessert plates and serve with the cream on the side.

Makes 6 cakes · Prep: 15 min. · Cooking: 10–12 min. · Level: 2 · Keeps: 1 day

CREAM PUFFS IN CHOCOLATE SAUCE

Assemble the cream puffs just before serving so that they don't get soggy.

1	recipe Choux Pastry (see page 308)

CREAM TOPPING

1	cup heavy cream
1	tablespoon granulated sugar
$^1/_4$	cup milk chocolate, grated
2	cups firmly packed vanilla ice cream
2	cups Quick Chocolate Sauce (see page 353)

Preheat the oven to 400°F. • Fit a pastry bag with a $^3/_4$-inch tip and fill the bag half full with batter. Pipe the batter out onto the baking sheet in 24 small mounds. If you don't have a piping bag, spoon scant tablespoons of the batter onto the sheet. •

Bake for 20–25 minutes, or until lightly browned. • Transfer to a rack to cool. • *Cream Topping*: Beat the cream and sugar in a medium bowl with an electric mixer at high speed until stiff. • Leave the ice cream at room temperature to soften, 10 minutes. Cut a "lid" off each cream puff. Use a teaspoon to hollow out the larger piece, if necessary. Fill with ice cream. Cover each puff with its lid and place on a large serving plate with 1-inch sides. Spoon a little cream onto the top of each. Sprinkle with the chocolate. • Pour $^3/_4$ of the chocolate sauce into the base of the serving plate and drizzle the rest over the top, taking care not to dismantle the cream puffs.

Makes about 24 cream puffs · Prep: 45 min. · Cooking: 20–25 min. · Level: 3 · Keeps: 1 day

APRICOT UPSIDE-DOWN CAKES

18	drained canned apricot halves
6	tablespoons firmly packed brown sugar
1	cup all-purpose flour
$1^1/_2$	teaspoons baking powder
$^1/_4$	teaspoon salt
$^1/_4$	cup ($^1/_2$ stick) butter, softened
$^1/_2$	cup granulated sugar
1	teaspoon vanilla extract
1	large egg, at room temperature
$^1/_4$	cup milk
$^3/_4$	cup heavy cream

Preheat the oven to 375°F. • Butter six 6-oz custard cups. • Slice the apricot halves and arrange them in the custard cups. Dust with 1 tablespoon sugar. Place the custard cups on a jelly-roll pan for easier handling. • Sift the flour, baking powder, and salt into a large bowl. • Beat the butter,

sugar, and vanilla in a medium bowl with an electric mixer at medium speed until creamy. • Add the egg, beating until just blended. • With mixer at low speed, gradually beat in the dry ingredients, alternating with the milk. • Spoon the batter into the cups. • Bake for 25–30 minutes, or until a toothpick inserted into the center comes out clean. • Cool the cakes in the cups for 10 minutes. Invert each onto a dessert plates. • With mixer at high speed, beat the cream in a small bowl until stiff. Spoon the cream over the cakes.

Makes 6 small cakes · Prep: 20 min. · Cooking: 25–30 min. · Level: 1 · Keeps: 1–2 days

FRUITY PUFFS

1	recipe Choux Pastry (see page 308)
1	cup frozen or fresh mixed berries, thawed if frozen
1	cup Chantilly Cream (see page 345)

Use the instructions for Cream Puffs in Chocolate Sauce (see recipe right) to prepare the choux puffs to the stage that they have cooled completely. • Use a large rubber spatula to fold the berries into the chantilly cream. Cut a "lid" off each puff. Use a teaspoon to hollow out the larger piece, if needed. Fill with the berry cream. Top each puff with its lid and arrange on a serving plate.

Makes about 24 puffs · Prep: 45 min. · Cooking: 20–25 min. · Level: 3 · Keeps 1 day

Coffee éclairs

LEMONY MINI PEACH CAKES

- 1 cup (2 sticks) butter, softened
- 1⅔ cups confectioners' sugar, + extra to dust
  - pinch of salt
- 4 large eggs, at room temperature
- 1⅓ cups all-purpose flour
- 1 teaspoon baking powder
- 1 teaspoon vanilla extract
  - grated zest of 1 lemon
- 8 oz peaches, peeled, pitted, and chopped
- 1 cup crushed pineapple, peeled and cut into pieces

Preheat the oven to 325°F. • Butter and flour 16 individual 4-inch pie plates. • Beat the butter, 1⅔ cups confectioners' sugar, and salt in a large bowl with an electric mixer at medium speed until creamy. • Add the eggs, one at a time, until just blended after each addition. • Use a large rubber spatula to fold in the flour and baking powder. Stir in the vanilla and lemon zest. • Arrange the fruit in the prepared pans. Spoon the batter over the fruit. • Bake for 25–30 minutes, or until golden brown. • Cool the cakes in the pans for 15 minutes. Invert onto individual serving plates to cool completely. Dust with the confectioners' sugar.

Makes 16 cakes · Prep: 30 min. · Cooking: 25–30 min. · Level: 1 · Keeps: 2 days

PENNSYLVANIA DUTCH FUNNEL CAKES

These little cakes taste a bit like donuts.

- 1⅔ cups all-purpose flour
- ¾ teaspoon baking soda
- ½ teaspoon cream of tartar
- ½ teaspoon ground cinnamon
- ¼ teaspoon salt
- 2 tablespoons granulated sugar
- 1 large egg

- 1 cup milk
  - vegetable oil, to fry
- ¼ cup confectioners' sugar, to dust

Sift the flour, baking soda, cream of tartar, cinnamon, and salt into a large bowl. Stir in the sugar. • Beat the egg and milk in a large bowl with an electric mixer at high speed until well blended. • With mixer at low speed, gradually beat in the dry ingredients. • Pour about 1 inch of oil into a large skillet over medium heat and heat until the oil reaches 365°F. • Pour ½ cup batter through a funnel into the skillet with a circular motion to form a spiral. Fry until golden brown, turning over once. Remove from the pan and drain on paper towels. • Dust with confectioners' sugar.

Makes 4 cakes · Prep: 20 min. · Cooking: 20 min. · Level: 1 · Keeps: 1 day

MINI MANDARIN SOUFFLÉS

Clementines, tangerines, and satsuma oranges are all types of mandarin oranges.

- 2 cups milk
- ¾ cup superfine sugar
  - grated zest of 1 mandarin orange (reserve 16 mandarin segments)
- ½ cup all-purpose flour
- ¼ cup (½ stick) + 1 teaspoon cold butter, cut up
- 5 large eggs, separated
  - pinch of salt
- 2 teaspoons firmly packed dark brown sugar
- 1 teaspoon orange liqueur
  - confectioners' sugar, to dust

Preheat the oven to 400°F. • Butter eight individual ramekins. • Bring the milk, ½ cup superfine sugar, and mandarin zest to a boil in a saucepan. • Remove from the heat. Use a large rubber spatula to fold in the flour and ¼ cup butter. Add the egg yolks, one at a time, until just blended after each addition. • Return to the heat and bring to a boil. • Set aside to cool completely. • Beat the egg whites and salt in a large bowl with an electric mixer at high speed until frothy. With mixer at high speed, beat in the remaining ¼ cup superfine sugar, beating until stiff, glossy peaks form. Use a large rubber spatula to fold them into the cooled egg yolk mixture. • Heat the remaining 1 teaspoon butter and brown sugar in a skillet. Sauté the mandarin segments until softened, 5 minutes. Drizzle with the liqueur. • Place 2 segments in each prepared ramekin. Spoon the batter evenly into the ramekins. • Bake for 15–18 minutes, or until lightly browned. • Dust with the confectioners' sugar. Serve warm.

Makes 8 soufflés · Prep: 30 min. · Cooking: 18 min. · Level: 2 · Keeps: 1 day in the refrigerator

SPICY SLICES

- 5 large eggs, at room temperature
- 1 cup granulated sugar
- 1 teaspoon vanilla extract
- 1 cup vegetable oil
- ¼ cup milk
- 2 cups all-purpose flour
- ½ cup hazelnuts, finely ground
- 1 tablespoon unsweetened cocoa powder
- 1 teaspoon ground allspice
- 1 teaspoon ground cinnamon
- ½ teaspoon baking powder

FILLING

- 1 cup Vanilla Pastry Cream (see page 342)
- 1 tablespoon dark rum
- 3 tablespoons red currant jelly

FROSTING

- 2 tablespoons apricot preserves
- ½ cup confectioners' sugar
- 4 oz almond paste

- 2 tablespoons confectioners' sugar
- 2 teaspoons water
- ½ teaspoon red food coloring, to decorate
  - silver balls, to decorate

Preheat the oven to 350°F. • Butter a 13 x 9-inch baking pan. Line with waxed paper. Butter the paper. • Beat the eggs, sugar, and vanilla in a large bowl with an electric mixer at high speed until pale and thick. Beat in the oil and milk. • Use a large rubber spatula to fold in the flour, hazelnuts, cocoa, allspice, cinnamon, and baking powder. • Spoon the batter into the prepared pan. •

Spicy slices

Bake for 25–30 minutes, or until a toothpick inserted into the center comes out clean. • Cool the cake in the pan for 10 minutes. Turn out onto a rack. Carefully remove the paper and let cool completely. • *Filling*: Flavor the Vanilla Pastry Cream with the rum. • Split the cake horizontally. Place a layer on a serving plate. Warm the jelly in a small saucepan. Brush a layer with the jelly. • Spread the filling over the jelly. Top with the remaining layer. • *Frosting*: Warm the preserves in a saucepan until liquid. • Use your hands to knead the confectioners' sugar into the almond paste on a surface dusted with confectioners' sugar. Roll out a rectangle to the size of the cake. • Brush the cake with the warmed preserves. • Cover with the rectangle of almond paste. • Slice the cake in half lengthways and cut into 1$^1/_2$-inch slices. • Mix the confectioners' sugar, water, and red food coloring. Spoon into a pastry bag and pipe over the slices in a decorative manner. Decorate with the silver balls.

Makes 16 cakes · Prep: 60 min. · Cooking: 25–30 min. · Level: 1 · Keeps: 2 days

MOCHA SNACKING CAKE

  8 oz semisweet chocolate, coarsely chopped
$^3/_4$ cup (1$^1/_2$ sticks) butter
$^3/_4$ cup granulated sugar
  1 tablespoon freeze-dried coffee granules
  1 tablespoon lukewarm water (105–115°F)
  3 large eggs
1$^1/_2$ cups all-purpose flour
     confectioners' sugar, to dust

Preheat the oven to 350°F. • Butter an 8-inch square baking pan. Line with waxed paper. Butter the paper. • Melt the chocolate and butter in a double boiler over barely simmering water. • Remove from the heat. Stir in the sugar. • Mix the coffee and water in a small bowl until the coffee has dissolved and add. • Add the eggs, one at a time, until just blended after each addition. • Use a large rubber spatula to fold in the flour. • Spoon the batter into the prepared pan. • Bake for 35–40 minutes, or until a toothpick inserted into the center comes out clean. Cool completely in the pan on a rack. • Cut into squares to serve. • Dust with confectioners' sugar.

Makes one 8-inch cake · Prep: 20 min. · Cooking: 35–40 min. · Level: 1 · Keeps: 3–4 days

Double chocolate brownies

NUTTY CARAMEL SLICE

  8 oz semisweet chocolate, coarsely chopped
  1 tablespoon butter
  2 cups graham cracker crumbs, lightly crushed

TOPPING

1$^1/_4$ cups light cream
  1 teaspoon vanilla extract
  1 tablespoon butter
$^1/_2$ cup honey
  1 cup firmly packed dark brown sugar
$^1/_2$ cup macadamia nuts, coarsely chopped
$^1/_2$ cup pine nuts
$^1/_2$ cup pecans, coarsely chopped
$^1/_2$ cup pistachios, coarsely chopped

Line a 9-inch square baking pan with plastic wrap. • Melt the chocolate and butter in a double boiler over barely simmering water. Spoon into the prepared pan. • Sprinkle the crumbs on top and press down lightly. Set aside at room temperature. • *Topping*: Mix the cream, vanilla, butter, honey, and brown sugar in a saucepan over low heat until the sugar has dissolved. Boil for about 20 minutes, without stirring, until caramel in color. Stir in the nuts. • Use a thin metal spatula to spread the topping over the chocolate base. • Refrigerate for 6 hours, or until set. • Turn out onto a plate to serve.

Makes one 9-inch cake · Prep: 30 min. + 6 hr. to chill · Level: 1 · Keeps: 3–4 days

SUNFLOWER SNACK SLICE

  3 large egg whites
$^1/_2$ cup granulated sugar
  1 cup all-purpose flour
$^1/_3$ cup pine nuts
$^1/_3$ cup pumpkin seed kernels
$^1/_3$ cup sunflower seed kernels
  2 tablespoons sesame seeds

Preheat the oven to 350°F. • Butter a 10-inch springform pan. • Beat the egg whites in a large bowl with an electric mixer at medium speed until frothy. With mixer at high speed, gradually beat in the sugar, beating until stiff, glossy peaks form. • Use a large rubber spatula to fold in the flour, pine nuts, pumpkin seed kernels, sunflower seed kernels, and sesame seeds. • Spoon the batter into the prepared pan. • Bake for 40–45 minutes, or until lightly browned. Cool the cake completely in the pan on a rack. • Loosen and remove the pan sides. Wrap the cake tightly in aluminum foil. • Set aside to rest for 24 hours. • Preheat the oven to 350°F. • Cut into wedges. Place the slices on baking sheets. Bake for 12–15 minutes, or until crisp.

Makes about 40 slices · Prep: 20 min. + 24 hr. to rest · Cooking: 52–60 min. · Level: 1 · Keeps: 3–4 days

DOUBLE CHOCOLATE BROWNIES

  4 oz semisweet chocolate, coarsely chopped
$^1/_2$ cup (1 stick) butter
1$^1/_4$ cups granulated sugar
  1 cup all-purpose flour
  1 teaspoon baking powder
$^1/_4$ teaspoon salt
  2 large eggs, lightly beaten
  3 oz bittersweet chocolate, coarsely grated

Preheat the oven to 325°F. • Butter a 13 x 9-inch baking pan. • Melt the semisweet chocolate and butter in a double boiler over barely simmering water. Set aside to cool for 10 minutes. • Stir in the sugar, flour, baking powder, salt, and eggs. • Spoon the batter into the prepared pan. • Bake for 20–30 minutes, or until a toothpick inserted into the center comes out clean. • Sprinkle the hot cake with the grated bittersweet chocolate. Cool the cake in the pan on a rack for 15 minutes. • Cut into 20 squares.

Makes 20 brownies. · Prep: 15 min. · Cooking: 20–30 min. · Level: 1 · Keeps: 2 days

YEAST CAKES

Yeast cakes require time—to rise and bake. But most of that time requires little from you, so you are free to pursue the rest of your preparations for holidays and family celebrations. Yeast cakes are indeed associated with celebrations, when the warm scent of cinnamon and baking cakes fills the house with the holiday spirit.

SPICED BREAD TWIST

1	package (¹/₄ oz) active dry yeast
¹/₄	cup granulated sugar + 2 tablespoons sugar crystals
¹/₄	cup lukewarm water (105°–115°F)
4	cups all-purpose flour
1	teaspoon salt
4	large egg yolks
¹/₄	cup (¹/₂ stick) butter, softened
¹/₂	cup granulated sugar + 2 tablespoons extra
1	tablespoon orange liqueur
1	teaspoon vanilla extract
1	teaspoon ground nutmeg
1	teaspoon ground ginger
¹/₄	teaspoon ground cloves
1	cup all-purpose flour
8	oz fresh or frozen puff pastry, thawed if frozen
2	large eggs, lightly beaten
¹/₂	cup golden raisins

Line a baking sheet with waxed paper. Butter the paper. • Stir together the yeast, ¹/₄ cup sugar, and water. Set aside for 10 minutes. • Sift the flour and salt into a large bowl. • Place the dough in a large bowl and, using your hands, work in the egg yolks. Work in the butter, ¹/₂ cup sugar, liqueur, vanilla, nutmeg, ginger, and cloves. Knead in the flour until the dough is smooth and elastic. Cover with a clean kitchen towel and let rise in a warm place, 1 hour. • Unfold or unroll the puff pastry on a lightly floured surface. Cut into two 10 x 4-inch rectangles. Brush with a little beaten egg. Sprinkle ¹/₄ cup raisins over one of the rectangles. • Turn the dough out onto a lightly floured surface and knead briefly. Shape it into a sausage about 9 inches long. Place on the pastry sprinkled with raisins. Sprinkle with the remaining raisins. Top with the remaining piece of pastry. Pull the pieces of pastry together along the sides and at the ends of the bread and pinch them together to seal. Brush with a little beaten egg and prick lightly with a fork. • Twist the whole pastry slightly. • Brush with the remaining egg and place on the prepared sheet. Sprinkle with the sugar crystals and cover with a kitchen towel. Let rise 1 hour. • Preheat the oven to 400°F. • Bake for 45–55 minutes, or until golden brown. Serve warm.

Makes one 10-inch loaf · Prep: 75 min. + 2 hr. to rise · Cooking: 45–55 min. · Level: 2 · Keeps: 2–3 days

◄ Lemon rum savarin (see page 328)

⊼ Spiced bread twist

MAKING YEAST CAKES

Active dry yeast comes in packages of ¹/₄ oz, which is normally sufficient to make a yeast cake.
Active dry yeast is now widely available in the refrigerated section of your local supermarket.

The yeast

To prepare the yeast, you will need a small bowl, a wooden spoon, warm water, and a little sugar. Exact quantities are given in each recipe.

1 Put the fresh or active dry yeast in a small bowl. If using fresh yeast, crumble it with your fingertips.

2 Add the sugar and half the warm water and stir with a fork until the yeast has dissolved.

3 Set the mixture aside for about 10 minutes. It will look creamy when ready. Stir again before proceeding to make the dough.

The dough

To prepare the dough, you will need a bowl, flour, salt, the yeast mixture, a wooden spoon, and the remaining water. Some recipes use slightly different ingredients.

1 Place the flour in a mixing bowl and sprinkle with the salt. Make a hollow in the center and pour in the yeast mixture, the remaining water, and any other ingredients listed in the recipe. Use a wooden spoon to stir the mixture. Stir well until the flour has almost all been absorbed.

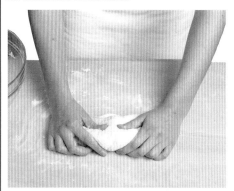

4 When the dough is kneaded, place it in a large well-oiled bowl and cover with a cloth. Most of the breads in this book have two rising times, while the pizzas are left to rise just once. The dough should double in volume during rising. To test whether it has risen sufficiently, poke your finger gently into the dough; if the impression remains, then the dough is ready. The rising times given in each recipe are approximate; remember that yeast is a living ingredient and is affected by air temperature and humidity, among other things. Some days it will take longer to rise than others.

2 The dough will be a rough and shaggy ball in the bottom of the bowl. Sprinkle a work surface, preferably made of wood, with a little flour. Note that the flour used to prepare the work surface is not included in the quantities given in the recipes. You will need about half a cup extra for this. Use a spatula (or your hands) to transfer the dough to the work surface. Curl your fingers around the dough and press it together to form a compact ball.

3 Press down on the dough with your knuckles to spread it a little. Take the far end of the dough, fold it a short distance toward you, then push it away again with the heel of your palm. Flexing your wrist, fold it toward you again, give it a quarter turn, then push it away. Repeat these motions, gently and with the lightest possible touch, for about 8–10 minutes. When the dough is firm and no longer sticks to your hands or the work surface, lift it up and bang it down hard against the work surface a couple of times. This will develop the gluten. When ready, the dough should be smooth and elastic. It should show definite air bubbles beneath the surface and should spring back if you flatten it with your palm.

BASIC SAVARIN

- 1 package (¹/₄ oz) active dry yeast
- ¹/₄ cup granulated sugar
- ¹/₄ cup lukewarm water (105°–115°F)
- 1²/₃ cups all-purpose flour
- 1 teaspoon salt
- 3 large eggs, at room temperature
- ¹/₂ cup (1 stick) butter, softened
- ¹/₄ cup dark rum

Butter a 10-inch savarin mold. • Stir together the yeast, sugar, and water. Set aside for 10 minutes. • Sift the flour and salt into a large bowl. • Beat the eggs, butter, and rum in a large bowl with an electric mixer at high speed until creamy. • Stir in the yeast mixture. Use a large rubber spatula to gradually fold in the dry ingredients. • Knead until a smooth dough is formed (see page 316). • Cover with plastic wrap and let rise in a warm place for 1 hour, or until doubled in bulk. • Punch down the dough, transfer to the prepared pan, and let rise for 40 minutes, or until doubled in bulk. • Preheat the oven to 375°F. • Bake for 35–40 minutes, or until golden. • Cool the savarin in the pan for 15 minutes. Turn out onto a rack to cool completely.

Makes one savarin · Prep: 30 min. + 1 hr. 40 min. to rise · Cooking: 35–40 min. · Level: 2 · Keeps 3 days

BASIC BRIOCHE

- 2 packages (¹/₄ oz) active dry yeast
- 2 tablespoons lukewarm water (105°–115°F)
- 2 large eggs
- 1¹/₂ cups bread flour
- ¹/₂ teaspoon salt
- 1 tablespoon superfine sugar
- ¹/₄ cup (¹/₂ stick) butter, melted

Butter a 2-quart brioche mold. • Stir together the yeast and water. Set aside for 10 minutes. • Sift the flour and salt into a large bowl. Stir in the sugar. Use your fingers to rub in the butter. • Knead until a smooth dough is formed (see page 316). • Cover with a clean kitchen towel and let rise in a warm place for 1 hour, or until doubled in bulk. • Break off a small ball of dough. Set aside. • Punch down the larger piece of dough, transfer to the prepared pan, and let rise for 40 minutes, or until doubled in bulk. • Make a hole in the center of the dough and press in the small ball of dough. Cover with a kitchen towel and let rise in a warm place for 30 minutes, or until the dough has risen just above the top of the mold. • Preheat the oven to 450°F. • Bake for 15–20 minutes, or until golden. • Cool the brioche in the pan for 15 minutes. Turn out onto a rack to cool completely.

Makes one brioche · Prep: 30 min. + 2 hr. 10 min. to rise · Cooking: 15–20 min. · Level: 2 · Keeps 3 days

SAFFRON TEA LOAF

- ¹/₈ teaspoon crumbled saffron
- 1¹/₂ cups lukewarm milk (105°–115°F)
- 1 package (¹/₄ oz) active dry yeast
- 1 tablespoon superfine sugar
- 4 cups bread flour
- 1 tablespoon butter, softened
- ¹/₂ tablespoon cardamom seeds
- ¹/₃ cup raisins
- 1 tablespoon honey
- 1 large egg, lightly beaten

Butter a 9 x 5-inch loaf pan. • Mix the saffron and 1 tablespoon milk in a small bowl. Let stand 10 minutes. • In another bowl, mix the yeast, superfine sugar, and the remaining milk. Let stand 10 minutes. • Sift the flour into a large bowl. • Use your fingertips to rub in the butter. • Stir in the cardamom and raisins. • Use a fork to beat the honey and egg into the yeast mixture. • Use a large rubber spatula to fold the egg mixture and saffron mixture into the batter. • Knead until a smooth dough is formed (see page 316). Shape into a ball and place in a well oiled bowl. Cover with a clean kitchen towel and let rest in a warm place for about 1 hour, or until doubled in bulk. • Preheat the oven to 400°F. • Punch the dough down. Place the dough in the prepared pan, spreading it evenly. Cover with plastic wrap and let rise in a warm place for 30 minutes more, or until it begins to rise. • Bake for 20–25 minutes, or until golden. • Turn out onto a rack to cool completely.

Makes one loaf · Prep: 30 min. + 1 hr. 30 min. to rise · Cooking: 20–25 min. · Level: 3 · Keeps 3 days

APPLE BREAKFAST CAKE

- 1 package (¹/₄ oz) active dry yeast
- 6 tablespoons honey
- 1 cup lukewarm water (105°–115°F)
- 3 cups whole-wheat flour
- ¹/₄ teaspoon salt
- ³/₄ cup raisins
- ¹/₂ cup pecans, coarsely chopped
- 1¹/₂ teaspoons ground cinnamon

TOPPING

- ¹/₂ cup whole-wheat flour
- ¹/₂ teaspoon ground cinnamon
- ¹/₄ cup honey
- ¹/₄ cup firmly packed dark brown sugar
- 2 tablespoons coarsely chopped pecans
- 2 large apples, cored, peeled, and thinly sliced

Set out a 13 x 9-inch baking pan. • Stir together the yeast, honey, and water. Set aside for 10 minutes. • Sift 1¹/₂ cups flour and salt into a large bowl. Stir in the yeast mixture. • Cover with a clean kitchen towel and let rise in a warm place for 30 minutes, or until foamy. • Soak the raisins in enough warm water to cover for 10 minutes. Drain well and pat dry with paper towels. • Stir the batter and add the raisins, pecans, and cinnamon. • Gradually stir in the remaining flour a little at a time until a smooth dough is formed. • Knead until a smooth dough is formed (see page 316). Add more flour if needed. (It should be soft but not sticky.) • Shape into a ball and place in a clean bowl. Cover with the kitchen towel and let rise in a warm place for about 1 hour, or until doubled in bulk. • Punch down the dough. Place in the pan, spreading it out. Cover and let rise for 15 minutes more. • *Topping*: Stir together the flour, cinnamon, honey, brown sugar, and pecans in a medium bowl. Arrange the apple slices on top of the dough. Sprinkle the pecan mixture over. • Preheat the oven to 350°F. • Cover and let rise in a warm place for 30 minutes. • Bake for 25–30 minutes, or until golden brown. • Serve warm.

Makes one 13 x 9-inch cake · Prep: 1 hr. + 2 hr. 15 min. to rise · Cooking: 25–30 min. · Level: 2 · Keeps: 2–3 days

RAISIN KUGELHOPF

This recipe comes from Alsace, a region in northeastern France. Serve with strong coffee.

- 3 packages (1/4 oz each) active dry yeast
- 1/2 cup lukewarm milk (105°–115°F)
- 1/2 cup granulated sugar
- 3 1/3 cups all-purpose flour
- 1/2 teaspoon ground nutmeg
- 1/2 teaspoon salt
- 3/4 cup (1 1/2 sticks) butter, melted and cooled
- 3 large eggs + 2 large egg yolks, lightly beaten
- 3/4 cup raisins
- 1/3 cup almonds, finely ground
- 3 tablespoons heavy cream
- 2 tablespoons grated lemon zest
- 1 tablespoon rum
- 1/4 cup confectioners' sugar, to dust

Butter and flour a 9-inch kugelhopf pan. • Stir together the yeast, water, and 1 teaspoon sugar. Set aside for 10 minutes. • Stir together the flour, remaining sugar, nutmeg, and salt in a large bowl and make a well in the center. Stir in the yeast mixture, butter, eggs, and egg yolks. • Stir in the raisins, almonds, cream, lemon zest and rum • Knead to form a smooth dough (see page 316). • Cover with a clean kitchen towel and let rise in a warm place for 1 hour, or until doubled in bulk. • Punch the dough down gently and knead again for 2–3 minutes. Place the dough in the prepared pan, spreading it evenly. Cover and let rise in a warm place for about 30 minutes, or until doubled in bulk. • Preheat the oven to 375°F. • Bake for 40–45 minutes, or until golden brown and a toothpick inserted into the center comes out clean. • Cool the kugelhopf in the pan for 10 minutes. Turn out onto a rack to cool completely. • Dust with confectioners' sugar.

Makes one 9-inch cake · Prep: 30 min. + 1 hr. 30 min. to rise · Cooking: 40–45 min. · Level: 2 · Keeps: 3–4 days

AUSTRIAN APPLE CAKE

- 1/2 cup milk
- 1/4 cup (1/2 stick) butter, cut up
- 1/4 cup + 2 tablespoons granulated sugar
- 1 package (1/4 oz) active dry yeast
- 1 large egg, at room temperature
- 2 cups all-purpose flour
- 1/2 teaspoon salt

APPLE-CREAM CHEESE FILLING

- 3 cups peeled and chopped tart apples (Granny Smiths are ideal)
- 1/4 cup firmly packed brown sugar
- 2 tablespoons fresh lemon juice
- 1 teaspoon ground cinnamon
- 1/2 teaspoon ground nutmeg
- 1 package (8 oz) cream cheese, softened
- 1/2 cup granulated sugar
- 1 large egg, at room temperature

Butter and flour a 10-inch springform pan. • Stir the milk and butter in a small saucepan over low heat until the butter has melted. Remove from the heat and cool to lukewarm (105°–115°F). Stir the sugar and yeast in a large bowl. Gradually stir in the milk mixture until the yeast and sugar have dissolved. • Beat in the egg, 1/2 cup flour, and the salt with an electric mixer at high speed. With mixer at low speed, beat in enough of the remaining flour to make a soft dough. Knead briefly in the bowl. Transfer to a lightly floured surface and knead until smooth (see page 316). • Cover with a clean kitchen towel and let rise in a warm place for 1 hour, or until doubled in bulk. • Punch down the dough. • Place the dough in the prepared

pan, pressing it halfway up the pan sides. • *Apple-Cream Cheese Filling*: Place the apples in a large bowl and stir in the brown sugar, lemon juice, cinnamon, and nutmeg until well coated. Sprinkle over the dough. • With mixer at medium speed, beat the cream cheese, granulated sugar, and egg in a medium bowl until smooth. Sprinkle over the apples. • Cover with plastic wrap and let rise in a warm place for 1 hour, or until almost doubled in bulk. • Preheat the oven to 350°F. • Bake for 35–40 minutes, or until golden. • Cool in the pan on a rack. Loosen and remove the pan sides. Serve warm.

Makes one 10-inch cake · Prep: 30 min. + 2 hr. to rise · Cooking: 35–40 min. · Level: 2 · Keeps: 1–2 days

TRENTINO CAKE

Trentino is an area in northern Italy where the lifestyle and language are distinctly more German than Italian.

- 1 tablespoon active dry yeast
- 1 cup lukewarm milk (105°–115°F)
- 4 cups all-purpose flour
- 1/2 cup (1 stick) butter, softened
- 3 large egg yolks + 1 large egg, lightly beaten
- 1 cup superfine sugar
- 1/8 teaspoon salt
- 1 cup golden raisins
- 1 1/2 cups candied lemon peel
- 1 teaspoon coriander seeds, crushed
- 2/3 cup pine nuts
- 1 cup dark rum
- 2 tablespoons finely grated orange zest
- 1 cup mixed nuts, finely chopped

Raisin kugelhopf

Butter a 10-inch round cake pan. • Stir together the yeast and milk. Set aside for 10 minutes. • Place 1⅓ cups flour in a large bowl and make a well in the center. Mix in the yeast mixture to form a smooth batter. • Cover with a clean kitchen towel and let rest in a warm place for 1 hour, or until doubled in bulk. • Stir 1¼ cups flour into the batter. Gradually mix enough of the remaining flour until a soft dough is formed. • Transfer to a lightly floured surface and knead until smooth (see page 316). • Cover with a clean kitchen towel and let rise in a warm place for 1 hour, or until doubled in bulk. • Beat the butter with an electric mixer at medium speed until creamy. Gradually add the egg yolks, one at a time, until just blended after each addition. Beat in the superfine sugar. Knead the butter mixture, half of the remaining flour and salt into the dough on a lightly floured surface. Knead the dough for 5 minutes and shape into a ball. • Return to the bowl. Cover with a kitchen towel and let rest for 1 hour, or until doubled in bulk. • Mix the raisins, lemon peel, coriander seeds, pine nuts, and rum in a large bowl. Cover and soak for 15 minutes. • Mix the orange zest and remaining flour into the soaked fruit. • Knead the fruit mixture into the dough on a lightly floured surface until well blended. Shape the dough into a long rope and join the two ends to form a ring. • Transfer to the prepared pan, cover with a kitchen towel, and let rise for 1 hour. • Preheat the oven to 375°F. • Brush with the beaten egg and sprinkle with the nuts. • Bake for 60–70 minutes, or until golden. Cool the cake completely in the pan. • Turn out into a storage container. Store for at least 1 week.

Makes one 10-inch cake · Prep: 2 hr. + 4 hr. to rise · Cooking: 60–70 min. · Level: 3 · Keeps: 2 weeks

BRAIDED SPICED COFFEECAKES

    1   package (¼ oz) active dry yeast
    ¼   cup lukewarm water (105°–115°F)
    ¾   cup granulated sugar
        about 6 cups all-purpose flour
    1   teaspoon salt
    1¼ cups lukewarm milk (105°–115°F)
    ½   cup (1 stick) butter, softened
    3   large egg yolks
    1   teaspoon ground cardamom
    1   teaspoon ground cinnamon
    ½   teaspoon ground nutmeg
    ½   teaspoon ground ginger

Trentino cake

TOPPING
    2   tablespoons milk
    ¼   cup granulated sugar
    1   teaspoon ground cinnamon
    ½   teaspoon ground nutmeg

Butter two baking sheets. • Stir together the yeast, water, and 1 teaspoon sugar. Set aside for 10 minutes. • Stir together 3 cups flour and the salt in a large bowl. Make a well in the center. Beat in the milk and the yeast mixture. Cover with a clean kitchen towel and let rise in a warm place for 90 minutes, or until doubled in bulk. • Punch the dough down. Stir in the butter, egg yolks, cardamom, cinnamon, nutmeg, ginger, remaining sugar, and remaining flour to form a soft dough. • Transfer to a lightly floured surface and knead until smooth (see page 316). • Cover with a clean kitchen towel and let rise in a warm place for 1 hour, or until doubled in bulk. • Cut the dough in half and cut each half into 3 pieces. Use the palms of your hands to roll each piece into a long rope, about 16 inches long. Arrange these ropes next to each other on the prepared sheet. Pinch the ends together at the top. Braid the ropes.

Pinch the loose ends together and tuck all ends underneath the loaf. Repeat with the other three ropes. Cover each loaf loosely with plastic wrap and let rise in a warm place for about 30 minutes. • Preheat the oven to 375°F. • *Topping*: Brush each braid with 1 tablespoon milk. Mix the sugar, cinnamon, and nutmeg in a cup. Sprinkle over each braid. • Bake for 25–30 minutes, or until lightly browned and they sound hollow when tapped on the bottom. Transfer onto racks to cool. • Serve warm or at room temperature.

Makes two loaves · Prep: 45 min. + 3 hr. to rise · Cooking: 25–30 min. · Level: 2 · Keeps: 2–3 days

Sweet poppy loaf

SWEET POPPY LOAF

- 1 package (¹/₄ oz) active dry yeast
- ³/₄ cup lukewarm milk (105°–115°F)
- 3²/₃ cups all-purpose flour
- ¹/₂ cup granulated sugar
- ¹/₂ teaspoon salt
- 3 large egg yolks + 1 large egg
- ¹/₄ cup vegetable oil
- 1 teaspoon anise extract
- 1 cup raisins
- 1 cup anisette
- ¹/₂ cup poppy seeds
  butter, to serve

Butter and flour a baking sheet. • Stir together the yeast and milk. Set aside for 10 minutes. • Place the flour, sugar, and salt in a large bowl and make a well in the center. Stir in the yeast mixture, egg yolks, oil, and anise extract. • Transfer to a lightly floured surface and knead until smooth and elastic. • Cover with a clean kitchen towel and let rise in a warm place until doubled in bulk, about 1 hour. • Soak the raisins in the anisette for 15 minutes. • Punch the dough down and roll out on a lightly floured surface to about ¹/₄

inch thick. • Drain the raisins. Do not squeeze out all the liqueur; it will add to the flavor of the bread. • Sprinkle the raisins over the dough and roll it up. • Beat the remaining egg and brush it over the surface of the rolled dough. Sprinkle with the poppy seeds. • Place the roll on the baking sheet. Cover with a clean kitchen towel and set aside in a warm place to rise for about 90 minutes. • Preheat the oven to 350°F. • Bake for 35–45 minutes, or until golden brown. • Cool the loaf on a rack. Serve lightly buttered slices at room temperature.

Makes one loaf · Prep: 30 min. + 2 hr. 30 min. to rise ·Cooking: 35–45 min. · Level: 2 · Keeps: 1–2 days

CANDIED FRUIT AND PINE NUT BUNS

- 2 packages (¹/₄ oz each) active dry yeast
- ³/₄ cup lukewarm water (105°–115°F)
- ¹/₄ cup granulated sugar
- 2 cups all-purpose flour
- ¹/₄ teaspoon salt
- 2 tablespoons extra-virgin olive oil
- ¹/₂ cup golden raisins, plumped in warm water for 15 minutes, well drained
- 3 tablespoons pine nuts
- 2 tablespoons chopped mixed candied orange and lemon peel

Oil a baking sheet. • Stir together the yeast, ¹/₄ cup water, and 1 teaspoon sugar. Set aside for 10 minutes. • Place 1²/₃ cups flour in a large bowl and make a well in the center. Stir in the yeast mixture, remaining ¹/₂ cup water, remaining sugar, and oil. Cover with a clean kitchen towel and let rise in a warm place for 2 hours, or until doubled in bulk. • Transfer the dough to a lightly floured surface. Knead in the remaining ¹/₃ cup flour, raisins, pine nuts, and candied fruit. Knead thoroughly. Roll the dough into a fat sausage and cut into 12 even pieces. Shape each into a smooth ball. Arrange the dough balls, well spaced, on the prepared baking sheet. Cover with a kitchen towel and let rise in a warm place for 2 hours, or until doubled in bulk. • Preheat the oven to 375°F. • Bake for 12–15 minutes, or until golden. Transfer onto racks to cool.

Makes 12 buns · Prep: 30 min. + 4 hr. to rise · Cooking: 15 min. · Level: 2 · Keeps: 3–4 days

RUM BABA CAKES

The word "baba" is of Polish origin, and so, it seems, are these small cakes. But in Italy where this recipe comes from, the baba is just one more exquisite Neapolitan treat. There are many different versions of the rum baba. This one is easy to make and guaranteed to be a great success.

- 2 packages (¹/₄ oz each) active dry yeast
- ¹/₄ cup lukewarm water (105°–115°F)
- 2 tablespoons granulated sugar
- 5 large eggs, at room temperature
- ¹/₂ cup extra-virgin olive oil
- ¹/₄ cup (¹/₂ stick) butter, melted and cooled
- 2¹/₃ cups all-purpose flour
- ¹/₄ teaspoon salt

RUM SYRUP

- 2 cups water
- 1¹/₂ cups granulated sugar
- ¹/₂ cup rum
- 1 lemon, sliced

Butter twelve 2 x 3-inch baba molds. • Stir together the yeast, water, and 1 teaspoon sugar. Set aside for 1 minute. • Beat the eggs and remaining sugar in a large bowl with an electric mixer at high speed until pale and thick. • Stir in the oil, butter, and the yeast mixture. • Stir in the flour and salt. • Transfer to a lightly floured surface and knead until smooth (see page 316). • Roll the dough into a fat sausage and cut into 12 even pieces. Place in the prepared molds.

Cover with plastic wrap and let rise in a warm place until the dough has risen to just below the top of each mold, about 30 minutes. • Preheat the oven to 350°F. • Bake for 12–15 minutes, or until lightly browned. • *Rum Syrup*: Stir the water and sugar in a saucepan over medium heat until the sugar has dissolved and the mixture comes to a boil. Boil for about 10 minutes, or until syrupy and thick. • Stir in the rum and lemon. Set aside to cool. • Cool the babas in the molds for 15 minutes. Soak in the rum syrup and let drain on racks.

Makes about 12 baba cakes · Prep: 25 min. + 30 min. to rise · Cooking: 12–15 min. · Level: 2 · Keeps: 1–2 days

SWEET PIZZA CAKE

  3   packages (¼ oz each) active dry yeast
 ⅓   cup lukewarm water (105°–115°F)
 ¾   cup granulated sugar
  3   cups all-purpose flour
  7   large eggs, separated
 ½   cup milk
 ⅓   cup rum
 ¼   cup ricotta cheese
  2   tablespoons grated lemon zest
  1   teaspoon ground cinnamon
 ½   teaspoon crushed anise seeds
 ⅓   cup lard or butter, softened
 ¼   cup confectioners' sugar, to dust

Stir together the yeast, water, and 1 teaspoon sugar. Set aside for 10 minutes. • Place ⅔ cup flour in a large bowl and make a well in the center. Stir in the yeast mixture. Transfer to a lightly floured surface and knead until smooth (see page 316). Shape into a ball and place in a bowl. Cover with a clean kitchen towel and let rise in a warm place overnight. • The next day, beat 6 egg yolks and the remaining sugar in a large bowl with an electric mixer at high speed until pale and thick. • With mixer at high speed, beat the egg whites in a large bowl until stiff peaks form. • Use a large rubber spatula to fold the egg whites, milk, rum, ricotta, lemon zest, cinnamon, and anise into the egg yolk mixture. • Stir in the dough, remaining 2⅓ cups flour, and lard. Knead for 10 minutes. Shape into a ball and place in a large clean bowl. Cover with a clean kitchen towel and let rise in a warm place for 2 hours, or until doubled in

German jam doughnuts

bulk. Punch the dough down. Knead again for a few minutes and shape into a ball. Let rise for 1 hour. • Preheat the oven to 325°F. • Butter and flour a 10-inch springform pan. Place the dough in the prepared pan. Beat the remaining egg yolk and pour it over. Dust with the confectioners' sugar. • Bake for 35–45 minutes, or until golden. • Turn out onto a rack to cool completely.

Makes one 10-inch cake · Prep: 30 min. + 15 hr. to rise · Cooking: 35–45 min. · Level: 3 · Keeps: 3–4 days

GERMAN JAM DOUGHNUTS

  1   package (¼ oz) active dry yeast
  1   cup lukewarm milk (105°–115°F)
4⅓   cups all-purpose flour
 ¾   cup granulated sugar
 ½   teaspoon salt
  2   large eggs, at room temperature
 ½   cup (1 stick) butter, softened
  4   tablespoons cherry jelly
      vegetable oil, to fry
      confectioners' sugar, to dust

Stir together the yeast and milk. Set aside for 10 minutes. • Stir together the flour, yeast mixture, sugar, salt, and eggs in a large bowl. Transfer to a lightly floured surface and knead until smooth (see page 316). • Beat the butter in a medium bowl with an electric mixer at medium speed until creamy. Work the butter into the dough and continue kneading until well mixed. Set aside to rest in a large bowl for about 30 minutes, or until doubled in bulk. • Roll the dough out on a lightly floured surface to about ½-inch thick. Using 2½–3-inch pastry cutters, cut out disks. • Brush half the disks with the jelly. Place the remaining halves on top and seal the edges well. • Pour enough oil into a large skillet to cover the doughnuts by ½ inch and heat to 365°F. • Fry the doughnuts in small batches until golden brown on both sides. Drain on paper towels. • Dust with the confectioners' sugar.

Serves 4 · Prep: 40 min. + 30 min. to rest · Cooking: 10 min. · Level: 2 · Keeps: 1 day

FRESH FRUIT PIZZA

CRUST

- 1 package (1/4 oz) active dry yeast
- 1/2 cup lukewarm water (105°–115°F)
- 1 tablespoon granulated sugar
- 3 cups all-purpose flour
- 1/2 teaspoon salt
- 2 1/2 tablespoons extra-virgin olive oil
  cornmeal, to dust

TOPPING

- 1 1/3 cups ricotta cheese
- 1/2 cup mascarpone cheese
- 1 1/2 oz mixed fresh or frozen blackberries, blueberries, and raspberries
- 1/4 cup confectioners' sugar, to dust

Dust a large baking sheet or 15-inch round pizza pan with cornmeal. • *Crust*: Stir together the yeast, 1/4 cup water, and the sugar. Set aside for 10 minutes. • Sift the flour and salt into a large bowl and make a well in the center. Stir in the yeast mixture and the olive oil, adding as much of the remaining 1/4 cup water as needed to make a smooth dough. • Transfer to a lightly floured surface and knead until smooth (see page 316). Cover with a clean kitchen towel and let rise in a warm place for about 1 hour, or until doubled in bulk. • Preheat the oven to 400°F. • Roll the dough out on a lightly floured surface into a 15-inch round, about 1/8-inch thick. Roll the dough onto the rolling pin and uncoil it onto the prepared sheet. • *Topping*: Mix the ricotta and mascarpone in a medium bowl. Spread the cheese mixture over the pizza dough, leaving a 1-inch border. • Stir the fruit and confectioners' sugar in a large bowl. • Spread the fruit over. • Bake for 15–20 minutes, or until the crust is crisp and the filling hot. • Serve hot or warm.

Makes one 15-inch cake · Prep: 25 min. + 1 hr. to rise · Cooking 15–20 min. · Level: 2 · Keeps: 1–2 days

APPLE PIZZA

CRUST

- 1 package (1/4 oz) active dry yeast
- 1/2 cup lukewarm water (105°–115°F)
- 1 tablespoon granulated sugar
- 3 cups all-purpose flour
- 1/2 teaspoon salt
- 2 1/2 tablespoons extra-virgin olive oil
  cornmeal, to dust

TOPPING

- 1 1/3 cups ricotta cheese
- 6 tablespoons granulated sugar
- 1 teaspoon grated lemon zest
- 1/4 teaspoon ground nutmeg
- 2 large tart apples (Granny Smiths are ideal), cored and thinly sliced
- 2 tablespoons fresh lemon juice
- 2 teaspoons ground cinnamon
- 2 tablespoons cold butter, cut up

Prepare the Crust following the instructions for Fresh Fruit Pizza (see recipe left). • *Filling*: Mix the ricotta, 3 tablespoons sugar, the lemon zest, and nutmeg in a medium bowl. Spread the ricotta mixture over the pizza dough, leaving a 1-inch border. • Arrange the apples in circles over the ricotta. Sprinkle with the lemon juice. • Mix the cinnamon with the remaining sugar and sprinkle over the pizza. Dot with the butter. • Bake for 20–25 minutes, or until the crust is crisp and the apples tender. • Serve warm.

Makes one 15-inch pizza · Prep: 25 min. + 1 hr. to rise · Cooking 20–25 min. · Level: 2 · Keeps: 1–2 days

PEAR PIZZA

CRUST

- 1 package (1/4 oz) active dry yeast
- 1/2 cup lukewarm water (105°–115°F)
- 1 tablespoon granulated sugar
- 3 cups all-purpose flour
- 1/2 teaspoon salt
- 2 1/2 tablespoons extra-virgin olive oil
  cornmeal, to dust

TOPPING

- 1 1/3 cups ricotta cheese
- 6 tablespoons granulated sugar
- 1 teaspoon grated lemon zest
- 1/4 teaspoon ground nutmeg
- 2 large pears, cored and thinly sliced
- 2 tablespoons fresh lemon juice
- 2 teaspoons ground cinnamon
- 2 tablespoons cold butter, cut up

Prepare the Crust following the instructions for Fresh Fruit Pizza (see recipe left). • *Filling*: Mix the ricotta, 3 tablespoons sugar, the lemon zest, and nutmeg in a medium bowl. Spread the ricotta mixture over the pizza dough, leaving a 1-inch border. • Arrange the pear slices in circles over the ricotta. Sprinkle with the lemon juice. • Mix the cinnamon with the remaining sugar and sprinkle over the pizza. Dot with the butter. • Bake for 20–25 minutes, or until the crust is crisp and the pears tender. • Serve warm.

Makes one 15-inch pizza · Prep: 25 min. + 1 hr. to rise · Cooking 20–25 min. · Level: 2 · Keeps: 1–2 days

PANETTONE

- 1/2 cup golden raisins
- 1 cup lukewarm water (105°–115°F)
- 2 tablespoons candied lemon peel
- 2 tablespoons candied orange peel
- 3 tablespoons dark rum
- 1 package (1/4 oz) active dry yeast
- 1/2 cup lukewarm milk (105°–115°F)
- 2 cups all-purpose flour
- 1/3 cup + 1 tablespoon granulated sugar
- 1 large egg + 2 large egg yolks
- 1 teaspoon vanilla extract
  grated zest of 1 lemon
  grated zest of 1 orange
- 1 teaspoon salt
- 1/3 cup butter, softened + 2 teaspoons, melted

Place the raisins and water in a medium bowl. Let stand 1 hour. • Drain the raisins and add the candied lemon and orange peel. Sprinkle with the rum. Cover and soak for 30 minutes. • Sprinkle the yeast over the milk. Let stand until foamy, about 10 minutes. • Stir together 1 cup flour and 1 tablespoon sugar in a large bowl and make a well in the center. Stir in the yeast mixture. • Knead the dough on a lightly floured surface until smooth and elastic, about 10 minutes. Shape into a ball and return to the bowl. Cover with a clean kitchen towel and let rise in a warm place until doubled in bulk, about 90 minutes. • Beat the remaining sugar, egg and egg yolks, vanilla, lemon and orange zests, and salt in a large bowl with an electric mixer at low speed. • Knead the mixture and the flour into the dough on a lightly floured surface until a smooth dough is formed, about 7 minutes. • Knead in the softened butter and raisin mixture until well blended. Cover with the kitchen towel and let rise until doubled in bulk, about 90 minutes. • Butter a 6-cup panettone mold or an 8-inch round cake pan. Punch the dough down gently and knead again gently for 2–3 minutes. Place the dough in the prepared pan, spreading it evenly. • Cover and let rise in a warm place until almost doubled in bulk, 60 minutes. • Preheat the oven to 350°F. • Brush with the melted butter. • Bake for 45–55 minutes, or until golden brown and a toothpick inserted into the center comes out clean. • Cool the panettone in the pan for 5 minutes. Turn out onto a rack to cool completely.

Makes one panettone · Prep: 40 min. + 4 hr. to rise · Cooking: 45–55 min. · Level: 3 · Keeps: 3 days in the refrigerator

FILLED STRAWBERRY BRIOCHE

- 1 recipe Basic Brioche (see page 317)
- 1 large egg, lightly beaten
- 3 cups fresh strawberries, hulled
- 1/3 cup confectioners' sugar
- 2 tablespoons fresh lemon juice
- 1 cup amaretto
- 2 cups Classic Bavarian Cream (see page 341)

Prepare the dough according to the recipe directions through punching down the dough after the first rise. • Preheat the oven to 400°F. • Butter a 2-quart brioche mold. • Shape the dough into a ball and place in the prepared pan, punching down once. • Brush with the beaten egg. • With a sharp knife, make several cuts at regular intervals in the dough. • Bake for 40–50 minutes, or until golden. • Turn out of the pan and let cool on a rack. • Set aside 6 perfect strawberries for decoration and slice the remainder. Mix the strawberries, confectioners' sugar, lemon juice, and amaretto in a large bowl. • Fold the strawberries and their juice into the Bavarian cream • Cut the top off the brioche and hollow out the inside. (Serve the insides, toasted, for breakfast.) • Fill with the cream. Decorate with the reserved strawberries and replace the top.

Makes one 2-quart brioche · Prep: 45 min. · Cooking: 40–50 min. · Level: 2 · Keeps: 1 day

FILLED RASPBERRY BRIOCHE

- 1 recipe Basic Brioche (see page 317)
- 1 large egg, lightly beaten
- 3 cups fresh raspberries, hulled
- 1/3 cup confectioners' sugar
- 2 tablespoons fresh lemon juice
- 1 cup lemon liqueur
- 2 cups Classic Bavarian Cream (see page 341)

Prepare this following the instructions for Filled Strawberry Brioche (see recipe above), replacing the strawberries with the raspberries and the almond liqueur with the lemon liqueur.

Makes one 2-quart brioche · Prep: 45 min. · Cooking: 40–50 min. · Level: 2 · Keeps: 1 day

Filled strawberry brioche

Easter bunny cake

EASTER BUNNY CAKE

- 2 (¹/₄ oz) packages active dry yeast
- 1¹/₄ cups lukewarm milk (105°–115°F)
- 4 cups all-purpose flour
- ³/₄ cup granulated sugar + 2 tablespoons
- 1 teaspoon salt
- 1 teaspoon ground nutmeg
- 1 teaspoon ground ginger
- ¹/₃ cup butter, cut up
- 1 teaspoon vanilla extract
- 1 cup raisins
- 1 cup Vanilla Frosting (see page 347), colored with ¹/₂ teaspoon red food coloring
     candy, to decorate

Butter a baking sheet. Line with waxed paper. Butter the paper. • Stir together the yeast and milk. Set aside for 10 minutes. • Stir together the flour, ³/₄ cup sugar, salt, nutmeg, and ginger in a large bowl. Use a pastry blender to cut in the butter. Stir in the yeast mixture, vanilla, and raisins until blended. Shape into a ball and place in a large bowl. Cover with a clean kitchen towel and let rise in a warm place until doubled in bulk, about 1 hour. • Knead on a lightly

floured surface. Divide into three portions. • Shape two portions into a head and a body of a rabbit, reserving a small piece for the nose. Shape the third portion into legs and ears. Assemble the rabbit on the prepared pan. (See photo.) Spread the frosting all over the cake and use the candy to make the eyes and whiskers. • Cover with a clean kitchen towel and let rise in a warm place for 1¹/₂ hours. • Sprinkle with the remaining sugar. • Preheat the oven to 350°F. • Bake for 40–50 minutes, or until lightly browned. Cool the cake in the pan for 15 minutes. Turn out onto the rack to cool completely.

Makes 1 cake · Prep: 30 min. + 2 hr. 30 min. to rise · Cooking: 40–50 min. · Level: 2 · Keeps: 1 week

FLORENTINE CARNIVAL CAKE

In Florence this dish is traditionally eaten on the Thursday before Lent. If there is any left the day after, cut the cake horizontally and fill with whipped cream.

- 1 (¹/₄ oz) package active dry yeast
- 1 cup lukewarm water (105°–115°F)
- 3¹/₄ cups all-purpose flour
- 1 cup granulated sugar

- 4 large egg yolks
- ¹/₃ cup butter, melted
- 2 tablespoons finely grated orange zest
- ¹/₄ teaspoon salt
- 6 tablespoons confectioners' sugar, to dust

Butter a 9 x 13 inch baking pan. Line with waxed paper. Butter the paper. • Stir together the yeast and ¹/₂ cup water. Set aside for 10 minutes. • Mix the flour and sugar in a large bowl and make a well in the center. • Mix in the yeast mixture until the flour has all been absorbed, adding enough of the remaining ¹/₂ cup water to obtain a smooth dough. • Transfer to a lightly floured surface and knead until smooth (see page 316). Shape into a ball and place in a clean bowl. Cover with a clean kitchen towel and let rise in a warm place for about 1 hour. • Knead the dough again, and gradually work in the eggs, butter, orange zest, and salt. • Place the dough in the prepared pan, spreading it evenly. Let rise for 2 hours more, or until doubled in bulk. • Preheat the oven to 350°F. • Bake for 25–35 minutes, or until a toothpick inserted into the center comes out clean. • Cool the cake in the pan for 15 minutes. Turn out onto a rack to cool completely. Dust with confectioners' sugar.

Makes one 9 x 13-inch cake · Prep: 20 min. + 3 hr. to rise · Cooking: 25–35 min. · Level: 2 · Keeps: 1–2 days

VERONESE CHRISTMAS CAKE

- 2 cups all-purpose flour
- 1¹/₂ packages (¹/₄ oz each) active dry yeast
- 1 large egg + 5 large egg yolks
- ³/₄ cup granulated sugar
- 1 cup milk, warmed
- ³/₄ cup (1¹/₂ sticks) butter, softened
- ¹/₂ cup light cream
- 1 tablespoon grated lemon zest
- 1 teaspoon vanilla extract
- ¹/₃ cup confectioners' sugar + ¹/₄ cup, to dust

Sift ¹/₄ cup flour into a small bowl. Add the yeast, 1 egg yolk, and 1 tablespoon of the sugar. Stir together, adding the milk to form a soft dough. Shape into a ball. Cover with a plastic wrap and let rise in a warm place for 2 hours. • Sift half the remaining flour into a large bowl. Place the dough in the bowl. Stir in half the remaining sugar, 3 egg yolks, and 3 tablespoons butter. • Transfer to a lightly floured surface and knead until smooth (see page 316). Return to the bowl. Cover with a kitchen

towel and let rise for 2 hours more. •
Knead the remaining flour, remaining
sugar, remaining egg yolk, and the whole
egg into the dough. Shape into a ball and
return to the bowl. Cover and let rise for 2
hours more. • Knead in the cream, lemon
zest, and vanilla. • Roll the dough out into
a rectangle. Place the remaining butter in
the center and fold over first $\frac{1}{3}$ of the
rectangle, then the other so that you have a
3-layered "sandwich" of dough. Roll it out
again and fold again in the same way. Roll
it out more gently into a smaller rectangle.
Cover and let rest for 30 minutes. Repeat
the folding and rolling stage once more.
Cover and let rest for a final 30 minutes. •
Preheat the oven to 375°F. • Butter a fluted
turban mold and dust with confectioners'
sugar. Add the dough (it should half-fill
the mold). Cover and let rise until it has
reached the top of the mold, about 20
minutes. • Bake for 30 minutes. Reduce
the oven temperature to 350°F and
continue baking for 20–30 more minutes,
or until golden. • Turn out onto a rack to
cool completely. Dust with the
confectioners' sugar.

*Makes one cake · Prep: 1 hr. + 7 hr. 20 min. to rise ·
Cooking: 50–60 min. · Level: 2 · Keeps: 1–2 days*

TUSCAN HARVEST GRAPE BREAD

This recipe for sweet focaccia comes from
Tuscany, where it is made every year throughout
the grape harvest using the small black grapes
used to make the local Chianti wines.

- 2 ($\frac{1}{4}$ oz) packages active dry yeast
- $\frac{2}{3}$ cup lukewarm water
- 3$\frac{1}{4}$ cups all-purpose flour
- $\frac{1}{4}$ teaspoon salt
- $\frac{1}{4}$ cup granulated sugar

TOPPING

- 1 lb black grapes, crushed
- $\frac{3}{4}$ cup granulated sugar

Butter a large baking sheet. Line with waxed
paper. • Stir together the yeast and $\frac{1}{3}$ cup
water. Set aside for 10 minutes. • Stir
together the flour, sugar, and salt in a large
bowl and make a well in the center. Stir in
the yeast mixture until the flour has all been
absorbed, adding enough water to obtain a
smooth dough. • Transfer to a lightly floured
surface and knead until smooth (see page
316). Shape into a ball. Cover with a clean
tea towel and set aside to rise in a warm

place for about 1 hour, or until doubled in
bulk. • Divide the dough in two. Roll out the
dough into two sheets about 1-inch thick.
Place a dough sheet in the prepared pan.
Cover with half the grapes and half the
sugar. Top with the remaining dough sheet
and seal the edges thoroughly. • Spread the
remaining grapes over the top, pressing
them down into the dough. Sprinkle with the
sugar and set aside to rise for 1 hour. •
Preheat the oven to 350°F. • Bake for 40–50
minutes, or until lightly browned.

*Makes one large cake · Prep: 15 min. + 3 hr. to rise ·
Cooking: 40–50 min. · Level: 2 · Keeps: 1 day*

RASPBERRY FOCACCIA

- 2 ($\frac{1}{4}$ oz) packages active dry yeast
- $\frac{2}{3}$ cup lukewarm water
- 3$\frac{1}{4}$ cups all-purpose flour
- $\frac{1}{4}$ teaspoon salt
- $\frac{1}{4}$ cup granulated sugar

TOPPING

- 1 lb raspberries
- $\frac{3}{4}$ cup granulated sugar

Butter a large baking sheet. Line with
waxed paper. • Stir together the yeast and

$\frac{1}{3}$ cup water. Set aside for 10 minutes. •
Stir together the flour, sugar, and salt in a
large bowl and make a well in the center.
Stir in the yeast mixture until the flour
has all been absorbed, adding enough
water to obtain a smooth dough. •
Transfer to a lightly floured surface and
knead until smooth (see page 316).
Shape into a ball. Cover with a clean
kitchen towel and set aside to rise in a
warm place for about 1 hour, or until
doubled in bulk. • Divide the dough in
two. Roll out the dough into two sheets
about 1-inch thick. Place a dough sheet
in the prepared pan. Cover with half the
raspberries and half the sugar. Top with
the remaining dough sheet and seal the
edges thoroughly. • Spread the remaining
raspberries over the top, pressing them
down into the dough. Sprinkle with the
sugar and set aside to rise for 1 hour. •
Preheat the oven to 350°F. • Bake for
40–50 minutes, or until lightly browned.

*Makes one large cake · Prep: 15 min. + 3 hr. to rise ·
Cooking: 40–50 min. · Level: 2 · Keeps: 1 day*

BABKAS WITH STREUSEL TOPPING

- 2 packages (¼ oz each) active dry yeast
- ½ cup lukewarm water (105°–115°F)
- ⅓ cup granulated sugar
- ⅔ cup lukewarm milk (105°–115°F)
- ½ teaspoon salt
- 1 teaspoon vanilla extract
- ⅓ cup butter, softened
  about 4 cups all-purpose flour
- 3 large eggs

CHOCOLATE FILLING
- ⅓ cup unsweetened cocoa powder
- ¾ cup granulated sugar
- 1 cup walnuts, coarsely chopped

STREUSEL TOPPING
- ¾ cup firmly packed brown sugar
- ½ cup all-purpose flour
- 1 teaspoon ground cinnamon
- ½ teaspoon ground nutmeg
- ¼ cup (½ stick) butter, softened

Preheat the oven to 350°F. • Butter and flour two 4½ x 8½-inch loaf pans. • Stir together the yeast, water, and 1 teaspoon sugar in a large bowl. Set aside for 10 minutes. • Stir in the remaining sugar, milk, salt, vanilla, and ¼ cup butter. • With mixer at low speed, gradually beat in 2 cups flour until smooth, about 5 minutes. • Separate one egg, reserving the white for the glaze. • With mixer at medium speed, beat in the egg yolk and remaining eggs, one at a time, until just blended after each addition. • Stir in enough of the remaining flour to make a smooth dough. • Transfer to a lightly floured surface and knead until smooth (see page 316), adding the remaining flour if the dough is too sticky. • Shape into a ball and place the dough in a bowl. Cover with plastic wrap and let rise in a warm place about 45 minutes, or until doubled in bulk. • *Chocolate Filling*: Stir together the cocoa and sugar in a small bowl. • Punch the dough down. • Divide the dough in half. Roll out each half into a 10 x 20-inch rectangle. • Melt the remaining ¼ cup

butter and brush over the dough, leaving a ½-inch border around the edges. • Sprinkle half of the filling and walnuts over the butter. • Starting with the long side, roll each rectangle up tightly, squashing the ends to seal. Fit into the prepared pans and set aside in a warm place about 45 minutes, or until doubled in bulk. • *Streusel Topping*: Stir together the brown sugar, flour, cinnamon, and nutmeg in a large bowl. Use a pastry blender to cut in the butter. • Beat the reserved egg white and brush over. Sprinkle with the topping. • Bake for 30–40 minutes, or until browned. • Cool the loaves on racks.

Makes two loaves · Prep: 35 min. + 1hr. 30 min. to rise · Cooking: 30–40 min. · Level: 2 · Keeps: 1–2 days

LEMON CURD BREAKFAST CAKE

- 1 tablespoon active dry yeast
- ¼ cup lukewarm water (105°–115°F)
- ⅓ cup granulated sugar
- ½ cup sour cream
- 1 tablespoon grated lemon zest
- ¼ teaspoon salt
- 2⅔ cups all-purpose flour
- 2 large eggs, lightly beaten + 1 large egg
- ⅓ cup butter, softened
- 1 cup Lemon Curd (see page 345)
- ¼ cup slivered almonds

Stir together the yeast, water, and 1 teaspoon sugar. Set aside for 10 minutes. • Beat the sour cream, remaining sugar, lemon zest, and salt with an electric mixer at high speed in a large bowl until well blended. • Place

Babkas with streusel topping

the flour in a large bowl and make a well in the center. Stir in the yeast mixture and the beaten eggs. Use a large rubber spatula to gradually fold the flour into the sour cream mixture. • Beat in the butter, making a firm, slightly sticky dough. • Transfer to a lightly floured surface and knead until smooth (see page 316). Shape into a ball and place in a bowl. Cover with a clean kitchen towel and let rise in a warm place for about 1 hour, or until doubled in bulk. • Line a baking sheet with parchment paper. • Punch the dough down and roll out on a lightly floured surface to an 18 x 12-inch rectangle. Spread the lemon curd on the dough, leaving a ¾-inch border on all sides. Carefully roll up the dough from a short side. • Use a sharp knife to cut the roll into 1½-inch thick slices. Arrange the slices in a round ¼ inch apart on the prepared sheet. Cover with plastic wrap and let rise in a warm place for 30 minutes. • Preheat the oven to 375°F. • Beat the remaining egg and brush over the rolls. Sprinkle with the almonds. • Bake for 25–35 minutes, or until browned. • Serve hot or at room temperature.

Makes one 10-inch cake · Prep: 30 min. + 1 hr. 30 min. to rise · Cooking: 25–35 min. · Level: 2 · Keeps: 2–3 days

ALMOND BREAKFAST BRAIDS

- 1 cup sour cream
- ½ cup (1 stick) butter, cut up

- 1/2 cup granulated sugar
- 1 teaspoon salt
- 2 packages (1/4 oz each) active dry yeast
- 1/2 cup lukewarm water (105°–115°F)
- 2 large eggs, at room temperature, lightly beaten
- 4 cups all-purpose flour + 1/4 cup more, if needed
- 1/2 cup flaked almonds

CREAM CHEESE FILLING
- 2 packages (8 oz each) cream cheese, softened
- 3/4 cup granulated sugar
- 1 large egg, beaten
- 1/4 teaspoon salt
- 2 teaspoons vanilla extract

GLAZE
- 1 cup confectioners' sugar
- 1 teaspoon vanilla extract
- 1 1/2–2 tablespoons milk

Line 2 baking sheets with parchment paper. • Stir the sour cream and butter in a saucepan over low heat until the butter has melted. Stir in the sugar and salt. • Mix the yeast and water in a large bowl. • Use a large rubber spatula to fold in the sour cream mixture, eggs, and 4 cups flour, adding additional flour until the dough is no longer sticky. • Transfer to a lightly floured surface and knead until smooth (see page 316). Shape into a ball and place in a large bowl. Cover with a clean kitchen towel and let rise for 30 minutes. • *Cream Cheese Filling*: Beat the cream cheese and sugar with an electric mixer at medium speed until creamy. Beat in the egg, salt, and vanilla. • Divide the dough into eight equal parts. Roll each on a lightly floured surface into a 9 x 6-inch rectangle. Spread the filling on top of each rectangle, leaving a 1/2-inch border around the edges. Starting with a long side, roll each rectangle tightly. Pinch the ends to seal. Place the rolls seam-side down on the baking sheets. Make diagonal cuts over the dough, alternating sides, to resemble a braid. Cover with a kitchen towel and let rise for another hour, or until doubled in bulk. Sprinkle with the almonds. • Preheat the oven to 375°F. • Bake for 25–30 minutes, or until browned. Cool on racks. • *Glaze*: Mix the confectioners' sugar, vanilla, and milk in a small bowl. Drizzle the glaze over.

Makes 8 braids · Prep: 20 min. + 1 hr. 30 min. to rise · Cooking: 15–20 min. · Level: 2 · Keeps: 1–2 days

SWEDISH BREAKFAST CAKE
- 1 tablespoon active dry yeast
- 1/2 cup lukewarm milk (105°–115°F)

- 1/2 cup granulated sugar
- 1 2/3 cups all-purpose flour
- 1/2 teaspoon vanilla extract
- 1/4 teaspoon salt
- 4 large egg yolks + 1 large egg, lightly beaten
- 1/2 cup (1 stick) butter, melted
- 1 cup golden raisins

Preheat the oven to 350°F. • Butter a 10-inch springform pan. Sprinkle with dry bread crumbs. • Stir together the yeast, milk, and 1 teaspoon sugar. Set aside for 10 minutes. • Stir together the flour, 1 tablespoon sugar, vanilla, and salt in a large bowl. Add the egg yolks, one at a time, until just blended after each addition. Stir in the yeast mixture until a smooth dough is formed. • Transfer to a lightly floured surface and knead until smooth (see page 316). • Break off a piece slightly larger than an egg and knead for a few seconds. • Knead the remaining dough for a few seconds. • Shape each piece of dough into a ball and place in two separate bowls. Cover with a clean kitchen towel and let rise in a warm place until doubled in bulk, about 30 minutes. • Roll out the smaller dough ball on a lightly floured surface to 1/8 inch thick. Fit the dough into the prepared pan. • Roll out the larger dough ball to 1/8 inch thick to make a 16 x 7-inch rectangle. • Brush with the melted butter and sprinkle with the remaining sugar and raisins. • From a long side, roll up the dough jelly-roll fashion. Cut into 1 1/2-inch thick slices. Arrange the slices evenly on the

dough base. • Cover with a kitchen towel and let rest in a warm place until the slices have expanded to fill the pan, about 1 hour. • Brush with the beaten egg. • Bake for 30–35 minutes, or until golden brown. • Cool the cake in the pan for 10 minutes. Loosen and remove the pan sides and bottom.

Makes one 10-inch cake · Prep: 30 min. + 1 hr. 30 min. to rise · Cooking: 30–35 min. · Level: 2 · Keeps: 2–3 days

PEAR BREAKFAST CAKE
- 1 package (1/4 oz) active dry yeast
- 6 tablespoons honey
- 1 cup lukewarm water (105°–115°F)
- 1/4 teaspoon salt
- 3 cups whole-wheat flour
- 3/4 cup raisins
- 1/2 cup pecans, coarsely chopped
- 1 1/2 teaspoons ground cinnamon

TOPPING
- 1/2 cup whole-wheat flour
- 1/2 teaspoon ground cinnamon
- 1/4 cup honey
- 1/4 cup firmly packed dark brown sugar
- 2 tablespoons walnuts, coarsely chopped
- 2 large pears, cored, peeled, and thinly sliced

Use the instructions for Apple Breakfast Cake (see page 317), replacing the apples with the pears, and the pecans with walnuts.

Makes one 13 x 9-inch cake · Prep: 1 hr. + 2 hr. 15 min. to rise · Cooking: 25–30 min. · Level: 2 · Keeps: 2–3 days

Apricot rum savarin

RASPBERRY CREAM SAVARIN

1 recipe Basic Savarin (see page 317)
2 cups raspberries
2 tablespoons fresh orange juice
1/2 cup dark rum
2/3 cup heavy cream

Prepare the dough according to the recipe directions through punching down the dough after the first rise. • Butter a 9-inch savarin pan. • Place the dough in the pan. Set aside in a warm place to rise for 1 hour. • Preheat the oven to 400°F. • Bake for 25–30 minutes, or until golden. • Cool the savarin in the pan for 15 minutes. • Place the cake on a large plate and poke holes all over with a fork. • Mix the orange juice and rum in a small bowl. Drizzle over the cake. • Fill the center of the savarin with the raspberries. • Beat the cream in a large bowl with an electric mixer at high speed until stiff. • Spoon the cream into a pastry bag and pipe in a decorative manner. • Decorate with the raspberries.

Makes one 9-inch cake · Prep: 25 min. · Cooking: 25–30 min. · Level: 2 · Keeps: 2 days in the refrigerator

APRICOT RUM SAVARIN

1 recipe Basic Savarin (see page 317)
1 1/2 cups granulated sugar
2 cups cold water
1/2 cup dark rum
2 cups apricot preserves or jam
1 1/2 cups heavy cream
1 teaspoon vanilla extract
apricot halves, to decorate

Prepare the dough according to the recipe directions through punching the dough down after the first rise. • Butter a 9-inch springform pan. • Place the savarin dough in the pan. Set aside in a warm place to rise for 1 hour. • Preheat the oven to 400°F. • Bake for 20–25 minutes, or until golden brown. • Turn out onto a rack and let cool. • Bring 1 1/4 cups sugar and water to a boil in a saucepan. • Place the cake (still on the rack) on a large plate. Drizzle the hot syrup over the cake. Scoop up any excess syrup with a spoon and drizzle over the cake. • Drizzle with the rum. • Heat the apricot preserves in a saucepan until liquid. Pour half the hot jam over the cake. Set aside to cool. • Repeat with the remaining jam and set aside to cool.

• Beat the cream, remaining 1/4 cup sugar, and vanilla in a medium bowl with an electric mixer at high speed until stiff. • Split the cake horizontally, making sure that the bottom layer is thicker than the top layer. • Place the bottom layer on a serving plate. Spread with the cream. Place the remaining layer on top. • Decorate with the apricot halves.

Makes one 9-inch cake · Prep: 45 min. + 1 hr. to rise · Cooking: 20–25 min. · Level: 2 · Keeps: 1 day in the refrigerator

LEMON RUM SAVARIN

1 recipe Basic Savarin (see page 317)
1 1/2 cups granulated sugar
2 cups cold water
2 tablespoons finely grated lemon zest
1 cinnamon stick
2 cups rum
1/2 cup apricot preserves
1 1/2 cups heavy cream
1/3 cup confectioners' sugar
candied cherries and almonds, to decorate

Prepare the dough according to the recipe directions through punching down the dough after the first rise. • Butter a 10-inch tube pan. • Place the savarin dough in the pan. Let rise in a warm place for 1 hour. • Preheat the oven to 400°F. • Bake for 20–25 minutes, or until golden brown. • Turn out onto a rack to cool. • Bring the sugar, water, lemon zest, and cinnamon stick to a boil in a saucepan. • Place the cake (still on the rack) on a large plate. • Remove the cinnamon stick from the syrup. Drizzle the hot syrup over the cake. Scoop up any excess syrup with a spoon and drizzle over the cake. • Drizzle with the rum. • Heat the apricot preserves in a saucepan until liquid. Pour over the cake and set aside to cool. • Beat the cream and confectioners' sugar in a medium bowl with an electric mixer at high speed until stiff. • Spoon the cream into the center. • Decorate with the cherries and almonds.

Makes one 10-inch cake · Prep: 45 min. + 1 hr. to rise · Cooking: 20–25 min. · Level: 2 · Keeps: 1 day in the refrigerator

JAMAICAN SAVARIN

1/3 cup lukewarm milk (105°–115°F)
1 1/2 packages (1/4 oz each) active dry yeast
2 tablespoons granulated sugar
2 cups all-purpose flour
1/2 teaspoon salt

¹/₃ cup butter, softened
4 large eggs, lightly beaten, at room temperature

SYRUP

1 large orange
2 cups water
1¹/₄ cups granulated sugar
1 cup dark Jamaican rum

¹/₄ cup strawberry jelly
1 tablespoon dark Jamaican rum
3 cups fresh strawberries, hulled and halved

Stir together the milk, yeast, and 1 teaspoon sugar. Set aside for 10 minutes. • Sift the flour and salt into a large bowl and make a well in the center. Stir in the yeast mixture. • Add the eggs, butter, and remaining sugar until well blended. • Transfer to a lightly floured surface and knead until smooth (see page 316). • Shape into a ball and place in a bowl. Cover with a clean kitchen towel, and let rise in a warm place for about 1 hour, or until doubled in bulk. • Butter a 9-inch savarin pan. • Punch down the dough. Place in the prepared pan, spreading it evenly. Cover with the kitchen towel and let rise in a warm place for 30 minutes, or until almost doubled in bulk. • Preheat the oven to 375°F. • Bake for 35–45 minutes, or until golden brown. Cool the savarin in the pan for 15 minutes. • *Syrup*: Remove the zest from the orange. • Bring the water, sugar, and orange zest to a boil in a saucepan over medium heat, stirring constantly, until the sugar has dissolved. Boil for 8 minutes. Remove from the heat and add the rum. • Spoon the syrup over the cake until all the syrup has been absorbed. Cool the savarin completely in the pan on a rack. • Heat the jelly and rum in a saucepan over low heat. • Turn the savarin onto a serving plate and spread with the warm jelly. • Decorate with the strawberries.

Makes one 9-inch cake · Prep: 25 min. + 1hr. 30 min. to rise · Cooking: 35–45 min. · Level: 2 · Keeps: 2–3 days

PLUM SAVARIN

1 recipe Basic Savarin (see page 317)
1 cup granulated sugar
1 cup water
3 cups plums, pitted and thinly sliced
¹/₄ cup apricot preserves or jam
¹/₂ cup brandy

Prepare the dough according to the recipe directions through punching down

Jamaican savarin

the dough after the first rise. • Butter a 9-inch savarin pan. • Place the savarin dough in the pan. Set aside in a warm place to rise for 1 hour. • Preheat the oven to 400°F. • Bake for 25–30 minutes, or until golden brown. • Cool the savarin in the pan for 15 minutes. • Place the cake (still on the rack) on a large plate and poke holes all over with a fork. • Bring the sugar and water to a boil in a saucepan. Boil for 5 minutes, or until syrupy. Stir in the fruit until well coated. • Remove the fruit and set aside. • Stir in the preserves and brandy. Spoon the syrup over until the syrup has been absorbed. • Arrange the fruit in the center of the savarin.

Makes one 9-inch cake · Prep: 25 min. · Cooking: 25–30 min. · Level: 2 · Keeps: 2 days in the refrigerator

PEACH SAVARIN

1 recipe Basic Savarin (see page 317)
1 can (15 oz) peach slices, drained (reserve the juice)

¹/₂ cup dark rum
²/₃ cup heavy cream

Prepare the dough according to the recipe directions through punching down the dough after the first rise. • Butter a 9-inch savarin pan. • Place the savarin dough in the pan. Set aside in a warm place to rise for 1 hour. • Preheat the oven to 400°F. • Bake for 25–30 minutes, or until golden brown. • Cool the savarin in the pan for 15 minutes. • Place the cake (still on the rack) on a large plate and poke holes all over with a fork. • Mix the peach juice and rum in a small bowl. Drizzle over the cake. • Chop half the peaches coarsely. Fill the center of the savarin with the chopped peaches. • Beat the cream in a large bowl with an electric mixer at high speed until stiff. • Spoon the cream into a pastry bag and pipe in a decorative manner over the top. • Decorate with the remaining peach slices.

Makes one 9-inch cake · Prep: 25 min. · Cooking: 25–30 min. · Level: 2 · Keeps: 2 days in the refrigerator

SPECIAL CAKES

This chapter contains a dazzling array of cakes from all around the world. Some contain unusual ingredients and flavors, some are quite simple to prepare. Guests will enjoy their special flavors and exciting, even whimsical, presentations.

GREEK RICE CAKE

Make this cake with arborio rice.

- 2 cups milk
- ³/₄ cup short-grain rice
- 4 large eggs, separated
- ³/₄ cup granulated sugar
- ¹/₂ cup (1 stick) butter, softened
- ¹/₂ cup chopped mixed candied fruit
- 2 oz bittersweet chocolate, chopped
- ¹/₄ cup confectioners' sugar, to dust
    candied cherries and angelica, to decorate

Bring the milk and rice to a boil in a saucepan over medium heat. Lower the heat and cook until the rice is tender, about 20 minutes. Remove from the heat and set aside to cool. • Preheat the oven to 350°F. • Butter a 9-inch round cake pan. Line with waxed paper. Butter the paper. • Process the rice mixture in a food processor until smooth. • Transfer to a large bowl and beat in the egg yolks, sugar, and butter. • Stir in the candied fruit and chocolate. • Beat the egg whites in a large bowl with an electric mixer at high speed until stiff peaks form. Use a rubber spatula to fold them into the rice mixture. • Spoon the batter into the prepared pan. • Bake for 35–45 minutes, or until a toothpick inserted into the center comes out clean. • Cool the cake in the pan for 15 minutes. Turn out onto a rack. Carefully remove the paper and let cool completely. • Dust with the confectioners' sugar. Decorate with the candied cherries and angelica.

Makes one 9-inch cake · Prep: 25 min. · Cooking: 35–45 min. · Level: 1 · Keeps: 3–4 days

◄ Almond and pistachio baklava
(see page 339)

➢ Greek rice cake

Peruvian baba

ARMENIAN NUTMEG CAKE

- 2 cups all-purpose flour
- 2 cups firmly packed dark brown sugar
- 2 teaspoons baking powder
- 1 teaspoon ground nutmeg
- 1 teaspoon ground cardamom
- 1/2 teaspoon ground cloves
- 1/2 teaspoon salt
- 1/2 cup (1 stick) butter, cold cut up
- 1/2 cup milk
- 1 large egg, at room temperature
- 1 teaspoon baking soda
- 3/4 cup assorted unsalted nuts, coarsely chopped

Preheat the oven to 350°F. • Butter a 13 x 9-inch baking pan. • Stir together the flour, brown sugar, baking powder, nutmeg, cardamom, cloves, and salt in a large bowl. • Use a pastry blender to cut in the butter until the mixture resembles fine crumbs. • Press half the mixture into the prepared pan. • Beat the milk, egg, and baking soda in a medium bowl. Stir the milk mixture and nuts into the remaining dry ingredients. Spoon over the crumb mixture. • Bake for 50–60 minutes, or until a toothpick inserted into the center comes out clean. • Cool the cake completely in the pan on a rack.

Makes one 13 x 9-inch cake · Prep: 20 min. · Cooking: 50–60 min. · Level: 1 · Keeps: 2 days

PERUVIAN BABA

Pisco is a Peruvian grape brandy.

- 18 large egg yolks + 1 large egg
- 2 tablespoons pisco or brandy

SYRUP

- 2 1/4 cups granulated sugar
- 2 cups pisco or brandy
- 2 cups water
- 1 1/3 cups slivered almonds, toasted
- 1/2 cup raisins

Preheat the oven to 300°F. • Line an 11 x 7-inch baking pan with waxed paper. Butter the paper. • Beat the egg yolks, egg, and pisco with an electric mixer at medium speed until pale and thick. • Pour the batter into the prepared pan. • Cover with foil and place in a roasting pan. Pour enough boiling water into the roasting pan to come halfway up the sides. • Bake for 35–40 minutes, or until set. Remove the cake from the waterbath and remove the foil. • Cool the cake for 20 minutes in the pan on a rack. Invert onto a large plate. • *Syrup*: Bring the sugar, pisco, and water to a boil in a saucepan. Boil until the mixture thickens to a syrup, about 10 minutes. Set aside to cool. • Cut the cake into squares. Soak in the syrup, about 5 minutes. Transfer to a serving plate. Drizzle with the remaining syrup. • Decorate with the almonds and raisins.

Makes one 11 x 7-inch cake · Prep: 30 min. · Cooking: 35–40 min. · Level: 2 · Keeps: 4–5 days

SANDY CAKE WITH LEMON PASTRY CREAM

Rice flour may be found in the health or natural foods section of your supermarket.

- 1 1/2 cups all-purpose flour
- 3/4 cup rice flour
- 2 teaspoons baking powder
- 1/4 teaspoon salt
- 1 cup (2 sticks) butter, softened
- 1 cup granulated sugar
- 1 tablespoon grated lemon zest
- 1 teaspoon vanilla extract
- 1 teaspoon lemon extract
- 4 large eggs, at room temperature
- 2 tablespoons Limoncello (Italian lemon liqueur)
- 1/2 cup flaked almonds
- 1 cup Lemon Pastry Cream (see page 346)

Preheat the oven to 350°F. • Butter two 9-inch round cake pans. Line with waxed paper. Butter the paper. • Sift both flours, baking powder, and salt into a medium bowl. • Beat the butter, sugar, lemon zest, and vanilla and lemon extract in a large bowl with an electric mixer at medium speed until creamy. • Add the eggs, one at a time, until just blended after each addition. • With mixer at low speed, gradually beat in the dry ingredients and liqueur. • Spoon half the batter into each of the prepared pans. Sprinkle one cake with the almonds. Bake for 35–40 minutes, or until a toothpick inserted into the center comes out clean. • Cool the cakes in the pans for 5 minutes. Turn out onto racks to cool completely. Carefully remove the paper. • Place the cake without the almonds on a serving plate and spread with the Limoncello cream. Place the remaining cake almond-side up on top. • Refrigerate for 30 minutes.

Makes one 9-inch cake · Prep: 25 min. + 30 min. to chill · Cooking: 35–40 min. · Level: 1 · Keeps: 1–2 days

SWEET POLENTA CAKE

This unusual recipe comes from Bergamo, in northern Italy, where polenta was once a staple food. In this version, the birds (along with mushrooms and other woodland plants and animals) are formed from a mixture of almond paste and cocoa. The decorations are optional.

- 6 large eggs, separated
- 2 1/4 cups confectioners' sugar
- 1 cup finely ground yellow cornmeal
- 1 cup cornstarch
- 2 tablespoons finely grated lemon zest
- 1/4 teaspoon salt

Preheat the oven to 375°F. • Butter and flour an 8-inch pudding mold. • Beat 3 egg yolks and 2 cups confectioners' sugar in a large bowl with an electric mixer at medium speed until pale and thick. Add the remaining egg yolks, one at a time, until just blended after each addition. • With mixer at low speed, gradually beat in the cornmeal, cornstarch, and lemon zest. • With mixer at high speed, beat the egg whites and salt in a medium bowl until stiff peaks form. Use a large rubber spatula to fold them into the mixture. • Spoon the batter into the prepared mold and smooth the top. • Bake for 35–40 minutes, or until lightly browned and a toothpick inserted into the center comes out clean. • Cool the cake in the pan for 10 minutes. Turn out onto a rack to cool completely. • Dust with the remaining 1/4 cup confectioners' sugar.

Makes one 8-inch cake · Prep: 30 min. · Cooking: 35–40 min. · Level: 1 · Keeps: 3–4 days

DECORATED SWEET POLENTA CAKE

- 1 Sweet Polenta Cake (see page left)
- 1/3 cup vanilla liqueur
- 1/3 cup rum
- 3/4 cup apricot preserves or jam
- 1 lb yellow marzipan
  yellow food coloring
- 2 tablespoons granulated sugar
- 2 tablespoons unsweetened cocoa powder

Use a sharp knife to trim the crisp crust off the sweet polenta cake. Slice the cake in three horizontally. Place the largest layer on a plate. • Mix the liqueur and rum in a small bowl. • Brush some of the liqueur mixture over the cake layer. Spread with a layer of preserves. Top with another layer of cake and repeat. Top with the remaining cake layer and spread with the preserves. • Work enough yellow food coloring into the almond paste to match the color of polenta. Shape the paste into a disk. Roll the almond paste out on a surface sprinkled with confectioners' sugar into a large disk large enough to cover the cake. • Wrap the almond paste around the rolling pin and place it over the cake, pressing it down so that it sticks to the preserves. There should be plenty of extra paste at the bottom of the cake. Trim it off evenly, leaving a 1-inch border. • Place one hand on top of the cake and turn it upside down. Tuck the extra almond paste underneath. Place the cake on

Decorated sweet
polenta cake

a serving plate. • Brush the cake with a little of rum mixture and sprinkle with the sugar. • Place the extra pieces of almond paste in a small bowl with the cocoa and work until the cocoa is blended. Shape the chocolate paste into birds or mushrooms. Spoon the remaining preserves onto the top of the cake and place the decorations on top.

Makes one 8-inch cake · Prep: 1 hr. · Level: 2 · Keeps: 1–2 days

PEANUT CAKE

If you can't find ground peanuts, grind them yourself in a food processor, adding 2 tablespoons of sugar from the recipe so they don't become greasy.

- 3 large eggs, at room temperature
- 3 tablespoons boiling water
- 1 cup granulated sugar
- 2 teaspoons baking powder
- 1 teaspoon vanilla extract
- 1/2 teaspoon salt
- 1 lb unsalted toasted peanuts, finely ground
- 1/4 cup confectioners' sugar, to dust

Preheat the oven to 350°F. • Butter a 9-inch square baking pan. Line with waxed paper. Butter the paper. • Beat the eggs in a large bowl with an electric mixer at high speed until pale and thick. Gradually beat in the boiling water and sugar. • With mixer at low speed, beat in the baking powder, vanilla, and salt. Use a large rubber spatula to fold in the peanuts. • Spoon the batter into the prepared pan. • Bake for 45–50 minutes, or until a toothpick inserted into the center comes out clean. • Cool the cake completely in the pan on a rack. • Dust with the confectioners' sugar.

Makes one 9-inch cake · Prep: 25 min. · Cooking: 45–50 min. · Level: 1 · Keeps: 3–4 days

TUSCAN CHESTNUT CAKE

Chestnuts grow wild throughout Tuscany. In the fall, people in the country gather the chestnuts and grind them into flour. This is an unusual recipe for those unaccustomed to unsweetened cakes. Chestnut flour can be obtained in many health-food stores and in some Italian markets.

- 4 cups chestnut flour, sifted
- 3 1/4 cups cold water
- 1/4 teaspoon salt
- 3 tablespoons pine nuts
- 2 tablespoons extra-virgin olive oil
- 1 tablespoon fresh rosemary

Preheat the oven to 400°F. • Oil a baking sheet. Place the chestnut flour in a large bowl and gradually beat in the water, taking care that no lumps form. • Stir in the salt and 2 1/2 tablespoons pine nuts. • Spread the chestnut mixture about 1/2-inch thick on the prepared sheet. Drizzle with the oil and sprinkle with the rosemary and remaining pine nuts. • Bake for 50–60 minutes, or until a toothpick inserted into the center comes out clean. • Serve warm.

Makes one cake · Prep: 15 min. · Cooking: 50–60 min. · Level: 1 · Keeps: 3 days

BUTTERLESS, EGGLESS CAKE

- 3 1/3 cups all-purpose flour
- 1 tablespoon baking powder
- 1 teaspoon baking soda
- 1/4 teaspoon salt
- 2 cups granulated sugar
- 2 cups buttermilk
- 2/3 cup vegetable oil
- 1 tablespoon white wine vinegar
- 2 teaspoons vanilla extract
- 1 cup semisweet chocolate chips

Preheat the oven to 350°F. • Butter and flour a 13 x 9-inch baking pan. • Sift the flour, baking powder, baking soda, and salt into a large bowl. Stir in the sugar. • Mix the buttermilk, oil, vinegar, and vanilla in a medium bowl. • Beat the buttermilk mixture into the dry ingredients with an electric mixer at medium speed until smooth. Stir in the chocolate chips. • Spoon the batter into the prepared pan. • Bake for 40–50 minutes, or until golden and a toothpick inserted into the center comes out clean. • Cool the cake completely in the pan on a rack.

Makes one 13 x 9-inch cake · Prep: 15 min. · Cooking: 40–50 min. · Level: 1 · Keeps: 3–4 days

Italian rice cake

Preheat the oven to 350°F. • Butter and flour a 9-inch square cake pan. • Chop the dates in a food processor with the milk. • Add the oil, egg yolks, and applesauce and blend until smooth. • Stir together both flours, dry milk, cinnamon, baking powder, baking soda, cloves, nutmeg, and salt in a large bowl.• With an electric mixer at low speed, gradually beat in the date mixture and banana. • With mixer at high speed, beat the egg whites in a large bowl until stiff peaks form. Use a large rubber spatula to fold them into the batter. • Spoon the batter into the prepared pan. • Bake for 45–55 minutes, or until a toothpick inserted into the center comes out clean. • Cool the cake in the pan on a rack. Serve warm.

Makes one 9-inch cake · Prep: 30 min. · Cooking: 45–55 min. · Level: 1 · Keeps: 2–3 days

FRUIT-SWEETENED CARROT LOAF

2	cups whole-wheat flour
1¹/₂	teaspoons baking powder
1	teaspoon baking soda
1	teaspoon ground cinnamon
¹/₂	teaspoon ground ginger
¹/₄	teaspoon salt
¹/₂	cup (1 stick) cold butter, cut up
1	cup chopped walnuts
2	medium Granny Smith apples, peeled, cored and grated
2	large carrots, grated
³/₄	cup raisins
2	large eggs, lightly beaten
2	tablespoons grated orange zest
¹/₄	cup fresh orange juice

Preheat the oven to 350°F. • Butter a 9 x 5-inch loaf pan. Line with foil, letting the edges overhang. Butter the foil. • Sift the flour, baking powder, baking soda, cinnamon, ginger, and salt into a large bowl. Use a pastry blender to cut in the butter until the mixture resembles coarse crumbs. • Stir in the walnuts, apples, carrots, raisins, eggs, and orange zest and juice. • Spoon the batter into the prepared pan. • Bake for 65–70 minutes, or until a toothpick inserted into the center comes out clean. • Cool the loaf in the pan for 30 minutes. Using the foil as a lifter, remove from the pan. Carefully remove the foil and let cool completely.

Makes one 9 x 5-inch loaf · Prep 20 min. · Cooking: 65–70 min. · Level: 1 · Keeps: 2–3 days

ITALIAN RICE CAKE

1¹/₄	cups raisins
2	cups milk
1	cup granulated sugar
¹/₄	teaspoon salt
1	cup short-grain rice (preferably Italian arborio rice)
3	tablespoons butter, cut up
¹/₂	cup pine nuts
²/₃	cup candied orange peel
2	tablespoons grated lemon zest
3	large eggs, separated

Plump the raisins in 2 cups lukewarm water in a small bowl for 30 minutes. Drain well and pat dry with paper towels. • Preheat the oven to 350°F. • Butter and flour a 9-inch springform pan. • Bring the milk, sugar, and salt to a boil in a saucepan over medium heat. Add the rice. Simmer over low heat, stirring frequently, until the rice is tender, about 15 minutes. • Remove from the heat and stir in the butter, pine nuts, orange peel, lemon zest, and raisins. Cool for 15 minutes. • Stir the egg yolks into the rice. • Beat the egg whites in a medium bowl with an electric mixer at high speed until stiff. Use a large rubber spatula to fold them into the rice. • Spoon the batter into the prepared pan. • Bake for 40–50 minutes, or until lightly browned. • Cool the cake completely in the pan on a rack. Loosen and remove the pan sides to serve.

Makes one 9-inch cake · Prep: 25 min. + 45 min. to soak + cool · Cooking: 40–50 min. · Level: 1 · Keeps: 1–2 days

FRUIT-SWEETENED BANANA SPICE CAKE

¹/₂	cup chopped dates
¹/₂	cup milk
¹/₄	cup vegetable oil
2	large eggs, separated
³/₄	cup unsweetened applesauce
1³/₄	cups whole-wheat flour
2	tablespoons soy flour
2	tablespoons nonfat dry milk powder
2	teaspoons ground cinnamon
2	teaspoons baking powder
1	teaspoon baking soda
¹/₂	teaspoon ground cloves
¹/₂	teaspoon ground nutmeg
¹/₂	teaspoon salt
1	cup mashed bananas

FRUIT-SWEETENED APPLE AND SPICE CAKE

2½ cups all-purpose flour
1 tablespoon baking soda
2 teaspoons ground cinnamon
1 teaspoon ground nutmeg
½ teaspoon salt
¼ cup granulated fructose
1 cup (2 sticks) butter, melted
2 large eggs, at room temperature
2 teaspoons vanilla extract
4 cups grated apples
1 cup chopped walnuts

Preheat the oven to 350°F. • Butter and flour a 9-inch springform pan. • Sift the flour, baking soda, cinnamon, nutmeg, and salt into a large bowl. Add the fructose. • Beat in the butter, eggs, and vanilla with an electric mixer at medium speed. • With mixer at low speed, beat in the apples and nuts. • Spoon the batter into the prepared pan. • Bake for 40–50 minutes, or until a toothpick inserted into the center comes out clean. • Cool the cake completely in the pan on a rack. Loosen and remove the pan sides to serve.

Makes one 9-inch cake · Prep: 30 min. · Cooking: 45–55 min. · Level: 1 · Keeps: 3–4 days

BASIC CREPES

3 large eggs
1 cup all-purpose flour
2 tablespoons granulated sugar
¼ teaspoon salt
1½ cups milk
¼ cup (½ stick) butter

Beat the eggs in a large bowl with an electric mixer at medium speed until pale and thick. • Stir together the flour, sugar, and salt in a large bowl. Gradually pour in the milk, beating constantly so that no lumps form. Beat the batter into the eggs until smooth. • Cover with plastic wrap and refrigerate for 30 minutes. • Melt 1 tablespoon of the butter in an 8-inch crepe pan or skillet. Pour a ladleful of batter into the pan. Rotate the pan so that the batter covers the bottom in an even layer. • Place over medium heat and cook until golden brown. Use a wooden spatula to flip the crepe. Brown on the other side, then transfer to a serving plate. • Add a little more butter, and prepare another crepe. Continue until all the batter is used up. Pile the crepes up in a warm place.

Makes about 12 crepes · Prep: 20 min. + 30 min. to chill · Level: 1 · Keeps: 1 day

Pancake layer cake

PANCAKE LAYER CAKE

1 recipe Basic Crepes batter (see recipe left)
1 cup cherry or black raspberry ice cream
1 cup heavy cream
1 cup strawberry ice cream
6 oz fresh strawberries, hulled and sliced

Prepare the crepe batter and use it to make 7 thick pancakes, following the instructions for Basic Crepes. • Leave the ice cream at room temperature to soften, 10 minutes. • Beat the cream in a medium bowl with an electric mixer at high speed until stiff. • Place one pancake on a serving dish. Spread with half the cherry ice cream. Place another pancake on top and spread with half the whipped cream. Place another pancake on top and spread with half the strawberry ice cream. • Repeat so that all the pancakes and ice cream are stacked, finishing with a pancake. • Decorate with the strawberries.

Makes one 8-inch cake · Prep: 20 min. · Level: 1 · Keeps: 1 day in the freezer

PINEAPPLE CREPE LAYER CAKE

2 cups heavy cream
12 Basic Crepes (see recipe left)
1 cup orange liqueur
1 can (8 oz) crushed pineapple, drained
⅓ cup granulated sugar
1 cup fresh orange juice
6 tablespoons heavy cream

Beat the cream in a large bowl with an electric mixer at high speed until stiff. • Place a crepe on a serving dish and spread with a layer of cream. Drizzle with a teaspoon liqueur and sprinkle with some pineapple. Place another crepe on top and repeat until all the crepes have been stacked and layered. • Cook the sugar in a saucepan, stirring until the sugar has dissolved. Continue cooking, without stirring, over low heat until deep gold. Stir in the orange juice and cook until reduced. • Add the cream and bring to a boil. Boil for 2–3 minutes. Set aside to cool. • Stir in the remaining liqueur. Pour over the crepes and serve.

Makes one 8-inch cake · Prep: 20 min. · Level: 2 · Keeps: 1 day

GLUTEN-FREE CAKE

1½ cups rice flour
⅔ cup tapioca flour
1 tablespoon baking powder
1 teaspoon baking soda
¼ teaspoon salt
⅔ cup butter, softened
1¼ cups granulated sugar
2 teaspoons vanilla extract
4 large eggs, at room temperature
1 cup milk

Preheat the oven to 350°F. • Butter two 9-inch round cake pans. Line with waxed paper. Butter the paper. • Sift the rice flour, tapioca flour, baking powder, baking soda, and salt into a medium bowl. • Beat the butter, sugar, and vanilla in a large bowl with an electric mixer at medium speed until creamy. • Add the eggs, one at a time, until just blended after each addition. • With mixer at low speed, gradually beat in the dry ingredients, alternating with the milk. • Spoon half the batter into each of the prepared pans. • Bake for 20–30 minutes, or until the cakes shrink from the pan sides and a toothpick inserted into the center comes out clean. • Cool the cakes in the pans for 10 minutes. Turn out onto racks. Carefully remove the paper and let cool completely.

Makes two 9-inch cakes · Prep: 20 min. · Cooking: 20–30 min. · Level: 1 · Keeps: 3–4 days

LEMON CURD TORTE

Semolina flour may be found in supermarkets or health-food stores.

6 large eggs, separated
1 cup granulated sugar
2 tablespoons grated lemon zest
¼ cup + 2 tablespoons fresh lemon juice
1 cup semolina flour
3 cups Lemon Curd (see page 345)
2 tablespoons candied lemon peel, finely chopped (optional)

Preheat the oven to 350°F. • Butter two 9-inch cake pans. Line with parchment paper. Butter the paper. • Beat the egg yolks and sugar in a large bowl with an electric mixer at high speed until pale and very thick. • With mixer at low speed, gradually beat in the lemon zest and juice and semolina flour. • With mixer at high speed, beat the egg whites in a large bowl until stiff peaks form. Use a large rubber spatula to fold them into the batter. • Spoon half the batter into each of the prepared pans. • Bake for

30–40 minutes, or until springy to the touch and a toothpick inserted into the center comes out clean. • Cool the cakes in the pans for 10 minutes. Turn out onto racks. Carefully remove the paper and let cool completely. • Place one cake on a serving plate. Spread with ⅔ of the lemon curd. Top with the remaining cake and spread with the remaining lemon curd. Decorate with the lemon peel, if desired.

Makes one 9-inch cake · Prep: 30 min. · Cooking: 30–40 min. · Level: 1 · Keeps: 2–3 days

ST. ANTHONY'S SLIPPER

1½ cups almonds, finely ground
1 cup superfine sugar
2⅓ cups all-purpose flour
zest of 1 lemon
¼ teaspoon salt
3 large eggs + 2 large egg yolks
¾ cup (1½ sticks) cold butter, cut up
2 oz semisweet chocolate, coarsely chopped

Preheat the oven to 375°F. • Butter and flour a baking sheet. • Use a pencil to sketch the outline of a slipper on parchment paper and cut it out to make a template. • Stir together the almonds and 1 teaspoon superfine sugar. • Mix the flour, remaining sugar, almond mixture, lemon zest, and salt in a large bowl. Make a well in the center and beat in 2 eggs and the egg yolks, one at a time, until just blended after each addition. Use a pastry blender to cut in the butter to make a smooth dough. • Shape the dough into a ball. Cover with a clean kitchen towel and let rest in a warm place for 1 hour. • Divide the dough into two balls, one twice

White chocolate thousand-layer cake

the size of the other, and shape into flattened disks. • Roll the larger disk out on a lightly floured surface to 2-inches thick to make the raised part of the slipper, using the template as a guide. • Roll the remaining dough out to ½-inch thick and, using a knife, cut to fit the sole of the slipper, using the template as a guide. Transfer the dough onto the prepared sheet. • Roll out the remaining dough into 3 thin strips and twist the strips together to resemble a braid. Place the braid along the edges of the raised part of the slipper. • Beat the remaining egg and brush over the dough. • Bake for 40–45 minutes, or until golden. Cool the pastry completely on the sheet. • Melt the chocolate in a double boiler over barely simmering water. Spread the sole of the slipper with the melted chocolate and set aside to dry.

Makes one slipper-shaped cake · Prep: 30 min. + 1 hr. to rest · Cooking: 40–45 min. · Level: 2 · Keeps: 2–3 days

RASPBERRY THOUSAND-LAYER CAKE

2 lb fresh or frozen puff pastry, thawed if frozen
1 cup confectioners' sugar
1 cup Zabaglione (see page 348), cooled
1 cup heavy cream, whipped
8 Basic Meringues rosettes, crumbled (see page 212)
1 cup raspberries
⅔ cup flaked almonds, toasted

Preheat the oven to 400°F. • Line 2 baking sheets with waxed paper. • Unfold or unroll the pastry on a lightly floured surface. Roll into four equal squares. • Place on the prepared sheets and prick all over with a fork. • Bake for 15–20 minutes, or until golden brown. • Sprinkle each with 1 tablespoon confectioners' sugar and return to the oven to caramelize, about 5 minutes. • Cool the pastry on racks. • Use a large rubber spatula to fold the cream and crumbled meringues into the zabaglione. • Place one pastry layer on a serving plate and spread with half the zabaglione. Sprinkle with raspberries and almonds. Cover with another pastry layer and repeat with the remaining zabaglione, raspberries, and almonds. • Dust with the remaining confectioners' sugar.

Makes one 9-inch square cake · Prep: 15 min. · Cooking: 20–25 min. · Level: 2 · Keeps: 1 day

Chestnut thousand-layer cake

WHITE CHOCOLATE THOUSAND-LAYER CAKE

1½ lb fresh or frozen puff pastry, thawed if frozen
3 tablespoons confectioners' sugar
3 cups Vanilla Pastry Cream (see page 342)
8 oz white chocolate, coarsely chopped
1 oz bittersweet chocolate, coarsely chopped
1 cup flaked almonds

Preheat the oven to 400°F. • Line 2 baking sheets with waxed paper. • Unfold or unroll the pastry on a lightly floured surface. Cut into three equal squares. Place on the prepared sheets and prick all over with a fork. • Bake for 15–20 minutes, or until golden brown. Sprinkle with 1 tablespoon confectioners' sugar and return to the oven for 5 minutes to caramelize, about 5 minutes. • Cool the pastry on racks. • Place one pastry layer on a serving plate and spread with half the pastry cream. Cover with another pastry layer and repeat with the remaining cream and pastry. • Melt the white chocolate in a double boiler over barely simmering water. Set aside to cool. Spread over the cake. • Melt the bittersweet chocolate in a double boiler over barely simmering water. Set aside to cool. Spoon into a pastry bag. • Pipe lines of dark chocolate into the white chocolate and draw a knife through the lines to create the pattern shown in the photo (left). Press the almonds onto the sides of the cake.

Makes one cake · Prep: 45 min. · Cooking: 10–15 min. · Level: 2 · Keeps: 1 day in the refrigerator

STRAWBERRY THOUSAND-LAYER CAKE

2 lb fresh or frozen puff pastry, thawed if frozen
1 cup confectioners' sugar
1 cup Zabaglione (see page 348), cooled
1 cup heavy cream, whipped
8 Basic Meringues rosettes (see page 212)
1 cup strawberries, hulled and thinly sliced
⅔ cup flaked almonds, toasted

Use the instructions for Raspberry Thousand-Layer Cake (see page left), substituting the strawberries for the raspberries.

Makes one 9-inch cake · Prep: 15 min. · Cooking: 20–25 min. · Level: 2 · Keeps: 1 day

PEACH THOUSAND-LAYER CAKE

2 lb fresh or frozen puff pastry, thawed if frozen
1 cup confectioners' sugar
1 cup Zabaglione (see page 348), cooled
1 cup heavy cream, whipped
8 Basic Meringues rosettes (see page 212)
1 cup peaches, peeled, pitted, and thinly sliced
⅔ cup flaked almonds, toasted

Use the instructions for Raspberry Thousand-Layer Cake (see page left), substituting the peaches for the raspberries.

Makes one 9-inch cake · Prep: 15 min. · Cooking: 20–25 min. · Level: 2 · Keeps: 1 day

APPLE THOUSAND-LAYER CAKE

2 lb fresh or frozen puff pastry, thawed
1 cup confectioners' sugar
1 cup Zabaglione (see page 348), cooled
1 cup heavy cream, whipped
8 Basic Meringues rosettes (see page 212)
2 medium apples, peeled, cored, and thinly sliced
⅔ cup flaked almonds, toasted

Use the instructions for Raspberry Thousand-Layer Cake (see page left), substituting the apples for the raspberries.

Makes one 9-inch cake · Prep: 15 min. · Cooking: 20–25 min. · Level: 2 · Keeps: 1 day

CHESTNUT THOUSAND-LAYER CAKE

2 lb frozen puff pastry, thawed
2–3 tablespoons confectioners' sugar, to dust
   candied chestnuts, to decorate
   chocolate leaves (see page 55), to decorate

CHESTNUT CREAM FILLING

12 oz candied chestnuts, coarsely chopped
2 tablespoons rum
⅓ cup milk
1¼ cups heavy cream

Preheat the oven to 400°F. • Line a baking sheet with waxed paper. • Unfold or unroll the pastry on a lightly floured surface. Place on the prepared sheet and prick all over with a fork. • Bake for 10–15 minutes, or until golden brown. • Cool the pastry on a rack. • Use a sharp knife to cut into 4 rectangles, measuring about 4 x 9 inches. • *Chestnut Cream Filling*: Puree the candied chestnuts, rum, and milk in a food processor until smooth. • Place one pastry layer on a serving plate. Spread with a ¼-inch layer of chestnut cream. Cover with another pastry layer and repeat until all the pastry and cream has been used up. • Finish with a pastry layer. Dust with the confectioners' sugar. Decorate with the candied chestnuts and chocolate leaves.

Makes one 4 x 8-inch cake · Prep: 30 min. · Cooking: 10–15 min. · Level: 1 · Keeps: 1–2 days

Apple and bread cake

WHOLE-WHEAT CEREAL CAKE

1 1/2 cups all-purpose flour
2 teaspoons baking powder
1/4 teaspoon salt
1/2 cup granulated sugar
1/2 cup (1 stick) butter, cut up
1 large egg, lightly beaten

TOPPING

1 2/3 cups fruit-flavored yogurt
1/3 cup superfine sugar
2 large eggs, lightly beaten
1 cup crushed wheat flake cereal

Preheat the oven to 350°F. • Butter a 9 x 13-inch baking pan. Line with waxed paper. Butter the paper. • Sift the flour, baking powder, and salt into a large bowl. Stir in the sugar. Use a pastry blender to cut in the butter until the mixture resembles coarse crumbs. Mix in the egg. • Spread the batter into the prepared pan and smooth the top. • Bake for 15–20 minutes, or until lightly browned. Cool the cake completely in the pan on a rack. • *Topping*: Mix the yogurt, superfine sugar, and eggs in a large bowl. Spread the topping over the cake. Sprinkle

with the cereal. • Bake for 40–45 minutes, or until lightly browned. Cool completely in the pan on the rack. • Refrigerate for 30 minutes. • Cut into squares to serve.

Makes one 9 x 13-inch cake · Prep: 20 min. + 30 min. to chill · Cooking: 55–65 min. · Level: 1 · Keeps: 1 day

MODENA CAKE

Basic and filling, this is a traditional recipe from the northern Italian town of Modena.

3 cups all-purpose flour
3/4 cup granulated sugar
1/4 teaspoon salt
1 1/2 teaspoons grated lemon zest
1 tablespoon + 1/2 teaspoon baking powder
1/2 cup (1 stick) cold butter, cut up
3 large eggs, lightly beaten
2–3 tablespoons milk
1/2 cup sugar crystals

Preheat the oven to 350°F. • Butter and flour a baking sheet. • Stir together the flour, sugar, baking powder, lemon zest, and salt in a large bowl. • Shape into a mound and make a well in the center. Add the butter and eggs (reserving 1 tablespoon beaten egg to glaze the cake). • Use your fingers to work the ingredients and enough milk until a dough is

formed. Knead until smooth. • Shape into a long, thick sausage. Arrange it in an S-shape on the prepared sheet. • Brush the surface with the reserved egg. Sprinkle with the sugar crystals. Use a sharp knife to make an incision along the center of the length of the cake. • Bake for 35–45 minutes, or until a toothpick inserted into the center comes out clean. • Cool in the pan on a rack for 10 minutes.

Makes one large S-shaped cake · Prep: 20 min. · Cooking: 35–45 min. · Level: 1 · Keeps: 3–4 days

APPLE AND BREAD CAKE

1 1/2 cups milk
3/4 cup granulated sugar
10 large hard bread rolls, cut into 1/4-inch slices (reserve the crumbs)
3 large eggs
2 tablespoons finely grated lemon zest
1 teaspoon ground cinnamon
1 1/4 lb tart apples, such as Granny Smiths, peeled, cored, and thinly sliced
2/3 cup raisins
2/3 cup almonds, coarsely chopped
1/2 cup (1 stick) cold butter, cut up

Preheat the oven to 350°F. • Butter a 9-inch springform pan. • Heat the milk and sugar in a saucepan over medium heat until the sugar has dissolved. Set aside to cool. • Sprinkle the bread crumbs in the prepared pan. • Lightly beat the eggs, lemon zest, and cinnamon. Stir into the cooled milk. • Place a layer of bread in the prepared pan and pour in enough of the milk and egg mixture to soak. Cover with a layer of apple slices. Sprinkle with the raisins, almonds, and butter. Repeat until all the ingredients are in the pan, finishing with a layer of bread and topping with butter. Do not soak the last layer of bread. • Bake for 30–35 minutes, or until golden brown. • Loosen and remove the pan sides. Transfer onto a serving plate. Serve warm.

Makes one 9-inch cake · Prep: 30 min. · Cooking: 30–35 min. · Level: 1 · Keeps: 1–2 days

BAKLAVA (GREEK PASTRIES)

This is the traditional recipe of the famous Greek specialty.

14 sheets phyllo dough, thawed if frozen
2 1/2 cups almonds, finely ground
2/3 cup granulated sugar
2 teaspoons ground cinnamon
1 cup (2 sticks) butter, melted

HONEY SYRUP

1 cup honey
1/4 cup water

1/4 cup granulated sugar
1 1/2 tablespoons rose water
2 tablespoons almonds, coarsely chopped, to decorate

Preheat the oven to 325°F. • Butter a 9-inch square baking pan. • Lay the sheets of dough out flat and cover with waxed paper and a damp kitchen towel. (This will stop them from drying out.) • Stir together the almonds, sugar, and cinnamon in a large bowl. • Fit one phyllo sheet in the pan and brush with butter. Fit the remaining sheet on top and brush with butter. Sprinkle with a scant 1/4 cup almond filling. Place another sheet on top, brush with butter, and sprinkle with filling. Repeat until all the almond mixture is used up. You should have about 12 layers of filled dough. • Fold the remaining sheets and place on top. Brush with butter. • Use a long knife to cut the pastry into diamond shapes about 2 inches square or in rectangles about 1 1/2 x 2 1/2 inches. Be sure to cut through all the layers to the bottom of the pan. • Bake for 40–50 minutes, or until golden brown. • *Honey Syrup*: Bring the honey, water, and sugar to a boil in a saucepan over low heat until the sugar has dissolved. Remove from the heat and add the rose water. • Drizzle the syrup over the baklava after removing it from the oven. Sprinkle with almonds. • Cool the cake completely in the pan on a rack.

Makes one 9-inch cake · Prep: 45 min. · Level: 2 · Keeps: 2–3 days

ALMOND AND PISTACHIO BAKLAVA

Orange-flower water may be found in gourmet food stores.

12 sheets phyllo dough
5 cups almonds
2 cups pistachios
1 cup confectioners' sugar
3 tablespoons orange-flower water or rose water
1 teaspoon ground cardamom
1 cup (2 sticks) butter, melted
1 cup whole almonds
1 1/4 cups honey
1/2 cup candied cherries, to decorate

Preheat the oven to 350°F. • Lay the sheets of phyllo out flat and cover with waxed paper and a damp kitchen towel. (This will stop them from drying out.) • Butter a baking sheet. • Process 4 cups almonds, pistachios, confectioners' sugar, orange-flower water, and cardamom in a food processor until very finely chopped. • Place a phyllo sheet on the

Baklava

prepared sheet and brush with butter. Cover with 6 more sheets, brushing each one with butter. • Spread the almond mixture over and top with the remaining 5 sheets, brushing each with butter. • Use a knife to cut into diamond shapes. Don't separate the diamond shapes into pieces. Sprinkle with the remaining almonds and brush with butter. • Bake for 50–60 minutes, or until browned. • Heat the honey in a saucepan until liquid. Drizzle the honey over. • Split into diamonds and rest overnight. Decorate with cherries.

Makes 20–25 cakes · Prep: 2 hr. + 24 hr. to rest · Cooking: 50–60 min. · Level: 2 · Keeps: 3–4 days

PECAN BAKLAVA

1 lb sheets phyllo dough, thawed if frozen
2 cups (4 sticks) butter, melted
1 lb pecans, coarsely chopped
1/2 cup sugar
2 teaspoons ground cinnamon

SYRUP
2 cups granulated sugar
2 cups water
juice of 1/2 lemon

Preheat the oven to 350°F. • Butter a baking sheet. • Lay the sheets of phyllo out flat and cover with waxed paper and a damp kitchen towel. (This will stop them from drying out.) Place the first sheet on the prepared pan and brush with butter. Sprinkle with pecans. Top with another sheet and brush with butter. Repeat with 10 more sheets. • Mix the pecans, sugar, and cinnamon in a large bowl. • Spoon half the pecan mixture over. Top with five more buttered layers of phyllo. Spoon the remaining pecan mixture over. Top with the remaining buttered layers of dough until it is all used up. • Refrigerate for 30 minutes. Cut the pastry in rows lengthwise and cut diagonally to make diamond shapes. • Pour the remaining butter over. • Bake for 45–50 minutes, or until golden. • *Syrup*: Bring the sugar, water, and lemon juice to a boil in a saucepan over medium heat. Boil for 20 minutes. Set aside to cool. • Pour the syrup over the hot cake until absorbed.

Makes one cake · Prep: 50 min. + 30 min. to chill · Cooking: 45–50 min. · Level: 2 · Keeps: 1–2 days

FILLINGS & FROSTINGS

Many cakes can go from ordinary to extraordinary simply by adding a filling or a frosting. Creamy custards, dreamy chocolate frostings, and rich ganaches are ideal to finish a cake. Fruity sauces, liqueur creams, and glazes can even provide an edge of professionalism to many cakes.

CLASSIC BAVARIAN CREAM

Versatile Bavarian cream can be used to fill or top many different cakes. It can also be served on its own or with whipped cream or fruit.

1	tablespoon unflavored gelatin
1/4	cup cold water
5	large egg yolks
1/2	cup granulated sugar
1/8	teaspoon salt
1 1/2	cups milk
1 1/2	teaspoons vanilla extract
1	cup heavy cream, chilled

Sprinkle the gelatin over the cold water in a saucepan. Let stand 1 minute. Stir over low heat until the gelatin has completely dissolved. • Beat the egg yolks, sugar, and salt in a saucepan until well blended. • Bring the milk and vanilla to a boil in a saucepan. Remove from the heat and stir about 1/4 cup hot milk into the yolk mixture. Cook over low heat, stirring constantly with a wooden spoon, until the mixture lightly coats a metal spoon or registers 160°F on an instant-read thermometer. Gradually pour in the remaining milk, stirring constantly. • Pour through a strainer into a large bowl and add the gelatin mixture. Immediately plunge the bowl into a bowl of ice water until the mixture has cooled, stirring occasionally. • Beat the cream in a medium bowl with an electric mixer at high speed until stiff. • When the custard has cooled, but not set, fold in the cream. • Refrigerate for 4 hours.

Makes about 4 cups · Prep: 30 min. · Chilling: 4 hr. · Level: 2 · Keeps: 1–2 days in the refrigerator

‹ Simple chocolate frosting (see page 349)

➤ Classic Bavarian cream

MAKING FILLINGS & FROSTINGS

*Fillings and frostings provide that edge, which can make a cake perfect in every way.
Knowing the basics of how to create pastry cream and using a pastry bag will give
your cakes an air of professionalism with very little effort.*

Making vanilla pastry cream

Vanilla pastry cream is used as a cake filling or as a basic ingredient in many desserts.

5   large egg yolks
²/₃ cup granulated sugar
¹/₃ cup all-purpose flour
2   cups whole milk
    pinch of salt
4   drops vanilla extract

*Makes: about 2 cups · Prep: 10 min. ·
Cooking: 10 min. · Level: 1*

1 Beat the egg yolks and sugar until pale and thick.

2 Bring the milk to a boil with the salt and vanilla, then stir it into the egg and sugar.

3 Cook over low heat, stirring constantly with a wooden spoon, until the mixture lightly coats a metal spoon or registers 160°F on an instant-read thermometer.

VARIATIONS

• Hazelnut or Almond Cream: Add 2 tablespoons ground hazelnuts or almonds to the cream while still hot.

• Liqueur Cream: Add one or two tablespoons rum, cognac, or other liqueur to the cream while still hot.

• Lemon Cream: Boil the finely grated zest of 1 lemon in the milk and omit the vanilla extract.

Using a pastry bag

Many people regard the use of a pastry bag as a tricky task, but using the instructions below you can add the perfect finish every time.

1 Fit the required nozzle into a muslin pastry bag, making sure it fits snugly into the opening without any gaps.

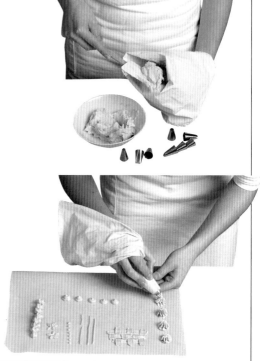

2 Fold the pastry bag over and lightly place in the palm of your hand. Spoon the frosting into the bag, filling it no more than ¼ full.

3 Still holding the bag lightly in the palm of your hand, turn over the fold and lightly twist the fabric.

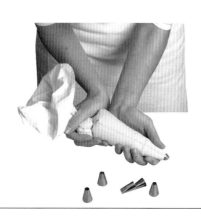

4 Slide your hand down and thread the fabric between your thumb and first finger. Squeeze the bag very lightly and begin to pipe.

CHOCOLATE MOUSSE

- 12 oz bittersweet chocolate
- $^1/_2$ cup milk
- 6 large eggs, separated
- $^1/_2$ cup confectioners' sugar
- $^3/_4$ cup heavy cream
- $^1/_4$ teaspoon cream of tartar
- 2 tablespoons granulated sugar

Melt the chocolate with the milk in a double boiler over barely simmering water. • Beat the egg yolks and sugar in a double boiler until well blended. Stir in the chocolate mixture. Cook over low heat, stirring constantly with a wooden spoon, until the mixture lightly coats a metal spoon or registers 160°F on an instant-read thermometer. Immediately plunge the pan into a bowl of ice water and stir until the egg mixture has cooled. • Beat the cream in a large bowl with an electric mixer at high speed until stiff. Fold it into the chocolate mixture. • Stir the egg whites, cream of tartar, and sugar in a double boiler until blended. Cook over low heat, beating constantly with an electric mixer at low speed until the whites register 160°F on an instant-read thermometer. Beat at high speed until stiff peaks form. • Fold them into the chocolate mixture. • Refrigerate for 4 hours.

Makes 3 cups · Prep: 20 min. + 4 hr. to chill · Level: 2 · Keeps: 1 day in the refrigerator

BASIC ICE CREAM

This basic recipe can be flavored with vanilla extract, coffee, chocolate, or many different spices, flavorings, and liqueurs to make a wide variety of ice creams.

- 4 large egg yolks
- 1 scant cup granulated sugar
- 2 cups milk
- 1 cup light or heavy cream

Beat the egg yolks and sugar until pale and thick. • Bring the milk and cream to a boil in a saucepan. Remove from the heat and let cool slightly. Gradually stir into the egg and sugar. • Cook over low heat, beating constantly with a wooden spoon, until the mixture lightly coats a metal spoon or registers 160°F on an instant-read thermometer. Immediately plunge the pan into a bowl of ice water and stir until the egg mixture has cooled. • If you have an ice cream maker, pour the mixture into it and follow the instructions. • If you don't have an

Ricotta vanilla cream

ice cream maker, pour into a large bowl and freeze. After 3 hours, stir the mixture well. After another 3 hours, stir for a few minutes and freeze for 3 hours more.

Makes 1 quart · Prep: 30 min. + 9 hr. to freeze (without ice cream maker) · Level: 2

STRAWBERRY ICE CREAM

This is a basic recipe for fruit-flavored ice cream. They should all be pureed before adding to the ice cream mixture.

- 2 cups milk
- 1 cup light cream
- 1 scant cup granulated sugar
- 3 cups strawberries + about 12 extra, cut in half, to decorate

Bring the milk and cream to a boil in a saucepan. Boil for 4 minutes. • Dissolve the sugar in the mixture and set aside to cool. • Puree the strawberries and stir into the milk and cream mixture. • Follow the instructions for Basic Ice Cream (see recipe left) to finish.

Makes 1 quart · Prep: 20 min. + 9 hr. to freeze (without ice-cream maker) · Cooking: 5 min. · Level: 1

HEAVENLY CREAM

- 1 cup milk
- 4 large egg yolks
- $^1/_3$ cup granulated sugar
- $^1/_3$ cup sweet white dessert wine

Bring the milk to a boil in a saucepan over medium heat. Remove from the heat. • Beat the egg yolks and sugar in a large bowl with an electric mixer at high speed until pale and thick. • Pour the milk into the eggs. • Transfer to a double boiler over barely simmering water. Stir until the mixture lightly

coats a metal spoon or registers 160°F on an instant-read thermometer. Remove from the heat and stir in the wine.

Makes 1$^1/_2$ cups · Prep: 15 min. · Level: 1 · Keeps: 2–3 days

RICOTTA VANILLA CREAM

For chocolate ricotta cream, add 2 tablespoons of unsweetened cocoa powder.

- 1$^1/_4$ lb very fresh ricotta cheese
- 1 cup confectioners' sugar
- 1 teaspoon freshly ground cinnamon

Mix the ricotta, confectioners' sugar, and cinnamon in a large bowl until smooth. • Refrigerate for 1 hour before serving.

Makes 2 cups · Prep: 5 min. + 1 hr to chill · Level: 1

STRENGTHENED WHIPPED CREAM

Heavy cream with 40 percent butterfat can be whipped and will stay firm enough to fill a cake or jelly roll for several hours without leakage. However, not all heavy cream contains that amount of butterfat and you may sometimes need to "strengthen" your cream to be sure it will hold.

- $^3/_4$ teaspoon plain unflavored gelatin
- 2 tablespoons cold water
- 1 cup heavy cream
- 2 tablespoons confectioners' sugar
- $^1/_4$ teaspoon vanilla extract

Sprinkle the gelatin over the cold water in a saucepan. Let stand 1 minute. • Stir over low heat until the gelatin has completely dissolved. • Beat the cream, confectioners' sugar, and vanilla in a large bowl with an electric mixer at high speed until it begins to thicken. Add the gelatin until stiff.

Makes about 2 cups · Prep: 10 min. · Level: 1 · Keeps: 1–2 days

Mock cream

ORANGE MASCARPONE CREAM

This delicious cream can be flavored with all sorts of other liqueurs, not just fruit-flavored ones. Try it with coffee or chocolate liqueur.

- 6 large eggs, separated
- 3/4 cup granulated sugar
- 1 2/3 cups mascarpone cheese
- 1 cup orange liqueur

Beat the egg yolks and 1/2 cup sugar in a large bowl with an electric mixer at high speed until pale and thick. • With mixer at low speed, gradually beat in the mascarpone and liqueur. • Stir the egg whites and remaining sugar in a saucepan until blended. Stir over low heat, beating constantly, until the whites register 160°F on an instant-read thermometer. Transfer to a bowl and beat at high speed until stiff peaks form. Use a large rubber spatula to fold them into the cream.

Makes 2 cups · Prep: 15 min. · Level: 1 · Keeps: 2–3 days in the refrigerator

LEMON OR LIME MUFFIN BUTTER

Muffin butters set off the flavors in the muffins.

- 3/4 cup (1 1/2 sticks) butter, softened
- 2 tablespoons finely grated lemon or lime zest
- 1 tablespoon fresh lemon or lime juice
- 1 cup confectioners' sugar

Beat the butter, zest, and juice in a small bowl with an electric mixer at low speed until smooth. • Beat in the confectioners' sugar.

Makes about 1 cup · Prep: 5 min. · Level: 1 · Keeps: 1–2 days in the refrigerator

SPICED MUFFIN BUTTER

- 3/4 cup (1 1/2 sticks) butter, softened
- 1 teaspoon ground cinnamon
- 1 teaspoon ground ginger

- 1/2 teaspoon ground nutmeg
- 2 tablespoons honey
- 1 cup confectioners' sugar

Beat the butter, cinnamon, ginger, nutmeg, and honey in a small bowl with an electric mixer at low speed until smooth. • Gradually beat in the confectioners' sugar.

Makes about 1 cup · Prep: 5 min. · Level: 1 · Keeps: 1–2 days in the refrigerator

VANILLA MUFFIN BUTTER

- 1/2 cup (1 stick) butter, softened
- 2 teaspoons vanilla extract
- 1 1/3 cups confectioners' sugar

Beat the butter and vanilla extract in a small bowl with an electric mixer at low speed until smooth. • Beat in the confectioners' sugar.

Makes about 1 cup · Prep: 5 min. · Level: 1 · Keeps: 1–2 days in the refrigerator

VANILLA CUSTARD

- 2 cups milk
- 3/4 cup granulated sugar
- 6 large egg yolks
- 1 teaspoon vanilla extract

Bring the milk and 1/4 cup sugar to a boil in a saucepan. • Beat the egg yolks and remaining 1/2 cup sugar in a large bowl with an electric mixer at high speed until pale and thick. • Stir the milk into the yolks. Return to the saucepan. Cook over low heat, stirring constantly with a wooden spoon, until the mixture lightly coats a spoon or registers 160°F on an instant-read thermometer. Remove from the heat and add the vanilla. Set aside to cool.

Makes about 2 cups · Prep: 25 min. · Level: 1 · Keeps: 1 day in the refrigerator

MAPLE MUFFIN BUTTER

- 1/2 cup (1 stick) butter, softened
- 2 tablespoons pure maple syrup
- 1 cup confectioners' sugar

Beat the butter and maple syrup in a small bowl with an electric mixer at low speed until smooth. • Beat in the confectioners' sugar.

Makes about 1 cup · Prep: 5 min. · Level: 1 · Keeps: 1–2 days in the refrigerator

ORANGE MUFFIN BUTTER

- 3/4 cup (1 1/2 sticks) butter, softened
- 2 tablespoons finely grated orange zest
- 1 tablespoon orange liqueur
- 1 cup confectioners' sugar

Beat the butter, orange zest, and liqueur in a small bowl with an electric mixer at low speed until smooth. • Beat in the confectioners' sugar.

Makes about 1 cup · Prep: 5 min. · Level: 1 · Keeps: 1–2 days in the refrigerator

MOCK CREAM

This looks like the real thing but lasts longer.

- 1/2 cup (1 stick) butter, softened
- 1/2 cup granulated sugar
- 1/2 cup boiling water
- 1 teaspoon vanilla extract

Beat the butter, sugar, water, and vanilla in a medium bowl with an electric mixer at high speed until creamy. • The mixture may curdle as you beat; continue beating until smooth.

Makes 1 cup · Prep: 5 min. · Level: 1 · Keeps: 2–3 days

COFFEE CUSTARD

- 2 cups milk
- 3/4 cup granulated sugar
- 1 tablespoon freeze-dried coffee granules
- 6 large egg yolks

Bring the milk and 1/4 cup sugar to a boil in a saucepan. • Add the coffee and remove from the heat. Cover and set aside for 25 minutes. • Beat the egg yolks and remaining 1/2 cup sugar in a large bowl with an electric mixer at high speed until pale and thick. • Stir in the milk. • Return to the saucepan. Cook over low heat, stirring constantly with a wooden spoon, until the mixture lightly coats a spoon or registers 160°F on an instant-read thermometer. Remove from the heat and set aside to cool.

Makes about 2 cups · Prep: 25 min. + 25 min. to cool · Level: 1 · Keeps: 1 day in the refrigerator

ELYSIAN CUSTARD

1¼ cups milk
¾ cup heavy cream
½ cup honey
6 large egg yolks
½ cup granulated sugar

Bring the milk, cream, and honey to a boil in a saucepan. • Beat the egg yolks and sugar in a large bowl with an electric mixer at high speed until pale and thick. • Stir the milk into the egg yolks. • Return to the saucepan. Cook over low heat, stirring constantly with a wooden spoon, until the mixture lightly coats a spoon or registers 160°F on an instant-read thermometer. Remove from heat and set aside to cool.

Makes about 2 cups · Prep: 25 min. · Level: 1 · Keeps: 1 day in the refrigerator

LEMON CURD

3 large eggs
½ cup granulated sugar
3 tablespoons grated lemon zest
⅓ cup fresh lemon juice
½ cup (1 stick) butter, cut up

Beat the eggs, sugar, and lemon zest and juice in a saucepan until well blended. Cook over low heat, stirring constantly with a wooden spoon, until the mixture lightly coats a wooden spoon or registers 160°F on an instant-read thermometer. • Add the butter, stirring until it has melted before adding more. Immediately plunge the pan into a bowl of ice water and stir until the mixture has cooled. • Transfer to a bowl, cover with plastic wrap, and refrigerate.

Makes about 1½ cups · Prep: 25 min. · Level: 1 · Keeps: 5 days in the refrigerator

PASSION FRUIT CREAM

Spread this divine cream on muffins fresh from the oven or on slices of plain tea or coffee cake.

10 large passion fruit
2 tablespoons fresh lemon juice
2½ cups granulated sugar
3 tablespoons butter
4 large eggs, lightly beaten

Cut the passion fruit in half and scoop out the pulp. • Beat the pulp, lemon juice, sugar, butter, and eggs in a double boiler until well blended. Place over barely simmering water, stirring constantly with a wooden spoon, until the sauce lightly coats a metal spoon or registers 160°F on an instant-read

thermometer. Set aside to cool.

Makes about 2 cups · Prep: 20 min. · Level: 1 · Keeps: 1–2 days in the refrigerator

CHANTILLY CREAM

This French cream is a lightly sweetened cream used to fill a cake.

2 cups heavy cream
¼ cup granulated sugar

Beat the cream and sugar in a large bowl with an electric mixer at high speed until stiff.

Makes about 4 cups · Prep: 5 min. · Level: 1 · Keeps: 1 day

FLAVORED CHANTILLY CREAM

Chantilly Cream can also be flavored with liqueur. Choose a liqueur that will highlight the flavor of your cake.

2 cups Chantilly Cream (see recipe above)
1 tablespoon liqueur

Beat the liqueur into the chantilly cream.

Makes about 2 cups · Prep: 10 min. · Level: 1 · Keeps: 1 day in the refrigerator

CHOCOLATE CHANTILLY CREAM

4 oz bittersweet chocolate, coarsely chopped
2 cups Chantilly Cream (see recipe above)

Melt the chocolate in a double boiler over barely simmering water. • Set aside to cool. • With mixer at low speed, beat the chocolate into the chantilly cream.

Makes about 2¼ cups · Prep: 15 min. · Level: 1 · Keeps: 1 day in the refrigerator

COCOA CHANTILLY CREAM

3 tablespoons heavy cream
2 tablespoons unsweetened cocoa powder
½ teaspoon unflavored gelatin
2 tablespoons cold water
2 cups Chantilly Cream (see recipe above)

Warm the cream in a saucepan over low heat. • Stir in the cocoa until dissolved. • Sprinkle the gelatin over the water in a small bowl. Let stand 1 minute. Stir the gelatin mixture into the cream until dissolved. Set aside to cool. Beat the cocoa mixture into the chantilly cream.

Makes about 2 cups · Prep: 15 min. · Level: 1 · Keeps: 1 day in the refrigerator

VIENNA CREAM

A wonderfully light, fluffy filling.

½ cup (1 stick) butter, softened
1½ cups confectioners' sugar
2 tablespoons unsweetened cocoa powder
2 tablespoons milk

Beat the butter in a medium bowl with an electric mixer at high speed until creamy. • Gradually beat in the confectioners' sugar and cocoa until smooth. Add the milk and beat for 3 minutes more.

Makes 1½ cups · Prep: 15 min. · Level: 1 · Keeps: 1–2 days

FRUIT AND WINE EGG CREAM

5 large egg yolks + 1 large egg
½ cup dry white wine
½ cup granulated sugar
1 cup fresh raspberries

Stir together the yolks, egg, wine, and sugar in a double boiler over barely simmering water until the mixture lightly coats a metal spoon or registers 160°F on an instant-read thermometer. Plunge the pan into a bowl of ice water and stir until cooled. • Beat until tripled in volume and thick, about 10 minutes. • Remove from the heat and add the raspberries.

Makes about 2 cups · Prep: 15 min. · Level: 1 · Keeps: 1–2 days

Passion fruit cream

Lemon pastry cream

ITALIAN BUTTERCREAM

Add 1 teaspoon vanilla extract for Vanilla Buttercream or $^1/_2$ teaspoon almond extract for an Almond Buttercream.

- $^1/_2$ cup water
- $^3/_4$ cup granulated sugar
- 3   large egg yolks
- 1   cup (2 sticks) butter, softened

Stir the water and sugar in a saucepan over medium heat until the sugar has dissolved. • With a pastry brush dipped in cold water, wash down the sides of the pan to prevent sugar crystals from forming. Cook, without stirring, until the mixture reaches 238°F, or the soft-ball stage. • Beat the egg yolks in a double boiler with an electric mixer at high speed until pale. • Gradually beat the syrup into the beaten yolks. • Place over barely simmering water, stirring constantly with a wooden spoon, until the mixture lightly coats a metal spoon or registers 160°F on an instant-read thermometer. • Immediately plunge the pan into a bowl of ice water and stir until cooled. • Beat the butter in a large bowl until creamy. Beat into the egg mixture.

Makes about 2 cups · Prep: 25 min. · Level: 1 · Keeps: 5–6 days in refrigerator, 5–6 months in freezer

CHOCOLATE PASTRY CREAM

- 2   cups Vanilla Pastry Cream (see page 342)
- 7   oz bittersweet chocolate, coarsely chopped

Prepare the Vanilla Pastry Cream, but do not cool. • Melt the chocolate in a double boiler over barely simmering water. • Stir the chocolate into the hot pastry cream. • Press waxed paper directly on the surface to prevent a skin from forming. Refrigerate.

Makes: about 2$^1/_2$ cups · Prep: 30 min. · Level: 1 · Keeps: 1–2 days

CHANTILLY PASTRY CREAM

- 2   cups Vanilla Pastry Cream (see page 342)
- 1   cup Chantilly Cream (see page 345)

Prepare the Vanilla Pastry Cream and set aside to cool. • Prepare the chantilly cream. • Use a large rubber spatula to fold the chantilly cream into the pastry cream. • Refrigerate for 1 hour.

Makes about 3 cups · Prep: 15 min. + 1 hr. to chill · Level: 1 · Keeps: 1 day

COFFEE PASTRY CREAM

- 2   cups Vanilla Pastry Cream (see page 342)
- 1   tablespoon freeze-dried coffee granules

Prepare the Vanilla Pastry Cream, adding the coffee to the yolks and sugar.

Makes: about 2 cups · Prep: 30 min. · Level: 1 · Keeps: 1–2 days

LEMON PASTRY CREAM

- 2   cups Vanilla Pastry Cream (see page 342)
- 1   tablespoon grated lemon zest

Prepare the Vanilla Pastry Cream, adding the grated zest to the egg yolks and sugar.

Makes about 2 cups · Prep: 15 min. · Cooking: 15 min. · Level: 1 · Keeps: 1–2 days

LIQUEUR PASTRY CREAM

- 2   cups Vanilla Pastry Cream (see page 342)
- 2   tablespoons fruit liqueur

Prepare the Vanilla Pastry Cream, adding the liqueur to the egg yolks and sugar.

Makes about 2 cups · Prep: 15 min. · Cooking: 15 min. · Level: 1 · Keeps: 1–2 days

COFFEE BUTTERCREAM

- 2   cups Italian Buttercream (see recipe above)
- 2   tablespoons very strong lukewarm coffee

Prepare the buttercream, replacing the coffee for the water.

Makes about 2 cups · Prep: 5 min. · Level: 1 · Keeps: 5–6 days in refrigerator, 5–6 months in freezer

SIMPLE ALMOND BUTTERCREAM

- $^3/_4$ cup (1$^1/_2$ sticks) butter, softened
- $^3/_4$ cup granulated sugar
- 1$^1/_3$ cups finely ground almonds
- 1   teaspoon vanilla extract

Beat the butter and sugar in a medium bowl with an electric mixer at high speed until creamy. • Add the almonds and vanilla.

Makes 2 cups · Prep: 30 min. · Level: 1 · Keeps: 2–3 days

CHOCOLATE BUTTERCREAM

- 2   cups Italian Buttercream (see recipe above)
- 8   oz bittersweet chocolate, coarsely chopped

Melt the chocolate in a double boiler over barely simmering water. • Cool andbeat into the cream.

Makes about 3 cups · Prep: 10 min. · Level: 1 · Keeps: 5–6 days in refrigerator, 5–6 months in freezer

ORANGE LIQUEUR BUTTERCREAM

For different flavors, vary the liqueur.

- 2 tablespoons orange liqueur
- 2 cups Italian Buttercream (see page left)

Beat the orange liqueur into the buttercream.

Makes about 2 cups · Prep: 5 min. · Level: 1 · Keeps: 5–6 days in refrigerator, 5–6 months in freezer

VANILLA FROSTING

- $2/3$ cup confectioners' sugar
- $1/2$ tablespoons water
- $1/2$ teaspoon vanilla extract

Sift the confectioners' sugar into a large bowl. • Stir in the water and vanilla until smooth.

Makes 1 cup · Prep: 5 min. · Level: 1 · Keeps: 1 day

PASSION FRUIT BUTTER

- 10 large passion fruit, pulped
- 2 cups granulated sugar
- 2 tablespoons butter
- 4 large eggs, lightly beaten

Beat the pulp, sugar, butter, and eggs in a double boiler until well blended. Stir over low heat, stirring constantly, until the mixture lightly coats a metal spoon or registers 160°F on an instant-read thermometer. Immediately plunge the pan into a bowl of ice water and stir until cooled. • Serve warm.

Makes 2 cups · Prep: 15 min. · Level: 1 · Keeps: 1 day in the refrigerator

PASSION FRUIT FROSTING

Excellent flavor with a wild orange color.

- 2 cups confectioners' sugar
- $1/4$ cup passion fruit pulp
- 3 tablespoons butter, softened
- 1–2 tablespoons hot water

Beat the confectioners' sugar, passion fruit pulp, butter, and 1 tablespoon water in a medium bowl until creamy. Beat in extra water to make a spreadable frosting.

Makes about $1^1/4$ cups · Prep: 10 min. · Level: 1 · Keeps: 1–2 days

FUDGE FROSTING

- 2 cups granulated sugar
- 3 oz bittersweet chocolate, coarsely chopped
- $3/4$ cup milk
- 2 tablespoons light corn syrup
- 2 tablespoons butter, cut up
- 1 teaspoon vanilla extract

Place the sugar, chocolate, milk, and corn syrup in a saucepan over low heat and stir until the sugar has dissolved. Wash down the

Passion fruit butter

sides of the pan with a brush dipped in cold water to prevent sugar crystals from forming. • Cook, without stirring, until the mixture reaches 238°F, or the soft-ball stage. Add the butter and remove from the heat. • Plunge the pan into a bowl of ice water and stir until lukewarm. Add the vanilla and continue stirring until cool. Use immediately as a glaze.

Makes about $2^1/2$ cups · Prep: 20–25 min. · Level: 1 · Keeps: 2–3 days

SOFT FUDGE FROSTING

- 8 oz bittersweet chocolate, coarsely chopped
- 1 cup (2 sticks) unsalted butter, softened
- 2 cups confectioners' sugar
- $1/4$ cup hot water
- 2 teaspoons vanilla extract

Melt the chocolate and $1/2$ cup butter in a double boiler over barely simmering water. Set aside to cool. • Beat the remaining butter, confectioners' sugar, water, and vanilla in a medium bowl with an electric mixer at high speed. • Beat in the chocolate mixture.

Makes 3 cups · Prep: 10 min. · Level: 1 · Keeps: 1–2 days

CHOCOLATE–WALNUT FROSTING

- 4 oz semisweet chocolate, coarsely chopped
- $1/3$ cup butter, cut up
- $2^1/2$ cups confectioners' sugar
- 1 teaspoon vanilla extract
- 1 tablespoon fresh lemon juice
- 1 cup walnuts, coarsely chopped

Melt the chocolate and butter in a double boiler over barely simmering water. Set aside to cool. • Beat in the confectioners' sugar, vanilla, and lemon juice. Add the walnuts. Use immediately.

Makes 2 cups · Prep: 10 min. · Level: 1 · Keeps: 2–3 days

CHOCOLATE CREAM FROSTING

- 6 oz bittersweet chocolate, coarsely chopped
- $1^1/2$ cups heavy cream
- 1 teaspoon vanilla extract

Melt the chocolate with the cream in a double boiler over barely simmering water. Add the vanilla. Transfer to a medium bowl. Cover and refrigerate until thick and spreadable, about 12 hours.

Makes 2 cups · Prep: 15 min. + 12 hr. to chill · Level: 1 · Keeps: 2–3 days

Zabaglione

ZABAGLIONE

Use as a cake filling or spoon over ripe berries or sliced peaches.

4 large egg yolks
1/4 cup granulated sugar
1/2 cup dry Marsala wine or dry sherry or vin santo (a Tuscan sweet dessert wine)

Beat the egg yolks and sugar in a double boiler with an electric mixer at high speed until pale and very thick. • Gradually add the Marsala. • Place the bowl over barely simmering water. Place over low heat and cook, beating constantly, until very thick, about 10 minutes, making sure that the mixture cooks to 160°F. Serve right away or place plastic wrap directly on the surface and refrigerate until ready to serve.

Makes 1½ cups · Prep: 20 min. · Level: 1 · Keeps: 1 day

POIRE WILLIAM ZABAGLIONE

6 large egg yolks
1 cup granulated sugar
1/2 cup Champagne
1/2 cup Poire William liqueur
1/3 cup whipped cream

Beat the egg yolks and sugar in a double boiler with an electric mixer at high speed until pale and thick. • Place over barely simmering water and gradually beat in the Champagne and liqueur. Continue cooking until the mixture lightly coats a metal spoon or registers 160°F on an instant-read thermometer. • Remove from heat and set aside to cool. • Use a large rubber spatula to fold in the whipped cream.

Makes about 2 cups · Prep: 25 min. + 25 min. to cool · Level: 1 · Keeps: 1 day

APRICOT GLAZE

1 cup apricot preserves or jam
2 tablespoons cold water or liqueur

Stir the preserves in a saucepan over low heat until it becomes slightly more liquid. • Strain the mixture and return to the heat. • Add the water or liqueur and boil gently for 2–3 minutes.

Makes about 1 cup · Prep: 15 min. · Level: 1 · Keeps: 1–2 days

RASPBERRY GLAZE

2/3 cup raspberry preserves
2/3 cup confectioners' sugar
1–2 tablespoons fresh lemon juice

Stir the raspberry preserves, confectioners' sugar, and 1 tablespoon lemon juice in a saucepan over low heat until it becomes slightly more liquid. • Strain the mixture and return to the heat. Cook for 2–3 minutes. Set aside to cool. • Add the extra lemon juice for a more liquid glaze.

Makes: about 1 cup · Prep: 10 min. · Cooking: 10 min. · Level: 1 · Keeps: 1–2 days

LEMON GLAZE

This simple glaze can also be made with orange or lime juice and zest.

2 cups confectioners' sugar
4–5 tablespoons fresh lemon juice
1½ teaspoons finely grated lemon zest

Place the confectioners' sugar in a medium bowl. Beat in 4 tablespoons lemon juice and zest until smooth, adding the additional tablespoon of lemon juice as needed to make a good spreading consistency.

Makes about ¾ cup · Prep: 5 min. · Level: 1 · Keeps: 1–2 days

LADY BALTIMORE FROSTING

4 large egg whites
2 cups granulated sugar
1/3 cup water
1/4 teaspoon cream of tartar
1/4 cup light corn syrup
1/8 teaspoon salt
1 teaspoon vanilla extract

Stir the egg whites, ½ cup sugar, 4 teaspoons water, and cream of tartar in a saucepan until blended. Cook over low heat, beating constantly with an electric mixer at low speed until the whites register 160°F on an instant-read thermometer. • Transfer to a bowl and beat at high speed until the egg whites form stiff peaks. • Stir the remaining sugar, remaining water, corn syrup, and salt in a saucepan over medium heat. Wash down the sides of the pan with a pastry brush dipped in cold water to prevent sugar crystals from forming. Cook, without stirring, until the mixture reaches 238°F, or the soft-ball stage. • Pour the sugar mixture in a thin stream over the egg whites, beating continuously. Add the vanilla and continue beating until the frosting has a good spreading consistency.

Makes about 4 cups · Prep: 55 min. · Level: 1 · Keeps: 2–3 days

SEVEN-MINUTE FROSTING

1½ cups granulated sugar
2 large egg whites
1/3 cup water
1/4 teaspoon salt
1/4 teaspoon cream of tartar
1 teaspoon vanilla extract

Stir the sugar, egg whites, water, salt, and cream of tartar in a saucepan until blended. Cook over low heat, beating constantly with an electric mixer at low speed until the whites register 160°F on an instant-read thermometer. Transfer to a bowl and beat at high speed until the egg whites form stiff peaks. • Remove from the heat and stir in the vanilla. • Beat until smooth and spreadable.

Makes about 5 cups · Prep: 10 min. · Level: 1 · Keeps: 2–3 days (in the refrigerator)

FONDANT

2 cups granulated sugar
3/4 cup cold water
1/4 teaspoon cream of tartar
1/4 cup confectioners' sugar, to dust

Bring the sugar, water, and cream of tartar to a boil in a saucepan over medium heat.

Wash down the sides of the pan with a pastry brush dipped in cold water to prevent sugar crystals from forming. Cook, without stirring, until the mixture reaches 238°F, or the soft-ball stage. • Sprinkle a marble slab or lightly oiled baking sheet with cold water. Pour the fondant syrup onto the slab or sheet and let cool until lukewarm, about 10–15 minutes. When ready, the fondant should hold an indentation made with a fingertip. • Use a large spatula to work the fondant, lifting from the edges toward the center, folding it until it begins to thicken, lose its gloss, and begin to turn pure white. • Dust your hands with confectioners' sugar and knead the fondant until smooth and creamy. Place in a bowl and cover with a clean cloth. Let stand overnight before using.

Makes about 1 cup · Prep: 35 min. + 12 hr. to rest · Level: 1 · Keeps: 1–2 days

FLUFFY MERINGUE FROSTING

Try this frosting on vanilla, butterscotch, or spiced cakes.

- 3 large egg whites
- 1³/₄ cups firmly packed dark brown sugar
- 1/₃ cup water
- 1/₂ teaspoon cream of tartar
- 1 teaspoon vanilla extract

Beat the egg whites, sugar, water, and cream of tartar in a saucepan until blended. Cook over low heat, beating constantly with an electric mixer at low speed until the egg whites register 160°F on an instant-read thermometer. Transfer to a bowl and beat at high speed until the egg whites form soft peaks. • Add the vanilla and continue beating until stiff peaks form, or until the frosting has a good spreading consistency.

Makes about 2 cups · Prep: 20 min. · Level: 1 · Keeps: 2–3 days

COFFEE MERINGUE FROSTING

This frosting is good with plain butter cakes, coconut cakes, and rich chocolate cakes.

- 1¹/₂ cups firmly packed light brown sugar
- 3 large egg whites
- 1/₄ cup very strong lukewarm coffee
- 1/₂ teaspoon cream of tartar
- 1 teaspoon vanilla extract

Beat the sugar, egg whites, coffee, and cream of tartar in a saucepan until blended. Cook over low heat, beating constantly with an electric mixer at low speed until the egg whites register 160°F on an instant-read thermometer. Transfer to a bowl and beat at high speed until the whites form stiff peaks. • Add the vanilla and beat until the frosting has a good spreading consistency.

Makes about 3 cups · Prep: 15 min. · Cooking: 10 min. · Level: 1 · Keeps: 2–3 days

SIMPLE CHOCOLATE FROSTING

- 2 cups confectioners' sugar
- 1/₄ cup unsweetened cocoa powder
- 2 tablespoons butter, softened
- 1 teaspoon vanilla extract
  about 2 tablespoons boiling water

Stir together the confectioners' sugar and cocoa in a double boiler. Add the butter, vanilla, and enough of the water to make a firm paste. Stir over simmering water until the frosting has a spreadable consistency, about 3 minutes.

Makes about 1¹/₂ cups · Prep: 5 min. · Level: 1 · Keeps: 2–3 days

RICH CHOCOLATE FROSTING

- 2 cups granulated sugar
- 1 cup heavy cream + 1–2 tablespoons as needed
- 8 oz bittersweet chocolate, coarsely chopped
- 2 tablespoons butter
- 1 teaspoon vanilla extract

Bring the sugar and 1 cup cream to a boil in a saucepan over medium heat. Boil for 1 minute, then remove from the heat. • Stir in the chocolate. • Return the saucepan to medium heat and cook, without stirring, until the mixture reaches 238°F, or the soft-ball stage. Remove from the heat. • Add the butter and vanilla, without stirring, and place the saucepan in a larger pan of cold water for 5 minutes before stirring. • Beat with a wooden spoon until the frosting begins to lose its sheen, 5–10 minutes. Immediately stir in 1 tablespoon cream. Do not let the frosting harden too much before adding the cream. • Let stand for 3–4 minutes, then stir until it has a spreadable consistency. Add more cream, 1 teaspoon at a time, if it is too stiff.

Makes about 2 cups · Prep: 15 min. · Cooking: 10 min. · Level: 1 · Keeps: 1–2 days

CHOCOLATE–SOUR CREAM FROSTING

- 8 oz semisweet chocolate, coarsely chopped
- 1/₄ cup (1/₂ stick) butter, softened
- 1/₂ cup sour cream
- 2²/₃ cups confectioners' sugar

Melt the chocolate in a double boiler over barely simmering water. Add the butter and set aside to cool for 5 minutes. • Stir in the sour cream. Beat in the confectioners' sugar until smooth and spreadable.

Makes 2¹/₂ cups · Prep: 15 min. + 5 min. to cool · Level: 1 · Keeps: 1–2 days

TANGY LEMON FROSTING

- 4 cups confectioners' sugar
- 1/₂ cup (1 stick) butter, softened
- 1 tablespoon grated lemon zest
- 4–6 tablespoons fresh lemon juice

Beat the confectioners' sugar, butter, lemon zest, and 4 tablespoons lemon juice in a large bowl with an electric mixer at medium speed until smooth. Add enough of the remaining lemon juice, a tablespoon at a time, to make a thick spreadable frosting.

Makes 2 cups · Prep: 10 min. · Level: 1 · Keeps: 1–2 days

SHERRY BUTTER CHRISTMAS CAKE FROSTING

- 5 cups confectioners' sugar
- 1 cup (2 sticks) butter, softened
- 3¹/₂ tablespoons dry sherry
- 2 teaspoons vanilla extract

Beat the confectioners' sugar, butter, sherry, and vanilla until smooth.

Makes about 3 cups · Prep: 10 min. · Level: 1 · Keeps: 1–3 days

SOFT LEMON FROSTING

- 2 cups confectioners' sugar
- 2 tablespoons butter, melted
- 2–3 tablespoons fresh lemon juice
- 1 tablespoon finely grated lemon zest

Beat the confectioners' sugar, butter, half the lemon juice, and the lemon zest until soft and spreadable, adding the lemon juice.

Makes about 1 cup · Prep: 5 min. · Level: 1 · Keeps: 1–2 days

Lemon butter frosting

LEMON BUTTER FROSTING

 2 cups confectioners' sugar
 1/4 cup (1/2 stick) butter, softened
 2 tablespoons fresh lemon juice

Beat the confectioners' sugar, butter, and
lemon juice in a medium bowl with an
electric mixer at medium speed until fluffy.

Makes 1 cup · Prep: 5 min. · Level: 1 · Keeps: 2–3 days

CHOCOLATE-PEPPERMINT FROSTING

 1/4 cup (1/2 stick) butter
 1/3 cup unsweetened cocoa powder
 2 cups confectioners' sugar
 3 tablespoons milk
 1/2 teaspoon vanilla extract
 1/4 teaspoon peppermint oil

Melt the butter in a saucepan over low heat.
Add the cocoa. • Add the confectioners' sugar
and milk until it has a spreading consistency.
Add the vanilla and peppermint oil.

*Makes about 1 cup · Prep: 5 min. · Level: 1 · Keeps:
1–2 days*

CARAMEL FROSTING

A soft frosting. If you'd like a more spreadable
consistency, refrigerate for 20-30 minutes, but no
longer, or it will develop a granular texture.

 2 cups firmly packed brown sugar
 1/3 cup granulated sugar
 1 cup heavy cream
 1/4 cup (1/2 stick) butter, cut up
 2 teaspoons vanilla extract

Stir both sugars, cream, and butter in a
medium saucepan over low heat until the
sugars have dissolved. • Increase heat to
medium. Wash down the sides of the pan
with a pastry brush dipped in cold water to
prevent sugar crystals from forming. Cook,
without stirring, until the mixture reaches
238°F, or the soft-ball stage. Remove from
the heat and set aside to cool for 15
minutes. • Transfer to a medium bowl, and
beat in the vanilla with an electric mixer at
low speed until the frosting loses its sheen
and thickens slightly.

*Makes about 2 1/4 cups · Prep: 30 min. · Level: 1 ·
Keeps: 1–2 days*

ALMOND BUTTER FROSTING

 2 cups (4 sticks) unsalted butter, softened
 2 teaspoons almond extract
 5 cups confectioners' sugar
 1/4–1/3 cup milk

Beat the butter and almond extract in a
large bowl with an electric mixer at medium
speed until creamy. Gradually beat in the
confectioners' sugar and enough of the milk
to make a smooth, spreadable frosting.

*Makes about 4 1/2 cups · Prep: 10 min. · Level: 1 ·
Keeps: 2–3 days*

WHITE CHOCOLATE GANACHE

 1/2 cup heavy cream
 13 oz white chocolate, coarsely chopped

Heat the cream almost to a boil in a small
saucepan over low heat. Place the chocolate
in a large bowl. Pour the cream over the
chocolate and stir until the chocolate is
melted and smooth. Refrigerate until
thickened and spreadable, about 30
minutes, stirring occasionally

*Makes about 1 1/2 cups · Prep: 15 min. + 30 min. to
chill · Level: 1 · Keeps: 2–3 days*

CHOCOLATE GANACHE

 1 1/2 cups heavy cream
 1 tablespoon corn syrup
 10 oz bittersweet chocolate, coarsely chopped

Bring the cream and corn syrup to a boil in
a medium saucepan over medium heat. •
Remove from heat. • Stir the chocolate into
the pan, then set aside for 2 minutes. • Beat
until the chocolate has melted and the
cream is thick.

*Makes about 2 cups · Prep: 20 min. · Level: 1 ·
Keeps: 2–3 days*

RASPBERRY PUREE

Serve with vanilla or raspberry ice cream, or spoon
over portions of rich chocolate cake (raspberries
and chocolate go very well together).

 2 lb fresh raspberries
 1/4 cup fresh lemon juice
 2–4 tablespoons superfine sugar

Process the raspberries, lemon juice, and 2
tablespoons superfine sugar until very finely
chopped. • Pass the mixture through a sieve.
• Taste and add the extra sugar, if needed.

*Makes about 4 cups · Prep: 10 min. · Level: 1 ·
Keeps: 1–2 days in the refrigerator*

RASPBERRY COULIS

 1 lb fresh raspberries
 3/4 cup granulated sugar
 2 tablespoons fresh lemon juice
 2 tablespoons kirsch or raspberry liqueur

Puree the raspberries, sugar, lemon juice,
and kirsch in a blender until smooth, about
1 minute.

*Makes about 2 cups · Prep: 15 min. · Level: 1 ·
Keeps: 2–3 days in the refrigerator*

STRAWBERRY COULIS

 1 lb fresh strawberries, hulled
 1/2 cup granulated sugar
 1/4 cup fresh lemon juice

Puree the strawberries, sugar, and juice in
a blender until smooth, about 1 minute.

*Makes about 2 cups · Prep: 15 min. · Level: 1 ·
Keeps: 2–3 days in the refrigerator*

BLACK CURRANT COULIS

Replace the black currants with red currants for a stunning red coulis.

- 1 lb fresh black currants
- 1 cup granulated sugar
- 2 tablespoons fresh lemon juice

Puree the currants, sugar, and lemon juice in a blender until smooth, about 1 minute.

Makes about 2 cups · Prep: 15 min. · Level: 1 · Keeps: 2–3 days in the refrigerator

SWEET WINE KIWI COULIS

- 1 lb ripe kiwifruit, peeled and roughly chopped
- ³/₄ cup granulated sugar
- 1 teaspoon ground cinnamon (optional)
- 2 tablespoons strong sweet dessert wine

Puree the kiwifruit, sugar, cinnamon, if desired, and wine in a blender until smooth.

Makes about 2 cups · Prep: 15 min. · Level: 1 · Keeps: 2–3 days in the refrigerator

TROPICAL COULIS

- 1 (7 oz) mango, peeled and coarsely chopped
- 1–2 (7 oz) papaya, peeled and seeded
- 2 passion fruit, pulped
- ³/₄ cup granulated sugar
- ¹/₄ cup dark rum

Puree the mango, papaya, passion fruit, sugar, and rum in a blender until smooth, about 1 minute.

Makes about 2 cups · Prep: 15 min. · Level: 1 · Keeps: 2–3 days in the refrigerator

PEACH COULIS

- 1 lb fresh peaches, peeled and coarsely chopped
- ³/₄ cup honey
- 1 teaspoon ground cinnamon (optional)
- 1 tablespoon dark rum
- 1 tablespoon fresh lemon juice

Puree the peaches, honey, cinnamon, if desired, rum, and lemon juice in a blender until smooth, about 1 minute.

Makes about 2 cups · Prep: 15 min. · Level: 1 · Keeps: 2–3 days in the refrigerator

APRICOT COULIS

- 1 lb fresh apricots, coarsely chopped
- ³/₄ cup granulated sugar
- ¹/₄ cup apricot brandy

Puree the apricots, sugar, and brandy in a blender until smooth, about 1 minute.

Makes about 2 cups · Prep: 15 min. · Level: 1 · Keeps: 2–3 days in the refrigerator

Raspberry puree

APRICOT SAUCE

- 1/2 cup granulated sugar
- 1 1/4 cups cold water
- 16–18 ripe apricots, pitted
- 2 tablespoons light rum

Cook the sugar and water in a saucepan over low heat until the sugar has dissolved. Add the apricots and cook over low heat until the apricots are completely tender and falling apart, about 25 minutes. • Remove from the heat and puree in a food processor until smooth. • Strain the mixture into a bowl and stir in the rum. Serve warm.

Makes about 2 cups · Prep: 35 min. · Level: 1 · Keeps: 1 day

APPLESAUCE

- 2 1/2 lb tart cooking apples (Granny Smiths are ideal) peeled, cored, and chopped
- 1 cup cold water
- 1 cup granulated sugar
- 1/3 cup fresh lemon juice
- 1 teaspoon vanilla extract

Cook the apples, water, and sugar in a large saucepan over low heat until the apples are mushy, about 20 minutes. • Remove from the heat and stir in the lemon juice and vanilla. • Strain the mixture in a food mill or puree in a food processor or blender.

Makes about 2 1/2 cups · Prep: 30 min. · Level: 1 · Keeps: 2–3 days

APPLE CHARLOTTE SAUCE

- 1 1/2 cups apricot preserves or jam
- 1/3 cup cold water
- 1/2 cup apple brandy

Heat the preserves in a saucepan over low heat until liquid. • Strain the preserves and return to the saucepan with the water. Cook over low heat until the mixture begins to thicken, about 15 minutes. • Remove from the heat and add the apple brandy. • Serve hot or cold.

Makes about 2 cups · Prep: 20 min. · Level: 1 · Keeps: 1 day

CARAMEL SAUCE

Spoon this sauce over plain butter cakes to turn them into mouthwatering desserts.

- 1 cup granulated sugar
- 1/3 cup + 1 tablespoon cold water

Hot chocolate sauce

- 1 1/4 cups heavy cream
- 2 tablespoons butter

Cook the sugar and water in a saucepan, stirring, over low heat until the sugar has dissolved. Continue cooking, without stirring, until deep golden brown. • Bring the cream to a boil in a separate saucepan. • Remove the caramel from heat and stir in the cream. • Return to medium heat for 3 minutes, beating constantly. • Remove from the heat and add the butter. Serve warm.

Makes about 2 cups · Prep: 25 min. · Level: 1 · Keeps: 1 day

ORANGE CHAMPAGNE SAUCE

- 3/4 cup granulated sugar
- 1 cup fresh orange juice
- 1/4 cup orange liqueur
- 1/4 cup Champagne
- 1/3 cup butter

Bring the sugar, orange juice, orange liqueur, and Champagne to a boil in a saucepan. Continue cooking over low heat until the sauce is reduced by half, about 20 minutes. • Remove from the heat. • Beat in the butter. • Serve hot or cold.

Makes about 2 cups · Prep: 30 min. · Level: 1 · Keeps: 1 day

CITRUS SAUCE

- 1 1/2 cups granulated sugar
- 1 cup fresh orange juice
- 1/2 cup fresh lemon or lime juice
- 2 tablespoons finely grated orange zest
- 2 tablespoons finely grated lemon zest
- 1/3 cup orange liqueur

Bring the sugar, orange juice, lemon juice, orange zest, and lemon zest to a boil in a saucepan. Continue cooking over low heat until the sauce becomes syrupy, about 10 minutes. • Remove from the heat and stir in the orange liqueur. • Strain the sauce into a bowl. • Serve hot or cold.

Makes about 2 cups · Prep: 15 min. · Level: 1 · Keeps: 1 day

HOT CHOCOLATE SAUCE

- 1/2 cup (1 stick) butter
- 2/3 cup water
- 5 oz bittersweet chocolate, coarsely chopped
- 1 1/4 cups granulated sugar
- 1/4 cup corn syrup
- 1/4 teaspoon salt
- 2 teaspoons vanilla extract

Melt the butter with the water in a saucepan over medium heat. Bring to a boil, stirring constantly. • Stir in the chocolate until melted. • Add the sugar, corn syrup, and salt. Bring to a boil and simmer for 5 minutes. Remove from the heat and add the vanilla. • Serve hot or warm.

Makes about 2 cups · Prep: 15 min. · Level: 1 · Keeps: 1–2 days

QUICK CHOCOLATE SAUCE

- 8 oz bittersweet chocolate, coarsely chopped
- 1/2 cup milk
- 1/2 cup heavy cream

Melt the chocolate with the milk and cream in a double boiler over barely simmering water. Serve warm.

Makes about 2 cups · Prep: 5 min. · Cooking: 10 min. · Level: 1 · Keeps: 1–2 days

LOWER-FAT CHOCOLATE SAUCE

This sauce has a deep chocolately flavor without being too sinful.

- 2 oz bittersweet chocolate
- 3 tablespoons unsweetened cocoa powder
- 1 teaspoon freeze-dried coffee granules
- 3/4 cup light corn syrup
- 1 tablespoon orange liqueur
- 1 teaspoon butter
- 2 teaspoons vanilla extract

Melt the chocolate with the cocoa, coffee, corn syrup, and butter in a saucepan over low heat. • Remove from the heat and add the vanilla and orange liqueur. Serve warm.

Makes 1 generous cup · Prep: 15 min. · Level: 1 · Keeps: 1–2 days

RUM SAUCE

- 1/2 cup granulated sugar
- 3 tablespoons cold water
- 2 cups heavy cream
- 1/4 cup rum

Cook the sugar and water in a saucepan, stirring, until the sugar has dissolved. Continue cooking, without stirring, over low heat until deep golden brown. Set aside to cool for 5 minutes. • Bring the cream to a boil in a separate saucepan. • Return the caramel to the heat and beat in the cream. • Remove from the heat and add the rum.

Makes 1 generous cup · Prep: 15 min. · Level: 1 · Keeps: 1–2 days

INDEX

C

Candied fruit
-Candied fruit and pine nut buns, 320
-Candied fruit sponge cake, 166
-Candied orange and white chocolate
   cheesecake, 251
-Candied orange wheel cake, 104

Caramel
-Caramel cheesecake, 248
-Caramel chocolate-chip cake, 248
-Caramel-filled coconut cake, 32
-Caramelized fresh fruit upside-down
   cake, 96
-Caramelized Venetian Christmas
   cake, 192
-Caramel layer cake, 34
-Caramel pound cake, 44
-Caramel sponge cake, 170
-Caramel vacherin, 214
-Caramel walnut tart, 289
-Saint-Honoré gâteau, 178

Carrots
-Best-ever carrot and walnut cake, 119
-Carrot and walnut cake with orange
   cream cheese frosting, 120
-Carrot cake with ginger cream cheese
   frosting, 122
-Carrot cheesecake, 263
-Carrot, date, and walnut cake, 120
-Carrot muffins with lemon frosting, 301
-Carrot spice cake, 122
-Fruit-sweetened carrot loaf, 334
-Low-fat carrot cake, 122
-Quick carrot and raisin loaf, 120
-Quick mix carrot, nut, and raisin
   cake, 121
-Spicy carrot cheesecake, 263
-Sunflower carrot cake with orange
   cream cheese frosting, 120
-Swiss carrot cake, 122
-Yogurt carrot cake with lemon cream
   cheese frosting, 120

Charlottes
-Apple charlotte with caramel sauce, 234
-Apple sorbet charlotte, 229
-Apricot charlotte, 231
-Baked apple charlotte, 234
-Banana charlotte, 233
-Chestnut charlotte, 232
-Chocolate mousse charlotte, 232
-Creamy coffee charlotte, 230
-Fresh fruit charlotte, 230
-Fresh fruit and cream charlotte, 231
-Grandma's charlotte cake, 230
-Hazelnut pumpkin charlotte, 233
-Lemon charlotte, 234
-Maple syrup charlotte, 232
-Marbled mascarpone charlotte, 232
-Mini fruit charlottes, 235
-Pear molds with citrus sauce, 231
-Raspberry mousse cake, 235
-Rosita charlotte, 230
-Spicy mini apple charlottes, 234
-Strawberry charlotte, 233

Cheesecakes
-Almond cheesecake, 242
-Amaretto cheesecake, 245
-Apple crunch cheesecake, 260
-Apple streusel cheesecake, 260
-Autumn cheesecake, 260
-Berry cheesecake with wine, 257
-Bitter orange cheesecake, 251
-Blackberry cheesecake, 258
-Black forest cheesecake, 250
-Candied orange and white chocolate
   cheesecake, 251
-Cappuccino cheesecake, 249
-Caramel cheesecake, 248
-Caramel chocolate-chip cake, 248
-Carrot cheesecake, 263
-Chocolate almond cheesecake, 242
-Chocolate cheesecake, 245
-Chocolate-bottom cheesecakes, 248
-Chocolate-cherry cheesecake, 250
-Chocolate-chip amaretto cake, 245
-Chocolate coffee cheesecake, 242
-Chocolate cream cheesecake, 246
-Chocolate hazelnut cream cake, 242
-Chocolate and lemon cheesecake, 250
-Chocolate liqueur suicide cake, 244
-Chocolate-mascarpone cake, 241
-Christmas eggnog cheesecake, 244
-Citrus fruit gâteau, 253
-Coconut cheesecake, 255
-Coconut mango cheesecake, 255
-Cornflake cheesecake with Champagne
   filling, 256
-Cranberry cheesecake, 257
-Crème de cassis and white chocolate
   cheesecake, 246
-Crystallized ginger cheesecake, 261
-Easy mini-cheesecakes, 239
-Family favorite cheesecake, 238
-Fruits of the forest tofu cake, 258
-Fudge brownie cheesecake, 241
-Ginger almond cheesecake, 261
-Ginger-apple cheesecake, 262
-Ginger pumpkin cheesecake, 262
-Irish cream cheesecake, 243
-Italian black currant cake, 258
-Italian ricotta cake, 263
-Key lime cheesecake, 237
-Kids' favorite cheesecake, 238
-Lemon and lime cheesecake, 253
-Lemon-vanilla cheesecake, 239
-Light chocolate almond cake, 242
-Light coffee cheesecake, 249
-Light ricotta cheesecake, 259
-Marbled chocolate and raspberry
   cheesecake, 247
-Mascarpone mold, 247
-Mocha cheesecake, 243
-Neapolitan ricotta cheesecake, 240
-New-York style cheesecake, 238
-No-bake lime cheesecake, 254
-Nutty caramel cheesecake, 248
-Orange chip cheesecake, 253
-Orange chocolate chip cheesecake, 251

-Orange cream cheesecake, 243
-Passion fruit cheesecake, 254
-Peanut chocolate cheesecake, 240
-Peanut-chocolate cheesecake, 240
-Quick pineapple cheesecake, 255
-Rice and berry cake, 256
-Ricotta cake with berries, 259
-Ricotta peach cake, 259
-Rum-raisin cheesecake, 244
-Spicy blueberry cheesecake, 256
-Spicy carrot cheesecake, 263
-Spicy pumpkin cheesecake, 262
-Spicy sweet cheesecake, 239
-Sweet potato cheesecake, 262
-Tiramisu cheesecake, 250
-Toffee-topped cheesecake, 249
-Treasure island cheesecake, 254
-Tutti-frutti cheesecake, 255
-Vanilla cheesecake with Chantilly and
   raspberries, 239
-Vanilla crumble cheesecake, 238
-White chocolate and raspberry
   cheesecake, 246

Cherries
-Black forest cake, 70
-Black forest cheesecake, 250
-Cherry-almond muffins, 302
-Cherry-apple strudel, 226
-Cherry choc meringue cake, 212
-Cherry and cream sponge, 166
-Cherry jelly tart, 287
-Cherry mille-feuille, 185
-Cherry and raisin loaf, 138
-Cherry tart, 288
-Cherry tartlets, 307
-Cherry tea cake, 27
-Easy jam strudel, 221
-Frozen cherry gâteau, 115
-No-bake cherry cake, 274
-Sour cream cherry cake, 115
-Wild cherry tart, 288

Chestnuts
-Chestnut charlotte, 232
-Chestnut crostata, 280
-Chestnut thousand-layer cake, 337
-Tuscan chestnut cake, 333

Chocolate
-Baked meringue with chocolate
   filling, 213
-Bavarian zabaglione cake, 271
-Checkerboard cake, 72
-Children's birthday cat cake, 186
-Children's party cake, 188
-Chilled chocolate citrus cake, 169
-Chocoholic supreme, 69
-Chocolate almond cake, 80
-Chocolate almond cake with marbled
   frosting, 80
-Chocolate almond cheesecake, 242
-Chocolate almond crostata, 286
-Chocolate angel food cake, 168
-Chocolate apple loaf with macadamia
   nuts, 94
-Chocolate applesauce cake, 65

-Chocolate apricot jam cake, 65
-Chocolate-banana cake with cream-
   cheese frosting, 67
-Chocolate berry crostata, 285
-Chocolate-bottom cheesecakes, 248
-Chocolate buttercream, 346
-Chocolate buttermilk cake, 56
-Chocolate butterscotch cake, 83
-Chocolate cake with Chantilly
   cream, 168
-Chocolate cantaloupe cake, 184
-Chocolate carrot cake, 64
-Chocolate Chantilly cream, 345
-Chocolate cheesecake, 245
-Chocolate-cherry cheesecake, 250
-Chocolate-cherry muffins, 304
-Chocolate cherry sponge, 168
-Chocolate chip-amaretto
   cheesecake, 245
-Chocolate chip cake, 58
-Chocolate chip loaf, 62
-Chocolate chip oatmeal cake, 57
-Chocolate chip pound cake, 44
-Chocolate coffee cake, 57
-Chocolate coffee cheesecake, 242
-Chocolate coffee cream roll, 171
-Chocolate coffee liqueur cake, 68
-Chocolate coffee yogurt cake, 57
-Chocolate cookie chill, 270
-Chocolate cream cheese and date
   cake, 60
-Chocolate cream cheesecake, 246
-Chocolate cream dacquoise, 215
-Chocolate cream dessert, 271
-Chocolate cream frosting, 347
-Chocolate crostata, 284
-Chocolate dacquoise, 203
-Chocolate Easter egg cake, 198
-Chocolate Easter muffins, 304
-Chocolate éclairs, 310
-Chocolate fudge nut snacking cake, 60
-Chocolate ganache, 350
-Chocolate hazelnut cake, 81
-Chocolate hazelnut cream cake, 242
-Chocolate hazelnut cream cake, 81
-Chocolate ice cream cake, 265
-Chocolate ice cream cake with figs and
   raspberries, 267
-Chocolate layer cake with fresh figs, 53
-Chocolate layer cake with truffles, 72
-Chocolate and lemon cheesecake, 250
-Chocolate liqueur suicide cake, 244
-Chocolate log, 191
-Chocolate-mascarpone cake, 241
-Chocolate meringue cake, 213
-Chocolate-mint cupcakes, 306
-Chocolate mint meringues, 212
-Chocolate mousse, 343
-Chocolate mousse cake, 86
-Chocolate mousse charlotte, 232
-Chocolate mousse mold, 87
-Chocolate mousse supreme, 87
-Chocolate muffins, 303
-Chocolate-nut cupcakes, 306

METRIC EQUIVALENTS

VOLUME

IMPERIAL	METRIC
1/8 teaspoon	0.5 milliliter
1/4 teaspoon	1 milliliter
1/2 teaspoon	2 milliliters
1 teaspoon	5 milliliters
1 tablespoon (1/2 fluid ounce)	1 tablespoon (15 milliliters)*
1/4 cup (2 fluid ounces)	2 tablespoons (59 milliliters)
1/3 cup (3 fluid ounces)	1/4 cup (90 milliliters)
1/2 cup (4 fluid ounces)	1/3 cup (120 milliliters)
1 cup (8 fluid ounces)	3/4 cup (235 milliliters)
1 quart (32 fluid ounces)	1 liter minus 3 tablespoons
1 gallon (128 fluid ounces)	4 liters minus 1½ cups

*The Australian tablespoon is 20 milliliters,
but the difference is negligible in most recipes.*

TEMPERATURE

IMPERIAL	METRIC
0°F (freezer temperature)	minus 18°C
32°F (temperature water freezes)	0°C
180°F (temperature water simmers)*	82°C
212°F (temperature water boils)*	100°C
250°F (low oven temperature)	120°C
350°F (moderate oven temperature)	180°C
425°F (hot oven temperature)	220°C
500°F (very hot oven temperature)	260°C

At sea level

WEIGHT

IMPERIAL	METRIC
1/4 ounce	7 grams
1/2 ounce	15 grams
3/4 ounce	20 grams
1 ounce	30 grams
6 ounces	170 grams
8 ounces (1/2 pound)	225 grams
12 ounces (3/4 pound)	340 grams
16 ounces (1 pound)	450 grams
35 ounces (2 ¼ pounds)	1 kilogram

BAKING PAN SIZES

IMPERIAL	METRIC
8 x 1½-inch round cake pan	20 x 4-centimeter cake tin
9 x 1½-inch round cake pan	23 x 3.5-centimeter cake tin
11 x 7 x 1½-inch baking pan	28 x 18 x 4-centimeter baking tin
13 x 9 x 2-inch baking pan	30 x 20 x 3-centimeter baking tin
15 x 10 x 1-inch baking pan (jelly-roll pan)	30 x 25 x 2-centimeter baking tin (Swiss roll tin)
9 x 5 x 3-inch loaf pan	23 x 13 x 7-centimeter loaf tin
9-inch pie plate	23 x 4-centimeter pie plate
7- or 8-inch springform pan or loose-bottom tin	18- or 20-centimeter springform

LENGTH

IMPERIAL	METRIC
1/2 inch	12 millimeters
1 inch	2.5 centimeters
6 inches	15 centimeters
12 inches (1 foot)	30 centimeters